Crisis and Constitutionalism

Crisis and Constitutionalism

Roman Political Thought from the Fall of the Republic to the Age of Revolution

BENJAMIN STRAUMANN

OXFORD
UNIVERSITY PRESS

OXFORD
UNIVERSITY PRESS

Oxford University Press is a department of the University of Oxford. It furthers the University's objective of excellence in research, scholarship, and education by publishing worldwide.Oxford is a registered trade mark of Oxford University Press in the UK and certain other countries.

Published in the United States of America by Oxford University Press
198 Madison Avenue, New York, NY 10016, United States of America.

Library of Congress Cataloging-in-Publication Data
Names: Straumann, Benjamin, author.
Title: Crisis and constitutionalism : Roman political thought from the fall of the republic to the age of revolution / Benjamin Straumann.
Description: New York, NY : Oxford University Press, 2016. | Includes bibliographical references and index.
Identifiers: LCCN 2015028298 |
ISBN 978–0–19–995092–8 (hardback) | ISBN 978–0–19–995093–5 (e-book)
Subjects: LCSH: Constitutional history—Philosophy. | Roman law—Influence. | Constitutional history—Rome. | Rome—Politics and government—265–30 B.C. Republicanism—History. | Political science—Philosophy. |
BISAC: HISTORY / Ancient / Rome.
Classification: LCC K3161 .S767 2016 | DDC 342.37—dc23 LC record available at http://lccn.loc.gov/2015028298

In memory of my parents,
Ruth Reichstein (1933–1989) and Bruno Straumann (1924–2000)

Contents

Preface and Acknowledgments ix

Introduction: The Fall of the Roman Republic and the Rise of Constitutional Thought 1

PART I: *Inchoate Constitutionalism in the Late Roman Republic* 23

1. "Not Some Piece of Legislation": The Roman Concept of Constitution 27
2. Infinite Power? Emergencies and Extraordinary Powers in Constitutional Argument 63
3. "The Sole Bulwark of Liberty": Constitutional Rights at Rome 118

PART II: *A Hierarchy of Laws: Roman Constitutional Theory* 147

4. Cicero and the Legitimacy of Political Authority 149
5. Greek vs. Roman Constitutional Thought 191

PART III: *The Limits of Virtue: The Roman Contribution to Political Thought* 239

6. The Roman Republic as a Constitutional Order from the Principate to the Renaissance 241

7. Neo-Roman Interlude: Machiavelli and the Anti-Constitutional Tradition 260

8. Jean Bodin and the Fall of the Roman Republic 278

Epilogue: Constitutional Republicanism, the "Cant-Word" Virtue and the American Founding 303

Bibliography 343

General Index 373

Index Locorum 403

Preface and Acknowledgments

THOSE LIVING IN political orders that are also constitutional orders tend to take the ideas developed by Roman constitutional thought for granted. Constitutionalism, like vaccination, perennially runs the danger of falling victim to its own success. But, as Roman writers and thinkers of the last century of the Republic knew all too well, political orders can and do collapse. The crises and eventual collapse of the Roman Republic were one of the pivotal moments in European political and intellectual history. How and why did this vast, successful republican political order fail? From Cicero and his contemporaries onward, this question has attracted the interest of some of the best and most interesting political thinkers. One influential answer, already put forward by some of the ancients, was that luxury, corruption, and the loss of virtue were to blame. A very different answer was lurking in Roman historiography, Polybius, and, more explicitly, in some of Cicero's philosophical works: the crises of the late Republic had been of a constitutional nature and could be solved by constitutional means alone. The idea of a constitutional order, that is to say, a political order based on rules and institutions that are themselves not subject to the political process; are more firmly entrenched than mere legislation; and rest on a normative justification that is substantive, not merely procedural—this idea found resonance in the history of political thought as a result of, and as an answer to, the crisis of the Roman Republic.

Roman constitutional thought could build on an inchoate constitutionalism already implicit in the Roman republican political order and its highly legalized political negotiations. It was further developed and made explicit in Cicero's works, and found a very perceptive audience in all those political thinkers from the fourteenth century onward who preferred the Roman republican order to the Empire. The fall of the Roman Republic remained the central point of interest for thinkers who sought constitutional remedies to problems of political order. Jean Bodin, usually misunderstood as simply an absolutist thinker, was really a key exponent of the tradition of Roman political thought emanating from the crisis of the Republic, and it was Bodin who established the very Roman terms through which Montesquieu and the thinkers of the Enlightenment started to investigate solutions to problems of stability and justice in large modern, i.e., commercial, republics. Even thinkers who are not usually thought to argue with historical examples, such as Hobbes or Locke, can be shown to exhibit features of the Roman tradition under consideration in the present book. The tension between those interested primarily in virtue (whether for instrumental-political reasons or for its own, eudaemonistic sake), on the one hand, and those focusing on constitutional ideas, on the other, never went away. Whatever the scholarly arguments over Rousseau's legacy eventually yield, there is an obvious overlap in the Genevan's attraction to virtue and the commitment, on the part of some of the French revolutionaries, especially the Mountain, to a doctrine of virtue that had only contempt for formal institutions and constitutional safeguards. But a surprisingly large number of thinkers who are conventionally thought to be champions of republican virtue, such as Marchamont Nedham, James Harrington, Walter Moyle, Trenchard and Gordon, or John Adams turn out to be the heirs to the influential strand of thought described in this book. For them, Roman political thought, properly understood, was constitutional thought. A fortiori this was the case for those, like Bodin, Montesquieu, and the Federalist framers of the U.S. Constitution, who had never shown too much enthusiasm for, let alone trust in, virtue.

The title of this book carries some overtones that will be particularly obvious to those who have been exposed to German-language scholarship in ancient and European intellectual history. It responds to, and argues against, however obliquely, some of the concerns and arguments that have been put forward in influential monographs by Christian Meier and Reinhart Koselleck. But this is by no means the main thrust of this book. Rather, I seek here to address a key topic in ancient history from a fresh angle and to connect it with the reception of classical antiquity. The reception provides the overarching framework and orientation, notwithstanding the fact that it takes up only one third of the book. This means that the book is at the same time an attempt to describe a key period in ancient history and the ideas it engendered as well as an attempt at writing a long-term intellectual history of constitutional thought that seeks to close some gaps and establish bridgeheads between classical antiquity, the Renaissance, and the Enlightenment. I hope that, rather than falling between several chairs, it will find audiences in ancient history, ancient philosophy, the history of political thought, legal history, and among early modernists and even early Americanists. A brief remark seems in order to explain the relationship between the ideas put forward in the present study and those explored in a previous book of mine, *Roman Law in the State of Nature*, that dealt with Hugo Grotius' use of Roman law. It was the claim of that earlier book that Grotius, along with other natural lawyers and some exponents of the Scottish Enlightenment, had drawn very extensively on Roman law and ethics in his attempt to construct and justify a secular, universal normative order. Grotius' was never meant to be a *political* theory in the narrow sense, i.e., a theory that dealt with the state, political institutions, and their justification, although it had, of course, very important ramifications that would bear directly on political theory more narrowly conceived. Rather, it was supposed to provide a theory of justice for the state of nature, that is to say, the pre- or *extra-political* realm. In contrast, the ideas explored in the present book are political in a narrower sense and stem directly from the crisis and fall of one of the most historically prominent political orders, the Roman Republic.

This study represents a revised version of my *Habilitationsschrift*, submitted to the Faculty of Arts and Social Sciences at the University of Zurich in the fall of 2015. I have incurred a great many debts to many people and institutions while writing this book. Reading the Aristotelian *Athenaion Politeia* at the University of Zurich in 1999 under the guidance of Christian Marek in a very small group that included Victor Walser left a lasting impression and reinforced my interest in constitutional issues. I owe a huge debt to Peter Garnsey and David Lupher, who provided very valuable comments on the whole draft. Andrew Lintott and Jürgen von Ungern-Sternberg have read and commented upon many chapter drafts and have been extremely helpful and encouraging. Benedict Kingsbury has offered unwavering support for my work, and New York University School of Law has been an intellectually stimulating institution to do research at. The Swiss National Science Foundation supported this project with a generous Fellowship for Advanced Researchers, and early on I profited from comments and correspondence with Elizabeth Meyer. Wilfried Nippel's invitation to a conference in Helsinki helped to articulate my ideas, and Pasquale Pasquino was an excellent person to talk to about dictatorship and emergency powers. I owe thanks to Christopher Brooke, Leslie Green, Andrew Lintott, and Fergus Millar for facilitating my stay in Oxford in 2009, and I was fortunate that Beat Näf, consistently supportive of my project, invited me back to Zurich to teach a seminar and give a series of lectures in 2012, which allowed me further to elaborate my views. Several chapters were written in the rich libraries of the École française and the American Academy in Rome in 2013. A meeting of the Association of Ancient Historians in Erie, Pennsylvania, as well as talks at the Universities of Basel and Bern provided interested and critical audiences for parts of this book. I would like to thank especially Ryan Balot, Stefan Rebenich, Alfred Schmid, Sebastian Schmidt-Hofner, Thomas Späth, and Lukas Thommen for discussions, criticism, and invitations to speak. Joy Connolly, Michèle Lowrie, Andrew Monson, Michael Peachin, and Kaius Tuori shared many of my interests and helped clarify my thoughts at our informal gatherings on Roman political thought and legal history at New York University's Department of Classics. Kinch Hoekstra, Martti Koskenniemi, Eric Nelson, Chris Warren, and Arthur Weststeijn answered questions, gave advice and offered feedback, and Frederik Vervaet and Tobias Schaffner have been encouraging and sharp colleagues to correspond with. Daniel Lee very generously shared the manuscript of his forthcoming book, *Popular Sovereignty in Early Modern Constitutional Thought*, with me; my interpretation of Bodin is obviously indebted to his insights. I should also mention the inspiration provided by David Dyzenhaus' work, above and beyond his scholarship on Hobbes cited in this study. David's scholarship on the constitutional thought of Weimar has been an important indirect influence, as was Karl Dietrich Bracher's work. Needless to say, none of the scholars named endorses all of my arguments; all remaining errors are my own. I owe further thanks to my editor, Stefan Vranka, who never ceased supporting the project. Further thanks are due to the anonymous readers and to my copy-editor, Andrew Dyck, whose erudition made this a much better book than it would otherwise have been. I am grateful for permission to reuse material previously published as "Constitutional Thought in the Late Roman Republic," *History of Political Thought* 32, 2 (2011): 280–292.

Anna-Maria von Lösch and Enzo Franco provided wine, meals, conversations and companionship in Rome, as did Jascha Preuss, Naomi Wolfensohn, Ariella and Tani in New York; Thömse, Jane, and Rowan Wolff in Basel; and the Diems in Aarau. Andreas Gyr's friendship has been a crucial and longstanding source of ideas, conversation, support, and exchange. My father Bruno gave me Leszek Kolakowski's *Main Currents of Marxism* for my sixteenth birthday, and Kolakowski's engrossing book persuaded me that the history of ideas, properly done, is where the action is. My dad intuited correctly that intellectual history was more congenial a field of activity for me than music, where his own interests and vast talent lay. His taste, unconventional magnanimity, warmth, and wit cannot be overstated. My mother Ruth was interested in and very supportive of everything to do with literature and ideas, and my brothers, Till and Patrick, helped sharpen my argumentative abilities early on. They, together with Adriana, Élie, Yael, and Abril have constantly provided friendship and sustenance notwithstanding the geographical distances involved. Eva and the new Bruno are simply the non plus ultra and the best company conceivable.

New York City, September 28, 2015 Benjamin Straumann

Crisis and Constitutionalism

Introduction

THE FALL OF THE ROMAN REPUBLIC AND THE RISE OF CONSTITUTIONAL THOUGHT

"Can anyone be so indifferent or lazy that he could fail to want to know how and thanks to what kind of constitution (τίνι γένει πολιτείας) almost the entire known world was mastered and brought under the single rule of the Romans, in less than fifty-three years—an unprecedented event?" (Polybius 1.1.5)

"[T]he successes of the Thebans were due not to the composition of their constitution (ἡ τῆς πολιτείας σύστασις), but to the virtue of their leading men (ἡ τῶν προεστώτων ἀνδρῶν ἀρετή). . . . We must hold very much the same opinion about the Athenian state." (Polybius 6.43.5–6.44.1)

THE EXTRAORDINARY INFLUENCE of the ancient Republic of Rome has not been limited to classical antiquity, or to the vast geographical area reached by its forces. Rome, not Athens, has had the deeper impact on Western political history both in the province of the history of events and institutions and in the realm of political and legal ideas. Rome, not Athens, was considered the epitome of an extraordinarily successful, enduring, stable and free republic. And it was Rome, not Athens, which gave rise to sustained constitutional thought about the proper limits of legislative authority and the power of magistrates. In short, in the subsequent history of Western political thought the Roman Republic, not any of the Greek *poleis*, with the exception of Sparta, was considered the proper object of study for thinking about constitutional government. This extraordinary prominence of Rome in political and legal thought remained until at least the rehabilitation of democracy, including Athenian democracy, in the nineteenth century.[1]

1. For Sparta, see Rawson, *Spartan Tradition*. For the afterlife of Athens, see Roberts, *Athens on Trial*. For a broad survey, see Nippel, *Antike oder moderne Freiheit;* cf. Straumann, "Review Nippel."

Beginning with Polybius, much of the attention paid to the Roman Republic in the history of political thought has been concerned with the Republic's constitutional design. Most importantly from the point of view of the present study, it was the constitution of the Roman Republic that became the focal point of a growing body of writing that centered, from the first century BC onward, on the crisis and downfall of the Republic, describing the end of the republican order in constitutional terms, the crisis as a constitutional crisis, and prescribing constitutional remedies. Cicero's theoretical writings as well as his forensic and deliberative oratory breathe this constitutional spirit and contain much that can only be described as constitutional argument; and Livy's and other historians' historiography can be interpreted as projecting back into the early Republic constitutional debates about the proper limits of the various powers and authorities contained in the republican constitution and about the proper application of emergency powers. It was the crisis of the Republic which sparked constitutional reflection concerning the precise boundaries between constitutional and extra-constitutional violence and authority. What had to be explained, from the point of view of contemporaries, was the failure of the republican constitution, and the subsequent constitutional change from Republic to Principate; and the explanation, for the Romans as well as for much of later Western political thought, had to be sought in the proper delineation of constitutional powers. Since the debates about the scope of such powers became especially relevant and heated in the face of real and alleged emergencies, the constitutional debates centering on emergency powers and extraordinary competencies will have a central claim on our attention. We will not be concerned, then, with a "republican" interest in the uncorrupted virtue of the early Republic, but rather with the keen interest in the constitutional crises and eventual failure of the late Republic.

The distinctive contributions of Roman republican institutions and, most importantly, Roman republican political and constitutional thought, have been increasingly obscured by a lumping together of the various contributions of Greeks and Romans to political thought under the label of "classical republicanism." Since at least the interwar years there has been a comparable neglect of specifically Roman political ideas in the scholarly literature on the history of political thought.[2] What has been termed "classical republicanism" by historians

2. See Hammer, *Roman Political Thought*, ch. 1; Kapust, *Republicanism*, ch. 1; Hammer, *Roman Political Thought from Cicero*, for a very different approach from the one pursued here; cf. Straumann, "Review Hammer."

of political thought, and identified variously and promiscuously with a Platonic impulse for redistribution, Polybian doctrines of the allegedly mixed constitution, a Sallustian worry about corruption, and above all with an Aristotelian concern with virtue, has not been sensitive to Roman specificities and has thus blunted our conceptual instruments and muddied the waters considerably. With the important exception of a series of seminal works on republicanism and "neo-Roman" theories of the state by Quentin Skinner, Philip Pettit, Maurizio Viroli, Eric Nelson, and others, "classical republicanism" has often been used as an overly expansive term under which are subsumed not simply the institutional realities of the Greek city-states of Athens, Sparta, and lesser Greek *poleis* as well as of Rome, but also the political thought engendered by those commonwealths.

The origins of this lumping together may be found deep in the nineteenth century, in Benjamin Constant's famous speech, given 1819 at the Athénée Royal in Paris, on the "Liberty of the Ancients Compared with that of the Moderns," which itself was merely the most prominent and influential outgrowth of a tradition, starting with Adam Ferguson and the Marquis de Condorcet,[3] that would contrast the liberty of the ancients with the liberty of the moderns, drawing a sharp distinction between a perceived lack of individual rights in classical antiquity, on the one hand, and the modern conception of rights-based liberty, on the other. Constant, who was educated in Edinburgh, was drawing on the distinction, already embraced by his Scottish predecessors, between the martial polities of classical antiquity and modern commercial societies. For Constant, this corresponded to a distinction between ancient liberty, which really meant political participation, and modern liberty, which consisted in institutional safeguards for "individual enjoyments," i.e., individual rights limiting the reach of government. This distinction was to have great impact on historical writing and on liberal political thought in the nineteenth and twentieth centuries, and its influence can be traced in the works of Fustel de Coulanges, Jacob Burckhardt, Lord Acton and Max Weber.[4] Constant differentiated the picture of classical antiquity somewhat by noting that Athens, by virtue of its openness to trade, allowed "its citizens an infinitely greater individual liberty than Sparta or Rome." However, this differentiation did not owe anything to Athens' constitutional features;

3. See Ferguson, *Essay*, p. 156; Condorcet, *Sur l'instruction publique*, p. 47. On Ferguson's use of classical antiquity, see McDaniel, *Ferguson*.

4. See Nippel, *Antike oder moderne Freiheit*, pp. 201–221; id., "Antike und moderne Freiheit," pp. 49–68. For the effects of this tradition, see Podoksik, "One Concept." Constant's view corresponds on some level with the history of ethics put forward by Alasdair MacIntyre: where Constant saw progress, MacIntyre sees decline and the loss of a pre-modern virtue ethics. See MacIntyre, *After Virtue*.

constitutionally speaking, the ancient polities were all lumped together, sharing according to Constant a lack of respect for the independence of individuals, subjecting instead virtually every conceivable action of the individual "to the empire of the legislator."[5] Constant thus presented a view of the basic unity of the classical constitutional world and equated the "liberty of the ancients" with "active and constant participation in collective power," thereby taxing the ancients as a whole with having mistaken "the authority of the social body for liberty" and with subjecting the citizens entirely "in order for the nation to be sovereign."[6] Amongst Constant's coevals, by contrast, "individuals have rights which society must respect."[7] This provides a constraint on the "empire of the legislator"—laws, although preferable to the arbitrary power of men, must have their limits too.[8]

Constant was by no means the first to present this monolithic view of classical antiquity, of course. One could cite Hobbes, to whom all the Greek and Roman polities were "popular states," and for whom the liberty described by the classical authors was not the liberty of "particular men," but the "Libertie of the Common-wealth."[9] Out of this tradition liberal constitutionalism grew, aiming to safeguard individual rights, chief among them the right to private property. These safeguards were to be instituted against Constant's "empire of the legislator," whether that legislator be democratic, aristocratic, or monarchic.

In something akin to a new *querelle des anciens et des modernes* the term "classical republicanism" has thus been attached to many ancient things and ideas, usually with a slight bent towards the *poleis* of ancient Greece. Paul Rahe, an ancient historian by education, in his magisterial *Republics Ancient and Modern* (1992), an extensive essay in comparative politics, arrives at a very Constantian emphasis on the "depths of the chasm that separates the republics of Greek antiquity from those of recent modernity."[10] Rahe arguably arrives at his Constantian conclusion by considerably loading the dice, however—that is, by leaving out the one ancient republic that might have bridged that chasm: Rome. Although acknowledging two years later in the introduction to the first volume of the paperback edition of *Republics Ancient and Modern* that one cannot "make full sense of the history of the struggle for self-government in early modern Europe

5. Constant, "Liberty," p. 319.

6. Ibid., p. 318.

7. Ibid., p. 321.

8. Ibid., p. 320.

9. Hobbes, *Leviathan*, vol. 2, ch. 21, p. 332.

10. Rahe, *Republics*, p. 19.

without referring to the influence of Roman institutions and law," and conceding that a "case can no doubt be made for according priority" to ancient Rome, Rahe concludes by stating that to "the extent that modern political reflection draws on and responds to the political thought of the ancient Greeks, Hellas must be accorded primacy."[11] But this is surely to beg the question, as this "extent" is precisely what is at issue: to what extent did modern political thought draw on and respond to the political thought of the ancient Greeks, and to what extent did it draw on and respond to that of the ancient Romans? Furthermore, might the deeply antidemocratic character of virtually all of Greek political thought have had a hand in directing Western political theory towards the example and ideas of the Roman Republic? And if so, should not Rome be accorded primacy?

While Rahe, avoiding the Roman Republic, presents us with a view of "republics ancient and modern" so much akin to Constant's that it represents, in the words of one critic, a voluminous "reprint"[12] of Constant's slim text, the prominent ancient historian Fergus Millar has given us what promised to be a much needed study of the history of the Roman Republic in Western political thought. In *The Roman Republic in Political Thought* (2002), Millar attempts a selective survey of the legacy of the Roman republican constitution from contemporary writers up to some very recent works of political theory, discussing what Aristotle might have said about the Republic, Polybius, later Greek writers, Machiavelli, Marchamont Nedham, James Harrington, John Milton, Montesquieu, Rousseau, and the American Founders along the way. Since Millar is above all concerned with finding traces of his own views on the democratic character of the Roman Republic, however, and since very few of the writers he discusses subscribe to such views, his book has a very idiosyncratic flavor to it—indeed, Millar's attempt at explaining why so few thinkers thought of the Republic as a democracy amounts, as one reviewer has sardonically remarked, to "Sherlock Holmes's curious incident of the dog in the night on a very large scale."[13]

The present study might thus be helpfully conceived of as supplementing Fergus Millar's as well as Paul Rahe's important work. As opposed to Millar I will not be concerned with trying to find resonances of the Republic's supposedly democratic institutions. Rather, my aim is to give an account of what I take to be the chief Roman contributions to political thought: constitutionalism, a concern with both pre-political and civil rights, and a corresponding idea of

11. Id., *The Ancien Régime*, p. xxiii.

12. Nippel, *Antike oder moderne Freiheit*, p. 335 ("Neuauflage").

13. Zetzel, "Review Millar."

political justice that is conspicuously distinct from Greek thinking on the subject. In the same vein the present work might be thought of as adding Roman political thought to the Greek examples discussed in Paul Rahe's *Republics Ancient and Modern*. Contrary to Rahe's "reprint" of Constant, however, I will try to show how the constitutional crises that attended the fall of the Roman Republic engendered constitutional thought that exhibited a deep proto-liberal concern with Constantian themes such as the limits of legislation and popular sovereignty. Indeed, one of the most interesting, and most distinguishing, features of Roman constitutional thought in the late Republic is its concern with sovereignty—its sources, its limits, its institutional locus, and the consequences of its breakdown. Millar's emphasis on the democratic element in the late republican constitution is attractive insofar it gives due attention to Polybius' interpretation of the constitution—but Polybius' own conclusion was of course very pessimistic,[14] and normatively perfectly at odds with Millar's; Polybius anticipated that "when Rome was most democratic, it was also most corrupt."[15]

This aspect of Roman constitutional argument becomes particularly salient in discussions that concern emergency powers: whenever the constitutionality of states of emergency is at stake, whenever the lawfulness of extraordinary commands, of dictatorships, or of the violation of civil rights is contested, constitutional argument and the underlying constitutional theory try to determine where sovereignty lies. This will require us to discuss the institution of dictatorship, irregular commands (*imperia*), and attempts to legitimize the violation of the right of appeal (*provocatio*).

Constant had associated the revival of classical constitutional ideals with the period of the Terror after the French Revolution and with the Jacobins' revival of Greek and Roman models. With his speech on the "Liberty of the Ancients Compared with that of the Moderns" he had aimed to curb whatever enthusiasm was left in post-Napoleonic times for imitating the republics of antiquity or at least certain "republican usages" such as Athenian ostracism or the Roman censorship. The thrust of Constant's argument thus exhibits very clearly what has become by now an all too often repeated cliché, namely the dichotomy between ancient republicanism and liberalism, a dichotomy that was to feature prominently in the historiography of political thought in general and that can also be profitably demonstrated in the historiography of the American revolutionary and early republican periods.

14. Polyb. 6.57.9.

15. Zetzel, "Review Millar."

The historiography of American political thought has indeed drawn on the dichotomy between ancient republicanism and liberalism to a considerable extent, using the two concepts in order to describe the American Founding in terms of a shift in political thought from classical republicanism to modern liberalism. Historians have differed over the question of where to draw the line in the chronology of late colonial and early American political thought, but the integrity of the concepts has never been called into question. While Bernard Bailyn in *The Ideological Origins of the American Revolution* (1967) had insisted on a minor role for classical republicanism in the Founders' political thought, a role confined to providing an indirect source mediated by the British Whig tradition,[16] other historians have followed Gordon Wood in conceding far more weight to ancient republicanism in the revolutionary period,[17] at least up to 1787, when a "transformation" took place "from a republican to a liberal . . . culture,"[18] where liberty meant personal or private liberty.[19] A few years later, John Pocock further extended the importance of the classical republican tradition into the early national period.[20] And as we have seen, in his *Republics Ancient and Modern*, Paul Rahe, while acknowledging "a deliberately contrived mixed regime of sorts,"[21] between ancient and modern republicanism, in the end remained attached to the broad dichotomy between "ancient republican" and "modern liberal."

A similar description can be given of the historiography of republican thought in general, showing that the dichotomy between classical republicanism and

16. Bailyn, *Origins*, pp. 22–54.

17. Wood, *Creation*, pp. 48–53.

18. Ibid., p. xii.

19. Ibid., p. 609. Cf. Shalev, *Rome Reborn*, p. 113, for a distinction between a Southern "classical" republicanism and a "modernity-embracing" New England republicanism.

20. Pocock, *Machiavellian Moment*. For criticism, stressing the importance especially for Harrington of republican Rome as opposed to "Aristotle's Greece," see Fukuda, *Sovereignty*, pp. 8, 123–126; Hexter, "Review Pocock," pp. 330–337. Hexter points to the the language of the liberty and property of Englishmen and situates this kind of "ancient constitutionalism" in a tradition reaching back to Magna Carta as its "medieval version" (p. 333) and, ultimately, to a "convergence of Stoic ideals and Roman law practicalities" (p. 332). It is true that this tradition is conceptually close to the Roman one under investigation here, but historically they are separate; see the differentiation in Appleby, *Capitalism*, pp. 16–22, where the American colonial rebels are said to have first appealed to the rights of Englishmen and then to have shifted to a more abstract notion of constitutionalism—one described in this book as inspired by the fall of the Roman Republic; see Epilogue.

21. Rahe, *Republics*, p. x. For a salutary corrective of the republican-liberal distinction, see Sullivan, *Machiavelli*. Shalev, *Rome Reborn*, convincingly shows the debt American revolutionaries owed to the classics, especially in terms of their historical thought.

modern liberalism is at work here too. Indeed, as Stephen Holmes has noted, "the history of modern political theory has recently been reconstructed as a running battle between two supposedly rival traditions: liberalism vs. republicanism."[22] In Quentin Skinner's work, the battle has been reconfigured as a debate about whether the constitutional framework of a society has a bearing upon the individual liberty of its members, with what Skinner calls the "neo-Roman theorists" maintaining that it does, and their critics, such as Thomas Hobbes and later Isaiah Berlin, that it does not. In Skinner's account, the republican camp has thus been broadened and made to include adherents of all sorts of constitutional arrangements short of absolutism, not just republican writers in a strict sense. These "neo-Roman theorists"—among whom Skinner counts Harrington, Machiavelli, Milton, More, Nedham, Neville, and Sidney—saw individual liberty as conditioned upon the existence of a "free state," drawing upon an analogy between individual freedom as non-slavery and the freedom of states as not being subject to tyrannical rule.[23]

Reinforcing the dichotomy between Hobbes' and the republican, "neo-Roman" conception of liberty Skinner, in *Hobbes and Republican Liberty* (2008), deepens his claim that what Hobbes was fundamentally opposing was the view, defended by certain "Democraticall Gentlemen," that to live freely is to live in a republic as opposed to a monarchy—that to live freely is impossible in a monarchy. Skinner's interpretation of Hobbes' conception of liberty as it appears in *Leviathan* seems strained and narrow in giving too much weight to what Hobbes calls "the proper sense" of liberty, and in neglecting the fact that Hobbes, when talking about the liberty of subjects, and political liberty, does not seem to adhere to this "proper sense," but rather to a view of liberty as consisting in liberty from the "artificial chains" of laws and covenants—in liberty from Constant's "empire of the legislator," in short.[24]

The conception of liberty in *Leviathan* constrains the sovereign, moreover, in various ways: subjects are at liberty to disobey the sovereign's command to abstain from the use of food, air, medicine, "or any other thing, without which he cannot live."[25] Subjects are free to refrain from accusing themselves, and are of course free to exercise self-defense and defend their own lives against the sovereign absent an

---

22. Holmes, *Passions*, p. 28.

23. Skinner, *Liberty, passim*. See also id., "Negative Liberty," p. 203.

24. See Gert, "Review Skinner."

25. Hobbes, *Leviathan*, vol. 2, chap. 21, p. 336. For a convincing constitutionalist interpretation of Hobbes, see Dyzenhaus, "Hobbes' Constitutional Theory"; and see Chapter 7 and the Epilogue.

offer of pardon.[26] Thus nothing may be interpreted according to *Leviathan* as the subject's consent to giving up these liberties—indeed, there is a very strong constitutionalist conception of inalienable rights derived from an a priori view of the state of nature. But while it might be accurate to interpret Hobbes' conception of liberty as a rather narrow one, Skinner's account is much less convincing with regard to his opposition between the so-called "neo-Roman" theorists on the one hand and liberals "after liberalism," such as Benjamin Constant, on the other. It seems that, although deliberately allowing for a wide range of constitutional make-ups, the writers he calls "neo-Roman" are in fact united, not so much by their fierce resistance to monarchy (as in Hobbes' caricature of their stance),[27] but rather by a commitment to constitutional safeguards limiting the authority of government. Skinner does mention this aspect briefly, but without paying sufficient attention to it; his "neo-Roman" theorists, in permitting for "a monarch to be the ruler of a free state," surely qualify as proponents of "self-rule" and liberty only through their commitment to safeguards which deprive the "head of state . . . of any power to reduce the body of the commonwealth to a condition of dependence."[28]

But if this is so, what distinctly "neo-Roman" properties remain? Or, to put it differently, do not these theorists themselves seem to be subscribing to an ideal of liberty "after liberalism" after all? In stressing constitutional safeguards and elevating them to the status of necessary and sufficient conditions of liberty, are these writers not in fact giving up anything distinctly "neo-Roman" in favor of the liberal view, shared by Hobbes and Constant, according to which it is not the "source of the law but its extent"[29] that matters? If safeguards are key, regardless of the precise constitutional structure surrounding them, it would seem that the distinction between neo-Roman and liberal collapses, opening up

26. *Leviathan*, vol. 2, ch. 21, pp. 336–337.

27. Ibid., vol. 2, chap. 29, pp. 506–507.

28. Skinner, *Liberty*, pp. 54–55. For criticism of Skinner and Pettit's views, stressing the compatibility of Roman republican liberty with a certain amount of paternalism, see Kapust, "Skinner, Pettit and Livy." It is noteworthy that Pettit's stress on "non-domination" as the crucial feature of republicanism does give constitutionalism its due; his republicanism is, however, consequentialist in orientation, unlike the Roman tradition discussed here (*Republicanism*, pp. 99–102). Moreover, Pettit seems to glide from a "Roman," constitutionalist standard of justice (that verges on collapsing into liberalism) to a Rousseauvian account where well-designed democratic processes are sufficient to guarantee freedom as non-domination. See Pettit, *Republicanism*; id., *On the People's Terms*. Cf. Dyzenhaus, "Critical Notice of *On the People's Terms*." Non-domination resembles at times Hobbesian peace and security; *pace* Pettit, it may best be achieved by Hobbesian means.

29. Skinner, *Liberty*, p. 85. See Hobbes, *Leviathan*, vol. 2, chap. 21, p. 332.

once again the gap between liberalism, neo-Roman or not, and republicanism of the narrow sort which is concerned with participation, virtue, and self-rule rather than constraints on the sovereign authority—"Athenian republicanism," as it were, in keeping with a view of Athens prevalent until at least George Grote and John Stuart Mill in the nineteenth century. Ironically, the historical and institutional reality of Athens—as opposed to the view of Athens propounded in theoretical and normative texts—especially from the late fifth century BC onwards would actually hold much interest for those interested in constitutionalism and its institutions. This has been obscured by the fact that at least until Grote, interest in Greek history did not extend chronologically beyond the Arginusae trial, to put it crudely. The Athenian institutions most pertinent to a history of constitutionalism—a sort of judicial review (the *graphe paranomon*) and the distinction between higher-order norms (*nomoi*) and mere decrees (*psephismata*)—remained thus largely hidden from view for most of the history of political thought.[30] By contrast, Greek political *thought* (as opposed to constitutional reality) has of course had immense impact over the centuries. The institutional and historical realities of late republican Rome, on the other hand, remained much closer to, and indeed provided the impetus for, the specifically Roman kind of political and constitutional thought that is going to interest us in the course of this book.

Wherever historians were inclined to draw the distinction, and whatever the differences between the various scholarly approaches described, a belief in the basic dichotomy between ancient republicanism and modern liberalism is common to all of them. The belief seems to rest on two, usually implicit assumptions: first, the assumption that there is such a thing as "ancient republicanism," i.e., that the various versions of classical republicanism and instances of actual republics as evidenced by classical literature, philosophy, and historiography can be said to share a sufficient number of properties to make the unifying concept meaningful; and second, the assumption that the concept of liberty as based on individual rights and on constraints on public powers is a distinctly modern idea, liberty after liberalism as it were, paying less attention to self-government but stressing the limits of Constant's "empire of the legislator."

Republicanism has been the Roman legacy most emphasized in the historiography of political thought; at times, a certain kind of republicanism has also influentially been taken to have some normative upshot, as in Quentin Skinner and Philip Pettit's work on freedom as non-domination. This view

30. Except for Hume, who showed interest in these institutions, as we will see in Chapter 5. Cf. Ostwald, *Popular Sovereignty*.

has been criticized, both on normative and on historical grounds.[31] My book seeks to be read as a contribution to that literature, from both an ancient historian's and an intellectual historian's point of view, and I hope that it will be read by historians of political thought as well as by classicists. The legacy of Roman political thought as stressed in my account is not to be confounded with that focused on by Skinner and Pettit; rather, it is the Roman contribution to a specific view of politics that centers on certain rights and norms achieved and guaranteed by a set of higher-order constitutional rules, rules that are understood to have legal character. This I take to be an extremely influential as well as rather specific outgrowth of the crises of the late Roman Republic that can profitably be contrasted with Greek political thought. That the institutional arrangements of the Roman Republic were highly successful and therefore noteworthy is a view that was advanced already in classical antiquity by the Greek historian Polybius, and it has since had its share of important adherents, first among them Machiavelli.[32] This view, however, is one that subscribes to a highly pragmatic, if not outright cynical, position on the criteria for success: Roman imperial expansion was thought to be the chief achievement of the republican constitutional order. As such it is a rather odd candidate to serve as a model for the theory of "freedom as non-domination," as Clifford Ando has pointed out. But there has always been another, less empirically minded interpretation of the constitutional setup of the Roman Republic, and it is this *normative* view of the Roman model that will interest us here.

Due to Benjamin Constant's ancient-modern dichotomy, a distinct Roman constitutional tradition, not to be confused with Skinner's "neo-Roman" republicanism, has been lost from sight. For us to see it again, it will be necessary to disassemble the far too broad concept of "ancient republicanism" by paying close attention to its Roman parts. Much progress has already been made in this regard in recent years. A certain reorientation, increasingly skeptical of the unifying concept "ancient republicanism" and more sensitive to differentiation, is already visible in the historiography of political thought. Earlier research that had assumed "classical republicanism" *tout court*[33] has given way to studies focusing on the substantial differences between Greek and Roman political thought

31. See, e.g., Ando, *Law*, ch. 5.

32. However, as we will see Polybius, unlike Machiavelli, offers a genuinely normative justification for Roman constitutionalism, above and beyond the prudential aspects of his admiration for Rome.

33. See, e.g., Pocock, *Machiavellian Moment*.

and institutional legal history.[34] Much of the progress was made possible by paying increased attention to the ancient world itself, to its institutions and its political thought, and to the rich literature developed by ancient historians, classicists, and historians of Greek and Roman philosophy.

Manifestations of this can be found in the work of ancient historians and classicists who focus on the legacy of classical antiquity in the later history of political thought, such as that of Peter Garnsey, Fergus Millar, Wilfried Nippel, Paul Rahe, Elizabeth Rawson, and Jennifer Tolbert Roberts. In tandem with this development, historians of political thought—of the so-called Cambridge School and beyond—have been giving increasing attention to the rich and relevant body of scholarship produced by classicists, such as Chaim Wirszubski's seminal monograph on Roman *libertas*, Andrew Lintott's work on the Roman republican constitution, Robert Morstein-Marx's innovative scholarship on the *contiones* of the late Republic, Claude Nicolet's on Roman citizenship, Wilfried Nippel's work on *Mischverfassungstheorie* or Kurt von Fritz's book on *The Theory of the Mixed Constitution in Antiquity*. Moreover there is a marked tendency, at least in American academia, for classicists and ancient historians to work not only on the history of (ancient) political thought, but increasingly on problems in political theory proper. Examples for this tendency are not hard to find—Josiah Ober, Ryan Balot, Kinch Hoekstra, and, most recently, Jed Atkins account for some of the most interesting and visible scholarship in this regard.

My book seeks to make a contribution to this kind of literature by practicing the history of political thought as the history of the reception of classical antiquity. I hope that this will be of interest to ancient historians, historians of political thought, legal historians, early modernists, and political theorists alike. Furthermore, it is hoped that the ideas, institutions, and historical development explored in this study may have something to offer even to those of a more empirical bent. In the last forty years economists, economic historians, and political scientists, especially scholars associated with neo-institutional economics, have shown a keen interest in the development of institutions and their relevance for the behavior of historical agents.[35] Constitutional thought as discussed in this book is shown to have arisen against the background of late republican

---

34. See Millar, *Roman Republic*; Nelson, *Greek Tradition*; Hammer, *Roman Political Thought*; id., *Roman Political Thought from Cicero*; and Skinner's and Pettit's work on republicanism.

35. See North, *Institutions*; North, Wallis and Weingast, *Violence*; and North and Weingast, "Constitutions and Commitment," for an application of neo-institutionalism to English constitutionalism after 1688. Cf. also Acemoglu and Robinson, *Nations*, pp. 158–164 for an account of the institutions of the Roman Republic as "inclusive" and thus providing economic incentives.

institutions and politics, but it also testifies to the historically powerful effect of ideas and to the large body of thought that is presupposed by the constitutional institutions we inhabit in the West. Constitutionalism as investigated here is, furthermore, not just one institution among many; rather, it is the basis and fundamental framework on which all other institutions rest. Institutions matter, but they presuppose constitutionalism. Constitutionalism is pivotal, but it presupposes a particular political theory. To explain the emergence of Roman constitutional thought against the backdrop of the fall of the late Republic is not to reduce these constitutional ideas to their historical context. Constitutionalism, understood as political theory and remedy against republican decline, is not merely epiphenomenal but can be shown empirically to have acquired causal force of its own over the long term. Having a normative constitution in the relevant sense is, on the view of the tradition described in this book, a necessary condition for a political order that is both stable and just.[36]

As for the set of problems I am setting out to deal with in the present book, the political ideas on constitutionalism and emergencies arising out of the constitutional crises of the late Roman Republic, and their legacy in the history of Western political and constitutional thinking, these have not been dealt with comprehensively or even coherently in the literature.[37] On the ancient side of things, there is no comprehensive scholarly work dealing with the constitutional history of the late Republic's various emergency institutions and exceptional powers.[38] One reason for this might be an increased skepticism among scholars towards the effectiveness of legal rules in classical antiquity in general, and increased interest and sensitivity towards the role of forces other than law in fostering social cohesion.[39] Moreover, ever since Ronald Syme's path-breaking *Roman Revolution* (1939)[40] there has been a strong tendency to describe the development from Republic to Principate in terms of the disintegration of the old

36. My thinking about constitutionalism and its importance owes an obvious debt to a body of scholarship by Jon Elster and Stephen Holmes. See Elster, *Ulysses and the Sirens*; id., *Ulysses Unbound*; Holmes, *Passions*.

37. For the fall of the Republic, see Bleicken, *Geschichte*, pp. 242–246; id., *Gedanken*; Bringmann, *Krise und Ende*, esp. pp. 93–95; Christ, "Untergang," esp. pp. 150–157; id., *Krise und Untergang*. See also Beard and Crawford, *Rome in the Late Republic*; Meier, *Res publica amissa*; Deininger, "Zur Kontroverse"; Gruen, *Last Generation*.

38. But see Nippel, *Aufruhr*; Lintott, *Violence*; id., *Constitution*Arena, *Libertas*, pp. 179–220; Golden, *Crisis Management* (cf. Straumann "Review Golden"); Vervaet, *High Command*, ch. 7.

39. See, e.g., Nippel, *Public Order*; for a similar view of Athens, see Cohen, *Law*.

40. Syme famously referred to the republican constitution as "a screen and a sham": *Roman Revolution*, p. 15.

nobility and with prosopographical means,[41] a tendency that has been complemented, and to a degree superseded, by attempts to describe the institutions of the Roman Republic—seemingly inspired by approaches developed in political science—in structural terms by reference to their underlying social forces.[42] While few scholars during the last thirty years were prepared to ascribe crucial causal force to the constitutional makeup of the Roman Republic, and although some have indeed declared Roman constitutional law a non-entity,[43] an enduring belief in the "centrality of the legal and constitutional machinery at Rome"[44] can still be found in relatively recent scholarly work, and Theodor Mommsen's *Römisches Staatsrecht* continues to exert a defining influence on the literature[45]—all the while never having been translated into English.

Indeed, the most provocative and influential recent account of the late Roman Republic's constitutional setup that has shaped the debate in the field for the last twenty years, that of Fergus Millar, has been subjected to severe criticism precisely due to its alleged adherence to an ideal-typical, meta-historical conceptual framework in the tradition of nineteenth-century *Begriffsjurisprudenz*.[46] Karl-Joachim Hölkeskamp and, with a different emphasis, Martin Jehne have instead proposed to approach the Roman Republic through a description in terms of its "political culture," comprehensively understood, rather than in narrowly legal terms.[47] Jochen Bleicken, who in his *Lex Publica* had discussed and

41. Wiseman, *New Men*, and Gruen, *Last Generation*, are best seen in this tradition, which has emerged out of the early prosopographical works by Drumann and Groebe and the later contributions especially by Münzer and Gelzer to *Paulys Realenzyklopädie*; see, e.g., Drumann, *Geschichte Roms*; Münzer, *Adelsparteien*; id., "Ti. Sempronius Gracchus"; Gelzer, *Pompeius*. For important criticism, see Brunt, "Fall"; North, "Politics and Aristocracy."

42. Meier, *Res publica* has inspired and influenced research ever since its publication in 1966 and could be described as initiating the program of examining the "political culture," rather than the constitution, of the Republic. For the research of the last decades, see Hölkeskamp, *Rekonstruktionen*, see for Meier's impact especially pp. 31–56.

43. For an ascription of this view to Eduard Fraenkel, see Daube, "Das Selbstverständliche," p. 10.

44. Lintott, *Violence*, p. xxvii.

45. On Mommsen's *Staatsrecht* and its continuing impact, see the contributions in Nippel and Seidensticker, *Mommsens langer Schatten*. Cf. also Grziwotz, *Verfassungsbegriff*, pp. 25–284.

46. See especially Millar, *Crowd*. For criticism of Millar, see Hölkeskamp, *Senatus*, pp. 257–277 (review of Millar, *Crowd*); id., *Reconstructing*, pp. 12–14; Jehne, *Demokratie*, p. 8. See also Mouritsen, *Plebs*. For the role of the *contiones*, see Morstein-Marx, *Mass Oratory*; see also the important study of elections in late republican Rome by Yakobson, *Elections*; cf. Harris, "On Defining."

47. Hölkeskamp is indebted to Christian Meier's work. See Hölkeskamp, *Rekonstruktionen*, pp. 57–72; id., "Ein 'Gegensatz'"; Jehne, "Die Volksversammlungen," pp. 149–160, with further references.

fundamentally criticized Mommsen's approach, can be seen as staking out a middle ground: the role of the *mos maiorum* and other not prima facie normative sets of legal rules is taken into account, without, however, underestimating the importance of specifically constitutional and legal arguments in the late Roman Republic and thus without collapsing the distinction between the *mos maiorum, leges*, and other broadly constitutional sets of rules on the one hand and political practices in general on the other.[48]

For the purposes of the present work it will be crucial to acknowledge, with Bleicken, the importance of a concept of constitutional rules distinct from other action-guiding norms but inclusive of rules such as those contained in the *mos*.[49] The concept of constitution applied will thus be broader than Mommsen's yet narrower than Martin Jehne's concept of *Institutionalität*.[50] This is necessary because it is one of the working assumptions of this book that certain rules that can be reasonably termed "constitutional" did have that distinct status in the minds of the crucial actors in the late Republic, and that certain actions and arguments cannot be completely described without reference to the concept of constitutional rules;[51] reducing the "constitutional" to "political culture" might leave one unable to account adequately for the specific normative weight and juridical quality of certain rules in the late Roman Republic. Institutions and the ideas motivating them are "a peculiar organism with a life of their own: they are in their essence the creations of the dead and they weigh on the living; they are like a coral reef, part petrified, part alive, and on that solid rock often crush those who wish to reform or reject them, as the Gracchi and Caesar were to find."[52] As Jochen Bleicken put it in his review of Christian Meier's *Res publica amissa*, this resulted in a view that endowed the state with a *legal* nature, a view that was still alive and well in Augustus' principate.[53] It is well worth stressing, moreover, that Mommsen was not as anachronistic a *Begriffsjurist* as is commonly assumed: his terminology in the *Staatsrecht* is largely taken from the sources, and he is in fact highly

48. Bleicken, *Lex Publica*, pp. 16–51; 432–439; id., *Verfassung*, pp. 12–14; Bleicken uses the term *Verfassung* without scare quotes. See also Grziwotz, *Verfassungsverständnis*; id., *Verfassungsbegriff*. For discussion of Mommsen's conceptual categories, see Kunkel, "Bericht"; Wieacker, *Rechtsgeschichte*, pp. 343–345, 353–354; Kunkel and Wittmann, *Staatsordnung*, p. 15; Thomas, *Mommsen*.

49. Cf. Hölkeskamp, *Reconstructing*, p. 17.

50. Jehne, "Die Volksversammlungen," pp. 155–158, esp. p. 156.

51. For the reasons given by Raz, *Practical Reason*, pp. 108–111.

52. Linderski, "Review Lintott," p. 591.

53. Bleicken, "Rezension Meier," p. 460. Indeed, a certain juridical constitutionalist mindset was absolutely central to Roman political culture.

sensitive to political and social context, as Aloys Winterling has recently pointed out.[54] It is precisely one of the defining features of the political culture of the late Republic as evidenced by the sources that this was a culture where political institutions and procedures were expressed in *juridical norms*, and that these norms, whose existence and relevance are indeed "undeniable,"[55] developed a normative pull quite independent of purely political or purely economic considerations. When in 133 BC murder became for the first time a prominent tool of domestic politics and Tiberius Gracchus' discharge of his colleague in office was being viewed even by the many with skepticism and outright disapproval,[56] it would seem to be incumbent upon us to focus our scholarly attention on the *violation of norms* on which the interest of our sources seems to center. It is common to interpret the resistance to Gracchus as the reaction of economic interests to his agrarian policies; however, both recent research and the language of the sources suggest that it was not so much Gracchus' redistributive policies—which in any case continued for years, probably concerned much less land than the pro-Gracchan accounts assume, sought to distribute land possessed by Italian allies, not citizens, and which can be seen, at least to some extent, as successful[57]—but rather his violation of constitutional norms that provoked resistance even among the many. Cicero pointed out that it was not the agrarian issue nor any other policy-related question that had ruined Tiberius Gracchus, but his exalted view of the power of the comitia and his violation of the constitutionally guaranteed sacrosanctity of a tribune: "What else was there that brought him down, if not the abrogation of the power of a colleague who intervened?"[58] It may well be that Cicero exhibited blindness to the social realities of his time, but this should not blind us to the very real constitutional issues that troubled the late Republic.

This book is thus committed to a belief in the centrality of the republican constitution and its normative character; the fact that the major political actors during the Republic's last hundred years were expressing their conflicting views and attitudes as conflicting interpretations of the republican constitution, expressed in legal terminology, must be taken seriously. The late Republic knew, at the very least, an inchoate constitutionalism.[59] The various crises the late Roman Republic endured were invariably accompanied by,

54. Winterling, "Dyarchie," p. 193.

55. Ibid.

56. Plut. *Ti. Gracch.* 15.1.

57. Bringmann, *Agrarreform*; Lintott, *Judicial Reform*, pp. 45–58; Roselaar, *Public Land.*

58. Cic. *Leg.* 3.24. Trans. Zetzel. But cf. the utterly orthodox and Sallustian interpretation of the Republic's fall by Wiseman, "The Two-Headed State."

59. Cf. Nippel, "Gesetze," p. 97.

and to a degree the expression of, radically diverging interpretations of the Republic's constitution. It was these *constitutional interpretations*, that is to say, legal arguments, that seemed to have resonance among the followers of the various leaders and yield the support needed, and the arguments made for or against emergency measures and for or against the qualification of circumstances as exceptional were arguments for or against the *constitutionality* of such measures, or lack thereof—in short, these protagonists did indeed have a (however inchoate) normative concept of a constitution.[60] Similarly, the theoretical remedies presented for the reform of the Republic, successful or not, were of a constitutional nature, as were the institutional remedies eventually imposed by Octavian. Accusations by political protagonists of the late Republic that their antagonists are misinterpreting the constitutional norms of their commonwealth, e.g., the claim that some course of action or a particular piece of legislation is in fact everything but *iure*, do not imply that there are no such constitutional norms operating in the background—on the contrary, the intensity of these arguments in fact presupposes the assumption of such norms, as we will see in Chapters 2 and 3.

Part of the reason for classicists' skepticism when it comes to the use of the terms "constitutional" or "constitution" lies, I suspect, in a largely implicit conception of constitution that these scholars bring to their sources: are not constitutions written documents? Do they not supply clear textual guidance on constitutional questions? Do they not provide for enforceable basic constitutional rights? And do they not foresee a final arbiter where the constitutional buck stops and where constitutional decisions are taken once and for all: judicial review? This is largely a semantic issue; we are of course completely free to raise these elements to the status of essential criteria, but we must be aware that this would effectively dismiss most historical phenomena ever addressed under the label "constitutionalism" and bring a rather provincial, recent concept to the historical problem. From the English constitutional model admired by Montesquieu to the early American constitution to the Weimar constitution—to name but the most glaring examples—none would qualify under the rigid criteria sketched above, be it for a lack of judicial review (as in the early American republic), a lack of writtenness (as in the British case), or a lack of enforceable basic rights (Weimar). Indeed, these criteria turn out to be rather naïve even when applied to much more recent examples. Scholars of the jurisprudence of the US Supreme Court are well aware of the difficulties that a lack of textual evidence can pose in adjudicating constitutional issues, but that can hardly

---

60. On the applicability of such concepts to historical and alien cultures, see Raz, "Theory of Law."

be taken as evidence for the United States' lacking a normative constitution; and the fact that in most of today's legal systems writtenness is neither a necessary nor a sufficient condition for constitutional norms is not to be interpreted as proof that these systems are constitutionless.

To explain the normative weight of certain rules in the late Roman Republic, the specifically Roman and significantly juridical flavor encountered in the late republican sources, I propose the following criteria for a working concept of constitutionality in the late Republic: a) *entrenchment*, i.e., rules that are considered more entrenched, harder to change, and thus less malleable than other rules; b) *political importance*, i.e., rules that are of great importance in that they govern the institutions through which political power is exercised; c) *normative importance*, i.e. rules that betray the political system's and its protagonists' underlying political theory; and d) that the rules in question are assigned a *juridical quality*, that is to say, they are part of recognizably legal arguments.

It is crucial to bear in mind, however, that I am not concerned to argue that there was, or was not, in fact a constitution in late republican Rome; rather, it is my aim to show, in the first part of this study, that Romans in the last century of the Republic were highly sensitive to the necessity of being able to assess the legitimacy of emergency measures, magistracies, and certain legislation, with reference to higher-order and more firmly entrenched norms. My argument operates, that is, primarily on the plane of constitutional *thought* and argument, not of institutions—although of course a fair amount of institutional and historical context will need to be discussed, especially in Part I of the book. I wish to insist that diverging interpretations of the constitution were at the center of the crisis of the late Republic, something that emerges both in the political debates and conflicts of the period and, as we will see in Part II, in the theoretical, more properly philosophical reflections of Cicero. The Roman concept of constitution developed out of the crises of the Republic—the birth of constitutionalism out of the spirit of the late Republic, as it were—and Cicero and others were convinced by these crises and the increasing emergence of extraordinary commands and emergency measures that there was a need for constitutional norms. In his works of political theory, Cicero can be seen to search for and develop the norms and rights that he thought should provide the substance of this constitutionalism. It is above all this constitutional focus, I shall argue, which is unique to Roman political thought, and which distinguishes it crucially from its Greek predecessor. This constitutional focus is itself to be seen in the context, and indeed as an integral part, of the intellectual revolution Claudia Moatti has termed Rome's "age of reason."[61]

61. Moatti, *Raison de Rome*, p. 54.

Part III will be concerned with the afterlife of these Roman ideas. For many thinkers from the Renaissance onward, it was Roman constitutional thought, an understanding of the higher-order norms that set limits on government, which set the Republic apart, not Roman virtue, as Sallust or Augustine had suggested. Most importantly, the anxieties provoked by the Republic's fall, and the insight that the crises that had brought about this fall were of a constitutional nature, proved to be the well from which sprang, from Bodin onward, the idea of constitutionalism as a remedy to the problems that had plagued the Republic. Bodin is indeed crucial to this perspective; from him there can be seen to emanate a tradition of concern with the fall of the Roman Republic that does not trust the Sallustian cliché of the Republic's demise as the effect of a lack of virtue. Constitutionalism and constitutional design, not virtue, constitute the answer for this tradition, which starts with Bodin and leads, by way of Montesquieu, to John Adams and the new, large republic across the Atlantic. The inchoate constitutionalism of the last century of the Roman Republic met with the interest of these early modern authors, who, under Bodin's influence, started to describe the constitutional conflicts of the late Republic in terms of sovereignty. There was always a question of sovereignty lurking implicitly in the constitutional debates of the late Republic; Bodin, and Pomponius before him, brought this out and made their readers and intellectual successors see the crises of the Republic through the prism of sovereignty, and sovereignty through the prism of Roman republican history. Theirs was a new, constitutional republicanism, "short on virtue,"[62] but dedicated to avoiding the Roman Republic's fate—military despotism. While the natural lawyers from Gentili and Grotius onward may be said to have provided an ever more detailed and extremely influential normative picture of a pre- or extra-political state of nature, the constitutional tradition followed here was concerned with the fragility of self-government and the constitutional institutions thought key to keeping republics both just and stable.[63] This tradition culminates in the *Federalist Papers* and, especially, John Adams' political thought—indeed, looking at the differences between late eighteenth-century French and American approaches to sovereignty and constitutionalism through the framework of their respective notions of the Roman Republic is particularly instructive: while virtue lies at

62. Shklar, "Montesquieu," p. 279.

63. The two traditions are distinct, but complementary; for the natural law tradition and its reliance on a tradition of private Roman law, see Kingsbury and Straumann, "State of Nature"; eid., "Introduction"; Straumann, "*Corpus iuris* as a Source of Law"; id., *Roman Law in the State of Nature*.

the heart of the rhetoric of the Mountain and the *Comité de salut public*, Adams, suspicious of virtue, recognizes the *constitutional* nature of the crises and failure of the Roman Republic. Thus Bodin, Cato, Montesquieu, Adams, and the *Federalist* did not simply limit their attention to "early Rome as the repository of republican *uirtus*."[64] Rather, they were interested in the constitutional aspects of the *fall* of the Republic and united in the thought that constitutional remedies, not republican *virtus*, could have prevented the Republic from falling.

Methodologically, I hope that the survey offered in this book may serve as an example for the kind of *longue durée* intellectual history David Armitage has recently called for.[65] Prompted by the historical experience of the fall of the Republic, Cicero and his contemporaries sought to give a constitutional answer to the crises of their age. This inchoate constitutionalism, refined by Cicero in his more theoretical works, was then taken up by those thinkers who struggled to develop answers to problems of their own, but the "unit-ideas," or basic conceptual components, developed in the Roman sources were put to use, not unlike *spolia*, to build political orders that could escape the fate of the Roman Republic.[66] As Jerzy Linderski has observed, in "history there is no end," and the end of the Republic, "the decay of this great republican (though by no means democratic!) system was a defining event in Western history until the rise of American republicanism."[67] The crises of the late Roman Republic were the experimental political context within which there took shape an extremely influential response to what the relevant writers assumed were perennial problems of self-governing republics.[68] This response, although first formulated inchoately in a specific setting, proved so deep, interesting, and convincing that many later thinkers took the propositional content and universalizability of the Roman texts under serious consideration and elaborated the constitutionalism they found there. Out of this engagement with a longstanding problem, the decay of the paradigmatic republic, they drew certain conclusions that were characterized by their distrust of virtue and their

64. Zetzel, "Review Millar."

65. Armitage, "Big Idea."

66. For a convincing attempt at rejuvenating Lovejoy's unit-ideas, and an equally convincing defense of Lovejoy's contextualist credentials, see Knight, "Unit-Ideas Unleashed." See also McMahon and Moyn, *Rethinking*, esp. ch. 1.

67. Linderski, "Review Lintott," p. 592.

68. See the methodological views offered in my *Roman Law in the State of Nature*, pp. 19–23; see also Steinberger, "Analysis and History."

reliance on higher-order rules and institutions, conclusions that came to be grouped under the label "constitutionalism."

To sum up: the Constantian dichotomy between ancient and modern liberty, while conceptually coherent, has obscured the historical fact that there was a distinct Roman tradition of constitutional and political thought, arising in the late Roman Republic and springing to life again in the Renaissance, which concerned itself primarily with constitutional safeguards and limits to government—a concept of constitution that had emerged out of the crises of the late Republic. Intensely preoccupied with the precise extent of legitimate government power, constitutional and political thought as exhibited in Cicero's works and forensic speeches and as reflected in Livy's historiography was sparked by the constitutional crises that led to the Republic's end, and originally focused above all on emergency powers, dictatorship, and extraordinary measures which were thought necessary to save the Republic's constitution or to precipitate the demise of the republican order. In the context of the collapse of the republican institutions, however, both the arguments and debates on the ground as well as—especially—Cicero's mature political theory assumed a new quality. The dysfunctional institutions of the Republic came to resemble, suggestively, a state of nature; the recourse to emergency measures and the emergence of big men with extraordinary powers convinced Cicero and likeminded politicians of the need for a normative constitution grounded in natural law and natural justice, and set them searching for the norms and rights which would be its substance. The result, a specifically Roman, normative concept of constitution was very different from anything Greek political thought had ever produced.

PART I

Inchoate Constitutionalism in the Late Roman Republic

One of the goals of this book is to convince its readers that Roman political thought, as encapsulated most conspicuously in the works of Cicero, must be construed as a radical departure from Greek thinking on the subject of politics. It will be suggested that Roman political thought should be interpreted against the backdrop, and as the result, of the crises of the late Roman Republic; and that those crises should properly be understood as the expression of radically diverging interpretations of the Republic's most fundamental norms, that is to say, constitutional norms. The political conflicts from the Gracchi onwards and the civil wars triggered by them were characterized, first and foremost, by the "antinomy between the authority of the senate," on the one hand, "and the rights of the people,"[1] on the other, where both the *auctoritas patrum* and the rights of the Roman People functioned as constitutional concepts and where the proper limits of the legislative reach of the popular assemblies were no less contested than the legitimate scope of the Senate's authority. At least from the Gracchi onwards, then, there existed *two* rival, mutually exclusive and at least prima facie equally plausible interpretations of the republican constitution, one popular, and one from the senatorial viewpoint.[2]

The existence of these two rival interpretations required, however, a concept of constitution presupposed by all the political actors of the time. In the following chapter I will argue that such a concept can for the late Republic be applied to a set of rules that were thought to be both more entrenched and more important than other legal rules, and I will attempt to show how that concept

1. Brunt, "Fall," p. 34.

2. See Nippel, "Roman Notion," p. 21; Grziwotz, *Verfassungsverständnis*, pp. 311–349.

was worked out, and increasingly appealed to, in the context of the crises[3] and violent contests of the late Republic. One might say that appeals to such a body of constitutional norms were assuming all the more urgency the less the normal institutions of the Republic proved workable, and that such appeals were at their height precisely when the rival interpretations of the constitution, of that "something," in John Stuart Mill's words, "which is settled, something permanent, and not to be called in question," had become too divergent for the constitutional and institutional apparatus to adjudicate and were thus settled by force. Indeed, when reading Mill on those necessary background assumptions that guarantee the functioning of any constitutional order, and his description of their decay, it is hard not to be reminded of the late Roman Republic:

> [I]n all political societies which have had a durable existence, there has been some fixed point: something which people agreed in holding sacred; which wherever freedom of discussion was a recognised principle, it was of course lawful to contest in theory, but which no one could either fear or hope to see shaken in practice; which, in short (except perhaps during some temporary crisis) was in the common estimation placed beyond discussion. . . . A state never is, nor until mankind are vastly improved, can hope to be, for any long time exempt from internal dissension; for there neither is nor has ever been any state of society in which collisions did not occur between the immediate interests and passions of powerful sections of the people. What, then, enables nations to weather these storms . . .? Precisely this—that however important the interests about which men fell out, the conflict did not affect the fundamental principle of the system of social union which happened to exist . . .. But when the questioning of these fundamental principles is . . . the habitual condition of the body politic, and when all the violent animosities are called forth, which spring naturally from such a situation, the state is virtually in a position of civil war; and can never long remain free from it in act and fact.[4]

It could be said that such questioning of the "fundamental principle," the constitution, of the Roman Republic became its "habitual condition" from the Gracchi onward; and that the strain put on the functioning of the Republic by that questioning led to a consciousness of the importance and necessity of a "fixed point"; so that when what had been largely an "implicit constitution" until the late second

3. See, on the application of the term "crisis" to the decline of the Republic, the discussion in Flower, *Roman Republics*, pp. ix–x. See also the contributions in Hölkeskamp, *Politische Kultur.*

4. Mill, *System of Logic*, Part II, VI.10.5.

century BC became contested, the need to engage in explicit constitutional argument and, on the level of political philosophy, constitutional theory, made itself felt. The appeal, in an institutional setting before the Roman People or before the Senate, to norms beyond and above mere legislation led increasingly to the development of what one might call a specifically Roman "jural" conception of politics. This conception acknowledged, both in practice and in constitutional theory, the necessity of an "explicit constitution," a fundamental, permanent "fixed point," and in Cicero's speeches and in particular in his philosophical works this conception culminated in a constitutionalism based on natural law.

In this jural conception of politics the idea of entrenched constitutional norms occupied center stage. Unlike eudaemonistic Greek theorizing about politics, the Roman jural conception did not put the main emphasis on the need for laws to create virtuous citizens and thus create the conditions for the good life; rather, it sought constitutional remedies for a situation characterized by decaying institutions and civil war. More often than not, the perceived need for such remedies was brought into focus by seemingly boundless legislative activity. At the same time, the decay of institutions and the loss of the Republic posed the question of what norms, if any, held in a state where the institutions and positive laws had been destroyed.[5] When one of the chief protagonists of the constitutional debates evolving around emergency powers, Cicero, came around to formulating treatises on political philosophy, these expressed many of the views that had dominated the constitutional debates and the jural conception of politics inherent in these views. The backdrop of the failing Republic, with its hectic lawmaking and increasingly unenforceable written laws, posed the very real question of the locus of sovereignty and its limits and could serve as a vivid and frightening model of the state of nature. Roman political thought, especially as it appears in Cicero's theoretical work, has consequently developed a concern with the idea of the state of nature and its relation with the state; this concern led to the development of a concept of entrenched principles that hold even if not expressed as the people's will in legislation; and thus a jural view of politics as limited by law-like constitutional principles emerges which bears no similarity with the Aristotelian view of the continuity between ethics and politics, with the natural priority of the *polis* to the individual, and with politics as—at best—ensuring virtue.

5. Cic. *Phil.* 11.28. See Girardet, "Rechtsstellung," pp. 227ff.

I

"*Not Some Piece of Legislation*"

THE ROMAN CONCEPT OF CONSTITUTION

DID THE ROMANS have the concept of constitution? This chapter presents the case for thinking that the Romans were in fact perfectly capable of thinking in terms of higher-order constitutional norms, norms that are in effect being presupposed by any attempt at formulating emergency powers. First a positive answer is given to the question of whether in the late Roman Republic the concept of constitution can be found in the realm of political ideas. Then it is shown how the protagonists in the constitutional conflicts of the late Republic appealed to the sources of constitutional norms. It will be suggested that by evoking the concepts of *mos maiorum* and, most importantly, *ius*, the participants in constitutional debates were gesturing at sources of constitutional law above and beyond mere legislation.[6]

Although there is no dearth of scholarship dealing with the constitution of the Roman Republic or with certain constitutional features of the republican order, there is little literature—apart from Jochen Bleicken's work and important remarks by P. A. Brunt and Andrew Lintott—that confronts the fundamental issue of whether the Roman republican order can be profitably described in constitutional terms or not. More surprisingly, as Wilfried Nippel has pointed out in a recent essay, Christian Meier's important *Res publica amissa* does not contain much in the way of a principled discussion of the nature of Roman constitutional norms either[7]—a circumstance acknowledged by Meier.[8] There is of course much

6. For an argument against the existence of a hierarchy of norms in the late Republic, see Lundgreen, *Regelkonflikte*.

7. Nippel, "Regel," p. 121. See for a summary of Meier's remarks ibid., pp. 123–124.

8. Meier, "Antworten," p. 279. But see, for a recent attempt to show that we can meaningfully speak of Roman constitutionalism, Pani, *Costituzionalismo*.

scholarly debate about constitutional issues, but the participants in this debate have mostly made up their minds as to the applicability of the term "constitution" to the Roman Republic—either the term is applied without much further ado, or it is applied with scare quotes.

A screen and a sham? Tacitean views

The view that republican Rome did not have anything resembling a constitutional order with discernible, effective constitutional norms is one that is expressed with the utmost clarity by Ronald Syme: "The Roman constitution was a screen and a sham." Real causal importance could, on Syme's view, be ascribed only to the "forces that lay behind or beyond it,"[9] which leads effortlessly to a conception of Roman politics as representing mere "struggles for power within the ruling élite."[10] This view can be traced back at least to Tacitus. Turning against those who, like Polybius and Cicero in their different ways, had described the Roman republican constitution as a constitutional order where the popular element, the elite, and a monarchical element were joined together in a normative system, Tacitus seems to be denying not only the possibility of an enduring mixed constitution but, even more radically, the very possibility of *any constitutional order* with real normative pull; the model of a commonwealth joined together by selecting the elements of popular rule, the rule of a nobility, or of one man is more easily praised than achieved, according to Tacitus, and even if achieved cannot be lasting.[11] Tacitus does not deem a system of normative constitutional rules viable—what he thus has in mind instead is a description of actually obtaining power relations, that is to say, his student Syme's "forces that lay behind or beyond it," as opposed to a set of norms.

This seems prima facie consistent with Tacitus' view of the history of the Roman Republic, although Tacitus in an earlier passage in the *Annals* on republican history also leaves room for the view that a proper constitutional order can exist for a certain time, and subsequently undergo corruption. In his brief outline of the history of the Republic given in the third book of the *Annals*, describing the period from the expulsion of the kings to the Republic's downfall in the last century BC, Tacitus assigns the legislative activities of the People directed by the

9. Syme, *Roman Revolution*, p. 15. Cf. with Syme's terminology Luc. *Phars*. 9.207.

10. These words are Brunt's, who identifies as the mistaken basis of this conception the modern tendency to give too much importance to patronage: "Fall," p. 32. See also North, "Politics and Aristocracy."

11. Tac. *Ann*. 4.33.

tribunes of the plebs a key role in the fall of the Republic: while explicitly stating merely a strong correlation between the enactment of laws and the corruption of the Republic, Tacitus in fact invites the much stronger conclusion that legislation was the single most important *cause* of the Republic's fall. After Tarquinius' banishment, Tacitus writes, the People had made arrangements to protect liberty (*libertas*); the Twelve Tables represented the "greatest degree of just and equal law" (*finis aequi iuris*). However, subsequent laws (*secutae leges*) were carried by force (*per vim*) to "acquire illegal honors" or for other "crooked reasons." Sulla's reforms brought brief respite, but afterwards the tribunes' "license to drive people in whatever direction they themselves wished" was restored, and "now legal proceedings were instituted not only in general but against individual men, and, with the infection in the state at its peak (*corruptissima re publica*), the number of laws was at its greatest."[12]

Far from simply representing the history of the Republic as a series of power struggles within the elite, Tacitus gives an account of the Republic that is very much an account of functioning constitutional "arrangements" established to protect liberty and stability; the gradual demise of this functioning constitutional order is on this view brought about much later, through bad, unconstitutional legislation. By "subsequent laws" Tacitus refers, not to all and sundry legislation from the Twelve Tables to the end of the Republic, but rather to the legislation from 133 BC onward.[13] In Tacitus' polemical view, not only were these laws enacted by violence but also with base legislative intent (*ob prava latae sunt*). If this mainstream interpretation is correct and Tacitus is indeed confining his view of the corrupting impact of legislation to the period from the Gracchi onward, the historical development from the Twelve Tables to the late second century would seem to have been quite uneventful, constitutionally speaking, due to the fact that there were indeed constitutional rules that were being upheld and that provided not only stability over more than 300 years but also the protection of liberty and equality before the law. Tacitus implies that not only did the Twelve Tables themselves constitute just law to the highest degree, but the legislation following the Twelve Tables too seems to have given

12. Tac. *Ann.* 3.27. Trans. A. J. Woodman, except for my rendering of *finis aequi iuris* as "the greatest degree of just and equal law" rather than "culmination of fair legislation." *Aequum ius* has here the connotation of "equality before the law"; see Wirszubski, *Libertas*, p. 13; cf. Cic. *Off.* 2.41–42. Moreover, *ius* need not refer to statutory law, but can also have the meaning of non-statutory constitutional law; see Bleicken, *Lex Publica*, pp. 348–354 and my discussion below, pp. 54–62. Cf. also Livy 3.34.6.

13. See Woodman and Martin, *The Annals*, p. 251. See also Ungern-Sternberg, "Wahrnehmung," p. 96. On the reaction of jurists to the crisis of 133, see Behrends, "Tiberius Gracchus."

expression to *aequum ius*.[14] The crises brought about by legislative overreach are presented as constitutional crises—the legislation in question is not simply presented as morally bad, or as a mere instrument in a struggle for power within the elite à la Syme, but it is described as violating the constitutional arrangements established in the early Republic in several respects.

Indeed, contrary to the Symean views he expresses at 4.33, Tacitus in the passage just discussed does allow for the existence of a genuine constitutional order. This is borne out most conspicuously by his reference to the subsequent, post-133 BC legislation being carried by violence (*per vim*) and with the purpose of acquiring "illegal" honors (*inlicitos honores*), and by his emphasis on the distinction between legal proceedings addressed to legal subjects in general and those focusing on individuals. Measured against which yardstick would legislation carried by force be illegitimate? How could any honors be *inlicitos* (a term with strong juridical overtones, meaning "illicit" in the sense of "against the law") according to Tacitus? And on what basis does he discredit proceedings (*quaestiones*) or legislation (*leges*) directed against (prominent) individuals (bills of attainder, as opposed to norms addressed to the polity at large)? A large proportion of legislation between the Gracchi and the end of the Republic was not simply morally bad, or imprudent, thus corrupting and undermining the stability and longevity of the republican order—rather, the purposes served by some of the legislation as well as the way these laws came about were *unconstitutional*.

The crises of the late Republic as constitutional crises

In the following paragraphs I will try to give a sense of how Tacitus' presentation of the dissolution of the republican order as a constitutional crisis can serve as a roadmap, as it were, for the treatment of the issues with which this book is concerned. The first important point to note is that even the constitutional skeptic Tacitus could not but describe the crisis of the late Roman Republic as a *constitutional crisis*; second, Tacitus points to the importance of the constitutional arrangements, produced as a consequence of the Conflict of the Orders, that guarantee liberty and a basic unanimity regarding the foundational constitutional principles; and third, by drawing attention to the role played by illegitimate legislation and by hinting at the granting of extraordinary, unconstitutional

14. This interpretation would of course be further strengthened if Tacitus, in keeping with and based on Livy 3.34.6, really wrote *fons aequi iuris*, conveying a sense of the Twelve Tables as the "source of equal and just law," rather than *finis aequi iuris*. But see Woodman and Martin, *The Annals*, pp. 250–251. *Fons* would further strengthen the interpretation of the Twelve Tables as a foundational *constitutional* statute.

powers through legislation as a major cause of the Republic's disintegration, Tacitus describes in brief what transpires at length from the sources on which we draw for the last century of the Republic. The interpretation of the violent seditions and civil wars from the Gracchi to Augustus as constitutional crises[15] is one that can be gleaned from much of the contemporary thought and writing on the issues, especially of course from Cicero's works on political philosophy and from his speeches. Moreover, the political ideas and constitutional arguments triggered by the constitutional crises of the last century of the Republic were arguably highly original and of fundamental importance in that they exhibit for the first time in the history of political thought a concern with constitutionalism, the constitutional guarantee of individual rights and certain procedures—that is to say the crisis of the late Republic sparked a normative, not merely descriptive concern with the very purpose of a constitutional order, a concern that lay not exclusively with prudential criteria such as stability and peace, but also prominently with negative liberty and procedural safeguards.

It is questionable whether there ever existed, in the constitutional reality of the late Roman Republic, a statutory or customary basis for the annulment of laws passed by force (*per vim*).[16] The annulment of Sulpicius' laws after Sulla's march on Rome in 88 on the ground of having been passed by violence[17] looks very much like an attempt at establishing such a customary basis for the Senate's authority to annul legislation carried by violence; and it is probably this instance Tacitus has in mind when inveighing against post-133 legislation passed *per vim*—certainly the pro-Sullan sentiment expressed by him in this very passage would recommend such an interpretation. Apart from the institutional realities in the late Republic, however, there certainly existed a very strong desire for the authority to curtail laws that had been passed by violent means, a desire expressed not only by Tacitus but also in the constitutional thought of the late Republic; Cicero, in his codification of what I am going to argue are constitutional rules in *On the Laws*, puts forward the rule "Let there be no violence in public,"[18]

---

15. For a fresh periodization, see Flower, *Roman Republics*; cf. Yakobson "Review Flower."

16. I follow Lintott, *Violence*, pp. 140–143. Lintott may be too restrictive in rejecting violence as a "technical ground for annulment" (p. 145). Violence may not have been "by statute an offence," but by non-statutory *ius*. Sulla took issue with Sulpicius' laws on the ground of their having been "unlawful" (Cic. *Phil.* 8.7)—to say that this *ius* may not have been statutory begs the question as to whether it was constitutional non-statutory law which was at stake. The Senate seems to have annulled about ten *leges* from 100 BC onwards: see Heikkilä, "*Lex non iure rogata*."

17. Cic. *Phil.* 8.7.

18. Cic. *Leg.* 3.11.3. Trans. Zetzel.

referring to violence used to influence the decision-making in legislative popular assemblies. He goes on to offer the following comment on this rule:

> Then come dealings with the people, in which the first and most important provision is 'let there be no violence.' There is nothing more destructive for states, nothing more contrary to law and statutes (*contrarium iuri ac legibus*), nothing less civil and humane, than the use of violence in public affairs in a duly constituted commonwealth. The law ordains obedience to someone interposing a veto, and there is nothing more valuable than that: it is better for a good thing to be blocked than to give way to a bad one.[19]

Tacitus, in line with the constitutional thought of the late Republic, acknowledges both the problem of legislation passed by violent means and the need for a constitutional solution, that is to say, for higher-order norms capable of providing criteria for the validity of legislation. Similarly, his constitutional account of the downfall of the Republic cited above criticizes in a strongly Ciceronian vein[20] the use of legislation and law-courts against individuals, as opposed to generally applicable legal rules that promote equality before the law (*aequum ius*). Most telling is Tacitus' invocation of legislation carried by violence aimed at "illicit honors" (*inlicitos honores*), which goes to the heart of our investigation. This kind of legislation is problematic not merely on account of its procedural defects, but also in its substance. Tacitus here seems to suggest that there are certain substantive limits on what the People can and cannot pass as legislation in the popular assemblies.

Tacitus could have been thinking of the "pernicious" or "unlawful" laws, put forward by the tribune P. Sulpicius Rufus, which took the command against Mithridates away from the consul L. Cornelius Sulla, to whom it had been granted by the Senate, and transferred it to the private citizen C. Marius instead.[21]

---

19. Cic. *Leg.* 3.42. Trans. Zetzel; I translate *contrarium iuri ac legibus* "contrary to law and statutes" as opposed to "contrary to right and law," to convey that *ius* here refers to the legal order of the duly constituted commonwealth as a whole, including non-statutory constitutional law, while *leges* refer to statutory laws.

20. He has the events leading up to Cicero's exile in mind; for Cicero's own constitutional remedies to the use of *privilegia*, see *Leg.* 3.11.9; 3.44. On the legal facts, see Dyck, *Commentary*, p. 17, with n. 71.

21. Livy, *Per.* 77 (*perniciosas leges*); Diod. Sic. 37.29.2 (παρανόμως); Vell. Pat. 2.18.5–6; Val. Max. 9.7, ext. 1; Plut. *Mar.* 34–35; *Sull.* 8.2: App. *BCiv.* 1.55–56; Broughton, *Magistrates*, vol. 2, p. 41.

This law had been passed by violence,[22] but the command given to Marius under it was held to be unconstitutional not only on account of the violence but also because of the fact that Marius was, as a private individual, not eligible for the command, which had moreover already been granted regularly to Sulla. Sulla's subsequent march on Rome with his troops, his coup, occupation and military rule of the city in 88 introduced both the novelty of a Roman army invading Rome and the further novelty of designating certain Roman citizens as *hostes* or "foreign enemies of the Roman people."[23] The revolutionary character of Sulla's coup d'état, the idea that "conventional republican government did indeed collapse in 88," with the consequence that afterward the "previous republican rules" no longer held,[24] was pointed out forcibly by Appian, who stressed the year 88 as a caesura in the history of the downfall of the Republic.[25]

Tacitus could not but address some of the features of the late Republic in constitutional terms, and he recognizes the importance of foundational constitutional principles. How about modern-day scholars of republican Rome? Both adherents of the idea that the Romans had a constitution in some strict sense of the term and scholars who believe that they had better hedge their bets by applying the term in scare quotes do not usually bother to justify their position; rather, the correctness of either point of view is often simply and more or less implicitly assumed. Lintott, in his work on *The Constitution of the Roman Republic*, does not address the question;[26] and scholars who are more comfortable with the scare quotes version[27] seem to rely on the implicit assumption that, given the differences between paradigmatic constitutional orders such as the American or French ones on the one hand and the Roman Republic on the other, it would be preposterous to use the term outright. Here it would seem that features of modern-day constitutions such as writtenness, judicial review, and the guarantee

22. Cic. *Phil.* 8.7.

23. Vell. Pat. 2.19.1; App. *BCiv.* 1.57–60. See Ungern-Sternberg, *Untersuchungen*, pp. 74–75. Did the *quaestio* of Popillius Laenas in 132 BC declare Ti. Gracchus' followers to be *hostes*? See Lintott, *Violence*, pp. 162–164; but (p. 164, my emphasis), "for Popillius to justify his *quaestio* on this count would involve *assuming* the verdict that a legitimate trial would give."

24. For Sulla's march on Rome as a watershed leading to the "complete collapse of the traditional republican culture," see Flower, *Roman Republics*, pp. 91–92. See also Keaveney, "What Happened"; Levick, "Sulla's March"; Volkmann, *Sullas Marsch*; Dahlheim, "Staatsstreich."

25. App. *BCiv.* 1.60.

26. Lintott, *Constitution*. Cf. also, e.g., Brennan, *Praetorship*; Martino, *Storia*; Bleicken, *Verfassung*, pp. 12–14.

27. E. g., Hölkeskamp, *Reconstructing*, pp. 12–22; cf. also Syme, *Roman Revolution*.

of certain individual rights serve as the defining, if implicit, features of a real constitutional order.

A working concept of constitution

As pointed out in the Introduction, the matter is one of definition. If judicial review is a necessary feature of a constitution, then a great many institutional arrangements throughout history would not qualify as constitutional orders—including, for that matter, the early constitution of the United States, before the Supreme Court asserted its competence to pronounce on the constitutional validity of statutes. Equally, if writtenness is supposed to be the essential criterion, then many a political order would remain outside the boundaries of the term, including the English constitution.

The revolutionary pamphleteer Thomas Paine pointed this out when in his *Rights of Man* (referring to the English Septennial Act of 1716) he wrote that the "act by which the English parliament empowered itself to sit for seven years, shews there is no constitution in England. It might, by the same authority, have sate any greater number of years, or for life."[28] For Paine, the defining feature of a constitution *stricto sensu* is that it is "a thing *antecedent* to a government; and a government is only the creature of a constitution,"[29] which leads him to the view that "a government without a constitution, is power without a right."[30] Accordingly, Paine viewed the English institutional order as "merely a form of government without a constitution, and constituting itself with what power it pleases."[31] So Paine may side with the scare-quotes faction of ancient historians with regard to the constitution (or, rather, "constitution") of the Roman Republic. A more useful concept of constitution, closer to the one we should use preliminarily for the Roman case, was put forward by Henry St John, Viscount Bolingbroke, in 1733:

> By constitution we mean, whenever we speak with propriety and exactness, that assemblage of laws, institutions and customs, derived from certain fixed principles of reason, directed to certain fixed objects of public good, that compose the general system according to which the community hath agreed to be governed.[32]

---

28. Paine, *Rights of Man*, p. 311.

29. Ibid., p. 310.

30. Ibid., p. 428.

31. Ibid., p. 373.

32. Bolingbroke, *Dissertation*, p. 88.

Incidentally, it would seem that the British case is actually fairly well suited to our purposes, both as an example of what kind of concept of constitution we should be looking for when trying to apply that concept to the Roman Republic and as a gateway, as it were, into a historical situation and constitutional debate that is close to the late Roman republican one. It is worth bearing in mind the occasion that had given rise to Paine's remarks—namely the Septennial Act of 1716, which had postponed the parliamentary election after the Jacobite Rebellion of 1715. The Whigs justified this expansion of parliamentary power as a necessary, albeit extraordinary, emergency measure—and they did so, interestingly, by reference to Cicero's famous maxim in *De legibus*, that *salus populi suprema lex esto*. John Selden (1584–1654) had protested this use of the Ciceronian maxim in the previous century thus:

> There is not any thing in the World more abused than this Sentence, *Salus populi suprema Lex esto*, for we apply it, as if we ought to forsake the known Law, when it may be most for the advantage of the People, when it means no such thing. For first, 'tis not *Salus populi suprema Lex est*, but *esto*; it being one of the Laws of the Twelve Tables, and after divers Laws made, some for Punishment, some for Reward; then follows this. *Salus populi suprema Lex esto*: That is, in all the Laws you make, have a special Eye to the Good of the People; and then what does this concern the way they now go?[33]

Selden's claim that the *salus populi suprema lex esto* phrase constituted one of the laws of the XII Tables is, of course, wrong. The phrase is Ciceronian and is spelled out in its entirety for the first time in Cicero's *De legibus*. The shorter phrase *salus populi Romani* is often found in Cicero's speeches and letters.[34] Now both Selden's misunderstanding of the origin of the phrase as well as his interpretation of it are quite interesting for our purposes here. As for the first point, Selden seems to think that by virtue of being part of the XII Tables the principle of *salus populi suprema lex esto* is somehow endowed with legal authority of a special and presumably more important kind than any other legislation. Secondly, with regard to Selden's interpretation of the principle, I think he is wrong in establishing a relationship between the process of legislation ("in all the laws you make") and the conduct of the consuls in office; however, I believe Selden to be quite

33. Selden, *Table Talk*, s.v. People, p. 112.

34. Eighteen times in the speeches (fifteen times during and after the Catilinarian affair) and twice in the letters: Dyck, *Commentary*, p. 459.

correct in assuming that the phrase in question put forward a supreme principle for the conduct of consuls in office, rather than placing the consuls above the law. This can be borne out, I believe, by looking more closely at the actual context of the principle, Cicero's *De legibus*, which I shall do shortly.

To establish whether or not the Romans in the late Republic had the concept of constitution, we need to circle back to the initial question of what the defining features of that concept are. Neither writtenness nor judicial review seem to be essential features, *pace* Thomas Paine. Bolingbroke's "assemblage of laws, institutions and customs," by contrast, composing a "general system according to which the community hath agreed to be governed,"[35] seems a much more promising a candidate for our purposes, as long as we do not make the mistake of thinking that the customary part of Bolingbroke's "assemblage"—what corresponds roughly with the Roman *mos maiorum*, and probably non-statutory *ius*—means simply actual practice and behavior, utterly devoid of any normative force.

A working definition of constitutionality in the late Roman republican context is required. The following two criteria seem to me both individually necessary and jointly sufficient for the concept of constitution: a) *entrenchment*, i.e., the fact that certain rules are more entrenched than other rules and less susceptible to change, and b) political *importance*, that is to say, rules that are of great substantive importance in that they govern the institutions through which political power is exercised. The first criterion, entrenchment, establishes a *hierarchy* of norms in that the more entrenched rules have to be seen to stand above the less entrenched ones and should thus prevail over these in case of a conflict between norms.

Now quite obviously, in a very narrow sense, even an institutional setup which does not allow for any norms of a higher order than whatever the legislature provides for would seem to rely on at least one higher-order norm: the rule that "whatever the legislature provides for, is binding law." This, incidentally, has been the view of the British constitution held by more than a few prominent constitutional lawyers; "What the Queen in Parliament enacts is law" has been held to be the most fundamental rule of the British constitution, meaning that "there are no fundamental constitutional laws that Parliament cannot change," *other than the fundamental rule of parliamentary sovereignty itself*, that is.[36]

This is analogous to what Livy held to be a norm laid down in the Twelve Tables: *ut quodcumque postremum populus iussisset id ius ratumque esset*.[37] The

35. Bolingbroke, *Dissertation*, p. 88.

36. See Goldsworthy, *Sovereignty*, p. 1 and *passim*.

37. Livy 7.17.12 (= Tab. XII.5, Crawford, *Roman Statutes*, vol. 2, p. 721).

historicity of Livy's remarks on the Twelve Tables here is more than doubtful,[38] as the clause was probably "invented during the controversies of the first century BC,"[39] but this leaves us perfectly free still to use them as an expression of the political and constitutional thought of Livy's own time. Although it is maintained by Livy that the Twelve Tables had been passed as a law (*lex*) by the *comitia centuriata*,[40] this is almost certainly a construct of later historiography—the Twelve Tables were a statute given by the ten law-commissioners (*decemviri*), an arbitration body chosen precisely because of its constituent power which reached beyond any existing legal and political institutions.[41] So to the extent that the Twelve Tables contain any public-law provisions, which is admittedly very little, they can properly be described as a constitutional document.

The rule of what Livy takes to be Table XII "that whatever was the last order that the People made that should have the force of law (*ius*)" is thus analogous to the most fundamental rule of the British constitution just alluded to—it could be called the fundamental constitutional principle of the sovereignty of the Roman People and can be interpreted to mean that there are no fundamental constitutional rules that the *populus Romanus* cannot change, that is, *other than the fundamental constitutional rule of the sovereignty of the Roman People* ("that whatever was the last order that the People made that should have the force of law"). It has been argued that this clause should be taken to state merely that *ubi duae contrariae leges sunt, semper antiquae obrogat nova*,[42] rather than expressing the principle of popular sovereignty.[43] But surely the power to abrogate and override earlier, conflicting legislation must count as an expression of the principle of popular sovereignty.

This is important because if it is right, then we have a constitution at Rome at the time of the Republic, or at least at the time of the late Republic, without scare quotes, a constitution containing at least one constitutional rule.[44] This is certainly not to say that this is all there was to the Roman republican constitution; rather, it is to say that there must have been such a thing in the first place. I will now try to offer some discussion of the Roman republican constitution as it appears primarily in political

---

38. See Oakley, *Commentary*, vol. 2, p. 191.

39. Crawford, *Roman Statutes*, vol. 2, p. 721.

40. Livy 3.34.6.

41. Bleicken, *Lex Publica*, p. 91.

42. Livy 9.34.7.

43. Crawford, *Roman Statutes*, vol. 2, p. 721.

44. For an interpretation as a rule of recognition in H. L. A. Hart's sense, see Lundgreen, *Regelkonflikte*, pp. 259–273.

thought, as this will allow me to flesh out the concept of the Roman constitution beyond just that one constitutional rule of the sovereignty of the Roman People.

But first, let us consider an example provided by Livy that shows this one fundamental constitutional principle at work—on the ground, as it were—in a description of the election of P. Cornelius Scipio (the later Africanus) to the aedileship in 213 BC. It reads like a pure expression of a very narrow view of the Roman constitution where everything is susceptible to change by the *populus Romanus*, everything but the fundamental rule of the sovereignty of the *populus*. Livy tells us that Scipio's seeking the aedileship was opposed by the tribunes of the plebs, on the ground that he had not yet reached the required age—Scipio was about twenty-two years old at the time, and although it is by no means clear whether there was at that time a minimum legal age for the curule aedileship, it would seem that Scipio's age was even by mere customary standards very young. Again, it is important to keep in mind that what follows should be cautiously interpreted as a reflection of the political thought of the last century BC, rather than as an historical account of what Scipio actually said in 213 BC:

> When [Scipio] offered himself as a candidate, the tribunes of the plebs objected, and said that he could not be allowed to stand because he had not yet reached the legitimate age. His reply was: 'If the Quirites are unanimous in their desire to appoint me aedile, I am quite old enough.' On this the people hurried to give their tribal votes for him with such eagerness that the tribunes abandoned their opposition.[45]

Universal support in the popular assembly, on this view, trumps any other rule, is more firmly entrenched and of a higher order. It is sufficient even to bestow pro-consular *imperium*—not merely the petty *potestas* of the aedile—for Spain on Scipio three years later:

> The eyes of the whole assembly were directed towards him, and by acclamations and expressions of approbation, a prosperous and happy command were at once augured to him. Orders were then given that they should proceed to vote, when not only every century, but every individual to a man, decided that Publius Scipio should be invested with the command (*imperium*) in Spain.[46]

45. Livy 25.2.6–7. Cf. Polybius 10.4–5. Translations of Livy are by Canon Roberts, in Everyman's Library (London, 1912), by D. Spillan and Cyrus Edmonds, *The History of Rome by Titus Livius* (London, 1849), or by myself.

46. Livy 26.18.8–9.

This text too seems to indicate that far from lacking any constitutional higher-order norms, the republican order is based on at least one such norm, namely that whatever the assemblies decide holds, even if it may run counter to certain provisions enacted by earlier legislation, custom, *mos*, or non-statutory *ius publicum*.[47]

Above the law: a more ambitious constitutionalism

A further important and arguably more interesting example for a view of the republican constitutional order can be found in the Greek historian Appian's description of Scipio Aemilianus' election to the consulship in 148 BC.[48] Prima facie this view seems similar to the one just put forward in Livy; yet it introduces, as we shall see, a much richer constitutional argument than the one found in Livy, going beyond the narrow view of the Roman constitutional order as consisting merely of the absolute legislative sovereignty of the People. Appian, the Alexandria-born author of a Roman history from the regal period down to the second century CE, writes that Scipio Aemilianus was seeking election not as a consul, but merely as an aedile; the People, however, proceeded to elect him to the consulship, notwithstanding the fact that according to statute Scipio was too young to be elected consul:

> The election was drawing near and Scipio was a candidate for the ædileship, for the laws did not permit him to hold the consulship as yet, on account of his youth; yet the people elected him consul. This was illegal (*paranomou*), and when the consuls showed them the law (*ton nomon*) they became importunate and urged all the more, exclaiming that by the laws handed down from Tullius and Romulus (*ek ton Tulliou kai Rhomulou nomon*) the people had the authority over the elections (*kurion ton archairesion*), and that, of the laws pertaining thereto (*ton peri auton nomon*), they could set aside or confirm whichever they pleased.[49]

The historical accuracy of this passage, once again, is immaterial for our purposes.[50] But what is being shown here, to the extent that Appian's writing can be interpreted as an expression of Roman political thought, and we have good reason

---

47. The constitutional status of non-statutory *ius* has received less attention than *mos* but deserves a closer look; see Bleicken, *Lex Publica*, pp. 348–354, and below, pp. 54–62.

48. See Ungern-Sternberg, "Romulus-Bilder," p. 39.

49. App. *Pun.* 112.531. Trans. Horace White, slightly modified.

50. Cf. Astin, *Scipio Aemilianus*, p. 67, who takes the events to be historical.

to think that it can,[51] is highly pertinent to our search for a constitutional mindset, the consciousness of operating within the constraints of higher-order norms, in late republican Rome. It seems in fact to indicate that a distinction is being drawn, in a constitutional argument put forward by the People, between the law shown to them by the consuls, on the one hand, and the "laws handed down from Tullius and Romulus," on the other. It is these latter laws that provide the constitutional yardstick needed to undermine the validity of the later law, shown to the People by the consuls, which seeks to tie eligibility for office to a certain age.

Most importantly, Appian's account does not simply put forward a view of popular sovereignty indebted to a Greek mindset; unlike the examples from Livy shown above, Appian's actually conveys a self-conscious constitutional argument by the People relying on a differentiation between two hierarchically separate kinds of law. The laws "handed down from Tullius and Romulus" carve out, according to this argument, a sphere where the People have supreme authority: the elections as well as all "the laws pertaining thereto." This is unlike the elections described by Livy which we have discussed above, where the reference to a higher-order norm is only made implicitly and certainly is not argued for. Here, by contrast, we have the Roman People[52] exclaiming that it is on the ground of laws dating from the regal period that they should have the authority to set aside any earlier law pertaining to elections (and pertaining to elections only).[53]

This implies that in the absence of the laws "handed down from Tullius and Romulus," no such authority would pertain to the assembly; more generally it would seem to imply that without a constitutional justification, the assemblies lack the competence to legislate on the issue at hand. If followed to its logical conclusion, this would yield the mildly paradoxical doctrine that the assembly, were it not for certain very old laws from the regal period, is barred from "setting aside or confirming" an older law it has itself passed; and that there was a view of the constitution that did not simply elevate the legislative process over and above all the other elements of the constitution—did not, in short, hold Mommsen's view of popular sovereignty and of the "absolute" character of the legislative will.[54]

---

51. See Ungern-Sternberg, "Romulus-Bilder," pp. 39–40.

52. *Auct. ad Her.* 3.2 credits the Senate with the initiative in exempting Scipio from the statutes barring his election to the consulship.

53. Cf. Livy, *Epit.* 50: Scipio Aemilianus was eventually exempted from the relevant laws and made consul, but there is no reference to constitutional principle. Cf. also Cic. *Phil.* 11.17; Vell. Pat. 1.12.3. For the credible historical substance of Appian's account, see Bleicken, *Lex Publica*, p. 136, n. 111.

54. See Mommsen, *Staatsrecht*, vol. 3.1, pp. 300–368, esp. 313–314. Cf. Bleicken, *Lex Publica*, pp. 292–293, esp. n. 100. On *Gesetzesabsolutismus*, see Bleicken, *Lex Publica*, pp. 342–343 (against Mommsen).

Of course, this invites the danger of pressing the example of constitutional argument by the People in Appian too far. The passage cannot bear nearly enough weight to be cited as evidence for constitutional limits on the potential reach of legislation, much less as evidence in favor of a set of laws from the regal period which would as a matter of constitutional fact have constrained the assemblies down to the second century BC. At the very least, however, we may admit it as evidence of a late republican constitutional mindset which, confronted with absolutist claims made on behalf of the popular assemblies,[55] was increasingly aware of their ability to declare certain legislation as unlawful, by reference to higher-order and more firmly entrenched norms. The crucial aspect that has to be noted is that the People's constitutional argument in the cited passage is that the assembly is not constrained by previous legislation governing the eligibility for office,[56] and it proceeds not by asserting the People's absolute sovereignty, but by reference to an even older set of laws, which themselves severely constrain the legislative authority of the People by confining that authority to the specific domain of laws pertaining to elections.

In a very similar vein, some of the constitutional views put forward in Livy's first decade also show that the political thought of the late Republic expressed a well formulated sensitivity to the scope of the authority of the assemblies under the constitution. Let me briefly touch upon two of them. In the tenth book there is the example, which is not historical, of Q. Fabius Maximus Rullianus, who is portrayed as actively resisting, in 298 BC, his being elected prematurely again as consul in violation of the laws regulating the annuity of that office (this is, of course, an anachronism, the prohibition of the iteration of the consulship not being introduced by legislation until the mid-second century BC[57]). Livy writes that in the context of an imminent threat, with the Etruscans and Samnites levying huge armies, the People turned to Fabius Maximus, who, however, did not want to stand for election:

> This display of modesty and unselfishness only made the popular feeling all the keener in his favour by showing how rightly it was directed. Thinking that *the best way of checking it would be to appeal to the instinctive reverence for law,* he ordered the law to be rehearsed which forbade

55. See Chapter 3 below, pp. 119–129.

56. I.e., against the consuls' argument that their electing Scipio was illegal (*paranomou*).

57. See, for the date of the *lex annalis*, the discussion in Brennan, *Praetorship*, vol. 2, pp. 647–652, esp. p. 650; see also Bleicken, *Volkstribunat*, p. 58, n. 1.

> any man from being re-elected consul within ten years. Owing to the clamour the law was hardly heard, and the tribunes of the plebs declared that there was no impediment here; they would make a proposition to the Assembly that he should be exempt from its provisions. He, however, persisted in his refusal, and *repeatedly asked what was the object in making laws if they were deliberately broken by those who made them*; '*we*,' said he, '*are now ruling the laws instead of the laws ruling us*.' Notwithstanding his opposition the people began to vote, and as each century was called in, it declared without the slightest hesitation for Fabius. At last, yielding to the general desire of his countrymen, he said, 'May the gods approve what you have done and what you are going to do'.[58]

Fabius' point illustrates an awareness, in Livy's own time, of the problem posed by an unconstrained legislature. Let me now adduce again a passage from Livy, from the first decade, which is certainly not historical but should again be interpreted, even to a greater extent than the examples cited just before, as an expression of the political thought of Livy's own time. This passage provides us with a view of the republican constitution that is more fleshed out, making a substantive commitment to republican and against monarchical government. Describing Brutus' actions after the expulsion of the kings and the liberation of Rome, Livy says that "it is of a Rome henceforth free" that he is writing the history, with "the authority of her laws more powerful than that of men."[59] The origin of this newly gained freedom is said by Livy to lie in the term limits of the consular office, "because the consular power was limited to one year."[60] Apart from the general commitment to the rule of law, it is noteworthy that Livy here alludes to a constitutional feature, namely the term limits, which were not part of any statutory act at that point. Livy then goes on to say that Brutus, a zealous guardian of liberty (*custos libertatis*), "impelled the people to take an oath that they would suffer no one to be king in Rome."[61]

Although the oath seems extracted almost under duress (*populum . . . adegit*), the content of the oath as well as the very idea of a binding formula such as an oath (*iusiurandum*) both would seem to indicate a *constitutional rule* that there not be a kingly government in Rome.[62] The rule is constitutional in living up to our two

---

58. Livy 10.13.8–12 (my italics).

59. Ibid. 2.1.1.

60. Ibid. 2.1.7.

61. Ibid. 2.1.9.

62. See Bleicken, *Lex Publica*, p. 341.

criteria, importance and entrenchment; it is constitutional in the sense that it is of political importance, and in the sense that it seems to be on a higher hierarchical plane than mere legislation—indeed, any kind of legislation exercised by the *populus* as referred to in the Twelfth Table presupposes a constitutional rule that there not be a monarchy. At least according to Livy's (certainly mythical) account, the constitutional rule against monarchy was incorporated into legislation (*lex*) by Valerius Publicola in the first year of the Republic.[63] This does not contradict the claim that the ban on monarchy was perceived, by the time of the late Republic, as constitutional in nature; rather, it should be interpreted as an attempt by Livy to endow the legislation in question with longevity, which itself could be taken as an expression of the rule's entrenchment. Moreover, incorporating a constitutional rule into a statute does not make it any less constitutional.

Let us move on to the phrase criticized by Selden, *salus populi suprema lex esto*, and to Cicero's dialogue *De legibus*, from which it is taken. Selden had erroneously ascribed it to the Twelve Tables; the context in which it appears in the *De legibus* is Cicero's law code, the part on magistrates. Cicero introduces the consulate thus: "Let there be two men with royal power of command. . . . On military service let them have the highest authority, and let them obey no other. For them let the safety of the people be the highest law (*lex*)."[64] The first question this raises is whether Cicero meant this to place the consuls beyond, and above, the law and any constitutional norm (other than the norm that "for them let the safety of the people be the highest norm"), in the sense of a dispensation from constitutional and moral constraints in extraordinary circumstances such as states of emergencies. The second is what status the phrase itself, and the law code it is a part of, is supposed to have.

As for the first, internal, question it would seem that read as an invitation to the consuls to behave in any potentially illegal or unconstitutional way the provision conflicts with another principle expressed earlier in the *De legibus*, namely that "[j]ust as the laws are in control of (*praesunt*) the magistrates, so the magistrates are in control of the people."[65] This principle—reminding one strongly of Livy—prohibits us from reading the phrase on *salus populi* as in some way giving the consuls emergency authority to subvert the existing norms. Rather, it would seem that in their conduct of office, they are legally constrained by the safety of the people, without being given authority to go beyond fundamental norms.

63. Livy 2.8.2; cf. Dion. Hal. *Ant. Rom.* 5.19.4; Plut. *Publ.* 12.1.

64. Cic. *Leg.* 3.8. Trans. Zetzel.

65. Ibid. 3.2. Trans. Zetzel, slightly adapted.

Cicero's written constitution

At first sight, Cicero's use of the term *leges* for the norms he is proposing in *De legibus* seems to lend some plausibility to the claim that we are dealing here, not so much with a constitutional framework, but merely with a written law code reflecting a superior natural law. But since Klaus Girardet's important 1983 book on *De legibus* the mainstream interpretation of that dialogue has changed. We now tend—rightly so, I believe—to think that Cicero did not put forward a mere reflection of a hierarchically higher natural law, but instead was intent on writing up a code of norms which actually *was* natural law.[66] More recently Elizabeth Asmis has argued that the laws of books two and three of *De legibus* were merely "sharing in" natural law, but were not actually natural law themselves, thus upholding a distinction between natural law and the norms proposed in *De legibus* while acknowledging the constitutional nature of Cicero's body of rules, which was "conceived as a written constitution."[67] Her argument assumes that Cicero's account needs to be seen in a Stoic framework, where human legislation is excluded from being "law" and where natural law embodies perfect rationality, something only accessible to the Stoic wise man (*sapiens*). On this view, Cicero's laws are merely guides for *all* humans towards "intermediate actions" (*kathekonta*) as opposed to guiding the wise towards "perfectly appropriate actions" (*katorthomata*). Asmis' argument succeeds to the extent that it shows the real difficulties that lie in Cicero's attempt to reconcile Stoic natural law theory, with its emphasis on the wise and perfect rationality, with the constitutional framework of the Roman Republic. Jed Atkins, in a stimulating book, has argued, not unlike Asmis, that books two and three of *De legibus* are not intended to be natural law as book one expounds it. Rather—and here Atkins parts company with Asmis—in books two and three Cicero is following the Platonic rather than the Stoic model. This entails that books two and three present only the closest approximation to natural law that is practically possible given the constraints of human nature and contingency.[68]

---

66. Girardet, *Ordnung der Welt*. Cf. Rawson, "Review Girardet"; Dyck, *Commentary*, pp. 103–104. For a subtle, differentiated view, stressing Cicero's goal of insulating law from politics, see Sauer, "Dichotomie." For a defense of the dichotomy between natural law and Cicero's code, see Asmis, "Cicero on Natural Law." For Cicero's mature political philosophy, see Chapter 4.

67. Asmis, "Cicero on Natural Law," 25. See also Griffin, "When is Thought Political," esp. pp. 272–273.

68. Atkins, *Cicero on Politics*, chs. 5 and 6, esp. pp. 195–208.

According to Cicero, the Roman republican constitution as laid out in the *De legibus* either is identical with natural law or—on Asmis' reading—it merely partakes in natural law. For our purposes what matters is that even if Asmis or Atkins were right, and Cicero in his code presented only the closest possible approximation to natural law, he would still be looking for a higher standard, a "body of constitutional law"[69] with permanent validity. If in what follows I tend to side with Girardet on this question, it is because it seems that Cicero—quite purposefully—in his natural law doctrine is self-consciously moving away from the Greek Stoic distinction between perfectly appropriate actions and intermediate actions, in favor of a view that collapses the distinction and gives far more importance to what the Greek Stoics would have termed merely preferable indifferent things (*adiaphora proegmena*), especially to private property, which plays a pivotal role in Cicero's theory of justice, as will be seen in Chapter 4.[70] Analogously, Cicero's natural law holds not exclusively for the wise men, but for all of humankind.[71]

Cicero's language certainly bears out the view that the laws put forward in the *De legibus* are either themselves natural law or at least derived from it and thus hierarchically superior to mere legislation. For example, although Cicero is somewhat misleadingly using the term *leges* for "laws," evoking ideas about lawmaking and popular legislation, he makes it very clear that that is not what he has in mind. Unlike certain legislation passed in the assemblies of the Roman Republic but subsequently deemed invalid by the Senate and annulled, the code Cicero proposes will not be subject to annulment. "[I]n a single moment," Cicero says in the dialogue—and we are not concerned here with the somewhat dubious historicity of his claim—in a single moment certain laws (*leges*) "were removed by a single word from the Senate." He goes on to say that "[t]he law whose force I have explained, however, *can be neither removed nor abrogated*."[72] To which his brother Quintus replies: "So the laws that you will pass, I imagine, are never to

69. Asmis, "Cicero on Natural Law," p. 31.

70. See, for an attempt to differentiate more strongly than the Greek Stoics would have between *adiaphora*, Cic. *Fin.* 3.50; in Cic. *Off.* 3.17 the relevance of the distinction between *kathekonta* and *katorthomata* seems to be called into question; for this Romanized view of Stoic natural law and its influence on early modern natural law, see Straumann, "*Appetitus societatis*," pp. 58–62.

71. Although Cicero's definitions continue to equate natural law with the *recta ratio* of the Stoic wise man (Cic. *Leg.* 1.18–19; 2.8), he removes all generic distinctions between human beings (Cic. *Leg.* 1.29–30). See Vander Waerdt, "Philosophical Influence," p. 4872. Cf. also Sauer, "Dichotomie," who takes this to support Girardet's view.

72. Cic. *Leg.* 2.14. My emphasis.

be abrogated."[73] Marcus confirms this.[74] Here Quintus and Marcus are obviously referring to the code of norms contained in *De legibus*.

That Cicero is not using the term *lex* in the sense of (popular) legislation, legislation susceptible to changes and referring to contingent historical and geographical circumstances, becomes clear also from the following passage where he makes the point explicitly: law (*lex*), Cicero says, "was not thought up by human minds; . . . *it is not some piece of legislation by popular assemblies*."[75] And in a following chapter Cicero points out that the term *lex* is often used differently from his own use of the term: "The legislation that has been written down for nations in different ways and for particular occasions has the name of law (*leges*) more as a matter of courtesy than as a fact."[76]

It is therefore quite clear that we cannot draw a strong distinction between Cicero's Romanized Stoic account of natural law in the first book of *De legibus* on the one hand[77] and the content of his so-called laws in books two and three on the other; these laws are natural law, not legislation in the sense known from law-making in the popular assemblies of the Roman Republic. This entails, however, that the norms contained in *De legibus* are intended by Cicero to be hierarchically superior to mere positive legislation: what Cicero is thus engaged in in the *De legibus* is the drafting of a set of constitutional norms. The scholarly debate over the extent to which the work constituted a concrete political program as opposed to a theoretical endeavor in Plato's vein situated on a higher level of abstraction need not preoccupy us here.[78] The important point is that as a matter of political thought Cicero did have a concept of constitution and, what is more, formulated a set of constitutional norms that, by virtue of their constituting *natural law*, were supposed to be more firmly entrenched than mere normal legislation and superior in case of conflict.

This is expressed most clearly in two of the so-called laws concerning magistrates in the third book of *De legibus*, where a bar on legislation is provided on substantive grounds: the first provision prohibiting magistrates from proposing legislation that affects single individuals (bills of attainder, as opposed to laws with a universal scope), the second insisting on capital cases being brought

---

73. Ibid.

74. It is, of course, true that this partly amounts to jocular banter; however, as Asmis points out, behind it lies a serious purpose: "Cicero on Natural Law," p. 24.

75. Cic. *Leg.* 2.8.

76. Ibid. 2.11.

77. Esp. ibid. 1.17.

78. See Rawson, "Review Girardet," p. 311; for literature, see Dyck, *Commentary*, pp. 15–20.

exclusively before one of the popular assemblies, the assembly of the centuries.[79] Cicero claims that these two provisions had been part of the Twelve Tables, but this is not the justification for their being adopted in his code; rather, Cicero argues normatively by pointing out that "nothing is more unjust" than laws "against private men," that is to say, *privilegia*, "since it is the essence of law to be a decision or order applying to all." As for the second provision, the one prohibiting magistrates from deciding on capital penalties or from bringing them before any assembly other than the *comitia centuriata*, Cicero argues that "the distribution of the people by wealth, rank, and age brings greater wisdom to the ballot than when they are summoned broadly by tribes."[80] Both of these provisions, expressing natural law, are of a higher order than legislation passed by the assemblies and thus able to constrain it.

Cicero's Roman constitution as presented in *De legibus* is, qua natural law, presented as universal, permanent, and not historically contingent. It entails a concept of a pre-political moral order that supplies the rules incorporated in such a constitution. And indeed, Cicero, both in some of his forensic speeches (especially *Pro Sestio* and *Pro Milone*) and in the *De legibus* and the *De officiis*, provides exactly that: a picture of natural justice apt to inform higher-order constitutional norms and, as a corollary, the limits of popular legislation and the positive legal system. We will turn to the substance of Cicero's constitutional theory in Chapter 4; in the remainder of this chapter we will turn our attention to the sources of constitutional law as they appear "on the ground," as it were, in our historical evidence and in the constitutional conflicts that sparked Roman constitutional thinking in the first place.

The sources of constitutional norms: mos

This view of higher-order hierarchically superior and more entrenched constitutional norms found its way also into forensic argument, which provides a bridge for constitutional argument to cross from political thought into the institutional reality of the Roman republican ancestral constitution, "constituted in the wisest possible way by our ancestors."[81] Cicero's speeches allow us, not only to hear appeals to the republican constitution "in action," as it were, but also to glimpse parts of the institutional order that provided the background to his legal and

79. Cic. *Leg.* 3.11.

80. Ibid. 3.44. On *privilegia*, see also Cic. *Sest.* 73.

81. Cic. *Sest.* 137. This stands in obvious tension with the constitutional reality of the late Republic. The underlying ideal, however, that the Senate in principle is to be recruited *ab*

constitutional arguments. In 56 BC, Cicero defended Publius Sestius, who had been a tribune of the plebs the year before, before a standing criminal court (*quaestio*) against a charge of public violence (*de vi*). In the defense speech *Pro Sestio*, Cicero gives what sounds like an exclusive enumeration of the possible sources of constitutional law: constitutional law, broadly understood (*ius*), ancestral custom (*mos maiorum*), and the laws (*leges*).[82]

We will turn to *ius* in a moment. First, *mos maiorum*, or the "ways of the ancestors." The term denotes custom, the "way things happened to be done at the time."[83] Jochen Bleicken has discussed the development of this concept, claiming an increasingly normative function of the term.[84] While *mos* at first—that is to say, in the early Republic—simply denoted practice, without any normative pull, in private, religious and public law, the term more and more came to adopt the meaning of a norm that potentially could conflict with other legal norms, such as laws (*leges*), since *mos* was from the second century on understood to be itself a legal concept. According to Bleicken, this led to an assimilation of those parts of *mos* amenable to being subsumed under public law (*ius*) generally speaking with constitutional law.[85] By the time of the late Republic *mos* had developed into a source of constitutional law that often competed with other such sources such as new statute. In the context of the constitutional crises from the Gracchi onward and the struggle between *optimates* and *populares, mos* could thus become the optimates' favorite constitutional source, in the face of unwelcome popular legislation.[86] This entailed, however, that *mos, ius*, and *leges* were all seen as potentially equally valid sources of constitutional norms and that *mos* had become a normative juridical concept, which could also be given positive expression in statute.[87]

---

universo populo, should be taken seriously; it lends support to Millar's view that "no one became a member of the Senate by right of birth," and that consequently the term "aristocracy" cannot strictly be applied to the republican elite: *Crowd*, p. 5. As Brunt points out, it was not until "the Principate that the *ideal* was discarded; the hierarchical order was then strengthened, and eventually equality before the law was lost." Brunt, "Fall," p. 338.

82. Cic. *Sest.* 73.

83. Lintott, *Constitution*, p. 4. On *mos*, see Linke and Stemmler, *Mos maiorum*.

84. Bleicken, *Lex Publica*, pp. 354–396; Nippel, "Gesetze." See also the older dissertations, Plumpe, *Wesen*; Roloff, *Maiores*; Rech, *Mos maiorum*; and Grziwotz, *Verfassungsverständnis*, pp. 219–310.

85. *Lex Publica*, p. 371–377.

86. On the *populares/optimates* dichotomy, see Robb, *Beyond Populares*, where it is argued that these labels did not denote different categories of politicians. But see Yakobson, "Review Robb," p. 214.

87. See Cic. *Pis.* 50.

Bleicken's view of the development of *mos* is highly conjectural.[88] It is conspicuous that *mos*, whenever it is being adduced in the sources, is nearly always used for normative purposes, usually in the context of attacks on the constitutionality of extraordinary commands or emergency powers or, conversely, in the justification of such powers. It is thus plausible that *mos maiorum* really came into its own as a rhetorical and constitutional term of art only in the oratory and in the constitutional debates of the last century of the Republic.[89] In Ennius' famous verse of the early second century, "the Roman state stands upon the morals and men of old,"[90] the *mores* lack any kind of constitutional connotation, nor do they assume a constitutional sense in Plautus' late third century comedy *Trinummus*, where *mos* and *mos maiorum* appear as the custom and behavior of individual families' ancestors, which are explicitly contrasted with law and public sanction.[91] On the other hand, in the revolutionary period after the Gracchi, the term is used overwhelmingly to appeal to constitutional norms in a public setting, be it in speeches before the People, in court, or before the Senate. *Mos maiorum* may thus be seen as a constitutional term of relatively late coinage that acquired its salience and relevance in the context of the late republican constitutional crises; it is safe to say that it is only with Cicero that the concept acquires this constitutional emphasis.[92]

The sources bear this out. In his speech in 66 BC before a popular meeting (*contio*) supporting a bill by the tribune C. Manilius which entrusted an important military command against Mithridates of Pontus to Pompey, Cicero discusses the constitutional arguments that had previously been put forward against the bill. Quintus Catulus, one of the respected adversaries of the bill, makes the point that against ancestral precedents (*exempla*) and practices (*instituta*) no innovations should be introduced, and that the bestowal of the command against Mithridates constituted precisely such a constitutional innovation, implying as it did such far-reaching and extraordinary powers as *imperium* for the provinces of Bithynia and Pontus and Cilicia as well as a command competing with the governors of the adjacent provinces (*imperium maius*), subjecting all troops in the East to Pompey's authority. This combined several

88. See Lintott, *Constitution*, p. 6. For earlier interpretations from Mommsen to Kunkel and Wittmann, see Nippel, "Gesetze," pp. 89–96.

89. See Blösel, "*Mos maiorum*," p. 85.

90. Enn. *Ann.* 467 Warmington.

91. Plaut. *Trin.* 1046. See Earl, *Political Thought*, pp. 25–26.

92. For the evidence, see Blösel, "*Mos maiorum*."

powers that were felt to be extraordinary (*extra ordinem*)[93] and thus potentially unconstitutional. In particular the fact that these powers were bestowed, not by the Senate as a prorogation of the command of a regular magistrate, but by the popular assembly upon a single person who had previously (i.e., in 65) been a private citizen[94] and who was given consular power,[95] aroused the opposition of the optimates. We will get to the question of the contested constitutionality of such emergency powers in a later chapter; what is of interest here is the argument concerning *mos* as a source of constitutional norms. To Catulus' claim that the command is violating established precedent, Cicero replies that

> our ancestors (*maiores*) invariably followed custom (*consuetudo*) in time of peace, but expediency in war, and that they invariably responded to emergencies with new ways of doing things.[96]

This well-known, ingenious claim amounts to saying that far from adhering slavishly to custom, the "ways of the ancestors" were in fact to change the ways of the ancestors. In emergencies, there is thus a higher-level custom to be observed, namely to break with peacetime custom. To disregard custom in times of emergency can *itself* lay claim to be the *mos maiorum*, in other words, the putting aside of ordinary constraints in times of emergency is elevated to the status of *mos*.

In order to buttress his argument Cicero points out, speciously, that the Punic and Spanish wars too had been accomplished by a single general[97]—the issue with Scipio Aemilianus' election to the consulship of 147 BC and his command in that year in the Punic war, as we have seen above, was not collegiality (he had a colleague in office after all), but rather the fact that he had been elected consul before reaching the required age. If slightly odd in emphasis, Cicero's claim does point here to a constitutional irregularity apt to strengthen his argument about *mos*. He goes on to remind his audience that in the case of Marius Rome had put the command against Jugurtha, the Teutoni, and the Cimbri all in the hands of one man, Marius (alluding further to the fact that Catulus' father had been politically linked with Marius, had

93. Cic. *Dom.* 18.

94. Pompey's equally extraordinary three-year command of the previous year (67) against the pirates was still ongoing and added to his authority, so that strictly speaking he was not at this point a *privatus*; however, the resistance to the earlier command was based partly on the view that such bestowal upon a *privatus* was unconstitutional. See Gelzer, "Das erste Konsulat."

95. Vell. Pat. 2.31.2–4.

96. Cic. *Leg. Man.* 60. Trans. D. H. Berry.

97. Ibid.

held the consulship with him in 102, and had triumphed with him the following year).[98] The constitutional issue Cicero is raising here is that of the iteration and even continuation of the same office.[99] Marius had after all been elected to the consulship seven times, and five times in a row, with reelections in absentia and, most importantly, in violation of a law that prescribed a ten-year interval between holding the same office.[100] The evidence for this law is shaky,[101] and it seems to be in conflict with another law prohibiting anyone from holding the consulate twice,[102] but that there was at the very least strong customary opprobrium attached to the iteration let alone continuation of the consulship is quite clear. It is unclear whether Catulus in fact invoked any legal basis (in the sense of a *lex*, statute) for his claim that the award of the command to Pompey would be unconstitutional; if so, it was only by implication (if *exempla* and *instituta* are taken to imply statutory regulation).

The concept of *mos* as it appears in Cicero is inextricably tied up with the constitutional debates of the post-Gracchan time. Constitutional discussions of emergencies rarely go without it, and appeals to *mos* are appeals to constitutional norms. The contested nature of *mos* as a source of constitutional norms becomes particularly conspicuous when Cicero in his first Catilinarian speech addresses the potential concerns with putting Catiline to death—might this not violate *mos maiorum*? Interestingly, *mos* here is given pride of place; the potential violation of statute comes only second, and concerns about his own reputation last.[103] Cicero makes his country (*patria*) rhetorically ask him: "Surely you are going to give orders that he [Catiline] be cast into chains, led away to execution, and made to suffer the ultimate penalty? What on earth is stopping you? The tradition of our ancestors (*mos maiorum*)?" But in this case, *mos*, far from being a constraint, would according to Cicero allow, if not demand, that Catiline be put to death:

> But in this country it has very often been the case that even private citizens have punished dangerous citizens with death.[104]

---

98. Ibid.

99. See Brennan, *Praetorship*, vol. 2, pp. 647–652; Kunkel and Wittmann, *Staatsordnung*, pp. 6–8; Lundgreen, *Regelkonflikte*, pp. 85–97.

100. Plut. *Mar.* 12 offers the fullest discussion of the constitutional issues. See also Plut. *Mar.* 14.6–8; Livy, *Per.* 67.

101. Livy 7.42.2. Meier, *Res publica amissa*, p. 309 is skeptical; Rilinger, "Ausbildung" is less so. On term limits, see Coli, "Sui limiti."

102. Livy, *Per.* 56. See Broughton, *Magistrates*, vol. 1, p. 490, n. 1 for further references. For Scipio's elections to the consulship, see Astin, *Scipio Aemilianus*, pp. 61–69, 135.

103. Cf. the similar hierarchy at Cic. *Rab. Perd.* 17.

104. Cic. *Cat.* 1.27.12–28.2. Trans. D. H. Berry.

"Very often" is, of course, an exaggeration. The examples (*exempla*) that buttress this claim—in accordance with rhetorical theory[105]—are few, and Cicero mentioned earlier the only obvious one, the killing of Tiberius Gracchus by Publius Scipio Nasica when the latter was a private citizen.[106] Here *mos* appears fully as constitutional precedent, and Cicero's argument hinges on the empirical point—whether or not it has indeed "very often" been the case that private citizens have punished seditious citizens with death. But is that all there is to it, is this empirical-historical question the only one worth asking when it comes to *mos*? Can *mos* itself be normatively evaluated?

What, in other words, gives the *mos maiorum* its validity in Cicero's view? What are the grounds of obligation to it? Is the mere fact of "the way things happened to be done at the time"[107] sufficient for *mos* to set valid precedent, to become the source of constitutional norms and develop normative force? From a discussion in his rhetorical treatise *Partitiones oratoriae* it becomes clear that the validity of both custom (*mores*) and laws (*leges*) are based on natural law, that is to say, the primary ground of obligation, the reason why we are expected to adhere to *mos* and *lex*, is that the natural law prescribes this. This is to say that natural law, not mere custom or the "way things happened to be done," provides the ultimate criterion: it is "prescribed" or "commanded" by natural law that we should uphold and look to custom.[108]

The last word, then, rests with natural law; with a moral evaluation, not with custom. In the *De legibus*, Cicero makes the claim with clarity, and although the discussion here deals with religious customs, its elucidation of *mos* is not confined to custom in the religious domain:

> What follows in the law [i.e., in Cicero's proposed religious legislation in *De legibus* 2.22.3] is that the best of ancestral rites should be cultivated. When the Athenians consulted Pythian Apollo to ask what religions they should particularly preserve, the oracle came back: those which are part of ancestral custom (*mos maiorum*). When they came back and said that ancestral custom had changed frequently (*saepe mutatum*), and asked which of the various customs (*quem morem e variis*) they should

105. Quint. *Inst.* 5.11.6. Cf. Lausberg, *Handbuch*, §§ 410–425.

106. Cic. *Cat.* 1.3.1. The killings of L. Appuleius Saturninus and C. Servilius Glaucia (Cic. *Cat.* 1.4.5–7) were by private citizens, but under the authority of the consuls and a senatorial decree.

107. Lintott, *Constitution*, p. 4.

108. Cic. *Part. or.* 130.

> follow, he answered: the best. And in fact it is true that whatever is best should be considered oldest and closest to the god.[109]

Mos, then, does not provide an independent criterion for goodness—rather, what is good determines what is to be considered old. Cicero in fact says that nothing is good because it is old, but vice versa what is to be considered old is so to be considered because it is good.[110] What grounds our obligation to *mos* and *lex* is thus an independent, natural-law criterion of goodness. Antiquarian research cannot therefore yield the solution to problems of a normative, constitutional character; in the last resort only natural law can. Even if *mos* were less malleable and had not changed so frequently, one may suppose, Cicero would not concede normative force to custom unsanctioned by natural law. Rather, we are to pick those ancestral *exempla* that are constitutionally salient in light of prior natural-law reasoning. As we will see in Chapter 4 on Cicero's constitutional theory, it is this crucial move, founding the Roman *mores* and the republican constitution on natural law, that gives Cicero's thought its typical and highly original character.[111]

Now one might suppose that all of this is just so much rhetoric, mere foam thrown up by power politics and floating on the waves of *exempla* of the ancestors. But this would be to miss the point. Cicero's constitutional thought as detailed in his philosophical works and the reasoning exhibited in his speeches in the heat of politics are, in this regard, of a piece: they all presuppose, rather than simply rhetorically conjure up, the concept of a constitution founded, in the last resort, on objective natural law. The fact that the speeches in particular are highly rhetorical and tendentious does not mean that the *ars dicendi* is to have the last word. Nor does it mean that their appeal to constitutional principle—be it in the form of *mos*, or *ius*, or incorporated in legislation—is qua rhetoric not to be taken seriously and to be dismissed. Rather, the speeches show us constitutional argument in action, always presupposing, as they do, that what audiences have to be convinced of is a certain interpretation of the republican constitution. In this regard, and to the extent that the courts, the assemblies, and the Senate were still functioning, the late Roman Republic might be said to have exhibited a system of what constitutional lawyers in the United States would call "diffuse judicial review." That is

---

109. Cic. *Leg.* 2.40. Trans. Zetzel.

110. *Pace* Dyck, *Commentary*, p. 361.

111. Cf. Xen. *Mem.* 4.3.16, where custom or law (*nomos*) is the standard prescribed by the Pythian god.

to say, in any given forum, any given audience might be called upon to decide on the constitutionality of an issue, be it of a highly concrete kind (as in cases before criminal courts, or when dealing with emergencies) or of an abstract kind (as in deliberative speeches before meetings of the Senate or assemblies of the People).

The sources of constitutional norms: ius

In an attempt to flatter Pompey, Cicero in his speech *Pro Milone* in 52 BC calls him an expert in "public law (*ius publicum*), the custom of our ancestors (*mos maiorum*), and in all things to do with the Republic."[112] This kind of *ius*, often mentioned in one breath with *mos*, was not based on statute, nor was it perceived to be identical with *mos*.[113] According to Bleicken, *ius*, juxtaposed with statute (*lex*), was used to refer to all legal norms of the Republic in their entirety.[114] Bleicken appreciates that *ius* denotes the foundational institutions of public life.[115] Bleicken observes that Cicero's use of the term often excludes references to statutory law, as if *ius* and *lex* were distinct.[116] In my view, he should have gone further and recognized that *ius*, when in conflict with statute, assumes the rank of a source of superior constitutional norms, norms that win out against statutory law. In what follows I will try to substantiate this claim.

Early in the civil war between Caesar and Pompey, on March 25 in 49, Cicero speculated in a letter to his friend Atticus about Caesar's intentions and next moves:

> I imagine he [Caesar] will want a decree of the Senate and another from the Augurs . . . allowing a Praetor either to hold consular elections or to nominate a Dictator, neither of which is legal (*neutrum ius est*). But if Sulla could arrange for a Dictator to be nominated by an Interrex, and a Master of the Horse, why not Caesar?[117]

112. Cic. *Mil.* 70. Cf. Luc. *Phars.* 9.190–191.

113. See Schanbacher, "Ius und mos."

114. Bleicken, *Lex Publica*, pp. 348–354, esp. 349; 359–362.

115. Ibid., p. 349.

116. See ibid., especially p. 361, n. 68.

117. Cic. *Att.* 9.15.2. Trans. Shackleton Bailey. Cf. *Att.* 9.9.3.

The last sentence, far from expressing a view on valid precedent, is laced with bitter irony. Cicero's position is rendered in the first sentence—consular elections could only be held by a consul (or a dictator), and a dictator (the magistracy Caesar was, of course, going on to hold, after an enabling statute was carried by a praetor) could only be nominated by a consul. Everything else was not according to *ius*, and "neither of which is legal" here must mean that the procedures favored by Caesar are *unconstitutional* according to Cicero.[118]

Similarly, in two earlier letters to Atticus, Cicero makes it clear that acting *iure* means acting legally, but legally on a higher plane, as it were, than merely acting according to *leges*—again, it must mean acting according to the higher-order rules embodied in the republican constitution. In a letter from Formiae dated March 17, 49 BC, Cicero tells Atticus that he suspects Caesar might aim at having consuls elected under a praetor (instead of under a consul). Such a course of action, however, would not be constitutional (*non esse ius*). How does Cicero know this? The passage is extremely instructive as it gives us a rare glimpse into what must have been a rich antiquarian literature consisting of commentaries on constitutional practice, to be found mainly in the books of the religious colleges, especially the augurs (a college of which Cicero himself was a member from 53 onwards).[119] In his letter to Atticus, Cicero points out that "we have it in our books" (i.e., we, the augurs) that it is not according to *ius* "not only for Consuls but even Praetors to be elected under a Praetor, and that such a thing is without precedent."[120] In what must have been Cicero's source, Messalla's otherwise lost work on auspices, Messalla had explained that

> the praetor, although he is a colleague of the consul, cannot *iure* propose either a praetor or a consul, as indeed we have learned from our forefathers, or from what has been observed in the past, and as is shown in the thirteenth book of the *Commentaries* of C. Tuditanus; for the praetor has inferior authority (*imperium*) and the consul superior, and a higher authority cannot be proposed *iure* by a lower, or a superior colleague by an inferior.[121]

---

118. For a discussion too forgiving of Sulla, see Hurlet, *La dictature*, pp. 30–49, esp. pp. 48–49; see also Hinard, "De la dictature," p. 89 and n. 15.

119. See Linderski, "Augural Law," esp. pp. 2241–2256. See also Premerstein, "Commentarii"; Heuss, "Zur Thematik."

120. Cic. *Att.* 9.9.3. Trans. D. R. Shackleton Bailey.

121. Gell. 13.15.4. Trans. J. C. Rolfe, with some emendations.

Tuditanus' work on constitutional law, lost as well, thus also dealt with *ius* and with what could be done *iure*. The same use of the term can be found in Cicero's next letter to Atticus, where Cicero lumps together Sulla, Marius, and Cinna as having acted "rightly" (*recte*), even—perhaps!—constitutionally (*immo iure fortasse*): this is, however, no longer of any relevance, as their actions, however *iure*, yielded "the cruellest and most sinister episodes in our history."[122] Shackleton Bailey in his commentary rightly says that this "must mean that they could plead some constitutional justification, Sulla and Cinna as having been wrongfully deprived of a command and a Consulship respectively, Marius as Cinna's associate and as wrongfully exiled."[123]

This corresponds as well to the concept of *ius* employed by Cicero almost six years later in his *Philippic Eight*, delivered before the Senate on February 3, 43 BC. The speech, delivered in the context of the break between Cicero and Antonius and the ensuing civil war, was part of an attempt by Cicero to oppose the project of an embassy to the enemy. Cicero is trying to show that the present struggle with Antonius does indeed qualify as a war, and should be distinguished from earlier civil wars on the grounds that in the conflict with Antonius, all citizens present a united front against the opponent, who is set on the violent overthrow of the republican constitution with the goal of plundering and redistributing the private property of the citizenry. By contrast, earlier civil wars had been fought over constitutional interpretation:

> Is this not war, or is it even the greatest war that ever was? For in other wars, and particularly civil wars, a political reason (*rei publicae causa*) caused the conflict: Sulla <fought> Sulpicius about the validity of laws (*de iure legum*) which according to him [*sc.* Consul Sulla] had been passed by violence. Cinna fought Octavius about voting rights for the new citizens. Sulla again fought Marius and Carbo to put an end to the rule of the unworthy and to avenge the terribly cruel deaths of illustrious men. The causes for all these wars originated in political dispute (*ex rei publicae contentione*).[124]

---

122. Cic. *Att.* 9.10.3. Trans. D. R. Shackleton Bailey.

123. Shackleton Bailey, *Cicero's Letters*, p. 378. On the potential legitimacy of Sulla's actions in 88, see already Meyer, *Römischer Staat*, p. 315; Meier, *Res publica amissa*, p. 237; similarly, Robert Morstein-Marx, "Consular Appeals." Legitimacy, however, must here mean "constitutional legitimacy." Cf. Straumann, "Review H. Beck, *Consuls*"; Ungern-Sternberg, "Legitimitätskrise."

124. Cic. *Phil.* 8.7. Ed. and trans. Gesine Manuwald.

According to Cicero, the war with Antonius is much closer in character with a war against an outside enemy (*hostis*); the previous civil wars, on the other hand, were in effect fought over constitutional interpretation. When Cicero says that Sulla was driven to launch civil war (and to occupy Rome with his troops) because in his view the laws (*leges*) passed by the tribune of 88 BC, P. Sulpicius, were lacking in validity, he renders this as a struggle *de iure legum*.[125] The validity in question means constitutional validity—Sulpicius' legislation was unconstitutional, and this is what caused Sulla to march against Rome. All these wars were fought *rei publicae causa*, Cicero maintains, but the reason is not merely "political," as Manuwald's translation has it; it is clearly constitutional. As Cicero explicates, whether or not legislation and other acts were constitutionally valid, that is to say, *iure*, was at the center of those wars.[126]

This passage from *Philippic Eight* underscores not only the role of *ius* as a body of constitutional norms, but it also gives us a good sense of how Cicero, in my view convincingly, appraised the crises and civil wars of the late Republic as conflicts over constitutional interpretation. At least from Sulla onward, Cicero maintains, political struggles tended to find expression in two rival, mutually exclusive interpretations of the constitution, one popular, as in the case of Sulpicius, Cinna, Marius, and Carbo, the other senatorial or optimate, as in the case of Sulla and Octavius. Rather than as expressing any kind of "party" label, this is how the *populares-optimates* dichotomy is best understood: as expressing two mutually exclusive interpretations of the republican constitutional order.[127]

Let me give an example of the senatorial interpretation of the republican constitution very much in line with Cicero's interpretation of late republican history, an example that will also serve to reinforce our view of *ius* as a body of constitutional legal norms. When the Senate in 121 BC for the first time used its so-called "last decree" (*senatus consultum ultimum*) in order to declare a state of emergency, urging the consul Lucius Opimius to execute the former tribune of the plebs Gaius Gracchus, this was interpreted as an attempt of the Senate to undermine Gracchus' civic right of appeal (*provocatio*); and when Opimius was prosecuted the following year for killing a Roman citizen, the fact that he had acted in accordance with a decree of the Senate did not prevent his prosecution

125. For *de iure legum* denoting "the constitutionality of statutes," see also Cic. *Dom.* 71 (the Senate has authority to exercise some sort of judicial review).

126. See Manuwald, *Cicero*, vol. 2, p. 939: *de iure legum* "means 'how far the laws were constitutional/valid.'"

127. See Arena, *Libertas*, ch. 3, for the philosophical traditions behind these interpretations. Cf. also Robb, *Beyond Populares*; Perelli, *Il movimento*.

and was thus not seen in itself as giving sufficient legal justification for the execution.[128] When Cicero framed the issue in *De oratore*, writing years after having famously acted under a similar "last decree" against the Catilinarians, he stresses the conflict between the Senate's authority, as expressed in its *consultum ultimum*, and the rights of the People, as expressed in the laws that codify the Roman citizens' right of appeal: should a punishment be inflicted upon someone who had killed a citizen in conformity with a decree of the Senate (*ex senatus consulto*) for the preservation of his fatherland (*patriae conservandae causa*), when this was not permitted by the laws (*leges*)?[129] The issue, according to Cicero, is in short whether the killing "was permitted (*licueritne*) on account of the senate's decree for the rescue of the commonwealth (*servandae rei publicae causa*)."[130] "Permitted" here obviously cannot mean permitted by statute (*per leges*); rather, it must mean permitted by some higher norm. This higher norm presumably would make allowance for illegal killings—if at all—only if there was a decree of the Senate "for the rescue of the commonwealth," and, this being a necessary but not a sufficient condition, if in addition this argument would prove persuasive in a People's court in case of a prosecution of the magistrate accused of the unlawful killing.

This is precisely the way Opimius' case was dealt with. Opimius was prosecuted for the unlawful killing of C. Gracchus in a trial before the People and acquitted. If Cicero's account is correct,[131] the argument of the prosecution put forward by the tribune of the plebs P. Decius was that the Senate's decree *itself* was unlawful by virtue of being inconsistent with and contrary to statute (*contra leges*).[132] The consul C. Carbo, who defended Opimius, argued that the killing had been lawful (*iure*) on the grounds that it had been done "for the public safety" (*pro salute patriae*).[133] The argument was apparently convincing; Opimius was acquitted by the People.[134] In his speech on behalf of P. Sestius (56 BC), Cicero said that Opimius had "brilliantly

128. See Ungern-Sternberg, *Untersuchungen*, pp. 68–71.

129. Cic. *De or.* 2.134.

130. Ibid. 2.132.

131. Cicero's trustworthiness should not be impaired by his favorable view of the *SCU*. Rather, the question arises whether Cicero here projects back views about the *SCU* from his own time.

132. Cic. *De or.* 2.132.

133. Ibid. 2.106.

134. See Cic. *Brut.* 128; *Sest.* 140; Liv. *Per.* 61.

earned the republic's gratitude" and that "the Roman people itself rescued him from peril at a time when he was engulfed in a blaze of ill-will because of Gaius Gracchus' death,"[135] notwithstanding the fact that Opimius had the reputation of having over the course of his career constantly sided against the preferences of the People.[136]

Opimius' acquittal suggests that Carbo's argument must have prevailed at trial. The acquittal has been interpreted by scholars as setting a crucial, authoritative precedent (an *exemplum*) in favor of the validity of the "last decree" and thus of the senatorial interpretation of the constitution.[137] This is arguably borne out by the further history of the *senatus consultum ultimum*, a history that is one of further entrenchment and, until the trial of C. Rabirius in 63 BC, did not see any further prosecutions for violations of statute and the *ius provocationis*. Such a view may also find support in Cicero's account, in his fourth *Catilinarian*, of Caesar's stance on the matter—the phrase "the man who carried the Sempronian law himself paid the penalty to the state by the will of the people (*iussu populi*)" may seem to refer to Opimius' acquittal.[138] Then again, Cicero may simply have reported Caesar's view that not even C. Gracchus himself, who had carried the law concerning the requirement of *provocatio*, had been covered by its provisions—since he was a traitor not worthy of the law's protection.[139] Either way, we should keep in mind that notwithstanding the relatively frequent recourse to the Senate's "last decree" and the popularity of the use of martial means even within the city among both adherents of the popular as well as the senatorial view of the constitution, there were still attempts to deal with emergencies by way of statute and the establishment of a permanent court (*quaestio*

---

135. Cic. *Sest.* 140. Trans. Kaster, *Cicero: Speech*, slightly adapted.

136. Cic. *Brut.* 128.

137. See, e.g., Ungern-Sternberg, *Untersuchungen*, p. 70.

138. Cic. *Cat.* 4.10. Trans D. H. Berry. See Dyck, *Cicero: Catilinarians*, p. 224. The words imputed to Caesar by Cicero may refer to a *contio* held by Opimius and his supporters in 121: see Lintott, *Violence*, p. 170. Cf. also Livy, *Per.* 61. Cicero's wording (*iussu populi*) however suggests that he is here aiming to conjure up Opimius' acquittal as a precedent. Opimius may have held some sort of *quaestio* in order to give his actions at least the veneer of legitimacy; see August. *De civ. D.* 3.24; Rödl, *Senatus consultum ultimum*, pp. 73–78.

139. This depends on Cic. *Cat.* 4.10; all manuscripts have *iussu populi*, but there is reason to think that Cicero is making his case by pointing out that not even C. Gracchus, the author of the Sempronian law, would have been protected by it and had thus constitutionally been put to death even though the People had not been asked (*iniussu populi*). For the conjecture *iniussu*, see Ungern-Sternberg, *Untersuchungen*, p. 100, n. 86; similarly Drummond, *Law*, p. 44, n. 127. But see Lintott, *Violence*, p. 170.

perpetua) before which political violence could be prosecuted.[140] The use of the Senate's last decree with the specific aim of getting around the right of appeal (as opposed to declaring a state of emergency more generally) went arguably out of fashion after it was thus used in 100 BC.[141] Furthermore, while it seems that Opimius' acquittal did as a matter of fact entrench the Senate's last decree as an increasingly regular institution of the republican constitution, the trial of Opimius itself might as well be interpreted as setting a slightly different precedent: the introduction of a new constitutional device was subject to the People's imprimatur (it was a trial *before the People*, after all, that created the precedent in the first place), and although Opimius' acquittal entailed that acting *pro salute patriae* could be lawful even *contra leges*, it did by no means guarantee freedom from prosecution in general and for all time.

For our purposes most important, however, is that the argument of the prosecution, as represented here, insisted on the illegality of the decree of the Senate by pointing to norms of higher standing—namely statutory law (*leges*). This invited the defense's counterargument that there was yet an even higher-order criterion that could trump statute: if public safety required it, statute could be temporarily suspended, rendering any action undertaken *pro salute patriae* at least potentially lawful. The term used in Cicero's account for "lawful" is *iure*; that is, actions that are in accordance with this kind of *ius* are lawful even when conflicting with statute! What is more, this was accepted as an argument in a trial before the People. Since we do not know exactly what argument it was that swayed the People when they acquitted Opimius, the acquiescence of the *populus Romanus* in the superiority of *ius* as a body of constitutional law should not be made to bear too much weight. Still, the appeal to *ius* in an attempt to argue on the basis of rules that stand hierarchically above mere legislation should alert us to the use of that term in constitutional contexts; *ius* could, in the context of the constitutional conflict of the late Republic, apart and independently from *mos maiorum*, be the term of choice in constitutional arguments when alluding to constitutional norms.

To give a particularly salient example, Cicero, in his early speech for Caecina,[142] claimed that all laws passed in the assemblies contained a clause saying "that if anything were enacted in this statute contrary to law (*ius*), to that extent this statute was to have no validity." Apart from the more than dubious

140. For the establishment of the court and the legislation against public violence surrounding it (*lex Lutatia* and *lex Plautia*), see Lintott, *Violence*, pp. 112–123.

141. Cf. Drummond, *Law*, p. 108; Ungern-Sternberg, *Untersuchungen*, p. 84. On the *SCU*, see Chapter 2.

142. The speech was probably delivered in 69 BC; see Lintott, *Cicero*, p. 80.

historicity of this claim, the passage must interest us on the plane of constitutional thought as it differentiates starkly between *ius* on one hand, meaning the legal order as a whole and especially the constitutional provisions, and legislation on the other. Cicero goes on to ask, rhetorically, "what is there which is contrary to law which the Roman People is unable to command or to prohibit? Not to digress too far, this very additional clause proves that there is something. For unless there were, this would not be appended to all statutes." And now Cicero makes the crucial constitutional argument:

> But I ask of you whether you think, if the people ordered me to be your slave, or, on the other hand, you to be mine, that that order would be authoritative and valid? You see and admit that such an order is worthless. Hereby you first allow this, that it does not follow that whatever the people orders ought to be ratified.[143]

Of course, Cicero's argument here is as rhetorical as it is tendentious; it provides us, however, with a good example of the wide currency of constitutional arguments in institutional or forensic contexts and of the status *ius* enjoyed in those contexts as a body of constitutional, higher-order law.[144] How *ius* and its role as a body of constitutional law sanctioned by natural law came to occupy a crucial status in Cicero's more theoretical writings of political philosophy will be dealt with in the second part of this book on Roman constitutional theory. We may already hint however that in the central piece of Cicero's political theory, his definition of *res publica* in the *Republic, ius* comes to have precisely the function already adumbrated in his speeches, such as *Pro Caecina*. In the *Republic* no less than in the *Pro Caecina ius* serves as a constitutional constraint underwritten by natural law upon the otherwise tyrannical aspirations of the People. When Cicero says in his famous definition, widely circulated via Augustine[145] and widely read in the history of political thought, that *res publica* is *res populi* and that *populus* here, far from designating any gathering at all, means a "society by virtue of agreement with respect to constitutional rules (*iuris consensu*) and sharing in advantage,"[146] he is not merely giving constitutional rules (*ius*) their due as a necessary criterion for the existence of a *populus* (and of a *res publica*), but he also intends this to

143. Cic. *Caec.* 95–96. Trans. Yonge, slightly modified.

144. Cf. Cic. *Sest.* 61: Cato swore allegiance to a *lex* he thought was *non iure rogata* (Caesar's agrarian law of 59 BC), because it had been carried *vi* and against the auspices.

145. August. *De civ. D.* 2.21.

146. Cic. *Rep.* 1.39. My translation.

have a decidedly anti-democratic slant (as in *Pro Caecina*), with *ius* again acting as both constraint on the People's will and as a criterion for there being a people in the required sense in the first place. Later in the dialogue, Laelius refers back to the definition, and argues that a *res* that is under the sovereignty of the masses (*in multitudinis potestate*) cannot by the definition given earlier qualify as a *res publica*. This is because when everything is in the power of the People (*in populi potestate omnia*), an assembly (*conventus*) of the People is "as much a tyrant as if it were a single person."[147]

In the present chapter I have left out many important constitutional institutions such as the (constitutional) right of *provocatio*, the appeal to self-defense, or the annulment of legislation by the Senate provided for in the *lex Caecilia Didia* (98); these will be dealt with below. Instead I have focused on the development of the Roman concept of constitution out of a historical situation of constitutional crisis; or, to put it more strongly, on the origins of the very idea of the necessity of such a thing as a higher-order, entrenched set of norms able to constrain, and normatively judge, ordinary legal rules. These origins, I suggested, can be found in the last years of the Republic, when in so much forensic, deliberative and theoretical writing the idea of a normative yardstick applicable to statute and the political order was conjured up out of the matrix of the crises of the late Roman Republic as an expression of radically diverging interpretations of the Republic's fundamental rules. Most importantly for the history of political thought, this led to the essentially Roman formulation of what constitutes the constitutional criteria of legitimacy of government. Malcolm Schofield had it right when he pointed out, against Moses Finley, that Cicero raised "fairly explicitly a question about legitimacy that is never broached in Greek political philosophy."[148] The Ciceronian answer, as essentially constitutional and legal as it was Roman, was the outcome of what could only in retrospect be recognized as a constitutional crisis, and came, of course, too late for the Republic. But as we will see in the last part of this book on the afterlife of Roman constitutional thought, it did not come too late for Renaissance and early modern Europe.

---

147. Ibid. 3.45. For a more oratorical anti-democratic, anti-Greek view, see Cic. *Flacc.* 15–17 and 57. James Harrington used *Pro Flacco* to argue against democracy: *Oceana*, p. 132.

148. See Schofield, "Cicero's Definition," p. 66. Cf. ibid., pp. 64–65.

2

Infinite Power? Emergencies and Extraordinary Powers in Constitutional Argument

Such being the power that each part has of hampering the others or cooperating with them, their interplay is adequate to all emergencies, so that it is impossible to find a better constitutional order than this.

(POLYB. 6.18.1)

EMERGENCIES PROVIDE THE context for the invocation of higher-level constitutional norms. When ordinary legislation does not seem to suffice, and extralegal measures are said to be needed, these are both defended and argued against in the name of rules that have a higher degree of validity than mere laws. For this reason the many controversies about the bestowal of extraordinary powers that are so typical of the late Republic offer an ideal window into the inchoate constitutionalism of late republican political thought and practice.

The need for a clearer conceptual distinction between the sphere of the "constitutional" and the "extra-constitutional" becomes particularly salient in connection with issues raised by the bestowal of extraordinary powers and the passing of emergency measures. In the last century of the Republic questions of the constitutional locus of sovereignty and of the authority to suspend ordinary constitutional constraints assumed an urgency unheard of either before 133 BC or after Actium. Arguments surrounding emergencies are thus particularly well suited for our purpose and will bring the diverging interpretations of the constitutional order most clearly into focus. Most importantly, in emergencies appeals to a higher-order set of constitutional norms gain enormously in importance—what constitutes an emergency and thus justifies resort to extraordinary measures in the first place cannot be decided without an appeal to higher-order rules.

There are several candidates for extra-constitutional powers that are of interest to us.[1] The three main instruments that provided for exceptional powers and irregular measures in times of crisis were the dictatorship, the so-called "last decree of the Senate" (*senatus consultum ultimum*), and extraordinary commands (*imperia extraordinaria*). Further instances of extraordinary powers can be found in the competencies given to the ten law-commissioners (*decemviri*) who drafted the Twelve Tables in the fifth century BC, and in the powers accorded to the agrarian commissions intended to implement and adjudicate various agrarian reform proposals. Pompey's sole consulship in 52 belongs here as does his emergency administration of the grain supply of the city of Rome (*cura annonae*). In line with the overall ambition of this book, the main emphasis of this chapter will be not so much on the institutional framework of the late Roman republican constitution nor on the political history of the late Republic but rather on how these institutions are reflected in political thought and constitutional argument as represented in historiography. The crucial question will be how, in the constitutional and political thought of the epoch, the distinction between the constitutional and the extra-constitutional was construed.

The dictatorship

The dictatorship as an institution of the republican constitution was abolished in 44 BC by a statute put forward by M. Antonius.[2] Cicero, pointing out that this had been Antonius' most crucial measure, tells us in his first *Philippic* that this *lex Antonia* had "completely" (*funditus*) abolished the dictatorship, which had by then acquired the quality of a regal power.[3] Indeed, it was in order to prove his hatred of kingship (*odium regni*) that Antonius had, according to Cicero, done his best deed, the abolition of the dictatorship, designed to ban fear of kingly power for good.[4] Appian describes Antonius' abolition of the dictatorship as mere gamesmanship aimed at appeasing the Senate and achieving his

1. See von Fritz, "Emergency Powers"; Nippel, "Emergency Powers."

2. On the dictatorship, see Bandel, *Die römischen Diktaturen*; Keyes, "Constitutional Position"; Kellett, *Story*; Wilcken, "Entwicklung"; Rossiter, *Constitutional Dictatorship*; Cohen, "Origin"; Nolte, "Diktatur"; Irmscher, "Diktatur"; Hofmann, "Diktatur"; Hartfield, *Dictatorship*; Morgan, "Q. Metellus"; Münkler and Llanque, "Diktatur"; Nicolet, "Dictatorship"; Kalyvas, "Tyranny"; Nippel, "Saving." Cf. also the tendentious and disingenuous Schmitt, *Diktatur*; on Schmitt, see Nippel, "Carl Schmitts 'kommissarische' und 'souveräne Diktatur.'"

3. Cic. *Phil.* 1.3.

4. Ibid. 2.91.

real aim, the Macedonian command; having abolished the dictatorship, Appian writes, Antonius went on to be chosen as "autocratic" or dictatorial commander (*στρατηγὸς αὐτοκράτωρ*) of the Roman forces in Macedonia.[5] Cassius Dio offers a similarly skeptical view of the abolition of the dictatorship. The *lex Antonia* assumed wrongly, Dio writes, that the problems of the late Republic had been caused by constitutional positions and titles and could thus be remedied by the abolition of those positions and titles; but as a matter of fact, the problem lay with the actions themselves, which had not arisen as a consequence of the constitutional or institutional structure, but rather from opportunity: Dio mentions the availability of armed forces and says that the deeds in question had arisen *ἐκ τῶν ὅπλων*, or from the character of the individual officeholder.[6]

The accounts we have of the origin of the institution of the dictatorship are not historical. They represent all too transparent attempts, especially in the case of Livy and Dionysius of Halicarnassus, to retroject the problems and issues of the last century of the Republic back into early republican history.[7] It is striking that the dictatorship is presented as an institution designed to override the constitutional right *par excellence*, the right of appeal (*provocatio*), which guaranteed that a Roman citizen could not be executed without trial. Livy thinks that external military threats, especially the Sabines, motivated the creation of the dictatorship. The magistracy of the dictator, Livy tells us, was created by law—an assembly, however configured, must thus have instituted the dictatorship by means of a *lex de dictatore creando*.[8] Once created, the novel institution instilled fear in the plebs, precisely because there was no right of appeal against it:

> When, for the first time, a Dictator was created in Rome, a great fear fell on the people (*plebs*), after they saw the axes borne before him, and consequently they were more careful to obey his orders. For there was not, as in the case of the consuls, each of whom possessed the same authority, any chance of securing the aid of one against the other, nor was there any right of appeal (*provocatio*), nor in short was there any safety anywhere except in punctilious obedience.[9]

5. App. *BCiv.* 3.25. Cf. Luce, "Appian's Magisterial Terminology."

6. Dio Cass. 44.51.2–3.

7. See Gabba, "Dionigi," p. 217: the speeches concerning the origins of the dictatorship are full of "toni graccani ed echi dell'episodio catilinario." The same can be said of Livy and, to some extent, of Appian.

8. Livy 2.18.6.

9. Ibid. 2.18.8–9.

When confronted with the impossibility of holding a levy in the face of external military threats in 494 BC, and in the face of open resistance to the command of the consuls and the attempted enforcement of the levy by a lictor, the Senate and the consuls resolve to appoint a dictator. The decisive argument that convinces them to do so is said by Livy to have been given by the hardliner and ex-consul Appius Claudius:

> Appius Claudius, harsh by nature, and now maddened by the hatred of the plebs on the one hand and the praises of the senate on the other, asserted that these riotous gatherings were not the result of misery but of licence, the plebeians were actuated by wantonness more than by anger. This was the mischief which had sprung from the right of appeal (*provocatio*), for the consuls could only threaten without the power to execute their threats as long as a criminal was allowed to appeal to his fellow criminals. 'Come,' said he, 'let us create a Dictator from whom there is no appeal, then this madness which is setting everything on fire will soon die down. Let me see any one strike a lictor then, when he knows that his back and even his life are in the sole power of the man whose authority he attacks.'[10]

The dictator they end up nominating, Manius Valerius, manages to convince the People that they do not have anything to fear from him, notwithstanding his dictatorial powers—he actually goes on to support some of the plebs' demands for debt relief and successfully holds a levy, resulting in the largest army enrolled until then. This is important: although the motivation to introduce the dictatorship in general and nominate Manius Valerius in particular is said by Livy to lie at least partly in the dictator's immunity to *provocatio*, the dictator is not being shown to make use of his emergency powers by executing or flogging citizens freely. Rather than behaving like the consul Opimius in 121 or like Cicero in 63 in violation of the right of appeal, the dictator Manius Valerius is shown in action as a moderate mediator who even steps down from his dictatorship when it becomes clear that his attempt at debt relief finds no support in the Senate. That is to say that although the magistracy itself is introduced by Livy in a way perfectly suitable for protagonists of the crisis of the late Republic like Opimius or Cicero, Livy's early dictators themselves are almost never shown to use their allegedly fearsome coercive powers to suppress sedition.

In one case, however, Livy has a dictator and his *magister equitum* suppress a *coup d'état* allegedly aimed at kingship in 439 BC. Having discovered the designs of one Spurius Maelius to overthrow the republican order and to make himself

10. Ibid. 2.29.9–12.

king, the Senate accuses the consuls of having failed to punish the conspirators. The consul T. Quinctius defends himself by pointing out that he and his colleague were constrained by the right of appeal, which had been enacted by statute precisely in order to "destroy" their power to command (*ad dissolvendum imperium*). There was therefore a need, Quinctius states, for a man who was not only brave, but who was also "free and unfettered by the laws"—unfettered by the laws guaranteeing the right of appeal, that is.[11] The consul goes on to nominate Lucius Quinctius Cincinnatus as dictator. His master of the horse, trying to summon a recalcitrant Maelius before the dictator, proceeds to kill Maelius. Maelius is shown to have tried, to no avail, to appeal to the bystanders for physical support and protection against the *magister equitum*; he uses the language of *fidem plebis Romanae implorare*, of crying for help to the surrounding crowd, which, although not directly invoking *provocatio* or *auxilium*, is standard language for the invocation of the right of appeal.[12] As Maelius is appealing—*vociferans*—, he is killed by the master of the horse Servilius Ahala.[13] It is unclear whether the bystanders acknowledged that the dictator's summons would have voided any right of appeal or whether they simply chose not to help Maelius or were physically unable to do so. Livy's point seems to be that the bystanders were at least unsure about the legitimacy of Maelius' right of appeal vis-à-vis the command of a dictator or even tacitly acknowledged that there was no appeal against a dictator. When told that his master of the horse had killed Maelius when Maelius had resisted arrest, the dictator L. Quinctius Cincinnatus lauds him for having liberated the Republic.[14]

Cincinnatus then goes on to give his view of the legal situation. He does this by calling an informal assembly, a *contio*, acknowledging thus the political need for justification before the People but not conceding to the assembly any formal legal powers of adjudication with regard to the killing of Maelius. Maelius had been killed in a constitutional way—once again: *iure*—Cincinnatus maintains, not primarily on account of his plotting the overthrow of the Republic and aspiring to kingship, but because he had resisted the dictator's summons and had thus tried to avoid trial.[15] Cincinnatus here has in mind a trial where he himself, the

---

11. Ibid. 4.13.11.

12. See Lintott, "*Provocatio*," pp. 228–231.

13. Livy 4.14.3–6. Cf. Cic. *Sen.* 56. John Adams, too, followed this account: *Defence*, vol. 3, pp. 241–244.

14. An earlier tradition (Dion. Hal. *Ant. Rom.* 12.4.2–5) has Maelius being killed by Servilius Ahala as a private citizen; on this tradition and its relation to Livy, see Lintott, "Tradition," pp. 13–18.

15. Livy 4.15.1.

dictator, would have sat as judge, emphatically not a trial before the People.[16] He reaffirms, then, in a *contio* before the People, the constitutionality of the killing of a citizen by the dictator given the absence of a right of appeal against the dictator.

What are we to make of this? It is reasonably clear that the tradition which maintains that the dictatorship had been created primarily as a measure against sedition and in direct opposition to the right of appeal is marked by highly anachronistic echoes stemming from the Gracchan and Catilinarian conflicts.[17] This is precisely the kind of magistracy that would have been of use to Opimius in 121 and to Cicero in 63. It is this tradition which much later forced the historian Appian to ask himself why it was that nobody had thought of nominating a dictator in the year 133,[18] during the crisis which ensued after Ti. Gracchus tried to get himself elected tribune for a second consecutive year:

> In these circumstances the Senate assembled at the temple of Fides. It is astonishing to me that they never thought of appointing a dictator in this emergency, although they had often been protected by the government of a single ruler (*autokrator*) in such times of peril. Although this resource had been found most useful in former times few people remembered it, either then or later.[19]

The episodes related by Livy are said to have occurred in the context of a debt crisis, in the case of the dictator Manius Valerius, and of problems concerning the grain supply of Rome, in the case of Maelius' attempted *coup d'état*. This is the context within which Appian locates the Gracchan crisis, when he explains the motivation of Tiberius Gracchus' supporters as lying chiefly in their fear of no longer being able to live under equal laws, but of being reduced to servitude by the rich.[20] Similarly, in his retrojection of the traditions deriving from the Gracchan reforms and from the social problems of the 60s BC, Dionysius of Halicarnassus establishes the origins of the dictatorship in the context of the problems of conducting a levy in a citizenry riddled with debt. Exactly as in the passages of Livy, the solution is found in a magistracy immune to the right of appeal, which will allow for the coercion of unwilling poor citizens. The

16. Ibid. 4.15.2.

17. See Gutberlet, *Die erste Dekade*.

18. Cf. Golden, *Crisis Management*, p. 40.

19. App. *BCiv.* 1.16. Trans. Horace White.

20. App. *BCiv.* 1.15.

chief reason, according to Dionysius, for the establishment of what he calls a "voluntary tyranny" (αὐθαίρετος τυραννίς), was the law ascribed by the annalistic tradition to P. Valerius Publicola which had established the right of appeal—this (mythical) early law had, according to Dionysius, made the decisions and judgments of the consuls void.[21] For this reason the new magistracy, the dictatorship, had to have absolute power over every matter and could not be accountable for either its deliberations or its actions,[22] so that all would have to obey orders. This of course amounted to an at least temporary repeal of the right of appeal (temporary because Dionysius does insist on the six-month time limit for the dictator). Instead of trying to repeal the Valerian law openly, which would never have gone through the assembly, the Senate, according to Dionysius, did so surreptitiously by introducing the dictatorship, which amounted to the same thing:

> The senate reasoned that while this law remained in force the poor could not be compelled to obey the magistrates, because, as it was reasonable to suppose, they would scorn the punishments which they were to undergo, not immediately, but only after they had been condemned by the people, whereas, when this law had been repealed, all would be under the greatest necessity of obeying orders. And to the end that the poor might offer no opposition, in case an open attempt were made to repeal the law itself, the senate resolved to introduce into the government a magistracy of equal power with a tyranny (ἰσοτύραννος ἀρχή), which should be superior to all the laws. And they passed a decree by which they deceived the poor and, without being detected, repealed the law that secured their liberty. The decree was to this effect: that Larcius and Cloelius, who were the consuls at the time, should resign their power, and likewise any other person who held a magistracy or had the oversight of any public business; and that a single person, to be chosen by the senate and approved of by the people, should be invested with the whole authority of the commonwealth and exercise it for a period not longer than six months, having power superior to that of the consuls. The plebeians, being unaware of the real import of this proposal, ratified the resolutions of the senate, although, in fact, a magistracy that was superior to a legal magistracy was a tyranny; and they gave the senators permission to deliberate by themselves and choose the person who was to hold it.[23]

---

21. Dion. Hal. *Ant. Rom.* 5.70.2.

22. Ibid. 5.70.1.

23. Ibid. 5.70.3–5.

Thus the many are fooled and abrogate their own liberty. What makes the dictatorship in Dionysius' eyes tantamount to a tyranny is its power over the established right of appeal—it is an established republican trope that liberty consisted first and foremost in the right of appeal. The introduction of this new tyrannical magistracy, which is said to be above the laws and especially above the law enshrining *provocatio*, itself presupposes the passing of a law in the assembly: for this reason the Senate is portrayed as tricking the People by means of a ruse. The dictatorship appears as little more than the abrogation of *provocatio*, notwithstanding the strictly limited term of the office. We have here prominently the late republican themes of *provocatio* and the repression of internal strife, well known to Dionysius, writing in the Augustan era, hand in hand with the attested features of the historical republican dictatorship, namely the time limit. It is not overly fanciful to detect, in Dionysius' insistence that the dictatorship was created with authority "superior to all the laws," a reflection of the title that seems to have gone with Sulla's dictatorship in 82: *dictator legibus scribundis et rei publicae constituendae*.[24] As we will see, this aspect of the dictatorship has its analogue, not in the historical republican dictatorship, but in the powers of the *decemviri* as they appear in the annalistic tradition.[25] On the other hand, apart from the insistence on the dictatorship being above all the laws and above *provocatio*, that is, apart from the insistence on the dictatorship being tailored to emergencies within the city, there is the familiar view that ultimately the dictatorship is needed to deal with external military threats.

As with Livy's *lex de dictatore creando* there is a constitutional need, for Dionysius, to establish the dictatorship as an institution by means of a comitial statute (*lex*). As will be seen when we discuss the quintessential late republican constitutional emergency device, the so-called *senatus consultum ultimum*, this perceived need to legitimize the violation of *provocatio* by passing a law in the assembly cannot be shown still to have existed in the late Republic. Similarly, in the late Republic *provocatio* is usually undermined or violated not by means of the dictatorship, but by extra-legal means. This should alert us to the most plausible explanation of the early republican examples in the annalistic tradition, of dictators being empowered *seditionis sedandae causa*: that these are simply not historical, and that in the one plausible case where a dictator *seditionis sedandae causa* appears in the *fasti*, namely Publius Manlius Capitolinus in 368,[26] his

24. See App. *BCiv.* 1.99.

25. See Bellen, "Sullas Brief," pp. 557–560. Appian's wording (παυσάμενον ἔθος ἐκ τετρακοσίων ἐτῶν) may indeed have been taken from Dionysius 5.77.4: Gabba, *Appiani*, p. 269.

26. Degrassi 32–33, 103–104, 398–399; Livy 6.39.1. Broughton, *Magistrates*, vol. 1, p. 112.

dictatorship had not been in conflict with the right of appeal. Indeed, Manlius' predecessor as dictator that same year, M. Furius Camillus, is said by Livy to have been challenged by a tribunician law declaring him to be subject to a fine resulting from his actions as dictator. Livy wonders if this can be true: cannot a dictator, Livy asks himself, resist a measure put forward by the tribunes that is designed to limit his authority?[27] His successor Manlius Capitolinus, far from acting contrary to the right of appeal, even appoints a plebeian, C. Licinius, as his master of the horse, according to Livy very much to the chagrin of the patrician elite.[28]

The idea that the dictator was able to suppress seditions and internal unrest by virtue of his having *imperium* even within the city and, most importantly, by virtue of there being no right of appeal against him is one of the crucial features ascribed to the earlier republican dictatorship by our sources. This shows a deep constitutional tension between the dictatorship and the liberty of the People—Livy has the patrician leader of the plebs Manlius Capitolinus urge the People, in the context of another debt crisis in the early fourth century, to abolish the dictatorship and the consulate altogether.[29] Curtailing civil rights in the face of an emergency seemed to fit the dictator's sphere of competence, especially in the eyes of historians writing after Sulla's dictatorship, but the desire to have an instrument against *provocatio* must have been salient at least from the time of the Gracchi onward (as Appian[30] correctly intuited). That early republican dictators held *imperium domi* is something even the ancient historian Fred Drogula acknowledges in his revisionist account of *imperium*.[31] Drogula, arguing that there never was such a thing as *imperium domi* in the first place, holds that the dictatorship, endowed with *imperium domi* in order to be able to face down *provocatio*, was the exception that confirms his rule; however, his argument can be strengthened once it is acknowledged, as I shall argue here, that dictatorship *sine provocatione* is a construction of the last century of the Republic, fabricated under the influence of Sulla's dictatorship on the one hand and the annalistic tradition concerning the Decemvirate on the other.

In other words, what is presented to us by the annalistic tradition as one key feature of the early republican magistracy, its power to abrogate the right of appeal, in all likelihood was not one of its formal features at all before Sulla (to the extent that *provocatio* is thus presupposed for a time before 300 BC, this is

27. Livy 6.38.12.

28. Ibid. 6.39.3. Cf. Meloni, "'Dictatura popularis'," p. 82.

29. Livy 6.18.14.

30. App. *BCiv.* 1.16.

31. Drogula, "Imperium," pp. 446–447. Cf. Giovannini, *Consulare imperium*.

a quite glaring anachronism in any case). This gives us a plausible explanation for the fact that was so astonishing to Appian—that during the Gracchan crisis no one in the Senate seems to have thought of having the consul nominate a dictator.[32] No one thought of it because at that time it must still have been well known that dictators simply did not have *imperium sine provocatione*; whether they ever had it, or lost it later on, is immaterial for our purposes.[33] Andrew Lintott draws attention to the fact that at one point Livy seems to demonstrate that "the dictator's supreme power did not necessarily extend into the city, the realm of *provocatio*."[34] Livy in this passage describes a conflict between the dictator L. Papirius Cursor, appointed dictator *rei gerundae causa* in the Samnite war, and his master of the horse Q. Fabius in 325 BC. After the conflict escalates and Papirius Cursor orders "the Master of the Horse to be stripped and the rods and axes to be got ready,"[35] Q. Fabius' father, M. Fabius, proceeds to appeal to the People against the dictator:

> I claim the intervention of the tribunes of the plebs and appeal to the people. As you are seeking to escape from the judgment which the army has passed upon you and which the senate is passing now, I summon you before the one judge who has at all events more power and authority than your Dictatorship. I shall see whether you will submit to an appeal to which a Roman king—Tullus Hostilius—submitted.[36]

The episode related by Livy is ambiguous. Q. Fabius and his father proceed to appeal to the People, but their competence to judge in this matter does not seem to be acknowledged by the dictator; he does acknowledge, however, the power of the tribunes to interfere and lend *auxilium*. It seems as if the People had the last word on the question whether there was *provocatio* against the dictator in the first place, and decide to plead with him rather than formally take up Q. Fabius' appeal. At the very least the ambiguity shows that the right of appeal against a dictator was not believed in principle to be excluded (indeed, this is underlined by the fact that M. Fabius himself had been a dictator once).[37] As

---

32. For another reason, see Gabba, "Dionigi," p. 220, n. 15.

33. Kunkel and Wittmann speculate that *provocatio* was not valid against a dictator before 287 BC: *Staatsordnung*, p. 169, n. 261; pp. 672–673. Cf. Festus 216L.

34. Lintott, *Constitution*, p. 111.

35. Livy 8.32.10.

36. Ibid. 8.33.7–9. Trans. Canon Roberts.

37. But cf. Kunkel and Wittmann, *Staatsordnung*, p. 673.

we shall see in Chapter 8, Jean Bodin in his *Six livres de la République* was to make much of this example when setting out to show that the Roman dictator had by no means been sovereign.

This is supported by epigraphic evidence: the *lex repetundarum* suggests that a dictator could be prosecuted after his term of office.[38] This is something that would also seem to tie in with the way Polybius deals with the magistracy in his third book. It is to be noted that in Book 6 he notoriously fails even to mention the dictatorship as an element of the Roman constitution—a further indication that the office was not perceived as an instrument to suppress domestic unrest but exclusively as a command in the field. In Book 3 Polybius does say that the dictator was an "absolute commander" (αὐτοκράτωρ στρατηγός) and has the other magistrates abdicate their offices during a dictator's appointment as if to illustrate the dictatorship's autocratic character. Interestingly, however, and crucially, Polybius thinks that the tribunes would continue in office during a dictatorship,[39] a clear indication that neither *auxilium* nor *provocatio* were touched by that institution.[40] A further indication that the dictatorship had always been an institution tailored to wage external wars rather than suppress civil unrest lies in its abandonment after 202 BC: as the prorogation of commands was institutionalized after 146 BC, dictators were no longer necessary.[41]

It is difficult to know with any certainty, but both the case of Polybius, on the one hand, and the tensions surrounding the actions of the Gracchi, on the other, suggest that the idea, so prominent in later history and historiography as well as political thought, that the dictatorship had the power to coerce citizens in the city without their being able to resort to appeal may have arisen as a consequence of the killing of C. Gracchus by L. Opimius. Both Cicero's allusion to the possibility of Scipio Aemilianus assuming a dictatorship *rei publicae constituendae* in 129[42] as well as Plutarch's hint that Opimius in 121 had been the first as consul to exercise the *power of a dictator* (ἐξουσία δικτάτορος) when

---

38. *lex rep.* 8–9. See Lintott, *Judicial Reform*, p. 114.

39. Polyb. 3.87.7–8.

40. *Pace* Drogula, "Imperium," p. 445, n. 163. Polybius' remarks in Book 3 are not primarily aimed at the dictator's powers in the city, and his mention of the tribunes' staying in office shows that the dictator cannot possibly have been taken to act as αὐτοκράτωρ in Rome. See also Livy 9.26.7–20; 27.6.3–5.

41. See Hartfield, *Dictatorship*, pp. 252–255; Kunkel and Wittmann, *Staatsordnung*, pp. 701–702. For the dictatorships of the last two centuries, see Nicolet, *Rome*, pp. 393–455.

42. Cic. *Rep.* 6.12. See Nicolet, "Le *de re publica*."

putting C. Gracchus and other Roman citizens to death without trial[43] indicate that this view of the dictatorship may have taken shape late in the last third of the second century BC.[44] Emilio Gabba rightly points out that late in the second century BC "a relatively new idea of dictatorship was gaining ground," which "must have influenced the historiographical interpretation of the origins and historic development of the office, for example by underlining its interventions in internal politics in contrast to its original military role."[45] Alternatively, this new view of the dictatorship might reflect the terms of Sulla's dictatorship.

Sulla, the decemviri*, and Caesar*

It is certainly not until Sulla that the dictatorship is actually exercised in this way.[46] Dionysius, who had earlier committed himself to the view that dictators had always been able at least in principle to quell civil unrest with whatever means without having to face *provocatio*, now seems to allow that Sulla had in fact been the first so to use the institution:

> But in the time of our fathers, a full four hundred years after the dictatorship of Titus Larcius, the institution became an object of reproach and hatred to all men under L. Cornelius Sulla, the *first and only* dictator who exercised his power with harshness and cruelty; so that the Romans then perceived for the first time what they had all along been ignorant of, that the *dictatorship is a tyranny* (τυραννίς ἐστιν ἡ τοῦ δικτάτορος ἀρχή).[47]

Dionysius' view that the dictatorship had all along been a potential tyranny is something that follows from the annalistic rendering of the dictatorship as an institution overriding the right of appeal.[48] It also ties in with the view, put forward eloquently by Manius Valerius in an important speech written for him by Dionysius, that the dictatorship was a senatorial instrument against a people gone wild and enthralled by demagoguery, an instrument suitable for restoring

---

43. Plut. *C. Gracch.* 18.1.

44. See Rawson, "Interpretation," p. 350, n. 54.

45. Gabba, *Dionysius*, pp. 142–143.

46. For Sulla, see the biographies by Christ, *Sulla*; Hinard, *Sylla*; Keaveney, *Sulla*; Lanzani, *Silla*; for a recent bibliography, see Santangelo, *Sulla*.

47. Dion. Hal. *Ant. Rom.* 5.77.4. Trans. Ernest Cary, my italics. I take the "harshness and cruelty" to refer to, among other things, a disregard for *provocatio*.

48. Kalyvas, "Tyranny," takes this at face value.

the mixed constitution. In M'. Valerius' speech this restoration even takes on the character of a constitutional break with the past, in a very Sullan vein.[49] If we take the view I have been arguing for, however, and realize that in all likelihood such an overriding authority had never been formally part of the dictatorship and the right of appeal had always remained an option—however ambiguous—available *domi* even against a dictator, then Dionysius' statement that Sulla had been the first and only dictator to exercise his powers tyrannically starts to make sense. Not realizing that the dictatorship traditionally had not allowed for the violation of citizen rights within the city, Dionysius must have assumed that Sulla, rather than changing the institutional parameters of the office, was simply exhibiting cruel character traits. Appian, too, exhibits sensitivity to the novelty of Sulla's powers and explains them in a way more attuned to the constitutional changes. Under Sulla, the Romans had returned to "kingly government"; and although there had been tyrannical rule of the dictators before, it had at least been limited to short periods. But with Sulla, whom they chose as "absolute tyrant for as long as he liked," it for the *first time* became unlimited "and so an absolute tyranny."[50] Appian correctly points out that Sulla had done away with the constitutional limit of six months and thinks that therein lay the crucial institutional change. It is Appian too who gives us the formula or title under which Sulla became dictator: Sulla had been chosen "dictator for the enactment of such laws as he might deem best and for the regulation of the commonwealth."[51]

With this formula, retranslated into Latin as *dictator legibus scribundis et rei publicae constituendae*, we find ourselves thrown back into the fifth century BC and to another emergency institution, that of the *decemviri*, the so-called Ten Men. Both the apparent authority to write laws (perhaps even without the need to have them ratified in the assembly),[52] and the abrogation of the right of appeal make it very likely that Sulla's dictatorship in fact resembled, not the *historical* dictatorship of the early and middle Republic, but rather the board of *decemviri* of the fifth century BC as they were described in the—largely invented[53]—historical record. Both elements are contained in Cicero's rendering

49. Dion. Hal. *Ant. Rom.* 7.54–56, esp. 7.56.2.

50. App. *BCiv.* 1.99.

51. Ibid. See Nicolet, "Dictateurs romains," 37–39; Hahn, "Appians Darstellung." For Appian's interest in Roman constitutional matters, see Ungern-Sternberg, "Appians Blick," 208ff. Cf. Luce, "Appian's Magisterial Terminology."

52. Vervaet, "*Lex Valeria*," p. 69, n. 24, believes that the Ten had the authority to give laws.

53. Except that the Twelve Tables must have been proposed by a college of Ten, for reasons pointed out by Eugen Täubler; see Ungern-Sternberg, "Dezemvirat," pp. 79–80.

of the Decemvirate: "a board of ten would be elected with supreme authority and without the right of appeal from their decisions. These men were to have the chief power and were to write the laws."[54] These two elements, especially the abrogation of the right of appeal, are something we are already familiar with from Dionysius' account of the creation of the dictatorship and are clearly owed to Sulla's dictatorship.[55] Further Sullan elements can be found in the Ten Men's attempt to hold office without any time limit and in the suspension of the power of the tribunes of the plebs. Cicero's account mentions the unwillingness of the (second) panel of Ten Men to have others elected in their stead,[56] and Livy associates tyranny with the breach of the time limit—that is to say, in the Roman context, kingship (*regnum*):

> The greater part of the year had now elapsed; two tables had been added to the ten of the previous year; if these additional laws were passed by the 'Comitia Centuriata' there was no reason why the decemvirate should be any longer considered necessary. Men were wondering how soon notice would be given of the election of consuls; the sole anxiety of the plebeians was as to the method by which they could reestablish that bulwark of their liberties, the power of the tribunes, which was now suspended. Meantime nothing was said about any elections. . . . The fifteenth of May arrived, the decemvirs' term of office expired, but no new magistrates were appointed. Though now only private citizens, the decemvirs came forward as determined as ever to enforce their authority and retain all the emblems of power. It was now in truth undisguised monarchy (*regnum*).[57]

This bid for kingship resulted in Livy's view in the abolition of the Republic's constitutional order; here again, we see the language of *ius*, constitutional law, in opposition to mere legislation, when Livy writes that the men who had been "appointed to draw up laws (*leges*)," left "nothing constitutional (*nihil iuris*)" in the city. Livy goes on to enumerate the content of this constitutional order, and of its goal: voting in assemblies, the annual magistrates, the regular change of rulers, these alone guarantee liberty, which has to be equal for all.[58] A further, absolutely

---

54. Cic. *Rep.* 2.61. Trans. Zetzel.

55. See Dion. Hal. *Ant. Rom.* 5.70. On Sulla's dictatorship as a model for the accounts of the Decemvirate, see Ungern-Sternberg, "Dezemvirat," p. 88.

56. Cic. *Rep.* 2.62. Cicero takes this as the expression of a pure (i.e., unbalanced), increasingly oligarchic order, which cannot therefore last long.

57. Livy 3.37.4–38.1. Trans. Canon Roberts.

58. Ibid. 3.39.8.

central concern was the right of appeal. After Verginia is killed by her father, the only thing that is being discussed, especially by her husband-to-be Icilius, is the abolition of the tribunician power and of the right of appeal.[59] The latter, referred to as the "sole bulwark of liberty (*unicum praesidium libertatis*)," was, according to Livy, restored immediately after the overthrow of the Ten and further strengthened by a provision, enacted as a new law (*lex*), which "forbade the appointment of any magistrate from whom there was no right of appeal, and provided that any one who did so appoint might be rightly and lawfully put to death, nor should the man who put him to death be held guilty of murder."[60] Once again, the language used here to indicate the constitutionality of such a killing is that it shall be constitutional in the sense of conforming to *ius* to put to death anyone appointing a magistrate from whom there is no right of appeal (*ius fasque esset occidi*). Notwithstanding the fact that *provocatio* was here underwritten by a mere *lex*, the alleged statute itself contained the familiar language of constitutionality, of *ius*, pointing to the higher-order norms the *lex* is supposed to codify. Voting and legislating in assemblies, time limits on magistracies, and above all the right of appeal as the only protection of liberty: this sums up perfectly the constitutional commitments Livy thought the Roman Republic presupposed in order to continue in existence as a constitutional order.[61] To speculate about the historicity, or some putative historical core, of Livy's account of the strengthening of the right of appeal in the mid-fifth century BC would be rather to miss the point. It is the crisis of the last century of the Republic, understood as a constitutional crisis, which had given rise to the constitutional categories Livy resorts to when describing the reign and fall of the Ten. As Cicero writes very clearly, there were no magistrates whatsoever *sine provocatione* after the Ten, not even dictators.[62]

Back to Sulla. In 88 BC he had marched on Rome in order to oppose the tribune Sulpicius, who had taken control of the city and introduced legislation to take away the command in the East from Sulla, the consul, and give it to the private citizen Marius instead.[63] Sulpicius had expelled the consuls from the city,

59. Ibid. 3.48.9.

60. Ibid. 3.55.4–8. Trans. Canon Roberts, slightly adapted. On the very dubious authenticity, see Ogilvie, *Commentary*, pp. 499–500.

61. For time limits, see Livy 4.24.4, where the dictator of 434 BC, Mamercus Aemilius Mamercinus, is said to have limited the duration of the censorship to great popular acclaim. Both Machiavelli and Harrington quoted this. Machiavelli thought that prolonged commands and magistracies had ruined the Republic, and Harrington thought the principle applied especially to the dictatorship itself: *Discorsi* 3.24; *Oceana*, p. 296.

62. Cic. *Rep.* 2.54.

63. See Levick, "Sulla's March."

had used violence to promulgate his legislation and given *imperium* to a *privatus*, thus effectively "throw[ing] republican norms aside in his bid to control the political scene in Rome." Sulla's subsequent march on Rome and military occupation of the city in turn "overthrew republican government,"[64] and his army, consisting of troops "bound to their *imperator*" and "officers hand-picked for personal loyalty above constitutional scruples" lay "outside the framework of Roman politics as it had been known. In a truer sense (perhaps) than even Caesar or Octavian, Sulla stood against the Republic."[65] However, while it cannot be doubted that Sulla's actions were indeed unprecedented, especially his marching on Rome and the use of armed force within the city, Robert Morstein-Marx has cogently argued that more weight should be given to the claims of legitimacy made by the major protagonists in 88 and 87. In Chapter 1 we have already mentioned Cicero's remark, in a letter to Atticus, that Sulla, Marius, and Cinna had acted "rightly" (*recte*), perhaps even constitutionally (*iure*);[66] this view is confirmed by the "disinterested and relatively dispassionate"[67] Asconius, who writes that Sulpicius had passed his legislation "at a time when he had taken control of the state by violence (*per vim rem p. possedisset*) and after starting with good measures had gone on to bad. This was the start of the civil wars, and the reason why Sulpicius himself was regarded as having been crushed *iure* by the consuls' arms."[68]

Asconius here makes an interesting historical observation: the civil wars of the late Republic had started, not with the Gracchi, nor with Sulla's march on Rome, but with Sulpicius' taking control of the Republic by violence.[69] This had provoked Sulla's march on Rome and his counterattack on Sulpicius and Marius, which itself Asconius does not hesitate to describe as "constitutional"—once again, *iure*. As Morstein-Marx observes, this is not presented as Asconius' own opinion, but as the general one.[70] This reading could already be found in Cicero, especially in a passage from his *Eighth Philippic* touched upon already in the first

64. Flower, *Roman Republics*, pp. 91–92.

65. Badian, "Waiting for Sulla," p. 55. For a similar view, cf. Meyer, *Römischer Staat*, pp. 318–324.

66. Cic. *Att.* 9.10.3. Cf. Cic. *Leg.* 3.20.

67. Morstein-Marx, "Consular appeals," p. 262. Similarly, on Caesar's *dignitas* claims in 49 BC, id., "*Dignitas* and *res publica*."

68. Asc. 64C. Trans. R. G. Lewis.

69. Similarly App. *BCiv.* 1.55; Appian's account becomes increasingly critical of Sulla, however. Cf. Sall. *Iug.* 95.4; Luc. *Phars.* 9.204–205. (Sulla and Marius blamed for the demise of republican liberty).

70. Morstein-Marx, "Consular appeals," p. 262, n. 14. However, the claim may have originated with Sulla's memoirs: Marshall, *Commentary*, p. 233.

chapter: here Cicero claimed that Sulla had been driven to civil war and the occupation of Rome by the fact that Sulpicius' laws had been invalid; he describes their clash as a struggle *de iure legum*.[71] In the same vein, we have Diodorus describing Sulpicius' transfer of the command against Mithridates from the consul Sulla to the *privatus* Marius as unconstitutional (παρανόμως).[72] Sulla's occupation of Rome in the wake of Sulpicius' actions, albeit itself unprecedented and unconstitutional (the army stood *within* the city),[73] was thus generally seen as to some extent justifiable in light of Sulla's holding of the consulship[74] and Sulpicius' violations of the background norms of *ius* and *mos*.[75] This is a prominent example of how crises of the late Republic were interpreted as constitutional conflicts (*de iure legum*) and of how, ultimately, a Roman concept of constitution emerged out of the crises of the Republic. Sulla himself justified his actions by branding Sulpicius and his friends as armed rebels[76] aiming at tyranny.[77]

The assessment of the events of 88 differs markedly from the way Sulla's dictatorship of 82 is described. While Sulla already in 88 had tried to establish constitutional changes and entrench them beyond the reach of the tribal assembly,[78] formally by virtue of his consular authority but with his troops as onlookers, he must have felt that the consulship was insufficient for the far-reaching reforms he had in mind when he captured Rome for the second time after his return from the East.[79] This time, he aimed at the dictatorship.

As we saw before our digression into the annalistic episode on the *decemviri*—an episode probably modelled on Sulla's dictatorship—Dionysius described Sulla as "the first and only dictator who exercised his power with

---

71. Cic. *Phil.* 8.7. But cf. Cic. *Cat.* 3.24, delivered at a *contio*, where Sulla's actions mark the beginning of the civil wars. For *de iure legum*, see Cic. *Dom.* 71, with the dubious attribution to the Senate of some sort of judicial review.

72. Diod. Sic. 37.29.2; App. *BCiv.* 1.59. See Morstein-Marx, "Consular appeals," p. 263. Cf. also Vell. 2.18.5–20.2, esp. 2.18.6 for Sulpicius' legislation.

73. Constitutional criticism of Sulla's occupation of Rome: Cic. *Att.* 8.3.6; App. *BCiv.* 1.60; Plut. *Sull.* 9.6–7; Val. Max. 3.8.5. For Cinna's attempt to put Sulla on trial in 87, see Plut. *Sull.* 10.4; Broughton, *Magistrates*, vol. 2, p. 47.

74. Morstein-Marx, "Consular appeals," p. 275.

75. Cf. Livy, *Per.* 77. See Meier, *Res publica amissa*, pp. 224–225.

76. App. *BCiv.* 1.60. Cf. Nippel, *Aufruhr*, p. 91.

77. App. *BCiv.* 1.57.

78. Ibid. 1.59. Given the armed pressure applied to the Senate (Val. Max. 3.8.5), it is likely that the popular assembly summoned by Sulla as described by Appian was equally put under pressure by Sulla's troops.

79. On Sulla's reforms, see Hantos, *Res publica constituta*.

harshness and cruelty,"[80] and Appian suggested that the Romans under Sulla had returned to "kingly government." Choosing Sulla as an "absolute tyrant for as long as he liked," the Romans subjected themselves for the first time to unlimited dictatorship, which amounted to "an absolute tyranny."[81] Sulla was nominated to the dictatorship by the *interrex* L. Valerius Flaccus,[82] by means of a law (the *lex Valeria*).[83] This was procedurally dubious not simply because *interreges* were not considered eligible to nominate dictators (only consuls were), but also because Sulla *made* Flaccus nominate him, thereby effectively dissolving one of the crucial features of the traditional dictatorship: the separation between the magistrate competent to declare an emergency (the consul) and the magistrate charged with dealing with the emergency. As for the first, procedural point, scholars such as Keaveney, Seager, Hinard, and Hurlet who underline the traditional aspects of Sulla's dictatorship have tried to explain away Cicero's considered view, expressed to Atticus, that nomination of a dictator by an *interrex* did not conform with *ius*.[84] On the second issue, it was the fact that Sulla all but nominated himself that provoked Appian's most pointed criticism. Sulla commanded (προστάσσω) the Senate to choose an *interrex* and would afterwards direct Flaccus in a letter to nominate Sulla himself.[85] Plutarch, knowing perfectly well that formally Sulla had been nominated,[86] stated it even more succinctly: Sulla "proclaimed himself dictator."[87] There are problems with Appian's account in that he seems to maintain, incorrectly, that Sulla was actually elected, rather than nominated, to the dictatorship. However, in view of the most significant aspect of Sulla's dictatorship, the fact that Sulla's whole political program including his proscriptions were pushed through the assemblies and thus took the form of legislation, Appian is surely right to claim that it was the Roman *People* who ratified Sulla's policies. The Roman People "welcomed

---

80. Dion. Hal. *Ant. Rom.* 5.77.4.

81. App. *BCiv.* 1.99. Cf. Hahn, "Appians Darstellung."

82. On Asc. 37C, see Hurlet, *La dictature de Sylla*, pp. 45–47.

83. App. *BCiv.* 1.99.

84. Cic. *Att.* 9.15.2. See Keaveney, *Sulla*, p. 137; Seager, "Sulla's Monarchy," p. 347; Hinard, "De la dictature," p. 89; Hurlet, *La dictature*, p. 49. See also Vervaet, "*Lex Valeria*," pp. 80–81, who believes with Hurlet that it is Cicero's point that Sulla was rightfully appointed by the *interrex*. This strikes me as a far-fetched interpretation of Cicero's words.

85. App. *BCiv.* 1.98.

86. Plut. *Pomp.* 9.1.

87. Plut. *Sull.* 33.1.

this pretence of an election as an image and semblance of freedom and chose Sulla their absolute master for as long a time as he pleased."[88] While almost certainly wrong on the procedural details, this does capture the underlying theme of Sulla's reign: this was a tyranny established *by law* (*lege*), as Cicero was to put it polemically yet accurately in 63 BC.[89] By law, but not by higher-order constitutional law—*lege*, not *iure*.[90]

If we believe Appian and translate back into the Latin, Sulla's title in 82 must have been *dictator legibus scribundis et rei publicae constituendae*,[91] which, as has been pointed out, is a close parallel to the title of the Ten Men. There has been some scholarly controversy as to whether Sulla was indeed appointed *dictator legibus scribundis*, or simply *rei publicae constituendae*. The arguments against assuming a mandate *legibus scribundis* seem difficult to maintain;[92] in any case, far more important is its interpretation. Was Sulla authorized to legislate by edict, without having to ratify his decrees in the assembly? Or was he still bound to bring his laws before the People? In an incisive article, Frederik Vervaet has argued that "Sulla's capacity to promulgate laws without any intervention on the part of the comitia should not be questioned,"[93] pointing out that in the light of the accounts of Appian, Plutarch, and especially Cicero[94] Victor Ehrenberg had been correct in thinking that Sulla "was to give Rome a new constitution and new laws and . . . therefore stood above all existing laws."[95] However, as Ehrenberg also saw and Kunkel and Wittmann convincingly stress, there is no evidence whatsoever for any Sullan laws promulgated without ratification by the

88. App. *BCiv.* 1.99. Trans. Horace White.

89. Cic. *Leg. Agr.* 3.5.

90. Sulla's approach was unprecedented. Hurlet, *La dictature*, pp. 36–41, claims that Q. Fabius Maximus' (217) and Q. Fulvius Flaccus' (210) dictatorships show the increasing weight of the popular assembly in choosing a dictator, but the cases are unlike Sulla's: unlike Sulla, Fabius Maximus in 217 was probably *elected* by the People (Livy 22.8.5–6; Kunkel and Wittmann, *Staatsordnung*, p. 705), and Fulvius Flaccus in 210 was ultimately nominated by a consul (Livy 27.5.15–19).

91. See App. *BCiv.* 1.99.

92. Kunkel and Wittmann, *Staatsordnung*, pp. 703–704 interpret the phrase as an authorization to promulgate laws without the comitia. Even if Sulla did not have the authority to legislate without popular ratification, *dictator legibus scribendis* might still have been his mandate and semi-official title, as Kunkel and Wittmann's own example (Livy 3.34.6; 3.37.4) shows: the *decemviri legibus scribendis* had the Twelve Tables ratified by the assembly. Cf. Vervaet, "*Lex Valeria*," p. 41; Bringmann, "Das zweite Triumvirat," p. 26.

93. Vervaet, "*Lex Valeria*," p. 42.

94. App. *BCiv.* 1.99; Plut. *Sull.* 33.1; Cic. *Leg. Agr.* 3.5 and especially *2 Verr.* 3.82.

95. Ehrenberg, "*Imperium maius*," p. 126.

People.[96] Whether or not the Valerian law had established that Sulla's "absolute will should be the law to the Roman people," as Cicero put it in one of his speeches against Verres, it seems to have been crucial to Sulla's dictatorship that all his policies be ratified by the assemblies and enacted as legislation. Not only was Sulla given *imperium sine provocatione* by Valerius Flaccus' law, that is, by the People, but this law and further laws brought before the comitia by Sulla himself ratified Sulla's mass killings and attendant confiscations, his proscriptions, both retrospectively and prospectively.[97] The right of appeal was thus doubly undermined, and this attack on *provocatio* was sanctioned by legislation. Although the Senate might have ratified Sulla's proscriptions as well,[98] there is convincing evidence for at least some resistance on the Senate's part.[99] Sulla's dictatorship thus combined several distinguishable and distinctly novel elements.[100] His was a power *sine provocatione*, within the city,[101] there was no time limit set to this magistracy, and his changes to constitutional norms, such as the limitations of the tribunes' authority sanctioned by the popular assembly, were made through the legislative machinery. Under Sulla, constitutional amendment was done by law.

The fact that Sulla based the legitimacy of his reign and, particularly, of the proscriptions on legislation did not go unnoticed: indeed, it is this issue which was to serve as Cicero's best argument for a normative constitutional order as put forward in *De legibus*. Here he flags precisely the Valerian law as the chief example for his *reductio ad absurdum*: if all things were considered just "which have been ratified by a people's institutions and laws," then even the Valerian law would have been just, "that the dictator could put to death with impunity whatever citizens he wished, even without trial."[102] We will discuss Cicero's constitutional theory in depth in Part II, but it is obvious from Cicero's earlier speeches that the proscriptions and the laws justifying them were in tension with the norms established by *ius*, chief among them *provocatio*. Already in his speech for Roscius of Ameria, delivered in a murder trial before a permanent jury court (*quaestio perpetua de sicariis*) early in 80 BC, just after the proscriptions had ended, there

96. Ibid., p. 126, n. 28; cf. Vervaet, "*Lex Valeria*," p. 42. Similarly already Mommsen, *Staatsrecht* vol. 2.1, p. 726.

97. See Hinard, *Les proscriptions*, pp. 17–143.

98. If App. *BCiv.* 1.97 refers to a *senatus consultum*.

99. Cic. *Rosc. Am.* 153.

100. *Pace* Keaveney, Seager, Hinard, and Hurlet.

101. See Vervaet, "*Lex Valeria*," pp. 51–56.

102. Cic. *Leg.* 1.42. Trans. Zetzel. Cf. *Rosc. Amer.* 125, *Dom.* 43, *Leg. Agr.* 3.5. *Leg.* 1.42 is analogous to, but more refined than, Cic. *Caec.* 95–96.

are veiled hints of criticism of the proscriptions on constitutional grounds, notwithstanding Cicero's general appreciation of the new Sullan order.[103] Cicero makes room for the possibility that crimes were committed in connection with the proscriptions, even if not by Sulla himself,[104] and plays on the distinction between older legislation and Sulla's, on the one hand, and between legislation and *ius*, on the other.[105] In later speeches this constitutional criticism is undisguised and explicit,[106] culminating in the parallel he draws after his return from exile, in his speech *De domo sua*, between Clodius' law exiling him and the Sullan legislation enabling the proscriptions:

> You may have been tribune as constitutionally (*iure*) and legally (*legeque*) as the present P. Servilius Rullus himself, a man most illustrious and honourable on every account—still, by what *ius*, or in accordance with what tradition (*quo more*) or what precedent (*quo exemplo*) did you pass a law (*lex*) explicitly aimed, by name, against the civil rights (*de capite*) of a citizen who had not been condemned? . . . That horrible term 'proscription' and all the bitterness of the time of Sulla: what is it that is calling to mind cruelty most distinctly? I submit that it is punishment meted out against Roman citizens without trial.[107]

What this amounts to, whether or not we believe that *legibus scribundis* is to be interpreted as an inherent power of Sulla's dictatorship, is a view of Sulla's powers at odds with early emergency institutions and thus apt to be described, in Mommsen's terms, as an "extraordinary constituent power." Sulla used the assemblies to establish his political and constitutional program, which made it into something constitutionally novel—at least if we hold on to a distinction between *ius* and *leges*. In some sense, Sulla implicitly subscribed to a view of the Roman constitutional order as enunciated, as we have seen in Chapter 1, at various points in Livy's work. The view attributed to Scipio in 213 BC on the occasion of his under-age election to the aedileship—"If the Quirites are unanimous in their desire to appoint me aedile, I am quite old enough"[108]—is a view one may cautiously describe as tending toward

---

103. See Dyck, "Evidence and Rhetoric"; Lintott, *Cicero*, pp. 425–427.

104. Cic. *Rosc. Am.* 91. See also ibid. 143.

105. Ibid. 126.

106. Cic. *Leg. Agr.* 3.5.

107. Cic. *Dom.* 43. My translation. Cf. Cic. *Lig.* 12. This shows the nature of the proscriptions as "legalized murder": Bringmann, "Caesar als Richter?," p. 76.

108. Livy 25.2.7.

ascribing sovereignty to the comitia.[109] This is not to say that we should expect to find anything resembling the concept of popular sovereignty in the Roman sources. But we should acknowledge that in the surviving evidence considerable weight is assigned to the comitia and their decisions, and, as will become apparent in Part III below, it was out of these very materials that the early modern thinkers started constructing their conceptions of popular sovereignty.

On this vexed issue, the authority of the assemblies, we will say more in Chapter 3; for now suffice it to say that with regard to Sulla's dictatorship, it can indeed plausibly be seen as an extraordinary constituent power ("ausserordentliche constituirende Gewalt")[110] insofar as it was the logical extension of ascribing very far-reaching authority to the comitia.[111] Mommsen thought that Sulla's dictatorship was akin to the earlier regal period in Rome, in that both were based on the "freie Verpflichtung der Bürgerschaft, einem aus ihrer Mitte als absolutem Herrn zu gehorchen," and saw in Sulla's use of the assemblies an interesting parallel to C. Gracchus' methods.[112] The fact that Sulla's powers derived their validity from legislation was crucial to their quality as a constituent power ("constituirende Gewalt") in Mommsen's view,[113] a category he thought was difficult to pin down and in the *Staatsrecht* oscillates between extra-constitutional and constitutional.[114] This ambiguity follows from the fact that although nominally these powers were given validity by the comitia, the comitia themselves were according to the "predominant view" among the Romans supposed to be subject to constitutional constraints.[115] Although Mommsen, because he thought of the Principate as ultimately operating within constitutional limits,[116] was reluctant to think of Sulla's dictatorship as outright unconstitutional, he did—as had before him already a long line of scholars beginning with Machiavelli and Sigonio—mark them off very clearly from the traditional dictatorships.[117]

---

109. See below, pp. 119–129.

110. Mommsen, *Staatsrecht* vol. 2.1, pp. 702–742.

111. Cic. *Leg. Agr.* 3.5; *Leg.* 1.42.

112. Mommsen, *Römische Geschichte*, vol. 2, p. 337.

113. Mommsen, *Staatsrecht* vol. 2.1, p. 711. See Bringmann, "Das zweite Triumvirat," *passim* and esp. p. 37.

114. See Mommsen, *Staatsrecht* vol. 2.1, pp. 709–710.

115. Mommsen, *Abriß*, p. 188.

116. The Principate was much more constitutionally limited according to Mommsen than any of the republican constituting magistracies: *Staatsrecht* vol. 2.1, pp. 709–710.

117. For Sigonio's continuity between Sulla, Caesar, and Augustus, anticipating Mommsen's "ausserordentliche constituierende Gewalten," see McCuaig, *Sigonio*, pp. 171–172. Sigonio

Mommsen's oscillations pinpoint the fault line I am concerned with in this book. Mommsen was heir to a strand of scholarship beginning with Sigonio. This strand was sympathetic to the sentiment ascribed by Livy to Scipio in 213 and thus to the sovereignty of the comitia, and it can clearly be seen operating in the *Staatsrecht*: Mommsen is committed to the constitutionality of the "constituent powers."[118] Yet at the same time, his was a view which sharply distinguished between the traditional dictatorship and Sulla's extraordinary powers. On Cicero's interpretation, focusing on Sulla's abolition of constitutional rights through legislation, Sulla's powers and the legislation sanctioning them could not be described as *iure*.[119] It is important that Cicero, in his political and constitutional thought, does not simply reiterate the *veteres mores*, thus adding to a sense of Christian Meier's "crisis without alternative." Rather, he shone the light—first "on the ground," as it were, in his speeches, then more clearly in his mature political theory—on what he thought could resolve the crisis: a clearer sense of the entrenched norms that could limit political decision making and legislation. For Cicero, it would have been out of the question that Sulla's abolition of the right of appeal *by law*[120] had become part of *mos maiorum* and did not present any break with the republican tradition.[121] Rather, this abolition represented the triumph of a particular, quite novel conception of the authority of the comitia[122] and is indeed best interpreted as an extraordinary constituent power far beyond *ius* and *mos*. The manner of his nomination, the fact that there was no time limit set to his powers, and, most importantly, the fact that his dictatorship was *sine provocatione*, all of these elements bespeak a rupture with the republican constitutional tradition. The novel view of the authority of the comitia expressed in the abolition of the *ius provocationis* will be discussed in the next chapter; a crucial early modern analysis of this new weight of the assemblies, the one by Jean Bodin, will be treated in Chapter 8.

---

and Sieyès must have been among Mommsen's most important models; on Mommsen's use of Mably, Rousseau, and Sieyès, see Flaig, "Volkssouveränität"; on Mommsen and Carl Schmitt, see Nippel, "Schmitts 'kommissarische' und 'souveräne Diktatur'."

118. See, e.g., *Staatsrecht* vol. 2.1, pp. 711–712. Sigonio ascribed a very far-reaching decision-making authority to the assemblies: McCuaig, *Sigonio*, pp. 208–219.

119. Cic. *Leg.* 1.42.

120. See Cic. *Leg. Agr.* 3.5: *hic* [*sc.* Valerius] *rei publicae tyrannum lege constituit.*

121. *Pace* Hurlet, *La dictature*, p. 170.

122. See Mommsen, *Römische Geschichte*, vol. 2, p. 337: "Es war gar viel Niederlage in diesem letzten Siege der Oligarchie." For the increasing importance of the popular assemblies, see Magdelain, *Recherches*; and below, Chapter 3, pp. 119–129.

Between Sulla and the abolition of the dictatorship in 44 BC Caesar alone held the dictatorship. In 54 BC, in view of the looming *interregnum* for 53, the idea was floated to have the dictatorship bestowed on Pompey,[123] even to have him elected dictator by the People.[124] Pompey ultimately declined.[125] Caesar in 49 BC was nominated for the dictatorship by the praetor M. Aemilius Lepidus, on the basis of a law passed in the assembly and in the absence of the anti-Caesarian consuls.[126] Caesar resigned from his first dictatorship, probably *comitiorum habendorum causa*, after eleven days. While adhering to the traditional time limit, the nomination by a praetor was obviously not in accordance with constitutional norms.[127] The next year, after his victory at Pharsalus, Caesar had himself nominated for the dictatorship by the consul P. Servilius Isauricus, but on the basis of legislation and for the unprecedented duration of one year (unlike Sulla's dictatorship, Caesar's was limited but exceeded the time limit of six months), which raised eyebrows.[128] His mandate must have been (civil) war (*rei gerundae causa*),[129] not *dictator rei publicae constituendae* (*legibus scribundis*).[130] Caesar probably resigned from his dictatorship after the year was up. He was elected consul for 46 BC,[131] but was then given the dictatorship for ten years by the Senate after his victory at Thapsus in April 46.[132] This was designed as a succession of ten dictatorships each limited to a one-year duration, each of which Caesar was supposed to give up before taking up the next one.[133] There is an obvious escalation here, clearly

---

123. Cic. *Qfr.* 2.14.5; *Att.* 4.18.3; *Qfr.* 3.6.4; *Fam.* 8.4.3; *Qfr.* 3.7.3 (only *comitiorum habendorum causa*). See Borle, "Pompée et la dictature."

124. Plut. *Pomp.* 54.2.

125. Dio Cass. 40.45.5–46.1.

126. Caes. *BCiv.* 2.21.5; Dio Cass. 41.36.1. Cf. App. *BCiv.* 2.48; Plut. *Caes.* 37.1 (Caesar appointed by the Senate). Out of Caesar's nomination Mommsen constructed a specious rule, based on the conjecture that Q. Fabius Maximus in 217 too had been appointed by a praetor, that such an appointment was legal if sanctioned by the People. Mommsen, *Staatsrecht* vol. 2.1, p. 147.

127. Cic. *Att.* 9.15.3; Dio Cass. 41.36.1; Kunkel and Wittmann, *Staatsordnung*, p. 713.

128. Dio Cass. 42.21.1–2; Plut. *Caes.* 51.2.

129. Wilcken, "Zur Entwicklung," pp. 18–19.

130. The inscription from Tarentum, mentioning a power *rei public[ae con]/[stit]uendae*, probably refers to Octavian as triumvir: Sordi, "Ottaviano"; *pace* Gasperini, "Alcune epigrafi." Sigonio in his commentary on the *Fasti* of 1559 assumed that Caesar, like Sulla and later Augustus, had operated under the title of *dictator rei publicae constituendae*; see McCuaig, *Sigonio*, p. 172, n. 184.

131. See Broughton, *Magistrates*, vol. 2, pp. 284–285, n. 1.

132. Dio Cass. 43.14.4.

133. Kunkel and Wittmann, *Staatsordnung*, p. 715.

crossing the boundaries of the higher-order rules of the Republic governing magistracies: the irregular nomination, the highly irregular duration and iteration of office and the affected legalism reflected in the yearly abdication. It may be assumed that this was a *dictatura sine provocatione*,[134] operating without the right of appeal under a legal cover bestowed by the assembly (probably by a *lex Hirtia* in 48 BC),[135] reminiscent of Sulla's use of the *lex Valeria*.[136] The constitutional rights of the tribunes, having served their purpose as a constitutional argument at the outbreak of the civil war in 49 BC, were flouted as much by Caesar as by Sulla, and it bears mentioning that Cicero in his *Thirteenth Philippic* was to declare himself skeptical of the legal character of the *lex Hirtia*, again on constitutional grounds.[137] The climax was reached when Caesar accepted, in early 44 BC after having resigned from his fourth dictatorship, a completely unprecedented dictatorship for life.[138] While Sulla's dictatorship had been limited in duration at least in principle (that is to say limited by the duration of the mandate), Caesar's was entirely revolutionary. With his dictatorship, *ius* and *mos* lost any normative pull they had ever exhibited.[139]

Eduard Meyer saw in this the main reason for his distinction between Caesar's monarchy, on the one hand, and Pompey's and Augustus' principate, on the other: having rejected the constitutional trajectory presented to him in Cicero's speech on the occasion of Marcus Marcellus' recall in 46 BC,[140] Caesar's goal is absolute monarchy.[141] In a lucid essay Klaus Bringmann has convincingly argued that Caesar's dictatorship, with its lifetime monopoly of government, does not really fit Mommsen's category of an extraordinary constituent power—there was

134. It is plausible to assume that there was no right of appeal against the dictator's coercive measures. As Bringmann points out, Cic. *Lig.* 11–12 does not lend support to a view of Caesar exercising criminal jurisdiction—Caesar merely exercises *clementia*, as he was empowered by law to deal with his enemies as he saw fit: "Caesar als Richter?," *passim*, esp. p. 77.

135. Dio Cass. 42.20.1.

136. Dio Cass. 43.19.2–3 gives additional support to the conclusion that Caesar's powers were *sine provocatione*; on the connection between the number of lictors and the dictatorship *sine provocatione*, see Vervaet, "*Lex Valeria*," pp. 51–56. But see also Cic. *Att.* 10.4.9–10 on the loss of importance of constitutional norms in Caesar's autocracy, allegedly confirmed by Caesar himself: Suet. *Iul.* 77.

137. Cic. *Phil.* 13.32.

138. Ibid. 2.87; Livy *Per.* 116; Dio Cass. 44.8.4; see for the sources Broughton, *Magistrates*, vol. 2, pp. 317–318.

139. See Kunkel and Wittmann, *Staatsordnung*, p. 716.

140. Cf. Cic. *Fam.* 13.68.

141. Meyer, *Caesars Monarchie*, p. 410.

nothing to be constituted in Caesar's reign, unlike in Sulla's.[142] What does unite them, however, is the fact that both dictatorships—as well as the powers of the triumvirs later—were constituted by popular legislation and, being equipped with the *ius agendi cum populo*, continued to operate through popular legislation.

The senatus consultum ultimum *and* hostis *declarations*

There has been ample scholarly discussion concerning the constitutional aspects of the so-called "last decree" of the Senate,[143] a discussion which has mostly focused on the precise constitutional status of the *senatus consultum ultimum* (*SCU*).[144] The standard approach has been to ask whether this decree of the Senate, "that the consuls should take heed that the Republic suffer no harm,"[145] gave any formal powers to the consuls above and beyond their normal *potestas* and *imperium*. More specifically, the question has been whether the *SCU* should be interpreted as giving rise to special emergency powers on the part of magistrates, especially the consuls, which would suspend the statutory law guaranteeing the right of appeal to all citizens and would thus allow the consuls to put citizens to death without trial. Scholars have given various answers to these questions, ranging from Mommsen's view that the *SCU* was merely declaratory of an emergency which itself amply justified self-help on the part of all citizens (and not merely the magistrates), to Hugh Last's position that the *SCU* was "no more than an exhortation to the executive to attend to the business which it was appointed to perform,"[146] to T. N. Mitchell's strained interpretation that in emergencies the Senate assumed sovereignty over both magistrates and the citizens.[147]

---

142. Bringmann, "Das zweite Triumvirat," pp. 37–38.

143. It is not until Caes. *BCiv.* 1.5.3 that we find this terminology in the sources; it has become a technical term for good reason, however, as the sources view all the instances of this decree in the same light.

144. See Mommsen, *Staatsrecht* vol. 1, pp. 690–697; vol. 3.2, pp. 1240–1251; Plaumann, "Das sogenannte *senatus consultum ultimum*"; Last, "Gaius Gracchus," pp. 82–89; Bleicken, *Senatsgericht*, p. 23; Crifò, "Attività," pp. 61ff.; id., "In tema"; Guarino, "Senatus Consultum Ultimum"; Ungern-Sternberg, *Untersuchungen*; Mitchell, "Cicero and the *Senatus Consultum Ultimum*"; Burckhardt, *Politische Strategien*, pp. 88–110; 121–123; Ungern-Sternberg, "Verfahren"; Duplà Ansuategui, Videant consules; Lintott, *Violence*, pp. 149–174; id., *Constitution*, pp. 89–93; Drummond, *Law*, pp. 79–113; Arena, *Libertas*, pp. 200–220. See also Last, "Review Haskell," pp. 94–95; Nippel, *Public Order*, p. 63.

145. Sall. *Cat.* 29.2.

146. Last, "Gaius Gracchus," p. 84.

147. Mitchell, "Cicero and the *Senatus Consultum Ultimum*"; similarly, Lübtow on a latent *imperium* of the Senate: *Das römische Volk*, pp. 334–341.

It has been argued that the *SCU* implied the power to put citizens to death by suspending *provocatio* statutes, or by itself implying a declaration to the effect that the citizens in question were from now on to be treated as public enemies (*hostes*). Hugh Last thought as much, but there is no evidence of such declarations with the attending names of enemies; recognizing this, Wirszubski put forward the view that "the S.C. Ultimum itself, despite the fact that as a rule no names were mentioned in it, pointed out the quarters from which the State was threatened, and implied that certain citizens . . . should be treated as hostes."[148] This is seen by von Ungern-Sternberg as merely the first stage in the development of the *SCU*, which in his view came increasingly to be applied to cases of looming, as opposed to acute, danger and which thus increasingly relied on explicit *hostis*-declarations, issued by the Senate independently from the *SCU*, but somehow reliant on it.[149]

The best view is that the *SCU*, far from simply declaring an emergency, was indeed an exhortation addressed to the magistrates, usually the consuls, to do what they see fit "that the Republic suffer no harm"; that these magistrates themselves, rather than the Senate, were ultimately the authors of and responsible for whatever they proceeded to do; that the *SCU* itself "made no pretence of setting the law aside, or even of encouraging the magistrates to disregard the legal limitations of their power"[150] and did nothing whatsoever to change the constitutional situation, let alone suspend the right of appeal; and finally that the *SCU* neither implicitly declared citizens *hostes* nor necessarily operated in conjunction with a *hostis* declaration. It seems, furthermore, that the *SCU* was strictly confined to the city while the *hostis* declaration, by its very nature, could and did extend beyond the city to wherever the armed *hostes* were to be found.

According to both Cicero and Sallust, the *SCU* purported to constitute *mos*. In an elucidating passage in his *First Catilinarian* speech, held on November 8, 63 BC,[151] Cicero gives a brief historical sketch of the *SCU* as he sees it:

> The senate once decreed that the consul Lucius Opimius should see to it that the state came to no harm. Not a night intervened. Gaius Gracchus, despite his illustrious father, grandfather, and ancestors, was killed on suspicion of stirring up dissension; and the ex-consul Marcus Fulvius was also

148. Wirszubski, *Libertas*, p. 57.

149. Ungern-Sternberg, *Untersuchungen*, pp. 117–122; but see id., "Verfahren," esp. p. 353.

150. Last, "Gaius Gracchus," p. 84.

151. Asc. 6C. For a discussion of the date, see Dyck, *Cicero: Catilinarians*, pp. 243–244.

> killed, together with his children. A similar senatorial decree put the state into the hands of the consuls Gaius Marius and Lucius Valerius—and did even a single day then elapse before death and the state's vengeance overtook the tribune of the plebs Lucius Saturninus and the praetor Gaius Servilius? But we for twenty days now have been allowing the edge of the senate's authority to become blunt. We have a senatorial decree like those earlier ones (*habemus enim eius modi senatus consultum*), but it is filed away, as if hidden in sheath—but on the strength of that decree, you, Catiline, should have been instantly killed.[152]

This puts forward a strange view of the historical precedents of the *SCU*; on the one hand, there is the attempt to claim constitutional validity for the *SCU* as an instrument for the suspension of the right of appeal; on the other, it would seem to blame implicitly Cicero's own inactivity—given his view that the *SCU* had suspended, in a constitutionally valid way, Catiline's right of appeal, why not proceed in the manner of Opimius and Marius? Cicero's argument amounts to the rather transparent attempt to claim constitutional validity for the *SCU* as an institution established by *mos*, while at the same time implicitly conceding—by remaining inactive—the rather fanciful and precarious status of that claim. This very view of the *SCU* as having constitutional validity by virtue of having been established by *mos* is held by Sallust when he writes that the *SCU* conferred "according to Roman *mos*" a supreme power upon a magistrate, allowing him to "exert any kind of coercion" on allies and citizens alike, a right (*ius*) the consul would otherwise lack "without the order of the people (*sine populi iussu*)."[153]

In an insightful discussion of this Sallustian passage, Drummond has shown that Sallust's interpretation of the *SCU* as "by custom (*more Romano*) enabling the magistrate if he wished to assume certain specific powers" is fallacious, not least because there was simply not much of a constitutional tradition to draw upon: "Opimius' actions remained isolated and the growing appearance of *crudelitas* as a political reproach after the Sullan era could only reinforce such caution."[154] Drummond rightly says that in presenting the powers of the consul

---

152. Cic. *Cat.* 1.4. Trans. D. H. Berry. On the use of the *SCU* in 100 BC, see Badian, "Death of Saturninus," pp. 118f. Badian treats its use against a sitting tribune and praetor as a novelty, but given the novelty of the *SCU* itself, this may not be that astonishing.

153. Sall. *Cat.* 29.3. See on "new *mos maiorum*" Nippel, "Gesetze," pp. 95–96.

154. Drummond, *Law*, p. 93. However, by choosing the Temple of Concord for the Senate meetings of December 3 and 5, Cicero must have aimed to place his views and actions in the tradition of Opimius: Burckhardt, *Politische Strategien*, pp. 70–85.

under the *SCU* as "existing *more Romano* Sallust does not imply that they enjoy an inferior status vis-à-vis statute"; he should have gone further and made it clear that in fact Sallust's as well as Cicero's aim is precisely to give the *SCU* qua *mos* the status of a constitutional instrument which could be used to undermine the right of appeal; the attempt is to establish the *SCU more Romano* as constitutionally *superior* vis-à-vis statute. Drummond confusingly thinks that there are no genuine constitutional norms in play here, only pseudo "constitutional" norms; nonetheless, he correctly points out that such norms, establishing what could or could not be done *iure* or *more*, had a legal quality to them in the "language which Romans used" in this regard, and, effectively conceding the constitutional character of the arguments used, Drummond writes that "jurists and laymen alike sometimes use the concept of *ius publicum* . . . to embrace . . . what would now be categorized as constitutional norms."[155]

The *SCU*, resting at best on very recent *mos*, thus represented an attempt to get around the constitutional right of appeal. The attempt cannot be said to have been successful as a matter of constitutional innovation, but it does show us that all the protagonists involved in the Catilinarian emergency made constitutional arguments and were highly conscious of the utility of appeals to constitutional norms.[156] The *mos* the *SCU* was supposed to rest on was very young indeed, not even forty years old at the time of the Catilinarian conspiracy.[157] Invented with the intention of circumventing the citizens' right of appeal in the city, the *SCU* never in any straightforward way legitimized the killing of citizens: the trial of Opimius, Rabirius, Cicero's own contorted rhetorical maneuvers, Caesar's and someone else's[158] resistance in the Senate debate of December 5, 63, and not least Cicero's exile all testify to this. Drummond argues that constitutional issues need not have been at the center of Opimius' and Rabirius' trials and that we do not know on the strength of what arguments Opimius was acquitted; but then he goes on to concede that—referring to Opimius' trial—"the killing of citizens without proper trial must have lain at the heart of the case,"[159] and the evidence of course shows that the killing of citizens in violation of *provocatio* was indeed at the heart of a great many, if not most, of the constitutional disputes of the last century of

155. Drummond, *Law*, pp. 86–87.

156. Arena, *Libertas*, p. 202 claims that the *SCU* was "void of any strictly legal force," but this begs the question.

157. Counting from its use in the year 100 BC onward.

158. Probably Q. Metellus Nepos or L. Calpurnius Bestia: Drummond, *Law*, p. 15.

159. Drummond, *Law*, p. 91.

the Republic. In reference to the killing of C. Gracchus[160] Cicero adduces both the legitimacy of killing Gracchus *conservandae rei publicae causa* and the *SCU* as constitutional justification,[161] showing that there was at least a vigorous attempt to develop the *SCU* into an instrument of constitutional argument.

Doubts concerning its constitutional status never went away, however, and Cicero himself did not ultimately rely on it for his execution of the Catilinarians in the city, but on an independent senatorial decree which he tried to justify by arguing that the accused conspirators by virtue of their own actions no longer qualified as citizens. Once again, we find at the center of the debate the constitutionality of putting citizens to death: in his *Fourth Catilinarian* Cicero writes that "[i]n fact I notice that one of those who wish to be considered popular politicians is absent from our meeting, evidently so as not to have to vote on the life or death of Roman citizens (*de capite civium Romanorum*),"[162] an obvious allusion to the possible violation of *provocatio*. His own failed attempt to have the jailed conspirators declared "enemies" (*hostes* rather than *cives*) by the Senate[163] was aimed at putting both himself and the whole Senate in a position "so as not to have to vote on the life or death of Roman citizens." Had the attempt succeeded, the issue of a violation of citizens' right of appeal could have been at least sidestepped, if in a rather question-begging way. I shall deal with this issue—whether citizens could legitimately be turned into enemies—below. As far as the *SCU* itself is concerned, however, it seems reasonably clear that although it was originally, in 121 and 100 BC, developed and used with the aim of suspending the right of appeal, or at least thus interpreted by the leading protagonists, it was no longer so used afterwards. The *SCU* was declared against Sulla in 83,[164] against Lepidus in 77,[165] against Catilina and Manlius in 63,[166] against Metellus Nepos in 62,[167] after Clodius' death in 52,[168] and against Caesar's tribunes in 49[169]; none

160. Who had committed suicide, but the responsibility for his suicide was seen to have rested with Opimius.

161. Cic. *De or.* 2.132. See Drummond, *Law*, p. 92; Lintott, *Constitution*, p. 92.

162. Cic. *Cat.* 4.10.

163. See now Allély, *Déclaration*, p. 62. Cf. Straumann, "Review Allély."

164. Iul. Exup. 7.

165. Sall. *Hist.* 1.77.22

166. Sall. *Cat.* 29.2; Cic. *Cat.* 1.4.

167. Dio Cass. 37.43.3.

168. Cic. *Mil.* 70; Asc. 34C; Dio Cass. 40.49.5.

169. Caes. *BCiv.* 1.5; 1.7; Livy *Per.* 109; Dio Cass. 41.3.3.

of these instances was aimed at suspending anyone's *ius provocationis*.[170] In fact, most of these decrees had been issued against the background of armed threats from outside the city, rather than against internal sedition or violence within the city.[171] It is only in Cicero, and to some small extent in Livy, that we find, not surprisingly, the attempt to firmly link the *SCU* and the violation of the right of appeal, with the former justifying the latter. While the prosecution against Rabirius did not directly attack the constitutional validity of the *SCU*, but rather denied that Rabirius' actions had been covered by it,[172] Cicero in his defense of Rabirius raised the stakes and portrayed the charges against Rabirius as charges against the constitutionality of the *SCU*, understood as a device to suspend, if necessary, the right of appeal.[173] Cicero clearly tried, in this speech, or at least in the version published in 60 BC, to lend constitutional validity *more maiorum* to the *SCU* when he said, addressing the People:

> There is no foreign or external evil which can insinuate itself into this republic. If you wish this state to be immortal, if you wish your empire to be eternal, if you wish your glory to continue everlasting, then it is our own passions, it is the turbulence and desire of revolution engendered among our own citizens, it is intestine evil, it is domestic plots that must be guarded against. And your ancestors have left you a great protection against these evils in these words of the consul, "Whoever wishes the republic to be safe." Protect the legitimate use of these words, O Romans. Do not by your decision take the republic out of my hands; and do not take from the republic its hope of liberty, its hope of safety, its hope of dignity.[174]

170. A possible exception is the *SCU* of 62 BC, when the tribune Metellus Nepos' office was suspended and he was driven out of the city. The background for this *SCU*, however, was Pompey's return from the East, so that here too the potential threat from outside the city may have been more important. Moreover, Metellus Nepos was not ultimately deprived of his office (Plut. *Cat. Min.* 28–29); much less was his *ius provocationis* ever endangered.

171. The decrees of 63 and 62 had aspects of exterior armed threats to them, and the *SCU* of 52, although clearly aimed at violence and disorder within the city after Clodius' death, did not serve to justify violence or the suspension of *provocatio* against Milo, who was charged before the People. However, Pompey's presence in early 52 *in urbe* as proconsul (as well as in 51 and 50) with troops was arguably in tension with the exercise of tribunician rights: Lintott, *Violence*, pp. 200–201. Nor do the cases of Caelius Rufus in 48, Dolabella and Trebellius in 47, Antonius and Octavian in 43 (41) or Sextus Pompeius in 40 have the suspension of *provocatio* as their aim.

172. See Ungern-Sternberg, *Untersuchungen*, pp. 83–84.

173. Cic. *Rab. Perd.* 2.

174. Ibid. 33-34. Trans. C. D. Yonge, with slight changes.

Ironically, Rabirius himself had, of course, made use of *provocatio*. Cicero's reference to the curbing of civic passions is interesting;[175] is suspension of *provocatio* really what is at stake here, or rather the use of arms against *hostes* by everyone, including the people? If the latter, this could make one think that Cicero's argument was that in the events of 100 BC *provocatio* had not been violated because implicitly the People, by morphing into a lynch mob, had been asked and subsequently declined the appeal by Saturninus. In 63 BC, on the other hand, Labienus was the only one to have tried to violate *provocatio*.[176] This reading is supported by a later passage of Cicero's speech for Rabirius, where the lack of violence does not allude—*pace* Lintott—to the situation with the Catilinarians, but where it is used to make the point that *provocatio* can be granted when there is no ongoing civil war in the city: a parallel is drawn between the People in arms against an (internal) *hostis* and the People in assembly judging at Rabirius' trial.[177]

This view Cicero still embraced in his *First Catilinarian* speech, it is true, but in the subsequent *Catilinarians* he was to sever the connection between the *SCU* and the execution of the Catilinarians in the city,[178] basing the latter on a senatorial decree which was in turn argued for by Cicero by saying that the Catilinarians were not really citizens any longer, but enemies.[179] Cicero must have realized that his attempt, based on very few precedents and very recent *mos*, to fashion out of the *SCU* a constitutional instrument sanctioned by *mos* and apt to suspend *provocatio*, had failed. The *hostis* argument, on the other hand, was far more promising: never had anyone been prosecuted, let alone condemned, for killing someone previously declared a *hostis*.[180]

Before we get to *hostis* declarations and Cicero's *hostis*-argument, let me mention that Cicero was not the only one to try to lend pedigree and constitutional legitimacy to the *SCU*. Livy injects the *SCU* into the early history of the Republic (very implausibly, needless to say), with a first instance of its use in 464 BC and a second in 384 BC. Livy assimilates the *SCU* to the dictatorship: the first time an *SCU* is declared in 464 it is to counter a military emergency and the second time, in 384 to deal with domestic unrest, the two traditional occasions giving rise to the dictatorship, as we have seen above. Livy's account of the

---

175. On the Stoic background, see Arena, "Consulship."

176. Cic. *Rab. perd.* 11–12. See Arena, *Libertas*, pp. 207–208.

177. Cic. *Rab. perd.* 35.

178. See Drummond, *Law*, p. 96; Nippel, *Aufruhr*, p. 103.

179. They were, however, never formally declared *hostes*.

180. But see Plut. *Sull.* 10.4; Cic. *Brut.* 179.

SCU of 384 BC is particularly instructive. M. Manlius Capitolinus, the savior of the Capitol from the Gauls, stands accused of aspiring to kingship (*regnum*), an aspiration evidenced solely by his (privately) supporting distressed debtors. The Senate, looking for a means to kill him without violating the right of appeal, makes it clear that it thinks of Manlius as a public enemy (*hostis publicus*); looking for a means "milder in its terms but with the same force" as the dictatorship, the Senate decides to issue an *SCU* against Manlius.[181] While the passage leaves no doubt that this would have been sufficient to kill Manlius constitutionally,[182] Livy also tells us that in this particular instance, the tribunes align themselves with the Senate and seek charges against Manlius before the People, thus leaving the right of appeal untouched: as soon as the People recognize that Manlius was aiming at *regnum*, they will be more inclined to protect their own liberty and charge him rather than let him exercise his right to an ordinary trial.[183]

There are quite a few instances of Roman citizens being declared *hostes*, public enemies, from 88 BC onward, with the legal implication that those declared enemies could be legitimately killed by anyone.[184] It is not until Cicero, however, that there is an elaborate theory of how citizens could be turned into *hostes* and thus lose their constitutional rights or indeed how this could be legitimate in the first place. This seems due to the fact that Cicero for the first time tried to achieve the application of the term *hostis* to citizens not currently under arms and not currently involved in violent acts. His incentive for doing so is obvious: as the Catilinarian crisis progressed, the importance of the *SCU* faded away and a decree of the Senate to the effect that the Catilinarians in the city were *hostes* would have had a much better chance than the *SCU* to convince Cicero's opponents of the constitutional legitimacy of the executions. Such declarations had previously gone uncontested and had the advantage of skirting, rather than violating, the right of appeal—if the people in question were indeed acknowledged to be *hostes* rather than *cives*, there were simply no citizen rights to be violated and *provocatio* became a moot point.

The first time Roman citizens were declared *hostes*, or at least the first time we have any clear-cut evidence for it,[185] was in 88 BC when Sulla, after entering the

181. Livy 6.19.3.

182. Lintott, *Constitution*, p. 36.

183. Livy 6.19.7.

184. App. *BCiv.* 1.60; *Rhet. Her.* 1.25. See Bauman, "*Hostis* Declarations."

185. Val. Max. 4.7.1 supplies very weak evidence for a *hostis* declaration in 132 BC in the wake of the killing of Ti. Gracchus. According to Cic. *Amic.* 37, an extraordinary court (*quaestio*) was set up in 132 BC to deal with Ti. Gracchus' remaining friends, but it is unlikely that the Gracchans were on this occasion declared *hostes*; the whole case for such a declaration rests on

city with troops—an unprecedented event[186]—had the Senate declare Marius, his son, the tribune Sulpicius Rufus as well as nine other men enemies.[187] It was thus Sulla "who on this occasion introduced the new custom of openly designating a Roman citizen a *hostis*."[188] Neither in this case nor in the following year, when Sulla was himself declared an enemy, was there any use of the *SCU*. The independent status, both historically and conceptually, of the *hostis* declaration and the *SCU* is well attested.[189] In fact, in the nine or so cases when citizens were declared *hostes* by the Senate down to 43 BC,[190] the citizens targeted were almost always armed rebels in the field. Of course, the relative frequency of such declarations from 88 onward testifies vividly to the truth of Harriet Flower's claim that Sulla's taking of Rome militarily marked the end of "the era of republican politics that gave all citizens a share in the political arena."[191] In the one case where we do have some evidence, exclusively from Appian, of a *hostis* declaration targeting citizens in the city (senators supporting Sulla in 83 BC), this happened in the context of Sulla's second march on Rome and with the memory of his military occupation of the city in 88 still fresh.[192] *Hostis* declarations, issued at times in conjunction with the proclamation of war around the city (the *tumultus* decree)[193] were not deemed extraordinary or unconstitutional; and even the ones

---

interpreting Plut. *C. Gracch.* 4.1 (especially the verb ἐκκηρύττω) as referring, not to outlawry and banishment (*aquae et ignis interdictio*), but to a *hostis* declaration. This is not the most natural interpretation of the term (cf. also *C. Gracch.* 4.2; *Ti. Gracch.* 20.3), and Lintott's ingenious argument that it cannot have possibly meant banishment because *aquae et ignis interdictio* had to be voted by the People seems to beg the question: surely, if the *quaestio* of 132 BC deemed itself competent to declare the Gracchans *hostes*, an *aquae et ignis interdictio* would *a fortiori* have been deemed a legitimate outcome of the *quaestio* procedure. Cf. Ungern-Sternberg, *Untersuchungen*, pp. 38–43.

186. See Flower, *Roman Republics*, p. 92. For an argument against the conventional notion of Sulla acting illegitimately, see Morstein-Marx, "Consular Appeals."

187. Livy *Per.* 77; Cic. *Brut.* 168; App. *BCiv.* 1.60; Val. Max. 1.5.5, 3.8.5; Florus 2.9. Vell. Pat. 2.19 does not say that Marius and his followers were declared *hostes*, he merely says they were exiled; Plut. *Sull.* 10.1 does not say so either; and Val. Max. 3.8.5 merely says that Sulla was driven by the desire to have Marius declared an enemy as soon as possible.

188. Flower, *Roman Republics*, p. 92.

189. See the discussion in Lintott, *Violence*, pp. 155–158; and the chart in Allély, *Déclaration*, p. 151.

190. See the list in Allély, *Déclaration*, p. 151.

191. Flower, *Roman Republics*, p. 92.

192. Given all the other instances of the *hostis* declaration, used exclusively against military threats, App. *BCiv.* 1.86 may not be trustworthy.

193. See Lintott, *Violence*, pp. 153–155; Golden, *Crisis Management*, pp. 42–86.

without *tumultus* seem to have been uncontroversial as long as the enemies in question were bearing arms or were posing a clear military threat.

It is not overly fanciful to draw an analogy between the Roman republican practice of declaring citizens *hostes* and the practice of the United States government to designate certain citizens "enemy combatants" in the wake of the September 11, 2001 terror attacks.[194] Citizens deemed to be enemy combatants by the executive branch of government can be preventively detained without the protections of an ordinary criminal trial, and citizens determined to be enemy combatants can probably be lawfully executed without trial.[195] The parallels to the Roman republican arguments are instructive. In the United States, the constitutional validity of executive detention of enemy combatants (both foreigners and, a fortiori, citizens) was challenged on the grounds that such detention violated constitutional rights to an ordinary trial (*habeas corpus* rights granted under the US Constitution). The executive had originally advanced the argument that the president of the United States during wartime and emergencies had the constitutional power as commander-in-chief to detain whomever he determined to be an enemy combatant. As the courts started to consider the issue and the arguments evolved, the following picture emerged: the executive did indeed have the power to detain citizens deemed enemy combatants, but this power rested, not on the president's constitutional wartime powers, but on the authority conferred to the president by Congress "to use all necessary and appropriate force . . . in order to prevent any future acts of international terrorism against the United States."[196] This implied that Congress could constitutionally bar the executive from detaining citizens. But the validity of the power to designate citizens enemy combatants does not preclude such enemy combatants from seeking some sort of judicial review of their enemy combatant status: increasingly courts have required that the government present "some evidence"[197] to support the enemy combatant designation, and that there be a substitute for an ordinary criminal trial where such designation could be reviewed.[198] In

---

194. See Issacharoff and Pildes, "Emergency Contexts."

195. See the speech by Attorney General Eric Holder of March 5, 2012: http://www.justice.gov/iso/opa/ag/speeches/2012/ag-speech-1203051.html

196. Authorization for Use of Military Force, Pub. L. No. 107–40, § 2(a), 115 Stat. 224, 224 (2001).

197. *Padilla v. Bush*, 233 F. Supp. 2d 564, 607 (S.D.N.Y. 2002), at 608.

198. It remained thus only partly true, as Issacharoff and Pildes maintain ("Emergency Contexts," p. 322), that the courts "resolved the issues by focusing more on questions involving the institutional allocation of authority than directly on issues of 'individual rights.'" Subsequent decisions, after Issacharoff and Pildes' article was published, did indeed focus on individual rights, especially *habeas corpus*.

the absence of an adequate substitute for an ordinary trial—and some of the procedures established subsequently have indeed been found to be wanting[199]—enemy combatants were granted access to the US justice system.

Without pressing the analogy too hard, it could be argued that in cases where the "enemy" designation is straightforward, as with armed rebels or combatants in the field, the constitutionality of declaring even citizens *hostes* is uncontroversial and thus not deemed a violation of *provocatio* or *habeas corpus* rights. More constitutionally controversial issues arise when the citizens in question are unarmed, like the arrested Catilinarians, and have not been picked up on the battlefield. In these cases, given the existence of higher-order constitutional norms, some extraordinary substitute for an ordinary trial may be called for in order to review the *hostis*/enemy combatant designation. Seen in this light, Jochen Bleicken's view of the Senate as having sat as a court during the debate concerning the fate of the arrested Catilinarians[200] may not be quite as far-fetched as hitherto assumed. The Senate session of December 5, 63, may not have constituted a proper judicial proceeding, but Cato and Cicero must nonetheless have felt that it provided some veneer of constitutionality, an adequate substitute for an ordinary trial, perhaps even a "most generous set of procedural protections"[201] afforded those who had been "proven guilty" (*convicti*) by "some evidence" (*indicio*), "have confessed" (*confessi*), and are thus to be treated "as though caught in the act."[202] The force of this argument was called into question only later, due to the success of Clodius' constitutional argument as evidenced by his legislation and by the effect this legislation—and the popular pressure generated by it—had on Cicero. Similar issues of whether due process has been applied arise in the context of the targeted killing of US citizens deemed enemy combatants. These concern, not *habeas* rights, but the potential violation of

---

199. See *Boumediene v. Bush*, 553 U.S. 723 (2008), where the Military Commisssion Act of 2006 was held to to have constituted an unconstitutional suspension of the right of *habeas corpus*. It is the position of the Obama administration that Military Commissions cannot be used to try US citizens: see Attorney General Holder's speech of March 5, 2012: http://www.justice.gov/iso/opa/ag/speeches/2012/ag-speech-1203051.html

200. Bleicken, *Senatsgericht*, pp. 21–27; similarly Lübtow, *Das römische Volk*, p. 346.

201. Chief Justice Roberts, dissent to *Boumediene v. Bush*, 553 U.S. 723 (2008), at 1.

202. Cato's *sententia*, which was adopted by the Senate: Sall. *Cat.* 52.36. On Bleicken's thesis, see Sherwin-White, "Review Bleicken," where formal elements of a judicial proceeding are denied; see Ungern-Sternberg, *Untersuchungen*, pp. 115–117; Nippel, *Public Order*, pp. 68–69. These discussions are governed by hindsight, Cicero's exile, and by the fact that the Senate decision did not put the issue to rest. However, this might be asking too much: the Military Commissions Act of 2006 did not put the issues to rest either. Both are best seen as constitutional experiments.

the Due Process Clause as incorporated in the Fifth Amendment of the US Constitution; and the less obviously such citizens designated enemies pose an immediate armed threat, the more constitutional controversy does their execution invite.

It was not until Cicero developed his theory of citizens becoming enemies by virtue of their behavior, *ipso facto*, that the *hostis* declaration turned into a constitutionally contested issue. Cicero's view was that the *hostis* decree was not constitutive but merely declaratory of someone's status as a public enemy. This was a normative constitutional theory and never fully accepted, mostly due to Cicero's novel attempt to subsume under the term *hostis* citizens who were not posing an armed threat. The first time Cicero put forward this view was in his *First Catilinarian*, where he suggested that Catiline, although present in the Senate during the speech, was a public enemy. The whole commonwealth (*res publica*), Cicero claimed, was wondering why he, Cicero, after "discovering" (*comperisti*) Catiline to be a public enemy (*hostis*), did not give orders that he "be cast into chains, led away to execution, and made to suffer the ultimate penalty."[203] He further imagines the Republic asking him: "What on earth is stopping you? Constitutional tradition (*mos maiorum*)? . . . Or is it the laws that have been passed relating to the punishment of Roman citizens?" This affords Cicero the opportunity to make his dubious constitutional argument, eliding any distinction between armed rebellion and the mere suspicion of conspiring to rise in arms: "But at Rome people who have rebelled against the state have never retained the rights of citizens."[204] Again, the main obstacle this argument was designed to overcome was the right of appeal (*provocatio*). But this theory did not convince: a *hostis* decree by the Senate remained constitutive of that status, and Catiline was not declared a public enemy until he had joined his armed co-conspirators in the field.[205] Cicero tried again, subsuming the arrested Catilinarian conspirators in the city under the label *hostis*, but this in itself hardly convinced anyone.[206] Twenty years later, in the contest with Antonius Cicero put the argument forward for the last time by associating Antonius with others such as the Gracchi, Saturninus, Catiline, and Clodius, whom Cicero deemed "citizens by birth but public enemies by choice" (*natura cives, voluntate hostes*).[207] Apart from Catiline, none of the named persons had, in fact, ever formally been declared a *hostis* by

---

203. Cic. *Cat.* 1.27.

204. Ibid. 1.28. Trans. D. H. Berry, slightly adapted.

205. Sall. *Cat.* 36.1–2.

206. Cic. *Cat.* 4.10. See Drummond, *Law*, pp. 44, 96–102; Nippel, *Public Order*, p. 68.

207. Cic. *Phil.* 8.13–14. Trans. Shackleton Bailey.

the Senate,[208] and Antonius had not yet been declared an enemy when Cicero delivered his *Philippics*. Interestingly, Cicero himself seems to undermine his *hostis* theory in his speech in defence of Rabirius from early 63 BC, where he clearly acknowledges the taking of arms as a necessary condition for the declaration of someone as a *hostis*.[209]

It is thus indeed the case that "the *hostis* argument in this form probably owed its birth to Cicero and died with him."[210] However, it is significant that this constitutional theory did not develop until the political context and the republican institutions had deteriorated to a hitherto unknown extent; and in the context of such deterioration, constitutional conflict and argument started turning into natural law argument. This was especially the case in Cicero's theoretical works, but had already been more or less inchoately present in some of his speeches, owing to the fact that the late Republic came increasingly to resemble a state of nature. From arguing about the (constitutional) rights and norms that were supposed to hold under the Republic's higher-order legal norms (*ius*), Cicero more and more developed arguments concerning much more abstract, more entrenched, and higher-order norms (many of which, however, still suspiciously resembled the Roman ones he was acquainted with), those constituting a natural constitutional law, as it were. Below in Chapter 3 I will try to track this development in Roman constitutional thought and argument from political and forensic arguments about the Republic's constitutional norms toward the more recondite views on political and constitutional theory Cicero was to develop in his mature philosophical work. But first let us consider constitutional argument surrounding emergency powers of another kind, extraordinary commands. At first intended to be deployed outside the city in theaters of war, these powers were to have an impact on politics within the city as well.

Extraordinary commands (imperia extraordinaria)

> *[T]hat fatal neglect in the observance of all the laws, so essential to their constitution . . . made way for the seven consulships of Marius, the early and multiplied honours of Pompey, and the long continuation of Caesar's command in Gaul; which are on all hands allowed to have been the direct and immediate causes of the ruin of the commonwealth.* (*Walter Moyle,* An Essay upon the Constitution of the Roman Government)

208. But for Clodius as at least a potential *hostis*, see Cic. *Pis.* 35.

209. Cic. *Rab. Perd.* 35.

210. Drummond, *Law*, p. 44.

There is a venerable tradition in scholarship blaming the extraordinary military commands of the late Republic for its fall. In some sense since Machiavelli,[211] and certainly since Mommsen, such *imperia* have been identified as an anticipation of the Principate and as the single most important factor in the Republic's demise.[212] Indeed, Mommsen was of the opinion that the Principate was nothing but an extraordinary command.[213] Despite their crucial role in the crises of the late Republic there has not been a recent monographic treatment of *imperia extraordinaria*[214] except within the context of biographical works on holders of such powers, such as Pompey, Caesar, or Crassus.[215] It is important to note, from the outset, the crucial distinction we find in the sources between the prorogation of an existing command, usually decided by the Senate, as were other issues to do with *provinciae*, and the bestowal of *imperium* by the People on someone who is a mere private citizen (*privatus*). It was the latter which was felt to be extraordinary (*extra ordinem*) and thus constitutionally problematic. The differentiation is reflected in Mommsen's usage, where "exceptional" *imperia* are treated separately from "extraordinary" ones, where the latter form a more limited category, and alone comprise commands for private individuals.[216] This led Mommsen to view Caesar's ten-year *imperium* in Gaul as a case of prorogation (albeit a rather exceptional one), rather than an extraordinary command in the strict sense.[217] The term *extra ordinem* is also used in the sources, as Mommsen, of course, knew full well,[218] in a less strict sense

211. Cf. *Discorsi* 3.24 ("la prolungazione degli imperii," however, subsumes both prorogation and *privati cum imperio*).

212. Representative is Bleicken, *Geschichte*, 229. See also id., "*Imperium consulare/proconsulare*," p. 720. Cf. Brunt, *Social Conflicts*, pp. 152–153: the urban plebs "carried the Gabinian law by violence and thus gave Pompey his great command which proved fateful for the Republic."

213. Mommsen, *Staatsrecht* vol. 2.1, p. 662.

214. See the 1918 article by Boak, "Extraordinary Commands," the 1926 monograph by Wiehn, *Heereskommanden*; Kloft, *Prorogation*; Giuffrè, *Aspetti costituzionali*; and now Hurlet, "Pouvoirs extraordinaires"; Vervaet, "Praetorian Proconsuls"; id., *High Command*, ch. 7; Arena, *Libertas*, pp. 179–200. For the development of the promagistracy, see Jashemski, *Origins and History*.

215. See, e.g., Gelzer, *Pompeius*; Seager, *Pompey*; Gelzer, *Caesar*; Chr. Meier, *Caesar*; Jehne, *Caesar*; Ward, *Crassus*.

216. See Mommsen, *Staatsrecht* vol. 2.1, pp. 646–662; but see ibid., pp. 651–652, where Mommsen is ambiguous. Kloft, *Prorogation*, neglects the differentiation: Badian, "Review Kloft," p. 793.

217. Mommsen, *Staatsrecht* vol. 2.1, pp. 646.

218. See ibid. vol. 1, p. 20, at n. 2.

in order to describe any office bestowed in a way that violates or bypasses legislation,[219] be it legislation dealing with the *cursus honorum*,[220] with the interval between offices,[221] with sortition,[222] or with *imperia* altogether unforeseen by the constitution,[223] such as military commands *extra ordinem* in the strict sense. In this section we will pay particular attention to extraordinary military commands and their various deviations from constitutional principles such as annuity, collegiality, and geographical constraints. The aim is to show that the distinction between notions such as "constitutional," "*extra ordinem* but perhaps still constitutional" and "unconstitutional" constituted one of the key battlegrounds of constitutional argument in the late Republic.[224] This conflict yielded, over time, a shift of authority from the Senate to the tribal assembly.

If one were to list broadly exceptional powers in the late Republic one should mention the irregular bestowal of the consulship on Marius in late 105 BC;[225] the powers bestowed by the fragmentary *lex de provinciis praetoriis* from Delphi and Cnidos;[226] Marius' extraordinary command of 88;[227] Antonius' of 74;[228] Pompey's various commands in 81–80, 77–71, 67, 66, and 55, his *cura annonae*

219. Dio Cass. 36.39.

220. Cic. *Brut.* 226; Tac. *Ann.* 2.32; 13.29.

221. Caes. *BCiv.* 1.32.

222. Cic. *Dom.* 24.

223. Cic. *Phil.* 11.20; Suet. *Iul.* 11.

224. Arena, *Libertas*, p. 190, points out that resistance to extraordinary powers was always exercised in the name of *libertas*, while acknowledging that those resisting such powers also voiced concern about (p. 198) "the distribution of power amongst different institutional bodies." See Vervaet, *High Command*, ch. 7, on the gradual eclipse of the constitutional principle of "shared supremacy of the consuls in Rome and the principle that in Italy and beyond every *imperator cum provincia* normally held the supreme command ... in his offical province" (p. 289).

225. Cic. *Prov. cons.* 19 (Marius' re-election as consul in his absence *extra ordinem*); Plut. *Mar.* 12. At least since 330 BC there was legislation prescribing a ten-year interval between consulships: Livy 7.42; 10.13; Caes. *BCiv.* 1.32; Dio Cass. 40.51.

226. Crawford, *Roman Statutes*, vol. 1, pp. 231–270. The Delphi inscription is in Pomtow, "Neufunde"; the Cnidos fragment is in Hassall et al., "Rome and the Eastern Provinces," and a translation with commentary is offered by Sherk, *Rome*, no. 55. See also Hinrichs, "Tafel."

227. App. *BCiv.* 1.56; Plut. *Mar.* 35.4; Val. Max. 9.7. ext.1; for additional sources, see Broughton, *Magistrates*, vol. 2, p. 40.

228. Cic. *2Verr.* 2.8; 3.213; Livy *Per.* 97; Lactant. *Div. inst.* 1.11.32; Vell. 2.31.3–4; for additional sources, see Broughton, *Magistrates*, vol. 2, pp. 101–102.

in 57, and his sole consulship in 52;[229] Caesar's commands in Gaul (59 and 55);[230] Crassus' command against the Parthians of 55;[231] the bestowal by legislation of both Gauls on Antonius in 44; and the *imperia* Cicero sought to award to Octavian, M. Brutus, and C. Cassius in 43. In what follows, we will discuss those examples of extraordinary commands that are most salient for us, that is to say, those where we have good evidence for the constitutional arguments involved. First we need to have before us the distinction already introduced between prorogation, the extension of an existing command, usually by the Senate, and the bestowal of *imperium* on a *privatus* by the comitia. Both were resorted to often in the extraordinary circumstances of the Second Punic War, but the distinction remained crucial. When L. Cornelius Lentulus in the late third century BC asked the Senate for a triumph, this was considered unconstitutional, notwithstanding his achievements, given that he had been granted *imperium* as a mere private citizen in 206 BC.[232] By contrast, by 146 BC, when Africa and Macedonia were organized without adding any more praetors, prorogation by the Senate was completely regularized and became indeed a necessity.[233]

There is some debate as to the role of the popular assembly in the prorogation of commands; it seems reasonably clear, however, that at least from the second century BC onwards, prorogation became the exclusive domain of the Senate, notwithstanding the etymology suggesting a *rogatio* put to the People.[234] The etymology here is misleading when it comes to technical usage at least in the middle and late Republic; the technical term for reelecting magistrates for a second consecutive year in office, that is to say for continuation, is in fact *reficere*.[235] While continuation was always felt to be constitutionally problematic

229. Livy *Per.* 89; 91; 97; 99; 100; 105; *CIL* I², 178; Granius Licinianus 36; Cic. *Leg. Man.* 52, 62, and *passim; Phil.* 11.18; Val. Max. 8.15.8; Vell. 2.31.3; 2.33; App. *Hisp.* 76; *Mith.* 94 and 97; *BCiv.* 2.18; Dio Cass. 36.23–24; 36.36–37; 36.42; 39.33; 40.56.2; Plut. *Luc.* 34–35; *Crass.* 15–16; *Caes.* 28; *Cato Min.* 45–47; *Pomp.* 54.

230. Cic. *Att.* 8.3.3; *Fam.* 1.10; *Prov. cons.* 15, 17, and 42; *Vat.* 36; *Phil.* 2.24; Caes. *BGall.* 1.10.5; 1.21; 7.1; 7.6; Livy *Per.* 103; Suet. *Iul.* 22.1 and 24; Dio Cass. 37.57.2; 38.8.5; 39.33; Plut. *Caes.* 14 and 21; *Crass.* 15; *Pomp.* 48.3; 51–52; *Cato Min.* 33.3; Zonar. 10.6; App. *BCiv.* 2.13; 2.17–18; Vell. 2.44.5; 2.46; Oros. 6.7.1; Eutrop. 6.17.1.

231. Liv. *Per.* 105; App. *BCiv.* 2.18.65; Suet. *Iul.* 24; Plut. *Pomp.* 51–52; *Cato Min.* 41.1; *Crass.* 15; Dio Cass. 39.33.2.

232. Livy 31.20.3–4. Cf. Kloft, *Prorogation*, p. 70.

233. See Badian, "Review Kloft," pp. 793–794.

234. Cf. Livy 27.22.4–6 (prorogation decreed by the Senate and also confirmed by the People). See Richardson, *Empire*, pp. 17–22; cf. Oakley, *Commentary*, vol. 2, pp. 660–661.

235. Brennan, *Praetorship*, vol. 2, p. 651.

and was used only in military emergencies, often under additional emergency legislation,[236] prorogation by the Senate was routine. This suggests that prorogation was not felt to add the same prestige as being re-elected to the same office; prorogation was merely "folded into" the office that had been prorogued.[237] It also suggests that the danger inherent in the continuation of office, the danger of tyranny, was associated with the authority of the assemblies freely to reelect the same magistrates over and over again, not with the prorogation in office effected by the Senate. At the same time, the various prohibitions on iteration and continuation in office were—albeit vaguely understood to belong to norms of a higher order—enshrined in legislation in the way by now familiar to readers of this book. This entailed that these prohibitions themselves were felt to be subject to being abolished by emergency legislation:[238] what we witness in the evidence describing the arguments put forward "on the ground" is again a grappling with, or reaching for, the notion of a constitutional order governing such legislation, without arriving at a proper conceptualization.

More unusual commands, including *imperia* bestowed on private citizens, or commands bestowed in violation of constitutional principles such as annuity and collegiality of office, age limits, geographical limits, or prohibitions of iteration and continuation of the same office, were created and given by the assemblies. This accounts for Cicero's description of them in his *Eleventh Philippic*, delivered in early 43 BC before the Senate, as smacking "of 'popular' politics and inconsistency," unsuited for the gravity of the Senate.[239] Cicero here is particularly concerned to restrict the term "extraordinary command" to the bestowal of *imperium* on a *privatus* by the People. In an interesting and telling survey of the history of such commands, he claims that "no extraordinary command was required for that war [against Antiochus III in 190 BC] any more than in the two great Punic Wars earlier on, which were waged and brought to their conclusions by consuls or dictators, or in the war against Pyrrhus, in the war against Philip, and later in the Achaian War, or in the Third Punic War."[240] Prima facie this is a rather tendentious claim; for in the second Punic War (218-201 BC) and the years succeeding it roughly fifteen *privati cum imperio* can be counted.[241] About three of those were

236. Ibid., p. 652.

237. Kloft, *Prorogation*, pp. 64–66.

238. This must have been the case during Marius' repeated consulships: Brennan, *Praetorship*, vol. 2, p. 652.

239. Cic. *Phil.* 11.17.

240. Ibid.

241. Kloft, *Prorogation*, pp. 29–30.

mere legates without a command of their own, six or seven had had *imperium* at some point before but were private citizens when given a command in the war context, and the rest had never before been in office. Does Cicero here simply make a false claim for rhetorical effect? This has to be part of the explanation, but there is a second aspect that deserves consideration: given his claim that extraordinary commands are "popular and inconsistent" (conveniently forgetting his support for Pompey's command in 66, on which see below), and given that in the context of the *Eleventh Philippic* it is the Senate that is called upon, here Cicero may only be counting those *imperia* bestowed on *privati* by the Senate. He in effect seems to be saying that it was never the *Senate's* business to bestow such commands (thus at the same time inconsistently undermining his earlier claim that extraordinary commands are by definition bestowed by the People).

Speaking directly to Pompey's commands, Cicero in this late speech blames the assemblies: "As for the commands of Gnaeus Pompeius, a great man, indeed the first of men, the legislation was put through by troublemaking tribunes of the plebs, except that the war against Sertorius was assigned to him as a private citizen by the Senate because the consuls declined."[242] Cicero justifies the election of Scipio Aemilianus, who had not reached the required age, to the consulship in 147 BC by pointing out that at least he was elected to an ordinary magistracy, rather than an extraordinary one.[243] Cicero's arguments here are all the more acrobatic given his aim in the *Eleventh Philippic*: to extend a command to C. Cassius Longinus, one of the liberators, who had been praetor in 44 BC but who did not have *imperium* any longer and was thus a mere private citizen.[244] Cicero's arguments here are veering into the domain of natural law, a move we will further discuss in Chapter 4. It is instructive, however, to compare his historical survey of extraordinary commands as presented in the *Eleventh Philippic* with the review given in his speech *On the Manilian Law* (*De imperio Gnaei Pompeii*)—in the speech, that is, Cicero had delivered to the People in 66 BC in order to support Pompey's extraordinary command against Mithridates, support he obviously was not keen to stress in the passage cited from the *Philippic*.

In 67 BC, the *privatus* Pompey had been given an unlimited command over the whole Mediterranean and its coasts up to fifty miles inland for at least three years with the mandate to wipe out piracy.[245] Pompey's command,

---

242. Cic. *Phil.* 11.18.

243. Ibid. 11.17.

244. Cassius' *imperium* had not been prorogued; by leaving the city without the necessary rituals, he did not have authority *militiae*.

245. Vell. 2.31.2–4;

modeled on an earlier one bestowed on M. Antonius in 74 BC, which Cicero called *imperium infinitum* shortly thereafter,[246] was to be equal to that of the governors in the surrounding provinces and entailed the right to levy troops, raise at least 300 ships, and appoint at least fifteen legates with *imperium*.[247] This law, moved by the tribune A. Gabinius, had been subjected to heavy criticism. The main issue was that the law gave too much power to a single man, unconstrained by annuity, collegiality, or geographical boundaries; the example of M. Antonius' behavior will have been detrimental, too.[248] Q. Hortensius, the famous orator, had attacked Gabinius' bill in 67 by putting forward the same argument he was to repeat in 66: that "if everything is to be put in the hands of one man, then Pompeius is the most appropriate person; but that everything should *not* be handed over to one man."[249] Against this view, Cicero argued that there was constitutional precedent for entrusting everything to one man, adducing Scipio Aemilianus' destruction of Carthage and Numantia (146 and 133 BC) and, more to the point, Marius' repeated election to the consulship (104–100 BC) which clashed with constitutional norms of iteration and continuation. Unlike the previous ones, Marius' sixth consulship in 100 was not even a response to a military emergency: it was simply given him by the People due to his merits.[250] Cicero in his historical survey tellingly fails to mention that in 77 BC, Q. Catulus (*cos.* 78), the key opponent of the Manilian law, had already opposed Pompey, ordering him to disband his army (to no effect),[251] and that Catulus and Hortensius as well as other senators had vigorously opposed Pompey's command against the pirates in 67 on constitutional grounds.[252]

246. Cic. *2Verr.* 2.8, 3.213; Ps.-Asc. pp. 202, 239, 259; *Schol. Bob.* p. 96 Stangl. M. Antonius Creticus, the son of M. Antonius (*cos.* 99), seems to have been praetor: Livy *Per.* 97. See Broughton, *Magistrates*, vol. 2, pp. 101–102 and 108, n. 2; Brennan, *Praetorship*, vol. 2, pp. 406–407; Linderski, "Surname"; Vervaet, *High Command*, p. 218.

247. For the sources, see Broughton, *Magistrates*, vol. 2, pp. 144–145.

248. Cic. *2Verr.* 3.213–218.

249. Cic. *Leg. Man.* 52. Trans. D. H. Berry. For the argument that Cicero should be given preference over Dio when it comes to chronology (Catulus' objections as recorded by Dio should be placed in 66, not 67 BC), see Rodgers, "Catulus' Speech." This is overlooked by Arena, *Libertas*, pp. 187–188. Cf. also Vervaet, *High Command*, pp. 216–219, who believes that Catulus' speech as paraphrased by Dio would be pointless in the context of the *lex Manilia*.

250. Vell. 2.12.6.

251. Liv. *Per.* 91; Plut. *Pomp.* 17.1–4; for additional sources, see Broughton, *Magistrates*, vol. 2, p. 90.

252. Cic. *Leg. Man.* 52; Plut. *Pomp.* 25.4.

Cicero defends Pompey's command on the grounds that Pompey's whole career was littered with unprecedented actions and commands, all of which had been supported by the very people who now stood opposed to the command against Mithridates. Enumerating these departures from constitutional tradition, Cicero mentions Pompey's raising of an army as a mere *privatus* in 83, his commands in Sicily and Africa in 82 and 81, the command against Sertorius in 77/76, and his under-age consulship in 70 BC.[253] He concludes, strikingly, that "if you count up all the departures from precedent that have been allowed to everyone in history, there are fewer of them than we have witnessed in the case of this one man."[254] It has often been observed that this argument rested on the principle, or rather sophism, that "our ancestors invariably followed custom in time of peace, but expediency in war, and that they invariably responded to emergencies with new ways of doing things."[255] Yet this is not in fact meant to enunciate a constitutional principle—indeed, Cicero's list of precedents would hardly make sense if it were. Later in the speech, Cicero unveils the crucial principle at work: the Roman People can by its own right (*suo iure*) grant extraordinary commands, at least when the assembly acts in the interest of the Republic; the senatorial opposition cannot oppose the People on this on pain of appearing as

> unjust and intolerable, particularly given that the Roman people are now in a strong position to defend their own decision about Pompey in the face of all who disagree. Indeed, you have every right to defend that decision, seeing that when you chose him, and him alone, out of many possible contenders, to appoint to the war against the pirates, a chorus of protest was heard from precisely the same people who are protesting now. If you appointed him to that command for frivolous reasons or without considering the national interest (*rei publicae parum consuluistis*), then those men are right to try to use their wisdom to temper your enthusiasm. But if it was in fact you who had a clearer view of the national interest . . ., then these leading men should finally admit that they and everyone else have now no option but to defer to the unanimous authority of the Roman people.[256]

253. Cic. *Leg. Man.* 61–62. Omitting the junior magistracies, Pompey had risen to the consulship directly from equestrian status—a further irregularity.

254. Ibid. 62.

255. Ibid. 60.

256. Ibid. 63–64.

While the opponents of Pompey's command put forward constitutional claims against extraordinary commands rather than merely prudential ones, Cicero here argues solely from prudence and with the implicit constitutional assumption that "whatever the People orders ought to be ratified,"[257] a position obviously at odds with his considered views as expressed in his late speeches and his philosophical work. The only consideration tempering this assumption is something we may anachronistically term "national security." On this view, concern for the Republic's national interest may yet limit the decision-making authority of the assembly, while principles such as annuity, collegiality, and geographical limits do not.

That Cicero was able to defend, if not sincerely hold, this view is apparent from Asconius' commentary on Cicero's speech in defense of C. Cornelius, who had been tribune in 67 BC together with A. Gabinius, the sponsor of Pompey's extraordinary command against the pirates. Both Cornelius and Gabinius—and probably Manilius in 66 BC—had faced resistance to their legislation and had not shied away from attempting to use violence and to override vetoing tribunes, following Tiberius Gracchus' example. Cornelius was subsequently prosecuted for treason, on the grounds that his "conduct was highly relevant to the charge of impairing the *maiestas* of the tribunate, for, if this were to be allowed to individual tribunes, the veto was all but eliminated."[258] In Cornelius' case, where violence induced him to abandon his effort,[259] Cicero clearly is prepared to argue that a tribune's veto could indeed be overridden.[260] Comparing Cornelius' conduct with Gabinius', Cicero stresses the similarities and holds that for reasons of "national security" Gabinius' violation of the tribunician veto was indeed justified: "All these things a gallant person, this man's colleague A. Gabinius, did in an excellent cause, and in bringing salvation for the Roman people and for all nations an end to longstanding disgrace and servitude [i.e. piracy], did not permit the voice and preference of one single colleague of his to prevail over those of the state as a whole."[261]

That there were constitutional qualms about entrusting the enormously far-reaching command against the pirates to Pompey became a topos in later

257. Cic. *Caecin.* 96, where the point, of course, is to prove the exact opposite, that "not everything the people orders ought to be ratified." Cf. Livy 7.17.12 (= Tab. XII.5); and pp. 45f. in Chapter 1 above.

258. Asc. 61C.

259. Ibid. 58C.

260. Ibid. 61C. Cf. Lewis, *Asconius*, p. 268.

261. Ibid. 72C.

historiography. Velleius Paterculus, who could avail himself of many sources, Sallust and the rhetorical tradition chief among them,[262] observes that by the legislation of Gabinius, "the command of almost the entire world was being entrusted to one man." This was constitutionally problematic, for Pompey's power was unchecked: "men shrink from conferring extraordinary powers upon those who seem likely to retain them or lay them aside only as they themselves choose, and whose inclinations are their only check."[263] There was resistance from the optimates on constitutional grounds: Velleius imputes to Q. Catulus the view that Pompey's powers were becoming too expansive for a free Republic.[264] Similarly, Plutarch reports with regard to Pompey's command against Mithridates that it provoked fears among the ruling elite that he was in the process of establishing a tyranny and abolishing republican freedom.[265] Against Catulus' resistance, the People—all tribes—ratified the command, thus amplifying Pompey's powers almost to the level of Sulla's:[266] this was truly *extra ordinem*.[267]

The most explicit expression of political thought dealing with the constitutional implications of Pompey's extraordinary commands can be found in the speech given to Q. Catulus by Cassius Dio. In view of the conventions of ancient historiography this speech cannot be regarded as authentic; indeed, it cannot in all likelihood be regarded as anything but the historian's own invention.[268] While it is a bad source for the political history of the 60s BC, as an expression of a tradition of political thought preoccupied with the distinction between regular and extraordinary powers Catulus' speech must be taken seriously. Barbara Saylor Rodgers has argued persuasively that Dio must primarily have relied on Cicero's speech *On the Manilian Law* and on the rhetorical model of Demosthenes. She also shows that Catulus must have articulated his resistance to Pompey's powers in 66 and not in 67 BC as Dio would have it, and that Dio's Catulus channels arguments which must have been Hortensius'. Dio's overall goal is periodization—he aims to show that in hindsight Pompey's long-term commands marked the beginning of the end of the Republic,[269] a view

262. For Velleius' sources, see Rodgers, "Catulus' Speech," p. 303, n. 21.

263. Vell. 2.31.2–4. Trans. F. W. Shipley.

264. Ibid. 2.32.1. But Catulus' speech on balance probably belongs to 66 BC: see Rodgers, "Catulus' Speech," p. 298.

265. Plut. *Pomp.* 30.3.

266. Ibid. 30.5.

267. Asc. 65C.

268. Rodgers, "Catulus' Speech," *passim*, esp. p. 318; see also Millar, *Cassius Dio*, pp. 78–83.

269. Rodgers, "Catulus' Speech," p. 317; cf. Millar, *Cassius Dio*, p. 74–77.

shared by many modern scholars. For our purposes these points are immaterial; what counts is the constitutional argument contained in Catulus' speech to the People. The most important point is that annuity and the prohibition on the continuation of office are perceived as the key constitutional safeguards:

> I, for my part, assert first and foremost that it is not proper to entrust to any one man so many positions of command one after another.[270] This has not only been forbidden by the laws (ἐν τοῖς νόμοις ἀπηγόρευται), but has also been found by experience to be most perilous. What made Marius what he became was practically nothing else than being entrusted with so many wars in the shortest space of time and being made consul six times in the briefest period; and similarly Sulla became what he was because he held command of the armies so many years in succession, and later was appointed dictator, then consul. For it does not lie in human nature for a person—I speak not alone of the young but of the mature as well—after holding positions of authority for a long period to be willing to abide by ancestral customs (τοῖς πατρίοις ἔθεσιν). Now I do not say this in any disparagement of Pompey, but because it does not appear ever to have been of advantage to you in any way, and in particular because it is not permitted by the laws (μήτε ἐκ τῶν νόμων).[271]

By "laws," Dio is not merely referring to legislation, but to the *ius* embodied in such laws as the *leges annales*. It is their violation of such higher-order law that makes these commands extraordinary; Dio proposes either to stick with constitutional emergency powers such as the traditional dictatorship (as opposed to the Sullan one), or to let ordinary magistrates and promagistrates deal with the issue at hand. Dio, no less than his republican predecessors, differentiates between (constitutional) prorogation and (unconstitutional) extraordinary command:

> So long as consuls and praetors and those serving in their places [i.e., promagistrates] are receiving their offices and commands conformably to the laws (τεταγμένως ἐκ τῶν νόμων) it is in no wise fitting, nor yet advantageous, for you to overlook them and introduce some new office. To what end, indeed, do you elect the annual officials, if you are going to make no use of them for such occasions? Surely not that they may stalk about in

270. This position must have been articulated in 66, when Pompey received his command against Mithridates in addition to his previous command against the pirates.

271. Dio Cass. 36.31.3–32.1. Trans. E. Cary.

> purple-bordered togas, nor that, clothed with the name alone of the office, they may be deprived of its duties. How can you fail to arouse the enmity of these and all the rest who have a purpose to enter public life at all, if you overthrow the ancient offices, and entrust nothing to those elected by law (ἐκ τῶν νόμων), but assign some strange and hitherto unheard-of command (γεγενημένην ἡγεμονίαν) to a private individual?[272]

That Dio's *nomoi* are in fact equivalent to *ius* and thus cannot simply be identified with statutory law is a more than plausible assumption in light of the prehistory of the term; had Dio wished to refer narrowly to statutes he is likely to have chosen the term *psephisma*, a word he uses both for decrees of the Senate and popular legislation.[273] By contrast, *nomoi* for Dio means the same as it had meant for his Greek models including Thucydides, Lysias, and Demosthenes: not any specific statutes, but rather "the legal and social system as a whole,"[274] that is to say, the constitutional order or the set of higher-order legal norms referred to by the Romans as *ius*. The bestowal of a command on the private individual Pompey in 67 BC amounted thus to a violation of the *nomoi* understood as the constitutional order as a whole.

Pompey continues to provide us with the most instructive example of constitutional argument surrounding extraordinary powers. When an agrarian bill was proposed, unsuccessfully, in 60 to distribute public land to Pompey's veterans, the statute was opposed in the Senate—notwithstanding Cicero's qualified support for it—not so much on grounds of substance, but for fear of "some new powers for Pompey" that were connected with the bill.[275] New, extraordinary powers were a danger traditionally associated with agrarian legislation. In his speech to the People on the tribune Rullus' agrarian law delivered in 63 BC, Cicero invoked vague fears of "unprecedented despotism, extraordinary powers, suited for kings rather than magistrates"[276] and went on to denounce the commission envisaged under the bill that was to sell, buy, and distribute agrarian land as tyranny (*regnum*).[277] Worse, Cicero adds, the sweeping powers that would be

272. Ibid. 36.33.

273. See, e.g., ibid. 39.55.2. Cf. also fr. 57.16 (election to co-dictatorship); 37.26.1 (*SCU*); 45.44.3 (Antonius having overstepped the constitutional order—νῦν δ' ἅπαξ καὶ ἐκ τῶν νόμων καὶ ἐκ τῆς πολιτείας ἐκβάς—must be fought with all means); 46.23.4 (*SC*); 48.16.1 (declaration of war).

274. Ostwald, *Popular Sovereignty*, pp. 84–136; p. 127.

275. Cic. *Att.* 1.19.4.

276. Cic. *Leg. Agr.* 2.8.

277. Ibid. 2.32–34; 2.75.

given to the agrarian commission under the statute amount to even more than kingly authority:

> for there never was any kingly power that, if very little defined by some law (*ius*), was not at least understood to be subject to certain limitations. But this power is absolutely unbounded (*infinitum*); it is one within which all kingly powers (*regna omnia*), and your own authority (*imperium*), which is of such wide extent, and all other powers, whether freely exercised by your permission, or existing only by your tacit countenance, are, by express permission of the law (*permissu legis*), comprehended.[278]

These unchecked powers are the more tyrannical because they gave the commission the authority to sell private land—in this case including the property of the Roman People, that is to say, paradoxically, public land.[279] The agrarian bill was never passed, but this speech, from the advocate of Pompey's extraordinary command no less, must surely count among the most eloquent denunciations of such powers. Once again we encounter the by now familiar tension between *lex* and *ius*, with the powers of the agrarian commission as set up under Rullus' *lex* portrayed as going far beyond even the weak constitutional checks that usually confine kingly power, let alone the constitutional constraints (*ius*) that are considered fundamental to the Republic.

After Cicero's return from exile in 57 BC, he supported new powers for Pompey on a vast scale, comparable only to Pompey's commands in the 60s. His discussion of these powers gives us excellent evidence for the contentious character of the constitutional arguments deployed both for and against such extraordinary *imperia*. In response to unrest due to high grain prices "there was a general demand, not only from the populace but from the honest men (*boni*) too, that Pompey be asked to take charge of supplies."[280] The consuls and the Senate were willing to give Pompey fifteen legates and "control over all grain supplies throughout the world for a period of five years." A tribune of the plebs went even further and proposed a law giving him "control over all moneys and in addition a fleet, an army, and authority in the provinces superior to that of their governors."[281] The

278. Ibid. 2.35. Trans. C. D. Yonge, with slight changes.

279. Ibid. 2.38–41. Lintott, *Cicero*, p. 140: "A well-known characteristic of tyranny was that it seized private property—not usually a particular concern to the poor. However, the Rullan bill offered Cicero a magnificent alternative: the commission had powers to sell the public land of the Roman people."

280. Cic. *Att.* 4.1.6. Trans. D. R. Shackleton Bailey.

281. Ibid. 4.1.7.

senatorial resolution was passed, and Cicero shortly thereafter had to justify his support for such extraordinary powers in his highly instructive speech before the college of Pontiffs, *De domo sua*.

The crucial point is that Cicero, far from arguing that commands *extra ordinem* should really be considered constitutional, is forced to resort to the argument that his adversary, Clodius, is not a credible opponent of such powers. Clodius' argument—the very argument already put forward in the debates of the 60s—that no one person should be given extraordinary powers[282] is answered simply by considerations of *raison d'état* and by pointing out Pompey's great successes against the pirates and in the East,[283] on the one hand, and by pointing out *ad hominem* that Clodius himself had supported such commands in the past and was thus an unlikely defender of the constitutional order. This was an allusion to the strategy Clodius himself had used when in the previous year as tribune he passed a law giving Cato an extraordinary command[284] with the mission to annex Cyprus.[285] A clever move, this made it difficult for Cato, who had been an enemy of extraordinary commands of any kind, to continue opposing them: Clodius and his allies had boasted before the People that they "had torn from Marcus Cato's head the tongue that had always spoken freely against extraordinary commands."[286] According to Cicero, Cato had obeyed the statute giving him the command although he felt that it had been passed in violation of constitutional norms (*iniuste*).[287] And now Cicero uses the fact that Clodius had given Cato an extraordinary command to undermine Clodius' credibility: how can Clodius denounce extraordinary powers when just in the previous year he himself had given Cato an extraordinary command?[288] Cicero further points out that Clodius had bestowed various commands by legislation—*extra ordinem*, as this intruded on the Senate's authority—on his cronies.[289] Indeed, Cicero says, had Pompey not at last turned against Clodius[290] "would any corner of the earth

282. Cic. *Dom.* 18.

283. Ibid. 19.

284. Cato was sent *pro quaestore* with praetorian powers (*pro praetore*): Balsdon, "Roman History."

285. See Badian, "M. Porcius Cato."

286. Cic. *Sest.* 60. Trans. R. A. Kaster. Cf. *Dom.* 22.

287. Cic. *Sest.* 61.

288. Cic. *Dom.* 21.

289. Ibid. 23 and 24.

290. For Pompey's reasons, see Kaster, *Cicero: Speech*, p. 275.

have been spared the extraordinary *fasces* and the rule of Clodius?"[291] The very law Clodius had passed forcing Cicero into exile the previous year was itself an extraordinary measure, Cicero insists. Here Cicero is turning to his own advantage the fuzzy nature of the term *extra ordinem*. While he seeks to evade the conclusion that Pompey's extraordinary grain supply powers, which he supports, are in fact unconstitutional, when making his culminating point against Clodius Cicero uses *extra ordinem* in its meaning of "unconstitutional": Clodius' law, moved *extra ordinem*, was in fact no law at all.[292]

As an argument, this is not compelling, but it is telling nonetheless. Cicero implicitly admits that his support, both past and present, for extraordinary powers may be deemed unconstitutional, but he considers Clodius simply unqualified to criticize him on this account. Beyond that, Cicero's argument amounts to the claim that if reason of state demanded it, as in the present case of high grain prices, or as in the 60s when the pirates and Mithridates threatened Rome's interests, extraordinary commands were somehow constitutional; if not, not. The crux lies in the fact that Cicero's own point in the speech turns on his attempt to show that Clodius' legislation had been *extra ordinem* and thus invalid,[293] and on a less than charitable reading the argument seems to degenerate into an *ad hominem* attack on Clodius: whatever Clodius moved is extraordinary and thus unconstitutional, while Cicero's own support for extraordinary powers simply shows his steadfast adherence to principle (*constantia*, with a Stoic flavor).[294] It is salutary to keep in mind that Cicero himself was to see Pompey's use of extraordinary powers in a less benevolent and constitutional light, when he wrote to Atticus on February 27, 49 BC, that nothing really differentiated Pompey and Caesar: "Both of the pair have aimed at personal domination (*dominatio*)," and Pompey in particular had "been hankering for a long while after despotism (*regnum*) on the Sullan model."[295] This sharp contrast between despotism, servitude, and extraordinary powers

291. Cic. *Dom.* 24.

292. Ibid. 26.

293. Cicero knows, of course, that this alone would in all likelihood not suffice as an argument; otherwise the Pontiffs would hardly have needed to consider the case in the first place. He therefore needs to find fault with the religious procedure: see Stroh, "*De Domo Sua*," pp. 323–330.

294. Cic. *Dom.* 19 (contrasted with Clodius' *inconstantia* at 21).

295. Cic. *Att.* 8.11.2. Trans. D. R. Shackleton Bailey. Wirszubski argues that this provides ammunition against Ed. Meyer's view of a Pompeian principate as against a Caesarian monarchy: *Libertas*, p. 64.

on the one hand and constitutional liberty on the other is echoed, in similarly dire circumstances in 43 BC, by the tyrannicide Brutus in a letter to Cicero's friend Atticus: he will wage war against servitude, however agreeable, and that means war against despotism (*regnum*), against extraordinary powers (*imperia extraordinaria*), domination, and power that aims at being above the laws.[296]

Compared to the later accumulation of extraordinary powers by Pompey his five-year *cura annonae* may seem quaint. Pompey's combination of *cura annonae*, governorship of both Spains for five years as proconsul (from 54 onward), and the consulship (in 55 and as sole consul in 52 BC) anticipated the combination of powers within the city and *militiae* that was to become the hallmark of the Triumvirate and, eventually, of the Augustan order.[297] Especially the de facto invitation extended to him on the part of the Senate by way of an *SCU* in February of 52 to use troops if necessary even within the city and even before he became sole consul, on the basis of his proconsular powers alone, constituted an open invitation to reign, at least potentially, in the style of Sulla and eradicated the crucial constitutional status of the *pomerium*.[298] But while the political and constitutional history of Pompey's commands, the triumvirs, and of Augustus' powers in 27 and 23 are familiar,[299] there has been less discussion and analysis of the constitutional thought emanating from the ferment of these political events, and this is what interests us here.

Cicero's speech before the Pontiffs helps us understand what was at stake on the plane of constitutional argument. By the time Caesar occupied Rome in 49 and declared that "he had sought no extraordinary office"[300]

---

296. Cic. *Ad Brut.* 1.17.6.

297. See Bleicken, *Republik und Prinzipat*, pp. 59–60, esp. n. 174 for an argument for Pompey's accumulation of powers *domi* and *militiae* both in 55 and 52 BC; his arguments against Ridley, "Pompey's Commands," are compelling, and he rightly points out that such accumulation was already achieved by Caesar between March 1 and the end of 59 and aimed at by the commission envisaged under Rullus' agrarian law in late 64 BC. See also Bringmann, "Das zweite Triumvirat," p. 33; Gelzer, *Pompeius*, pp. 136–137, 147–148; Bleicken, "*Imperium consulare/proconsulare*," p. 708, n. 8; Vervaet, *High Command*, ch. 7.

298. Asc. 34C. Cf. Cic. *Mil.* 70; see ibid. 2 for the presence of troops at Milo's trial—troops requested, however, by Cicero himself (*Att.* 9.7b.2). For the trial, see Lintott, "Cicero and Milo."

299. See Boak, "Extraordinary Commands"; Ed. Meyer, *Caesars Monarchie*; Ridley, "Pompey's Commands"; Bleicken, *Republik und Prinzipat*; id., "*Imperium consulare/proconsulare*"; Bringmann, "Das zweite Triumvirat"; and now Vervaet, *High Command*, ch. 7.

300. Caes. *BCiv.* 1.32.2.

his lieutenant C. Scribonius Curio could display the current disregard for constitutional pretext openly,[301] and the debate concerning extraordinary commands had given way to their unchecked exercise. In 47 BC, in a letter to Cassius, Cicero expresses the hope that parts of the constitutional order can still be saved.[302] Four years later, in a letter to Brutus, this hope has given way to skepticism that any constitutional order could survive, no matter who will win the civil war. While previous civil wars had always seen some constitutional order survive (*aliqua forma futura rei publicae*), this time, even if the republican side should prevail, Cicero cannot be certain that this will guarantee a constitutional regime; he is quite certain, however, that there will not be anything constitutional left (*certe nullam umquam erit*) in case they should lose.[303] He was now reduced to a desperate, wholesale justification of extraordinary powers in the *Philippics*,[304] mostly appealing to natural law, culminating in the following justification of extraordinary commands for the *privati* Brutus and Cassius—a veritable obituary to the positive institutions of the Republic:

> Under what law, by what *ius*? By that *ius* which Jupiter himself established, that all things beneficial to the Republic be held lawful and constitutional (*iusta*). Law (*lex*) is nothing but a code of right conduct derived from the will of the gods, ordaining what is good and forbidding its opposite. This law, then, Cassius obeyed when he went to Syria; another man's province, if people were following written laws, but such laws having been overthrown, his by the law of nature (*lege naturae*).[305]

This is a conception of "law" completely divorced from the established usage during the Republic, but in tune with Cicero's terminology in *De legibus*. It is a notion of *lex* comparable to the way *ius* had been used in the constitutional arguments of the late Republic. The quoted passage demonstrates the extent to which Cicero was driven to come up with constitutional norms that would hold even in a state of nature; driven, that is, by the state of nature the overthrown

---

301. Cic. *Att.* 10.4.9–10.

302. Cic. *Fam.* 15.15.1. Cf. Cato's speech in Luc. *Phars.* 9.190–214, where 48 BC is the crucial caesura and at least a pretense of legal authority is said to have existed until Pompey's death.

303. Cic. *Ad. Brut.* 1.15.10.

304. *Phil.* 3; 5; 10; 11. See also *Ad Brut.* 1.3.3; 1.8.2; 1.10.1–2; 1.11.2; 1.15.10; 2.1.1ff.; *Fam.* 11.13a; 9.9.2–3; 12.14. Cf. Seneca's stance in Sen. *Ep.* 94, 64ff.

305. Cic. *Phil.* 11.28. Trans. Shackleton Bailey, slightly adapted.

Republic had left behind. There is no knowing what Cicero would have made of Augustus' new order, but there is reason to believe that he would have considered it at least *aliqua forma rei publicae*.[306] Cicero's more theoretical views on the kind of supreme authority he saw as a potential solution to situations of constitutional crisis will be considered in Part II; for now, let us turn in the following chapter to the origins, in political and forensic debate, of some of the more sophisticated views on political and constitutional theory Cicero increasingly developed.

306. Cf. Suet. *Aug.* 28.2, where Augustus in an edict aspires to be called *optimi status auctor* for having laid durable *fundamenta rei p.* This is very much in line with the constitutional character of the *Res gestae* (many thanks to Michael Peachin for discussion of these points).

3

"The Sole Bulwark of Liberty"

CONSTITUTIONAL RIGHTS AT ROME

IN THIS CHAPTER, I will lay out the constitutional safeguards and rights that were at stake in the constitutional crises of the late Republic. These safeguards and rights, especially the right of appeal (*provocatio*), were at the very heart of the inchoate constitutionalism of late republican politics. The chapter will describe a specifically Roman rights-based view of politics that will be further elaborated in the second part of this study, where we will be concerned with Roman constitutional thought as expressed in more theoretical and philosophical works.

The conditions of late republican tensions and civil wars caused three elements above all to crystallize into constitutional rights and safeguards guaranteed—or so it was argued—by higher-order norms. The first issue concerned the distribution of powers among the institutions of the Republic: were there any limits to what the People's assemblies could decide, or were the comitia sovereign?[1] The second concerned the procedural right to a regular trial, *provocatio*, which was key among the constitutional safeguards and in contemporary ideology almost tantamount to the constitutional order itself.[2] Its overwhelming importance is indicated by the fact that *provocatio* has already appeared on numerous occasions in the constitutional debates conducted in the context of emergency powers. The third issue was private property, which was thought to constitute a further constitutional right. Its importance would only be fully realized in Cicero's mature philosophical work, yet there are crucial traces of it in his earlier speeches that allow us some insight into the way his ideas developed. It was the experience of the deteriorating institutions of the Republic that set Cicero to

1. On some problems with the term "sovereignty" in pre-modern political contexts, see Meier, *Res publica amissa*, pp. 117–118.

2. See Wirszubski, *Libertas*, pp. 24–27.

thinking about the rights and norms that hold in a pre-political state of nature; the context of a declining proto-constitutional order provoked, perhaps paradoxically, the development of a political theory dedicated to establishing a constitutional order distinguished by its timeless quality and its explicit dedication to a hierarchy of legal norms. That political theory will be the subject of the next part of this book; in this chapter we still deal with the proto-constitutional order that gave rise to it.

The sovereignty of the People and its limits

> *In fact, Tiberius Gracchus himself was overturned by not only neglecting but removing the one who vetoed his actions. What else was there that brought him down, if not the abrogation of the power of a colleague who intervened? (Cic.* Leg. *3.24)*

> *[N]othing can be more certain, than that no constitution can subsist, where the whole frame of the laws may be shaken or suspended by the sudden temporary counsels of a multitude, and where the laws are governed by the people, instead of the people being governed by the laws. (Walter Moyle,* An Essay upon the Constitution of the Roman Government)

The competence of the popular assemblies is a key issue of this book. As we shall see in the next section, the right to a trial, *provocatio*, was not understood to be of normative importance simply because it was enshrined in legislation, but because it expressed a principle hierarchically superior to mere legislation. This would suggest that there were indeed thought to exist limits to the principle, expressed by Livy, which we encountered earlier: that "whatever was the last order that the People made, that should have the force of law (*ius*)."[3] That is to say that there was—at least on some interpretations—not just one higher-order norm, giving absolute power of disposition to the People, but rather a thicker, more substantial set of such norms, withdrawn from popular control, regulating and constraining the popular assemblies themselves. This constitutional issue was raised most forcefully when Tiberius Gracchus in 133 BC asked the People to depose his fellow tribune Octavius, who had vetoed Gracchus' agrarian bill. The event is described memorably in Plutarch's biography of Tiberius Gracchus, and the issue itself was to remain with the Republic until its very end. Were there any limits to the decisions of the People?[4]

3. Livy 7.17.12 (= Tab. XII.5, Crawford, *Roman Statutes*, vol. 2, p. 721).

4. For an overview of the issues involved, see Nocera, *Il potere*.

After the People deposed his colleague, Tiberius Gracchus is said by Plutarch to have put forward an interesting argument in defense of Octavius' dismissal, which was widely seen as unconstitutional. It is striking that Gracchus was forced to make his argument before the People, not before the Senate—the dismissal of Octavius, albeit sanctioned by the People and strictly made in the People's name, was "very displeasing, not only to the nobles, but also to the multitude."[5] The People seem to have had second thoughts, now deeming the tribune's deposition a violation of the tribunate's constitutional status. What gave rise to Gracchus' deference to the power of the assembly were two questions put to him by one Titus Annius,[6] in the form of a challenge with the wager (*sponsio*) "that he had indeed done dishonour to a fellow-tribune whom the laws (ἐκ τῶν νόμων) held sacred and inviolable."[7] Gracchus declined the challenge,[8] but sought instead to denounce Annius before an informal assembly of the people. Annius cleverly used the opportunity to put a further question to Gracchus: "If you wish to heap insult upon me and degrade me, and I invoke the aid of one of your colleagues in office, and he mount the rostra to speak in my defense, and you fly into a passion, come, will you deprive that colleague of his office?"[9] Plutarch tells us that Gracchus did not know how to answer the question, notwithstanding his eloquence. Annius had shown what the unprecedented deposition of the tribune Octavius entailed: the abolition of the tribune's *auxilium*, the institutionalized help tribunes were supposed to offer citizens against coercion by magistrates.[10] This help was considered the tribunes' chief function;[11] its abolition tantamount to the removal of a cornerstone of the Republic's constitutional order.[12] By deposing Octavius, the People had thus dangerously undermined some of the most important rights guaranteeing personal liberty.

The attack by Annius prompted Tiberius Gracchus to defend Octavius' deposition. Starting from the premise that a tribune was "was sacred and inviolable

5. Plut. *Ti. Gracch.* 15.1. Trans. Bernadotte Perin.

6. See Malcovati, *ORF*, pp. 104–105.

7. Plut. *Ti. Gracch.* 14.4. On the quasi-judicial procedure of *sponsio*, see Crook, "*Sponsione Provocare*," esp. p. 133.

8. Crook, "*Sponsione Provocare*," p. 133.

9. Plut. *Ti. Gracch.* 14.5.

10. On *auxilium* and its close connection with *provocatio*, see Lintott, *Constitution*, pp. 124–126.

11. Cic. *Leg.* 3.9. On the tribunate in the late Republic, see Thommen, *Volkstribunat*.

12. On the unintended consequences of deposing Octavius, see Ungern-Sternberg, "Die beiden Fragen," p. 268.

because he was consecrated to the people and was a champion of the people," Tiberius went on to develop an ingenious argument in favor of his colleague's deposition that is worth quoting in full:

> If, then, he [the tribune in question] should change about, wrong the people, maim its power, and rob it of the privilege of voting, he has by his own acts deprived himself of his honourable office by not fulfilling the conditions on which he received it; for otherwise there would be no interference with a tribune even though he should try to demolish the Capitol or set fire to the naval arsenal. If a tribune does these things, he is a bad tribune; but if he annuls the power of the people, he is no tribune at all. Is it not, then, a monstrous thing that a tribune should have power to hale a consul to prison, while the people cannot deprive a tribune of his power when he employs it against the very ones who bestowed it? For consul and tribune alike are elected by the people. And surely the kingly office, besides comprehending in itself every civil function, is also consecrated to the Deity by the performance of the most solemn religious rites; and yet Tarquin was expelled by the city for his wrong-doing, and because of one man's insolence the power which had founded Rome and descended from father to son was overthrown. Again, what institution at Rome is so holy and venerable as that of the virgins who tend and watch the undying fire? And yet if one of these breaks her vows, she is buried alive; for when they sin against the gods, they do not preserve that inviolable character which is given them for their service to the gods. Therefore it is not just (οὐδὲ δίκαιός ἐστιν) that a tribune who wrongs the people should retain that inviolable character which is given him for service to the people, since he is destroying the very power which is the source of his own power. And surely, if it is right (δικαίως) for him to be made tribune by a majority of the votes of the tribes, it must be even more right (δικαιότερον) for him to be deprived of his tribuneship by a unanimous vote.[13]

Gracchus argues that the People's deposition of Octavius had been merely declaratory, for by dismissing the People, that is to say by vetoing the bill, Octavius had ceased to be a tribune (ἐὰν δὲ καταλύῃ τὸν δῆμον, οὐ δήμαρχός ἐστι). Vetoing a bill, which was perfectly within the tribune's powers, is thus represented by Gracchus as an attempt to void the power of the People. It could be said that Gracchus here expresses a Burkean "delegate conception" of the tribunate, where

13. Plut. *Ti. Gracch.* 15.2–5. See Ungern-Sternberg, "Die beiden Fragen."

the tribune is to act on binding instructions from the assembly. Failing to do so will *eo ipso* depose him. Of course, this effectively meant the abolition of the veto. Gracchus does not seem to want to rely exclusively on the argument that Octavius had deposed *himself* by his actions; at the end of his speech he makes the crucial point that it lies well within the authority of the tribal assembly to depose a tribune. This last point, Gracchus' insistence on the overruling authority of the tribes, comes very close to establishing a principle of sovereignty of the comitia.[14] The idea of a tribune "wronging" the People (ἀδικῶν τὸν δῆμον) has a legal overtone and can be interpreted as a violation of contract.[15] It is, however, the People who have the last word on whether or not they consider themselves wronged, and it is they who can act without constraint even against a sacrosanct tribune. That this effectively meant the abolition not only of the tribunician veto but also of *auxilium* seems not to have disturbed Gracchus; Annius' second question remained unanswered. The procedural rights of Roman citizens guaranteeing their personal liberty depended thus no longer on the constitutional status of the tribunate, its inviolability, but on a majority decision of the People! The completely novel, revolutionary character of this view of the republican constitution comes to the fore in Gracchus' rhetorical question whether it is "not a monstrous thing that a tribune should have power to hale a consul to prison, while the people cannot deprive a tribune of his power when he employs it against the very ones who bestowed it?"[16] This derives its force from the fact that it describes the *existing* constitutional order, where the People could *not* simply deprive a tribune of his power. Gracchus' view that they could is revolutionary, but it carried the day, with enormous and largely unintended consequences. It could be said with little exaggeration that at least in this respect the People under Gracchus' guidance did more to undermine the rights of citizens than even Sulla did.[17] Sulla's dictatorship could be described as presenting the triumph of the very view Tiberius Gracchus put forward in Plutarch's speech: the tribune was sacrosanct only to the extent that he served the People.

---

14. *Pace* Ungern-Sternberg, "Die beiden Fragen," p. 269. Gracchus makes the People sovereign and ceases to rely exclusively on Octavius' actions—it is now the People who can depose whomever they have voted into office, regardless of behaviour. On the tension between Gracchus' speech and Roman sacral law, which based the tribunate and its sacrosanctity on the foundation of the *lex sacrata*, see Sordi, "La sacrosanctitas."

15. See Ungern-Sternberg, "Die beiden Fragen," p. 270.

16. Plut. *Ti. Gracch.* 15.3.

17. Not even Sulla abolished the tribunician veto (Caes. *BCiv.* 1.5.1; 1.7.3).

Gracchus' view boils down to a conception that the People were constitutionally unconstrained, master of the constitutional order. Of course, the People lacked initiative of their own, and it is true that, as Christian Meier has argued, there were "andere Organe *sui iuris*," apart from the assemblies, who had "überlegene Macht" vis-à-vis the comitia.[18] Yet Tiberius Gracchus' arguments as reported by Plutarch (as well as incidents reported by Livy) go to show that the standing and constitutional authority of these "other organs" was precisely what was at issue, and thus hardly uncontested. When Meier claims that it was only the individual magistrates who owed their magistracy to the People, while the office itself and associated *potestas* and *imperium* were insulated from the decision-making of the assemblies,[19] he cannot properly account for the *decemviri* and emergency powers in general, such as Sulla's: these were derived from the People, and their *Amtsgewalt* had been established *by law*, that is to say by the comitia—Cicero no less than Gracchus makes that point.[20]

The constitutional question of the limits of the authority of the People's assemblies remained latent. Overall, however, over the course of the last century of the Republic, Gracchus' position as laid out in his speech in Plutarch prevailed. The issue can be shown to underlie many of the key conflicts of that period: Marius' numerous consulships (especially that of 100), the transfer of the command against Mithridates in 88,[21] Cinna's consular status, the tribune Trebellius' recall from office in 67[22] and Pompey's command against the pirates, Pompey's command in 66, and above all Sulla's proscriptions and his dictatorship. Tiberius Gracchus' deposition of Octavius set in motion the constitutional conflict over the limits of the People's authority; and long after Tiberius' death, the unintended consequences of his constitutional arguments and actions provided the motor propelling the most important crises of the last century of the Republic and resulting in the destructive momentum that ultimately deformed the Roman Republic decisively.

Recent scholarship has undermined the conventional view of the Gracchan reforms as an attempt at solving a desperate agrarian problem; and while this lies outside my topic, it does bear mentioning that the argument I am pursuing here

18. Meier, *Res publica amissa*, p. 118.

19. Ibid., p. 117, n. 329.

20. Cic. *Leg. Agr.* 2.17 (on the extraordinary powers established by Rullus' agrarian law).

21. See Morstein-Marx, "Consular appeals."

22. Cic. *Corn.* 1, fr. 30; Asc. 72C; Dio Cass. 36.24.4; 36.30.1–2.

is entirely consistent with the skeptical attitude to the alleged large-scale agrarian crisis of the late second century BC.[23] Did the Gracchi provoke resistance more for constitutional than for agrarian and social reasons? Did their agrarian reforms, in conjunction with the agrarian law of 111 BC, actually work far better than is commonly assumed? And is it not the case that Gracchan agrarian legislation was "vigorously executed in a number of regions"?[24] It should give us pause that while the agrarian commission continued work unopposed at least until 129 BC and was likely to have continued even later, it was the constitutional issues raised by the Gracchans that survived and provided fuel for continuing conflict, more than the agrarian issue itself.[25] Plutarch himself, who is mostly responsible for the conventional view, reports in an oddly anticlimactic way that after the murder of Tiberius, "the Senate no longer opposed the distribution of public land, and proposed that the People should elect a commissioner in place of Tiberius."[26] Earlier, after Octavius had been deposed, we are told by Plutarch that Tiberius established a commission with far-reaching powers to distribute land under his agrarian law, consisting of himself, his brother, and his father-in-law.[27] Crucially, all of this was brought about with *no one* offering *any* resistance[28]—resistance and rage were focused on Tiberius and his violation of constitutional norms, not on his agrarian measure. Cicero, with the benefit of hindsight, reached precisely this conclusion: it was not the agrarian law which had cost Tiberius Gracchus his life, but his deposition of an interceding tribune.[29] This was reflected in the constitution put forward in the *Laws*, as we

23. Bringmann, *Agrarreform*; Lo Cascio, "Recruitment"; De Ligt, "Poverty"; Roselaar, *Public Land* (there was no demographic crisis in the second century, but growth, and much of the distributed *ager publicus* was in the periphery of Italy held by allies); Lintott, *Judicial Reform*, pp. 45–58, esp. 49 on the law of 111 BC: "a consolidation of the Gracchan achievement."

24. Lintott, *Judicial Reform*, p. 45. For the radicalism of Gracchus' proposal in actually distributing and privatizing *ager publicus* above 500 *iugera*, see Roselaar, *Public Land*, pp. 235–239.

25. Roselaar, *Public Land*, p. 241. Cf. Molthagen, "Durchführung." Indeed, while the agrarian problem continued to be an issue, there are signs that it was repeatedly dealt with in a largely successful way; Caesar's agrarian legislation of 59, while constitutionally faulty, must have been a success and may have "done more to revive the peasantry than Sulla had achieved." At least the veterans must have been satisfied: "on this point silence is proof": Brunt, *Social Conflicts*, p. 134.

26. Plut. *Ti. Gracch.* 21.1. Plutarch suggests that the Senate was interested in mending relationships with the People; but if the agrarian, not the constitutional, issue was primary, why all of a sudden give in after Tiberius' death?

27. Plut. *Ti. Gracch.* 13.1.

28. Plut. *Ti. Gracch.* 13.2.

29. Cic. *Leg.* 3.24; Cic. *Mil.* 72.

will see in Chapter 4.[30] Similarly, the Senate's opposition to the agrarian bill proposed by the tribune Flavius in 60 BC was due to its suspicion that the statute was really about new constitutional powers for Pompey.[31]

The issue of how to limit the power of the People is visible also in the position of the jurist P. Mucius Scaevola, who was consul in 133 BC. Prodded to take action against Gracchus, he was adamant that putting a citizen to death without trial was not within his authority[32] but insisted that there were limits to the authority of the People, too. Scaevola's view here counters Gracchus' argument about the limitless authority of the comitia and seems to allude to Octavius' deposition by the assembly. There are, Scaevola maintains, decisions that lie outside the People's authority because they are not constitutional (παρανόμων), and such decisions are not to be regarded as binding.[33] This must be interpreted, I think, as an expression of the hitherto prevailing view; a view of the limits as to what the popular assemblies could *iure* decide on, rendered obsolete with the deposition of Octavius.[34]

This remained very much a live issue. Tiberius Gracchus' example had an obvious effect; around 95 BC Cicero's mentor M. Antonius defended the former tribune C. Norbanus against a charge of having diminished the majesty of the Roman People (*de maiestate*). Almost ten years earlier Norbanus had presided over a popular assembly where two fellow-tribunes were prevented from vetoing a bill. Antonius, acknowledging that the tribunes had indeed been been prevented by violence from issuing their vetoes, argued along Gracchan lines that this could not possibly have diminished the People's *maiestas*: "If the magistrates ought to be in the power of the Roman People, of what do you accuse Norbanus, whose tribunate obeyed the will of the polity?"[35] Similarly, when in 67 BC the tribune Trebellius tried to veto Pompey's extraordinary command against the pirates, his colleague Gabinius, who had proposed the command, "began to call the tribes to vote in order to annul Trebellius' office, just as at one time Ti. Gracchus as tribune annulled the office of his colleague M. Octavius."[36] In Asconius' narrative,

30. Cic. *Leg.* 3.42 strengthens the veto power and constitutes a thinly veiled allusion to the deposition of Octavius.

31. Cic. *Att.* 1.19.4.

32. Plut. *Ti. Gracch.* 19.3; cf. Meier, *Res publica amissa*, p. 118–119.

33. Plut. *Ti. Gracch.* 19.3. *Pace* Meier, *Res publica amissa*, p. 119, this could mean legislation as well as voting.

34. Plut. *Ti. Gracch.* 11.2.

35. Cic. *De or.* 2.167. Cf. *Cic. Part.* or. 105. See Fantham, *Roman World*, pp. 37–38, 123–125.

36. Asc. 72C.

it is almost as if Trebellius was affirming the Gracchan interpretation of the authority of the comitia: after seventeen tribes voted in favor of deposing him, "Trebellius withdrew his veto." This amounts to an acceptance of the finality of the People's decision. Even Cicero himself, in that most *popularis* speech of his, the *pro Cornelio*, seems to have adopted Tiberius Gracchus' constitutional argument about the authority of the People.[37]

There were, however, strong institutional means as well as constitutional arguments against such an interpretation of the People's authority. Already in Mucius Scaevola's reaction to Gracchus' legislation as reported by Plutarch, we can catch a hint that magistrates themselves might withhold their backing for laws on the grounds of unconstitutionality.[38] A formal procedure for declaring laws unambiguously unconstitutional, however, did not come into being until in 98 BC under the *lex Caecilia Didia* "the senate was granted by statute the power to pass judgement on legislation."[39] The most important criteria of the constitutionality of any given statute were of a narrow, formal nature and included, apart from violation of the auspices (*contra auspicia*), the failure to heed a promulgation period (*trinundinum*) and the incorporation of diverse measures within one single law (*per saturam*).[40] On the basis of the *lex Caecilia Didia* the Senate in the following decades annulled legislation that violated these formal criteria. Apparently it was felt necessary to provide a legislative basis for the voiding of legislation. However, there was always a sense (quite similar to the way the *SCU* was argued for) that this power was not exclusively based on statute, but was also sanctioned under *ius* and *mos*.[41] Cicero tells us that the Senate had authority to pronounce on legislation *more maiorum* and was thus able to declare a law which had been passed as not binding;[42] Asconius comments that the Senate voted that certain "laws [the

37. See Lintott, *Cicero*, pp. 112–119.

38. Plut. *Ti. Gracch.* 19.3.

39. Lintott, *Violence*, p. 141. This bill probably reinforced earlier provisions contained in the *leges Aelia et Fufia* (mid-second century BC); see Astin, "*Leges Aelia et Fufia*." See also Heikkilä, "*Lex non iure rogata*."

40. See Lintott, *Violence*, pp. 132–148 (pp. 134–135 contain a list of voided legislation); Bleicken, *Lex Publica*, pp. 463–473. On the *auctoritas patrum* in the early Republic as a model for this power of annulment and for a convincing argument against Mommsen that it constituted a mere formality, see ibid., pp. 296–304; on *auctoritas patrum*, see Burckhardt, *Politische Strategien*, p. 233; Lundgreen, *Regelkonflikte*, p. 266. Cf. Cic. *Planc.* 8.

41. Cf. Cicero's ideal formulated in Cic. *Sest.* 137, where the Senate appears as *custos rei publicae*, and *Dom.* 71, with a kind of judicial review attributed to the Senate.

42. Asc. 68C. The other two kinds of Senate interference with legislation preserved in this passage still defer to the People and are ultimately *rogationes* (cf. Dio Cass. 36.38).

Livian laws of 91 BC] should be disallowed by a single senatorial decree. It was decided that they had been passed contrary to the auspices, and that the people was not bound by them."[43]

Were such laws void to begin with, or was a decree of the Senate necessary to annul them? Scaevola seemed to think the former to be true, and there is some evidence to back this up. We note that agrarian legislation carried in 100 BC by the tribune Appuleius Saturninus was probably never declared void by the Senate, but the magistrates simply refused to execute it, on the ground that it had been carried by violence (*per vim*).[44] This is perfectly in line with the view expressed by Scaevola, and it bears mentioning that this happened two years before the *lex Caecilia Didia* gave the Senate the power to void legislation. Overall, however, this interpretation never prevailed; a decree by the Senate was usually felt to be necessary. Although the argument was often made that certain legislation should not be regarded as binding on account of either formal or material deficiencies, this usually remained without effect in the absence of a decree by the Senate declaring the relevant legislation void. As we will see in the following section, Cicero after his return from exile argued that Clodius' bill exiling him should not be regarded as valid legislation—but for parts of that legislation to be formally declared invalid it still took a *senatus consultum*.[45] For our purposes it is important to note, however, that the constitutional argument that certain legislation was void regardless of any decree of the Senate could be and was made and was thus not deemed far-fetched. As the case of Saturninus' legislation seems to show, sometimes this argument had an effect in the realm of constitutional reality.

On what grounds could it be argued that legislation and other decisions by the People were invalid? There was a strand of constitutional thought that sought to show that certain legislation was void for material, *substantive* reasons, not only for the narrow procedural ones mentioned in the *lex Caecilia Didia*.[46] Mommsen for one thought that the annulment of statutes could be based on substantive reasons, and he mentions legislation establishing magistracies not

43. Asc. 69C.

44. I follow Lintott, *Violence*, p. 139; but see Bleicken, *Lex Publica*, pp. 464–465; Williamson, *Laws*, p. 389 (arguing that the Senate did in fact void Saturninus' agrarian bill). Cic. *Balb.* 48 is ambiguous, but seems to show that the Senate annulled the bill, but see Lintott, *Violence*, p. 138. Violence alone (without a violation of the auspices) was probably never a sufficient ground for annulment: ibid., p. 148. Similarly Nippel, "Gesetze," p. 88.

45. Cic. *Att.* 4.2.3–4.

46. For the procedural and religious limits imposed by the *lex Caecilia Didia*, see Cic. *Phil.* 5.7–10; the distinction between substantive and procedural criteria is well put at 5.10.

subject to the right of appeal as an example. Acknowledging such substantive constitutional restraints to the decision-making powers of the comitia pushes Mommsen's magnificent edifice of the *Staatsrecht* to its conceptual limits; as Mommsen, of course, realized, all norms governing the fundamental structure of the Republic such as the rules concerning legislation, magistracies and elections (annuity, collegiality, geographical limits, and so forth) must themselves be insulated from the decision-making authority of the People.[47] Yet this realization stood in tension with his conception of the "sovereign Comitia."[48] If the formulae *iure rogare* and *comitia iusta* had any meaning, they must have implied that laws carried other than *iure* were invalid.[49] There is little evidence, as a matter of institutional history, for material limits to popular decision making in the late Republic.[50] As a matter of constitutional *thought*, however, there is plenty of evidence for the concept of such limits. One example is provided by arguments concerning the right of appeal (*provocatio*), a cornerstone of republican constitutional thought; its potential to limit the People's decisions will be dealt with in the following section.

Another interesting example can be found in Cicero's speech *De provinciis consularibus* of 56 BC. Here Cicero argued, in a shameful change of course,[51] that Caesar should be entitled to keep his commands in both Gauls. Cisalpine Gaul had been given to Caesar by the *lex Vatinia*, which was held to have violated procedural and religious limitations on legislation; and Cicero manages to argue that Caesar should be allowed to hold on to this command while at the same time upholding the view that the *lex Vatinia* had indeed been invalid.[52] Given that, according to Caesar's enemies, both this law and legislation passed by Caesar himself during his consulship in 59 (such as his agrarian law) were unconstitutional (*non iure latas*) for procedural reasons[53] but valid on substantive grounds, the proposal seems to have been put forward to carry the same laws again but

---

47. Mommsen, *Staatsrecht*, vol. 3.1, p. 366–368.

48. Ibid., p. 334. These acrobatic considerations show that, ironically, Mommsen here is less constitutionalist than his sources. What is the "sovereign position" of the comitia owed to, if not a higher-order constitutional norm?

49. Ibid., p. 363.

50. Cf. Cic. *Planc.* 8 (on elections).

51. Cf. Cic. *Att.* 4.6.1 for his inner conflicts and feelings of shame.

52. Cic. *Prov. cons.* 39: the only "argument" put forward is that Caesar is unlikely to betray the Senate's trust.

53. Caesar's colleague in office, Bibulus, kept watching for omens and on this basis insisted on the legislation's unconstitutionality.

this time without the procedural flaws.[54] This is contrasted with Clodius' legislation which led to Cicero's exile. Clodius' bills were equally flawed on procedural grounds but, beyond this, they were also aimed at the overthrow of the state and thus unconstitutional on *material* grounds.[55] As intriguing as this argument is, it is of course highly rhetorical and should not be made to carry much weight as evidence for the constitutional order. As evidence of a constitutional theory, however, which increasingly looked to substantive criteria of constitutionality over procedural ones, this is a significant argument, providing a line of thought which was to gain importance in proportion as the institutions of the Roman Republic lost theirs and which culminated both in the natural-law constitutionalism of *De legibus* and in the arguments for extraordinary commands that can be found in the *Philippics*.[56]

The right of appeal (provocatio)

> *For you believe that the rights of freedom have to be retained not only here, where there are tribunes of the people, where there are other magistrates, where a forum is filled with lawcourts, where there is the authority of the Senate . . . but wherever in the world the right of Roman citizens is violated.*
> *(Cic.* 2Verr. *5.143)*

In Chapter 2 we discussed the (largely failed) attempts at portraying the *SCU* as a legitimate constitutional instrument able to suspend the right of appeal. Now let us focus on the constitutional arguments put forward against the validity of suspending the right of appeal under its cover. In the first chapter we have already seen that at Opimius' trial in 120 BC the prosecution had argued that the Senate's decree *itself* was unlawful by virtue of being inconsistent with and contrary to statute (*contra leges*).[57] Opimius' defense had countered by pointing to higher-level constitutional norms, *ius publicum*. As we can readily see from the debates surrounding the Catilinarian affair, whether or not the execution of the Catilinarians could be deemed *iure* (be it under the *SCU* or for independent reasons) and thus constitutional was a highly contested issue: even Cicero

54. Cic. *Prov. cons.* 46.

55. Ibid.

56. Cf. *Phil.* 11.28.

57. Cic. *De or.* 2.132.

recognized that executing the unarmed Catilina may not be deemed *iure*,[58] and even Caesar at one point seemed to imply that the execution of the arrested Catilinarians may indeed be *iure*.[59]

The counterarguments against such a use of the *SCU* stressed the idea that *provocatio* was constitutionally valid not simply by virtue of being enshrined in statutory law, but, more importantly, because *provocatio* itself was supposed to have a very valid claim to being an institution enacted *more maiorum* and embodying higher-order *ius publicum*. The constitutional tradition behind *provocatio* is thus seen as much stronger, and closer to the essence of the republican constitutional order, than the much more recent idea that a decree of the Senate could potentially suspend the right of appeal or other protections of Roman citizens such as the right not to be scourged and the right to go into exile even if found guilty on capital charges. In Sallust's Senate debate about the fate of the Catilinarians, Caesar suggests that the *leges Porciae*[60] as well as other statutory protections of citizens' rights really constitute *mos*.[61] It is true, as Drummond maintains,[62] that *provocatio* is not crucial to Caesar's argument here, which already assumes that the guilt of the conspirators has been established in a valid procedure; however, the constitutional protections afforded citizens are, as Drummond concedes, "in fact central to the argument. Caesar is in no doubt that Silanus' proposal goes outside what the law prescribes and in the last analysis his objection to it rests on his view of the law as a check on abuse (and individual power). It is for that reason that the *maiores* introduced the *lex Porcia* and *aliae leges*, modifying an earlier penal regime, based on Greek models, that involved scourging and execution."[63] It is particularly interesting that in Caesar's argument the defense of these constitutional rights is based on a self-conscious contrast with and rejection of the Greek model of constitutional practice: "Our ancestors . . . were never lacking either in wisdom or courage, and yet pride did

58. Cic. *Cat.* 1.5.

59. Sall. *Cat.* 51.6. For a convincing argument for a strongly Sallustian coloring of Caesar's *sententia*, see Drummond, *Law*, pp. 47–50, but Sallust can hardly be accused of harboring sympathies for the case of the optimates.

60. These laws in the early second century BC extended the realm of *provocatio* beyond the *pomerium* into the sphere *militiae*, at least for private citizens not on military service, and banned the flogging of citizens. See Lintott, *Constitution*, p. 98; Kunkel and Wittmann, *Staatsordnung*, pp. 168–170; Lintott, "*Provocatio*"; Martin, "Provokation"; Nicolet, *World*, pp. 320–324.

61. Sall. *Cat.* 51.37–42.

62. Drummond, *Law*, p. 36.

63. Ibid., p. 37.

not keep them from adopting foreign institutions. . . . They took their weapons from the Samnites, the insignia of their magistrates for the most part from the Etruscans. . . . But in that same age, following the usage of Greece, they applied the scourge to citizens and inflicted the capital penalty upon those guilty."[64] The implication is that Greek polities, unlike the Roman Republic, did not know any constitutional citizen rights and safeguards.

Caesar's argument is based on the fear of these protections being undermined in a process which will, eventually, itself establish constitutional norms by diametrically opposed *mos*; he warns that "at another time, when someone else is consul," the Senate's extra-constitutional course of action may have become constitutional:

> When the consul, with this precedent (*exemplum*) before him, shall draw the sword in obedience to the senate's decree (*per senatus decretum*), who shall limit or restrain him?[65]

In the Sallustian rendering of the debate, *provocatio* is explicitly mentioned in Caesar's resistance against putting the arrested conspirators to death, but their execution is seen as unconstitutional for reasons to do with the protections afforded by the *lex Porcia* as well as other citizen rights, and Caesar probably played with the fact that mention of the Porcian law would evoke overtones of *provocatio*.[66] The stance imputed to Caesar by Cicero in his *Fourth Catilinarian* is somewhat different, with *provocatio* being more explicitly alluded to; here Cicero writes that Caesar "recognizes that the Sempronian law relates to Roman citizens," and that "someone who is an enemy of the state (*rei publicae hostis*) cannot conceivably be viewed as a citizen."[67] This would still imply that *provocatio* provided the main hurdle for Cicero's argument, but that Caesar had bought into the notion that the conspirators had forfeited their citizen rights by their actions. This is inconsistent with Caesar's emphasis, in Sallust's account, on the various statutes protecting citizen rights, and it is likely that Cicero here

---

64. Sall. *Cat.* 51.37–39. Trans. J. C. Rolfe, with changes.

65. Sall. *Cat.* 51.36. Caesar here is not referring to the much earlier *SCU*, but rather to the possible decree under discussion. There are distinct echoes of Sallust's time of writing (44/43 BC) in this passage; Cicero himself always stressed that he had saved the republican order in 63 *sine armis, sine exercitu*: Cic. *Sull.* 33; cf. *Mil.* 70. See Nicolet, "Consul togatus."

66. See for the tight connection between *provocatio* and the *leges Porciae* in the public consciousness Cic. *Rep.* 2.54.

67. Cic. *Cat.* 4.10. Trans. D. H. Berry.

cunningly exploits a gap in Caesar's position: while insisting on some citizen rights, such as the right not to be flogged and to choose exile over the death penalty, Caesar's own proposal as to how to deal with the conspirators—imprisonment and confiscation of property[68]—arguably violated their right of appeal.[69] By pointing this out, Cicero adroitly points to a possible implication of Caesar's position—Caesar may be willing to infringe on *provocatio* rights because he accepts Cicero's argument that the conspirators are *hostes*! This was probably mere rhetoric, but for our purposes it is crucial that, as we have seen in the previous chapter, the issue of the violation of the conspirators' right of appeal is approached by Cicero by means of a new constitutional theory: rather than justifying the suspension of *provocatio* by appealing to the *SCU*, Cicero argues that such suspension (and thus the *SCU*), albeit valid, is moot in this case, since the conspirators are no longer citizens and thus no longer enjoy the protection of the right of appeal.[70]

Two further aspects of Caesar's position as reflected in our accounts of the Senate debate deserve mention. First is his interesting way of arguing in a Stoic vein, and second his assimilation of the presumably extra-legal, if not unconstitutional, execution of the Catilinarian conspirators with Sulla's proscriptions. In an original recent article Valentina Arena has argued that many of the arguments put forward by the optimates—especially by Catulus and Philippus against Lepidus and Pompey in 78/77 and 67/66—were based on a "philosophical substrate" that was predominantly Stoic.[71] Her argument is convincing, especially with regard to the use of Stoic doctrine on emotions and the ascription of ambition and fear to the *populares*. However, when one turns attention to the arguments put forward by Caesar during the Senate debate of December 5, 63 BC as rendered by Sallust,[72] it becomes clear that such Stoicizing descriptions of the traits of the political enemy were by no means the exclusive province of the optimates.[73] While Cicero tends to describe the *populares* as *homines turbulenti atque novarum rerum cupidi*,[74] Caesar during the Senate

68. Cic. *Cat.* 4.7–8; Sall. *Cat.* 51.43.

69. See the discussion in Lintott, *Violence*, pp. 170–171; Drummond, *Law*, pp. 36–37.

70. See Mommsen, *Römische Geschichte* III, p. 191, on Cicero as the true undertaker of the Republic.

71. Arena, "Consulship," p. 317.

72. Sall. *Cat.* 51.1–4; 14; 27; 30; 33.

73. See Drummond, *Law*, pp. 51–56 on the Mytilenean debate (Thuc. 3.36–49) as a model for Sallust.

74. Cic. *Rab. Perd.* 33.

debate warns of the *genus poenae novum* proposed by Silanus and the optimates.[75] Incidentally, this turning of the tables may be one of the major reasons Caesar resorts to denouncing the proposed form of punishment—execution—as novel, as constituting a *novum exemplum/consilium*.[76] The *popularis* Lepidus, as Arena shows, could also be described as *cupidus rerum novarum*.[77] The other reason for describing the executions as novel was, as we have seen, their being in violation of statute, both *provocatio* legislation as well as the laws granting the right to exile. Caesar suggests, in a very Stoic vein indeed, that breaking the laws as supported by Silanus, Cato, and Cicero, would be licentious and tantamount to giving free reign to the passions (*lubido*) rather than to reason and self-interest.[78] Incidentally, Cicero himself would later be described by Plutarch as increasingly giving in to the emotions of the masses, while having been able earlier in his career—i.e., until the end of 63 BC—to resist the desires of the people and convince them to take unpleasant medicine, very much in the vein of Pericles.[79] In the case of the speech Sallust assigns to Caesar, the emotions that need curbing in light of the relevant constitutional norms—the right to a trial—are being shown, not by the masses, but by the debating senators. Adhering to reason, on the other hand, requires adherence to the rules of the constitution.

On this *popularis* account of Roman history, giving free reign to the passions was not a new danger: the precedent Caesar wishes to stress here lies in Sulla's proscriptions. After mentioning the tyranny of the Thirty at Athens as a Greek precedent, Caesar goes on to point out that while many had at first welcomed the execution of *some* of Sulla's Marian enemies, this had led to a dangerous loosening of the constitutional constraints on the killing of citizens:

> But that was the beginning of great moral corruption; for whenever anyone coveted a man's house in town or country, or at last even his goods or his garment, he contrived to have him enrolled among the proscribed. Thus those who had exulted in the death of Damasippus[80] were themselves

---

75. Sall. *Cat.* 51.18.

76. Sall. *Cat.* 51.25–43.

77. Florus 2.11.2; Arena, "Consulship," p. 306.

78. Sall. *Cat.* 51.1–4.

79. But Plutarch describes Pericles as developing in the opposite way, someone originally beholden to popular emotions who manages to free himself from catering to them. Cf. Plut. *Per.* 15.1–2 and *Cic.* 32.7. See Lintott, *Plutarch*, pp. 4–11.

80. L. Iunius Brutus Damasippus had been urban praetor in 82 BC and had executed various supporters of Sulla.

> before long hurried of to execution, and the massacre did not end until Sulla glutted all his followers with riches.[81]

The crucial point, according to this interpretation of the constitutional framework of the Republic, was the violation of constitutional citizen rights, both in the case of the proscriptions and in the case of the Catilinarians. This is interesting not least because Caesar, by assimilating the two, does not seem to give any weight to the fact that the Sullan proscriptions—unlike the decree of the Senate sought by Cicero in 63—were prima facie based on valid statute. Given that the People's assembly was the source of statutory law, the argument could be made that the proscriptions did not formally infringe on *provocatio*. Caesar would have none of this, and indeed was careful not to add to these precedents but rather show his *clementia Caesaris*, a program clearly reflected in the speech written for him by Sallust. The validity of the right of appeal is thus in the last resort based not on its statutory status, but on its status as a higher-order constitutional norm.

This view was broadly shared, across the *popularis*-optimate divide. Just a year before Caesar had engineered the prosecution of Rabirius, he had in 64 BC been in charge of the jury-court dealing with murder, or rather with armed gangs and killers (*de sicariis*),[82] and had tried to have people prosecuted who had partaken in and profited from the proscriptions.[83] Convictions ensued[84]—ironically, in a court which had been established under a law carried by Sulla (the *lex Cornelia de sicariis*). There is evidence, too, that before being prosecuted for murder, some were charged with profiting illegally (*de peculatu*) from the proscriptions; Marcus Porcius Cato as quaestor was instrumental in these trials.[85] In view of the fact that we know with certainty of only three people who were charged, these trials may indeed have been largely symbolic;[86] but they certainly indicate that constitutional arguments to the effect that the proscriptions had infringed on citizen rights carried weight and were put to use in forensic contexts. Cicero, too, emphasized the dubious constitutionality of the proscriptions on the grounds that they were carried out against citizens who had been deprived of their right

81. Sall. *Cat.* 51.33–34. Trans. J. C. Rolfe; I translate *clades* as "moral corruption," rather than Rolfe's "bloodshed."

82. See Cloud, "Constitution," p. 522.

83. Caesar was probably presiding over the court: Hinard, *Proscriptions*, p. 204, n. 223; but cf. Gruen, *Last Generation*, p. 76, n. 124 (Caesar as prosecutor).

84. Dio Cass. 37.10.2. See also Asc. 90–91C; Suet. *Iul.* 11.

85. Plut. *Cat. Min.* 15.4–5.

86. See Hinard, *Proscriptions*, p. 206.

to a regular trial (*provocatio*), describing them as *indemnati*, condemned without trial.[87] The same term, *indemnatus*, Cicero is fond of using when describing his own situation after having been forced into exile, thus assimilating his own situation to that of the proscribed.[88]

Cicero's view of the proscriptions as unconstitutional, notwithstanding their formal justification by statute, is particularly relevant for our topic. Cicero himself had been forced to go into exile in March 58 BC; his enemy Clodius had carried a bill imposing the status of an outlaw on anyone who had put citizens to death without a trial,[89] and Cicero, sensing that the political mood had turned against him and acknowledging that his acts in 63 against the Catilinarian conspirators could be interpreted as falling under the bill's provisions, chose to go into exile as a consequence. On this occasion Caesar seems to have restated his view that the execution of the Catilinarians in 63 had been unconstitutional; in Cassius Dio's words, a transgression of the law (παρανομία)[90]—which is best retranslated into Latin as a transgression of Rome's *ius*. In a second statute, carried after Cicero had already left, Cicero was exiled by name (the former *lex* had been general in character and had not named any individual).[91] Writing to Atticus in August 58, Cicero now claims that the first bill did not affect him[92]—presumably because he thought that the Catilinarians had been executed as *hostes*, not citizens, and additionally because the Senate as Cicero's *consilium* had acted in a quasi-judicial function, thus according the accused *some* procedural rights.[93] The second bill, however, constituted in Cicero's view an unconstitutional *privilegium*, a bill of

---

87. Cic. *Leg. agr.* 2.56; *Leg.* 1.42 (*indicta causa inpune posset occidere*); *Dom.* 43. The passages adduced by Hinard, *Proscriptions*, pp. 163–164 (Cic. *2Verr.* 5.12; *Leg. agr.* 2.10) to show that occasionally the proscribed were referred to as *damnati* are misleading; these passages do not speak of the proscribed. As Hinard concedes (p. 165), Cicero, when talking about the proscribed, never fails to label them *indemnati*. Florus' suggestion (2.11.3) that the confiscated goods of the proscribed constituted *damnatorum bona* and were somehow seen to have been held *iure*, notwithstanding their dubious acquisition (*quamvis male capta*), does not represent a technical use of the term but merely points out that for pragmatic reasons restitution may not have been feasible.

88. Cic. *Dom.* 43; *Pis.* 30. See *Red. sen.* 4, where he uses the term *proscriptio*.

89. Livy *Per.* 103. For the sources, see Broughton, *Magistrates*, vol. 2, p. 196.

90. Dio Cass. 38.17.1. Cf. Plut. *Cic.* 30.5–6. See also Cic. *Pis.* 33 and 53.

91. Cic. *Dom.* 44.

92. Cic. *Att.* 3.15.5.

93. For the implausible theory that the Senate in 63 BC had acted as a court, see Bleicken, *Senatsgericht*. On the theory of extraordinary senatorial *quaestiones*, see Lintott, *Constitution*, pp. 149–157; Cloud, "Constitution."

attainder, formal legislation (*lex*) directed against *individuals* (rather than at the citizens at large). It seems as if this argument—that Clodius' second statute had really been unconstitutional qua *privilegium*—had originally been suggested to him by Q. Terentius Culleo, a tribune of the plebs in 58 BC, and by his friend Atticus. At first Cicero was not wholly convinced by it: if the bill was invalid because it was directed against Cicero as an individual, a formal repeal by the People's assembly was presumably redundant, but Cicero insists on trying to get it repealed, thus at least implicitly acknowledging the possibility of its validity.[94]

It was only after his return from exile that Cicero adopted Culleo's argument, when trying to recover the property that had been confiscated and destroyed as a consequence of Clodius' second statute. Cicero's house on the Palatine had been burned down and Clodius had dedicated a shrine to Liberty (*Libertas*) on the site. This religious dedication proved an obstacle to the restitution of the site to Cicero—if Clodius' consecration of it was valid based on his legislation, restitution would be impossible. The case was brought before the relevant college of priests, the *pontifices*, and was ultimately decided by them in Cicero's favor on narrow technical grounds;[95] the Senate, basing its decision of the Pontiffs' stance, decreed in turn that the site be restored to Cicero with compensation. The case is of great interest to us for the many constitutional arguments made by Cicero on his own behalf; the fact that it was ultimately decided on rather narrow procedural grounds—which themselves were of a constitutional nature—did not keep Cicero from developing a much broader constitutional view of Clodius' legislation.

The first point that should be mentioned is that the decree of the Senate by which Cicero's property was ultimately restored effectively invalidated parts of Clodius' legislation;[96] the Pontiffs had provided mere counsel, but the Senate had authority to judge the constitutional validity of the relevant legislation: "the Pontiffs had been judges of the religious issue, but the Senate was judge of the law (*lex*)."[97] Secondly, Cicero in the first part of his speech *De Domo* before the Pontiffs adopted Culleo's point that Clodius' second bill, the one aimed explicitly at Cicero and outlawing him, was no law at all but an unconstitutional *privilegium*.[98] First among the criteria for legislation carried constitutionally,

94. Cic. *Att.* 3.15.5.

95. See Lintott, *Cicero*, pp. 188–189.

96. Cic. *Att.* 4.2.3.

97. Cic. *Att.* 4.2.4. Trans. D. R. Shackleton Bailey.

98. This would, of course, have made the narrower religious point irrelevant; but Cicero's anxiety (*Att.* 3.15.5) proved justified, and "although some had denied the validity of Clodius'

iure, is whether or not the *lex* in question contravened the auspices. Since Cicero allows that Clodius' bill had been carried *iure* in that it had not contravened the auspices,[99] he now needs to attack the constitutionality of the legislation on the grounds of its content:

> By what constitutional norm (*ius*), what constitutional tradition (*mos*), what precedent (*exemplum*) did you carry a law (*lex*) expressly concerning the status of an individual citizen (*nominatim de capite civis*) without according him a trial (*indemnatus*)? The *leges sacratae*[100] forbid it, the Twelve Tables forbid it: individuals cannot be targeted by legislation; this would constitute a *privilegium*. No one has ever put forward anything like it; nothing is crueller, nothing more pernicious, nothing less bearable for this state.[101]

Cicero's claim that "no one has ever put forward" a *privilegium* is a mere flourish, and is at once contradicted by himself: what is it about "that most wretched term, proscription, and the whole bitterness of the Sullan period" that evokes so strongly the memory of cruelty? "I think," Cicero answers himself, it is the fact "that punishment was enacted against individually named Roman citizens without trial."[102] Whether or not one accepts Cicero's claim that the Twelve Tables prohibited *privilegia*, it is clear that he could plausibly argue before the college of Pontiffs that *privilegia* were not *iure* and thus not valid law. Clearly, "there were limits to what even Cicero could get away with in a forensic speech."[103] Cicero flatteringly points out that the college of Pontiffs is immune to the inconstancy and arbitrary passion typical of the People's assembly; but there is probably something to his claim that the Pontiffs had expertise in a well-defined body of religious law, constitutional precedent, and antiquarian writing as well as knowledge of institutions.[104]

---

law, there had been no *senatus consultum* to this effect, merely an instruction to the consuls to reinstate Cicero in his former rights by legislation, which, inconveniently, could not in itself overrule the religious force of the consecration." Lintott, *Cicero*, p. 188.

99. Cic. *Dom.* 42. For the legal aspects, see Stroh, "*De domo sua*"; Tatum, *Patrician Tribune.*

100. Cf. Festus 278L.

101. Cic. *Dom.* 43. My translation.

102. Cic. *Dom.* 43.

103. Crawford, *Roman Statutes*, vol. 2, p. 699.

104. Cic. *Dom.* 4.

Cicero stresses the parallel between Sulla's proscriptions and Clodius' legislation throughout. He also makes an interesting connection with the term that was usually used—as we have seen in the previous chapter—for extra-constitutional acts or extra-constitutional powers—*extra ordinem*—when he points out that Clodius' bill prescribing Cicero's exile had been carried in an unconstitutional, or extra-constitutional, way.[105] *Extra ordinem* is appropriate, for Cicero had not even been accused, let alone stood trial, when the bill was passed, thus turning the bill into an illicit *privilegium*.[106] All of this Cicero pronounces, in line with the argument I put forward in Chapter 1, as part and parcel of the *ius rei publicae*, the constitutional law of the Republic.[107] Nowhere does Cicero in his forensic speeches bring out more clearly how essential the right of appeal or right to a trial was to the constitutional order of the Republic, and how much it was seen to derive its validity, not from its various enactments in statutes, but from its belonging to the higher-order norms of *ius*:

> I hold that under our constitution (*iure publico*) and under the laws (*legibus*) that are in force in our state no such injury (*calamitas*) may be inflicted on any citizen without trial (*sine iudicio*). I maintain that this had been constitutional (*iuris*) in this state even during the rule of the kings, that it was handed down to us by our ancestors, and lastly that this is the essential trait of a free state (*proprium liberae civitatis*): that nothing can be taken away from the status (*de capite*) or the property (*de bonis*) of a citizen without trial (*sine iudicio*) in the Senate, before the People, or before judges appointed for the issue at hand.[108]

The claim that the Senate could act as a court is of course self-serving;[109] yet the underlying point, that legislation may not infringe upon *provocatio*, be it a presumed *lex quae de proscriptione est* under Sulla's dictatorship or the second *lex Clodia* or indeed any other popular bill, must have been accepted by

105. Ibid. 26.

106. Ibid.

107. Ibid. 32: the issue at hand partly belonged to *ius religionis* and partly to *ius rei publicae*; Cicero claims, not entirely correctly, to speak only to its constitutional aspects: *de iure rei publicae dicam*.

108. Ibid. 33. My translation. Cf. Cic. *2Verr.* 5.141–143.

109. But see Bleicken, *Senatsgericht*, pp. 20ff. (similarly already Levy, *Römische Kapitalstrafe*, pp. 340–341). Against Bleicken, see Sherwin-White, "Review Bleicken."

Cicero's audience, who must have regarded *provocatio* as lying beyond the purview of ordinary legislation by virtue of its being guaranteed by fundamental *ius publicum*. It is telling that Cicero links here, as he does elsewhere,[110] the protection of the right of appeal with the protection of private property. Cicero explicitly resists the usual, Livian privileging of the authority of the People by drawing a straight line from the rule of the kings to the balanced. government of his own day. Regardless of the source of authority—be it kingly or popular—the extent of that authority is said to be limited by certain guarantees, namely the right of appeal and private property.

Private property

Cicero's ideas about property and its status in the free city envisaged by him will be discussed in Chapter 4. It is important to note, however, that Cicero's concern with property and the weight he will accord it in his mature political theory is a typical and very significant offshoot of the anxieties that prevailed in late republican politics around the issue of agrarian reform. Legislation that aimed to take public land (*ager publicus*) away from its possessors (if not owners) and distribute it to veterans or to the poor was not the only redistributive venture that caught Cicero's and other optimates' attention, it is true. Other measures such as the cancellation of debts and legislation providing for the distribution of grain to the urban poor were likewise suspect. But it is fair to say that the Gracchan legislation concerning public land did touch a nerve, all the more so as there was indeed something novel in it—never before "had *ager publicus* actually been taken away from its possessors and distributed to the poor."[111] As I have argued above, I do not think that this was the main stumbling block for the Gracchi themselves—the breach of fundamental norms (*ius*) contributed more decisively to their failure at the time.[112] What was perceived as the redistribution of landholdings, however, did later come to fuel Cicero's theorizing. The reasons for this are twofold. On one hand, private property in the strict legal sense provided a bedrock of Roman legal thought and can already be found embedded in the Twelve Tables; this is what mostly accounts for the prominence of private property in Cicero's *De officiis*, as we shall see. On the other hand, the somewhat murky legal status of originally public land that had been occupied by Roman

110. Cf., e.g., Cic. *Pis.* 30.

111. Roselaar, *Public Land*, p. 237.

112. See Cic. *Leg.* 3.24.

citizens as well as allies lent itself to broader normative theories concerning the very definition of property rights outside the *ius civile*, the justice of property holding in a state of nature—where property rights were supposed to be similarly ill-defined and at least not subject to the sharp rules of the *ius civile*—and it also lent itself to considerations about the proper limits of the authority of the commonwealth over such property holding.

Starting with Carlo Sigonio, scholars working on the agrarian laws of the late Republic have correctly recognized that the Gracchan program was, legally speaking, not in violation of private property and thus did not constitute redistribution in any strict sense; rather, it concerned exclusively *public* land.[113] By contrast, other writers, even if in agreement with the Gracchan stance and broadly sympathetic with what scholars as early as Machiavelli and Sigonio perceived as the plight of the landless peasantry victimized by the patrician state, did indeed think of the various *leges agrariae* as redistributive in nature and "characteristic of Utopia, the symbol of radically redistributive social legislation."[114] Livy's description of the aim of the Licinian agrarian law as "the restriction of land: that no one should hold more than five hundred *iugera*" (*de modo agrorum: ne quis plus quingenta iugera agri possideret*) proved influential, for all its ambiguity—nowhere does Livy say explicitly that only the possession of *public* land was thus limited.[115] This view, coupled with Livy's and Cicero's animosity against agrarian legislation, was to influence later thinkers such as Machiavelli, Vico, and especially Montesquieu and Adam Ferguson. Not all of these authors were arguing against what they thought Livy and Cicero had opposed, namely the distribution of private property—in fact, Machiavelli and Montesquieu, at least in the *Considérations*, were in broad agreement with the aim of limiting property in land. Had they consulted Appian and Plutarch, they might have arrived at a different, more accurate view, namely that it was simply the occupation of public land that the Licinian and then again the Gracchan law sought to limit.[116]

113. On scholars prior to Niebuhr, see Ridley, "*Leges Agrariae*." On Niebuhr's treatment of the agrarian laws and the influence of ideas about agrarian legislation on European history, see Heuss, *Niebuhrs wissenschaftliche Anfänge*. On Sigonio and the agrarian laws, see ibid., pp. 237–241; McCuaig, *Sigonio*, pp. 153–164.

114. McCuaig, *Sigonio*, p. 159.

115. Livy 6.35.5 (but cf. 4.48); see Ridley, "*Leges Agrariae*," p. 460. Cf. Rathbone, "Control and Exploitation," arguing that the Licinian law referred to private land only. This is convincingly refuted by Roselaar, *Public Land*, pp. 104–107.

116. Plut. *Ti. Gracch.* 8–9; App. *BCiv.* 1.7–9. For the complex legal situation, see Roselaar, *Public Land*, pp. 86–145. Cf. Machiavelli, *Discorsi* 1.37.

Such an assessment, however, may be rather to miss the point, at least Cicero's. Even when we consult Appian, who reports correctly that it was public land that was at issue, there is a sense that by the time of the distributive efforts of the Gracchan land commission the administration of *ager publicus* was severely lacking and in confusion. The main problem was caused by unclear demarcation of public versus private land and a lack of accuracy in the original surveys:

> As the original proclamation authorized anybody to work the undistributed land who wished to do so, many had been prompted to cultivate the parts immediately adjoining their own, till the line of demarcation between public and private had faded from view; the progress of time changed everything.[117]

Appian does not think that the passage of time had changed anything normatively; he thinks it poses merely an epistemological problem. The rich had committed an injustice in occupying more land than the 500 *iugera* the Licinian law had established as a limit, but the extent of the injustice was hard to identify.[118] He does seem to indicate some discomfort with the results of the work of the agrarian commission, however, stemming from the difficulty in ascertaining the precise demarcations between public and private land:

> Not all owners had preserved their contracts, or their allotment titles, and even those that were found were often ambiguous. When the land was resurveyed some owners were obliged to give up their fruit-trees and farm-buildings in exchange for naked ground. Others were transferred from cultivated to uncultivated lands, or to swamps, or pools.[119]

Presupposing a sense that the possessors had in fact gained something close to private property, Appian concludes that the outcome of the commission's work consisted in "nothing but a general turn-about, all parties being transferred and settled in what belongs to others (ἐς ἀλλότρια)." There is some tension here between this seeming acknowledgment of people being deprived of "what belongs to them" (which seems to recognize that some possessors had a legitimate claim to their land) and the assessment that the occupation of public land above 500 *iugera* had also constituted a "great injustice."

---

117. App. *BCiv.* 1.18. Trans. Horace White, with slight adaptations.

118. Ibid.

119. Ibid.

Legally speaking, possessors of public land held such land as a *precarium*, making it liable to being taken away from them by the state at any time. But the sense that after long possession, and after the investment of money and labor, some possessors had a legitimate claim to such land must have been strong and was in fact increasingly recognized by the time of the Gracchi. As Saskia Roselaar explains, the state was forced "to grant the possessors of *ager publicus* extensive rights of tenure on the land they had held only as a *precarium* before,"[120] and in 111 BC an agrarian law confirmed the public land assigned by the Gracchan law as private property free from rent, recognized holdings of prior possessors as private property free from rent (to the extent that they did not violate the old limit of 500 *iugera*), acknowledged title of those who had bought from such *veteres possessores*, and allowed for the conversion of up to 30 *iugera* of additional public land into private property by cultivation.[121] The Gracchan agrarian reforms probably did correct most illegal holdings, resulting in less demand for new allotments, and the law of 111 BC consolidated this achievement.[122]

The sense of entitlement eventually granted legal expression in the agrarian law of 111 BC[123] informed the viewpoint of Livy and, especially, Cicero. Long administrative neglect and, with time, an increased sense of entitlement to the possession of what had been public land made for conditions resembling those Cicero imagined in a natural state, where things became private "by long occupation, as when men moved into some empty lands in the past."[124] This deliberate effort to assimilate the holding of public land to *occupatio*, one of the ways of gaining title to things assumed "natural" by the Roman jurists,[125] is at the same

120. Roselaar, *Public Land*, p. 118.

121. Lintott, *Judicial Reform*, pp. 48–52. Cf. Roselaar, *Public Land*, pp. 236–237.

122. Lintott, *Judicial Reform*, pp. 48–49. Lintott argues convincingly that it was not until the Social War and Sulla's proscriptions and large-scale confiscations that the amount of available public land was greatly reduced and the luxurious villa emerged as a new model of agriculture (p. 58). This finds support in Roselaar, *Public Land*, pp. 284–288, where it is shown that in 59 BC Caesar privatized all remaining arable public land.

123. Although it bears mentioning that this law, albeit granting private property rights free from rent or tax in what had previously been *ager publicus*, respected no less than its Gracchan predecessors the limit on public land *veteres possessores* could retain: Lintott, *Judicial Reform*, p. 48.

124. Cic. *Off.* 1.21. Trans. M. Atkins. Of course, *ager publicus* did not strictly speaking allow for adverse possession.

125. See Buckland, *Roman Law*, pp. 205–208, with pp. 53f.; see on the later use of this concept in the context of empire, Benton and Straumann, "Acquiring Empire by Law."

time an effort to describe the *ager publicus* as a state of nature. Cicero thought that Tiberius Gracchus' agrarian legislation had already "dislodged the wealthy from their long-lasting possessions."[126] That there might have been some legitimate consternation at Gracchus' attempt to distribute such long-term holdings, especially in view of the investments that had flowed into these holdings over time, is something recognized even by Appian:

> The rich collected together in groups, and made lamentation, and accused the poor of appropriating the results of their tillage, their vineyards, and their dwellings. Some said that they had paid the price of the land to their neighbours. Were they to lose the money with the land? Others said that the graves of their ancestors were in the ground, which had been allotted to them in the division of their fathers' estates. Others said that their wives' dowries had been expended on the estates, or that the land had been given to their own daughters as dowry. Moneylenders could show loans made on this security.[127]

Cicero tried to exempt possessors of such public law as was left in 60 BC from redistribution, and privileged generally existing possession over any other claims; possessors who had been given land confiscated by Sulla were to remain in their possession, and possessors of land confiscated by Sulla but not yet distributed were equally to remain in possession: "I am standing for the confirmation of all private persons in their holdings."[128] This was Cicero's stance even more than the Senate's—the agrarian bill proposed by the tribune Flavius in 60 had the Senate worried above all because of its constitutional implications: "The Senate is opposing the whole scheme for land distribution, suspecting that some new powers for Pompey are in view."[129] But Cicero was not the only one to worry about redistribution aimed at land that was, in a narrow legal sense, public, but had been occupied, tilled, and invested in by its possessors for a long time. The imperial Roman historian Florus voiced a very similar awareness. How, Florus asks with regard to Tiberius Gracchus' agrarian law, "could the common people be restored to the land without expulsion (*sine eversione*) of those who were in possession of it, and who were themselves a part of the people and held (*possidebant*)

126. Cic. *Sest.* 103.

127. App. *BCiv.* 1.10.

128. Cic. *Att.* 1.19.4. Trans. Shackleton Bailey.

129. Cic. *Att.* 1.19.4.

estates bequeathed to them by their forefathers quasi-legitimately (*quasi iure*) for a long time?"[130]

The Gracchan reform itself seemed to grant, at least initially, that claims to land that was to be distributed under Tiberius' legislation were to an extent *iure* and thus constitutionally protected. This acknowledgment found expression in the original plan—later replaced by the more radical project that was passed in the assemblies—to compensate landholders for their losses so that "the possessors would at least have recouped the value of their investments, since the state would in effect buy back its own lands."[131] Under the actual law, however, the possessors incurred an unexpected loss. As Roselaar puts it, "although the state theoretically had the right to take away *ager publicus* from its possessors, the proposal of Gracchus actually to do this caused far more protest than would have been expected," especially in view of the long-term nature of these holdings: the land in question had been public for at least seventy years at the time of Gracchus' reform, so that "most people had not expected to be dispossessed after such a long time, and had invested anyway."[132]

It was thus a widely shared sense of legitimate possession, if not ownership, which surrounded the—strictly speaking precarious—landholdings subject to distribution. Cicero tapped into this shared sense and, as we shall see in the second part of this book, chose to give private property a foundational status in his political thought and his theory of justice. The main model and inspiration for his philosophical treatment of the subject can be found in the struggles surrounding the agrarian laws of the late Republic; here the archetype for legitimate possessions acquired in a state of administrative neglect and held over time could be seen in the long-lasting holdings of what originally had been public land; and the legitimacy of these possessions may, in Cicero's view, even rise to the level of property, worthy of protection rather than distribution. This shows that the early modern commentators from Machiavelli to Montesquieu to Ferguson were, after all, not completely misguided in equating the agrarian laws with distribution of and limits on private property after all. While technically false, this was a sentiment that can be grasped unmistakeably already in the ancient sources. At least one agrarian statute, that proposed by the tribune Philippus in 104 BC (the date is not entirely certain), may have explicitly aimed at the redistribution and "equalization of private property" (rather than *ager publicus*); we cannot know

130. Flor. 2.3.13.7. My translation.

131. Roselaar, *Public Land*, p. 238. For the original project to compensate the possessors, see Plut. *Ti. Gracch*. 9.2.

132. Ibid.

for sure, and the bill was never passed, but the possibility of an equalization seems at least to have been implied.[133] Be that as it may, it is obvious that the difficulty of ascertaining the precise status of the land that was to be distributed under the agrarian laws of the late Republic lent itself to a theory that looked at the relevant landholdings as if they had taken place in a pre-political state of nature and should thus be governed not by Roman civil law but by natural law.

---

133. Cic. *Off.* 2.73. Cf. Dyck, *Commentary*, p. 464; Millar, "Politics, Persuasion," p. 7.

PART II

A Hierarchy of Laws

Roman Constitutional Theory

Part I sought to describe the process by which the Roman concept of constitution emerged out of the context of the crises of the late Republic. The frequent recourse to emergency measures and the increasing importance of private individuals with extraordinary powers convinced Cicero and other protagonists of late republican politics of the need for a higher-order set of rules, i.e., a constitutional order, and set them on a search for the rights and norms that would form its substance. We saw in Part I how this resulted, especially in forensic rhetoric, in the attempt to flesh out the distinction between *ius publicum* as a set of higher-order norms and statutory law (*leges*). In this second part I will discuss more theoretical responses to the problem that the dissolution of the Republic had posed so forcefully ever since Tiberius Gracchus' deposition of his colleague Octavius. These responses, as they have come down to us in Cicero's mature philosophical works, differ markedly from anything Greek political theory had to offer. Intended as a constitutionalist alternative to the crisis of the Republic, Cicero's political thought took its starting point from the *ius-lex* distinction often gestured at in late republican oratory; out of this distinction Cicero built a political theory centered on the constitutionalist idea of a hierarchy of the sources of law and a concern with norms that could be justified *outside* the framework of any given polity—in a pre-political state of nature.

4

Cicero and the Legitimacy of Political Authority

IN AN IMPORTANT recent book the classicist Jed Atkins has put forward a fresh interpretation of Cicero's political philosophy, especially as contained in the *Republic* and the *Laws*. Cicero, in his view, was crucially influenced by Plato's *Laws* and sought to establish a new view of the relationship between what is ideal in light of rational investigation, on the one hand, and what is practical in light of human nature and the contingencies of history, on the other. In Atkins' view, Cicero negotiated a delicate balance between a utopianism understood "as a vital component of political philosophy," all the while "cautioning against utopia's implementation."[1] Cicero's achievement, on this interpretation, lies, not in a proto-Hegelian collapsing of reason with history, but rather in a political theory that seeks "to bring the natural, ideal, and rational to bear on the customary, contingent, and practicable without completely collapsing these different categories."[2]

But perhaps ironically given his emphasis on Cicero's sensitivity to history and contingency, Atkins fails to pay the appropriate attention to the fall of the Republic as the crucial historical background of Cicero's political theory, the very background, that is, of constitutional crisis and argument about emergency powers we have been concerned to explore in the previous chapters of this book. Disregard of this historical context amounts to neglecting the most important experience lying behind Cicero's theorizing—that of civil war and the disintegration of the constitutional institutions of the late Roman Republic. This decline was perceived by Cicero, not as the result of the triumph of natural-law

1. Atkins, *Cicero on Politics*, p. 230.

2. Ibid., p. 6.

reasoning, as Atkins' Burkean Cicero would have it, but rather as the result of a lack of higher-order constitutional norms that could have been appealed to in times of crisis. Later in this chapter I will argue that with his *De legibus*, Cicero advanced precisely such a set of higher-order rules, which were conceived to serve as natural constitutional law. This natural constitutional law, it is true, took the post-Twelve-Tables Roman Republic as described in book 2 of the *Republic* as its model, but the link between natural law and the historical Roman Republic had already been established by Scipio himself in the *Republic* (2.66); now the task for Cicero was to supply a higher-order set of rules for what had effectively descended into a lawless state of nature: the very late Republic with its imminent civil wars.

While I am convinced by Atkins' sensitive exploration of the tension between reason, its limits, and the contingency of history as a key topic in Cicero's political theory, it seems to me that a fundamental element is missing from his analysis. What Cicero sought to remedy was the decline of the Republic; the solution he put forward was of a constitutional nature. While I accept that there is indeed a kinship between the norms put forward by Cicero in *Laws* 2 and 3 and his Platonic model, making it plausible that the rules suggested in books 2 and 3 are simply the closest approximation to natural law permitted given the constraints of human nature and historical contingency, and not Stoic natural law itself, it remains a fact even under Atkins' interpretation that these rules represent a higher standard—higher than ordinary legislation. It is this aspect of Cicero's solution to the problem posed by the disintegration of the Republic that has been obscured by interpretations that seek to gauge the precise extent of Cicero's dependence on Greek models. And while Cicero's approach to political theory did indeed differ in important aspects from Polybius' views as propounded in the famous sixth book of the *Histories*, there is an overlap in that Polybius, too, had based his analysis on a *normative* (and not merely descriptive) notion of the Roman constitution he described. What Cicero provided, not only in the *Republic* and the *Laws*, but also in *On Duties* (*De officiis*), was a *constitutional* solution to the fall of the Roman Republic, and this constitutional solution depended on a normative criterion from which politics and ordinary legislation could be judged. Cicero allows contingency and a sense of the limits of reason a role, it is true, but for his strongest claims about the very purpose of the state and the validity of higher-order rules to stand, he must make reference to a foundation of natural-law norms that govern a supposed pre-political realm. The model for this pre-political state of nature, I suggest, Cicero found in the lawlessness of the late years of the waning Republic.

In what follows, I will present an interpretation of Cicero's political theory that gives the constitutional features of his thought their due weight. I will argue that the constitutional order as seen in Cicero's works is presented as permanent, universal and not historically contingent; I will also argue that this constitutional order implies a pre-political moral order, which gives the constitutional rules their validity. Cicero, both in some of his speeches and in his philosophical works, provided a picture of natural justice that could inform and validate the more detailed constitutional norms he presented in *De legibus*. Before that, by way of introduction, I will give an interpretation of Polybius' constitutional analysis of the Roman Republic that stresses those aspects of Polybius' view that show some similarities with Cicero's political theory. Polybius' constitutional thought too was of a "Roman," normative nature, I should like to argue, unlike that of his Greek predecessors, whose views will be described, by way of contrast, in Chapter 5 below.

The first Roman constitutionalist: Polybius' constitutional equilibrium

In an illuminating essay, Andrew Lintott has attempted a comparison between Polybius' and Cicero's respective accounts of the so-called mixed constitution. Lintott points out, convincingly to my mind, that it is less than helpful to argue that Polybius was "imprisoned in a straitjacket of Greek constitutional thought." While Polybius obviously based his doctrine on Greek concepts and on the basic Greek constitutional organs, he did so in a very untraditional way.[3] Lintott believes that Polybius' originality is owed, at least in part, to the influence of Roman political thought, his "contact with Roman politics and Roman ideas." The most striking effect of Polybius' novel constitutional analysis lies in the way he, unlike Greek models, "talks of the power of the various organs in relation to one another, and this is not merely the formal power deriving from law or constitutional tradition, but the secondary power accruing from the exploitation of formal power in the sectional interest of this particular element."[4] This is true and very well put, but it will be helpful to point out that both the "formal power deriving from law or constitutional tradition" and Lintott's "secondary power" are, in Polybius' analysis, not descriptive sociological categories, but *normative constitutional* ones. These powers do derive from the constitutional framework, and Polybius' famous emphasis on the relationship between these powers, their conflict and cooperation, what has been called his doctrine of

3. Lintott, "Theory of the Mixed Constitution," p. 78. See also Arena, *Libertas*, pp. 81–101, noting the parallels between Cicero and Polybius.

4. Lintott, "Theory of the Mixed Constitution," p. 79.

checks and balances, in effect presupposes a constitutional order based on the interplay of various formal legal powers.

This is something that the mainstream interpretation of Polybius as a theorist stressing the potentially benevolent nature of conflict tends to overlook: the conflict in question is institutionalized constitutional conflict, not social *stasis*. The institutionalization, or constitutionalization, requires a conception of constitutional norms which—prior to the conflict in question, albeit at times of course shaped by it[5]—give meaning to the institutionalized powers enjoyed by the People, the Senate, and the consuls. It is important to note that, as Wilfried Nippel has pointed out, Polybius does not in fact use the terminology of the "mixed" constitution at all; his is a language of interplay, obstruction, conflict, and cooperation between the constitutional powers.[6] Polybius privileges the language of "composition," "competition," "arrangement," "balance," or "equilibrium,"[7] and rightly so, since Polybius' legally defined powers that compose the constitutional order are strictly separated, i.e., precisely *not* mixed.[8] I find that expressions such as "constitutional equilibrium" or even "constitutional concert" convey Polybius' idea best, certainly much better than the conventional ascription of a "mixed" constitution to the historian. This should already alert us to the constitutional, rather than sociological, nature of Polybius' undertaking. As Lintott points out by way of contrast, Aristotle is concerned with socioeconomic

5. There is an enormous bibliography on Polybius' view of the historical emergence of the Roman constitution; see Hahm, "Kings and Constitutions"; id., "Political Theory"; and still von Fritz, *Mixed Constitution*. For Polybius' sources, see Cole, "Sources."

6. Nippel, *Mischverfassungstheorie*, p. 19, esp. n. 2.

7. Polyb. 6.3.5: "that which is put together," a "combination," πολιτείαν συνεστῶσαν; 6.10.6: Lycurgus "assembled," or "united" the best features of the simple constitutions, συνήθροιζε; 6.10.7: "equally balanced and in equilibrium," ἰσορροποῦν καὶ ζυγοστατούμενον . . . ἀεὶ τὸ πολίτευμα; 6.18.1: "arrangement," ἡ ἁρμογή, which can be used in connection with the tuning of a lyre and in other musical contexts can be synonymous with "harmony"; 6.18.3: "competition," ἁμιλλωμένων, contending (without necessarily implying rivalry); 6.43.5: "the composition of the constitution," is being opposed to "the virtue of the leading men," ἡ τῆς πολιτείας σύστασις versus ἡ τῶν προεστώτων ἀνδρῶν ἀρετή.

8. Atkins, *Cicero on Politics*, p. 92, points out, correctly, that "the way in which fundamental powers are kept separate" constitutes "a key innovation" by Polybius (but see Walbank, *Commentary*, vol. 1, pp. 640-41 for the view that the Pythagorean Archytas of Tarentum had described Sparta in such a way already in the fourth century). Atkins observes that the separation of powers on the one hand and the mixed regime on the other are conceptually distinct notions (while still erroneously ascribing to Polybius the notion of the "mixed" constitution). Walbank, though also maintaining the terminology of the mixed constitution, well describes Polybius' ideal constitutional arrangement thus: "It was not . . . like a cake made out of well-mixed ingredients. On the contrary, its three main elements remained separate, but exercised

"fusion," a "blend of oligarchic and democratic ideologies," and the conflict between constitutional organs would probably have been regarded by him as a form of *stasis*.[9] Polybius, on the other hand, is interested precisely in the interplay of the various *legally defined* constitutional powers,[10] and it is the legalized and institutionalized nature of the interplay that prevents it from descending into *stasis*.[11]

Jed Atkins draws an interesting parallel between Polybius and Machiavelli. Both rejected, Atkins argues, what he calls the "Platonic-Aristotelian framework." The framework consists in four principles, namely a) a belief in the normatively overriding idea of the perfectly just regime, even if it is merely utopian and cannot be implemented; b) a belief that historical contingency must be taken seriously and has to be accommodated; c) a particular political psychology, according to which human nature is malleable and given to irrationality; and d) the view that social conflict is dangerous and should be eliminated.[12] While I accept Atkins' characterization of Machiavelli as rejecting the four principles, I do not believe that Polybius' own stance is correctly rendered by this close parallel with the Florentine. Machiavelli, to the extent that he followed Polybius, did not show much interest in the normative, specifically constitutional nature of Polybius' undertaking.[13] As we will discuss in more detail in Chapter 7, he shared with Polybius one thing above all, the fascination with Rome's capacity for imperial expansion. Machiavelli was interested in expansion above all but, unlike Polybius, credited pagan *virtue* with it, not a legal-constitutional structure. The

---

a series of checks or restraints over each other, in such a way as to create a balance and ensure political stability." Walbank, "A Greek Looks at Rome," p. 283.

9. Lintott, "Theory of the Mixed Constitution," p. 72.

10. It is misleading to portray Polybius as merely interested in power, as Jed Atkins tends to do in order to make him seem less concerned with legitimacy than Scipio or Cicero (*Cicero on Politics*, p. 107); Polybius is interested in legally defined power, not mere power.

11. Note that actual *stasis* for Polybius, notwithstanding his allegedly favorable view of conflict (representative is, e.g., Atkins, *Cicero on Politics*, p. 93), is something to be deplored: see, e.g., Polyb. 6.44.6, or 6.46.7, where Lycurgus' composed constitution is said to have done away with *stasis*. The "constitutionalized" conflict Polybius has in mind is, rather, a form of equilibrium and peaceful competition.

12. Atkins, *Cicero on Politics*, pp. 82–83. For the purposes of the comparison attempted here, I accept Atkins' characterization of the framework. As I will argue in Chapter 5, different aspects of Plato's and Aristotle's thought strike me as more crucial, such as a virtue-ethical stance entailing a certain eudaemonistic view of the purpose of the state and a corresponding lack of the conception of higher-order constitutional norms.

13. See on Machiavelli's lack of interest in law, Riley, "(Non-) Legal Thought."

purpose of the state is for Machiavelli the state itself, its glory and its expansion; by contrast, Polybius shows a lively interest in justice (*pace* Atkins),[14] understood as constitutional order and the rule of law, underwriting not just expansion but also constitutional liberty, protected by institutional safeguards. Polybius develops a sophistic or Epicurean account of justice, but shows keen awareness that on this contractarian "bargain" interpretation of justice, justice is a key purpose of the state and a necessary attribute of any stable commonwealth.[15] Furthermore, justice is made possible for Polybius by a moral psychology that goes far beyond the Epicurean contractarian account by acknowledging a kind of moral sentimentalism: resentment at injustice plays an important role in getting a just constitutional order off the ground in the first place.

My own view of Polybius, then, diverges from Atkins' on several grounds. It will be helpful to discuss the points of disagreement, as this will allow for a useful contrast to my own interpretation of Polybius. The first disagreement concerns what I just said concerning Polybius' stance on the value of justice. Atkins thinks that Polybius arranges offices in the "mixed" constitution, "not according to justice, but according to an understanding of the best way to apportion power to achieve the desired equilibrium of forces."[16] This is a false contrast, however—the constitutional equilibrium Polybius is seeking to achieve stands ultimately in the service of justice. This becomes clear from the way Polybius sees, not only the origins, but also the purpose of the state. In a way reminiscent of sophistic or Epicurean doctrine,[17] he explains the origins of political order by natural human weakness; this only leads to a very rudimentary order, no different from flocks of animals subordinating themselves to leaders who are merely exceptionally strong.[18] Once human reason is being applied to social life, however, things change. Humans, when they see someone being wronged—in a way entirely amenable to description in terms of modern game theory—"will notice the thing and be displeased at what is going on, looking to the future and reflecting that they may all meet with the same treatment." They "will naturally be displeased and offended by such conduct, sharing the resentment of their injured neighbor and

14. Atkins, *Cicero on Politics*, pp. 86–87. Atkins is clearly influenced by Walbank's "Machiavellian" interpretation of Polybius; my own is closer to Kurt von Fritz's and Arthur Eckstein's *Moral Vision*, see esp. pp. 16–27.

15. Polyb. 6.6–7.

16. Atkins, *Cicero on Politics*, p. 93.

17. This naturalistic account of social development may originally derive from Democritus; see Cole, *Democritus*. For a more cautious approach, see Walbank, *Polybius*, pp. 138–139.

18. Polyb. 6.5.

imagining themselves in the same situation."[19] This process provides the natural motivation—note the sentimentalism akin to Francis Hutcheson and later Scottish writers—to bring about a state that conforms with justice, and the rule by the strongman yields "by insensible degrees" to rule by a just king, "ferocity and force having yielded the supremacy to reason."[20]

Thus begins Polybius' famous cycle of constitutions, but notice that the stability that is the hallmark of his balance between the three good and just forms is at the same time the guarantee, and necessary condition, for a just order to prevail. Without it, there would, according to Polybius, still be just orders such as just kingship, but they would be short-lived. It is ultimately an interest in justice, understood as the outcome of natural resentment at injustice,[21] which provides the purpose and motive of Polybius' balanced constitutional order, not Machiavellian admiration of *grandezza*. Moreover, it is important to bear in mind that Polybius' justice, although it comes into being as an institution more or less at the same time with his just kingship, is an achievement that not only is required by reason, but can also be brought to bear to judge the political order normatively. It is prepolitical in the sense that it is, if not historically prior, then at least prior to and independent of political order when it comes to the *justification* of political order. One crucial criterion for assessing the justice of a constitutional order, Polybius maintains, is voluntary consent.[22] Legitimate kingship diverges from illegitimate monarchy on precisely this point: legitimate kingship is "only that which is voluntarily accepted (μόνην τὴν ἐξ ἑκόντων συγχωρουμένην)" and which is governed "by an appeal to reason (τῇ γνώμῃ)" rather than "by fear and force."[23] By implication, in Polybius' ideal constitutional equilibrium, the monarchical power will seek to appeal to reason in governing, the aristocratic power will consist of the "justest men," and the democratic power will show obedience to laws (νόμοις πείθεσθαι).[24]

---

19. Polyb. 6.6.4–6. Trans. W. R. Paton, rev. F. W. Walbank, C. Habicht. Notice the similarities between this stress on resentment and Adam Smith's, leading in both writers to the idea of an "impartial spectator." See Smith, *Theory of Moral Sentiments*, p. 79 (on resentment as the natural safeguard of justice) and p. 218 (resentment for injustice approved by the impartial spectator). See Berry, *Social Theory*, p. 132, 162–163.

20. Polyb. 6.6.12.

21. Note that unlike the very first origins of politics and human society, which are described in a sophistic and Epicurean vein by Polybius, this later natural resentment vis-à-vis injustice has a more Stoic ring to it.

22. See Arena, *Libertas*, p. 95.

23. Polyb. 6.4.2.

24. Polyb. 6.4.3–5. Cf. Lycurgus' composition, his constitutional equilibrium, at 6.10, and 6.15–18 for the Roman equilibrium of checks and balances.

A further, independent, purpose of political order on Polybius' account is the preservation of *liberty* through stability. He makes this goal perfectly clear when he discusses Lycurgus' Spartan constitution, by which, he points out, Lycurgus preserved liberty (διεφύλαξε τὴν ἐλευθερίαν) longer than anywhere else.[25] The Romans achieved the same result, Polybius says, just by a different process. Stability guaranteeing justice and liberty, then, is the result of the specific constitutional arrangement of checks and balances Polybius advances, and it is not quite right to say that "each individual and each part" in this constitutional order is simply motivated by self-interest and fear.[26] This is too Machiavellian a rendering of Polybius;[27] rather, Polybius' constitutional composition keeps the powers institutionally separate and by this arrangement keeps the office-holders, senators, and citizens from moral and ultimately political-constitutional degeneration. They do not start out degenerate, but it is the constitutional balance that keeps them from giving in to their "congenital evils (τὰς συμφυεῖς κακίας)," with the balanced constitution thereby acquiring a distinct normative quality and moral significance.[28]

This ties in with my second disagreement with Jed Atkins, concerning Polybius' view of human nature. Atkins seeks to show, drawing a (in my view misleading) contrast between Polybius and the "Platonic-Aristotelian framework," that Polybius adheres to a "uniform view of human nature,"[29] with humans as "invariably rational and self-interested actors."[30] This is supposed to entail an account of politics that refuses to give contingency its due weight but, given a stable human nature, turns historical development into a predictable and manageable affair. On my reading, however, it is precisely the fickleness and instability of human nature, its being prone to degeneration and the fact that it is not amenable to being reliably guided by virtue, at least not in the long run, which makes Polybius think that entrenched constitutional rules are a necessity.[31] Indeed, as Frank Walbank has pointed out, thereby identifying the

---

25. Polyb. 6.10.11.

26. Atkins, *Cicero on Politics*, p. 93.

27. It is, in fact, precisely the way Philus seeks to discredit Scipio's, and by implication Polybius', notion of the balanced constitution at Cic. *Rep.* 3.23.

28. Polyb. 6.10.7.

29. Atkins, *Cicero on Politics*, p. 89.

30. Ibid., p. 104.

31. Rendering a familiar theme, Polybius writes that the many are "fickle, full of lawless desires, unreasoned passion, and violent anger" (6.56.11). Although this passage occurs in the context of his Machiavellian praise of Roman superstition, this view of human

prime driver of Polybius' constitutionalism, while the "circumstances leading to . . . violent change are of a moral nature, namely corruption in the rulers," Polybius "nowhere suggests that this 'inbuilt evil' (σύμφυτον κακόν) within the successive simple constitutional forms can be corrected by exercising *moral* pressure on the offending elements."[32] This is the crucial point which makes Polybius into the first—and indeed a prime—example of the distinct "Roman" strand of constitutional thought we are concerned with in this book: virtue does not help, the only real solution is a constitutional one. This is Polybius' reason for not discussing Athens and Thebes: they owed their successes, not to the composition of the constitution, but merely to the virtue of their rulers: ἡ τῆς πολιτείας σύστασις, which is the only thing of interest to Polybius, versus ἡ τῶν προεστώτων ἀνδρῶν ἀρετή, which does not interest him.[33] Polybius' complete lack of interest in virtue and eudaemonistic political theory, and his corresponding interest in constitutionalism, I submit, is what distinguishes Polybius most from the Platonic-Aristotelian framework.

Polybius' constitutional solution can be arrived at by reason, and Polybius famously offers two paths to the goal—the Spartan way, which proceeds by the lawgiver's *a priori* reasoning, and the Roman way, which is empirical. Both end up with the same result, however, which consists in a stable constitutional order underwriting justice and liberty. The fact that the constitutional order can be arrived at both empirically *and* by pure reason should make one suspicious of Atkins' claim that Polybius denied the relevance of the ideal constitution, of the "perfectly just regime" as a model.[34] It is not an ideal constitution it is true, in the sense that human beings would have to change radically in order to be able to be motivated to adhere by it. But the Polybian constitutional arrangement is an ideal in the sense that it is a model held up by Polybius that can be found out in principle by reason alone, and, once installed, Polybius' constitutional order *itself* could be equated with governing reason. The Romans, not by pure reason (οὐ μὴν διὰ λόγου), but still by a cognitive process of consistently choosing the better (αἱρούμενοι τὸ βέλτιον) in light of knowledge (ἐξ αὐτῆς τῆς ἐπιγνώσεως) gained in the contingent historical process, arrived at the same result as the lawgiver

---

nature informs Polybius' constitutionalism as well—the fact that the desires are said to be *paranomon* shows as much.

32. Walbank, "A Greek Looks at Rome," p. 281 (emphasis mine).

33. Polyb. 6.43.5. Polybius holds that in Athens both leading men and the people had extraordinary *virtue*, but due to the lack of *constitutional norms* the polity was akin to a ship without captain: 6.44.

34. Atkins, *Cicero on Politics*, pp. 82, 86-87.

Lycurgus did by unaided reason.[35] Polybius' constitutional order is thus an ideal, but one that underwent empirical testing.

It may help to clarify my interpretation of Polybius in the light of the following observations put forward by the American philosopher Thomas Nagel. Nagel points out that political theory "typically has both an ideal and a persuasive function." This means that it both formulates an "ideal of collective life, and it tries to show people . . . that they should want to live under it." The distinction most useful for our purposes is the one Nagel draws next, between utopian ideals, on the one hand, and the kind of ideal I believe Polybius holds up, on the other. An ideal, according to Nagel, "is utopian if reasonable individuals cannot be motivated to live by it." On the other end of the spectrum, Nagel writes, we find political systems that are "completely tied down to individual motives" and thus "fail to embody any ideal at all."[36] We may believe, with Atkins, that Plato's ideal state as contained in the *Republic* presents us with a utopian ideal;[37] this would be tantamount to saying, in Nagel's words, that the *Republic* gives us a political theory that concerns itself "exclusively with what is right, for if it can be shown that a certain form of social organization is the right one, that should be all the reason anyone needs to want it to be realized."[38] The problem with utopianism is that if "real people find it psychologically very difficult or even impossible to live as the theory requires, or to adopt the relevant institutions, that should carry some weight against the ideal." On the other end of the spectrum lies Atkins' Machiavellian Polybius: a constitutional order "completely tied down to individual motives," failing to "embody any ideal at all," or, in Malcolm Schofield's words, a mere "balance of fear."[39]

But this fails to capture Polybius' normative aim. As I have shown above, Polybius, when describing the development of justice and the transition from rule by power and strength alone to just rule, underlines the role of humans' natural resentment at injustice. This natural motivational basis is precisely why a just constitutional order is possible and desirable on Polybius' view. In a vein

35. Polyb. 6.10.14.

36. Nagel, *Equality and Partiality*, p. 21.

37. Atkins, *Cicero on Politics*, p. 82.

38. Nagel, *Equality and Partiality*, p. 21. Plato for all his radical utopianism in the *Republic* seems to think it possible to bring about his just regime by persuasion, the way Socrates persuades Glaucon and Adeimantus. Cf. Pl. *Resp.* 480a, 489a–b, 499e–501e; see Burnyeat, "Sphinx without a Secret," p. 35. Polybius' answer is that Plato's persuasion never went beyond Glaucon and Adeimantus, so that it never rose to the level of available alternatives: Polyb. 6.47.7–10.

39. Nagel, *Equality and Partiality*, p. 21; Schofield, "Social and Political Thought," p. 749.

reminiscent of the writers of the Scottish Enlightenment of the eighteenth century and their view of mankind's capacity for sympathy and resentment of injustice, Polybius recommends his preferred constitutional order, his equilibrium, precisely on grounds of justice and liberty, not simply on grounds of mutual fear and self-interest narrowly conceived. Given this natural motivational background, a just order formulated along Polybius' constitutional lines is not only conceivable, but, as Polybius is at pains to point out, is also empirically tested as the most stable order.[40] The reason Polybius rejects Plato's Kallipolis, then, lies in the fact that it is utopian in Nagel's sense. This does not imply, however, that Polybius' own model constitutional order fails to embody any ideal at all and constitutes a mere balance of fear. Polybius does put forward an ideal not simply of stability and security, but of legitimacy, in the sense that he separates the legitimate constitutional orders from the illegitimate ones. The criterion for this distinction lies in the ability of the order to provide just rule—giving institutional expression to the natural resentment at injustice—and thus giving the citizens reasons to consent voluntarily, as we have seen above.

Polybius' condition of empirical testability is intended to ensure that this order is not utopian in Nagel's sense, all the while holding up an ideal that does not simply consist in solving a cooperation problem by finding equilibrium conditions. If this were all there is to Polybius' constitutional model, he might as well propose to arrange or compose a constitutional balance out of the three simple *bad* constitutional forms—they would arguably guarantee an even more efficient balance of fear. But the reason to establish the composed constitution in the first place lies in the normative preference for a just order; and its empirical testability ensures that, while just, it is not a utopian order in the way Kallipolis is. How then can Polybius' order still embody an ideal without being psychologically unrealistic, without, in Nagel's words, putting "too much pressure on individual motives"? The answer lies in Polybius' political psychology: humans are *not* simply narrowly self-interested, rational, utility-maximizing beings, but rather, as pointed out above, naturally disposed to share "the resentment of their injured neighbor and imagining themselves in the same situation."[41] This motivational foundation makes Polybius' constitutional order *possible* in the first place. It is made *necessary*, however, by the fact that the passions and desires tend to encroach upon the moral motivations in the "simple" constitutional orders,

40. Polyb. 6.47.7–10: Kallipolis is likened to an untrained athlete; it cannot be admitted "to the competition for the prize of merit, unless it first give an exhibition of its actual working."

41. Polyb. 6.6.6.

an aspect of human psychology that has to find expression in political theory, too. Humans "are motivationally complex, and a moral argument cannot transform them into beings of a completely different kind." Political theory is, in Nagel's words, "hostage to human nature,"[42] and this sensibility Polybius certainly shared. His answer, and the attempt rationally to constrain the worst impulses of human nature in an endurable way, consisted in his constitutional composition.[43]

This yields an interpretation of Polybius that puts him, as we will see in the rest of this chapter, closer to Cicero. Polybius' "interplay" of powers, his checks and balances, are not as far from Cicero's "harmony" of the constitutional elements as commonly assumed, or so I will argue. Cicero's ideal, no less than Polybius', was a constitutional order based on checks and balances;[44] and Cicero's constitutional "harmony," while not as obviously the result of constitutional conflict, is at least at times portrayed by Cicero as the constitutional outcome of social conflict.[45] Add to this the fact that Polybius' own terminology is by no means always as far from Cicero's as we are often led to believe—Polybius "interplay" of constitutional powers can assume an undertone of, or allusion to, musical harmony, as we have seen above.[46] It is true that Polybius' anthropological underpinnings, his political psychology, differ from Cicero's; but it remains to be seen whether the way Cicero frames the purpose of the state is all that far from Polybius' at times Epicurean, at times Stoic account of the origin of the state and of justice. Both believe that a properly conceived constitutional order will be able to bring stability as well as a modicum of justice to the state; neither believes that virtue can do that by itself. Polybius stresses the role of consent, and at times seems to operate with a proto-Hobbesian assumption of enlightened rational self-interest as his paradigm of moral psychology, crucially supplemented with a role for natural resentment at injustice; other passages, however, do acknowledge the overwhelming role of immoral passions and desires,[47] as we have seen, and allow for optimism only

42. Nagel, *Equality and Partiality*, pp. 26–27.

43. In a way very much reminiscent of the thinkers portrayed in Holmes, *Passions*.

44. *Pace* Arena, *Libertas*, p. 93, where the mainstream view is argued (with additional literature).

45. The reasons usually offered against checks and balances in Cicero are weak: apart from the extremely prominent role played by checks such as *provocatio* (*Rep.* 2.54, 3.44; *Leg.* 1.42, 3.6), the tribunes (*Leg.* 3.16), and the veto (*Leg.* 3.42), the role of constitutional conflict in bringing these checks about is also stressed (*Rep.* 2.57–58; *Leg.* 3.16–26).

46. See, e.g., 6.18.1, τὴν ἁρμογὴν.

47. See, e.g., 6.56.11.

insofar as Polybius' constitutional engineering, embodying reason itself, checks these passions by countervailing powers.[48]

Cicero's own account of natural constitutional law, as elaborated especially in *De legibus*, relies on a Stoic doctrine of natural law, but he no less than Polybius thought that it was in the correct constitutional distribution of powers—that is to say, a distribution entrenched in higher-order constitutional law, in *ius*—that the solution to political order must be sought. While Polybius had only a very slight inkling of the beginning travails of the Roman Republic, Cicero's theory must be interpreted as a reaction, and attempted solution, to the already very palpable decline of republican institutions from the mid-50s BC onwards. Cicero's diagnosis of the underlying problems was not Sallustian, or indeed Machiavellian, and did not put a decline of virtue front and center, but it was Polybian in that the lack of a proper constitutional framework, of constitutional norms, was held responsible. Cicero's solution is thus properly seen, I will argue, as the proposition, put forward by himself in *De legibus* in his function as *tutor* or *rector* of the state,[49] of a constitution for the Roman Republic.[50]

Cicero's brutish state of nature

Cicero, no less than Plato or the Stoics or Polybius, entertained a moral and political psychology that was ultimately rationalist and committed to the rule

48. This tension between the role of rational self-interest and the acknowledgment of the crucial role of irrational passions and desires in Polybius' thought must, in my view, be resolved similarly to the way the tension can be resolved in Hobbes' thought: enlightened self-interest is indeed rational, but it is a *normative* aim, and cannot be assumed as empirically valid. Indeed, to a certain extent Polybius' aim in writing his *Histories* might be said to lie—again, similarly to Hobbes—in a normative attempt at educating his readers towards a more rational, enlightened self-interest. In this limited sense, then, Polybius cannot be said to be more "pragmatic" than his Greek predecessors. In this Polybius and Hobbes may be said to overlap, but Polybius' notion of natural resentment of injustice is quite different from Hobbes' anthropology and goes beyond it. In my interpretation, then, Polybius emerges as much more of a Smithian and even Hobbesian than a Machiavellian. See on the educational, normative aspect of Hobbes' doctrine Malcolm, "Hobbes and the European Republic of Letters," pp. 543–545; see also id., *Reason of State,* pp. 114–115; and Herzog, *Happy Slaves,* pp. 85–86: "Egoism . . . serves Hobbes as a reforming proposal. Men may not currently be egoists, but they should be: others would be better off if they were."

49. See Lintott, *Constitution*, p. 226.

50. On reform proposals from the 50s to the 30s BC, see Lehmann, *Politische Reformvorschläge*; Girardet, *Ordnung der Welt*; Podes, "Krise"; Zecchini, "Staatstheoretische Debatte"; Jehne, "Krisenwahrnehmung"; Meyer, *Vision zur Reform.* Heuss, *Ciceros Theorie*, p. 271, believes that Cicero with the *Laws* (especially book 3) sought to save the Republic from its "irreversible death."

of reason over the non-rational parts of the soul and over those parts of the citizenry that were ruled by their desires. But while the Greek Stoics took this to be, for the most part, a problem of individual moral psychology with little to no political implications, Plato and the Peripatetics, for all their differences, viewed it as a chief issue of political psychology and consequently of political theory. Cicero, and Polybius before him, was committed to a similar, in itself conventional account that aimed at the rule of reason—unlike Plato and Aristotle, however, but very much like Polybius, Cicero sought the solution for the rule of reason in politics in a set of higher-order constitutional norms. Reason was to rule, but it was amenable to being formulated as a set of constitutional norms proposed by Cicero himself. These norms were not merely ordinary *leges*, as Cicero was at pains to explain; their ground of validity was not found in the assembly's ratification, but rather in their consisting of, or closely approximating, what right reason demanded. The rule of reason could thus be provided for, but it had to assume the form of a constitution based on natural law. At the same time—and this was something that Cicero diagnosed and Polybius could not yet have—the lack of such an explicit set of constitutional norms had been the chief reason for the undoing of Scipio's otherwise admirable constitutional order as laid out in the *Republic*. Cicero's diagnosis, in a sense, relied on a historical continuation of Polybius' empirical test of constitutional orders. What history and historical contingency had erected—the constitution as portrayed in the *Republic*'s second book—was, to the extent that it was sanctioned by reason and natural law, to be entrenched by way of the constitutional proposal advanced in the *Laws*.

Before discussing the *Republic*, the *Laws*, and *On Duties*—a work not taken into account by Jed Atkins—we will have a look at Cicero's conception of the natural state of humankind as it is developed in his early *De inventione* and his speeches *Pro Sestio* and *Pro Milone*.

In his defense speech for Publius Sestius, who had been charged with public violence, *vis*, Cicero in March of 56 BC developed an argument that relied on a distinction between the state of nature and a political community governed by law. Sestius had been charged with engaging in violence "against the public order" (*contra rem publicam*) under a law governing such public violence, the *lex Plautia de vi*, and was brought to trial before a jury court, the *quaestio de vi*.[51] Arguing that Sestius had acted in justified self-defense given that there was no recourse to the courts of law, Cicero's defense turns on the idea that in the absence of courts

51. See, on the *lex Plautia*, Lintott, *Violence*, pp. 109–123; Hough, "The Lex Lutatia"; on Sestius' trial, see Kaster, *Cicero: Speech*, pp. 14–22.

and of a certain minimal amount of stability and constitutional order, society reenters the state of nature, and a different set of rules applies. Appealing to the judges, he says:

> For who among us does not know, judges, how in the state of nature (*natura rerum*), before the time when either natural or civil law had been codified (*neque naturali neque civili iure descripto*), human beings once wandered at random, dispersed over the earth, and possessed only the goods that murder and bloodshed enabled them to seize or retain through physical force (*manu*)? When, therefore, the first people of virtue and practical intelligence arose and came to understand that humankind was by nature teachable, they gathered the scattered people into one place and led them from their bestial state to practise justice (*iustitia*) and mildness (*mansuetudo*). Then the possessions and activities that bear on the common advantage (*res ad communem utilitatem*), which we call 'public,' then the human gatherings that later were labeled 'civil communities,' then the assemblages of dwellings that we call 'cities' were marked off by walls, when the principles of divine and human law (*divinum ius et humanum*) had been discovered (*inventum*).[52]

Here Cicero explains the origins of civilization, of justice and the state. To this end he deploys a conception of the state of nature, and, given that he can assume that the judges on the *quaestio* recognize this conception of the natural state and find it convincing, one may suppose that this was a view of the natural state of humankind that enjoyed wide currency among the elite. It has been correctly pointed out that the idea put forward of human beings wandering at random and possessing only what physical violence had enabled them to seize bears a strong resemblance with Epicurean views of the state of nature. Indeed, as Robert Kaster puts it, it "more closely resembles a Hobbesian state of natural aggression and hostility than it does the 'natural tendency of human beings to, as it were, form herds' . . . that C[icero] stresses a few years later" in the *Republic*, the *Laws*, and in *On Duties*.[53] It is a view that owes much more to Cicero's earlier rhetorical work *De inventione*, where beastly early humans are said to have roamed the earth, "accomplishing nothing by reason, but most things by force," and where "no one had grasped the utility of justice" yet. Only through the persuasive, rhetorical

52. Cic. *Sest.* 91. Trans. Kaster, slightly adapted.

53. Kaster, *Cicero: Speech*, p. 308.

application of education and reason could these first humans be brought to acknowledge the utility of justice and give up force.[54] Cicero's state of nature as depicted here is, of course, also closely related to Lucretius' Epicurean anthropology, as is the strong dichotomy between force and justice, yet there is also an important difference. While for Lucretius, all constitutional order and law is purely conventional and its establishment is said to be simply the outcome of human weariness and disgust at living a life of violence—anachronistically put, this weariness could be expressed as utility maximization—for Cicero, natural law has always been there.[55] This aspect is already present in the speech for Sestius, as indeed it had to be, for Cicero's whole argument before the court depended on some legal norms having validity in the state of nature. Cicero achieves a combination of the Epicurean view with his later, Stoic or Peripatetic, outlook by emphasizing human reason and the fact that humans can be taught.[56] This allows him to render the first, beastly humans in an Epicurean key, representing "mere nature"[57] as it were; once these humans develop reason, however—not unlike the development of individual human beings according to Stoic *oikeiosis*—they are now able to "discover" law, including natural law.[58] Natural law must already have existed even in the Epicurean, beastly stage, but had not been "copied," "transcribed" or "codified" (*descripto*) yet. It is important to note that natural law, on this view, is amenable to being codified and positivized.

Cicero says that in the natural state, humans "possessed only the goods that murder and bloodshed enabled them to seize" and they could retain those goods only through physical force. The focus is on private property rights, which are indeed described in a Hobbesian way—everyone seems to have a right to

54. Cic. *Inv. rhet.* 1.2–3; cf. *De or.* 1.33. Trans. Kaster.

55. Lucr. 5.1143–1160. After a Polybian rendering of the fall of the monarch, whose overwhelming ambition and, anachronistically put, *amour propre* had led to his fall *sub pedibus vulgi*, Lucretius describes the motivation for magistrates, *iura*, and *leges* as lying in humankind's weariness of violence and gives a proto-Hobbesian explanation of the self-interested reasons for upholding a social contract—an urge for peace and fear of punishment.

56. Thus there need not really be a tension between Cicero's beastly natural state in *Sest.* 91 and the human qualities described in *Sest.* 92, since humans are naturally teachable; cf. Kaster, *Cicero: Speech*, p. 310.

57. The term is Julia Annas'; she uses it to describe an Aristotelian developmental view of the transformation of a thing's mere nature, understood as a starting point, into a full display of the thing's nature. Annas, *Morality of Happiness*, pp. 142–158. See Chapter 5 below, pp. 211–214.

58. It is this kind of reason Claudia Moatti ascribes to Antiochus' influence on Cicero's *Laws* when she writes that Antiochus defined an order superior to mere nature: *Raison de Rome*, p. 164.

everything and there are no corresponding duties to refrain. Once reason develops, however, not only do people start recognizing, and presumably codifying, "divine and human law" (which must include natural law), but states or commonwealths (*res publicae*) also come into existence. Cicero says we call those things "commonwealths," or "common things" or republics, which concern the common advantage. There is a sense of purpose here, with *tum res ad communem utilitatem, quas publicas appellamus* coming shortly after Cicero's description of how goods could be possessed in the state of nature. The idea that states serve the common advantage because they serve the purpose of protecting private property is already here, inchoately, but it really is a tangential concern to Cicero's purpose at hand, which is self-defense. The Hobbesian state of nature and its opposite, the law-governed state, are elaborated upon first and foremost so that the jury court can be reminded that once the state breaks down, different rules apply. It is clear, however, that although Cicero wants to make the case that physical force can be used in self-defense in Sestius' (or Milo's) situation, they are not thrown back all the way into the Hobbesian-Epicurean state of nature, but into a later stage, a stage where natural legal rules have already been discovered and where they indeed apply, notwithstanding the temporary absence of law-courts and other trappings of the state.

Indeed, Cicero is arguing the case, obviously, in front of such a law-court, insisting that the court acknowledge the rules that must claim validity outside the state. Given that the court unanimously decided to acquit Sestius,[59] and to the extent that the acquittal was the outcome of Cicero's argument, the acquittal would have been based on the grounds that self-defense, protected by natural law, counts as a valid argument in the court—natural law becomes relevant, then, for adjudication, the best proof of its codification and validity. By exercising self-defense against violent assault in the absence of courts, Cicero argued, Sestius and Milo had acted according to natural law and had, in addition, contributed to the tranquility and order of the republic. Property is pre-political, Cicero is concerned to point out, even while straining standards of relevance, and so are the norms of natural law, norms which are brought to bear on everyone once the commonwealth is established, but existed prior to that establishment and re-emerge in times of collapsing institutions. By acquitting Sestius, and by giving force to the natural rules of self-defense as Cicero conceives them, the court in effect reestablishes constitutional order (*ius*) against force (*vis*): "if we want violence to be eradicated, then law must prevail," Cicero says, and the courts "embody the whole concept of law (*iudicia, quibus omne ius continetur*); but if

---

59. Cic. *Q.fr.* 2.4.1.

the courts fall out of favor or cease to exist, then violence necessarily holds sway." This is what happened to Sestius, who was "compelled to defend his well-being and acquire armed protection against violent assault (*contra vim et manum*)."[60]

Cicero's defense in 52 BC—against the background of Pompey's quasi-dictatorial sole consulship—of Titus Annius Milo was less successful. Milo was convicted of the murder of Clodius under Pompey's new law against violence, the *lex Pompeia de vi*, and went into exile at Massilia. In his published defense speech, which diverged from the speech he had actually delivered before the court,[61] Cicero made the case that Milo had acted in lawful self-defense and the murder of Clodius had been no less *iure factum* than the killing of Ti. Gracchus had been.[62] *Ius* means, as in the examples discussed in the first part above, the body of constitutional rules and is now explicitly said by Cicero to be underwritten by natural law:

> There is therefore a law, judges, not one written down anywhere but a natural law (*non scripta sed nata lex*), not one that we have learned, inherited, and read, but one that we have seized, imbibed, and extracted from nature herself (*ex natura ipsa*), a law for which we were not taught, but made, which we know not from instruction but from intuition, the law which states that, if any attempt is made upon our lives, if we encounter violence and weapons, whether of brigands or enemies, then every method of saving ourselves is morally justifiable.[63]

As Wilfried Nippel has observed, the argument gained natural-law support when Cicero suggested that in the face of the failure of political institutions, a *pre-political condition* is restored, in which force may be resisted by force.[64] In this state of nature, and this was a further argument Cicero made in his published speech,[65] it might turn out to be not only not *contra rem publicam*,[66] but actually

60. Cic. *Sest.* 92.

61. Asc. 41C.

62. Cic. *Mil.* 8.

63. Cic. *Mil.* 10. Trans. D. H. Berry, slightly adapted.

64. Nippel, "Macht, Machtkontrolle," p. 67. Cf. Cic. *Phil.* 11.28, where Cicero establishes a similar hierarchy of natural law over positive law.

65. But not in the one he actually delivered: Asc. 41C.

66. Although Cicero has, for reasons imposed on him by the exigencies of the case, to admit that any violence between citizens in a free state is, in a sense, against the constitutional order (*contra rem publicam*): *Mil.* 13.

in the interest of the constitutional order, or its restoration (*pro re publica*, as Asconius puts it, or *e re publica*, as Cicero himself does).[67] Alluding to the killing of Sp. Maelius and Ti. Gracchus, who is once again said to have been killed due to his violation of the constitutional order,[68] Cicero seeks to show that Clodius, although by no means in the league of those men, had still posed a threat to the constitutional order and was thus killed *e re publica*. Milo could therefore make a claim to have upheld single-handedly, by killing Clodius, the constitution (*ius*), justice (*aequitas*), the laws (*leges*), and liberty (*libertas*).[69] Clodius himself, in a mirror-image, is said to have respected no law and, crucially, no property boundaries (*possessionum termini*).[70] With Clodius alive, Cicero argues, no one (especially not the judges on the court!) "could expect to enjoy any permanent right of possession (*ius perpetuae possessionis*) over your own private property." Under Pompey's sole consulship, by contrast, the state will prosper, license will be halted, unruly passions constrained, and laws and courts re-established (*legibus et iudiciis constitutis*).[71] There is a distinctly Stoic flavor to this language of checked political passions, but the remedy—checks and constraints, legal institutions, a constitutional order—is Polybian. As in Polybius, humans are fickle and subject to being ruled by their passions and desires; also as in Polybius, virtue may not suffice to check the passions, which is why *ius*, a constitutional solution to the problem of virtue's propensity to degenerate, is seen as a necessity.

Constitutional order and stability serve the common advantage on the view Cicero puts forward in these speeches. They respond to human weakness in the state of nature. Human sociability is not mentioned at all. This is indeed an Epicurean picture, except for the appearance of natural law in the state of nature. For Lucretius, all law is conventional, but Cicero even in his most Epicurean moments had a need for non-conventional rules. It is unclear whether what Cicero is offering in *Pro Sestio* is an explanation of the *origins* of political society, based on the advantages the state offers to weak humans, or if he is merely suggesting a motivational basis for the state which is plausible and decidedly non-utopian. The two are not mutually exclusive, and Cicero may hint at both. The latter he certainly holds: "shared utility is one of the bonds that maintain societies,"[72] making the state possible even if humans were but narrowly

---

67. This thought is expressed at *Mil.* 13-14. and taken up at greater length at *Mil.* 72–78.

68. Not due to his agrarian legislation: Cic. *Mil.* 72. Cf. above, Chapter 3, pp. 119–125.

69. Cic. *Mil.* 77.

70. Ibid. 74.

71. Ibid. 78.

72. Zetzel, *Cicero: De Re Publica*, p. 129, on *Rep.* 1.39 (*utilitatis communione*).

self-interested creatures. Jed Atkins points out, convincingly, that in the *Pro Sestio* we already encounter two crucial elements of the later definition of the *res publica* as put forward by Scipio in the *Republic*: the presence of *ius* and the concern for utility or advantage (*utilitas*).[73] As I will argue, *ius*, both in the speeches for Sestius and Milo and in Scipio's definition of *res publica* in the *Republic*,[74] means a body of constitutional norms, hierarchically superior to mere legislation.

Both speeches represent attempts to convince the courts of the necessity of re-establishing constitutional order and the state, flattering the judges by suggesting that they could, simply by acquitting Sestius and Milo, prevent the Republic from slipping further into the vividly painted, violent Hobbesian state of nature which represents the only alternative to the state. (Natural) law is present in that natural state, according to Cicero, and can be discerned, but courts alone can enforce *ius*. Cicero's appeal to natural law norms is thus not corrosive to the state nor to the established legal order in the sense natural law is often perceived to be;[75] rather, it is the state and its institutions, especially the courts, which are called upon to guarantee and enforce the norms of natural law. The very purpose of the state lies in upholding *ius*, and *ius*, understood as valid qua natural law, provides the body of higher-order norms that governs and constrains politics and legislation. This, as we will now see when turning to Cicero's *Republic*, the *Laws*, and *On Duties*, is the key ingredient of Cicero's contribution to constitutional thought.

Private property and natural justice in Cicero

Cicero's constitutional thought, I will argue, gives content to a Stoic idea of justice as conformity to natural law. This is different from Platonic and Aristotelian views of natural justice, where—as we will see by way of contrast in Chapter 5—justice is not seen as consisting in conformity to a set of (natural) rules, but rather as action producing happiness for the agent and, secondarily, a good state of affairs.[76] In Cicero's constitutional theory, natural justice finds expression in a body of rules underwritten by natural law. These are rules that are held to be

73. Atkins, *Cicero on Politics*, p. 132.

74. No less than it does in the constitutional debates of the late Roman Republic, as we have seen. See Chapters 1 and 2.

75. See on this Atkins, *Cicero on Politics*, pp. 39–40, 195, 210. But Cicero's concept of the state of nature is of course anti-Aristotelian, and this was recognized early on: see Bellarmine, *De Laicis*, ch. 5, p. 22.

76. On the originality of the Stoics, see Striker, "Origins."

binding in a pre-political state of nature, as we have just seen in the previous section, and they are supposed to impose some normative consequences on the political, legislative and juridical activities of the Roman state. Neither the idea of a pre-political state of nature, governed by a law-like normative structure, nor the concept of civil rights that are not differentiated according to natural differences would fit into Plato's or Aristotle's political theories.

In the *Republic*, written between 56 and 51 BC and made public when Cicero departed for his governorship in Cilicia in the spring of 51, Cicero advanced a constitutional theory which was clearly intended to be understood as an answer to the deterioration of public institutions of the late 50s. The dialogue is set in early 129 BC and is meant to represent a moment in Roman history when the decline of the Republic could still have been halted. Publius Cornelius Scipio Aemilianus, the main character of the conversation and a leading anti-Gracchan politician who was to die shortly after the date of Cicero's fictitious dialogue, puts forward a constitutional theory of the just commonwealth that must be interpreted as Cicero's solution to the problems engulfing the Republic. Cicero's dialogue is modeled in certain regards on Plato's *Republic*, and is also followed by a sequel called the *Laws*; unlike Plato's *Laws*, however, Cicero's sequel supplies the ideal constitutional order as elaborated in the *Republic* with a theory of constitutionalism and with a concrete set of constitutional norms.

In what follows I will try to show that in these two dialogues, Cicero tried to formulate a specifically constitutional solution to what he perceived to be constitutional crises that had caused the decline of the Republic. In the *Republic*, Scipio puts forward a definition of the commonwealth which at first aims pragmatically at stability, but then comes to be redefined in light of a Stoic theory of natural law put forward by another participant in the dialogue, Gaius Laelius. Scipio's redefinition makes it clear that a commonwealth or *res publica* that lacks an entrenched constitution cannot properly be called a commonwealth or republic at all. It is this redefined constitutional republic that provides the model for which Cicero's *Laws* then formulated a set of constitutional norms.

In the first book, Scipio gives a famous foundational definition of the state, the *res publica*.[77] It is a definition that really hinges on a second definition, that of what makes the people in a state the people in the relevant sense:

77. On Scipio's definition, see Büchner, *Cicero*, pp. 122–124; Schofield, "Cicero's Definition"; Ferrary, "L'archéologie"; Asmis, "State as a Partnership"; Harries, *Cicero and the Jurists*, pp. 24–25; Arena, *Libertas*, pp. 95–96 (stressing the similarities with Polyibus' account); Atkins, *Cicero on Politics*, pp. 130–134 (where the state's character as a legal partnership, *societas*, is emphasized along with the general legal background of the definition).

> The commonwealth (*res publica*) is the concern/property of the people (*res populi*), but a people is not any group of men assembled in any way, but an assemblage/company (*coetus*) of some size associated (*sociatus*) with one another through agreement about law (*iuris consensu*) and community of interest (*utilitatis communione*). The first cause of its assembly is not so much weakness (*imbecillitas*) as a kind of natural herding together of men: this species is not isolated or prone to wandering alone, but it is so created that not even in an abundance of everything . . .[78]

First it is apparent that Cicero seems to have changed his view on the state of nature to some extent. The heavily Epicurean account we encountered especially in the *Pro Sestio* has now given way to a more Aristotelian or Stoic view of both the *purpose* of the state and its historical-biological *origins*. Before we get to the purpose of the state, let us note that now Cicero allows for a kind of natural sociability when accounting for the historical origins of political society.[79] Note also, however, that he—or Scipio, whose account it is in the dialogue—does not seem to be decided on the relative importance of (sophistic or Epicurean) weakness on the one hand and (Aristotelian or Stoic) natural sociability on the other. Weakness, which was prominent in the speech for Sestius, seems to recede into the background here, to be sure, and sociability gains in importance. Weakness still retains a role, however, and Cicero makes it clear that the two need not be mutually exclusive. This twofold account of the origin of political society is reflected by and corresponds to Scipio's twofold account of the reason for and purpose of the kind of association that forms a proper *populus* that is in turn constitutive of the state, or *res publica*. Not any kind of crowd or gathering amounts to a people in the relevant sense, Scipio maintains, but apart from a minimal size the people have to be associated with one another through an agreement about *ius* and, furthermore, through commonality of interest or utility (*utilitas*). Associating for the purpose of realizing and maximizing utility corresponds to weakness as the "first cause of assembly" (*prima causa coeundi*). Cicero therefore does not entirely lose sight of weakness, utility, and the realization of some common advantage but no longer seems to think it necessary for his account of the state.[80]

---

78. Cic. *Rep.* 1.39. Trans. Zetzel, adapted. The passage is incomplete and followed by a lacuna.

79. Cf. Cic. *Off.* 1.11–12, where a similar combination of human weakness and natural gregariousness provides the motive for the formation of political society, but where the emphasis is on reason (but it is *nature* working through reason; the account of *On Duties* is thus not as different from that in the *Republic* as Zetzel, *Cicero: De Re Publica*, p. 127, thinks).

80. Present, still, but no longer necessary; nature would compel us to congregate even in the absence of weakness and the common advantage: Cic. *Rep.* 1.39 (with Nonius 321.16).

What is indeed necessary, and what constitutes the new focus of Cicero's theory of the state, is what Scipio calls "agreement about *ius*."[81] The term *iuris consensus* is most probably Cicero's, and it appears only here and then again in the third book where Scipio takes the idea up again and proposes a redefinition of *res publica*.[82] This *consensus iuris* is thus the unifying element of both definitions of the state, and it propels Scipio to redefine and elaborate the earlier definition just quoted. Only agreement about a body of constitutional rules—that is to say, about *ius* as we encountered it numerous times in the context of late republican constitutional argument in the early chapters of this book, where it meant a body of (often non-statutory) law more firmly entrenched and of a higher order than mere legislation—only agreement about that body of law would transform a multitude into a people and the commonwealth into a constitutional order properly speaking. The "community of interest" is no longer mentioned, which corresponds to a general shift from an Epicurean emphasis on human weakness as the prime motivation for establishing political society to an Aristotelian or Stoic stress on sociability. In the sixth book, Africanus the Elder takes up the definition a third time and calls states companies of people associated by law (*concilia coetusque hominum iure sociati*).[83]

Elizabeth Asmis and Jed Atkins have convincingly drawn attention to the Roman legal background of Scipio's definition, to the fact that Cicero is here using the legal metaphor of partnership (*societas*) to describe the state.[84] A partnership under Roman law was a contractual agreement between associates for the purpose of pursuing something to their mutual advantage. So far, this serves to underline the contractual aspect of Cicero's account of the state, implying a certain distribution of rights and duties.[85] As Jed Atkins has argued, very convincingly, the rights involved in this account resemble modern liberal claim-rights "against governing authorities because the very concept of the *res publica* requires that they 'own' it." These rights do not, therefore, result from distributive justice operating according to merit, as in Aristotle, but rather "enter into the calculation of how to distribute goods according to justice at a different point," namely,

81. This must be an objective genitive; see Büchner, *Cicero*, p. 123.

82. Ibid.

83. Cic. *Rep.* 6.13. The second redefinition is in the third book: *Rep.* 3.43–45.

84. Asmis, "The State as a Partnership"; Atkins, *Cicero on Politics*, pp. 134–138. For *societas*, see Wegner, *Untersuchungen*.

85. Zetzel, *Cicero: De Re Publica*, p. 129.

they are pre-political trumps and must already be taken "into account as one performs the calculations."[86]

However, Roman law partnerships are governed by *ius*, and this body of law is not itself (and cannot be) subject to the contractual agreements that bring the state or partnership into being. Witness Gaius' description of such a partnership in his *Institutes*: "But the partnership (*societas*) of which we are speaking, that is, the one contracted by mere consent (*nudo consensu*), is governed by the *ius gentium*, and so prevails in accordance with natural reason (*naturali ratione*) among all men."[87] The pursuit of the common advantage by way of a contract is constrained by *ius*, then, and this law, as we are to find out first in the third book of the *Republic* and then in the *Laws*, is the *ius gentium*, which, in Cicero's view, is equivalent to natural law and will provide the norms Cicero is going to codify in books two and three of the *Laws*.[88] The obligation to live up to the duties the partnership imposes or to follow the normal legislation imposed by the state is created, as are the subjective rights enjoyed in the *res publica*, by this higher-order constitutional *ius*, which, as Cicero in the *Republic* and subsequent works assures us, is natural law.[89]

The benefits secured by the partnership that is the state consist, as we will see in more detail shortly, not only in the political and procedural rights Jed Atkins has drawn attention to, but also, and more importantly, in the protection and guarantee of private property rights—of those goods, which "murder and bloodshed" had enabled men to "seize or retain through physical force," as Cicero had had it in the *Pro Sestio*.[90] These rights are not simply up for grabs and cannot be contracted away, but constitute the reason the partnership of the state is contracted into in the first place; property rights provide therefore a substantive

---

86. Atkins, *Cicero on Politics*, p. 147. On the differences between Cicero and Aristotle, see below, Chapter 5, pp. 208–221. Arena draws attention to some features of distributive justice that Cicero has taken over from Aristotle: *Libertas*, pp. 101–111.

87. Gai. *Inst.* 3.154: *sed ea quidem societas, de qua loquimur, id est, quae nudo consensu contrahitur, iuris gentium est; itaque inter omnes homines naturali ratione consistit.*

88. I agree with Jed Atkins on his interpretation of Scipio's *res publica* as a partnership bestowing (subjective) rights, but I do not agree that *iuris consensus* should be rendered as agreement on (subjective) rights. Rather, the *ius* in question here is the *ius* we encountered first in Chapter 1; it is *ius* in the sense of governing constitutional norms which makes the partnership conceivable and bestows (subjective) rights in the first place.

89. Cf. Cic. *Part. Orat.* 37, written either in the late 50s or even later, where Cicero explains in a rhetorical context the meaning of *ius* and *ius naturale* and the need for natural law to create an obligation to follow *leges* and *mores*.

90. Cic. *Sest.* 91. Trans. Kaster.

constraint on the partnership. In the *Republic* Cicero wishes to go beyond the utilitarian, Epicurean account of his speech for Sestius—without giving it up entirely—and seeks to ground his partnership, the state, on a more Stoic foundation, that of natural reason and natural sociability. His reasons for doing so must lie in his insight, properly advanced in the third book of the *Republic* and then again in the *Laws*, that a merely prudential, Epicurean contractarianism could not ultimately generate and account for the kind of moral obligation his natural-law based constitutionalism demanded.[91]

The idea that the state comes into being by way of contract for the mutual benefit of society is therefore there in Cicero but it is constrained by an ideal of justice which gives some additional normative content and shape to the norms political society is governed by. This becomes apparent when Scipio takes up his definition of the state again in the third book. Before that, he had already made it clear, by giving as his chief historical example the "well-tempered" constitution of the Roman Republic after the Twelve Tables, that the constitutional order he took to be ideal was one that was balanced, or well-tempered, in broadly the way Polybius had described the Roman Republic of the late third century BC.[92] Diverging from Polybius somewhat, however, Scipio advances the view that the restrained, or temperate constitution Rome eventually became was entirely different in kind from Lycurgus' order, or from Rome under the kings.[93] This was because while Lycurgus' order or the Roman monarchy may have exhibited features of the *mixed* (*mixta*) constitution, they were not properly *restrained*, or properly regulated (*temperata*), as they maintained rule by "one person with

91. See Cic. *Leg.* 1.42 for the argument that contractarianism cannot explain why one should uphold contracts. This argues against E. M. Atkins' view that Cicero's theory of justice is an instrumental, Hobbesian one: "'Domina et Regina'." See, for a convincing argument against Atkins, Horn, "Politische Gerechtigkeit." For a recent, ultimately in my view unsuccessful, attempt to overcome this problem, see Mackie, *Ethics*, pp. 107–111. Mackie proposes falling back on Protagoras' view that a sense of shame, a moral sense, is needed to generate the necessary moral obligation that narrowly self-interested contractarians would fail to feel—but does this not show the limits of contractarianism?

92. I find more similarities between Polybius' and Cicero's constitutional theories than Lintott or Jed Atkins do; unlike Lintott, I do not think that Cicero neglects the contribution of *popularis* agitation and conflict ("Theory of the Mixed Constitution," p. 81), and I believe that the ideas of the separation of constitutional powers and of constraints and checks play an important role in Cicero's account as well—see esp. Cic. *Rep.* 2.53–63, *Leg.* 3.16–26 on the tribunate, *Leg.* 3.27 on *provocatio*, and my discussion below. Unlike Atkins, I think that a certain amount of constitutional "harmony" plays an important role in Polybius, too (see above, p. 160), and that Ciceronian justice is not in tension with Polybian checks and balances.

93. Cf. Cic. *Rep.* 1.45 and 54; and Scipio's first full description of the advantages of the temperate constitution at 1.69, where its extraordinary stability is praised and it is ranked above monarchy.

permanent power." Therefore, Rome under the kings or Sparta under Lycurgus remained essentially monarchical constitutions. As such, they were "highly unstable" (*mutabilis maxime*), because through a single person's lack of virtue (*unius vitio*) the whole commonwealth could be subverted.

Scipio's reason for not including Rome under the kings or Sparta under Lycurgus among the properly regulated, temperate constitutions, then, is properly Polybian and tantamount to Polybius' reason not to discuss Athens or Thebes; where only virtue stood between the commonwealth and its subversion, the constitutional order did not deserve the name; the composition of the constitution, not virtue on the part of the ruler, guaranteed stable order.[94] Cicero's preferred constitutional order, it turns out, is precisely not "mixed," but rather "tempered" in a specific way.[95] It is, as Scipio elaborates, the "just balance" (*aequabilis compensatio*) of rights and duties (*et iuris et officii et muneris*) between the constitutional powers that he is after. This just balance is achieved by a natural process[96] which finds expression in Rome's history of constitutional conflict and culminates in the checks imposed on the *imperium* of the consuls by the establishment of the tribunate.[97] The check or constitutional constraint *par excellence* is of course the right of appeal (*provocatio*), which Scipio places at the very center of his constitutional history that leads from the rule of the kings

94. Polyb. 6.43.5, 6.44, and see above p. 115. But cf. Cic. *Rep.* 1.69, where Scipio does seem to acknowledge "great vices" on the part of the rulers as a potential pitfall even for his favorite constitutional order; however, as Büchner points out, the *res publica temperata* does not really have rulers in the relevant sense (*Cicero*, p. 166).

95. Büchner, *Cicero*, p. 214.

96. Scipio here contrasts nature with reason, which leads Atkins to remark that according to Scipio, "political affairs do not yield to reason," recognizing the limits of reason in politics (*Cicero on Politics*, p. 61). There is something to this, but it could be said, *pace* Atkins (pp. 98–99), that according to Polybius, too, Rome's history is governed by contingency—yet this contingent history is open to rational investigation for both Cicero and Polybius. Büchner puts it well (*Cicero*, p. 235): there are for Cicero two *naturae*, which are in tension with one another: one, striving for self-preservation (akin to Julia Annas' "mere nature"), the other "eine höhere zur vernünftigen Lösung strebende" nature, which would have a proto-Hegelian flavor to it—if it was not for the fact that Cicero, writing in the 50s, is openly bemoaning the decline and fall of the constitutional order that must have occurred between the dramatic date of the *Republic* and his own time.

97. Cic. *Rep.* 2.57–58. Here Cicero does give constitutional conflict and popular resistance its due. Nor is a stark contrast between Cicero and Polybius justified when it comes to the language of checks and balances; Scipio bemoans Lycurgus' inability to constrain, or check, the Greeks (*ne Lycurgi disciplina tenuit frenos*) and says that the ephors at Sparta were constituted *contra vim regiam*, as were the Roman tribunes *contra consulare imperium*.

through aristocracy and the oligarchy of the *decemviri* to the best, well-tempered constitutional order of the early fourth century.[98]

How does this historical Roman order relate to the kind of a priori political ideal put forward, most prominently, by Plato in his *Republic*? Scipio, like Polybius before him, is after an empirically tested ideal, and the Roman Republic of the fourth century BC provides that. Scipio points out that history serves as a mere "example" of the kind of best constitution he has in mind, while the a priori best constitution is also amenable to being described as an "image given by nature" (*imago naturae*).[99] This *imago naturae* must mean a way of describing in the abstract something originally gained inductively.[100] When proceeding to give the *imago naturae*, Scipio gives an extremely interesting account of the soul of the prudent man of foresight, the *prudens*. The *prudens* has been identified with Scipio's ideal statesman, the *rector* or *moderator*, who in turn has been taken to stand in for a number of Cicero's contemporaries, especially Pompey.[101] The man of foresight, who manages to control his passions and irrational desires with his mind, that is, with reason, here serves as a model for how the state should be constituted.

However, far from recommending that an actual *prudens* take over government, Cicero here employs the soul of the *prudens* as a mere metaphor for his ideal well-tempered constitution.[102] As Jean-Louis Ferrary observes, the well-tempered constitution for Scipio governs "a city which is similar in character to the soul of the *prudens*."[103] The *prudens* is not, then, a potential ruler with

98. Cic. *Rep.* 2.53–63, esp. 2.54. Büchner argues convincingly that the end point of Scipio's account must lie after 367 BC, i.e., after the *leges Liciniae Sextiae: Cicero*, p. 245.

99. Cic. *Rep.* 2.66.

100. It seems to look ahead to Laelius' description of natural law in the third book; cf. Atkins, *Cicero on Politics*, p. 65, n. 51, who is also inclined to this view, although he is hampered by the implausible assumption that Scipio does not endorse Laelius' argument: ibid., pp. 41–42. See below, pp. 177–178.

101. See Atkins, *Cicero on Politics*, p. 73. I largely follow Lintott, *Constitution*, p. 226.

102. The kind hinted at in the Nonius fragment, Cic. *Rep.* 2.41 (=Nonius 342.39): "the best-constituted commonwealth (*optume constitutam rem publicam*), moderately blended (*confusa modice*) from the three primary types . . . which does not provoke by punishment the wild and savage mind . . ." Trans. Zetzel, slightly adapted. Cicero is moving in the same metaphorical way from the *prudens* to musical harmony to the balanced constitution at *Rep.* 2.69. *This* is the reason the "limits of reason" and the "failure of rational control that had plagued Scipio earlier in the dialogue" (Atkins, *Cicero on Politics*, p. 78) are absent here: once the balanced constitution rules, reason rules and so, metaphorically speaking, the *prudens* does.

103. Ferrary, "Statesman," p. 63.

extraordinary powers, but a metaphor for the state governed by the balanced constitution.[104] By the best, balanced constitution Scipio means a normative body of entrenched constitutional rules warranted by natural law. Far from knowing that such a constitution "will never be realized," however, as Atkins has argued, Scipio makes the case that the historical constitution of Rome is indeed "the empirical realization" of the best constitution.[105] According to Atkins, the cosmic model of the rational, ideal city cannot be realized due to the limits of (human) reason; but as he himself is forced to admit, the constitution of the historical Roman Republic *does* serve as "the empirical realization" of that ideal for Scipio. It seems to me that Scipio's way of dissolving the tension is to point out that Rome's fourth-century balanced constitution was an impersonal institutional mechanism to handle irrationality in society in a rational way, and that that kind of constitutional stability, of *iuris consensus*, could be achieved once again only by establishing explicitly, on the basis of natural law, the constitutional rules that had operated largely implicitly in the historical model.

The way to achieve the *iuris consensus* as required by Scipio's definition is to show that his *ius* can lay claim to being just and to constituting natural law. When Scipio takes up his definition of *res publica* again in the third book of the *Republic* and refines it, he crucially takes Laelius' speech for justice and natural law on board and argues, in effect, that there can be no *res publica*, properly understood, in the absence of justice, where justice is now understood to mean justice as codified in a set of constitutional norms (*ius*). Laelius had been pushed to show that the state "cannot possibly function without justice."[106] The trigger for this had been Scipio's own claim, at the end of the second book, that justice was necessary for the balanced constitution. This leads in the third book to what is in many ways the centerpiece of the whole work, the famous so-called Carneadean debate. Lucius Philus takes it upon himself to argue as Carneades' mouthpiece in a sophistic-Epicurean vein that all law is essentially conventional, as evinced by the fact that positive law is different everywhere; that there is no universal natural law, at least not in the sense of natural justice; that only the pursuit of self-interest is rational and indeed natural; that the only sort of justice that could be called self-interested and advantageous in this sense was obedience to law, understood as a conventional contractual bond with the power to punish;

104. Following Lintott, one might say that the giver of the constitution, such as Cicero himself in the *Laws*, is the *prudens*: Lintott, *Constitution*, p. 226.

105. Atkins, *Cicero on Politics*, p. 79. This tension is at the heart of Atkins' argument; ultimately he fails to dissolve it convincingly.

106. Cic. *Rep*. 2.70. Trans. Zetzel.

and that what the advocates of a universal natural law call justice is thus mere irrational foolishness. This line of thought, obviously dependent on Glaucon's argument in Plato's *Republic*, is then countered by Laelius, whose argument has, unfortunately, come down to us in a very fragmentary form. It is clear, however, that Laelius argued for a universal natural law in a Stoic vein:

> True law is right reason, consonant with nature, spread through all people. It is constant and eternal . . . it is not permitted to abrogate any of it; it cannot be totally repealed. We cannot be released from this law by the senate or the people.[107]

Laelius goes on, in the future tense, to outline the entirely anti-Carneadean consequences of adopting, at some unspecified point in the future, this kind of natural law regime:

> There will not be one law at Rome and another at Athens, one now and another later; but all nations at all times will be bound by this one eternal and unchangeable law.[108]

It is obvious that this speech, enthusiastically greeted, especially by Scipio—"Scipio above all seemed positively ecstatic"[109]—was meant to counter Philus' contention that the balanced constitutional order envisaged by Scipio was merely a utilitarian pact based on fear and weakness (with the implication that it could,

107. Ibid. 3.33 = Lact. *Inst.* 6.8.7–9. Trans. Zetzel. The conception of law is Stoic, but, as we will see, the way it is put to use is Cicero's own and very Roman; cf. Ferrary, "Statesman," pp. 67–68. Right reason dictates the content of natural law; this a) makes it possible to know it and b) provides reasons for finding its commands obligatory. Above and beyond its rationality, there are also motivational factors such as natural sociability which provide a non-cognitive motivation for following the dictates of natural law, reminiscent of the Scottish moral-sense philosophers of the eighteenth century. But unlike Stoic natural law, Cicero's consists of rules (not simply agent-centered virtue), provides for rights, and can be applied to the Roman Republic, not merely to the cosmic city of Stoic sages. See on the origins of rule-based natural law Striker, "Origins."

108. Ibid. See Girardet, *Ordnung der Welt*, pp. 129–131 on the importance of the change in tense.

109. Cic. *Rep.* 3.42. Trans. Zetzel. This runs counter to Atkins, *Cicero on Politics*, pp. 41–42, who unconvincingly claims that "it is impossible to know" whether Scipio accepts Laelius' argument and that Scipio's treatment of the necessity of justice for the state "makes no reference to the sort of natural law theory Laelius" presents. Scipio's redefinition of the state is obviously a direct consequence of Laelius' speech; Laelius' and Scipio's closeness is further underscored by *Rep.* 3.45.

and should, be broken in the absence of the credible fear of punishment),[110] and that Laelius' natural-law based counterarguments prodded Scipio to review his definition of the state from the first book. Now Scipio makes it clear that the constitutional order he has in mind provides for natural justice, that is to say, an order based on a substantive idea of justice and not simply on a balance of fear. This is what makes people agree to it in the first place, rationally so—*pace* Philus/Carneades—and it is this that leads to the *iuris consensus*. Without the unifying constitutional agreement, the *vinculum iuris*, the people are but a multitude, a crowd, and there can consequently be no *res publica*. Without an agreed upon body of constitutional norms, without *ius*, there cannot exist a state in the proper sense.

This body of constitutional norms, however, cannot be merely formally defined; it has to incorporate substantive norms of natural law in order to be able to command the kind of agreement necessary for its stability. This is made clear in Laelius' speech in a very dramatic way. Far from simply equating the Roman Republic with a constitutional order embodying natural justice, Laelius is at pains to stress that the Republic has in fact violated the constitutional norms at its own peril. His example, showing dramatically the breadth of the norms of natural justice he has in mind, equates unjust treatment of the Latins and allies—of non-citizens, nota bene—with the violation of the constitutional order and equates the breakdown of the constitutional order, the move from *ius* to violence (*vis*), with it.[111] Significantly, this unjust treatment consists in the disregard for what the allies and Latins must have thought of as property rights, and it was Tiberius Gracchus' agrarian commission which is considered by Laelius as violating constitutional norms by having excessive extra-constitutional powers. Scipio's redefinition of the state makes it clear that norms embodying constitutional justice will have to have a key role in any state that deserves the name. Such constitutional norms Cicero puts forward in his sequel to the *Republic*, the *Laws*.

Commentators on Cicero's *Laws* have always been torn over whether, or to what extent, the actual laws put forward in books two and three of that work are meant to *be* natural law or merely to reflect natural law, approximate it, or be based on it. This dispute has gained some renewed traction with Jed Atkins, who has challenged the new orthodoxy, established by Klaus Girardet, according to which the laws of books two and three are of a piece with the legal theory put forward in book one and are themselves natural law. Unlike the Greek Stoics, who would have denied any written concrete laws the status of real laws,

110. Cic. *Rep.* 3.23.

111. Ibid. 3.41.

Girardet's Cicero as *prudens* (or *sapiens*) in the *Laws* drafts norms that are themselves natural law because they emanate from the right reason of the *prudens*, and so from human reason and human nature, and so from nature, which is the source of law according to both the first book of the *Laws* and the third book of the *Republic*.[112] Atkins, on the other hand, argues that while the first book of the *Laws* does indeed put forward a Stoic conception of natural law, books two and three take into account the limits of reason and human nature and advance merely an approximation of natural law for the best practicable regime, on the model of Plato's *Laws*.[113] James Zetzel has advanced what appears at first sight to be a reasonable middle position, arguing that Cicero "vacillates between presenting his laws as the best absolutely (and thus embodiments of natural law) and the best possible; between seeing them as universal and seeing them as specifically related to the particular circumstances of Rome."[114]

This is, of course, true enough as a description of what Cicero in fact did; but I doubt it captures his ambition accurately. Nor am I convinced by Atkins' attempt to ascribe the norms of books two and three merely to a second-best, practicable regime, for the following reasons. It is the balanced constitution itself that assumes the function of the *prudens* and of right reason, and it is precisely the balanced constitution's embodiment of right reason that enables it to stabilize human irrationality in the first place.[115] What Cicero is after is a non-utopian political theory, it is true (in the sense discussed above); but that does not entail that it is not an absolute, universal, non-contingent ideal. Scipio's historical Roman Republic *is* the ideal, not a mere second best, and it can be reestablished if the constitutional norms implicit in it are made explicit, as they are in the *Laws*.[116] *This* is how Cicero prevents natural law from being a "solvent" of established norms—by endowing some of these norms with the quality of

---

112. Girardet, *Ordnung der Welt*, pp. 85–110. The view has been accepted by many scholars, Jean-Louis Ferrary, E. M. Atkins, and Andrew Dyck most prominent among them. For an interesting distinction between two slightly different conceptions of natural law in the *Republic* and the *Laws*, respectively, see Moatti, *Raison de Rome*, p. 164. For an interpretation stressing the juristic and original quality of Cicero's thought, see Fontanella, *Politica e diritto*, ch. 6. Stressing Platonic aspects is Neschke-Hentschke, *Platonisme politique*, p. 193; 200–201.

113. Atkins, *Cicero on Politics*, chs. 5 and 6. Cf. also Asmis, "Cicero on Natural Law," who argues for a Stoic model with the laws of books two and three aiming at, not the Stoic sage, but the moral progressor, enjoining him or her to perform *kathekonta* (rather than the wise man's *kathortomata*).

114. Zetzel, *Cicero: On the Commonwealth*, p. xxiii.

115. Cicero makes this clear at *Leg.* 3.12, where he explicitly equates the constitutional code put forward in the *Laws* with Scipio's balanced, well-tempered constitution of the *Republic*.

116. For the universalism of the *Laws*, see Moatti, *Raison de Rome*, pp. 293–298.

natural law. He could not do that, however, if history or convention had any normative weight of its own and could justify these norms. They must be validated by reason, and, to the extent, but only to the extent, that reason demands that they be empirically tested, they must be so tested, which is why, as in Polybius, Cicero and Scipio adduce the Roman Republic of yore: it has been empirically tested, but the criteria it has to live up to are not themselves deduced from that empirical history.

It is true, as Atkins observes, that Cicero acknowledges the limits of reason and the importance of contingency. But Cicero's solution to the limits of reason is itself of an entirely rational nature: right reason demands that the limits of reason be handled by entrenching a balanced constitution. It is precisely to stabilize contingency that Cicero's right reason qua balanced constitution must be brought in. Girardet has correctly pointed out that this future aspiration, of an expanding constitutional empire, is already implied in Laelius' conception of natural law in the *Republic*. Laelius accepts that currently Philus' (or Carneades') description of normative diversity holds, but that this will give way, in the future, to a convergence everywhere, to an imperial *iuris consensus* as it were. The norms in *Laws* 2 and 3 aim to bring about this convergence under a balanced constitutional order containing explicitly higher-order, more firmly entrenched constitutional norms. Since Cicero's natural law is natural law for human nature, and since human nature on Cicero's view contains both reason and irrational passions, natural law can be brought to bear only if it is made into permanent, entrenched norms that govern the balanced constitution; then reason rules qua constitution.[117]

In his late philosophical work *On Duties* Cicero expresses the relationship between natural law (which he throughout equates with *ius gentium*, the latter being the empirical expression of natural law) and the civil law of individual historical societies in an instructive way that is apt to illuminate the relationship between his constitutional norms as put forward in the *Laws* on the one hand and local civil law on the other. In a passage that is designed to show that *ius civile* and natural law can come apart and that if they do, natural law is hierarchically superior and needs to prevail, Cicero specifies the relationship between the two as follows. Civil and natural law are distinct, so that "everything in the civil law need not be in the law of nations, but everything in the law of nations must also to be a part of civil law."[118] Cicero puts the relationship in set-theoretical terms, with the natural law (or law of nations) being a subset and the civil law

117. As metaphorically depicted in *Rep.* 2.67.

118. Cic. *Off.* 3.69. Trans. E. M. Atkins.

the superset. This means that the civil law can regulate things beyond what natural law determines, but it *has to* incorporate and enforce all rules of natural law. Natural law, this makes abundantly clear, determines at a fundamental level what the civil law regulates. Less fundamental norms can be handled in a locally and historically specific, contingent way, but fundamental principles—what is governed by natural law—underlie all these less fundamental norms and constrain them. This relationship would not make sense if the fundamental norms of natural law themselves were not embodying the ideal of (natural) justice.[119]

For the purposes of this book, however, I need not take a stance in this dispute. Even if Atkins were correct and the laws of books two and three merely approximate natural law, they would still represent a higher standard, a body of constitutional norms aiming to govern and constrain normal legislation. Misleadingly, Cicero calls the norms in books two and three *leges*, as if they constituted the stuff of regular legislation put to the assemblies. This has contributed, I believe, to the misunderstanding that the validity of these rules, in Cicero's view, depends on the assent of, if not a popular assembly, then at least the approval of the other two protagonists in the *Laws*, Cicero's friend Atticus and his brother Quintus. Yet the validity of the norms put forward in these books is not, it is strenuously pointed out, dependent on this kind of assent. It is an ironical conceit, and nothing more, when Cicero asks for his friends' approval. Cicero is after natural-law criteria for validity, not the vote of an assembly.[120] This leads to a hierarchical relationship between Cicero's code of so-called laws, which are really to be understood as a body of higher-ranking constitutional *ius*, on the one hand, and actual legislation, passed by popular assemblies, on the other. There are clear attempts to establish mechanisms to enforce the hierarchical distinction between the constitutional norms contained in books two and three of the *Laws* and mere legislation. The most crucial such attempt—at odds with Roman

119. Otherwise an infinite regress looms; the norms of natural justice must themselves be oriented towards a still more fundamental set of norms, which may itself be contingent but is itself oriented toward another, still more fundamental ideal, etc.

120. Cic. *Leg.* 2.14. Atkins, *Cicero on Politics*, p. 207 makes much of the fact that Atticus and Quintus do not accept all proposed provisions of Cicero's code; according to this logic, at least the accepted provisions should qualify as natural and thus universal and eternal. But the logic fails. Cicero does indeed suggest, as Atkins writes (ibid.), that "some written law," if it "can meet certain criteria" is consequently to be regarded as valid—but the criteria are those put forward by *recta ratio*, and the validity is that of natural law. The distinction is made very clear at *Leg.* 1.42, and esp. *Leg.* 2.8–14. See Girardet, *Ordnung der Welt*, pp. 72–73. See also, for an interesting further view, Schofield, "Cosmopolitanism," p. 13, where it is the judgment of rational persons that provides the criterion, with contingent factors influencing the judgment; cf. also Ferrary, "Statesman and the Law," p. 69, n. 52.

historical practice—is Cicero's reform of the censorship, which was now to be entrusted with the protection of the "fidelity of the laws."[121]

Cicero leaves no doubt that the only possible solution to what Atkins correctly identifies as "the limits of reason" in politics lies in the checks and institutional structure of Scipio's balanced, well-tempered constitution. That in the *Laws* he is now providing the constitutional norms for this kind of balanced constitution he makes abundantly clear. When Quintus remarks on the similarity of his constitutional code as put forward in book three of the *Laws* with Rome's historical constitutional setup, Marcus replies:

> Your observation, Quintus, is quite right. This is the balanced commonwealth which Scipio praises in that other book and which he most approves of, and it could not be brought to pass without such a distribution of offices.[122]

The constitutional solution is thus self-consciously not virtue-oriented, but of an institutional nature. It is, as Cicero puts it in the *Republic*, to be accomplished "on the authority of the *res publica*" through institutions and laws (*partim institutis, alia legibus*),[123] serving the purpose of a happy and just life (*beate et honeste vivendi*) for the citizens. This makes it seem, at first sight, faintly Aristotelian; but as we will see shortly when discussing *On Duties*, it is actually quite far from the Peripatetic ideal of the state as an educational machine that shapes the citizenry to enable them to lead a virtuous life. Cicero's focus on the constitutional framework should already alert us to the fact that his is not a virtue-centered political theory. It is often claimed by commentators that for Cicero, constitutional harmony (*concordia*) is what checks and balances are for Polybius, but the history of the tribunate Cicero offers in the third book of the *Laws* shows that he, no less than Polybius, is keenly interested—over and against Quintus' resistance—in upholding institutionalized conflict and the constraints the

121. Cic. *Leg.* 3.11. Cf. also Cicero's attempt to reinforce the weight of the augurs, which is at odds with prevailing practice; the augurs would, as we saw above in Chapter 3 (pp. 95f.), refer a violation of the auspices to the Senate, and it was within the Senate's discretion to declare legislation void (cf. Lundgreen, *Regelkonflikte*, pp. 265–266). Here in the *Laws* Cicero seems to suggest (*Leg.* 2.21) that the augurs themselves should have this power, which would amount to a kind of judicial review: "Whatever an augur has declared to be unjust, wrong, flawed (*iniusta nefasta vitiosa*), or ill-omened, let those things be void; and let anyone who does not obey be put to death." Trans. Zetzel, except for *vitiosa*, which here must mean a technical procedural flaw: Dyck, *Commentary*, pp. 308–309. Cf. Nippel, "Gesetze," pp. 87–88.

122. Cic. *Leg.* 3.12. Trans. Zetzel, modified. Cf. Schofield, "Cosmopolitanism," p. 12.

123. Cic. *Rep.* 4.3.

constitutional powers impose on each other.[124] This finds further expression in Cicero's emphatic reinforcement of the tribunes' veto or power of intercession, which is of course perfectly in line with his view of Gracchus having violated the constitutional order by defying his colleague Octavius' veto power.[125]

It is often claimed—as we already saw in connection with John Selden's interpretation of the passage in Chapter 1 above—that Cicero in the *Laws* empowered the chief magistrates to break the constitutional code in the face of necessity. The passage inviting this interpretation is of course the famous *salus populi suprema lex esto.*[126] Clinton Walker Keyes has advanced this view, according to which Cicero "actually intended to place the consuls above the law," "to give the consul extraordinary powers in cases of emergency."[127] Keyes himself however points out that this interpretation actually stands in tension with the constitution advanced in the *Laws*, namely with its first provision: the powers of the consuls are supposed to be constitutional (*iusta imperia sunto*), which means that there are checks delimiting their extent, especially the right of appeal: "Let the magistrate check the disobedient and harmful citizen . . . if no equal or greater authority or the people forbid it; let there be the right of appeal (*provocatio*) to the people."[128] This is justified by the idea that "as the laws are in charge of the magistrates, so the magistrates are in charge of the people," which already encapsulates the hierarchy between constitutional norm and magistrates.[129] When Cicero elevates *salus populi* to the status of a constitutional norm, he puts forward a supreme constitutional principle for the conduct of consuls in office, rather than placing the consuls above the law or any constitutional norms. This principle must be read, in light of *iusta imperia sunto* and the constraint of *provocatio*, as a check on the consuls' power more than as license in cases of emergency.[130]

But what substantive content does Cicero give to *salus*, or to his notion of the citizens' happy life? Although the relevant passages at first do have an Aristotelian ring to them, one looks in vain for the kind of extended eudaemonistic apparatus elucidating the virtue-ethical goals of this aspiration. To be

---

124. Cic. *Leg.* 3.15–26.

125. Cic. *Leg.* 3.42. See also Cicero's reinforcement of the prohibition of iteration of offices and the *lex annalis* at *Leg.* 3.9.

126. Cic. *Leg.* 3.8.

127. Keyes, "Original Elements," p. 317.

128. Cic. *Leg.* 3.6.

129. Ibid. 3.2.

130. Cf. Dyck, *Commentary*, pp. 458–459: regarding *Leg.* 3.8, the "difficulty lies perhaps in the tendency to take *lex* in this sentence too literally."

sure, the conventional cardinal virtues receive a fair share of attention, but there is more emphasis placed on the rules that define justice (*iustitia*) as the avoidance of aggression towards others' private property than on the idea that virtue will make for the kind of character-shaping habit necessary for *eudaemonia* in the Peripatetics' eyes. The emphasis, in short, is on rules protecting private property, and not on virtue as the road to happiness or well-being.[131] There are important hints as to what Cicero has in mind when using this most Ciceronian phrase of his, *salus populi*.[132] One strand of his thinking concerns simply the survival of the state, with *salus populi* being the outcome of Cicero's own actions in 63 BC.[133] But one must also always keep in mind Scipio's definition of the *populus* as a people in agreement about what constitutes the constitution (*ius*). *Salus populi* on this view is the integrity of the people's agreement about *ius*.

When we now turn to Cicero's late work of practical ethics, his *On Duties*, we can see that Cicero develops an account of the Roman republican constitution as grounded in natural law—of a piece with his account in the *Republic* and the *Laws*—where the purpose of the state is said to lie in maintaining justice. Justice, however, is now very explicitly said to lie in the protection and guarantee of essentially pre-political property rights.

In the *On Duties* Cicero reintroduces human weakness into his account of the origins of political society, but natural sociability is more prominent and eventually is said to be able to motivate action on its own, with weakness dropping out of the picture, in a Stoic account of *oikeiosis* which is, at least in its outlines, owed to Panaetius.[134] Rational activity and the search for truth are singled out as necessities for a well-lived life, but so is "whatever may contribute to the comfort and sustenance" of man and those close to him.[135] In his precepts for

131. See Cic. *Off.* 1.20–60 on justice (20–40 in the narrow sense, and 41–60 on liberality). See the remarks by Dyck on the distinction between the (narrowly confined) scope of justice on the one hand and of *liberalitas/beneficentia* on the other: *Commentary*, pp. 106–107. Lip-service is occasionally paid to well-being (*eudaemonia*) as the goal: cf. *Leg.* 1.52.

132. The phrase occurs eighteen times in the speeches: Dyck, *Commentary*, p. 459.

133. Winkler, *Salus*, p. 31.

134. Cic. *Off.* 1.11f. Cf. Dyck, *Commentary*, pp. 88–92 on the Polybian echoes contained therein, and see Lefèvre, *Pflichtenlehre*, pp. 19–20, for a view that gives due weight to Cicero's own contribution. Cf. also *Off.* 1.158, for reasons against the Epicurean account.

135. Cic. *Off.* 1.13; 1.12. Trans. Atkins. This is very close to Hobbes' interpretation of *salus populi* (he quotes Cicero's phrase in his *Elements of Law* 2.19.1, p. 179: "*Salus populi suprema lex*; by which must be understood, not the mere preservation of their lives, but generally their benefit and good." He goes on to point to "commodity of living" as a key temporal good, subsumed under the phrase *salus populi: Elements* 2.19.3, p. 179; quoted in Malcolm, *Reason of State*, pp. 116–117.

governing advanced in the second book, which we are now, after the discussion of the *Republic* and *Laws*, in a position to assess as precepts the balanced *constitution* needs to embody, Cicero starts by saying that agrarian laws are wrong by virtue of depriving people of their property:

> The men who administer public affairs must first of all see that everyone holds on to what is his, and that private men are never deprived of their goods by public acts. Philippus acted perniciously in his tribunate in proposing an agrarian law . . .

Cicero—making it clear that this does not merely concern good policy but is a matter of fundamental importance to his political thought—then goes on to define the very *purpose* of the state:

> For political communities (*res publicae*) and citizenships were constituted especially so that men could hold on to what was theirs (*ut sua tenerentur*). It may be true that nature first guided men to gather in groups; but it was in the hope of safeguarding their possessions (*spe custodiae rerum suarum*) that they sought protection in cities.[136]

It follows that for Cicero there are pre-political property rights, and that the legitimacy of government depends on the extent to which these pre-political rights are guaranteed and upheld. Private property provides therefore a proto-Lockean criterion for the legitimacy of political regimes. It is this criterion which serves as a vantage point from which to judge the existing political order and which Cicero seeks to elevate to the status of a constitutional norm. Jed Atkins' view, according to which there are no *natural* rights to be found in Cicero's political theory, must therefore be contested.[137] Private property rights do not exist at first in the state of nature, it is true, but once they have come into existence, for example by way of first occupancy, they are protected by natural law and thus deserving of the protection of constitutional norms.[138] These norms do not aim at a just pattern of *distribution* of private property. Rather, reminiscent of the political philosopher Robert Nozick's deontological, property-centered theory

136. Cic. *Off.* 2.73. Trans. E. M. Atkins. See Wood, *Cicero's Social and Political Thought*, p. 132.

137. Atkins, *Cicero on Politics*, pp. 138–154. Atkins here is talking about the *Republic*, but Cicero's *On Duties* should be seen as making explicit and fleshing out his views on the purpose of the state already contained in the *Republic* and the *Laws*.

138. Cic. *Off.* 1.21.

of justice, distributive justice is dethroned entirely and replaced by corrective justice. Indeed, Cicero, in a radically anti-Aristotelian move, turns the guarantee of pre-political property rights into the very definition of political justice and constitutionality. As G. E. M. de Ste. Croix observed, there is no Greek writer we know of who elevates the guarantee of private property to the "prime function of the state."[139] The constitutional norms, *fundamenta rei publicae*, are violated by agrarian legislation, debt relief, or any attempt at redistribution alike; just political order lets everyone hold on to what they already have, and the *suum cuique* is no longer the outcome of deserved and just distribution, but the pre-political yardstick of political justice (*aequitas*) and constitutionality.[140] Cicero denounces, by way of example, especially Sulla's proscriptions and Caesar's debt relief measures. It is the prime function of the justice of constitutional norms (*aequitas iuris*) and of the law courts to "enable each man to keep that which is his (*suum quisque teneat*)," and to "stop the weak from being oppressed because of their lowly state and the rich from being prevented through envy from maintaining or recovering what is theirs."[141]

Cicero had already put forward this view of the essential purpose of the state very early, in 69 BC in his speech for Caecina. There he had pointed out that property rights needed the protection of the state or, more precisely, of the immutable legal norms that safeguard those rights. If these norms could be changed on any arbitrary consideration, there could be no property rights and ultimately no political order, as the law provides the bonds of that order (*vincula utilitatis vitaeque communis*).[142] It is through *ius* and *leges* that we get to enjoy property: "the property which any one of us enjoys is to a greater degree the legacy of our constitution and our laws (*maior a iure et a legibus*) than of those who actually bequeathed it to him."[143] This is owed to the crucial feature of immutability—jurors in a lawsuit may be corrupted, but the law cannot be changed ad hoc.[144] Thomas Hobbes was to seize upon this remark by Cicero, adducing it as proof that even Cicero was convinced that there could be no property rights in the absence of sovereignty. But this enlists Cicero too quickly in

139. Ste. Croix, *Class Struggle*, p. 426.

140. Cic. *Off.* 2.78. Cf. *Caec.* 70: a person with contempt for law (*ius*) *leges ac iura labefactat*. For *fundamenta rei publicae*, cf Suet. *Aug.* 28.2, where Augustus in an edict aspires to be called *optimi status auctor* for having laid durable *fundamenta rei publicae*.

141. Cic. *Off.* 2.85. Trans. E. M. Atkins.

142. Cic. *Caec.* 70–74.

143. Ibid. 74. Trans. Hodge, modified.

144. Ibid. 72.

the ranks of positivists beholden to sovereignty; unlike Hobbes, Cicero did not think that the state created property rights; rather, he thought that the state had the purpose of safeguarding them and could be judged by its success in doing so, while for Hobbes there were no pre-political claims other than self-preservation that could be used to judge the legitimacy of the sovereign.[145] Hobbes correctly saw that Cicero thought property depended on government guarantees to an extent, given the lack of security in the state of nature, but Cicero's position here is of course Lockean, not Hobbesian; for Locke, as for Cicero, it is the fact that in the state of nature, the enjoyment of man's possessions is "very uncertain, and constantly exposed to the Invasion of others" which provides the reason and normative justification for the state.[146]

Nor is Cicero's conception of private property rights narrowly positivistic, or legalistic; the rights he has in mind do not only have validity by virtue of positive law. When discussing, in *On Duties*, Aratus of Sicyon, who was confronted with the problem of adjudicating between property owners who had been dispossessed for fifty years and those who had been in occupancy since, Cicero rather obviously has the normative concerns that arose in the context of Roman agrarian legislation in mind. He makes it clear that even in cases where there could be no prescription by law, as in Sicyon, the more recent occupants may have just claims to their holdings deserving of constitutional protection, "because after so long a stretch of time much of it was held as a result of inheritance, much had been bought, and much had been given as a dowry, all without injustice (*sine iniuria*)."[147] Aratus had achieved peace and justice by acknowledging the claims of both groups of owners and by paying compensation to those who could not be reinstated. He had thus managed not to tear apart (*divellere*) the interests of the citizens (*commoda civium*), but to bind everyone under the same just norms (*aequitas*) and good faith (*fides*).[148]

---

145. Hobbes, *Leviathan*, vol. 2, ch. 24, p. 388: "[E]ven *Cicero*, (a passionate defender of Liberty,) in a publique pleading, attributeth all Propriety to the Law Civil." Hobbes thinks that "the Introduction of *Propriety* is an effect of Common-wealth," but this cannot be squared with Cicero's insistence that it is the very purpose of the state to protect property. There is, however, a formal parallel between Hobbes' self-preservation and Cicero's property rights.

146. Locke, *Second Treatise*, ch. 9, § 123. The state is instrumental in bringing about justice, not the other way around, *pace* E. M. Atkins, "'Domina et Regina.'" Cf. Horn, "Politische Gerechtigkeit."

147. Cic. *Off.* 2.81. Trans. E. M. Atkins. The parallels with those who held *ager publicus* for a long time are obvious. See the discussion in Chapter 3, pp. 105–109. Cf. Cic. *Sest.* 103.

148. Cic. *Off.* 2.82–84.

Importantly, when norms of justice (*aequitas* or *ius*) and positive legal norms (*ius civile*) collide, the norms of justice prevail, as did the constitutional norms contained in books two and three of the *Laws*. This hierarchy comes to the fore in the third book of *On Duties*, where a debate is staged concerning some cases from the Roman law of sale between the Stoic philosopher Diogenes of Babylon and his student Antipater of Tarsus.[149] They discuss legal issues involving concealment and fraud in the context of property transfers. The challenge is whether behavior can be qualified as right (*honestum*) or merely expedient or prudent (*utile*). The potential tension between the two, central already in the Carneadean debate in the *Republic*, constitutes, of course, the topic of book three of *On Duties*, where Cicero is intent on showing that any tension must be in appearance only, as nothing can be prudent that is not morally right.[150] Cicero engages, in other words, in a redefinition of *utile*, so that narrowly self-interested behavior no longer qualifies as real prudence.[151] Diogenes says that behavior that does not violate prevailing legal norms of the *ius civile* should be allowed, while Antipater seeks to show that asymmetries of information between seller and buyer need to be disclosed under the more morally demanding rules of the natural law (*ius gentium/naturae*). Julia Annas has argued that Cicero here is confusing moral obligations on the one hand and enforceable legal rights on the other,[152] and that the debate therefore represented a "non-existing conflict."[153] Yet it is very clear that what Diogenes is claiming is that acting according to the *ius civile* is *morally* right, not simply legally unobjectionable.[154] Diogenes believes that his legal arguments have moral relevance. Antipater agrees but deems the moral standard of the positive *ius civile* too low. The conflict is therefore real, and Cicero, siding with Antipater, seeks to dissolve it by giving natural law a higher, constitutional status vis-à-vis positive legal rules. This is the real import of his support of Antipater's position,

149. Cic. *Off.* 3.50–67. Lefèvre, *Pflichtenlehre*, pp. 164–167 shows that the debate does not owe anything to the historical Diogenes and Antipater. Rather, the passage is purely Roman and Ciceronian. Cf. also Dyck, *Commentary*, pp. 557–564. on the historicity and possible sources of the debate.

150. It is the Carneadean debate we encountered above, as it appears in Cicero that provides the model here; but cf. Dyck, *Commentary*, p. 563, n. 50.

151. Diogenes does not deny Antipater's view that true, enlightened self-interest (*utilitas sua*) is identical with the interest of humanity at large (*utilitas communis*); implicitly confirming Antipater's claim, he merely denies that the behavior he commends does in fact constitute fraudulent concealment (*celare*). For a different view cf. Dyck, *Commentary*, p. 561.

152. Annas, "Cicero on Stoic Moral Philosophy," p. 164; similarly Nörr, *Rechtskritik*, p. 43.

153. Annas, "Cicero on Stoic Moral Philosophy," p. 165.

154. Ibid., p. 161, concedes that Diogenes is aware of the moral nature of Antipater's argument.

which makes it much less "puzzling" that he should argue against Diogenes, who seems the more property-friendly of the two. Cicero's position is about the hierarchy of rules.[155]

It is no coincidence that the debate concerning the relation between the *ius civile* and natural law serves as the introduction to Cicero's fundamental discussion of natural law and justice (*aequitas*).[156] This is where Cicero, as already touched upon above, argues that in cases of tension between statute or *ius civile* on the one hand and natural law on the other, the former has to give way; the civil law can regulate things beyond what the natural law determines, but it *has to* incorporate and enforce all rules of natural law.[157] His own time, Cicero believes, is characterized by the decay of this hierarchical relationship between constitutional natural law and statute and *ius civile*. He proceeds to give an account of Roman justice (*aequitas*) as based on natural law; *aequitas* here is justice qua natural law with nature as the source of law, on the one hand, but also refers to the specifically Roman legal procedure, called "formulary," administered by the Roman praetor and, significantly, originally developed by the peregrine praetor, thus explaining its identification with the *ius gentium* and its superiority over the *ius civile*.[158] This ties in with Cicero's previous discussion of what this justice consists in substantively. Earlier in book three, he had developed a definition, called a *formula* echoing the praetor's formulary procedure, according to which it is theft, the violation of private property, which constitutes the most fundamental injustice, leading to the dissolution of society.[159] We have arrived at the heart of Cicero's political and constitutional thought: justice is defined, in Roman legal language, as the guarantee of existing property holdings, and given the status of a superior constitutional norm.

What does the substance of Cicero's constitutional thought tell us concerning the underlying political theory? Cicero's constitutionalism does not represent a contractarian justification for the state in the vein of Glaucon in Plato's

---

155. Arena, *Libertas*, p. 161, does not discuss the hierarchy of rules and is thus bound to find Cicero's position puzzling; she describes the implications of Cicero/Antipater's argument for private property very clearly though: "from the partnership in the community of men it is deduced that the interest that everyone shares is that of preserving what everyone happens to own. Ultimately, this legitimates the pursuit of private interests."

156. Cic. *Off.* 3.68–72. I am following Lefèvre, *Pflichtenlehre*, pp. 167–169.

157. Cic. *Off.* 3.69.

158. Cic. *Off.* 3.72.

159. Ibid. 3.21. The *formula* is the heart of 3.19–32 dealing with apparent conflicts between justice and self-interest. See Lefèvre, *Pflichtenlehre*, pp. 141–151 on the specifically Roman character of the passage, with further literature.

Republic, or in that of Epicurean political theory. Nor is it merely a Stoic or Aristotelian view of natural sociability and the naturalness of political associations. It is not contractarian in that it postulates private property rights which are not simply up for grabs, and it is not Aristotelian or Stoic in that it adds a crucial feature to the *justification* of the state (all the while accepting the naturalness of its *origins*). Adding the crucial justificatory feature of private property alters furthermore the theory of justice applicable to political institutions; Cicero is effectively replacing any distributive aspects of political justice with corrective ones, making the legitimacy, and constitutionality, of government dependent on its respect for existing, ultimately pre-political property distribution and constitutionally restraining its power to redistribute.

5

Greek vs. Roman Constitutional Thought

IN THIS CHAPTER I will seek to identify and describe the crucial differences that separate Greek political theory from Roman constitutionalism. As the historian of constitutionalism Charles H. McIlwain has pointed out, in Greek political thought, "the law in a state" is thought of "only as one part or rather as one aspect of the whole polity itself, never as something outside or apart from the state to which that polity must conform."[1] By contrast, Cicero, both in his speeches and in his philosophical works, identifies a law that is antecedent in time to the state and binding on it, a claim that "no Greek of the fifth or fourth century B.C. could have dreamt of making, even supposing that he could have understood it."[2]

The term *politeia* is accordingly not to be understood, either in Plato or in Aristotle, to denote a jural conception of a higher, more firmly entrenched normative pre-political constitutional code. Rather it is a *descriptive* term that denotes the actual framework of a given state. When Aristotle discusses the supreme authority in a state, *to kurion*, he means actual supremacy, rather than the kind of legitimate authority we have come to associate with the term "sovereignty." Aristotle's famous view of the *politeia* as the organization (*taxis*) of offices in the city[3] is not be interpreted as the notion of *politeia* as a normative constitution in the modern sense and needs to be supplemented with his claim that the *politeia* is "so to speak the life of the city."[4] For Aristotle, there is no stark separation

1. McIlwain, *Constitutionalism*, p. 37.

2. Ibid., p. 38. For a similar argument stressing the difference, see Pani, *Costituzionalismo*, pp. 46–47.

3. Arist. *Pol.* 4.1.1289a15.

4. Ibid. 4.11.1295a40.

between ethics and politics, and the *politeia* as the city's political system shapes the life of the city and its citizens.[5] The *politeia* is thus "a way of organizing all of the citizens, not merely those who have special powers of political office." This is because for Aristotle, "the question, 'how should we organize our offices?' cannot be answered in isolation from a discussion of the more basic question, 'how is it best to live?' "[6] In Plato's *Republic*, the ideal state Kallipolis can be called happy and just as a consequence of the unity that its ordering achieves; the happiness is predicated, not of its individual citizens, but of the city as a whole, and when ordering the ideal state the concern is not for the various classes in it to partake in *eudaemonia*: it is left to nature to see to it that that happens.[7]

Plato

In what follows I will first sketch Plato's views insofar as they are relevant to our topic and will then give a survey of Aristotle's political and constitutional theory. This Greek background will then be contrasted with Roman political thought the better to appreciate the crucial difference between the two strands of thought. I will start with Plato's characterization of justice in his ideal state as developed in the *Republic*. When we seek to give substance to the concept of justice today, we tend to resort to views on equality, the distribution of goods, or the protection of individual liberty. Plato, on the other hand, provided a highly counterintuitive rendering of justice as a natural balance between the various classes of his ideal state; as Eric Nelson points out, for Plato, "a person's 'due' is his natural place within a rationally balanced, organic whole," leading to a view of justice "as the natural ordering of elements."[8] The elements in question correspond to Plato's tripartite division of the city into guardians, auxiliaries, and producers. It is these three classes which have to be in a particular relation to each other in order to make the city just. But, as Julia Annas correctly objects, is not justice "normally taken to be concerned with one's relation with *others*"? But for Plato "the city is just, not because of its relations to other cities, but because of the relations of its own three parts."[9]

Indeed, it turns out that keeping the three classes distinct from each other—rather than simply not letting individuals try their hand at other individuals'

5. Cf. Newman, *Politics*, vol. 4, p. 210.

6. Kraut, *Aristotle*, p. 15.

7. Pl. *Resp.* 4.421c.

8. Nelson, *Greek Tradition*, p. 13, n. 53.

9. Annas, *Plato's Republic*, p. 119.

jobs—constitutes justice according to Socrates in the *Republic.* Individual members of any one class may, without great damage to the city, share other people's work or deviate from their specialized jobs, as long as nobody does so beyond the boundaries of the three classes:

> The proper functioning of the money-making class, the helpers and the guardians, each doing its own work in the state, being the reverse of that just described, would be justice and would render the city just.[10]

This is so because the individual constituents of the three classes are by nature different, making the classes natural kinds; not expressing this natural difference on an institutional level would be unjust.

> But now the city was thought to be just because the three natural kinds existing in it performed each its own function.[11]

Plato famously constructed his edifice of the ideal state on a parallel between city and individual soul: the goal is to show that justice is the same for both city and individual and is worth having both for itself—like health—and for its consequences, since it is according to Socrates conducive to happiness, again both on the level of the individual and on that of the state, where happiness finds expression as unity. Justice for the individual consists in the correct relationship between the parts of his or her soul. Reason rules, while spirit or will ensures motivation, and desire or appetite submits to the demands of reason, resulting in a healthy and harmonious condition of the soul equivalent to bodily health. It is obvious that Plato here seeks to give us as individuals a reason to be just—who would not want to be healthy in the relevant way, and who would not thus want to order the parts of the soul in the way indicated by Socrates? As commentators have pointed out, there are several problems with this account. The first is that it involves a rather paradoxical account of justice—while Socrates is challenged to produce reasons why one should want to be just as conventionally understood, he is instead setting out to develop a concept of justice quite unlike the conventional one. Instead of giving us reasons not to steal or lie, he motivates us to submit our desires to reason. The next problem concerns the parallel between individual and state; even if one were to accept Socrates' new unconventional concept of justice as somehow entailing conventional justice, it is by no means clear how justice

10. Pl. *Resp.* 4.434c. Trans. P. Shorey.

11. Pl. *Resp.* 4.435b.

thus understood can be reproduced in the state. It would seem to imply that the three classes of the state are, like the different parts of the soul, very different from each other, to the point that they no longer share any common traits.[12] The producers, representing desire, submit to the guardians only because their rule is being imposed on them with the help of the auxiliaries (who represent spirit, or pride);[13] but it follows from such a view that the auxiliaries themselves, let alone the producers, do not as individuals have any prospect of being just and thus achieving happiness; rather, the guardians, being the only individuals ruled by reason in the relevant sense, are the only ones who can achieve personal happiness, given the parallel between soul and state Socrates is anxious to establish. Happiness can thus be predicated of the guardians, on the one hand, and of the state as a whole, on the other, not, however, of any other citizens of the ideal state.[14]

Justice is worth having for its own sake according to Plato, but, as Socrates seeks to demonstrate in books 8 and 9 of the *Republic*, it is also worth having for its consequences.[15] For the individual, happiness results from justice, and for the state, unity results. In an interesting discussion of Plato's ideal of unity, Malcolm Schofield writes that the "Unity Principle," the claim that the "greatest good for a city is what unifies it" amounts to Socrates' formula for the good. Schofield goes on to argue, counterintuitively, that this view of unity as the overarching ideal to be achieved is not too far removed from modern political liberalism as expounded by John Rawls. There is "more in common between" Plato's unity principle "and principles to which Rawls would subscribe than might be supposed," Schofield writes, notwithstanding modern liberalism's insistence that "there are many *conflicting* comprehensive views of life, each with its own conception of the good."[16] But what is meant here is the good of political society, not a shared conception of the good life; and it can indeed be said that for Plato there is no such thing as a shared conception of the good life for the citizens of his ideal state either, for these citizens belong by nature to different classes of human beings, and neither producers nor auxiliaries seem remotely capable of achieving individual happiness. They are, however, instrumental in bringing happiness,

12. See Annas, *Plato's Republic*, p. 150.

13. The amount of coercion envisaged by Plato is unclear; see Annas, *Plato's Republic*, pp. 116–117; 172–174.

14. *Pace* Vlastos, *Studies*, pp. 80–84, and Taylor, "Plato's Totalitarianism"; I follow Brown, "How Totalitarian is Plato's *Republic*?"

15. See Annas, *Plato's Republic*, ch. 12.

16. Schofield, *Plato*, pp. 216–217.

that is to say unity, to the state—and it is in this sense that producers and auxiliaries (and even the guardians, to the extent that ruling is not what they would originally like to do) are expected to sacrifice their actual wants and desires to the state. If they don't, they may be coerced; Plato is often ambiguous about the level of coercion involved,[17] but in Socrates' sketch of the breakdown of unity in the ideal state he makes it completely clear that in the interest of unity the producers may be coerced and even enslaved in the case of conflict:

> When civil war breaks out, the classes or natures are divided into two. The iron and bronze draw the state towards commerce, and the possession of land and housing, of gold and silver. The other pair, by contrast, the gold and silver, since in their souls they are not poor, but naturally wealthy, lead the state towards virtue and the traditional order. In fighting and struggling against one another they arrive at a compromise. The land and housing is to be divided up and owned privately, and they agree to enslave those who were previously watched over by them as free men, friends and providers. They now hold them as serfs and slaves, while their role is to watch them, and conduct warfare.[18]

What becomes perfectly obvious from this is that conflict is regarded as thoroughly bad, and, crucially, Plato does not envisage any apparatus of *public or constitutional law* to regulate conflict. Freedom of the producers is guarded by the guardians' virtue exclusively, without any *formal* institutions to guarantee anything resembling rights. Julia Annas stresses correctly that in Kallipolis "all classes are protected in freely having and doing what is necessary for them best to fill their social role,"[19] but this protection does not extend beyond what is necessary for fulfilling the classes' overriding *social* role, nor does it rise to the level of *legal* protection. The character of the guardians, their virtue, is the sole constraint. In fact, the only legal rules that seem of any consequence in Plato's edifice of the ideal state are those dealing with education—not education for Kallipolis as a whole, but the education the guardians are supposed to receive.[20] There is a tension here between what Plato thinks are classes that are different

17. See on this Kahn, "From *Republic* to *Laws*"; and cf. Schofield, *Plato*, pp. 272–274, who stresses restraint and obedience over coercion.

18. Pl. *Resp.* 8.547b-c. Trans. T. Griffith.

19. Annas, *Plato's Republic*, p. 177.

20. Pl. *Resp.* 425a; 502b-c. The guardians' common consumption, however, is also to be regulated by legislation: *Resp.* 417b.

by nature, and the unity which constitutes the main end of the political theory of the *Republic.* The entrenched and institutionalized distinctions between the classes are paradoxically supposed to serve to achieve the unity of the state. It is precisely when the state is perfectly united that it resembles most the individual soul in harmony—but it follows from taking the state-soul analogy seriously that if "each class corresponds exactly to some limited function in the soul, then in an important way the citizens of the state will not share a common human nature."[21]

This leads to an additional issue: Plato's concept of justice, which amounts to harmony of the classes or of the parts of the soul, is hardly able to account for the conventional notion of justice as "giving any individual what was appropriate for him," or "what was owed" to him or her.[22] Justice in Kallipolis is not only consistent with, but seems positively to require, keeping the producers in a subdued position. And what makes the individual guardian, who is just in Plato's sense and thus capable of happiness, immune to committing conventionally unjust acts, such as theft or breaking promises? Socrates, of course, thinks that the guardians' education and the resulting order of their souls will take care of that.[23] This is the reason for the centrality of those legal, perhaps even para-constitutional norms dealing with the education of the guardians[24] and for the corresponding unimportance of institutions and legal norms otherwise. Such norms and institutions pale by comparison with the virtue and, of course, the knowledge of the ideal rulers. Plato's nonegalitarian anthropological theory, his view of humankind, supplies the foundation for his political theory: given the nature-given inequality of the citizens, justice demands that this inequality find expression in the structure of the ideal state.

It is instructive to compare this picture with our own, liberal views on political justice. We assume that we simply do not have any criteria which would enable us to differentiate between citizens, on the basis of relevant natural differences, awarding political power and the capability to lead happy existences to some while denying this to others. Note that Plato's insistence on having available such criteria rests on an anthropological foundation, on his theory of human nature: Plato thinks that as an empirical matter, not all human beings share in reason. This positively requires, in his view, that those not able to partake in reason and knowledge not share in governing as a matter of justice—indeed, those

21. Annas, *Plato's Republic,* p. 150.

22. As in Simonides' definition: Pl. *Resp.* 1.332c.

23. Pl. *Resp.* 4.443a; 6.485c-e.

24. Ibid. 5.458c-d; 502b-c.

not sufficiently rational are likened to the slave, with the intention of describing the whole class of producers as slavish and not in the relevant sense free. Here is the famous description of the psychological makeup of a member of the producer class:

> "Why do you think someone is looked down on for engaging in menial tasks, or working with his hands? Isn't the reason just this? The best element in him is naturally (φύσει) weak, and so he is unable to control the creatures within him, but instead becomes their servant. All he can do is learn how to appease them."—"Apparently."—"So if we want someone like this to be under the same kind of rule as the best person, we say he must be the slave (δοῦλος) of that best person, don't we, since the best person has the divine ruler within him? And when we say he needs to be ruled, it's not that we mean any harm to the slave, which was Thrasymachus' view of being ruled. It's just that it's better for everyone to be ruled by what is divine and wise. Ideally he will have his own divine and wise element within himself, but failing that it will be imposed (ἐφεστῶτος) on him from outside, so that as far as possible we may all be equal, and all friends, since we are all under the guidance of the same commander."[25]

It has been objected that what we have here is a description, not of Kallipolis, but of actually existing slaves or producers, giving us "no reason to think that the farmers and craftsmen and businessmen of the good city will be very like the menial or manual worker characterized here."[26] But, as Terence Irwin persuasively points out, there is no suggestion on Socrates' part that the members of the producer class in the ideal state of the *Republic* will ever be ruled by their own reason,[27] and the description above does indeed seem to be intended for the ideal state. The producers, both in Kallipolis and in Plato's own experience, are *by nature* serving the lesser parts of their souls, which is precisely why justice demands that the producer class be ruled by the guardians. Slavery is of course but a metaphor here, but that does not mean that the producers in the ideal state will have any share in ruling; it only means that they will not be slaves in the conventional sense of the term. To the extent that reason is "imposed" on them "from outside" the producers will be ruled by the guardians in a coercive way; but the aspect of friendship throughout the city is nonetheless guaranteed by the fact

---

25. Ibid. 590c-d. Trans. T. Griffith.

26. Schofield, *Plato*, p. 274.

27. Irwin, *Plato's Ethics*, p. 351; see also Reeve, *Philosopher-Kings*, pp. 48–49.

that the producers' own desires and ultimate goals—their appetites, especially money-making—will be achieved, not thwarted, by the rule of the guardians. Reeve describes this state of affairs as one where "the rulers benefit the producers by insuring the existence of a structure within which their desires will be reliably satisfied throughout life," so that the rulers' commands are not "constantly at odds with their own desires."[28] But this is consistent with, and actually required by, a political order where the class of producers does not have any share in governing the city; again, this is so because the producers are, empirically speaking, unfree, i.e., ruled by their desires, which makes it imperative that they be ruled by the guardians' reason. Interestingly, the producers are the only ones who can own the "means of production," or private property *tout court*, while property is wholly absent from the governing class.

For us, the following points are central. First of all, the power of Plato's philosopher-kings is absolute and the principles by which they exercise their power are subject to their own discretion. For the producer, there is no autonomy with regard to the way he conducts his own life—as we have seen, justice consists in his or her not going beyond the boundaries of the producer class—nor are there any public legal or constitutional remedies: there are simply no constitutional rights of any kind.[29] Of course, in fairness it has to be mentioned that Plato assumes that the education of the ruling class—which itself is, as we have seen, one of the only domains subject to legal rules of any importance—will act as a constraint by guaranteeing that reason will rule supremely ("constitutionally," as it were) over everyone, as it is "better for everyone to be ruled by what is divine and wise." Virtue, understood both as the means to individual happiness and to the unity of the state, is supposed to act as the sole constraint.

Plato's history of the corruption and decay of the ideal state in the eighth book of the *Republic* provides a good example of this lack of legal constraints. The decline of Kallipolis is described in terms of the decline of the character virtues of the ruling class, and there are no *institutional* or legal impediments to this decline. In Socrates' sketch of the breakdown of unity in the ideal state quoted above it is clear that once education and virtue in the guardians break down over

---

28. Reeve, *Philosopher-Kings*, p. 285, n. 3; cf. Kraut, "Reason and Justice," pp. 217–218, who argues that such an interpretation is not compatible with friendship between classes and doubts that the producers actually benefit from the guardians' rule given *Resp.* 590c-d. Cf. also Schofield, *Plato*, p. 275, who, although rejecting Irwin's and Reeve's interpretation and arguing that the producers "can come to internalize the restraint of appetite which reason would dictate," admits that "the reason in their own souls is never going to be in the driving seat."

29. See Annas, *Plato's Republic*, pp. 172–178; on the concept of rights in Greek thought, see Burnyeat, "Did the Ancient Greeks have the Concept."

the generations, there are no constraints on what the rulers can do—if they were to arrogate private property to themselves, and to enslave the producers, this could not be countered by reference to entrenched legal norms. It is striking that Plato himself does not draw the conclusion that legal institutions might provide a solution to civil discord. The reason seems to lie in the view—apart from the perceived inevitability of decline—that in the absence of the rule of reason both happiness for the individual guardian or unity for the state are impossible, thus removing what made the ideal order worthwhile in the first place. In any case, the guardians' character and education are the only guarantees of the political order of Kallipolis in the *Republic*.

We can conclude that Plato has a notion of human nature which he arrives at a priori, that is to say, without inquiring about actually existing, empirical interests and desires of people. According to this view, only a select few individuals are capable of developing their rationality and living according to reason; it follows that only this elite—which exists by nature—is capable of freedom, justice, and happiness. The implication is that the rest of the population can and should in principle be coerced to play the role intended for them by Plato; indeed, justice positively requires such coercion if it is necessary in the interest of unity. The point is that Plato starts out from the interests of individuals *normatively* (not descriptively) understood, and that the public good is thought to consist of the aggregate, or collective harmonization, of interests and desires people are *supposed* to have, if they are to play the role intended for them. As Julia Annas puts it, Plato

> does not hesitate to sacrifice the needs and interests of actual people to those of the ideal individuals of his theory of human nature. He began by setting up the state as a mechanism for bringing it about that all the natural needs of human nature, in its different forms, would be harmoniously fulfilled. But he ends up imposing on people demands that most of them will see as externally sanctioned and not fulfilling their nature as they see it.[30]

This is so because on Plato's view, "only a few have the qualities necessary for excellence, so that rational attainment of excellence will involve forcing most people to go along whether they like it or not."[31] By contrast, Malcolm Schofield takes a more charitable view, preferring an interpretation that does not rely on

30. Annas, *Plato's Republic*, p. 181.

31. Ibid.

coercion so much as on restraint and self-discipline (*sophrosune*), achieved by "cultural means: by a combination above all of ideology and law."[32] But given the limited importance assigned to law throughout the dialogue (except its importance in the case of education), and given that education in the relevant sense is available exclusively to the guardians in Kallipolis, it is difficult to escape the conclusion that Plato is here indeed "imposing on people demands" that they themselves will experience as "externally sanctioned." Law, too, has a coercive component, and the restraint demanded of the producers is very much one inspired by the fear of punishment. If producers are caught lying by one of the guardians, punishment looms for them, and restraint for the producers consists above all "in being obedient to their masters."[33] Suppression of their appetites seems ultimately to hinge on fear of punishment.[34]

The general outlook is one positing the interests of the state and its unity as paramount, while neglecting the interests and desires of actual human beings.[35] This outlook can be demonstrated even with regard to Plato's revolutionary arguments in favor of the natural equality of women. Plato is justly famous for the argument that there is nothing in nature requiring females to pursue different occupations from men, and that the biological differences between the sexes are simply irrelevant when it comes to the pursuit of an occupation.[36] The argument has very interesting implications for us in two ways. On the one hand, it is true that Plato's argument for the equality of women and for the inclusion of some qualified women among the guardian class, where they will enjoy the same education as the male guardians, is not based on a view of what the interests of actual females require. It is rather an instrumental view: women are an untapped resource *for the state*.[37] Equality is not due to females as a matter of right—let alone a human right—rather, the equality of *some* women, those possessing the qualities of guardians, is something that will benefit Kallipolis and its unity. If it happened not to benefit the ideal state, the problem would not arise in the first place.[38]

32. Schofield, *Plato*, p. 273.

33. Pl. *Resp.* 3.389d-e.

34. But cf. Kahn, "From *Republic* to *Laws*," pp. 350–353.

35. For criticism of Plato's notion of unity as too ambitious, see Arist. *Pol.* 2.1-6, esp. 2.1261a17-31: too much unity will destroy the *polis*, which consists naturally of a multitude, and reduce it to a household.

36. Pl. *Resp.* 5.453e-455a; cf. also 7.540c.

37. Ibid. 5.452d-e; 456c; 457a-c.

38. See Annas, *Plato's Republic*, pp. 181–185.

This criticism of Plato's argument, put forward by Julia Annas, is fair as far as it goes. However, and this leads us to our second implication: Plato's view is once again based on a particular theory of human nature; and it should be stressed that in the case of female eligibility and fitness for the guardian class Plato's a priori view of the natural equality of some women holds extraordinary revolutionary potential, on the one hand, but is no less paternalistic than his general views on the required obedience of the producers, on the other. The fact that we have come to share this view of female equality—and extend it to all women—should not obscure the important insight that in this case, too, Plato does not pay any heed to the desires and interests of actual female members of the city-states of his time; his is a normative vision of human nature, arrived at by a priori reasoning, and it is women as they should be according to this vision who are built into Kallipolis in a revolutionary way.

But Annas' criticism of Plato's argument on women is also misguided: our own reasons for giving women equal rights are, of course, not based on instrumental reasoning in favor of the unity of the (ideal) state, but is it not the case that they are also based on a specific theory of human nature? The view, which to some extent is also Plato's, that women share in relevant aspects naturally in the properties that qualify men to do certain things is a *necessary presupposition* for developing the rights-based theory that underlies modern liberalism. Without this view we could not possibly arrive at liberal, rights-based equality either. The difference comes to the fore when we ask whether or not, after asking everyone equally what their actual desires and interests are, some should be coerced to live up to their natural equality. Athenian women of Plato's day, when asked the question, may satisfy the liberal by replying that they would rather stay at home. Conversely, Plato would want to force some young women—who might find themselves in the equivalent of the producer class—into a guardian role, notwithstanding their actual desires.

The crucial difference is this: on the liberal view, equal rights for women would have to be insisted upon on grounds of justice *even* if this would create costs or jeopardize the state's unity. On Plato's view, as expressed in the *Republic*, justice requires equal rights and duties for *some* women, as this will lead to greater happiness and unity for the state.

To sum up: according to the *Republic*, individual happiness is possible exclusively for the ruling philosophers, and even the philosophers partake in happiness only to the extent that they are prepared to play their role in the city.[39]

---

39. On the deep difference between philosophers and non-philosophers in the account of the *Republic*, see Bobonich, *Plato's Utopia Recast*, pp. 67–72.

Further, for Plato the question as to what we should ultimately want, the question what happiness (*to agathon, eudaemonia*) consists in, admits of an objective answer—at least by those who have enjoyed the proper philosophical education and are thus capable of knowledge. It is this knowledge which enables answers as to what we should do when we want to act justly. This practical knowledge which deals with correct actions is secondary, however, while the objective answer to the question of human happiness is primary. It is crucial that there cannot be any space for extra- or *pre-political* happiness: the good life—for the few naturally capable of enjoying it—is possible only in the ideal state, and the ideal state is oriented towards the greatest good of any state, namely unity:

> Well, then, can we think of any greater evil (κακὸν) for a city than what tears it apart and turns it into many cities instead of one? Or any greater good (μεῖζον ἀγαθὸν) than what unites it and makes it one?[40]

We have seen that there are no institutional or legal obstacles to these ends of the ideal state; the individual is not entitled to any guaranteed positive rights vis-à-vis the ruling class. This follows not only from Plato's giving priority to the state and its unity, but also, independently, from his distaste for legal arrangements, which he deems—at least in the *Republic* and in the *Statesman*—improper and objectionable obstacles for the statesman equipped with knowledge. In the *Statesman* he has the Eleatic Stranger put forward the following view on the relationship between law and expertise:

> "But now it is clear that we shall have to discuss the question of the propriety of government without laws."—"Of course we shall."—"In a sense, however, it is clear that law-making belongs to the science of kingship; but the best thing is not that the laws be in power, but that the man who is wise and of kingly nature be ruler. Do you see why?"—"Why is it?"—"Because law could never, by determining exactly what is noblest and most just for one and all, enjoin upon them that which is best; for the differences of men and of actions and the fact that nothing, I may say, in human life is ever at rest, forbid any science whatsoever to promulgate any simple rule for everything and for all time. We agree to that, I suppose?"—"Yes, of course."—"But we see that law aims at pretty nearly this very thing, like a stubborn and ignorant man who allows no one to do anything contrary to

40. Pl. *Resp.* 5.462b. Trans. T. Griffith.

> his command, or even to ask a question, not even if something new occurs to some one, which is better than the rule he has himself ordained."[41]

The Stranger, after remarking that "certainly anyone who really possessed the kingly knowledge (τὴν βασιλικὴν ἐπιστήμην), if he were able to do this, would hardly, I imagine, ever put obstacles (ἐμποδίσματα) in his own way by writing what we call laws"[42] goes on to ask:

> "But he who has made written or unwritten laws about the just and unjust, the honorable and disgraceful, the good and the bad for the herds of men that are tended in their several cities in accordance with the laws of the law-makers, is not to be permitted to give other laws contrary to those, if the expert law-maker, or another like him, should come! Would not such a prohibition appear in truth as ridiculous. . .?"[43]

This argument leads the Stranger to the paternalistic point of view that "whatever the wise rulers do, they can commit no error . . . by always dispensing absolute justice,"[44] even if this will have to be based on coercion:

> "Now if people are forced, contrary to the written laws and inherited traditions, to do what is juster and nobler and better than what they did before, tell me, will not anyone who blames such use of force, unless he is to be most utterly ridiculous, always say anything or everything rather than that those who have been so forced have suffered base and unjust and evil treatment at the hands of those who forced them?"—"Very true."—"But would the violence be just if he who uses it is rich, and unjust if he is poor? Or if a man, whether rich or poor, by persuasion or by other means, in accordance with written laws or contrary to them, does what is for the good of the people, must not this be the truest criterion of right government, in accordance with which the wise and good man will govern the affairs of his subjects? Just as the captain of a ship keeps watch for what is at any moment for the good of the vessel and the sailors, not by writing rules, but by making his expertise (τέχνη) his law (νόμος), and thus preserves his fellow voyagers, so may not a

41. Pl. *Pol.* 294a-c. Trans. Harold N. Fowler.

42. Ibid. 295b.

43. Ibid. 295e-296a (I use "expert" for Fowler's "scientific"). Cf. the analogy with the physician at 295b-d.

44. Ibid. 297a.

> right government be established in the same way by men who could rule by this principle, making expertise more powerful than the laws?"[45]

This makes a state or government that is subject to the rule of law an impossibility to conceive. Mere lawfulness cannot, on Plato's view, be considered a merit; a fortiori the concept of constitution and constitutional rights cannot have a role in Plato's edifice. This becomes strikingly obvious when the Stranger develops his concept of the correct "constitution" (πολιτεία). There is but one correct, legitimate constitution, and it is the autocratic rule by the statesman with expertise.[46] It follows that the six-fold classification of constitutions with its hierarchy of political systems arranged according to constitutional form does not really yield much in the way of insight; rather, these six systems are all equally incorrect compared to the one correct *politeia*.[47] But this *politeia* is a constitution only in a narrow, merely descriptive sense. All the term amounts to is a description of the autocratic rule of the expert statesman, devoid of any normative content. Nothing the statesman does could coherently be described as unconstitutional; indeed, not even his changing the system of government could be said to be unconstitutional.

This is no different in the *Laws*, although at first sight in this late work there is a marked tendency for a rather striking emphasis on law and legislation, quite different from both the *Republic* and the *Statesman*. The skepticism toward law that characterizes the *Statesman* here seemingly gives way to a much more sympathetic approach; witness the extremely interesting attempt by Cleinias the Cretan to flesh out the views of the Athenian Visitor by giving the proposed legislation for the second-best city featured in the *Laws*, Magnesia, a natural-law flavor. The lawgiver needs to persuade the citizenry that the law (νόμος) as well as his expertise (τέχνη) "exist by nature" (φύσει) if indeed they are the product of reason.[48] This is the closest Plato comes to developing a *normative* concept of constitution based on natural law. However, this must be read in conjunction with the view, put forward a bit earlier in the *Laws*, that Magnesia's reliance on legislation is on the whole owed to a more pessimistic view of human nature and the boundaries imposed by human psychology on Kallipolis, not to a principled

45. Ibid. 296c-297a. Trans. Fowler (I use "expertise" instead of "science").

46. Ibid. 293d-e.

47. See Balot, *Greek Political Thought*, p. 213: "Plato's own chief comment, however, is that the entire discussion [of constitutional types] is nearly worthless, since the true criterion of constitutional 'correctness' is the knowledge of the ruler."

48. Pl. *Leg.* 10.890d.

change in attitude toward the relation between justice and legislation. The reason for the necessity of legislation for men has to be sought in human nature (φύσις ἀνθρώπων), or, more precisely, in the problem of motivation; in a seeming renunciation of the Socratic denial of incontinence or *akrasia*, Plato acknowledges that, quite apart from cognitive abilities which allow men to recognize what is conducive to the polity, there always remains the problem of *motivation*.[49] "The reason thereof is this—that no man's nature is naturally able both to perceive what is of benefit to the civic life of men and, perceiving it, to be alike able and willing to practice what is best."[50] Even given knowledge on the part of the ruler, there is now in the *Laws* a much more qualified trust in the motivational makeup of the ruler than in both the *Republic* and the *Statesman*. This skepticism is expressed in a way directly antithetical to the manner in which the *Statesman* had defended autocratic rule of a knowledgeable expert:

> [E]ven if a man fully grasps the truth of this as a principle of art, should he afterwards get control of the State and become an unaccountable autocrat, he would never prove able to abide by this view and to continue always fostering the public interest in the State as the object of first importance, to which the private interest is but secondary; rather, his mortal nature will always urge him on to grasping and self-interested action, irrationally avoiding pain and pursuing pleasure; both these objects it will prefer above justice and goodness, and by causing darkness within itself it will fill to the uttermost both itself and the whole State with all manner of evils.[51]

It is this skepticism that justifies the Athenian's choice of the second-best state, Magnesia, over the ideal state. It is still maintained, even here, that if by divine providence a man should arise fit by nature to rule, he would have no need for laws above him, for "no law or ordinance is mightier than knowledge, nor is it right for reason to be subject or in thrall to anything."[52] But no such man exists; hence the need for a legal framework that is more attuned to the motivational deficiencies of actually existing men. This is a considerable concession, but we have to decide whether it changes anything more fundamental with regard to

49. Ibid. 9.874e-875b. This seems to express an externalism about motivation rather untypical of Plato.

50. Ibid. 9.875a. Trans. Bury.

51. Ibid. 9.875b-c.

52. Ibid. 9.875c.

the idea of constitutionalism. The statement by Cleinias cited above concerning the need for the lawgiver to persuade the citizens of Magnesia that their legal code is the product of reason and thus exists by nature comes closest to a view of these laws as both more deeply entrenched than mere legal conventions and more deeply justified than other rules.[53]

Are we then justified in taking this to be an expression of the idea of natural law and of the concept of constitution? I do not think so. First of all, as we have just seen, even if reason could be expressed as rules in an entrenched and institutionalized way, this would still be considered a second-best solution. The ideal ruler would do without a rule-based framework, for the reasons expressed in the *Statesman*: general rules will not be able to do justice to particular circumstances. Second, the view that the laws of Magnesia "exist by nature" is something the lawgiver is encouraged to persuade the citizens of; it is by no means clear whether this is indeed the view the Athenian himself takes. Also, Cleinias wavers between the laws existing by nature and their existing by virtue of something equal to nature. Third, and most important, given that "no law or ordinance is mightier than knowledge" and reason, the status of the legal rules that obtain at Magnesia is bound to be precarious. In this Plato's view resembles utilitarian theories of our own time, as Gisela Striker has pointed out: "It would seem that for Plato laws have the kind of status that rules have in utilitarian theories—they are always just rules of thumb since the actual standard of rightness is the result to be achieved, and this will inevitably require an indefinite number of exceptions to the rules."[54] There is thus no concept of higher-order legal rules that are more firmly entrenched than other legislation, and there is no concept of constitution in any normative sense.

The legitimacy of government rests on the extent to which it succeeds in making the city's citizens virtuous. It can be argued that, compared to the *Republic*, the order of priority between state and citizen has been reversed in the *Laws* and that happiness is portrayed as achievable for all citizens, not just for the philosopher-kings. However, the latter claim depends on the view one takes of where Plato draws the boundaries of citizenship in the *Laws*, and the case made by Bobonich that citizenship in the later work is much more exclusive is sound: the *Republic*'s producers lose their citizenship in the *Laws*,[55] pointing

---

53. But cf. the attempt by Irwin to interpret the *Laws* as putting forward a notion of (internal) natural law: "Morality as Law."

54. Striker, "Origins," p. 214. Cf. also Rowe, "The *Politicus*"; Cooper, "Plato's *Statesman*"; Gill, "Rethinking Constitutionalism"; Lane, *Method and Politics*; and on the *Laws*, Morrow, *Plato's Cretan City*.

55. Bobonich, *Plato's Utopia Recast*, pp. 413–417.

ahead to an order that resembles, as we will see, Aristotle's views as put forward in the *Politics*.[56] But what about the order of priority between the city and its citizens? In the *Republic*, as we have seen, Kallipolis could be called happy as a consequence of its unity, and the happiness was predicated of the city as a whole, not of its citizens.[57] This looks quite different in the *Laws*; the unity of the state has given way to individual *eudaemonia* as the ultimate goal of statecraft:

> The sum and substance of our agreement was simply this: that whatsoever be the way in which a member of our community—be he of the male or female sex, young or old,—may become a good citizen, possessed of the excellence of soul which belongs to man, whether derived from some pursuit or disposition, or from some form of diet, or from desire or opinion or mental study, to the attainment of this end all his efforts throughout the whole of his life shall be directed; and not a single person shall show himself preferring any object which impedes this aim; in fine, even as regards the State, he must allow it to be revolutionized, if it seems necessary, rather than voluntarily submit to the yoke of slavery under the rule of the worse, or else he must himself quit the State as an exile: all such sufferings men must endure rather than change to a polity which naturally makes men worse.[58]

This is remarkable: the state has now been made entirely subservient to the happiness of its citizens, who—contrary to the starkly differentiated classes of the *Republic*—are in principle *all* capable of being educated to lead virtuous and thus genuinely happy lives. Indeed, the "entire law code of the city aims at fostering all the virtues in the whole citizen body."[59] However, this requires the redrawing of the boundaries of citizenship, as mentioned above, "so that the just political association has become a community of the virtuous."[60] Could it not be argued, then, that these rules concerning the qualification for citizenship in both the *Statesman* and the *Laws* as well as the norms providing for the education required by the ultimate goal of the state do indeed rise to the level of entrenched, higher-order constitutional norms? I think there is something to be said for this

---

56. Ibid., p. 576, n. 96.

57. Pl. *Resp.* 4.421c. See above, p. 199.

58. Pl. *Leg.* 6.770c-e.

59. Bobonich, *Plato's Utopia Recast*, p. 417.

60. Ibid., p. 416.

kind of argument, yet I strongly doubt that these rules themselves (in keeping with the logic of Plato's argument) would not also be subject to the will of those who govern; the rulers, both in the *Statesman* and in the *Laws*, are probably still ranked higher in the hierarchy of virtue than the rest of the citizens.[61] Second, as in the *Republic*, there is no space for any extra- or pre-political happiness nor for any normative claims vis-à-vis the state that are not themselves based on the rules of the polity: the good life—for the few naturally capable of enjoying it—is possible only in the ideal state. So even if the rules concerning citizenship and education do deserve to be called of a higher-order in that they are presupposed by the orders of Kallipolis and Magnesia, they are emphatically not constitutional in the sense of isolating an extra- or pre-political domain from politics. Such a confined sphere, demarcated from politics and protected from intrusion from the polity, cannot exist as a matter of principle. The rulers' rational insight may act as a constraint, but it is in the nature of things that it cannot be juridified in constitutional norms.[62]

Aristotle

Let us now turn to Aristotle. The *Politics*, of course, was conceived by Aristotle as a sequel to the *Nicomachean Ethics*, aiming at the realization of the goals argued for in the *Ethics*. The good life as fleshed out in the *Ethics* becomes, just as in Plato's *Laws*, the ultimate aim of politics, which thus turns into the means to reach ethical ends. It will become clear from what follows that Aristotle takes the prescriptions of his political theory to be a *necessary condition* for the achievement of the good life for human beings. Politics are thus not simply any means for the achievement of the goals of ethics, but the necessary means par excellence. Conversely, Aristotle sees his *Ethics* as a "political" work of sorts and insists on the systematic continuity between the two treatises.[63] Prima facie it would seem to follow that those of us who live in polities that are not ordered according to the principles laid out by Aristotle—that is to say, all of us today—are not capable of living good lives. This is so because for Aristotle, no less than for Plato, the successful, good life is inconceivable without the virtues which themselves are for Aristotle shaped by the state and its laws (very much akin to the view

61. Cf. ibid., p. 415.

62. It is unclear whether basic tenets such as the communism of the guardians or the education of women in the Republic are themselves protected from intrusion by the guardians; presumably Plato would argue that knowledgeable rulers would not want to change those basic tenets.

63. Arist. *Eth. Nic.* 1.1094b11.

in Plato's *Laws*) and are thus dependent on the state. The state, then, acts as an "educational machine" and is responsible for the good life.

One of the most influential ideas we encounter in Aristotle consists in his political anthropology, his considerations concerning the biological nature of man. From these considerations, famously, normative conclusions are drawn:

> When several villages are united in a single complete community, large enough to be nearly or quite self-sufficing, the state (πόλις) comes into existence, originating in the bare needs of life, and continuing in existence for the sake of a good life. And therefore, if the earlier forms of society are natural, so is the state (διὸ πᾶσα πόλις φύσει ἐστίν), for it is the end of them, and the nature of a thing is its end. For what each thing is when fully developed, we call its nature, whether we are speaking of a man, a horse, or a family. Besides, the final cause and end of a thing is the best, and to be self-sufficing is the end and the best. Hence it is evident that the state is a creation of nature, and that man is by nature a political animal. And he who by nature and not by mere accident is without a state, is either a bad man or above humanity . . .[64]

The claim that the good life for humans can only be achieved by human beings in the state is based on a particular view of human nature. Unlike other animals who also form "political" entities in order to cooperate, humans have language; this natural trait leads them to cooperate in a special way, namely by arguing about what is just and what is unjust. Such argument is given institutional expression in the *polis*, which can thus be said to allow humans to express their nature most fully and thus exists by nature:

> Now, that man is more of a political animal than bees or any other gregarious animal is evident. Nature, as we often say, makes nothing in vain, and man is the only animal who has the gift of speech. And whereas mere voice is but an indication of pleasure or pain, and is therefore found in other animals . . ., the power of speech is intended to set forth the expedient and inexpedient, and therefore likewise the just and the unjust. And it is a characteristic of man that he alone has any sense of good and evil, of just and unjust, and the like, and the association of living beings who have this sense makes a family and a state.[65]

---

64. Arist. *Pol.* 1.1252b28-1253a4. Revised Oxford translation, ed. by Jonathan Barnes. For Aristippus as the prototypical apolitical person, see Xen. *Mem.* 2.1.13.

65. Arist. *Pol.* 1.1253a7-a18.

Unlike Epicurus,[66] Aristotle does not, of course, equate utility and justice here, but he does mark them both as specifically human concerns. While pleasure may serve as the end for some societies, household and *polis* are "ethical unities."[67] This elucidation of his claim that human beings are by nature made for life in *poleis* serves as the background for his even bolder, famous claim that the state or *polis* is "by nature prior (πρότερον δὲ τῇ φύσει πόλις) to . . . the individual, since the whole is of necessity prior to the part." By way of analogy, Aristotle says that "if the whole body be destroyed, there will be no foot or hand." This is proven by the fact "that the individual, when isolated, is not self-sufficing." Justice, therefore, "is something political (ἡ δὲ δικαιοσύνη πολιτικόν); for the administration of justice, which is the determination of what is just, is the principle of order in political society."[68]

Aristotle is careful to make it clear that the state is prior to the individual not in a *genealogical* sense—the individual and the household have emerged, as a matter of fact, prior to the state—but in a conceptual sense. As W. L. Newman summarizes the argument, "when severed from the whole, the part loses its capacity to discharge its function"; the state "exists by nature and is prior to the individual, for if the individual is not self-complete when severed from the πόλις, he will be posterior to it just as any other part is posterior to its whole."[69] Newman points out, correctly, that the argument is not valid as it stands. The fact (if it is a fact) that the individual is not self-sufficient without the state "does not prove that he stands to it in the relation of a part to its whole." Even if one were to grant that the individual does indeed stand to the *polis* in the relation of a part to the whole, it still "does not follow that all parts of all wholes stand in the same relation to those wholes. A limb stands in a far more intimate relation to the body of which it is a part than a wheel does to a cart, or a portion of a rock does to that rock."[70] It is clear, however, that Aristotle takes his argument to prove that the individual, in order to perfect himself and lead the good life, is in need of the state as a matter of necessity. The key reason for this lies in the absence of virtue outside the state—indeed, Aristotle claims that the virtue of justice is inconceivable without the state: justice is *essentially* of a political nature.

---

66. Diog. Laert. 10.150. Cf. also Hor. *Sat.* 1.3.98.

67. Newman, *Politics*, vol. 2, p. 124.

68. Arist. *Pol.* 1.1253a19-a39. Trans. adapted.

69. Newman, *Politics*, vol. 2, p. 125.

70. Ibid., p. 126.

When Aristotle claims that the state exists by nature and is prior to the individual, and when he furthermore claims that the natural end of the individual lies in the good life, which is achievable exclusively in the *polis*, what conception of nature is he presupposing? Does what is natural simply consist in what is (empirically speaking) normal, what constitutes the usual pattern of behavior? At times we are led to believe that it does and that by "nature" Aristotle simply means "custom." In other cases, however, Aristotle denotes very unusual practices as "natural." Julia Annas has argued very convincingly that Aristotle operates with two distinct notions of nature; one that denotes "what we start from, but hardly serves as an ethical guide of any kind,"[71] and another one that is stronger and denotes "not a minimal starting point to improve on, but itself a desirable goal."[72] She calls the first, non-normative notion of nature "mere nature," as opposed to the normatively significant "full nature."[73] Aristotle's distinction between "natural" and "proper" virtue in book 6 of the *Nicomachean Ethics*, Annas argues, maps neatly onto the distinction between mere nature and nature in the normative sense.[74] Aristotle's well-known account of the purpose or function (*ergon*) of humans in the first book,[75] his account of pleasure in book 7 of the *Ethics*,[76] and the notion of nature used in the first book of the *Politics* are all examples of the stronger, normatively charged conception of nature. So when Aristotle claims that the state exists by nature, is prior to the individual, and that the natural end of the individual lies in the good life that can be achieved only in the *polis*, he seems to be using the second, normatively charged conception of nature. His view that only the *polis* represents the natural end point of social development toward the state is really a thesis about human nature[77]—human nature "is such

71. Annas, *Morality*, p. 143.

72. Ibid., p. 145.

73. Hobbes, e.g., seems to operate with a conception of "mere nature."

74. Arist. *Eth. Nic.* 6.1144b1-12. Annas, *Morality*, pp. 143–144.

75. Arist. *Eth. Nic.* 1.1097b21-1098a20. *Pace* Annas, *Morality*, p. 144, who thinks that "we cannot press this argument to show that Aristotle has a stronger notion of nature than mere nature in mind," because he "does not prominently present the argument as involving nature," only "somewhat casually." But Aristotle does seem to set out to show that humans do have a function by nature, by answering his own rhetorical question whether humans are naturally disposed to be without function (ἀργὸν πέφυκεν) in the negative. The teleology he develops by way of answering the question can certainly be interpreted as being based on the second, normative notion of nature.

76. Arist. *Eth. Nic.* 7.1152b33-1153a15; 1153b7-19.

77. One perfectly in tune with his biological views; see Arist. *Ph.* 193b3-12. For a discussion, see Everson, "Aristotle on the Foundations."

that people's needs will be met, and their interests catered to, only in the city-state form of community."[78] But there is some ambiguity here, as Aristotle oscillates between a normative conception of nature and "mere" nature. For him, the *polis* is not the product of force or of manipulation.[79] This view Aristotle forms on the basis of strong empirical evidence; his own historical context and the history of the Greek city-states gave him at least prima facie reason to think that *poleis* were the natural end point of state-building, and here "natural" has the empirical flavor of "mere" nature. Larger entities such as the Macedonian or Persian empires could be seen, by contrast, as merely based on force.[80]

The naturalness of Aristotle's state is thus based both—ambiguously—on "mere nature," insofar as the naturalness of the state is seen as what is normal or customary, and on a more normatively charged conception of nature. As Annas convincingly points out, there is another argument Aristotle puts forward where his conception of nature cannot rely on empirical evidence and must thus unambiguously rest on a normative conception of nature. He famously and influentially argued that certain ways of money-making were unnatural but these practices, such as trade, were, of course, by no means unusual. Both the *polis* and slavery seemed natural to Aristotle by virtue of being customary, but the kind of money-making he deemed natural—producing only to meet needs, with very little exchange—represents a certain primitivism and is of course opposed to his contemporary state of affairs, where trade was thoroughly normal.[81] If one were to introduce these "natural" money-making practices into the *poleis* of Aristotle's day, it would have made for a revolutionary break with the way these economies actually worked (although Aristotle's views were in fact aligned with aristocratic predilections for farming and prejudices against trading). His conception of nature in this example is thus clearly of a normative nature; and I think the same holds ultimately for his conception of nature throughout book 1 of the *Politics*, since even in the cases where Aristotle ostensibly relies on empirical evidence of Greek political development, he glosses over the fact that his preference for the *polis* requires some very strong normative assumptions about human nature that cannot rely on "mere nature" alone.

It will be instructive to offer a brief excursus here on the relation between Aristotelian and early modern political theory. Conventional accounts of the history of political thought usually emphasize prominently the differences between

---

78. Annas, *Morality*, p. 150.

79. Ibid., p. 152.

80. Ibid., pp. 151–152.

81. See ibid., pp. 156–157.

Aristotle and early modern political thought, especially what separates Thomas Hobbes' (1588-1679) work from Aristotle's. Without wanting to deny these fundamental distinctions, it seems to me that the interpretation of Aristotle's political thought has at times been influenced by Hobbes' own view of the Aristotelian viewpoint. When we think about what Aristotle says about human beings without the state, we realize to what extent we have an adumbration of the state of nature as explicated in the famous thirteenth chapter of *Leviathan*. Most interesting in this regard is Aristotle's thesis, cited above, that justice itself and the legal framework that expresses and undergirds justice are political things, that is to say, they are somehow essentially political (ἡ δὲ δικαιοσύνη πολιτικόν).[82] It is not entirely clear whether this should be understood merely as an empirical claim to the effect that justice and law as a matter of fact cannot be found without the state. Yet it seems that Aristotle's claim is a stronger one, saying that outside of the state we lack—as a matter of *principle*—the criteria that allow us to differentiate between just and unjust. According to this latter interpretation Aristotle comes all of a sudden to look much more Hobbesian, however: outside the *polis* there is but an amoral state of nature, inhabited by humans "full of lust and gluttony," resembling the "most savage of animals."[83] Compare this with Hobbes' famous account of the state of nature:

> Hereby it is manifest, that during the time men live without a common Power to keep them all in awe, they are in that condition which is called Warre; and such a warre, as is of every man, against every man. ... To this warre of every man against every man, this also is consequent; that nothing can be Unjust. The notions of Right and Wrong, Justice and Injustice have there no place. Where there is no common Power, there is no Law: where no Law, no Injustice.[84]

Maybe this softening of the distinctions between Aristotle and Hobbes amounts to too extreme an interpretation. What is important for Aristotle is the idea that the state comes about by nature, yet by "nature" we may not simply think of the biological nature of human beings (Julia Annas' "mere nature"). Hobbes' view is similar to a certain extent in that he also thinks that humans were placed into their "ill" natural condition by "meer Nature," but "with a possibility to come out

82. Arist. *Pol.* 1.1253a37-39.

83. Ibid. 1.1253a36-37.

84. Hobbes, *Leviathan*, vol. 2, ch. 13, pp. 192, 196.

of it, consisting partly in the Passions, partly in [their] Reason."[85] This "possibility to come out" of the natural state is natural too for Hobbes, and closer to "mere nature" than it is for Aristotle. We need to keep in mind, however, that Aristotle operates with a normatively charged notion of human nature which locates the essence of the good life in virtue and in habits developed under the guidance of reason. This is consistent with Aristotle's account of the end of the state, which is of course very different for him than it is for Hobbes. Aristotle's has been a very influential view of the good life, of course, but any political theory built on it is bound to have strongly anti-egalitarian tendencies, since it is only a minority that is adequately equipped and can afford the leisure to develop the relevant virtues. These tendencies have been pointed out and criticized with biting wit by Hobbes himself, in a passage from the fifteenth chapter worth quoting in full:

> The question who is the better man, has no place in the condition of meer Nature; where, (as has been shewn before,) all men are equall. The inequallity that now is, has bin introduced by the Lawes civill. I know that *Aristotle* in the first booke of his Politiques, for a foundation of his doctrine, maketh men by Nature, some more worthy to Command, meaning the wiser sort (such as he thought himself to be for his Philosophy;) others to Serve (meaning those that had strong bodies, but were not Philosophers as he;) as if Master and Servant were not introduced by consent of men, but by difference of Wit: which is not only against reason; but also against experience. For there are very few so foolish, that had not rather governe themselves, than be governed by others: Nor when the wise in their own conceit, contend by force, with them who distrust their owne wisdome, do they alwaies, or often, or almost at any time, get the Victory.[86]

Aristotle's political theory presupposes effectively a majority of economically active people which cannot have a place in his ideal state as described in books 7 and 8 of the *Politics*. This leads Aristotle to exclude this majority of farmers, traders, and craftsmen from political rights and from citizenship, an exclusion justified by reference to the doctrine alluded to by Hobbes, where some men are "by Nature, . . . more worthy to Command, . . . others to Serve (meaning those that had strong bodies, but were not Philosophers as he)." "Nature" here must presumably be understood as "mere nature." C. C. W. Taylor has described this

85. Ibid., p. 196.

86. Ibid., ch. 15, p. 234.

view incisively as follows, drawing attention to some internal inconsistencies of the Aristotelian picture:

> As it stands, the co-called ideal polis is not a political community at all, since it is not self-sufficient for life, much less the good life (1252b27-30). Rather, it is an exploiting elite, a community of free-riders whose ability to pursue the good life is made possible by the willingness of others to forgo that pursuit. Even leaving aside the question of slavery, the 'ideal' polis is thus characterized by systematic injustice.[87]

Given Aristotle's own criterion of self-sufficiency, the reliance of his ideal state on non-citizen labor is contradictory. The ideal state is supposed to make possible the objectively good and successful life and happiness, but it can do this exclusively for those of its inhabitants who already have the natural requirements at their disposal and who can, by virtue of their nature, develop the virtues necessary for the good life. The development of these virtues in turn requires leisure, which is incompatible with productive activity and money-making. The goods of the community, political rights as well as material goods, are thus only or mostly accorded to an elite.[88]

For our purposes the most important point lies in Aristotle's political anthropology and its claim to be able to determine what objectively constitutes the good life and what we should objectively want and aspire to (as opposed to what we ourselves may accidentally happen to want). This objective end, the good life, is what the ideal state is based on in Aristotle's account, with the result that the state can now be understood as a machinery achieving educational goals, namely the development of virtuous traits for the members of the citizen elite and ultimately the achievement of the good life for the elite. This educational machinery does not conflict with any human or constitutional rights on the part of the citizens, let alone the other non-citizen inhabitants of the ideal state; while the citizen elite do have political rights, there are no institutionalized rights apart from

87. Taylor, "Politics," p. 250.

88. It is instructive to realize that this anti-egalitarian distribution of goods would not be accepted by other philosophical schools of classical antiquity; but this is so both because they do not agree on what constitutes an actual good and because they do not agree on distribution. Stoics and Christians would oppose Aristotle on both counts: goods should be distributed equally, but since political rights and material goods do not constitute actual goods, their ability to live the good life may not be impeded in Aristotle's ideal state. Democrats, on the other hand, would largely agree with Aristotle on what constitutes the relevant goods, but would insist on the equal distribution of these goods.

rights to political participation for them or anyone else. Why not? What is the content, then, of the various "constitutions" (*politeiai*) described by Aristotle?

An answer to this question requires us to turn to Aristotle's conception of constitution. It is customary to translate the Greek term *politeia* with "constitution." If we seek to clarify Aristotle's conception of constitution we have first to pay attention to his use of this term and to the relationship between *politeia* and the state (*polis*) in his thought. Aristotle writes that the state is a collection or composite, made up of "the citizens, who compose it" (ἡ γὰρ πόλις πολιτῶν τι πλῆθός ἐστιν)[89] and that the essence of the state needs to be identified as a collection of citizens "sufficiently numerous to secure independence of life" (πόλιν δὲ τὸ τῶν τοιούτων πλῆθος ἱκανὸν πρὸς αὐτάρκειαν ζωῆς).[90] Aristotle goes on to ask the question whether the state (*polis*) itself changes when its *politeia* changes and develops his conception of constitution by means of this question. He answers the question in the affirmative and says that whether a given state is to be seen as the same or a different one has to be decided with a view to its *politeia* (εἰς τὴν πολιτείαν βλέποντας): "it is evident that the sameness of the state consists chiefly in the sameness of the constitution," regardless of whether the inhabitants change.[91] The constitution (*politeia*) is thus made the decisive criterion, in a departure from his earlier focus on the citizenry. Aristotle illustrates this by reference to an analogy, comparing the state to the chorus in a play, where the "tragic differs from a comic chorus, although the members of both may be identical."[92] The *politeia* thus characterizes the state in a decisive way—but what is it exactly that Aristotle means by *politeia*?

Here is Aristotle's well-known definition of *politeia*, which precedes the no less famous passage on the classification of constitutions:

> A constitution (πολιτεία) is the arrangement (τάξις) of magistracies in a state (πόλις), especially of the highest of all. The government (πολίτευμα) is everywhere supreme in the state, and the government virtually is the constitution. For example, in democracies the people are supreme (κύριος), but in oligarchies, the few; and, therefore, we say that these two constitutions also are different: and so in other cases.[93]

89. Arist. *Pol.* 3.1274b41. Trans. Rackham.

90. Ibid. 3.1275b20. Trans. Rackham.

91. Ibid. 3.1276b10-13. Trans. ed. J. Barnes.

92. Ibid. 3.1276b4-6.

93. Ibid. 3.1278b9-15. Trans. ed. J. Barnes, with some adaptations.

The passage is ambiguous. The arrangement or ordering of the magistracies in the state is said to *be* the constitution. The highest magistracy is the most important one, and it, the *politeuma*, is also identified with the constitution. It is thus the hierarchic ordering or arrangement of magistracies and political organs which determines what kind of constitution we have. This is consistent with the earlier chorus analogy, which also seemed to suggest that each constitution arranges the citizens of any given *polis* in a typical way.[94] Whatever authority gets to decide last—the decider of last resort, the supreme authority—determines what kind of constitution it is we are talking about. We would say that where the people are sovereign, we are dealing with a democracy. Yet Aristotle's classification of constitutions, while starting out by differentiating between the various *politeiai* merely on *formal* grounds (rule by many, by few, by one), is now enriched by an added layer of *normative* criteria, which yields three "correct" and three "incorrect" types of constitutions.[95] This move added the novel normative view that the orders that Plato had only deemed "lawful" were actually in Aristotle's view "correct" if and only if its rulers—its *politeuma*—aim at the common advantage of the city rather than their own potentially despotic factional interest. It is crucial to bear in mind, however, that for Aristotle it is ultimately the rulers' *ethical* qualities, not constitutional forms, that are decisive. And in the real world of "incorrect" constitutions, constitutional issues for Aristotle are mostly conceived of in terms of claims for honors and economic rewards of socioeconomic classes, not in terms of claims of individuals against the state.

Indeed, it should be noticed that ultimately economic and ethical criteria trump formal criteria. Undermining effectively his initial formal scheme, Aristotle implies that a state in which a poor minority rules over a rich majority is a democracy, and one where many rich rule over a minority of poor citizens is an oligarchy.[96] The ideal state presented in books 7 and 8 of the *Politics* is a eudaemonistic organization strongly reminiscent of Plato's *Laws* and aiming at the happiness of its exclusive citizenry; it is situated beyond the classification of constitutions developed in book 3 and cannot effortlessly be fitted into it. What kind of *politeia* (according to the scheme in book 3) the ideal state represents seems, astonishingly, of no interest. Even within the classification of *politeiai* in book 3 the normative differentiation between "correct" and "incorrect" constitutions is not really bound up with any one of the formal kinds of constitution. Ultimately for a constitution to qualify as "correct" it is irrelevant whether rule

---

94. Cf. Newman, *Politics*, vol. 3, p. 153.

95. Arist. *Pol.* 3.1279a22-1279b10.

96. Ibid. 3.1279b20-1280a6.

is exercised by one, by a few, or by many; all these types can be "correct" *without reference to* their legal or institutional framework, as long as it is the advantage of the whole state that is aimed at and not the interests of a faction or, as in the ideal state, as long as education, virtue, and thus happiness are being furthered.[97] This is so probably for the reason explained in book 3: men outstanding in virtue cannot be legislated for by the others; "there can be no law (*nomos*) dealing with such men as those described, for they are themselves a law (*nomos*)."[98]

It is crucial that Aristotle first uses descriptive criteria to differentiate between types of constitutions. Then, when judging normatively, he still considers various types that are formally distinct. It seems to me that this shows that Aristotle—much like a sociologist, anthropologist, or political scientist in our own time—is applying a conception of constitution (*politeia*) that is purely empirical and serves to describe the power relations that actually obtain. The fifth book of the *Politics* is replete with fine-grained historical-empirical descriptions of constitutional change, most of them motivated by socioeconomic interests. Whenever Aristotle judges city-states and their governments normatively, he does so not from the point of view of the constitutional form, but in terms of the ethical qualities of the rulers. It should be clear by now that this is a conception of constitution that is very different indeed from that we encountered in Cicero and in late republican Roman thought in Chapters 1 through4.

One might object that Aristotle elevates legality, or the rule of law (the observance of *nomos*), into a criterion for correct and stable constitutions and that in this we seem to encounter a conception of constitution much more akin to the Roman one described earlier. In the third book we find, for example, the famous remarks on why the rule of law should be preferred as more rational than the rule of one or even of the best.[99] But even here it seems to me that what Aristotle means by *nomos* is the actually existing order (*taxis*) rather than a *normative*, higher-order set of legal rules. The descriptive character of what is meant by "law" here becomes increasingly clear when we see that Aristotle goes on to base the law ultimately on custom (*ethos*) and that nowhere are there any specifications or requirements as regards the content of the *nomoi*—there are no substantive goals that the *nomoi* are asked to enforce. At most what is at stake is what we

97. In book 4 Aristotle characterizes the "polity," now qualified as a mix between democracy and oligarchy, as merely the second-best constitution, inferior to the ideal state (leaving the options of aristocracy and monarchy as ideal constitutions on the table: 1289a32f.). These doubts as to the "correctness" of the "polity" are very much connected with typically Aristotelian doubts concerning the ability and virtuousness of the many.

98. Arist. *Pol.* 3.1284a13-14.

99. Ibid. 3.1287a15-1287b35.

would call "rule of law," that is to say a formal preference for rule-guided over arbitrary behavior that is, however, empty in terms of content. This is, of course, highly important in its own right and differs notably from Plato's views, but it has absolutely no bearing on a normative conception of constitution beholden to the protection of pre-political rights. The specific function of Aristotle's state, the purpose of the *polis*, is the good life, and it can be achieved on a spectrum of legal-institutional arrangements; but a determination, on substantive grounds, of the legitimate scope of the authority of the state Aristotle does not give us. He admits as much when he writes:

> Someone may say that it is bad in any case for a man, subject as he is to all the accidents of human passion, to be supreme (κύριος), rather than the law. But what if the law itself be democratic or oligarchical, how will that help us out of our difficulties? Not at all; the same consequences will follow.[100]

Aristotle seemingly comes close to a stronger, normative conception of constitution when he qualifies the rule of the *nomoi* as follows:

> [L]aws, when good, should be supreme (τοὺς νόμους εἶναι κυρίους); and . . . the magistrate—whether it be one or several—should regulate those matters only on which the laws are unable to speak with precision owing to the difficulty of any general principle embracing all particulars. But what are correctly established laws (τοὺς ὀρθῶς κειμένους νόμους) has not yet been clearly explained; the old difficulty remains. The goodness or badness, justice or injustice, of laws varies of necessity with the constitution of states. This, however, is clear, that the laws must be adapted to the constitutions. But, if so, correct constitutions will of necessity have just laws, and perverted forms of government will have unjust laws.[101]

Correct *politeiai* produce just laws, with the justice of the laws determined relative to the constitution in question. But as we have seen, the correctness of a constitution is itself determined by the aims of the *politeuma*, that is to say by the ethical qualities of the rulers. Here too we ultimately arrive at a *descriptive*, positivist conception of constitution, where *politeia* means once again merely the correct ordering of magistracies, aimed at granting political

---

100. Ibid. 3.1281a35-39. Trans. ed. J. Barnes, with slight adaptation.

101. Ibid. 3.1282b1-14. Trans. ed. J. Barnes, with adaptations.

rights to those with the right character disposition, i.e., to the virtuous. The *nomoi* themselves are simply reflections of the kind of constitution they have been enacted under, which throws us back to the fact that we are not given any substantive criteria with which to mark the best constitutional order. Above the *nomoi*, in other words, there is the Aristotelian preoccupation with the good life, but there are no institutional restraints on the content of those laws themselves.[102]

Aristotle does broach the problem of restraining legislative activity on the basis of some substantive criteria—what might be called the problem of constitutionalism *tout court*—especially when he discusses the relationship between supreme authority (*to kurion*) and private property. I do not believe, however, that the solution envisaged by Aristotle to this problem is really a *constitutional* solution; rather, it relies on education and virtue. Here is the relevant passage, which resembles a public debate:

> There is also a doubt as to what is to be the supreme power in the state: Is it the multitude? Or the wealthy? Or the good? Or the one best man? Or a tyrant? Any of these alternatives seems to involve disagreeable consequences. If the poor, for example, because they are more in number, divide among themselves the property of the rich—is not this unjust (ἄδικον)? No, by heaven (will be the reply), for the supreme authority willed it in due form (δικαίως). But if this is not extreme injustice (ἀδικίαν), what is? Again, when in the first division all has been taken, and the majority divide anew the property of the minority, is it not evident, if this goes on, that they will ruin the state? Yet surely, virtue (ἀρετή) is not the ruin of those who possess it, nor is justice destructive of a state; and therefore this law (νόμον) of confiscation clearly cannot be just (δίκαιον). If it were, all the acts of a tyrant must of necessity be just; for he only coerces other men by superior power, just as the multitude coerce the rich.[103]

---

102. In more defective regimes, Aristotle appreciates (see *Pol.* 4.1292a5-7) the formal distinction between general *nomoi* and ad hoc *psephismata* and the hierarchy between the two—a feature of fourth-century Athens, as we shall see in the next section. But this, too, is merely positivist constitutionalism, if it is constitutionalism at all, and very different indeed from the natural law arguments on which Cicero had based his constitutionalism.

103. Arist. *Pol.* 3.1281a11-24. Trans. ed. J. Barnes, adapted. Newman points out, correctly, that the point made by the defender of the supremacy of the multitude amounts to the view that "what the supreme authority decides is *ipso facto* just." He thus wants to translate δικαίως as "justly," not as "with full legal validity." But that omits one step in the argument, which amounts to the claim that what is enacted in due form *is* just; the point trades on the ambiguity in the Greek. Newman, *Politics*, vol. 3, p. 210.

Here we see Aristotle approaching a constitutional viewpoint, yet we are bound to run into difficulties if we were to push this interpretation too far. First of all, we should notice that the claim that the described confiscation is an injustice relies on an empirical premise, namely that such confiscation would ruin the state. This premise is more than dubious, however. And suppose it did not ruin the state, then, on Aristotle's own view, the argument fails (though valid, it would not be sound), and a confiscation as described would have to be qualified as not only enacted in due form but also as just. It is important to note that this is so because the criterion of a pre-political inviolable right is absent in Aristotle's account. Second, apart from the problem with the empirical premise that private property is of some utility to the state and therefore deserving of protection, Aristotle's sympathies for private property are due to his particular views on the virtue of generosity. Without private property, generosity would lapse.[104] Therefore the protection of private property depends on a particular view of the state which sees the state as an educational organization charged with equipping the citizenry with the virtues necessary for the good life. If generosity were not a virtue, or if generosity were conceivable without private property, private property would not on this account be worthy of protection. Virtue, not property, is central.

A constitutionalist interpretation of the passage quoted above raises a third issue. The validity of confiscation based on a decree of the popular assembly is at least on a procedural level unassailable; although Aristotle polemically likens it to the coercion exercised by a tyrant by superior power, there surely is a difference between the duly enacted decree and the tyrant's raw power.[105] The fact that it has been "duly enacted" would seem to imply a higher-order rule that spells out the criteria for what is, and what is not, lawful (δικαίως). So in a very weak sense it might be said that Aristotle here implies a concept of constitution, but it would be a concept that is merely procedural, without specifying anything of substance beyond what is procedurally correct. It is only in this weak sense, then, that we may call this view a constitutionalist one; compared to the constitutionalism of the late Roman Republic this is a very thin constitutionalism indeed.

---

104. Arist. *Pol.* 2.1263b5-14. See the discussion, and criticism of Aristotle's defense of private property, in Irwin, *Aristotle's First Principles*, pp. 462–466.

105. Newman suggests that Aristotle here probably had Xen. *Mem.* 1.2.42-46 before him; there, too, any distinction between a procedurally valid enactment and brute force is leveled out. For Alcibiades, as portrayed by Xenophon, the crucial criterion is persuasion; enactments that do not persuade the citizenry as a whole are imposed by force (1.2.45). This contrast between force and persuasion is of course prominent in Plato's *Laws*, where it leads to his highly original idea of adding preambles to his laws, thus "mixing" persuasion with force: Pl. *Leg.* 722b4-c2. As Annas points out, persuasion is never to be used alone in the *Laws*, only mixed with force: "Virtue and Law in Plato," p. 76.

Greek constitutionalism?

There is an obvious objection to my line of reasoning. We have been comparing Greek political theory with Roman constitutional thought, treating the latter as it arose from the context of the conflicts of the late Republic, and tracing it both on the elevated level of political theory and, closer to the ground, on the level of arguments put forward from within the political conflicts. By contrast, we have looked at Greek political theory, which operates at a high level of abstraction; what about Greek institutions? Did not the Athenian city-state provide for procedures against those who tried to circumvent existing laws (*nomoi*)? Were not these laws, at least from the reestablishment of democracy in 403 BC onward, more firmly entrenched and of a higher order than mere decrees (*psephismata*)? And did not the fact that it was open to any citizen to prosecute the proposer of any law that the accuser deemed to be in conflict with existing *nomoi*, i.e., the *graphe paranomon*, entail the possibility of something similar to judicial review, where lower-level legislation is scrutinized as to its validity under higher-order norms?

Before we get to Athenian institutions and forensic oratory, let me address one further potential candidate for Greek constitutionalism: unwritten laws, or the related concept of natural justice, as it appears especially in the context of fifth century debates touching upon the notorious distinction between *nomos* and *phusis*.[106] Did not the idea of a natural law first arise in connection with this cluster of notions? Is constitutionalism, and the idea of higher-order legal rules, not something that can be traced back to earlier ideas of natural justice and, say, Antigone's concept of an unwritten law? I do not intend to spend much time dealing with these questions, for reasons put forward by Gisela Striker. In an important essay, Striker has argued very convincingly that the concept of natural justice, which was familiar to both Plato and Aristotle (and, one might add, some of the sophists), cannot be interpreted to imply the notion of natural law. This is so, Striker points out, because "the terms 'just' or 'justice' refer to certain states of affairs or ways of acting that ensure the stability and flourishing of communities," while it is not at all clear that those ways of acting "must necessarily be captured by a set of unchanging rules." She concludes that "there might be a concept of natural justice, but there need not be a corresponding notion of natural law." Crediting the Stoics with the innovation of the concept of natural law, she suspects that Plato and Aristotle "would have rejected the

106. See Hirzel, *Agraphos nomos*; Ehrenberg, *Rechtsidee*; Ehrenberg, *Sophocles*; Ostwald, *Nomos*; Ostwald, "Was There a Concept?"

idea of morality as natural law."[107] Striker thinks that both Plato and Aristotle "indeed hold that there is an objective, 'natural' standard of justice;" but they decidedly do "not believe that this standard is given by anything that could be called natural law." There is a natural quality to justice qua virtue, she argues, but "this virtue does not seem to be defined by reference to any natural *law*."[108] The sophist Callicles, who puts forward for the first time the phrase "law of nature" (νόμος τῆς φύσεως) in Plato's *Gorgias*,[109] is quite obviously trying to make a paradoxical, shocking point against the background of the sharp sophistic distinction between *nomos* and *phusis*; he is not, however, trying to give any rule-based content to this "law of nature" of his.[110] The key difference between the rule-based concept of natural law that originated with the Stoics and the idea of natural justice current earlier is captured succinctly by Striker: "while Plato and Aristotle start from the notion of justice as a good or right state of affairs, or action apt to produce such a state, and then describe good or just laws as necessarily imperfect prescriptions about how to achieve such a good state, the Stoics begin with the notion of goodness as rational order and regularity, and then define virtue and just conduct in terms of obedience to the laws of nature."[111] This key difference between the Stoic innovation and their predecessors leads Striker to see the Stoic conception of natural law as the true predecessor of modern, "deontological" theories of morality. While I agree with Striker that the Greek Stoics must have been the original innovators of such a natural law doctrine, it was not until Cicero's *Laws* that this doctrine was given detailed content and was formulated in a coherent way. It was in Cicero's formulation that the ideal of a system of natural legal rules, predestined for constitutionalism, gained the enormous influence it has exercised in the history of political and legal thought.[112]

What about the concept of "unwritten law" (ἄγραφος νόμος)? It has been argued that what is meant here is a universally valid divine law, and that this conception, conceived even before the sophists, is the legitimate precursor of natural law.[113] But it has been appreciated, rightly, by Martin Ostwald among

107. Striker, "Origins," pp. 210–211. For a summary of the debate on the origins of the concept of natural law, see Miller, "Stoics, Grotius and Spinoza," pp. 117–120.

108. Striker, "Origins," pp. 214–215. My emphasis.

109. Pl. *Grg.* 483e6.

110. Striker, "Origins," p. 212.

111. Ibid. p. 219.

112. See Watson, "Natural Law and Stoicism."

113. See, e.g., Pizzorni, *Diritto naturale*, pp. 19–20.

others, that what *nomos* means from Hesiod to the tragic poets,[114] is not "'law' or 'ordinance' which prescribes a certain kind of behaviour," rather, the term "designates the behaviour itself." It is "an order of living, a way of life, which Zeus has given to men," and that it is "god-given is only incidental." This is the sense of *nomos* we encounter in *Antigone* as well: the unwritten laws Antigone relies on against Creon's written rules are of divine origin, but here, too, what is meant is a certain kind of behavior that is sanctioned by them, the customs of a country.[115] Pindar's famous fragment declaring *nomos* to be "king of all, both mortals and immortals," is quoted in Plato's *Gorgias* by Callicles to support his notorious view of a "law of nature" which allows for violations by the strong of positive, man-made law. It has been argued that *nomos* here must be understood to mean the will of Zeus;[116] but as Guthrie has correctly pointed out, Pindar rather straightforwardly says that Zeus himself is subject to *nomos*, "which lords it over gods as well as men."[117] This leads Guthrie to the very plausible interpretation that what Pindar has in mind here is that "[r]ecognized custom (usage, tradition) has immense power. Both gods and men conform to it, and any act, however wrong or terrible it may seem in itself, will, if only it becomes sanctioned by *nomos*, appear to be justified."[118]

In sum, neither Pindar's *nomos*, nor Sophocles' *agraphos nomos*, nor the concept of natural justice put forward by Plato and Aristotle are candidates for the kind of rule-based natural law that provides the foundation, as we have seen, for Cicero's pre-political normative system that can be used to provide a constitutional yardstick for lower-level legal rules. The conceptions put forward by Plato and Aristotle do provide a normative order, it is true, and their "naturalness" fulfills the same function natural law proper provides, namely objectivity. This is not true for the other concepts of *nomos* we briefly discussed here, which are all ultimately used in order to describe customary arrangements that derive their validity from nothing deeper than having been in place for a long time and that do not exhibit any normative pull. However, while there is really nothing in

114. See, e.g., Hes. *Op.* 276-280; Thgn. 289-290; Soph. *Ant.* 450–460; Eur. *Hipp.* 98; Eur. *Supp.* 377–378; see also Ar. *Av.* 1344–1345; Pl. *Prt.* 337c-338b. See Ostwald, *Nomos*, pp. 20–22.

115. See Guthrie, *Fifth-Century Enlightenment*, pp. 119–129. Cf. Ehrenberg, *Rechtsidee*, p. 113, n. 6.

116. See, e.g., Gigante, *Nomos Basileus*, pp. 72–108.

117. Guthrie, *Fifth-Century Enlightenment*, p. 133. I follow his discussion at pp. 131–134.

118. Ibid., p. 134. This is very similar to Ehrenberg's position that Pindar here means "alte heilige Sitte," which sanctions even violence: *Rechtsidee*, p. 120. See Hdt. 3.38 for confirmation that Pindar was referring to the power of custom.

Greek thought that corresponds to the kind of natural-law based constitutionalism put forward especially by Cicero, there might have existed, in the institutional reality of fourth-century Athens, rudiments of entrenched, higher-order rules that would seem to qualify as constitutional in the relevant sense.

Let us now turn to these institutions and decide to what exent we can detect any constitutional aspects there. It is indeed perfectly true, as we shall see, that certain aspects of the institutional reality of Athenian democracy lend themselves to being described in constitutionalist terms, at the latest in the fourth century BC.[119] This institutional reality, however, unlike the Roman case, has hardly had any resonance in subsequent political *thought*. This holds for classical antiquity, where these constitutionalist aspects enter political rhetoric in the speeches of fourth-century orators, but do not take hold in political thought beyond those speeches. This holds even more for the later reception of Athenian history in European intellectual history, where the received wisdom on the history of the democratic regime of Athens usually ends with the Arginusae trial and where these constitutionalist aspects met with very little interest indeed. There are exceptions—David Hume, for one, thought that the law establishing the *graphe paranomon* had been "remarkable" and goes on to describe it as follows:

> By the *graphe paranomon*, or *indictment of illegality*, (though it has not been remarked by antiquaries or commentators) any man was tried and punished in a common court of judicature, for any law which had passed upon his motion, in the assembly of the people, if that law appeared to the court unjust, or prejudicial to the public.[120]

Hume is inaccurate in saying that only laws "which had passed" were potentially subject to an indictment under the *graphe paranomon*; in fact, the mover of a mere proposal could be so indicted, and the indictment itself was sufficient to

119. Even in the fifth century there are signs of entrenchment clauses in Athenian enactments seeking to protect these norms from being overturned; see, e.g., Hdt. 1.29, for time-limited entrenchment by oath of Solon's enactments. See Dem. 23.62 for an entrenchment clause presumably stemming from the time of Drakon. However, as Melissa Schwartzberg has argued, there are good reasons to think that entrenchment clauses were overwhelmingly used in an international setting in order to entrench alliances and conduct foreign policy more efficiently, rather than in domestic constitutional settings. In the domestic setting, Schwartzberg claims ("Athenian Democracy," p. 323), the "Athenians understood that the law would be unable to restrain a determined *demos*."

120. Hume, "Remarkable Customs," p. 180.

suspend proposals as well as laws which had already been passed in the assembly.[121] Hume, expressing perfectly conventional views on democratic Athens,[122] thought that the "Athenian Democracy was such a tumultuous government as we can scarcely form a notion of in the present age of the world," where the "whole collective body of the people voted in every law," without "controul from any magistracy or senate; and consequently without regard to order, justice, or prudence."[123] The "remarkable" *graphe paranomon* was in his view both an attempt to rein in demagogues, and thus provide a check on the legislative actions of the assembly, as well as a necessary condition for democracy to exist. Hume commented very wryly on the *graphe*'s function as a check. The Athenians did recognize the "mischiefs" and dangers inherent in the lack of control of the assembly in their constitution, according to Hume:

> But being averse to checking themselves by any rule or restriction, they resolved, at least, to check their demagogues or counsellors, by the fear of future punishment and enquiry. They accordingly instituted this remarkable law; a law esteemed so essential to their form of government, that Aeschines insists on it as a known truth, that, were it abolished or neglected, it were impossible for the Democracy to subsist.[124]

So what exactly was that "remarkable law"? The indictment *paranomon*, or charge of illegality or unconstitutionality (it is better at this point to leave this open in order not to prejudice the question), was a procedure that had first been established in the fifth century BC. The first time we have datable evidence for a *graphe paranomon* is in 415 BC, but the procedure is likely to be somewhat older than that.[125] With the *graphe* any citizen could prosecute the proposer of a law or decree of the people's assembly that was suspected of violating existing laws. The

121. On the *graphe paranomon*, see Wolff, *"Normenkontrolle" und Gesetzesbegriff*; Bleicken, "Verfassungsschutz"; id., *Demokratie*, pp. 385–389; Hansen, *Democracy*, pp. 161–162, 205–212; id., *Sovereignty of the People's Court*; Yunis "Law, Politics and the *Graphe Paranomon*"; Carawan, "Trial of the Arginousai Generals"; Lanni, "Judicial Review"; Schwartzberg, "*Graphe Paranomon*." On the suspension of proposed as well as enacted legislation, see Hansen, "*Graphe Paranomon*."

122. See Roberts, *Athens on Trial*.

123. Hume, "Remarkable Customs," p. 181.

124. Ibid.

125. Some scholars date it shortly after the reforms of Ephialtes (462/461 BC); see, e.g., Bleicken, *Demokratie*, p. 386. However, 415 is the only certain date we have (Andoc. 1.17), and Wolff, *"Normenkontrolle,"* pp. 15–22 convinces me that the *graphe* is not likely to have originated before 427 BC. See also Ostwald, *Popular Sovereignty*, pp. 135–136.

indictment had the effect of suspending the law in question and could be brought both against legislation that had already been passed in the assembly and against proposals. The charge was brought in a jury court and, if successful, had the effect of punishing the proposer of the legislation severely. If the proposer was acquitted and the legislation thus deemed consistent with existing *nomoi*, this resulted in the legislation being either reinstated (if it had already passed the assembly) or, remarkably, in the proposed legislation being enacted (without its having to pass the assembly at all and with the jury court thus acting as legislating sovereign).[126] As Hume noted, Aeschines in 330 BC thought the *graphe* constituted the bulwark of democracy; [127] this was indeed a topos of fourth-century rhetoric, and was certainly a plausible idea given that the oligarchic coup of 411 BC, amidst the Peloponnesian War, abolished the *graphe paranomon* as a preliminary to abolishing the democratic regime. It is still a widely held view among scholars today.[128]

In the fifth century, the *graphe* could be used against proposers of laws and decrees alike, as both *nomoi* and *psephismata* were passed in the people's assembly. After the reestablishment of democracy in 403 BC, surely as a consequence of the way the democratic regime had been subverted in both 411 and 404, important reforms of the legislative process took place which entailed some changes for the *graphe paranomon* as well. In 411, the oligarchs, according to Thucydides, had brought "no other measure" before the people "except the bare proposal that any Athenian should be permitted with impunity to offer any motion he pleased; and if anyone should move to indict the speaker for making an illegal proposal (γράψηται παρανόμων) . . . they imposed severe penalties upon him."[129] The people's assembly itself then proceeded without any opposition from anyone to ratify the abolition of the *graphe paranomon* as well as the entire democratic regime (ἡ ἐκκλησία οὐδενὸς ἀντειπόντος, ἀλλὰ κυρώσασα ταῦτα διελύθη).[130] The Aristotelian *Athenaion Politeia* also describes the abolition of the *graphe*, as well as of another legal device designed to protect the fifth-century democratic order, the charge (*eisangelia*) brought against citizens alleged to be guilty of treason (especially against the subverters of democracy).[131] Given the (however brief) success of the

126. Also, in order to prevent frivolous accusations from being filed, there was a fine for anyone who brought the charge *paranomon* without being able to convince at least a fifth of the jurors of his case.

127. Hume has in mind Aeschin. *In Ctes.* 5.

128. See, e.g., Hansen, *Democracy*, p. 211.

129. Thuc. 8.67. Trans. Charles Forster Smith.

130. Ibid. 8.69.

131. *Ath. Pol.* 29.4.

oligarchic coup of 411, and given that the assembly itself had sanctioned its own demise, there is good reason to think that the changes introduced when the democratic order was reestablished in 403 BC (after the second crisis in 404/403) were at least partly owed to the desire to prevent similarly self-undermining decisions from occurring in the assembly. It is to these changes that we now turn, and to the impact they had on the most important institutions of Greek constitutionalism: the *graphe paranomon* itself, a related charge introduced in or soon after 403 (the *nomon me epitedeion theinai*) and the procedure of legislation (*nomothesia*); procedures to hold magistrates accountable (*euthunai*) and impeachments for treason (*eisangeliai*), chief among them charges of the subversion of democracy (*katalusis tou demou*), also belong in this context.[132]

When democracy was restored in 410 after the first oligarchic coup, a major collection of all existing written laws (*nomoi*) was undertaken. After democracy was restored again in 403 after the rule of the Thirty, this project was resumed, and the laws were collected and scrutinized by commissions of legislators, so-called *nomothetai*.[133] Importantly, changes to this codification of written laws were henceforth to be subject to a new legislative procedure: amendments and changes of *nomoi* were no longer decided upon in the people's assembly, but rather in a new legislative body of 501, 1001 or more *nomothetai*, "lawgivers," who were chosen from among those who had taken the oath to serve in the jury courts.[134] As Jochen Bleicken and others have pointed out, this is unlikely to have been intended or perceived as a derogation from the people's assembly's sovereignty, but it certainly separated the legislative process on a procedural level from other

132. We shall not dwell on charges of εἰσαγγελία here, but it is clear—especially given the parallel abolition of *eisangelia* and *graphe paranomon* in 411—that charges of treason for the subversion of democracy could be used as a safeguard more effectively once the hierarchy between entrenched *nomoi* and *psephismata* was in place and once *eisangelia* was enshrined in statute (*nomos*) and thus entrenched. See Hyp. 4.7-8, and Hansen, *Eisangelia*; Harris, "Open Texture"; id., *Rule of Law*, pp. 233–241. For the accountability for officeholders by way of *euthunai*, see Bleicken, *Demokratie*, pp. 326–329. It bears mentioning that the *euthunai* procedure, while establishing accountability for magistrates, could not hold the sovereign itself accountable, i.e., the people and the jurors: Thuc. 3.43.4-5.

133. For an excellent brief account of the legal reforms of the late fifth century, see Hansen, *Democracy*, 162–165; see also Lanni, *Law and Justice*, pp. 142–148, with further literature. In my view her account suffers, however, from an exaggeration of the changing nature of the Athenian law code after the reforms; she claims that the laws (*nomoi*) were "in constant flux," but that seems untenable in light of the few new laws we actually possess from the fourth century and given the entrechment provided to *nomoi* by *nomothesia* and the *graphai paranomon* and *nomon me epitedeion theinai*.

134. On *nomothesia*, see now Canevaro, "*Nomothesia*," with the relevant literature and evidence. On the judicial oath, see Harris, "Rule of Law."

decisions of the assembly.[135] Henceforth the laws (*nomoi*) that were passed by the *nomothetai* were seen as dealing with general and constitutional subject matter and, most importantly, were considered *superior* to mere situational decrees (*psephismata*) passed in the assembly. This *hierarchy of norms* between *nomoi* on one hand and *psephismata* on the other is surely a major argument for the existence, on the institutional level, of constitutionalism in Athens in the fourth century. We find the underlying principle prescribing the hierarchy of norms in Andocides: "No decree (*psephisma*) either of the Council or of the Assembly shall have superior authority to a law (*nomos*)."[136] This principle was itself framed as a law (*nomos*). The hierarchy found expression in the fact that henceforth (i.e., from 403 onwards) the *graphe paranomon* could be brought against proposers of decrees passed by the assembly on the ground that these *psephismata* violated higher-order norms contained in the *nomoi*.

Many scholars have described this as an early version of judicial review, and while it is true, as Melissa Schwartzberg has argued, that the Athenian courts cannot be seen as analogous to constitutional courts in our own day in that they did not embody any particular kind of legal expertise,[137] there is still a case to be made that the Athenian courts dealing with charges of *paranomon* did exercise the functional equivalent of judicial review. It is true that the courts embodied simply the people in a different procedural setting,[138] but, as Harvey Yunis convincingly argues, these different settings mattered a great deal: "the setting in court was far less amenable to the demagogue than the assembly. The prosecutor had a captive audience and an allotted time to speak; he prosecuted in the name of the law; he could subject the decree to the legal and political scrutiny it may not have received in the assembly; the jurors rendered their decision by secret ballot; and the mere act of reconsideration might serve to dispel the demagogue's

135. Bleicken, "Verfassungsschutz," p. 394; Ober, *Mass and Elite*, p. 144; Schwartzberg, "Judicial Review," p. 1052.

136. Andoc. 1.87. Many orators cite this statute, see, e.g., Dem. 23.87.

137. Schwartzberg, "Judicial Review," *passim* and esp. pp. 1060-1061. While it is certainly true that judicial review in the US exhibits an almost Platonic concern with expertise, one should not entirely discount at least some expertise, or at least experience, on the part of the Athenian dikasts: unlike jurors in modern jury courts, the dikasts decided routinely on all sorts of cases. See Lanni, *Law and Justice*; and now Harris, *Rule of Law*.

138. Jurors had to be at least 30 years old, and Adriaan Lanni thinks that this amounted to "a significant difference" from the assembly "in a society like Athens, where age was very strongly associated with wisdom and rationality": Lanni, "Judicial Review," p. 19. I agree with Josiah Ober and Schwartzberg that this should not be overemphasized and that the average jury was likely to have been very similar in composition to the average council or assembly: Ober, *Mass and Elite*, p. 144; Schwartzberg, "Judicial Review," p. 1052.

influence."[139] Yunis goes on to remind us of an important example, an indictment of *paranomon* where the court reversed a unanimous decision of the assembly.[140] This shows that at least in principle the courts judging a charge of *paranomon* could exercise judicial review. The citizens acting as jurors were bound by oath to cast their votes "according to the laws" (ψηφιοῦμαι κατὰ τοὺς νόμους),[141] and the prosecution usually argued their case by directly comparing written copies of the allegedly violated law(s) with copies of the violating decree.[142] This produced a reliance on laws (*nomoi*) and, most importantly, served to enforce the hierarchy between laws passed by the *nomothetai* on the one hand and mere decrees of the assembly on the other. The oath of the jurors must have had particular weight in a case of *paranomon*, given that it was precisely a given decree's conformity with the laws that was at stake in these indictments.[143] Furthermore, political considerations and arguments from expediency certainly had much more weight than constitutional ones in an assembly setting. In the courts, legal considerations were pivotal and indeed necessary for a prosecutor to gain a conviction: whether or not the *psephisma* in question was according to the laws was the very focus of the procedure.[144] By contrast, in the assembly the focus would often lie with considerations far removed from these constitutional issues. As Yunis points out, the "*graphe paranomon* should be viewed in the context of the nomothetic reforms

139. Yunis, "Law, Politics," p. 379.

140. [Dem.] 59.5. Yunis, "Law, Politics," p. 379, n. 54.

141. On the oath of the jurors and its reconstruction, see Mirhady, "Dikasts' Oath." See also Harris, "Rule of Law."

142. Yunis, "Law, Politics," p. 365 gives a good description and evidence.

143. This is an argument against Schwartzberg's view that the people in the assembly were similarly bound by their ephebic oath to follow the laws ("Judicial Review," pp. 1054–1055); given the assembly setting, this was simply not the main focus of the proceedings. The oath was obviously equally crucial to proceedings in *graphai nomon me epitedeion theinai*, as we shall see below.

144. Siding with Wolff on this issue I am not convinced by Yunis' view that the "legal plea, although necessary, was not by itself sufficient to convince the jurors to condemn an indicted decree." As an empirical observation, this is certainly true; but as a matter of law, the jury courts in *paranomon* cases were supposed to cast their votes on the basis of the legal plea only. The question is an old one: Max Fränkel thought that "die einzige Norm für die Urteilsfindung" had been "das subjective Belieben des Richters": *Geschworenengerichte*, pp. 109–110. Lanni, without referencing Fränkel, adopts a similar view but her portrayal is much more sympathetic, emphasizing that Athenians *chose* a very discretionary take on justice in the courts to reflect their democratic commitments: Lanni, *Law and Justice*, esp. pp. 41–74; she admits, however, that "the treatment of legal and extra-legal arguments was not . . . entirely symmetrical: law court speakers do not explicitly urge jurors to ignore the law in favor of fairness and other extra-legal considerations" (pp. 72–73). See also Lanni, "Judicial Review."

instituted at the end of the fifth century," as a means to "prevent the assembly from enacting such fundamental, statutory measures as the reforms aimed to relegate to the more deliberate, orderly procedure of *nomothesia*."[145]

The *graphe* must itself have been enshrined in a law (*nomos*)[146] and was thus itself insulated from the assembly—an absolutely crucial point in light of the fact that the oligarchs, when abolishing democracy in 411 BC, had deemed it key in their endeavor first to abolish the *graphe* in the assembly.[147] After *nomothesia* was established as the only procedure to change or amend existing written laws, a proposal to abolish the charge of *paranomon* would have had to undergo all the steps required of the nomothetic process: proposal before the assembly, publication of the proposal, submission of a draft of the proposal to the assembly by the council (*probouleuma*), decision of the assembly to establish a commission of 501 or more *nomothetai* from the roster of jurors, and then something resembling a trial before the *nomothetai*, with prosecutors arguing for a change or amendment to existing *nomoi* and defenders of the old *nomoi* against.[148] The proposer of changing or amending one of the existing *nomoi* was himself potentially subject to being indicted under the *graphe nomon me epitedeion theinai*, a charge which, in close analogy to the *graphe paranomon*, provided the option of additional review of changes to the *nomoi* in one of the people's courts. The set of *nomoi*, therefore, was a set of *deeply entrenched* norms. This is reflected in the fact that for the last eighty years of Athenian democracy, between 403 and 322 BC, we have record of several hundred enactments of the assembly while there are but seven laws (*nomoi*) passed in *nomothetai* commissions.[149] It is quite true that in the context of emergencies the law courts seem to have decided on prudential, rather than legal, grounds; but this hardly goes to show that the laws were not entrenched, nor that the courts did not as a rule exercise some kind of functional

145. Yunis, "Law, Politics," pp. 377–378. See also MacDowell, *Law in Classical Athens*, p. 48, arguing convincingly that the experience of the coup in 404 showed that what "was needed was a more careful check on legal changes before they took effect."

146. We do not have this law, but it is clear that the *graphe* cannot possibly have rested simply on a *psephisma*, or on some unwritten law—applying ἄγραφος νόμος was prohibited by law: Andoc. 1.85, 87, 89.

147. For the prohibition against enacting laws (*nomoi*) in the assembly, see Dem. 24.25, describing the nomothetic procedure prescribed by the laws, which puts legislation of *nomoi* in the hands of *nomothetai* exclusively.

148. On the procedure, see Canevaro, "*Nomothesia*." For different views, see Rhodes, "*Nomothesia*"; Hansen, "Athenian *nomothesia*"; Bleicken, *Demokratie*, pp. 216–224.

149. Bleicken, *Demokratie*, p. 223.

judicial review.[150] All it shows is that jurors were amenable to arguments pleading exceptional circumstances and necessity in cases of real existential danger.[151] On one pressing issue, the proposal of help for the Olynthians against Philip of Macedonia in 348 BC, a charge of *paranomon* was brought against the mover of a *psephisma* which allocated funds to the military. In this case, the proposer of the decree was found guilty of *paranomon*.[152] We do not know to what extent extra-legal arguments played a role, but it surely is significant that at the same time the *graphe* was argued in court, Demosthenes, in the *Third Olynthiac*, tried in a constitutionally cleaner way to convince the assembly to have the relevant laws (which seemed to prevent the allocation of funds to the military) repealed by *nomothetai* so that the funds could be used to help the Olynthians against Philip.[153] The whole episode stresses the entrenchment of the higher-order laws.

These higher-order laws, the *nomoi*, were further entrenched by the *graphe nomon me epitedeion theinai*, which allowed any citizen to challenge in court changed or amended *nomoi* that had been either proposed to the *nomothetai* or already been passed by them; as in the *graphe paranomon*, this charge was also usually directed against the proposer of the law and resulted, in the case of a successful prosecution, in severe punishment for the proposer and repeal of the law in question. It seems as if such a charge could only be leveled against a law immediately after it had been passed, and only during a brief period; once a certain amount of time had passed, the law became part of the code of *nomoi* and, thus entrenched, was changeable only by the *nomothetai*.[154] As with the *graphe paranomon*, legislation could be challenged both on procedural and on substantive grounds.[155] Laws that had been passed in violation of the nomothetic procedure were subject to challenge, as were laws that contradicted other statutes;

---

150. Hyp. frr. 27–28 Jensen; cf. Yunis, "Law, Politics," p. 376.

151. Similarly, the US Supreme Court usually defers to other branches of government in times of crisis and emergency rather than simply protecting constitutional rights; see Issacharoff and Pildes, "Emergency Contexts."

152. See Hansen, "The Theoric Fund."

153. Dem. 3.10. Cf. Yunis, "Law, Politics," pp. 373–375, who cites the incident as an example for the relative importance of arguments from expediency over *nomos*; I do not think the evidence warrants his conclusion.

154. The assumption of a brief time period after the enactment of a law during which it is still subject to the *graphe* is necessary, since we know that usually *nomoi* could be abrogated exclusively by the *nomothetai*, not by a court: Hansen, "Athenian *nomothesia*," p. 350.

155. Wolff thought that general principles played an important role as well; however, Sundahl, "Living Constitution," shows that the speeches by and large deploy arguments from procedure and from conflicts with particular laws.

if a contradictory law was proposed, any contradicting laws would have to be repealed by the proposer before the new one could be enacted.[156] Coherence within the body of higher-order *nomoi* is absolutely crucial, Demosthenes reminds the jurors, as the jurors in popular courts would otherwise be forced to break their oath: since contradictory laws would be equally valid, jurors could not follow one without violating another and thus breaking the oath.[157]

In a stimulating article, Adriaan Lanni has put forward the argument that both *graphai* were intended first and foremost to protect the democratic legislative and judicial process. She believes that the constitutionality of laws and decrees was challenged on the basis of a) "an appreciation for an overarching set of abstract democratic principles to which legislation must conform, independent of individual existing statutes," and that b) those "principles seem to have been limited to protecting popular decision making in the legislative and adjudicative process."[158] She believes that in this way the popular courts when deciding these cases actually performed a kind of "democratic judicial review," which she recommends as avoiding the central paradoxes of our own present-day judicial review. The Athenian judicial review on this view avoided the counter-majoritarian difficulty, since the Athenian courts were composed simply of the people in a different setting and because "constitutional principles could be overridden by the popular jury to further current policy interests."[159] Lanni adduces the Arginusae affair, interpreting Euryptolemus' unsuccessful attempt to challenge a decree in the assembly with a charge of *paranomon*—the first surviving discussion of a *paranomon* charge—as an application of the democratic principle to a right to a trial in the popular courts.[160]

It seems to me, however, that the Arginusae affair is less than conducive to this line of argument. It is very doubtful that "if the Athenians had employed their

156. Dem. 24.34.

157. Ibid. 24.34-35. When Lanni, *Law and Justice*, p. 148, writes that the effect of *nomothesia* was rather limited, she does not pay sufficient attention to the hierarchy of norms established by *nomothesia*, their entrenchment, and their coherence as enforced by the looming threat of a potential *graphe nomon me epitedeion theinai*. Of course judicial verdicts remained discretionary, but coherence between *nomoi* and positivist *Normenkontrolle* were things clearly aimed at, as Demosthenes' hint at the dikasts' oath shows.

158. Lanni, "Judicial Review," p. 8. Contra Wolff, she thinks that this set of abstract principles did not include any substantive moral values.

159. Lanni, "Judicial Review," p. 21. I do not find this convincing—they doubtless were at times thus overridden, but this was hardly what the speeches argued for, except perhaps in extreme emergency situations such as those alluded to in Hyp. frr. 27–28 Jensen and described in Lycurg. *Leoc.* 36–49.

160. Xen. *Hell.* 1.7.16-33.

judicial review procedures in this case the disastrous decision might have been averted."[161] Yet the constitutionalist, counter-majoritarian changes introduced in 403-399—hierarchy of norms and the entrenchment of *nomoi*—were very probably owed to experiences such as the Arginusae affair in the first place. The strict hierarchy between nomothetic laws and assembly decrees must have been introduced to safeguard against hasty decisions in the assembly. This is suggested by a passage from Demosthenes' *Against Leptines*, where Demosthenes adduces, in a charge *nomon me epitedeion theinai*, a law that Leptines' enactment had allegedly violated.[162] Under this law it was prohibited "to be passed haphazardly" simply to meet some emergency, and equally prohibited for a *nomos* thus passed to be at once valid without passing scrutiny.[163] It is important, Demosthenes says, for these laws' validity, to be thoroughly scrutinized, heard many times before the proper authority, and examined at leisure. "The aim" of the lawgiver "was for each of you to hear the laws many times and have a chance to study them at leisure and then enact those that were just and in the public interest."[164] There seems to have been a preliminary debate about proposals concerning *nomoi* in the assembly before the proposal was referred to the *nomothetai*,[165] which additionally slowed things down.[166] Allowing time to pass before passing higher-order norms was obviously a crucial factor in preventing radical, passionate change from happening and in allowing counterarguments to be heard.

These were all post-403 BC procedural innovations intended to make the legislative process less ad hoc and less volatile, especially as far as general *nomoi* are concerned, which govern the political order itself. Whether this insulation of legislation from quick decisions in the assembly is an expression of a particularly democratic mindset, as Lanni claims, is not obvious to me[167]—what better way of avoiding the counter-majoritarian difficulty than proceeding exactly as the assembly actually did with the Arginusae generals? But it is clear that the narrow procedural focus of the institutions discussed here made for a very narrow, positivist constitutionalism. This holds especially for the two *graphai*—for "judicial

---

161. Lanni, "Judicial Review," p. 22, n. 105.

162. This *graphe* was unusual, as the charge was heard after the statutory year had lapsed. For the details, see Hansen, "Athenian *nomothesia*"; Harris, *Demosthenes*, pp. 15–21; and cf. Kremmydas, *Commentary*.

163. Dem. 20.90. Trans. E. M. Harris.

164. Ibid. 94.

165. Hansen, "Athenian *nomothesia*," pp. 354–355.

166. See Bleicken, *Demokratie*, p. 387.

167. Lanni, "Judicial Review."

review." When Demosthenes faults, e.g., in an entirely typical way, a decree of the assembly for having been passed without a formal draft proposal (*probouleuma*), the claimed lack of constitutionality for the decree is argued for in very narrow, positivist terms.[168]

In all the speeches reviewing either decrees or laws, their constitutionality or lack thereof is always the result of painstaking comparison of the enactment in question with the passages in established *nomoi* the enactment is alleged to violate. This essentially *formal* character of Athenian constitutionalism yields a constitutional positivism which would be inconceivable without the strict hierarchy of norms and the entrenchment of higher-order laws. When Euryptolemus in the Arginusae debate over the fate of the generals puts forward the view that their execution would be unconstitutional, he does so without any regard for existing, positive *nomoi* and without distinguishing between laws and decrees.[169] Fourth-century Athens, by contrast, certainly had a positive, entrenched constitution—its code of *nomoi*, as well as a way of enforcing its higher authority over enactments of the assembly—the *graphe paranomon*. This positivist constitutionalism is precisely in line with Aristotle's distinction between democracies where all citizens have a share in governing, but where the law remains above decisions of the assembly, and those where "the multitude is sovereign (*kurion*) and not the law." The latter kind of democracy is characterized by assembly decrees overriding law (τὰ ψηφίσματα κύρια ᾖ ἀλλὰ μὴ ὁ νόμος).[170] Aristotle, too, recognizes as crucial the formal hierarchy of *nomoi* and *psephismata*, at least for defective regimes. As we have seen in the section on Aristotle above, his view at times probably does qualify as a weak, positivist constitutionalism. It is very far removed, however, from Cicero's substantive constitutionalism based on natural-law arguments, as we have seen in the previous chapter. When Aristotle offers his view that certain outstandingly virtuous men cannot be subject to any *nomoi* because they are a *nomos* unto themselves, he does this, interestingly, in the context of yet another Athenian safeguard against unconstitutional behavior—ostracism.[171] Deficient,

---

168. Dem. 22.5-7.

169. Xen. *Hell.* 1.7.20-22. Yunis, "Law, Politics," p. 382: "By the standards observable in all fourth-century cases, Euryptolemus' legal plea would have to be judged utterly inept and especially confused in its failure to distinguish between statute and decree. In fact, Euryptolemus deserves no such censure because in all probability the standards adhered to by fourth-century pleaders had not yet been introduced."

170. Arist. *Pol.* 4.1292a5-7. Kraut, *Aristotle*, p. 454, points out that Aristotle is not merely criticizing unrestrained assemblies "for failing to make decisions of sufficient generality, and for being vulnerable to the distorting effects of emotion. He is also saying that such an assembly will do terrible things, just as a tyrant does terrible things."

171. Arist. *Pol.* 3.1284a13-14.

yet law-abiding regimes require institutional safeguards such as ostracism to keep such outstandingly virtuous men at bay. The Athenian democracy, which by the fourth century had replaced ostracism with the *graphai* just discussed,[172] surely amounts to such a deficient regime in Aristotle's view.

Hume's view, cited above, that the check instituted by the *graphe paranomon* was not ultimately aimed at the people is certainly correct; the jury courts which decided indictments *paranomon* were themselves simply the people in another guise, acting according to a different procedure.[173] Hume says that the *graphe paranomon* was aimed at laws passed in the assembly; but as we have seen, this was the case only in the fifth century. Had Hume been familiar with the sophisticated procedural safeguards instituted by means of the *nomothesia*, he might have been more lenient toward the Athenians and may have found the constitutional remedies the two *graphai* presented even more remarkable. Hume thought that the *graphe* was merely a weak attempt at reining in the "mischiefs," that is to say the proposers of unconstitutional enactments. Indeed, Hume thought that the reason it was not ultimately successful was that the assembly, "averse to checking themselves," remained ultimately unchecked. However, as we have seen, this is surely wrong for the fourth century, when a considerable amount of positivist constitutional thought emerged in the arguments before the people's courts, based ultimately on the hierarchy between norms introduced in the legal reforms at the end of the fifth century. As Hume's example shows, however, this indeed highly remarkable development did not have much of an impact on subsequent political thought and did little to dispel the notion of Athens as an unconstitutional, tumultuous democratic regime governed by the fickle passions of the demos. For most subsequent political thinkers, Athenian history ended with the Arginusae affair. That Arginusae would be very difficult indeed to conceive in the context of fourth-century institutions and constitutional argument is something that has left too little trace in the history of ideas.

To sum up: fourth-century Athens did clearly know a constitutional distinction between entrenched higher-order norms and more disposable lower-level decrees, and it did also have legal remedies in place that were capable of enforcing this distinction. Fourth-century forensic oratory shows us that this had become an important part of the political thought of that society. However, fourth-century Athenian constitutional thought never did have anything close to the kind of impact Roman political thought was to enjoy; the memory of the

172. For the replacement thesis, see Yunis, "Law, Politics," pp. 380-381.

173. See Bleicken, "Verfassungsschutz," p. 394. See also id., *Demokratie*, p. 388; Schwartzberg, "Judicial Review," pp. 1059–1061.

fourth century was eclipsed by the history of the fifth, and the anti-democratic animus underlying political thought, at least until the nineteenth century, was too overwhelming.[174] In addition, there is an important distinction to be made between the kind of Roman constitutionalism described in the previous chapters and the Athenian fourth-century version discussed here. The key difference lies in the latter's deeply *positivist* character—even a merely cursory reading of the speeches arguing charges *paranomon* or *nomon me epitedeion theinai* reveals the extent to which these arguments were all based, and had to be based, very explicitly and at times tediously, on positive laws and passages of laws that had to be adduced over and over in order to convince popular courts to abide by their oath and cast their votes κατὰ τοὺς νόμους. Unlike Roman constitutional argument in the last century of the Republic—not to mention Cicero's natural-law theory—fourth-century Athenian constitutional thought and constitutional institutions were firmly anchored in the body of positive laws collected and reformed in the period after 410 and after 403. In the late Republic there were cases, such as the *ius provocationis*, where the content of *ius* was elaborated by statutory law and was thus reasonably clear and positive. As we have seen, however, the validity of *provocatio* was ultimately thought to be based, not on its status as statute, but on its being part of higher-order *ius*.[175] This higher-order *ius* was not formally distinct from lower-level decrees in the way *nomoi* were differentiated from *psephismata*, if only because there was no positivist theory of higher-order law available. In this, Roman constitutionalism might have been closer to fifth-century Athens with its somewhat vague view of what the *nomos* as a whole may require.[176] Roman arguments *de iure legum* always presupposed the existence of higher-order norms in a way reminiscent of *paranomon* oratory, but unlike arguments *paranomon*, they left room for a more or less creative elaboration of what these higher-order norms might precisely consist in. These elaborations were to capture the imagination of Western political thinkers for many centuries after the fall of the Roman Republic.

174. Roberts, *Athens on Trial*.

175. See, e.g., Cic. *Dom*. 33. See above, Chapter 3, p. 130.

176. Where *nomos* embodies "a general consensus of values": Ostwald, *Popular Sovereignty*, p. 136. For the Greek conception of *nomos* and its change in meaning from denoting the conventional order of things to positive statute, see Ostwald, *Nomos*, pp. 26–54, 57–136.

PART III

The Limits of Virtue

The Roman Contribution to Political Thought

6

The Roman Republic as a Constitutional Order from the Principate to the Renaissance

Pomponius and the lex regia

Tacitus, as we saw in Chapter 1, had already drawn attention to the constitutional aspect of the crises of the late Roman Republic. A later author, the jurist Pomponius, writing in the second century AD, in his handbook, the *Enchiridion*, pointed to the crucial tension that existed in the history of the Republic between constitutional safeguards for individual rights on the one hand and the necessity imposed by emergencies on the other. Pomponius' focus is on *provocatio ad populum*, the specifically Roman institutional safeguard of the right of appeal. That he is retrojecting the right of appeal into the fifth century BC—an anachronistic staple of the late annalists, relied upon by Cicero, Livy, and Dionysius of Halicarnassus as well as by Plutarch—need not concern us here. When describing the Ten Men (*decemviri*) and their authority to give laws to the Roman Republic after the fall of the Kings, Pomponius portrays this authority as sovereign—that is to say, without the possibility of appeal against it:

> [I]t was decided that there be appointed, on the authority of the people (*publica auctoritate*), a commission of ten men by whom were to be studied the laws of the Greek city states and by whom their own city was to be endowed with laws. They wrote out the laws in full on ivory tablets and put the tablets together in front of the rostra, to make the laws all the more open to inspection. They were given during that year sovereign right

> in the *civitas* (*ius in civitate summum*), to enable them to correct the laws, if there should be a need for that, and to interpret them without liability to any appeal (*provocatio*) such as lay from the rest of the magistracy.[1]

The result of this procedure—the Twelve Tables—was of course to be of the greatest importance for the legal history of the Roman Republic, but the procedure through which the codification of the Twelve Tables came about—the Decemvirate and its extraordinary powers—was the subject of fierce criticism, as we have already seen above in Chapter 2 on emergency powers. Leaving aside the question of the (more than dubious) historicity of the Decemvirate (and the tangled issues surrounding the distinction between the First and the Second Decemvirate),[2] Pomponius' account of the commission of the Ten Men shows how, in the period of classical jurisprudence during the Principate, the lack of constitutional safeguards and the assumption of tyrannical, extra-constitutional powers were still taken to be causal forces in the conflicts undermining the Republican order.[3] The question at the heart of Pomponius' account is the question of sovereignty. "Sovereign right" (*summum ius*), uncurbed by any right of appeal or, we might say in this context, veto power, is given to the college of Ten "on the authority of the people." Sovereignty here seems almost defined by the absence of appeal (*provocatio*); it is, however, granted by the people on certain conditions—namely only for the duration of one year—and thus not absolute. Interestingly, Pomponius (as well as Livy, whom he is presumably following, and Cicero) does not take the right of appeal to have been brought into existence by the Twelve Tables; rather, *provocatio* must have existed before their codification, given that the Ten could be freed from it.[4]

Sovereignty thus rests ultimately with the People in Pomponius' view; the Ten serve at the pleasure of the People in their extraordinary capacity, and are given delegated sovereignty unimpeded by *provocatio* for a defined amount of time. Later in the *Enchiridion*, the consequences of overstepping the boundaries inherent in the delegation of sovereign power become apparent. Pomponius writes that

1. Pomp. *Dig.* 1.2.2.4. Trans. ed. A. Watson.

2. See still Beloch, *Römische Geschichte*, pp. 242–246; Täubler, *Untersuchungen*. For a commented edition of the Twelve Tables, see Flach, *Zwölftafelgesetz*. See also Crawford, *Roman Statutes*, vol. 2, pp. 555–721, esp. pp. 560–561.

3. For the role of popular sovereignty in Pomponius' text, see Millar's discussion in his *Roman Republic*, pp. 52–53.

4. Cf. Livy 3.32.6, where *provocatio* is also something pre-existing the Twelve Tables. See Cic. *Rep.* 2.54, where it is claimed in antiquarian fashion that *provocatio* already existed under the Kings; see Zetzel, *Cicero: De Re Publica*, pp. 209–210.

> [w]hen it had been resolved that statutes were indeed to be passed, it was proposed to the people that all the magistrates should abdicate their offices, in order that the Ten Men might be appointed to produce statute laws (*leges*) in writing. The Ten Men were accordingly appointed for one year. But when they prorogued the magistracy in their own favor (*magistratum prorogarent sibi*) and exercised unlawful power (*iniuriose tractarent*) and refused in due course to give way to the magistrates, aiming to keep possession of the Republic in perpetuity for themselves (*perpetuo rem publicam occupatam retineret*) and their faction, they brought matters to such a pass, by the excesses of their harsh despotism (*aspera dominatio*), that the army seceded from the Republic.[5]

Here the unconstitutionality of the rule of the Ten is seen in their violation of the time limit, that is to say, in the fact that the Ten themselves extended their term indefinitely, thereby inviting the charge that their authority had become illegitimate and despotic. Pomponius seems to assume that the People passed a decision in statutory form that authorized the establishment of the extraordinary magistracy of the Decemvirate, but that the People by the same statute that had given rise to the establishment of the Ten in the first place also set limits to their authority. He does not seem to consider the plausible argument that there is nothing, prima facie, that elevates the statutory establishment of the Ten and the term limit inherent therein above the legislative activity of the Ten (including their prorogation of their own magistracy). Implicitly, then, Pomponius, no less than his republican predecessors, appears as an adherent of the position that decisions by the Roman People have a higher (constitutional) status than the legal pronouncements of magistracies created by them.

The origin of the dictatorship is equally treated in the *Enchiridion* as a decision taken by the Romans (he does not mention the precise institutional source of the decision) under the pressure of emergencies.

> [S]ince wars were growing frequent and some were waged with abnormal ferocity by neighboring peoples, sometimes, under the pressure of events (*re exigente*), it was decided to establish a magistrate with greater power (*maioris potestatis*). Accordingly, dictators were put in office from whom there was no right of appeal (*nec provocandi ius fuit*) and to whom even the capital penalty was entrusted.

---

5. Pomp. *Dig.* 1.2.2.24. Trans. ed. A. Watson, slightly modified. Cf. Livy 3.36.5-9.

But, Pomponius adds, it was "not lawful for this magistrate to be kept in office longer than six months, since he had sovereign power (*summa potestas*)."[6] The consuls, by comparison, had, according to Pomponius, originally had "supreme authority" (*summum ius*) which had been accorded to them by statute (*lex*), but this authority had subsequently been limited by the right of appeal (*provocatio*), a limit introduced by statute (*lex*), lest the consuls "should claim for themselves kingly power (*regia potestas*) over all things."[7] Once again, as in the account of the Decemvirate, sovereign power (*summum ius/summa potestas*) is characterized by the absence of the right of appeal against it. If such power is uncurbed by either the right of appeal or a term limit, it assumes a monarchic flavor—*regia potestas*. The limitation of the consular "supreme authority" by *provocatio* is effortlessly achieved by statute, which demonstrates again that Pomponius, notwithstanding the strong words about *summum ius*, actually acknowledges a constitutional rule of popular sovereignty.

Setting aside once again the dubious historical reliability of the *Enchiridion*, we may still take away the impression that Pomponius, albeit writing under the Principate, has an understanding of the pivotal place that was accorded to the right of appeal under the constitution of the Republic, and that Pomponius in a Mommsenian way describes the relationship between sovereignty and *provocatio* as inversely proportional. The lawgiving commission of the Ten is on the one hand described as a constituent power, unfettered by the right of appeal; on the other hand, the Ten are still subject to a term limit, presumably a constitutional limitation of their time in office. What was the source of this constitutional limitation? Pomponius says that the Ten had been appointed "on the authority of the people" (*publica auctoritate*), for once not referring to obscure statute. When discussing the dictatorship and the way it was established, there is no mention of statute either. Other constitutional institutions however are based on and, presumably, justified by, statute in the *Enchiridion*. It seems fair to say that the constitutional rule consistently evoked here, albeit implicitly, is again that of popular sovereignty and of the potential applicability of *provocatio* to any magistracy. Both popular sovereignty and the right of appeal predate, in Pomponius' account, the Twelve Tables, and are thus felt to be of higher constitutional status compared to mere legislation.

Not unlike the protagonists of the constitutional crises of the late Republic, and *a fortiori* like the protagonists of Cicero's dialogues, then, Pomponius shows some dim awareness of a hierarchy between sources of constitutional

---

6. Ibid. 1.2.2.18. Trans. ed. Watson.

7. Ibid. 1.2.2.16.

and statutory legal norms, which, however, he never makes explicit. The philosophical natural-law basis for such a hierarchy, it is true, is missing entirely from Pomponius' historical legal handbook as excerpted in the *Digest*. But the crucial importance of the right of appeal is reflected in the important role of *provocatio* even for the period of the Decemvirate, and the awareness that in the context of emergencies this right could stand in tension with an emergency power such as the dictatorship is prominent in the *Enchiridion*. Emergency powers appear here as constitutionally hedged, and in the case of overreaching—when the Ten overstep the constitutional term limit—the response is swift and drastic. Ultimately, however, Pomponius needed to explain the transition from Republic to the imperial monarchy, and this he accomplishes by giving the following rather opaque pragmatic report. After decisions by the plebs had been given the force of statute by the *lex Hortensia* (287 BC), and laws and plebiscites had thus equal legal force,

> it grew hard for the plebs to assemble, and to be sure much harder for the entire citizenry to assemble, being now such a vast crowd of men . . . And thus did the senate come to exercise authority, and whatever it resolved was respected, and such a law was called a *senatus consultum*. . . . Most recently, just as there was seen to have been a transition toward fewer ways of establishing law, a transition effected by stages under dictation of circumstances (*rebus dictantibus*), it has come about that affairs of state have had to be entrusted to one man (for the senate had been unable latterly to govern all the provinces honestly). An emperor, therefore, having been established (*constituto principe*), to him was given the right (*ius datum est*) that what he had decided be deemed law (*ut quod constituisset, ratum esset*).[8]

Put briefly, in Pomponius' view the Principate had come about mainly due to the pragmatic difficulty of the growing Roman People to assemble.[9] The origin of the right of the Emperor to legislate seems to lie in a delegation of that right—via the Senate—to the Emperor, who is of course not constrained by either the right of appeal or any set term limit. Whether the Emperor's right to legislate could be revoked Pomponius does not say. From the above account it would appear

8. Pomp. *Dig.* 1.2.2.9-11. Trans. ed. A. Watson, with slight modifications.

9. This is reminiscent of the scholarly debate concerning the democratic aspects of the Roman Republic. Critics such as Ramsay MacMullen have argued that the various localities where the people's assemblies gathered could not have possibly contained a sufficient amount of people for the Republic to qualify as democratic. MacMullen, "How Many Romans Voted."

that the Emperor himself, being a source of law, absent the People's authority for revocation and absent any hierarchy of sources of legal rules, was not bound or limited by laws any more than the Roman People had been. Of the examples of sovereign power given by Pomponius, next to the college of the Ten Men the People's assembly was closest to being absolute in the sense of later legal theory—they are by virtue of their unlimited legislative authority not bound by previous legislation (given that previous legislation is always liable to abrogation), at least in the absence of any robust sense of superior constitutional norms (a sense indeed not palpable in the *Enchiridion* apart from the thin sense of popular sovereignty which seems to be underlying the transfer of power to the Emperor). By contrast, the sovereignty of the dictatorship and consulship were limited by term limits and, in the case of the latter, the right of appeal (Pomponius does not mention that these magistracies did not have the right to legislate: what they decided was not "deemed law"). Still, it would be a mistake to miss the constitutional flavor of Pomponius' account. The Emperor is granted a "right" to legislate, and without this grant his authority would not be legitimate; and his position had been established lawfully. Most importantly, it seems that for Pomponius the Senate and ultimately the Emperor came to have a representative function in view of the fact that the People, had it not been for the fact that the assemblies had become impossible for practical reasons, would still be legislating. Also, the Emperor's sovereignty is not God-given or theocratic on this account, unlike elsewhere in the *Corpus iuris*.

Is this an absolute conception of the sovereignty of the Emperor, or does it base the Emperor's authority in the last resort on the sovereignty of the People? It is clear that, genealogically, the Emperor's sovereignty is derived from that of the People; but do the People retain some of their authority? And if not, is the Emperor bound by earlier legislation or by his own? There is a distinct ambiguity in the *Corpus iuris*, the Roman law codification within which excerpts from Pomponius' handbook have survived, with regard to these questions. A contemporary of Pomponius, the second century jurist Julian, gives the People and its will a voice in legislation in that he sees the popular will at work in the making of custom and gives custom the power to abrogate legislation: statutes may be repealed "by the silent agreement of everyone expressed through desuetude."[10] And the classic statements in the *Digest* which have been taken to underwrite an absolute conception of the Emperor's sovereignty, that "what has pleased the Emperor has the force of law" and that he is "not bound by the laws (*legibus*

10. *Dig.* 1.3.32. Trans. ed. A. Watson. The passage may be interpolated; see, for a contrary later view expressed in a constitution of Emperor Constantine, *Const.* 8.52.2.

solutus)"[11]; these statements are counterbalanced by what follows immediately after the former one: "This is because the people commits to him and into him its own entire authority and power, doing this by the royal law (*lex regia*) which is passed anent his authority."[12] The Emperor's sovereignty may thus not be bound by any statute, but his authority is seen ultimately to rest on the authority of the People (on this view the People must have also been freed from the laws, *legibus solutus*).

The republican potential inherent in the idea of a transfer of sovereignty from the Roman People to the Emperors by way of a *lex regia* had also, on some interpretations, a constitutional dimension.[13] If the transfer had been revocable, or if it had been tied to certain conditions, this was apt to cast some doubt on the claim of the Emperor's absolute sovereignty. The problem with the idea of a transfer by *lex regia* was that no such statute is independently attested.[14] In 1344, however, a great bronze tablet was found on which something very much resembling a *lex regia* was inscribed: the so-called *lex de imperio Vespasiani*, a law detailing the powers conferred on Emperor Vespasian by statute in AD 69.[15] This inscription was discovered and then put on display in the Church of St. John Lateran in Rome by Cola di Rienzo, a champion of republican government, who subsequently used and interpreted it to reintroduce a republican constitution at Rome in 1347. Whether or not the law on the bronze tablet was actually a *lex regia* as described in the *Digest*, it certainly seemed to lend support to the idea that in the last resort the Emperor's authority was derived from, and depended on, the Roman People and was thus not absolute.

An early exclusive republican: Ptolemy of Lucca and his portion of the De regimine principum

Cola di Rienzo was not the first to take a friendlier attitude toward the Roman Republic as opposed to the Empire. Charles Till Davis has shown, arguing against Hans Baron's thesis of a decisive republican break occurring at the beginning of the *quattrocento*, that such a republican orientation could be traced back at least to

---

11. Ulp. *Dig.* 1.3.31.

12. Ibid. 1.4.1.pr. See also *Inst.* 1.2.6. But cf. *Cod.* 1.14.12.

13. For a brief account of the implications of the *lex regia* for the Middle Ages and for medieval ideas on the source of imperial authority, see Canning, *History*, pp. 7–9. For absolute sovereignty in the late Middle Ages, see Pennington, *Prince and the Law.*

14. On the *lex regia*, see Mommsen, *Staatsrecht*, vol. 2.2, pp. 876–879.

15. See on this the classic article by Brunt, "Lex de Imperio."

the early fourteenth century with the spread of Aristotelianism and the works of Latini, Marsilius of Padua, Dante, the commentator Bartolus of Sassoferrato, and the Dominicans Remigius of Florence and Ptolemy of Lucca.[16] Especially Ptolemy showed a very sustained interest in the history of the Republic and expressed an unmitigated preference for it as against the Empire in his *De regimine principum*. This work, long attributed to Thomas Aquinas (who probably wrote the first part of it), exhibits in the second part a very pointed "republican exclusivism";[17] that is to say that far from endorsing monarchy as the best form of government, as previous medieval thought routinely did, Ptolemy shows hostility to monarchy to the point of equating regal rule with despotism, and puts forward an equally strong preference for what the author takes to be the balanced constitution of the Roman Republic, which he describes in almost Polybian terms (without, of course, knowing Polybius' *Histories*) as an Aristotelian polity, a tempered government of the many and the few.[18]

Ptolemy has picked up some information about the institutions of the Roman Republic from the fourth-century historian Flavius Eutropius. His predilection for republican government to the exclusion of any other form comes to the fore when he reasons that

> [w]hen it comes to the parts of a polity having to do with government, I must especially use the Romans as exemplars, because the Roman Republic was very distinguished in its order, and because historians have described the hierarchy of officials after the expulsion of Tarquin from the kingdom.[19]

Ptolemy is impressed with the fact that after the expulsion of the kings, the Romans had two consuls,[20] equal in power, and with a limited term in office.

---

16. Davis, "Ptolemy of Lucca"; id., *Dante's Italy*.

17. The term is Eric Nelson's. What he asserts concerning seventeenth century political thinkers—that they made the "new and revolutionary argument" that "monarchy per se is an illicit constitutional form and that all legitimate constitutions are republican"—holds already of Ptolemy of Lucca. See Nelson, *Hebrew Republic*, p. 3.

18. See J. M. Blythe, "Introduction," in Ptolemy of Lucca, *Government of Rulers*, pp. 33–39. See also Millar, *Roman Republic*, pp. 59–61, who is however too focused on spotting democratic elements and does not pay attention to the constitutionalism of Ptolemy.

19. *On the Government of Rulers* 4.26.1. For his view of the development of the constitution of the Republic, and its gradually more "democratic" character, see also 4.19.5 and Millar, *Roman Republic*, p. 60.

20. Note the contradictory information that there was only one consul gleaned from the Bible (1 Maccabees 8.16), which Ptolemy also repeatedly relates, without noting the contradiction: see, e.g., *On the Government of Rulers* 2.8.1.

They were called consuls, he maintains based on the etymology of the word by Isidore of Seville, either from "their 'consulting the interests of' (*consulere*) the citizens, or from their governing everything by consultation."[21] The term limit the Romans instituted, according to Ptolemy, "so that no one could remain insolent for long."[22] He is also aware of the fact, based on Isidore and Eutropius, that the Romans in a time of military threat established the office of the dictator, "to greatly strengthen the nation, and it had a more extensive power and command than the consulate."[23] However, Ptolemy mistakenly believes with Isidore (who is by far the most important source for him on the subject of Roman republican magistracies)[24] that the dictator's term of office was longer than the consuls', "expiring after five years, whereas the consulate lasted only for one year."[25] He does correctly point out that Caesar had held the office.[26] Interestingly, he does not follow Eutropius in the mistaken belief that Emperor Augustus too had held the dictatorship, thus correctly confining the office to the domain of the republican constitution.[27] Finally, he relates how, "because the consuls excessively oppressed the plebs, tribunes were instituted by the people." The tribunes were called such "because they handed down rights to the people."[28] All of this suggests that Ptolemy has an implicit understanding of the higher-order norms that limit, e.g., the consuls' term in office and of the fact that these norms are of a constitutional character. It is this that distinguishes the Republic, not a zeal for grandeur and glory, as Augustine had maintained.

Claiming the church father's support, Ptolemy turns Augustine's ambiguity about Roman civic virtue into a plain affirmation of their virtues, which he chiefly finds represented in the Romans' "love of their fatherland," their "zeal for justice" and their "virtue of benevolence." To illustrate the first of these virtues,

---

21. Isid. *Etym.* 9.3.6. Trans. S. A. Barney/W. J. Lewis/J. A. Beach/O. Berghof.

22. *On the Government of Rulers* 4.26.1. This is a very close rendering of Isidore's description of the office, from whom he also takes the odd distinction between a "military" and a "civil" consul.

23. Ibid. 4.26.2.

24. Blythe's notes in general do not pay sufficient attention to Isidore as a source of Ptolemy.

25. *On the Government of Rulers* 4.26.2. Cf. Isid. *Etym.* 9.3.11.

26. Ibid.

27. Eutropius thinks that both Caesar and Augustus had been dictators, adding that the dictatorship was the power closest in character to the imperial office of Emperor Valens (to whom the *Breviarium ab urbe condita* is dedicated), thus continuing the illusion of the Principate as a continuation of the constitutional government of the Republic: Eutr. 1.12 (ed. Droysen).

28. *On the Government of Rulers* 4.26.3, quoting Isid. *Etym.* 9.3.29 and 9.4.18.

Ptolemy cites Sallust, who recalls nostalgically what had made the Republic great: "industry at home, just command abroad, a free spirit in counseling." Ptolemy also cites Sallust's rendering of a speech of Marcus Porcius Cato on the reasons for the decline of republican government at Rome: "But instead of these things we now have luxury and avarice, poverty in public but opulence in private; we praise wealth, we seek idleness, we make no distinction between the good and the evil, and ambition reaps all the rewards of virtue."[29] Another crucial Roman virtue, according to Ptolemy and his tendentious version of Augustine, is "their zeal for justice (*zelus iustitiae*)," which constitutes "another reason why the Romans were worthy of lordship"—and by "the Romans," the Roman Republic is meant. This zeal for justice made the Romans acquire their rule "by natural right (*iure naturae*), from which all just lordship (*iustum dominium*) originates." Because of "their exceptionally just laws (*iustissimae leges*), others spontaneously subjected themselves to their lordship."[30] Ptolemy goes on to cite the *Acts of the Apostles*:

> When Festus [the Roman procurator of Judea] was in Jerusalem, the ruling priests visited him and demanded that Paul be condemned to death. Festus answered that according to the way that individuals are subject to the Romans' laws, 'it is not the custom of the Romans to condemn them,' or to pardon them, 'unless their accusers are present and they have the chance to defend themselves and clear themselves of the accusation.' For this reason Augustine says: 'It pleased God that the Romans should conquer the world, so that it might be pacified by being brought far and wide into the single society of the Republic and its laws (*in unam societatem reipublicae legumque*).'[31]

From the last remark it becomes clear that, notwithstanding the episode from the *Acts of the Apostles*, it is the Roman Republic, not the Empire, which displays the legalistic and constitutional traits Ptolemy values. His whole discussion of the justification of Roman rule is dense with quotations, above all, from Augustine's *City of God*, which, in turn, relies heavily on Cicero's *Republic* in its argument about the justice of the Roman Empire and Roman virtues. The debate about imperial justice in book three of the *Republic* thus looms large, albeit by way of Augustine, in the background of Ptolemy's evaluation of the Roman Republic and its constitution.

---

29. Ptolemy of Lucca, *On the Government of Rulers* 3.4, p. 155, citing Sall. *Cat.* 52.21.

30. Ibid. 3.5, p. 157.

31. Ibid. 3.5, pp. 157–158, citing *Acts* 25.16 and August. *De civ. D.* 18.22.

Cicero, as we have seen, after discussing constitutional theory merely in terms of prudential criteria such as stability, effective rule, and longevity, in the third book of his dialogue moved towards a *moral* consideration of the Roman Republic, framing it as an exchange of arguments modeled on a pair of famous speeches given by the Academic skeptic Carneades in Rome in 155 BC, speeches in which Carneades had argued, first for and then, in the second speech, against the indispensability of justice in a polity. Cicero in the *Republic* turned the sequence of the speeches on its head, thus beginning with the skeptical challenge to justice and assigning the defense of justice the last word. Most importantly with regard to the use of the theme by Augustine and then Ptolemy, when adapting what he knew about Carneades' arguments for the *Republic*, Cicero applied the controversial discussion of the importance of justice for politics to the international realm, thus extending political theory beyond the *polis* and rendering Rome's acquisition of empire a subject fit for normative, moral consideration.[32] Cicero's *Republic* had thus brought moral philosophy in the form of natural law to bear on Rome's rule, beyond the borders of a given polity. Most importantly, the norms applicable in this realm could not possibly be the particular norms of just any state—they had to answer either to the criteria of utility and self-interest, as Philus (alias Carneades) is made to argue in the *Republic*, or to the criteria of justice, largely conceived in Stoic natural-law terms, as Philus' adversary Laelius, delivering the pro-justice speech in the *Republic*, maintains. Natural law in Cicero provides the yardstick for gauging the justice of imperial rule and conquest, and its provisions are of a moral kind, not, as Carneades would have it, merely prescribing self-preservation.

The Carneadean debate shines through—via Augustine—in Ptolemy's account. Unlike Augustine, who is highly ambiguous about the secular virtue of the Romans and what he takes in the last analysis to be their vain emphasis of glory and honor,[33] Ptolemy adopts a view perfectly akin to Cicero's (or Laelius') natural-law defense of the Republic and its imperialism. He then co-opts Augustine effectively into this view of the Republic having inherited imperial rule from Alexander the Great because of their "exercising lordship justly and exercising governance legitimately." Ptolemy here seems to imply that part of the problem with Alexander had been that he was a monarch, and thus

32. For the relation between Cicero and the original Carneadean debate, see Zetzel, "Natural Law and Poetic Justice."

33. On Ptolemy's transformation of Augustine's ambiguity about the Romans into straightforward praise, see Davis, "Ptolemy of Lucca"; on his use (and abuse) of Augustine and his efforts to reconcile him with Aristotle, see also Blythe, "Introduction," pp. 24–30; see also Blythe's note on the text, p. 153, n. 38.

not capable of the kind of rule by "most holy laws" and of directing "the people under the laws," thus preserving "the multitude of persons in civil society" for the "purpose of preserving the peace and justice." The monarch Alexander is not capable of that kind of constitutional justice, which Ptolemy calls "legal justice (*legalis iustitia*)" and which in his view is in the last resort based on natural law.

This defense of the Roman Republic's imperial rule by reference to the Republic's constitutional rule and the civilizing influence of the Roman law and the Romans' *legalis iustitia* was to become a topos in European political thought after the discovery of the Americas.[34] What is most interesting about its use in Ptolemy's work is not only its revolutionary, unabashed pro-republican (and effectively "exclusivist" republican) stance—which is interesting and revolutionary enough.[35] But there is an additional aspect, which has to do with the precise reasons for Ptolemy's interest in the Republic. Notwithstanding Ptolemy's frequent mention of Augustine and his attempts to masquerade his own views as those of the church father, his interpretation of the Republic really is closer to that of Cicero as presented in the *Republic* (which he knows through Augustine), the *Laws*, and *On Duties* (both of which he knows directly). It shows no awareness of Augustine's differentiation between *vera iustitia* and mere earthly justice; and although there is at times a broadly Aristotelian terminology at work in *De regimine principum*,[36] the outlook is that of the constitutional tradition of the Roman Republic. The constitutional rule spread by Roman republican imperialism simply *is vera iustitia* for Ptolemy, and the chief justification of their empire. The whole world should, by natural right, be governed by the Republic and pacified by being brought under the "single society of the Republic and its laws."

As an example for Roman benevolence, Ptolemy unwittingly cites Virgil and Sallust by way of Augustine—"it was characteristic of the Romans 'to spare their subjects and vanquish the proud, and they preferred to forgive injuries than to

34. See Kingsbury and Straumann, "Introduction"; Benton and Straumann, "Acquiring Empire by Law"; Lupher, *Romans*; Straumann, "*Ius erat in armis*." For an example of the use of Augustine by an anti-imperialist humanist jurist, see Vázquez de Menchaca's *Controversiae illustres* (1564). Vázquez explained Augustine's account by saying that the Romans were granted their empire by God not on grounds of their showing virtue in conquering it, but rather because, quite apart from their warfare, the Romans were excelling other peoples in terms of other virtues; vol. 2, c. 20, 31.

35. See on this Witt, "Rebirth."

36. See e.g. *On the Government of Rulers* 3.5.3, p. 158, alluding to Arist. *Pol.* 1.2, 1253a2-3: The "multitude of persons in civil society" is, "according to Aristotle," "a necessity for them as naturally social animals."

avenge them.'"[37] He further adduces Cicero's *On Duties* on the obligatory bond the Romans felt towards their Republic as additional justification of their rule.[38] Ptolemy betrays an affinity with a genuinely Augustinian view (and thus an awareness of the Republic's eventual degeneration and decline) only when he briefly imports Sallust and his theme of republican decline through avarice, luxury, and general loss of virtue;[39] but even then this does not seem to be designed to illustrate Augustine's point that "for one vice"—glory—the Romans overcame avarice and other vices.[40] The idea of one vice doubling as a virtue to the extent that it restrains and checks other vices is foreign to Ptolemy.[41] Hence *gloria* does not figure as an end in his account at all.

Ptolemy brings out very clearly the constitutional dimension of the Roman Republic and its mode of government in the following passage, where he contrasts the republican constitutional government ("political rule") with rule by one. He routinely conflates the Aristotelian distinction between regal and despotic rule, so that monarchy assumes overall a despotic character. Now the most interesting aspect of "political rule" is that, although Ptolemy is heavily inclined to praise it, and initially points out its stability, he also diagnoses a certain inferiority to monarchy, the government by one, or regal rule, by virtue of the fact that the "political" ruler is bound by law and thus not free to react as he wishes, e.g., in emergencies. "Political government," as exercised in the Roman Republic, is of necessity of a pleasant and mild (*suave*) character, and it is also

> a sure mode of governing because it is according to the form of the laws (*secundum formam legum*) of the commune or the municipality, to which the rector is bound. But for this reason the ruler's prudence is not free, and, therefore it is more remote from the divine and imitates it less. Although laws originate in natural law (*ius naturae*), as Cicero proves in his treatise *On Laws*, and natural law derives from divine law . . .; nevertheless they fail in particular acts (*in particularibus actibus*), for which legislators cannot provide, since they are ignorant of future events. Thus, political government results in a certain weakness, since political rectors

---

37. Ibid. 3.6.3, quoting August. *De civ. D.* 1.6, who is in turn quoting Verg. *Aen.* 6.853 and Sall. *Cat.* 9.5.

38. Ibid. 3.4.3, citing from Cic. *Off.* 1.57.

39. Ibid. 3.4.3, citing from Sall. *Cat.* 52.21.

40. Cf. August. *De civ. D.* 5.13. On glory and virtue, see Chapter 7.

41. On the idea of one vice or desire acting as a check on the others and thereby acquiring respectable status, see Hirschman, *Passions and the Interests*.

> judge the people by the laws alone. This weakness is eliminated in regal lordship since the rulers, not being obligated by the laws, may judge by what is in their hearts, and they therefore more closely follow divine providence . . .[42]

Ptolemy shows awareness, in a text very much given to his preference for republican government "according to the form of the laws," of the problem that this kind of government might actually end up being weaker than monarchy, or "regal" rule, where rulers are not bound by law and can thus answer particular contingencies not provided for in legal form according to their discretion. Whether this amounts to an awareness of what Carl Friedrich has called "constitutional reason of state," that is to say, reason of state in its application to a constitutional order,[43] is less clear. The legal limits and constraints to the capacity to act which plague the republican order are not here looked at from a moral point of view; however, given that Ptolemy is prone to thinking of all monarchy or "regal" rule as despotic, he does seem to point here to a tension between despotic government, lacking in justice but with a discretionary capacity to act in emergencies, on the one hand, and republican constitutional government, on the other. The status of natural law is ambiguous, as it does sanction—Cicero's name is not taken in vain here—for Ptolemy the legal order of the Roman Republic. On the other hand, as opposed to Cicero but in line with Greek thought, he seems to think that natural law is not really susceptible of being formulated in general legal rules. Rather, the virtue of the ruler might come closer to acting in accordance with it. But interestingly this perceived weakness of Republics does not lead Ptolemy to give up on republican rule in favor of monarchy. Whether or not Ptolemy has in mind here an idea akin to Cicero's *salus populi* cannot be decided on the evidence of his text. As we will see, a reconciliation of constitutional constraints and discretionary powers on the basis of Cicero's *salus populi* will be attempted by John Locke and his doctrine of the prerogative.[44]

Ptolemy's originality consists in his straightforward preference for the Roman Republic and his general preference for republican government. He exhibits many of the traits characteristic of the Roman constitutional tradition portrayed here. The expansion of the Republic is justified, according to him, not

---

42. *On the Government of Rulers* 2.8.6. Cf. also 4.16.3.

43. Friedrich, *Constitutional Reason of State.*

44. See Locke, *Second Treatise* §160: "This Power to act according to discretion, for the publick good, without the prescription of the Law, and sometimes even against it, *is* that which is called *Prerogative.*" See below, p. 318.

because striving for glory is a value, but rather due to the constitutional nature of Roman republican rule. This is an early example of what was to become a prominent strand in early modern natural law theories[45]—spreading the content of the natural law underlying their "most just laws," the Romans acquired their empire due to their "zeal for justice." Ptolemy does not put his faith in the virtuous disposition of the ruler. For better or worse, he prefers a system where the ruler is constrained by law and puts the emphasis on legal constraints, not on virtue. He does not seem to think that these constraining lower-order laws could be violated, or set aside, by reference to the higher-order natural law and in order to save the republican constitution; indeed, he does not seem to have given much thought to such an idea.

To sum up, Ptolemy has a normative preference for republican rule due to its natural justice and constitutional constraints, and he is thus not a Machiavellian republican in the sense of giving ultimate value to *grandezza* and glory. The liberty which is encouraged under republican rule recommends it as pleasant, or mild: because they exercise rule themselves when it is their turn, subjects (*subditi*, an strange term given the context) are "bold in pursuing liberty, so as not to be forced to submit and bow down to kings."[46] It is a liberty very much of the kind Benjamin Constant had in mind when describing "ancient liberty" and its distinguishing features, namely political participation and political rights.[47] This Aristotelian flavor can be detected throughout the work, and it is at odds with the kind of Ciceronian property-centered political and constitutional theory based on a state of nature (portrayed in earlier chapters above),[48] as is his Sallustian romantic glorification of public opulence and private poverty.[49] It is equally at odds, however, with Augustine's view of the Roman Republic as exhibiting but second-rate, pagan qualities (which are really vices). As opposed to Augustine Ptolemy thinks the justice demonstrated and spread by the Republic and its empire is the real (and only) thing, and thus agrees with Cicero (or Laelius) in the *Republic*. In this last regard, then, his views are indeed Ciceronian, as are his invocations of natural justice as contained in the Carneadean debate.

---

45. See, for the most elaborate take on this, Gentili, *Wars*.

46. *On the Government of Rulers* 2.8.5.

47. Constant, "Liberty of the Ancients."

48. See *On the Government of Rulers* 2.9.4. Here Ptolemy argues that republican government could already be found in the state of innocence, as opposed to monarchy; to render the state of innocence as "state of nature" as Blythe does is misleading.

49. Ibid. 3.4.3.

Mario Salamonio's early Roman constitutionalism

Ptolemy of Lucca with his predilection for the Roman Republic as opposed to the Empire did not pay attention to the problem of how the legal authority of the Emperor could be justified. In his view, the Republic ruled "through consuls, dictators, and tribunes" from Tarquin the Proud until it degenerated with the civil wars and ended with Julius Caesar's rule.[50] Thus, he did not pay attention to the *lex regia* or to Pomponius' account of how sovereignty had been transferred from the people to the Emperors. One of the earliest and, in their relevance to the constitutional tradition, most salient and sustained discussions of the *lex regia* and Pomponius' text can be found in the work of the Roman humanist lawyer Mario Salamonio. Salamonio, born of a Roman patrician family at Rome in the mid-fifteenth century, wrote his main work *Patritii Romani de principatu libri VI* (1544) between 1512 and 1514 in the context of the conflict between the papal curia and the Commune of the city of Rome. The book takes the form of a dialogue between a philosopher, a lawyer, a theologian, and a historian. The question at issue is whether or not the Roman Emperor can be said to be *legibus solutus*, that is to say whether he can be said to rule absolutely. The lawyer's rather impetuous claim is that there really isn't a question: the Emperor as a matter of course is absolute. The philosopher contests this claim and adduces Aristotle, arguing that the lawyer's stance would make it difficult to differentiate between tyrannical and imperial rule.[51] The lawyer responds by laying out a positivist theory of law, and by arguing that law (*lex*) is essentially a command, a prohibition, or a punishment, something in short which has force exclusively vis-à-vis subjects, not equals. The emperor can thus not command or prescribe anything to himself.[52]

This stance arouses the philosopher's decided resistance, and as the dialogue unfolds the philosopher manages to convince the lawyer that far from being above his own legislation, the Emperor is bound by it as the Roman People were bound by their own lawmaking before delegating this authority to the Emperor by means of the *lex regia*. The common assumption of all the participants in the dialogue is that natural (and divine) law constrains the legislative power of whoever holds that power; and it is conceded by the lawyer to the philosopher that the *lex regia* itself is outside the scope of the Emperor's lawmaking authority

50. Ibid. 2.9.6.

51. *De principatu* p. 3. I use the Paris 1578 edition, which is a republication of the *editio princeps* published at Rome in 1544. The Paris edition must have been published in the context of monarchomachic thought.

52. *De principatu* p. 5.

and thus immune to his sovereignty. Since the lawyer concedes that he is not sure as to the content of the historical *lex regia*, the debate proceeds, interestingly, by way of a priori argument, leading the philosopher to conclude that the People *could not possibly* have contracted to delegate its authority permanently and irrevocably. The way power was delegated—a revocable delegation, as the philosopher insists—to the Emperor is taken from Pomponius' *Enchiridion* in the Digest, which is cited word by word. The *lex de imperio Vespasiani*, too, is cited by way of support, and the historian betrays a quite detailed knowledge of the working of he Roman comitia and their role in legislation as well as elections. Interestingly, when discussing the constraints upon the Emperor's legislative powers, contract law is—as is the *lex regia*—taken to lie outside the scope of the sovereign's authority; the rules of contracts cannot be changed and are thus a constraint on the Emperor's lawmaking, a further (and as it turns out, crucial) element in the philosopher's argument that the *princeps* and his *imperium* are by no means *legibus solutus*.[53] The philosopher's motive in arguing for contract law enjoying this status is that he explicitly models the delegation of power from the People to the Emperor on the Roman legal institution of mandate (*mandatum*),[54] which is part of the Roman law of contract and was conceptualized in the Roman legal sources as a consensual contract, requiring for its conclusion but the tacit or explicit consent of the parties.[55] The mandator, in Salamonio's case the People, would mandate the mandatary, here the Emperor, with the discharging of legislation on his behalf. This kind of contract was entirely gratuitous and could be revoked at any time by the parties.

This contractual bent in Salamonio's thought is further supported by his use of Cicero's *Republic* and the widely known (via Augustine) definition of *res publica* stated therein.[56] Excluding societies that are formed with a view towards committing injustice, the philosopher uses Cicero's definition of the required kind of *populus* and renders it as the correct definition of a "civil people" (*civilis populus*). Cicero had said it well in the *Republic*, the philosopher says, when defining the *res publica* as a "collection of men which forms a society by virtue of agreement with respect to justice (*iuris consensu*) and sharing in advantage."[57] Seizing on the term *sociatus*, Salamonio goes on—in keeping with the essentially Roman and Ciceronian spirit—to ask the lawyer: "If the state

53. We will see in Chapter 8 that Bodin made use of this idea as well.

54. Gai. *Inst.* 3.162.

55. See, for the Roman law of mandate, Watson, *Contract of Mandate.*

56. Cic. *Rep.* 1.39. Cf. August. *De civ. D.* 2.21.

57. *De principatu* p. 38.

(*Civitas*) is nothing but a sort of civil partnership (*civilis quaedam societas*), can such a partnership be established without any contract (*sine pactionibus*)?"[58] He brings the lawyer to concede that the contracts of such a partnership are correctly called "laws." On this account the whole People acts as the legislator—akin to Marsilius of Padua's ideas—with the Emperor only being one partner (*socius*) among many acting on behalf of the People. As before with the Roman law of mandate, this builds on the Roman contract of partnership (*societas*), which, based on faith (*fides*), was not limited to Roman citizens, a characteristic useful for Salamonio's purpose of having a *societas* agreed upon in an essentially pre-political condition.[59] The partners (*socii*) in the partnership all had to consent to the partnership, and the consent had to be ongoing—one partner's lack of consent would effectively abolish the *societas* as a whole. Again, given the framing of the argument in terms of Roman contract law, and given that the philosopher had already established the essentially constitutional status of the rules of contract law and its immunity to the sovereignty of the legislator, this amounts to an implicit formulation of a set of immutable, entrenched higher-order rules, rules that turn out to be the rules of Roman contract law on the one hand and natural law norms on the other. As in Cicero's own political thought, there are certain substantive constraints on what can be agreed upon by means of contract; if it were not for the constitutional constraint of justice (*ius*), brigands too could qualify as a constitutional *societas*.

Neither Salamonio's stated preference for republican government nor his ideas of popular sovereignty were new. Legal and political thinkers of an Aristotelian bent such as Bartolus of Sassoferrato, Baldus de Ubaldis and Marsilius of Padua had already put forward arguments favoring popular sovereignty, and of the scholastic writers at least Ptolemy of Lucca had expressed views strongly favoring the Roman Republic over the rule of the Emperors, a judgment of the relative value of these periods of Roman history followed, of course, most prominently by the Florentine humanist Leonardo Bruni.[60] Quentin Skinner and before him Paul Oskar Kristeller have already shown that Hans Baron's view of a decisive change in outlook early in the *quattrocento*, the so-called "Baron thesis," according to which a civic-minded republican form of humanism first developed in the context of the conflict between republican Florence and autocratic Milan, cannot be upheld given that such views can be shown to have developed much

58. Ibid.

59. See Kaser, *Römisches Privatrecht*, § 43.

60. See, e.g., Bruni's *Laudatio Florentinae urbis* of 1403/1404, pp. 16–19; and his later *History of the Florentine People* (*Historiae Florentini populi*) 1.38, pp. 48–50.

earlier, in the twelfth and thirteenth centuries.[61] What distinguishes Salamonio is that, unlike Bartolus or Baldus, he uses the *lex regia* extensively in his argument about popular sovereignty and *imperium*, and unlike the scholastics, he imports into his eclectic mixture of elements of Aristotelian philosophy and legal humanism an important dose of Ciceronian thinking about the pre-political realm. His main concern is constitutionalist, the idea that not only did the *lex regia* as a matter of historical fact not irrevocably bestow absolute sovereignty on the Emperor, as Bartolus and Baldus had maintained,[62] but, crucially, no such bestowal could ever possibly convey sovereignty that is *legibus solutus* and the sovereignty of any *princeps* is always bound by the *lex regia* under which it was originally bestowed. There is thus a constraint on any sovereign, universally, to remain under the dictates of natural law. In case of conflict with natural law or with popular sovereignty, legislation by the sovereign can even be abrogated. This has led several historians of political thought to add Salamonio prominently to the tradition of the social-contract thinkers,[63] a characterization that is certainly not implausible in light of the passages quoted above.[64] More importantly, however, Salamonio also recognizes, with Cicero, certain substantive constraints on what can be contracted into, and it is this view of natural law made constitutionally relevant which makes him a Ciceronian in the sense specified in the second part of this book. The description of Salamonio as a social-contract theorist thus seems to miss the most important point, which lies in Salamonio's use of a Ciceronian concept of natural law and in the way this concept serves as a constitutional constraint even on certain contractual options.

61. See Skinner, *Foundations*, vol. 1, pp. 101–109; Baron, *Crisis*; see also Hankins, "The 'Baron Thesis'."

62. See on this Canning, *History*, p. 170; on Baldus, see id., *Political Thought of Baldus*, pp. 61–64. Bartolus struggled to establish a concept of tyranny flexible enough to accommodate cases of necessity, where tyranny was to be tolerated; see especially his *Tractatus de regimine civitatis* and the *Tractatus de tyranno*, available in Quaglioni, *Politica*, 147–170; 171–213.

63. Gough, *Social Contract*, pp. 45–47. See also d'Addio, *L'idea*, pp. 111–115, arguing convincingly that Salamonio is a Ciceronian who endows political society with a legal personality as well as an enemy of Machiavelli.

64. But see Skinner, *Foundations*, p. 132, esp. n. 1.

7

Neo-Roman Interlude

MACHIAVELLI AND THE ANTI-CONSTITUTIONAL TRADITION

BY WAY OF contrast, let us briefly consider an influential strand of thought no less dependent on Roman antecedents, but in many ways very much opposed to the constitutionalist tradition we are concerned with in this book: the anti-constitutionalism of Machiavelli and other "neo-Romans." This chapter revolves around what the traditional historiography of republicanism has often described as the quintessential "neo-Roman" theory of the state and of liberty.[1] I propose to interpret this tradition, not as part of the Roman constitutional tradition that is my subject in this book, but rather as a relic of an Augustinian tradition, based on the way Augustine in the *City of God* had portrayed so-called "pagan virtue." Machiavelli, applying Roman republicanism to contemporary issues in his *Discorsi* (1531), can be shown to have built on Augustine's distinction between pagan Roman virtue and Christian virtue. By assigning absolute value to the preservation of the state and its aggrandizement, Machiavelli aimed at a restoration of what Augustine had termed "pagan" virtue and developed out of it a concept of unconstrained reason of state.[2] The tradition discussed in this chapter is thus informed by an anti-constitutional view that had already been opposed by Cicero and that is ultimately Greek in origin—the arguments for it come from the Greek skeptic Carneades who in turn draws on Glaucon from Plato's *Republic*.

---

1. See Skinner, *Liberty*; Pettit, *Republicanism*.

2. *Avant la lettre*, it is true, as Friedrich points out in his illuminating book on *Constitutional Reason of State* (see pp. 15–17), but unlike Friedrich I think that Meinecke's take on Machiavelli in this respect still carries weight. See Meinecke, *Staatsräson*, pp. 29–56. Cf. Irwin, *Development*, ch. 28; Mehmel, "Machiavelli und die Antike."

The pagan virtue of glory

As we have just seen in Chapter 6, the Carneadean debate was a powerful undercurrent of normative political thought from Ptolemy of Lucca onward. Reverberations of it reappear in Virgil, and very prominently in the Christian writers Lactantius (*c.*240–*c.*320) and Augustine (354–430). The way these last two framed the debate proved particularly influential, for the simple reason that it was primarily in their texts that fragments of book 3 of Cicero's *Republic* have been preserved. It provided a model for Machiavelli (1469–1527) in the *Discourses* and for Alberico Gentili's (1552–1608) work on the justice of the Roman Empire, *The Wars of the Romans* (*De armis Romanis*, 1599). Repercussions of its effects can also be felt in Thomas Hobbes' thought.

In his influential interpretation of the Carneadean debate and its impact on later international thought, Richard Tuck has put forward the view that Cicero's "final message," his defense of the justice of Roman imperial rule, was "likely to have been . . . that the apparent injustice of an imperial hegemony could be defended as being in the necessary interests of Rome." This leads Tuck to claim that "the Romans were the most powerful voices in antiquity in defence of what we may reasonably term this *raison d'état* view," a view he sums up as the "idea that war could legitimately be made for imperial power and glory."[3] This is almost certainly wrong as an interpretation of Cicero and the Carneadean debate, although it is an influential view that has been held in various versions by Lactantius, Augustine, and Machiavelli. The idea that the Romans considered glory-seeking, *cupiditas gloriae*, as the driving force behind Rome's expansion can already be found in Roman writers, especially historians. It is expressed succinctly by Sallust, who wrote that once Rome lived under republican government, as opposed to kingly rule, "it is hard to believe how quickly the city grew once liberty had been gained: so much had the desire for glory triumphed (*tanta cupido gloriae incesserat*)."[4] But while Sallust famously explained the downfall of the Roman Republic by reference to a moralizing account of the corrupting effect of imperial rule and the attending luxury,[5] the Carneadean debate offered a very different way of accounting for the demise of the Republic, with constitutional justice (or lack thereof), not glory, being the chief ingredient. This distinction between pagan virtue, on the one hand, and juridical justice or constitutionalism, on the other, is the key to understanding the different paths that political

3. Tuck, *Rights of War and Peace*, pp. 22–23.

4. Sall. *Cat.* 7.3.

5. Ibid. 52.19–23 (Cato's speech). For Sallust's influence, see Osmond, "Princeps."

thought was to take up to the eighteenth century and the *Federalist Papers*: a concern with constitutionalism and constitutional rules united such diverse thinkers as Polybius and Cicero with later authors such as Bodin, Hobbes, Harrington, Trenchard and Gordon, Bolingbroke, Montesquieu, Hume, John Adams, and Madison. It separated them from Sallust, Machiavelli, and the eighteenth-century French proponents of virtue, whose language of virtue played a crucial role in the Revolution and came effectively to dominate the National Assembly.[6]

The classicist James Zetzel has argued that Cicero's account of the Carneadean debate profoundly influenced Virgil's vision of the Roman imperial order as it appears in the *Aeneid*. Zetzel draws attention to the fact that in Virgil as well as in Cicero the "Roman order may have triumphed, but not all the ways in which that triumph was achieved were admirable."[7] This has consequences for the imperial power, Rome, herself: far from advocating *raison d'état* and the seeking of *gloria*, Cicero in his answer to Carneades offers a very different vision.

One of the key texts for Tuck is a passage from Laelius' answer to Carneades in the *Republic* where the effect of death for states is contrasted with its effect on individuals:

> For the state (*civitas*) ought to be so established as to be eternal, and therefore there is no natural death of a state (*res publica*) as there is for a man, for whom death is not only necessary, but at times desirable. When a state (*civitas*) is removed, destroyed, extinguished, it is somehow similar (comparing small to great) to the death and collapse of the entire cosmos.[8]

Tuck thinks that this merely illustrates that "sacrifice of the citizen" was considered a "particularly glorious thing by all Roman writers."[9] However, as Zetzel shows, the passage is set in the context of an argument about justice and its being in harmony with natural law and its being eternal, which is all in a very Stoic vein. This, on the one hand, serves to justify the integration of formerly independent cities and states into the Roman imperial order.[10] On the other hand, however—and this is crucial

6. See the Epilogue; and Linton, *Politics of Virtue*, pp. 201–213; cf. Parker, *Cult of Antiquity*, pp. 8–34. For a slightly different view, see Armitage, "Empire and Liberty"; see also Shklar, "Montesquieu," and Rahe, "Montesquieu's *Considerations*," esp. p. 82.

7. Zetzel, "Natural Law and Poetic Justice," p. 312.

8. Cic. *Rep.* 3.34 = August. *De civ. D.* 22.6. Trans. Zetzel.

9. Tuck, *Rights of War and Peace*, p. 22.

10. Zetzel, "Natural Law and Poetic Justice," p. 316.

for my argument—Cicero seems to be implying that Rome and the Republican constitution itself, when failing to live up to the standards of natural law sketched in the Carneadean debate, will have to fear for its survival. At this point it bears repeating that Cicero's dialogue, albeit written in the late 50s BC in a context of looming civil war and highly dysfunctional constitutional institutions, is actually set in the year 129 BC—also in the context of constitutional conflict, this time over Ti. Gracchus' redistributive land reforms, especially over the judicial powers of the agrarian commission established under those reforms, when one of the protagonists of the dialogue, Scipio, must have been floated as a potential dictator to put the constitutional order back in place.[11] However, this came to nought when the real Scipio died only a few days after the dramatic date of Cicero's dialogue (a historical fact alluded to by Cicero). His death destroyed hopes of a return to the old constitutional ways, and serves as a watershed for Cicero: looking back to 129 BC from the late 50s, he suggests that roughly 70 years earlier, the constitution could still have been saved. How? Interestingly, this is where Cicero brings in the necessity of constitutional justice, even vis-à-vis non-citizens:

> Tiberius Gracchus . . . paid attention to citizens, but neglected the rights and treaties of the allies and the Latins. If that license should become customary and spread more widely, and should transform our power from *ius* to violence (*imperiumque nostrum ad vim a iure traduxerit*), so that those who are now our willing subjects be held by terror (*ut qui adhuc voluntate nobis oboediunt, terrore teneantur*), even if those of us who are getting on in years are finishing our watch, I am still concerned about our descendants and about the immortality of the republic, which could be eternal, if our life remained in accordance with ancestral institutions and customs (*institutis et moribus*).[12]

Of course, given the dramatic date of the dialogue and the time of its writing, this implies that, in Cicero's view, by the late 50s, the *imperium* of the Romans had been transformed from *ius* (constitutional justice) to *vis* (violence) and that the once willing subjects, non-citizens, who, according to Cicero, should nonetheless be entitled to certain constitutional rights (*iura*), are now simply ruled by terror.[13] This is not the language of someone devoted simply to *gloria*, necessity or *raison*

11. See Nicolet, "Le *De re publica*"; Ferrary, "Cicéron et la dictature"; Stevenson, "Readings."

12. Cic. *Rep.* 3.41. Trans. Zetzel (except he has "laws" instead of "institutions"). This part of the dialogue has been transmitted only in the palimpsest found in 1819 by Angelo Mai (first ed. Rome-Stuttgart 1822); the palimpsest starts abruptly.

13. Analogous to the relationship between *vis* and *ius* sketched in *Pro Sestio*; see above, pp. 165–166.

d'état. Almost 10 years later, Cicero makes this clear in the *De officiis*; here he unmistakably points to the tension between glory-seeking and justice, between especially military glory (*bellica gloria*) and the morally right (*honestum*), dissolving the former in favor of the latter.[14] Also, Cicero says, glory-seeking leads to injustice,[15] since "no one who has gained glory through bravery by treachery and cunning" can be lauded, for "nothing can be morally right that lacks justice."[16]

Virgil's *Aeneid* contains Jupiter's announcement that he had given the Romans *imperium sine fine*, "empire without limit or end,"[17] and Virgil was heavily influenced by Cicero. In the description of the shield of Aeneas, Rome becomes the cosmos; in James Zetzel's words, the victory of Augustus and the empire he pacified become "the goal of world history and the center of the universe," portraying "the end of history in both senses of the word 'end.'"[18] Zetzel shows, however, that Virgil's vision is ultimately not all that Hegelian, but rather contains strong ambiguities, proving any "end of history" to be a false, naïve hope. A further important strand of Virgil's propagandistic poem is the importance it attaches to the pacification of subjects through the imposition of the constitutional norms of *mos*. In one of the most famous passages[19] Anchises reminds Aeneas of the mission of the Romans:

> *You, Roman, be sure to rule the world*
> *(be these your arts)*
> *to impose order (*morem*) on the foundation of peace*
> *to spare the vanquished and to crush the proud.*[20]

14. Cic. *Off.* 1.68: "we must beware of ambition for glory; for it robs us of liberty." Cf. generally 1.62–69.

15. *Off.* 1.64.

16. *Off.* 1.62. For a real-world example of the problems of conscience involved with unjust empire, see *Tusc.* 5.102 (statues illicitly gained in the provinces; cf. also *2Verr.* 4).

17. Virg. *Aen.* 1.239. Cf. Gentili, *Wars* 2.2, p. 140/141, at n. 51, where the lines of Virgil are not quoted. There is an echo of these lines at *Wars* 2.13, p. 350/351, however, where peace and laws are said to have been the arts by which Rome grew: *Illis artibus Roma crevit: istis artibus Roma stetit.*

18. Zetzel, "Natural Law and Poetic Justice," p. 310. On the shield, see West, "Shield of Aeneas." 1975–76.

19. Which Augustine quotes as well (*De civ. D.* 5.12), but without stressing peace, order and the imposition of *mos*. But cf. *De civ. D.* 5.17.

20. Verg. *Aen.* 6.851-853. Trans. H. R. Fairclough, adapted.

This is not about glory, but about the pacifying imposition of a constitutional order. Similarly, a few lines earlier Virgil has Anchises express strong misgivings about glory-seeking,[21] and in book 7, when Aeneas' son Ascanius is said to be "inflamed with love of extraordinary praise," this makes him pursue Silvia's stag, which in turn triggers the war that lasts for the rest of the *Aeneid*, a catastrophic war very much modeled on the Roman civil wars of Virgil's youth.[22]

Once we get to the Carneadean debate as it appears in the Christian writers Lactantius and Augustine, we encounter additional layers added to it. Lactantius, in his *Divine Institutes*,[23] a work he was provoked to write by the emperor Diocletian's Great Persecution (which began in 303), quotes the central argument put forward in the *Republic* against Carneades' skeptical, anti-imperialist stance verbatim—Cicero's familiar Stoic[24] description of natural law as an objective yardstick for justice and a universal constitutional order:

> True law is right reason, consonant with nature, spread through all people. It is constant and eternal. . . . We cannot be released from this law by senate or people. . . . There will not be one law at Rome and another in Athens, one now and another later; but all nations at all times will be bound by this one eternal and unchangeable law.[25]

But Lactantius is not sympathetic to Cicero's theory of natural law. He cites this passage from the *Republic* only to go on to show that justice, properly understood, had, in fact, been absent from Rome. He is inclined to present Carneades' skeptical stance and his anti-Ciceronian arguments as effective as far as they go, both because he thinks that Cicero, as a pagan, could not possibly have refuted Carneades' skepticism, and because Lactantius is rather hostile to the Roman

---

21. Ibid. 6.817-23, on Lucius Iunius Brutus' killing of his own sons in the name of republican liberty. Virgil's discomfort shows in his calling Brutus' spirit "proud" (*animam superbam*), aligning him with Tarquinius Superbus. Augustine (*De civ. D.* 5.18) was to seize upon the passage, and so did Machiavelli, in *Discourses* 1.16.4; 3.1.5 and esp. 3.3.1. Machiavelli, of course, approved of Brutus. Gentili also adduced the passage; Picenus (*Wars* 1.4, p. 38) cites Anchises' claim that Brutus' glory-seeking made him unhappy (*infelix*). In book 2 (2.4, pp. 178–187) Brutus is defended, and the authority of Augustine doubted; the law of God has no claim to authority.

22. Verg. *Aen.* 7.496. Thanks to David Lupher for this hint.

23. On Lactantius and his work, see the Introduction in Bowen and Garnsey, *Lactantius: Divine Institutes*.

24. Although Carneades is portrayed by Lactantius as an enemy of Plato and Aristotle's ethical doctrines, Cicero claims that his main target were the Stoics: *Tusc.* 5.83.

25. Cic. *Rep.* 3.33 = Lact. *Inst.* 6.8.7-9. Trans. Zetzel.

Empire of his own day, which was persecuting Christians. Lactantius goes on to say that "if Cicero had also known or explained what instructions the holy law itself consists in as clearly as he saw its force and reason, he would have fulfilled the role not of a philosopher but of a prophet. That, however, he could not do, and so we must."[26]

With Lactantius tilting the Carneadean debate dangerously in favor of Carneades' skeptical stance (at least in the absence of Christianity), it remained for Augustine to explain how the Romans could have been given their empire by God in the first place.[27] Augustine, slightly more sympathetic to Cicero's defense against Carneades' skeptical argument than Lactantius had been, does not himself really try to refute Carneades.[28] Rather, he integrates the debate into a historical view that accords the Romans some virtues due to which they gained their empire—above all what Augustine thinks of as the pagan virtue *par excellence*, glory.

Augustine's account is ambiguous; given Rome's pagan nature, the Romans could never achieve true justice.[29] But when he discusses "by what virtues the ancient Romans gained the favour of the true God, so that he increased their empire although they did not worship him,"[30] Augustine quotes Sallust and answers that the Romans had been "eager for praise" and "sought unbounded glory."[31] Creating a highly influential legacy conspicuous in Machiavelli,[32] Augustine goes on to say that "this glory they [the Romans] most ardently loved. For its sake they chose to live and for its sake they did not hesitate to die. They suppressed all other desires in their boundless desire for this one thing."[33] A thirst for glory had first resulted in the Romans shaking off kingly rule and seeking liberty. "But once they had freedom, so great was the passion for glory which arose

---

26. Lact. *Inst.* 6.8.11-12. Trans. Bowen and Garnsey.

27. On Augustine's *City of God*, see O'Daly, *Augustine's* City of God; on his political thought, see Baynes, *Political Ideas*; Deane, *Political and Social Ideas*; Markus, *Saeculum*; Weithman, "Augustine's Political Philosophy."

28. On Augustine's use of Cicero, see Testard, *Saint Augustin et Cicéron*; Stock, *Augustine the Reader*; Hagendahl, *Augustine*, vol. 2, pp. 479–588, esp. 540–553 on the *Republic*.

29. August. *De civ. D.* 19.21. For an excellent comparison with Cicero's conception of justice, see Horn, "Politische Gerechtigkeit."

30. Ibid. August. *De civ. D.* 5.12. Trans. W. M. Green.

31. Ibid. 5.12, quoting Sall. *Cat.* 7.6.

32. For a good summary of the scholarly discussion of Augustine's influence on Machiavelli, with further literature, see Warner and Scott, "Sin City."

33. August. *De civ. D.* 5.12. Trans. W. M. Green.

that liberty seemed too little by itself unless they were also seeking dominion over others."[34] It was for this reason, Augustine maintains in an utterly Sallustian vein, that the Romans gained first liberty, and then empire. While the Romans were virtuous in this sense and not corrupted by wealth, while their treasury (*aerarium*) was filled and their private wealth small (*tenues res privatae*), the empire grew.[35] But glory and the love of praise are virtues only in a very tenuous sense. Augustine does call glory-seeking a virtue of sorts,[36] but then he almost immediately enters a caveat, quoting Sallust to the effect that glory-seeking was in fact "a vice," albeit one "that comes close to being a virtue,"[37] as opposed to avarice. At times Augustine makes it clear, unambiguously, that glory is but a name the Romans used to hide crimes motivated by their lust for domination (*libido dominandi*).[38] As soon as pagan virtue was replaced by greed and luxury, the state grew poor and the private citizens rich, leading to the downfall Cato outlines in Sallust, a description Augustine quotes in the *City of God*.

But, Augustine writes, developing an interesting and extremely influential idea,[39] glory-seeking and the love of praise can be "regarded as virtues" in the sense that they limit or restrain (*cohibentur*) the greater vices.[40] The Romans, Augustine states, "for one vice, that is, love of praise, . . . overcame the love of money and many other vices."[41] Importantly, Augustine imputes to Cicero this exact notion of glory as the chief pagan virtue. He argues that "men who do not obtain the gift of the Holy Spirit and bridle their baser passions by pious faith and by love of intelligible beauty, at any rate live better because of their desire for human praise and glory," and goes on to claim that Cicero also could not disguise this fact. "[N]ot even in his philosophical works," Augustine writes, "did Cicero shrink from this pestilential notion, for he declares allegiance to it in them as plain as day." By "philosophical works" the church father here means Cicero's *Tusculan Disputations*, a highly rhetorical work, where Cicero makes a throwaway remark on the motivational power of glory which Augustine fastens

34. Ibid.

35. Ibid.; cf. 5.15.

36. Ibid. 5.12.

37. Ibid. 5.12, quoting Sall. *Cat.* 11.1-2.

38. *De civ. D.* 3.14.

39. The idea of "countervailing passions," where one vice or passion weakens or tames the others; see Hirschman, *Passions*, esp. pp. 20–31.

40. August. *De civ. D.* 5.13.

41. Ibid.

upon.[42] Ultimately, glory-seeking remains a vice, or at best a pagan virtue; men "like Scaevola, Curtius, and the Decii" were merely "citizens of the earthly city," who, in the absence of eternal life, could not be motivated but by glory.[43] As Pierre Bayle was to put it in his *Dictionary*, solidifying this strand of interpretation of Augustine, "the good morals of some atheists" do not constitute "any real virtues"; rather, these "were only glittering sins, *splendida peccata*, as St Augustine has said of all the fine actions of the pagans."[44]

We are now in a position to see clearly a virtue-oriented tradition of thought, inspired by Sallust and given expression most prominently by Augustine, according to which glory-seeking was the true Roman virtue.[45] Augustine was helped in giving prominence to this idea by the contrast he could draw between it and his own Christian worldview. It is true that Augustine did mention the other, Ciceronian or Virgilian elements, such as the "imposition of laws on many nations" and the fact that "the Romans too were not exempt from living under their own laws, the same laws that they imposed on others."[46] But his emphasis, as well as his most important legacy, remained the focus on virtue, especially glory-seeking.

From Lactantius and Augustine to Machiavelli

This focus on virtue and the sharp dichotomy between pagan and Christian virtue was taken up and used very influentially by Machiavelli.[47] While for Augustine *gloria* remained ambivalent at best, Machiavelli gave it a straightforwardly sympathetic description.[48] Adopting Augustine's dichotomy, but appraising pagan virtue in a way diametrically opposed to the church father, Machiavelli

42. Ibid., citing Cic. *Tusc.* 1.4 (more representative, however, is *Tusc.* 5.102).

43. August. *De civ. D.* 5.14.

44. Bayle, *Dictionary*, p. 401 (*Dictionnaire*, p. 627). See Irwin, *Development*, pp. 418–420.

45. For guidance to Augustine's extraordinary and far-reaching influence on later Western thought, with literature, see now Pollmann, *Historical Reception*.

46. August. *De civ. D.* 5.17. Augustine quotes Virgil's verses on the mission of the Romans (*Aen.* 6.851–853), but does not dwell on the crucial aspect of the imposition of peace and constitutional order. On Augustine's use of Virgil, see MacCormack, *Shadows of Poetry*, ch. 5; see also Stock, *Augustine the Reader*.

47. For interpretations of Machiavelli's thought that differ in crucial ways from each other and from the line pursued here, see Rahe, *Against Throne and Altar*; Pocock, *Machiavellian Moment*.

48. My discussion is indebted to Irwin, *Development*, pp. 725–743, esp. pp. 729–731. See also Perreau-Saussine, "Skinner in Context," esp. pp. 117–118.

broaches the topic in a chapter designed to show how Roman virtue was instrumental in expanding the empire:

> If one asks oneself how it comes about that peoples of old were more fond of liberty than they are today, I think the answer is that it is due to the same cause that makes men today less bold than they used to be; and this is due, I think, to the difference between our education and that of bygone times, which is based on the difference between our religion and the religion of those days. For our religion, having taught us the truth and the true way of life, leads us to ascribe less esteem to worldly honour. Hence the gentiles, who held it in high esteem and looked upon it as their highest good (*il sommo bene*), displayed in their actions more ferocity than we do. . . . [T]he old religion did not beatify men unless they were replete with worldly glory: army commanders, for instance, and rulers of republics.[49]

Wordly honor or glory, Machiavelli holds, constituted the highest end, or greatest good for "the gentiles." This is perfectly Augustinian, but it is, of course, polemical to impute this view to Cicero, who introduced the notion of the greatest good into Latin to render the Greek *telos*: an end in itself, that for the sake of which everything else is ultimately done. The fact that Machiavelli chooses the term *il sommo bene* is significant and betrays the polemical thrust. The *summum bonum* in ancient ethics is usually held to be the individual's well-being or happiness, his or her *eudaemonia*. The final good is identified with virtue by various schools of ancient ethics, the aim being to dissolve any conflict between individual well-being and virtue, where virtue is understood as other-regarding morality. In line with this Cicero points out that "when the Stoics say that the greatest good (*summum bonum*) is to live agreeably with nature, this means, in my view, the following: always to concur with virtue; and as for other things that are in accordance with nature, to choose them if they do not conflict with virtue."[50] The point is that when writing on virtue, Cicero has in mind, not Augustine and Machiavelli's pagan virtue with its concern for glory, but other-regarding justice, what he calls the *honestum*.[51]

---

49. *Discourses* 2.2.6. Trans. Walker.

50. Cic. *Off.* 3.13. Trans. E. M. Atkins.

51. On Machiavelli's relationship to Cicero, see Skinner, *Machiavelli*, pp. 36–47; see also Colish, "Cicero's *De officiis*." Cf. also Isaiah Berlin, "Originality of Machiavelli," who takes Machiavelli's pagan-Christian dichotomy at face value.

Machiavelli extols glory-seeking as a virtue able to motivate citizens to preserve and expand their state.[52] For Machiavelli, therefore, virtue is not an end in itself, but is instrumental to what he perceives as the ultimate, highest end: the preservation and expansion of the state. Glory can and should be sacrificed to the safety and preservation of the state.[53] Machiavelli defends exceptional means to save the state and adduces as an illustration Romulus' murder of Remus. Any "action, however extraordinary, which may be of service in the organising of a kingdom or the constituting of a republic" is justified in Machiavelli's view, and in killing Remus Romulus exhibited pagan virtue.[54] Augustine had also discussed Romulus' example, and agreed with Machiavelli that Romulus had been motivated by the desire to rule by himself and to acquire glory.[55] Augustine, of course, did not think the deed justified, least of all on the grounds of glory. Notwithstanding Augustine's talk of pagan virtue, Cicero's take on Romulus also resulted in a condemnation, on grounds of Stoic moral philosophy. In Cicero's view, Romulus' killing illustrates a case of conflict between expediency and what is right, where what seemed expedient won out:

> [T]he appearance of benefit (*utilitas*) drove his [Romulus'] spirit; and when it seemed more beneficial (*utilius*) to him to rule alone than with someone else, he killed his brother. He abandoned both family obligation and humanity in order to secure something that seemed beneficial, but was not. . . . He did wrong, then.[56]

Machiavelli's defense of such extraordinary, extra-constitutional measures oscillates between the position that considerations of justice or constitutionality either do not apply to the kinds of emergency situations he discusses (because the preservation and expansion of the state overrides justice as an end) and the position that the preservation and expansion of the state is itself something that

52. *Discourses* 1.43. Cf. 2.2.9. For an interesting comparison between Machiavelli and Francis Bacon, see Clarke, "Uprooting Nebuchadnezzar's Tree." For a more pacifist Machiavelli, see Viroli, *Machiavelli*, pp. 101–102; 139–140; but see Sullivan, *Machiavelli*, p. 39, n. 8.

53. *Discourses* 3.41.

54. Ibid. 1.9.2. Cf. 1.18.5-7 on extraordinary means. See Warner and Scott, "Sin City," pp. 863–866, on Machiavelli's use of the Romulus example.

55. August. *De civ. D.* 15.5. Cf. *Discourses* 1.10.6.

56. Cic. *Off.* 3.41. Trans. E. M. Atkins. Romulus' course of action is only *seemingly* beneficial, as for Cicero there cannot be a real conflict between morality and expediency. The *honestum* is necessarily beneficial, while the reverse does not hold.

is required by justice, or by the constitutional order. Both positions cannot be maintained. As Terence Irwin has pointed out, "Machiavelli seems to argue that since extraordinary means are morally acceptable in emergencies, we ought to disregard morality altogether in all circumstances. The argument is not only unconvincing but also inconsistent; for if we think it matters to find moral grounds or permission for extraordinary means in emergencies, we cannot consistently suppose that moral considerations never matter."[57]

If his defense of "pagan virtue," glory, and the preservation of the state is not, however, built on grounds of justice or constitutionality, then how does Machiavelli justify the idea that the safety of the state and imperialism constitute the *summum bonum*? One way of interpreting Machiavelli is to claim that he in effect makes a Hobbesian argument here for the importance of the state as a necessary condition for human self-preservation.[58] His views on glory and pagan virtue, however, are in deep tension with Hobbes' views on individual prudence and practical rationality.[59] They are shaped by Augustine's description of pagan virtue, with which Machiavelli entirely agrees, while of course diverging from Augustine's bleak normative assessment; as Warner and Scott write in an illuminating essay, Machiavelli "celebrates Rome as unreservedly as Sallust while seeing it as clearly as Augustine."[60]

Machiavelli's brand of republicanism is not at all committed to any prepolitical norms; rather, the order of the state is itself permanently up for grabs, in the sense that most times seem extraordinary, the republic is permanently on the brink of corruption, and a (re)ordering of the "constitutional" order is often warranted. Such a reordering is not itself bound by any higher-order norms, except for the preservation of the state. Unlike in Cicero's formula, *salus populi suprema lex esto*,[61] which serves, as we have seen in Chapter 4, as a constitutional restraint on the chief magistrates and is not meant as an invitation to subvert existing constitutional norms, Machiavelli's position points to a much more malleable view of the "constitutional" order:

---

57. Irwin, *Development*, p. 739.

58. Irwin, *Development*, p. 734, suggests this.

59. Cf. for a different interpretation of the relationship between Machiavelli and Hobbes Rahe, *Against Throne and Altar*. On Machiavelli and imperialism, see Hörnqvist, *Machiavelli and Empire*; see also Armitage, *Ideological Origins*, pp. 125–145.

60. Warner and Scott, "Sin City," p. 862. Machiavelli does not believe Sallust's description of early, harmonious Rome, nor does he think harmony would have been desirable. In a Polybian way, he emphasizes the importance of conflict for stability.

61. Cic. *Leg.* 3.8.

> [S]hould a prince seek worldly glory (*la gloria del mondo*), he should most certainly covet possession of a city that has become corrupt, not, with Caesar, to complete its spoliation, but, with Romulus, to reform it (*riordinarla*). Nor in very truth can the heavens afford men a better opportunity of acquiring glory (*gloria*); nor can men desire anything better than this.[62]

Reordering the corrupt city with sole authority, regardless of higher-order constraints, is justified as long as the state is thus preserved. This stands in stark tension with the views held by Cicero and the Roman tradition of constitutional thought.

Gentili's Hobbesian alternative

We may usefully contrast Machiavelli's admiration of "pagan virtue" with Alberico Gentili's view, and rejection, of the virtue of glory. In his *Wars of the Romans*, we encounter a treatise very much in the mold of the Carneadean dialogue in Cicero's *Republic*.[63] The Augustinian emphasis on glory and Roman virtue is reflected, but—as opposed to Machiavelli's vision—ultimately clearly rejected. In the first book, which constitutes an attack on Roman imperialism from the viewpoint of justice very much in the vein of Carneades, glory-seeking is identified as the chief trait of the Romans in the very first sentence:

> There is a famous utterance of Cicero in a dispute about military affairs and political wisdom: 'Military excellence has engendered fame for the Roman people and eternal glory (*aeternam gloriam*) for the city; it has forced the whole world to obey this rule.'[64]

Similarly, referring explicitly to Cicero's *Republic* and to the distinction drawn in the Carneadean debate between civil justice, which is born of mere necessity and reflects simply a contractarian bargain, and natural justice, which, if it even exists, is identified by Carneades with foolishness, Gentili, or rather the Carneadean speaker of book 1, addresses Cicero directly, in an accusatory tone:

> Cicero, you will say and contend that civil—that is, cunning—justice existed in your state, but you will not persuade us that it was true, genuine

62. *Discourses* 1.10.9. Trans. Walker.

63. See Kingsbury and Straumann, "Introduction"; Lupher, "The *De armis Romanis*."

64. Gentili, *Wars* 1.1, p. 8/9, citing Cic. *Mur.* 22.

> justice, as Lactantius learnedly argues against you and as Augustine points out. 'A state cannot be enlarged without injustice'—among you Romans and for your benefit was that saying born.[65]

The quotation comes of course—by way of Augustine—from Carneades' skeptical attack as portrayed in Cicero's *Republic*. Gentili also gives an account of the essence of Carneades' point, which he knew via Lactantius:

> And thus Carneades quite properly told you, Romans, that if you wished to be just, you ought to return to those huts from which you first set forth, and you ought to surrender this empire of the world.[66]

Here, in book 1, Lactantius' sympathetic report of the Carneadean attack clearly serves as the model and sets the tone. Gentili, too, discusses the example set by Romulus and does not fail to point out that Cicero had condemned Romulus' deeds in *De officiis* (3.41). He adds a further reference to this treatise, as support for the thoroughly anti-Machiavellian point that "[r]epulsive and criminal acts ought not to be done even for the sake of saving one's country."[67]

Gentili's response in book 2 also follows the general path sketched by Cicero, namely a defense of Roman imperialism in terms of a universal natural law, which in Gentili's hands is now identified with the Roman law of the *Corpus iuris*. There was of course no *Corpus iuris* in Cicero's day, but Cicero too thought that the law in force at Rome during the heyday of the Roman Republic was identical with, or at least reflective of, natural law, as we have seen in Chapter 4.

Hence, the defense of the justice of Roman imperialism in the second book of *The Wars of the Romans* bases the justice of the Roman Empire on precisely the defense put forward in Cicero's *Republic* by Laelius, a defense known to Gentili through Augustine. The empire was "seized by force of arms, but without wrongdoing," Gentili writes, and, helped by Augustine's ambivalence, he goes on to enlist the Bishop of Hippo and other "theologians" for his cause:

> Thus the interpreters of the law call the Roman empire just, for it was obtained partly by agreement, partly by the sword. And the theologians and Augustine agree: 'It constitutes a just defense of the Romans for so many wars undertaken and waged that it was the necessity of protecting

65. Ibid. 1.13, p. 118/119, alluding to August. *De civ. D.* 2.21.

66. Ibid. 1.8, p. 68/69, citing Lact. *Inst.* 5.16.2-5.

67. Ibid. 1.2, p. 24/25. Gentili must have had Cic. *Off.* 1.159 in mind.

> their safety and liberty, not greed for acquiring human glory, that forced them to resist enemies who attacked them violently.'[68]

Defending Romulus, Gentili in book 2 first makes room for doubt that Remus had been killed at all.[69] He then goes on to assume for argument's sake that Remus had indeed been killed by Romulus, but defends this action—against Cicero—as a lawful deed, where violence had been countered with violence (*per quam vim propulsata vis*) and Remus' killing was thus "justifiable as an act of punishment."[70] Note that unlike Machiavelli, Gentili does not justify Romulus' act on the Machiavellian grounds of "reordering" the state in order to acquire glory; rather, he justifies the act on legal grounds, along the lines pursued by Cicero in his speeches in defense of Sestius and Milo.

In the culmination of the defense of Roman imperialism, the argument that the Romans had not had a temple dedicated to Peace is rejected.[71] Gentili could not have known emperor Augustus' altar to Peace, the *Ara Pacis*, which since the Fascist era has been so prominently on display in Rome—Augustus' propaganda would have vigorously enforced the point Gentili's defender of the justice of empire is trying to make, the point already made in Virgil's *Aeneid, viz.* that pacification and the imposition of constitutional order carry the main normative weight, not glory.[72] Given how well Gentili knew Virgil, it is somewhat astonishing that in the *Wars of the Romans* he nowhere quotes the famous lines from the sixth book of the *Aeneid* quoted above (6.851-853); there are, however, prominent allusions to and echoes of the *Aeneid* in that work, especially in the thirteenth chapter of the second book, where the imposition of peace and laws are said to have been the arts by which Rome grew.[73]

In the *Wars of the Romans* Gentili is also aligned with the almost Hegelian, teleological aspects of Virgil's view—the Roman Empire, or at least the spread of its constitutional order, is the goal of history, while any other outcome is tantamount to slipping back into a state of nature. The imposition of law and peaceful order as a defense of Roman imperial rule is supported by a quotation from Tacitus: "it

---

68. Ibid., p. 162/163, citing August. *De civ. D.* 3.10.

69. Ibid. 2.2, p. 140/141, referencing the late antique pastiche *De origine gentis Romanae* 23.6.

70. Ibid. 2.2, p. 142/143.

71. Ibid. 2.13, p. 334/335.

72. Augustus' *Res Gestae* includes not one mention of *gloria*.

73. *Wars* 2.13, p. 350/351; cf. *Aen.* 6.852.

is impossible to have peace among peoples without arms." The only alternative to such a Virgilian imposition of peace, Gentili thinks, is a state of nature, conceived in a proto-Hobbesian way as a war of all against all. The anthropological foundations for this view, highly skeptical of virtue, are taken from Tacitus: "There will be vices as long as there are men," hence, "should the Romans be driven out . . . what can result but wars between all these nations?"[74] The resulting state of nature and war of all against all Gentili describes by quoting Virgil:

> But at last the empire was overthrown, and along with all other mortal affairs it had its end. But what had been predicted so long before by wise men, behold, when the Romans had been driven away . . . But behold, . . . behold now the wars of all, of all peoples among themselves. "Neighboring cities, the laws among them burst asunder, take arms; impious Mars rages throughout the globe; as when chariots pour out from the starting pens, they go faster each lap; nor does anyone hold the halter; the chariot is carried along by the horses, and no one guides the reins."[75]

Glimpses of this Virgilian theme can, I believe, also be detected in Thomas Hobbes' interest in the imposition of legal order and his corresponding intense distrust of glory (or pride, as he often calls it). As we know from John Aubrey, although Hobbes in later life had few books, he could always be expected to have copies of Virgil on his table.[76] Christopher Brooke has made it very clear that there is an "Augustinian Hobbes,"[77] for whom glory was a central worry. In fact, this is why Hobbes called his book *Leviathan* in the first place; Leviathan is "King of all the children of Pride,"[78] and while it "might be God who humbles the proud, according to the text of the *Magnificat*, . . . Hobbes assigns this task to the secular sovereign."[79]

---

74. Tac. *Hist.* 4.74 (from the same speech by Cerialis quoted by Gentili, *Wars* 2.13, p. 346/347). On Gentili's use of Tacitus, Tacitean anthropology, and his conception of the state of nature, see Kingsbury and Straumann, "Introduction," esp. pp. xvi-xviii.

75. *Wars* 2.13, p. 355. The (sloppy) quotation is from Verg. *G.* 1.510–14.

76. Skinner, *Visions of Politics*, p. 42.

77. Brooke, *Philosophic Pride*, pp. 69–75.

78. Hobbes, *Leviathan*, vol. 2, ch. 28, p. 496.

79. Brooke, *Philosophic Pride*, p. 74. Hobbes' constitutional order, designed to humble the proud, bears, incidentally, a curious resemblance to Philip Pettit's non-domination, which can potentially even be secured by state interference (*On the People's Terms*, pp. 57–58; 159–160).

In Hobbes' famous suspicion that "there was never any thing so deerly bought" as the "learning of the Greek and Latine tongues"[80] there lies his rejection of Augustine's pagan virtues, and Hobbes is, of course, very much opposed to Machiavelli's embrace of glory. But Hobbes depends to a large extent on the Tacitean and Virgilian sentiments reported above.[81] With slight exaggeration it could be said that Hobbes' state of nature—as much as Gentili's dire world without Roman imperialism—bears a striking resemblance to Machiavelli's ideal of the conflicted, glory-seeking Roman Republic.[82] By contrast, Hobbes' state is really a constitutional mechanism to crush the proud and impose peace. This characteristic of his thought crucially sets him apart from Machiavelli and the entire reason-of-state tradition.[83] For Hobbes, reason of state is part and parcel of his science of prudence, where self-interest acts to restrain as much as to authorize. In some limited sense, then, Hobbes' willingness to breach conventional moral or legal norms is itself sanctioned by higher-level moral and constitutional norms.[84]

To sum up: there are two important strands of thought emanating from the Carneadean debate in early modern constitutional thought, one a Machiavellian anti-constitutional focus on republican expansion, self-interest, and glory, the other a constitutionalist concern with the expansion of law—one might say with the expansion of "natural constitutional law"[85]—and the imposition of order. Early modern anti-constitutional republicans who were marching in Machiavelli's

80. Hobbes, *Leviathan*, vol. 2, ch. 21, p. 334. Cf. *Leviathan*, vol. 3, ch. 46, p. 1097, where Hobbes cites from Virgil's fourth *Eclogue* (4.36) to warn of the future (civil) wars if the teaching of "Greek and Latin eloquence and philosophy" in universities is not going to be constrained.

81. Which, as Hobbes realized, were connected with the emperor Augustus' program. Hobbes writes that he "observed in *Virgil*, that the Honor done to *Aeneas* and his companions has so bright a reflection upon *Augustus Caesar* and other great *Romans* of that time": "Answer to Davenant's Preface to *Gondibert*," p. 58. I owe the hint to this passage to Chris Warren.

82. Putting it the other way around, one might say that, for Machiavelli, there is no stark separation between a state of nature and a political state, which is precisely why extraordinary means are always in order, justified by a pervasive lack of trust.

83. Justus Lipsius, as Brooke has suggested (*Philosophic Pride*, p. 36), is "poised theoretically as well as chronologically between Machiavelli and Hobbes," as his Machiavellian outlook is tempered by considerations of security and the common good.

84. On Hobbes' relationship with the reason of state tradition, see Malcolm, *Reason of State*, pp. 92–123. Malcolm argues (p. 120) that unlike "the 'ragion di stato' theorists, Hobbes did not have to juggle with two opposing value-scales that proceeded on fundamentally different bases; rather, he showed how they were necessarily related within a single overall system." See also Foisneau, "Sovereignty," esp. pp. 340–341; and the Epilogue.

85. This is the kind of constitutional legal order (*ius*) I argue Cicero is referring to in Scipio's famous definition (*iuris consensus*) at *Rep*. 1.39.

footsteps, beholden to *ragion di stato*, were also tracking the Roman historians, especially Sallust, Augustine's claims about glory as the chief Roman virtue, and Carneades' skeptical arguments. Ptolemy of Lucca, Alberico Gentili, the natural lawyers, and Hobbes, on the other hand, were much more interested in and convinced by the *refutation* of Carneades, a refutation Cicero had already sketched, based on a rebuttal of glory, a suspicion of virtue and an insistence on the value of pacification and the imposition of constitutional norms and order. The most influential thinker in this tradition, at least until Hobbes, was, however, Bodin.

8

Jean Bodin and the Fall of the Roman Republic

THE KEY PROTAGONIST in the constitutionalist strand of thought is Jean Bodin (1530–1596). The Roman republican constitution and its concept of dictatorship is the starting point from which he develops his highly influential concept of sovereignty in the *Six livres de la République* (1576).[1] Bodin's work achieved enormous prominence already in the late sixteenth century, with the *République* and its Latin version combined running through at least twenty-six editions, among them translations into other vernaculars, by the year 1606, and with the earlier *Methodus ad facilem historiarum cognitionem* (1566) reaching at least twelve editions.[2] Usually interpreted as the key theorist of absolutist sovereignty, Bodin has recently received a more fine-grained and sensitive interpretation in the work of Daniel Lee. Lee has paid due attention to Bodin's use of Roman law materials and has thus arrived at the conclusion that Bodin should really be seen, not as an absolutist, but as the preeminent early modern theorist of popular sovereignty.[3] According to Lee, Bodin developed a theory of popular sovereignty on the basis of a distinction between the level of the state and sovereignty, on the one hand, and the level of administration or government, on the other. This distinction, elaborated on the basis of a close study of the model of the Roman Republic,

1. Bodin, *République* 1.8, 123–124; see also 3.3, where the concept of *dictator* is philologically examined. For Bodin, see Franklin, *Jean Bodin*, Quaglioni, *Limiti*, and Quaritsch, *Staat*. The Roman foundations of Bodin's thought are severely understudied, with the important exception of Daniel Lee's work. Cf. also Grotius, *De iure belli ac pacis* 1.3.8.12; 1.3.11.1–2; Grotius is important, furthermore, with regard to his invention of the concept of *dominium eminens*, which allowed for emergency takings of private property by the sovereign; see *De iure belli ac pacis* 2.14.7–8; 1.1.6; 3.19.7; Boldt, "Ausnahmezustand," pp. 350–351. See also Hobbes, *De cive*, ch. 7, para. 16, 156–157; Pufendorf, *De iure naturae et gentium* 7.6.15; 8.6.14.

2. Blair, "Authorial Strategies," p. 138.

3. Lee, *Popular Sovereignty*, ch. 6.

allowed Bodin to divorce sovereignty from politics, thus "de-politicizing" sovereignty, and to argue for the "instrumental rationality of the constitutional strategy of precommitment and self-binding."[4] Bodin thus becomes a theorist of constitutionalism, where government is by legally constituted magistrates rather than by commissioners directed by the arbitrary will of the sovereign.

Bodin arrives at his concept of sovereignty by way of a close analysis of Roman legal materials and, most importantly, of the constitutional history of the late Roman Republic. Indeed, Bodin's view of the disintegration of the Roman republican constitutional framework traces the analysis put forward by Pomponius in his *Enchiridion* in important ways[5] and presupposes, as will be shown, a distinction between higher-order rules and normal legislation. Bodin developed his views on the late Roman Republic on the basis of antiquarian research, the most important authors being the humanist historians Carlo Sigonio and Nicolas de Grouchy. From Grouchy Bodin took the revolutionary view that the Roman Republic had in fact been neither an aristocracy nor a mixed constitution, but rather a democracy with undivided sovereignty residing in the assemblies.[6] Before 287 BC and the *lex Hortensia*, sovereignty (*summum imperium*) had been vested in the popular assembly. Afterwards, with the *lex Hortensia* declaring plebiscites, too, as binding, the plebeians had taken over sovereignty. Bodin, in his early *Methodus ad facilem historiarum cognitionem* (1566), took over Grouchy's original assessment of the Republic as a democracy and had proceeded to expound his views on the way this popular sovereignty had been administered in the Republic.

After briefly recounting Polybius' view of the Republic as a combination of kingly, aristocratic, and democratic elements, Grouchy went on to say that to him, the Republic looked like a democracy. Grouchy's reasoning was that notwithstanding the somewhat kingly power inhering in the consuls' *imperium* and the "optimate" power of the Senate, the People were really the locus of sovereignty (*maiestas*). The crucial criterion for this astonishing claim was the right of appeal, which proved that the legal power (*potestas*) of the People was ultimately greater than that of the magistrates.[7] Bodin agreed; in effect paraphrasing Grouchy, he

---

4. Lee, *Popular Sovereignty*, ch. 6, "The Problem of Popular Sovereignty."

5. Many thanks to Daniel Lee for this parallel.

6. Neither Grouchy nor Bodin find mention in Fergus Millar's *Roman Republic*, although they are clearly predecessors of his own views. Carlo Sigonio identified the last century of the Republic with the decline of the mixed constitution due to popular domination, qualifying *provocatio* as one of the crucial criteria of republican freedom; see Sigonio, *De antiquo iure* 1.6, pp. 46–52.

7. Grouchy, *De comitiis Romanorum*, p. 3.

wrote in the *Methodus* that the greatest legal power during the Republic had been the People's (*in plebe maxima potestas*).[8] Interestingly, his periodization of Republic and Principate is rather unorthodox, as he takes the Republic not to end with Augustus, but to endure up to the *lex de imperio Vespasiani*.

The Roman dictatorship, provocatio, *and sovereignty*

Bodin's *Methodus* as well as his main work, the *République* (1576), flesh out his conception of sovereignty by analyzing the institutions and constitutional arguments of the Roman Republic.[9] Most prominent are the ones discussed in the early chapters of the present book, namely the Roman dictatorship, the *decemviri*, and the late irregular dictatorships and extraordinary commands of the last century BC. His treatment of the Roman dictatorship is of particular importance as it enables Bodin to say with great clarity what exactly he has in mind when speaking of sovereignty (*maiestas, summum imperium*). Based on the account of Dionysius of Halicarnassus describing the origins of the dictatorship—discussed above in Chapter 2—Bodin writes in the *Methodus* that the dictatorship had been invented as an instrument by the Senate in order to deceive the plebs and to get rid of the right of appeal (*provocatio*).[10] Drawing on Dionysius, Bodin must have thought that the earliest dictatorship resembled Sulla's and must have been tyrannical in character; at least that is what Dionysius calls it, characterizing it as "a magistracy that was superior to a legal magistracy" and thus "a tyranny."[11]

8. *Methodus ad facilem historiarium cognitionem* (Paris, 1566), pp. 211–212. Cf. also p. 205: *Non enim Senatus Romanorum, inquit [Dionysius of Halicarnassus], arbiter est, id est κύριος earum rerum quas decrevit, sed populus.* In the *République*, Bodin reversed his position and attributed to the magistrates greater "dignity" than to the Senate: *Commonweale*, p. 274.

9. My interpretation follows those scholars, like Daniel Lee, Richard Tuck, or Preston King, who emphasize the basic continuity between the *Methodus* and *Les six livres de la République*; but see, for a diverging view, Julian Franklin's work. For the *Methodus* I am using the 1566 Paris edition, for the *République* the 1583 Paris edition, as well as the 1586 Paris edition of Bodin's Latin translation *De republica libri sex* and Richard Knolles' 1606 English translation in the 1962 edition by Kenneth Douglas McRae, *The Six Bookes of a Commonweale*. For the tension between Bodin's "anti-Roman" methodological protestations and the prominence of Roman law and Roman practice for his argument, see Lee, *Popular Sovereignty*, ch. 5.

10. Bodin sees the *SCU* in a similar light, and believes with Livy that it was an ancient institution (*Commonweale* 3.1, p. 274). This is evidence, for Bodin, that the "chiefe commaund" had been in the magistrates vis-à-vis the Senate; but the tribunes as representatives of the People were superior to everyone else. Cf. *Methodus*, pp. 210–211, where the *SCU* is mentioned and the Senate given more weight.

11. Dion. Hal. *Ant. Rom.* 5.70.3-5. See above, p. 69.

Bodin claims that the tribunes detected this *arcanum imperii* and easily realized that the plebs was being fooled.[12] Drawing on Festus, he goes on to say that the tribunes did not permit the dictatorship to exist to the full extent of its original authority, that is, they did not accept the dictatorship without the right of appeal (*sine provocatione*) for long.[13] With Plutarch, Polybius, and Cicero Bodin states, erroneously, that with the exception of the tribunes, all other magistrates abdicated as soon as the dictator was appointed. The crucial points, which are historically accurate, are that the tribunes could not be overridden by the dictator and were still able to intercede, thus considerably weakening the dictatorship; and, secondly, that the right of appeal was introduced at some point, constraining even the dictatorship, at least within the city limits. The emphasis on *provocatio* is reminiscent of, and to some extent owed to, Pomponius' *Enchiridion*.[14] Further limitations, apart from the veto (intercession) and the right of appeal, lie in the dictator's revocability and, most importantly, the term limit. There is no indication that dictators could actually be revoked by either the nominating magistrate, the Senate, or the People, but Bodin, on the basis of the Roman private-law institution of *depositum*, believes that dictators could be revoked in principle:

> But the dictator had the power of war, peace, life, death, and over the whole state by right of his office (*iure magistratus*), but still it was only as long as he was in office. He held, not actually an office, but a deposit. Even if the command (*imperium*) is peculiar to him, nevertheless no one has an office or honors in his own right (*suo iure*), but as a deposit (*veluti depositos*) until the term has elapsed or until he who has given it takes it away. Ulpian meant this when he said, "I have laid down the office which I once took up."[15]

---

12. This represents an interesting early use of *arcana imperii* (cf. Tac. *Hist.* 1.4), long before Arnold Clapmarius' *De arcanis rerum publicarum* (1605) or Christoph Besold's 1614 treatise of the same title. Unlike Clapmarius and Besold, however, Bodin does not recommend the *arcana* unambiguously; rather, they seem prone to being detected, as in the example here. Cf. Arist. *Pol.* 5.8.1307b40-1308a1, where *sophismata* are also prone to being unmasked.

13. The reference is to Festus 216L.

14. Bodin refers numerous times to the relevant passage, *de orig. Iuris* (*Dig.* 1.2.2).

15. *Methodus*, p. 204. It seems as if Bodin in the *Methodus* is using the language of *depositum* to cover both magistrates in the narrow sense and commissioners, a distinction which was to figure prominently in the *République*. In the later work, *depositum* as well as other Roman real contracts such as *mutuum* or *commodatum* that have a (however "imperfect") bilateral character, is used to describe only magistracies, while the more unilateral real contract of *precarium* applies to commissioners. See on this Lee, *Popular Sovereignty*, ch. 6, "Commissions and Offices." Many thanks to Dan Lee for discussion of this point.

Bodin seems to be wavering here over whether or not the Roman dictator deserved to be called a magistrate in the strict sense. As he would make clear in his later work, the *République*, there was in his view a very rigid distinction between regular magistrates established by higher norms, on the one hand, and mere commissioners, on the other, which latter were established arbitrarily by sovereign will and served at the pleasure of the sovereign. Bodin's choice of the term "magistrate" in the passage quoted seems to indicate that he thought the dictator did have some characteristics of a regular magistrate, but his view of the dictator as a commissioner is best expressed by the clause "until he who has given it takes it away." The distinction between term limits (*quousque tempus finiatur*), on the one hand, and serving at the sovereign's pleasure (*aut is qui dedit repetat*), on the other, is what counts for Bodin's dichotomy of magistrate and commissioner, which comes to the fore in connection with his discussion, not only of the dictator, but also of other extraordinary powers of the Roman Republic. That he views dictators as mere commissioners Bodin makes obvious in his later work, the *République*, when he says that the dictator, even in the earliest time when there was no right of appeal against him, was not sovereign, since (Bodin believed erroneously) he could be revoked at any time and was (Bodin correctly points out) subject to a term limit. This was so even though Bodin held the powers of the dictator to be far-reaching, subsuming even those, such as *constituere rempublicam*, which only Sulla and the *triumviri*, and perhaps Caesar, had held, and which had led Theodor Mommsen and Carlo Sigonio before him—and Carl Schmitt after him—to assume that Sulla, Caesar, and the second triumvirate were "constituent powers" without *any* constitutional limits.[16] Bodin, on the other hand, did not think this sufficient to attribute sovereignty to these dictators *reipublicae constituendae causa*, whom he does not sharply distinguish from the earlier, "ordinary" dictators; to him, all dictators were extraordinary commissioners, but still within the limits of the constitutional order, as they all served at the pleasure of the sovereign: the People.[17]

---

16. Sigonio thought that Sulla, Caesar, and the *triumviri* had all used the designation of *reipublicae constituendae causa*, which then served to inspire Mommsen's notion of these as "constituting powers" no longer subject to constitutional limitations; see above, Chapter 2; Sigonio, *In Fastos*, p. 312; Mommsen, *Staatsrecht*, vol. 2.1, pp. 702–742. This was eventually copied by Carl Schmitt, who mapped his distinction between "commissarial" and "sovereign" dictatorship onto Sigonio's and Mommsen's distinction between early, ordinary dictators on the one hand and late, extraordinary dictators *reipublicae constituendae causa* on the other. Bodin, unlike Schmitt, did not think that the latter were truly sovereign; he is much closer to Roman reality, too, in pointing out that Sulla et al. had acted at the pleasure of the people, not as "constituting" sovereigns. For the Mommsen-Schmitt trajectory, see Nippel, "Saving the Constitution."

17. Bodin is not always clear on whether or not the dictator was sovereign in the relevant sense. When discussing the advantages of monarchy vis-à-vis aristocracy or democracy, he

The same held for the Ten Men (*decemviri*), who in the French version are fittingly rendered as the "*dix Commissaires*" (ten commissioners); they were "established for the reforming of customes and lawes," and "albeit that they had absolute power, from which there was no appeale to be made, and that all offices were suspended, during the time of their commission; yet had they not for all that any Soveraigntie; for their commission being fulfilled, their power also expired; as did that of the Dictators."[18] The Ten had had absolute *summa potestas*, according to the Latin version—*summam ac legibus solutam potestatem haberent*—but they were still subject to a term limit, which made their power less than sovereign.[19]

The point here is that the crucial criteria for sovereignty—each necessary and jointly sufficient—are absolute power, irrevocability, and the absence of term limits. In Bodin's view, Roman dictators were subject (apart from the earliest time) to constraints in all three regards: *provocatio*, revocability, and the term limit of six months all undermined their sovereignty. The idea that the dictator was revocable is expressed in the Roman private law language of *depositum*, a real contract where a thing was handed over by the depositor to the depositee to be kept in his charge. The contract was gratuitous, and created a set of mutual rights and obligations, with little liability for the depositee in case of loss of the thing due to slight negligence, but with the obligation to restore the deposited thing on demand, even when there was a fixed term.[20] In his later work, the *République*, Bodin reserves the comparison with deposit, loan, and other Roman real contracts for magistracies only, with term limits, while the unilateral real contract of *precarium* is applied to the dictator as a commissioner, whose powers can always be revoked by the sovereign. The private-law nature of the contractual relationships Bodin alludes to cannot be stressed enough; for, as we will see, contractual obligations, even on the part of the sovereign, were binding on Bodin's account. Further, both the right of appeal and the term limit show, according to Bodin, that there were constitutional constraints on the dictator in the Roman Republic which made it by definition impossible to attribute any sovereignty to him: "Soveraigntie is not limited either in power, charge, or time certaine."[21]

---

contradicts himself and says that aristocracies or popular states in emergencies would "usually create a Dictator, as a soveraigne Monarch: knowing well that a Monarchie was the anckor whereunto of necessitie they must have recourse": *Commonweale* 6.4, p. 715.

18. Ibid. 1.8, p. 85.

19. *De republica*, p. 80.

20. Buckland, *Roman Law*, pp. 467–470.

21. *Commonweale* 1.8, p. 85; cf. *De republica*, p. 80.

In his chapter on citizenship, Bodin points to the crucial position that the right of appeal had enjoyed: *provocatio* had been "holy Law" for Roman citizens and scarcely anything "was so proper unto the Roman citizens in generall, as that the magistrats and governours might not proceed in iudgement against them in matters concerning their life and libertie, without the peoples leave."[22] This was "the greatest and chiefest priveledge (*summum ius*) proper to the citisens of Rome, That they could not by the magistrats be punished either with death or exile, but that they might still from them appeale; which libertie all the citisens of Rome enioyed."[23] The sanctions for violation of the *provocatio* norms were increasingly strengthened, with the result that "at such time as *Cicero* was about to have commaunded the Roman citisens privie to the conspiracie of Cateline to be strangled in prison," violation of the right of appeal came at a high cost, which had an interesting effect on the subsequent constitutional history of Rome: "Which law [*provocatio* statutes] *Cicero* having transgressed, was therefore not onely driven into exile, but also proscribed, his goods confiscated, his house . . . burnt, and a temple built in the plot thereof, which the people at the motion of *Clodius* their Tribune, commaunded to be consecrated to Libertie: wherewith the magistrats terrified, durst not but from that time forward with lesse severitie proceed against the Roman citisens, yea even after that the popular state was chaunged."[24] The right of appeal appears here as an enduring constitutional constraint, one that even survives the Roman Republic and continues to constrain magistrates' power during the Principate. It constitutes the *summum ius* of Roman citizens and has constitutional status; Sulla's proscriptions, even though based on popular legislation, were in violation thereof and constituted tyranny.[25]

Bodin gives an interesting account of Sulla's dictatorship, which, he says, did not amount to sovereignty either, for all its extreme concentration of power. It did not really constitute a dictatorship at all, Bodin claims, for reasons he says Cicero had already put forward; "if one should say, that *Sylla* was by the law

22. *Commonweale* 1.6, p. 55. This *lex sacrata* had been introduced, Bodin says following Livy, right after the expulsion of the kings: *De republica*, p. 53.

23. *Commonweale* 1.6, p. 57. Cf. *De republica*, p. 54 (note the use of *ius* in the sense of subjective right).

24. *Commonweale* 1.6, pp. 55–56. Cf. *De republica*, pp. 53–54. Bodin seems to have based his account of the Catilinarian affair largely on Sallust, from whom he cites parts of Caesar's speech without acknowledging the source (Sall. *Cat*. 51).

25. There is a slight ambiguity in Bodin's account here; although he explicitly describes Sulla's reign as a tyranny, rather than an actual dictatorship, he seems to allow for the possibility that Sulla's, no less than Caesar's and Augustus' position represented to some extent a commission, constitutionally granted by the people.

Valeria made Dictator for threescore yeares: I will aunswere as *Cicero* did, That it was neither Dictatorship nor law, but a most cruell tyrannie."[26] In the Latin edition, there is a reference to the first book of Cicero's *Laws*.[27] Bodin must have had the passage at 1.42 in mind, where Cicero, as we have seen in Chapter 2, attacks the legitimacy of Sulla's reign and of Sulla's legislation-based proscriptions, using the blatant injustice and violation of the spirit (if not letter) of the right of appeal during Sulla's dictatorship as an argument for the constitutional order he himself puts forward in the *Laws*. Cicero had, we remember, pointed to the Valerian law which made Sulla dictator as the key exhibit for his claim that if all things were considered just "which have been ratified by a people's institutions and laws," then even the Valerian law would have been just, "that the dictator could put to death with impunity whatever citizens he wished, even without trial."[28] Bodin completely misses (although it would have helped his argument) the novelty of a dictator being appointed under a law carried by an *interrex* (rather than being nominated by a consul).[29] Yet the injustice of the Valerian law and its implications, namely the violation of the right of appeal, were clear, and they were what mattered to Bodin. Describing Sulla's proscriptions, Bodin observes that nobody "could assure himselfe of his life, or of his goods in the time of the tyrannie of *Sylla*, who had proposed thirtie Sesterties unto free men, and unto bond men liberty, as a reward if they should discover their masters, or bring in the head of any one of them that were by him proscribed[.] In which fear the citizens were, untill that threescore thousand of them being slaine, and so the state in a manner againe appeased."[30] As Cicero had pointed out, in a speech known to Bodin but not cited here,[31] Sulla's dictatorship was a tyranny established *by law* (*lege*),[32] that is to say not by higher-order constitutional norms—*lege*, not *iure*.[33]

When discussing tyranny, and whether "a Tyrant who by force or fraud having oppressed the libertie of the people, and so aspired unto the soveraigntie, may be justly slaine," Bodin again turns to the example of Sulla. He considers

26. *Commonweale* 1.8, p. 86.

27. *De republica*, p. 80, n. 11.

28. Cic. *Leg.* 1.42, trans. Zetzel.

29. *Methodus*, p. 211. But cf. Cic. *Att.* 9.15.2. Bodin knew Cicero's correspondence with Atticus fairly well and quoted from it often; it is astonishing he missed this.

30. *Commonweale* 1.5, pp. 37–38. Bodin makes this point in connection with his argument against slavery.

31. Cf. *De republica*, p. 774, n. 3.

32. Cic. *Leg. Agr.* 3.5.

33. See also *Commonweale* 4.4, p. 481 (*De republica*, p. 434).

the possibility that Sulla's dictatorship may have been achieved legitimately, "confirmed by the voyces of the people" in a "solemn act," which may have represented a "true ratification of him in his tyrannie, the people consenting thereonto."[34] Still, Bodin is "neverthelesse of the opinion, that he may lawfully be slaine, and that without any lawfull processe or triall."[35] The wording in the Latin version is very revealing: the tyrant may be slain *iure*, without regard to any remedy at law (*legis actio*).[36] This is where the Ciceronian distinction between *ius* and *lex* carries most weight, as it allows for the *iure* killing of a tyrant even without resort to any statutory norms; incidentally, this invalidates the claim made by many scholars of Bodin, Carl Friedrich prominent among them, that Bodin's "citizen cannot appeal from the *loi* to the *droit*"—in the case of tyranny, Bodin actually explicitly recommends such an appeal.[37] Sulla serves as the key example: when Sulla "caused himselfe to be confirmed dictator for fourescore years, by the law Valeria, which hee caused to be published, having at the same time a strong and puissant armie of his own within the citie: *Cicero* said, That it was no law at all."[38] Both Sulla's and Caesar's dictatorships as well as extraordinary commands and other late republican emergency measures were symptoms, for Bodin, of a process that had to do with the way the People exercised their sovereignty in the Roman Republic—a republic that was, we remember, a democracy according to Bodin's constitutional categories.

Constitutional contract law and the ius-lex *distinction*

One of the most revealing aspects of Bodin's constitutional thought concerns his view of the delegation of powers. Such delegations are described by Bodin in the private-law language of mutually binding contracts such as bilateral real contracts, e.g. *depositum*, or the consensual contract of mandate (*mandatum*). For Bodin, then, as it had been for Mario Salamonio, contract law is beyond the scope of the sovereign's decision-making, or even his lawmaking. Unlike Salamonio, whose Philosopher had denied that the sovereign was *legibus solutus*, Bodin argued that the sovereign was indeed *legibus solutus*, while accepting that there were constraints on the sovereign that were of a *contractual* nature. The

34. *Commonweale* 2.5, p. 219; *De republica*, p. 208.

35. On tyrannicide, cf. also *Commonweale* 4.3, p. 475.

36. *De republica*, p. 208.

37. Friedrich, *Constitutional Reason of State*, p. 72.

38. *Commonweale* 2.5, pp. 219–220.

reason for these contractual constitutional constraints is deep and anticipates some of Hobbes' most profound ideas regarding the relationship between subjects and the sovereign:[39] given that it lies in the very essence of the sovereign to guarantee his subjects' mutual contractual relationships, the sovereign is, in a very strong sense, *necessarily* bound to keep the contracts he himself is a party too—even if these contracts are between him and a subject:

> the soveraigne prince is bound unto the contracts by him made, bee it with his subiect, or with a straunger: for seeing he is the warrant to his subiects of the mutuall conventions and obligations that they have one of them against another: of how much more reason is he the debter of iustice in his own fact, and so bound to keepe the faith and promises by himselfe given and made to others?[40]

From this the further consequence flows that magistrates in the strict sense (i.e., not mere commissioners) may not be deprived of their office by the sovereign: "For if a prince have once bestowed an honour or an office upon a man, it is deemed, that he may not without iust cause take it againe away from him."[41] As Daniel Lee has convincingly argued, this is because the office and legal authority of magistrates are bestowed upon them in the form of mutually binding contracts, that is to say, contracts that create rights and obligations both for the magistrate and for the sovereign. Bodin uses so-called bilateral contracts of Roman law as his model, such as *commodatum, pignus*, or *depositum*, while modeling extraordinary commissions on the unilateral contract of *precarium*, a gratuitous grant of a thing that was revocable at will.[42] The former contracts create duties on the part of the sovereign, too, such as a duty of non-interference with the magistrate for the duration of his term, while the latter only create obligations on the part of the commissioner. The transfer of sovereignty from

---

39. Hobbes, *Leviathan*, vol. 2, ch. 21, p. 342. Cf. Dyzenhaus, "How Hobbes Met the 'Hobbes Challenge,'" esp. pp. 496–502.

40. *Commonweale* 1.8, p. 106; *De republica*, p. 99.

41. *Commonweale* 1.8, p. 106. This reasoning will contribute to Bodin's ambiguity shown in his analysis of the deposition of the tribune Octavius; see below.

42. Lee, *Popular Sovereignty*, ch. 6, "Commissions and Offices." The contract of *depositum* would seem to be a bit of a stretch on Bodin's part; according to the *Digest*, the depositee seems to have been under a duty to return the thing on demand, which does not fit too well with term limits and the general framework Bodin has in mind for magistrates. This may be the reason why Bodin muddles this in the passage on the dictator in the *Methodus*, where he seems unclear whether or not *depositum* is a good analogy for the dictator, or for ordinary magistrates.

the People of Rome to the Emperors must have been of a third kind, as magistrates, and much less commissioners, were not sovereign on this model. It would seem that for Bodin the transfer of sovereignty effected by the *lex regia* must itself be valid on the basis of norms that are of necessity not subject to the power of the sovereign. While Bodin, unlike Salamonio, accepted that with the *lex regia* sovereignty could be alienated for good, he must still acknowledge, with Salamonio, that the rules governing the alienability (or lack thereof, as the case may be) under the *lex regia* themselves cannot be subject to the sovereign's lawmaking—they must be rules that exist, in a sense, prior to sovereignty. These rules are, once again, the rules of Roman property and contract law. Bodin observes that the *lex regia*, in order to transfer actual sovereignty—rather than simply delegating powers, e.g., to a magistrate, for a fixed term—has to amount to a gift (*donatio*) under Roman law:

> But what shall we then say of him to whom the people have given absolute power so long as he liveth? In this case we must distinguish: If such absolute power bee given him purely and simply without the name of a magistrate, governour, or lieutenant, or other forme of deputation; it is certaine that such an one is, and may call himselfe a Soveraigne Monarch: for so the people hath voluntarily disleised and dispoyled it selfe of the soveraigne power, to seasse and invest another therein; having on him, and upon him transported all the power, authoritie, prerogatives, and soveraignties thereof: as if a man should by pure gift deliver unto another man the propriety and possession that unto him belongeth: in which case such a perfect donation (*perfecta donatio*) admitteth no conditions. In which sort the regall law (*lex regia*) is by the lawyer said to have bene made in these words, *Cum populus ei & in eum omnem potestatem contulit.*[43]

A gift under Roman law requires a formal agreement or contract in order to be enforceable, and Bodin seems to believe that the *lex regia* rendered by Ulpian in the *Digest*, which he cites here, amounted to such a formal agreement. The key is that such a gift, once completed (*perfecta donatio*), does not admit of any further conditions, added later on, as stated in the passage of the *Code* referenced by Bodin in the Latin text.[44] Even Augustus, after his victory at Actium, had not been sovereign, but merely "chiefe of the Commonweale," and it was not until

43. *Commonweale* 1.8, p. 88; *De republica*, p. 82.

44. *Cod.* 8.54.4.

Vespasian had been empowered by the *lex de imperio Vespasiani* that the Roman Republic and its brand of democracy had ended.[45] It is only with a *lex regia* that the People can create a sovereign other than themselves; citing Ulpian, Bodin claims that the *lex regia* as described by Ulpian in the *Digest* is the only way, formally speaking, of creating a sovereign. It has to be "by pure gift," a "perfect donation" that "admitteth no conditions."[46]

"Lordly" vs. constitutional government

Famously, Bodin did not just acknowledge contractual constraints on sovereign power, but thought that the subjects' private property, too, could represent a constitutional limit on sovereignty. Whether or not the private property of the subjects is outside the reach of the sovereign is elevated by Bodin to the chief criterion in his important distinction between "lordly" or "seigneurial" rule, on the one hand, and "lawful" rule, on the other. The litmus test for lawfully exercised sovereignty lies in the limits private property imposes on sovereignty. It is precisely what defines the lawful exercise of sovereignty "that every subiect hath the true proprietie of his owne things, and may thereof dispose at his pleasure."[47] It is here that Bodin introduces a further crucial distinction, that between sovereignty or the state itself, on the one hand, and the administration of the state or exercise of sovereignty, on the other.[48] It is the way sovereignty is *exercised* that shows whether or not rule is "seigneurial" or "lawful." It is the exercise of sovereignty, or government, then, which can be called constitutional (i.e., "lawful") or despotic (i.e., "seigneurial") or tyrannical.[49] The criterion for distinguishing

45. *Commonweale* 1.8, p. 98. Although Bodin, similarly to Pomponius, seems to accept the formal caesura that the *lex de imperio* (which he identifies with the *lex regia*) had brought about, his attitude is one of ironic incredulity: "And after that *Vespatian* the emperour was also exempted from the power of the lawes, not by the Senat onely, but onely by the expresse law of the people as many thinke, and as yet it is to be found engraven in marble in Rome: which the lawyer calleth the law Royall, howbeit that it hath no great probabilitie, that the people which long time before had lost al their power, should give it to him that was stronger than themselves."

46. *Commonweale* 1.8, p. 88 (citing *Dig.* 1.4.1).

47. *Commonweale* 2.2, pp. 201–202; cf. *De republica*, p. 191. In Europe, there are, according to Bodin, no "lordly" sovereigns except for the "Princes of the Turkes, and of the Moscovits"; not even Augustus had been a lordly monarch.

48. Bodin thought that his was an original distinction, and it allowed him to acknowledge "tempered" regimes while adhering to his doctrine of the impossibility of mixed sovereignty: *Commonweale* 2.2, pp. 199–200.

49. See Turchetti, "'Despotism' and 'Tyranny.'"

between lawful and despotic government lies in the respect accorded, on the part of the sovereign, to natural law, contract law, and the protection of private property. It is not, strictly speaking, unconstitutional for the sovereign to exercise its sovereignty seigneurially or despotically, but Bodin seems unclear on the issue. At times, he claims that it is merely *imprudent* for the sovereign so to exercise its sovereignty, as in the case of the Gracchi and the subsequent takeover of the exercise of sovereignty by the sovereign, the Roman People, which led in Bodin's view to the fall of the Republic. But at times he seems to be making the stronger claim that despotic or seigneurial government is lawful by virtue of the rules of *ius gentium*, that is to say, because of customary rules.[50] This would imply that despotic government, while constitutional in Bodin's own time by virtue of the law of nations, might lose its constitutional status if the norms of the *ius gentium* were ever to rule it out—at the very least, the legitimacy even of seigneurial government is, on Bodin's account, governed by, and subject to, the rules of the law of nations. This is precisely what separates seigneurial from tyrannical government—the latter is not justified by the laws of war and characterized by "contemning the lawes of nature and nations," where the sovereign "imperiously abuseth the persons of his free borne subjects, and their goods as his owne." Precisely as for Cicero, for Bodin tyrannical exercise of government need not be confined to a single ruler either—whether sovereignty be with one, the few, or the many, its exercise can in each case be constitutional (lawful), or despotic, or tyrannical.[51]

There are, then, higher-order constitutional rules implicit in Bodin's legal thought, and they are the rules of the Roman law of obligations and of property. These must be more firmly entrenched and of a higher order than other statutes, as the sovereign could otherwise, not being bound by his own legislation, simply change the law of contracts; this is explicitly excluded by Bodin, however, leaving open only the solution just sketched: the Roman law of contracts is superior to the sovereign's legislation and cannot be abrogated by the sovereign, thus amounting to a set of constitutional norms. Even other legislation, not concerning

50. See *Commonweale* 2.2, p. 200, where Bodin states the conditions under which "lordly" government legitimately arises: "The lordly Monarchie is that where the prince is become lord of the goods and persons of his subiects, by law of armes and lawfull warre (*iure belli*); governing them as the master of a familie doth his slaves": *De republica*, p. 189.

51. Referencing Cicero, Bodin says that all states "may be lawful, lordly, and tirannicall, in such sort as I have said: for the greatest tyrannie of all other is of *Tully* called the rage of the furious and turbulent people": *Commonweale* 2.2, p. 200; *De republica*, p. 189. Cic. *Rep.* 3.45 would be the closest candidate for the reference, but Bodin could not have known the passage. Bodin must have taken the notion from the summary of Cic. *Rep.* 3 in August. *De civ. D.* 2.21 (see Isnardi Parente, *ad loc.*). Cf. also *De civ. D.* 19.21.1-33.

the law of contracts or of property, is subject to some substantive constraints, however, which Bodin interestingly elucidates with reference to Cicero's speech *Pro Caecina* and the idea contained therein, discussed in Chapter 1 above, that if legislation contained anything that was not *iure*, it was to be considered void. Bodin thus introduces Cicero's *ius-lex* distinction, as well as the idea that the former is hierarchically superior to the latter, into his discussion of sovereignty, undermining the *legibus solutus* claim considerably. After claiming that sovereigns could not abrogate the law of nature, Bodin goes on to observe that for the same reason,

> the Roman magistrats did notably, who unto the end of all their requests & laws which they propounded unto the good liking of the people, commonly annexed this clause, *Si quid ius non esset E. E. L. N. R. eius ea lege nihilem* [sic] *rogaretur*, that is to say, That if any thing were therein contained that was not iust and reasonable (*iure*), they by that law requested nothing.[52]

This claim is, as we know from Chapter 1, taken from Cicero's speech *Pro Caecina*, where Cicero had made the rhetorical point that the assemblies, although in a sense sovereign, could not simply legislate without any substantive limits: there was always *ius* to constrain *leges*. Here Cicero is referring to legislation passed by Sulla, which already makes it problematic; but Cicero is after a bigger claim:

> Oh, but Sulla passed a law. Without wasting time in making any complaints about that time, and about the disasters of the republic, I make you this answer—that Sulla also added to that same law, "that if anything were enacted in this statute contrary to *ius*, to that extent this statute (*lex*) was to have no validity." What is there which is contrary to *ius* which the Roman people is unable to command or to prohibit? Not to digress too far, this very additional clause proves that there is something. For unless there were, this would not be appended to all statutes. But I ask of you whether you think, if the people ordered me to be your slave, or, on the other hand, you to be mine, that that order would be authoritative and valid? You see and admit that such an order is worthless. Hereby you first allow this, that it does not follow that whatever the people orders ought to be ratified.[53]

---

52. *Commonweale* 1.8, p. 104; *De republica*, p. 97.

53. Cic. *Caec.* 95–96. Trans. C. D. Yonge, slightly modified. Sigonio had already made use of Cic. *Caec.*: *De antiquo iure* 1.6, p. 42.

This speech by Cicero is where Bodin finds the clause allegedly appended to all Roman legislation, leading him to introduce Cicero's *lex-ius* distinction into his own framework. By *ius* Bodin means, no less than Cicero, norms of a higher order than mere legislation (*lex*). He explains that "there is much difference betwixt" *ius*, on the one hand, and law, on the other; for *ius* "respecteth nothing but that which is good and upright; but a law importeth a commaundement. For the law is nothing els but the commaundement of a soveraigne, using of his soveraigne power." But natural law (which Bodin only by analogy calls at times *lex naturae*) does not even make an exception for the pope or the emperor when it comes to the protection of private property from sovereign confiscation. Even though some canonists maintained that the pope's sovereignty allowed him to encroach upon private property, this was, according to Bodin, "as if they should say it to bee lawfull (*fas*) for them to rob and spoyle their subiects, oppressed by force of armes: which law (*ius*), the more mightie use against them that be weaker than themselves, which the Germans most rightly call, The law of theeves and robbers (*praedatorium ius*)."[54] Seizures may only be done with just cause; and, alluding to the example of Aratus of Sicyon which had figured prominently in Cicero's discussion of private property in *De officiis*,[55] Bodin goes on to underline the importance of stability of possession and private property both from a utilitarian focus on political peace and from the viewpoint of justice and natural law.[56] Citing Seneca, he carves out a public sphere for the lawful or constitutional exercise of sovereignty and juxtaposes it with a private sphere, where property of subjects enjoys far-reaching protection:

> For that which the common people commonly saith, *All to be the princes*, is to be understood concerning power and soveraigntie, the proprietie and possession of everie mans things yet reserved to himselfe. For so saith *Seneca, Ad reges potestas omnium pertinet, ad singulos proprietas,* Unto kings belongeth the power of all things, and unto particular men the proprietie. And a little after, *Omnia rex imperio possidet singuli dominio,* The king in power possesseth all things: and privat men as owners.[57]

54. *Commonweale* 1.8, pp. 108–109; *De republica*, p. 102.

55. Cic. *Off.* 2.81. See above, Chapter 4, p. 187.

56. *Commonweale* 1.8, p. 110; *De republica*, p. 103.

57. *Commonweale* 1.8, p. 110; *De republica*, p. 104. The quotations are from Sen. *Ben.* 7.4.2 and 7.5.1.

It is important to note that Bodin is here less absolutist than Seneca, as Seneca seems to imply—akin to Alberico Gentili in his more absolutist work[58]—that the prince's sovereignty "can be used to expropriate or encumber private property."[59] The second citation from Seneca's *De beneficiis* was shortened by Bodin: Seneca wrote that *sub optimo rege omnia rex imperio possidet, singuli dominio,* thus qualifying the claim and reminding us, as Miriam Griffin observes, "that bad kings or tyrants often take possession of the private property of individuals without legal justification."[60] Bodin with his own formulation lessened Seneca's stress on the virtue of the prince, giving much more emphasis to constitutional constraints and institutions than to the prince's personal virtue. Claims by subjects against the sovereign do not have to rely on the king being *optimus* and virtuous. According to Bodin, private property claims against the sovereign can be enforced in court, and so can the sovereign's contractual obligations: "And if the king be debtor to any privat man his subiect, he is therefore oft times sued, condemned, and enforced to pay the debt."[61]

This is consistent with Bodin's stance on taxation and sovereign crown lands. He is somewhat ambiguous on the topic of taxation, but seems ultimately to believe that the sovereign—at least the lawful sovereign—cannot tax his subjects without their consent.[62] Unlike Hobbes, he does not think that this undermines sovereignty; ultimately sovereignty rests, not on the power to tax, but on the power to legislate. An even more important limit on the exercise of sovereignty is provided by Bodin's interesting belief that crown lands cannot be mortgaged or alienated by the sovereign. While sovereignty itself can, on Bodin's view, be alienated—as happened with the *lex regia*—there are constraints on crown lands, since these are not properly the prince's, but the *state*'s. There is, then, in Bodin's thought a separation between the person, or collective, that exercises sovereignty,

---

58. See on his *De potestate Regis absoluta* my remarks in "The *Corpus iuris* as a Source of Law," pp. 104–112; on Gentili's use of Bodin more generally, indeed as a major source for his *De iure belli,* see Quaglioni, "The Italian 'Readers' out of Italy." Gentili had carefully annotated Bodin's *République*; the annotations are among Gentili's papers in Oxford's Bodleian library; see Simmonds, "Gentili Manuscripts." Robert Filmer, too, used Bodin in a very one-sided way to emphasize an absolutism far more vulgar than anything Bodin had ever formulated: *Patriarcha*, pp. 172–183, esp. 173–179. See Burgess, "Bodin in the English Revolution," pp. 392–401, on the use of Bodin by English Royalist writers.

59. Griffin, *Seneca on Society*, p. 325. On the use of Seneca's formula in early modern political thought, see Burgess, *Absolute Monarchy*, pp. 74–76.

60. Griffin, *Seneca on Society*, p. 326.

61. *Commonweale* 1.8, p. 111; *De republica*, p. 104.

62. *Commonweale* 6.2, p. 665.

on the one hand, and the state, or sovereignty itself, on the other. The crown lands are attached to the latter, not to the natural person of the sovereign. Bodin draws an analogy with the Roman law of guardianship and of dowry, with the commonwealth or state (*res publica*) being equivalent to the ward (*pupillus*) or to the wife, and the sovereign assuming the role of the guardian or husband.[63] This implies high standards of care on the part of the sovereign, and obviously entails a fiduciary obligation for the sovereign to act in the best interest of the state, which Bodin took to mean that crown lands could not be mortgaged or alienated. There were remedies under Roman law against fraudulent guardians, and Bodin makes it clear that the sovereign's position vis-à-vis the commonwealth was even weaker than that of the husband under Roman rules governing the dowry:

> Neyther can the prince challenge that unto himselfe which belongs unto the publike, no more than a husband can his wives dowrie, wherin the prince hath lesse right; for the husband may abuse the fruits of his wives dowrie at his pleasure, but a prince may well use, but not abuse the fruits of a publike dowrie.[64]

Here Bodin extends the analogy to usufruct, and puts the prince in the position of a usufructuary, who could under Roman property law be held liable for wrongful damage. Bodin asserts that "[o]ur kings have and doe acknowledge, that the proprietie of the crowne lands is not the princes."[65]

Bodin's constitutionalism relies, then, on the protection of private property and contractual obligations under natural law, the hallmarks of "lawful" sovereignty. His chief illustration of his distinction between lawful and seigneurial exercise of sovereignty and the parallel distinction between ordinary magistrates and extraordinary commissioners is the late Roman Republic. The most important conclusion Bodin draws from his discussion of the constitutional history of the late Roman Republic is that it is not so much magistrates or commissioners who, by overstepping their competences and acting *ultra vires* represent a danger to the political order, but rather the *sovereign itself*, which, by ruling seigneurally rather than constitutionally, runs the risk of undermining its own position and of subverting the constitutional order as a whole. This, albeit formulated in prudential, rather than moral or constitutional terms, is the conclusion Bodin drew from the spectacle of the Roman People adhering increasingly to the

63. *De republica*, pp. 640–641, with references to the Roman law of dowry (*Dig.* 23.3.7pr.).

64. *Commonweale* 6.2, p. 652; *De republica*, pp. 640–641.

65. *Commonweale* 6.2, p. 652; *De republica*, p. 641.

doctrine Tiberius Gracchus seems to have expounded, and exemplified, for the first time—the doctrine of the comitia as sovereign. The danger, as Bodin saw it, did not lie in the principle of the comitia being sovereign itself; rather, it was the takeover by the assemblies of the daily *administration* of the state[66] that constituted overreach. That this overreach assumed the form of a violation of constitutional norms is something Bodin merely hints at, but is to some extent prevented from seeing; in his eyes, there is normative neutrality between seigneurial rule and rule by higher-order norms. The latter is overall to be preferred, however, if only for prudential reasons of stability.

Whenever Bodin adopts the Roman republican distinction between *lege* and *iure*, discussed in the first two chapters of this book, or when he argues for the insulation of the norms of Roman contract law from sovereign reach, or for the inviolability of natural law, property, and the limits imposed on the sovereign by the inalienability of crown lands—whenever these limits on sovereignty come into focus, the sources and arguments of the constitutional conflicts of the late Roman Republic assume pride of place. His most ingenious argument, which deserves to be taken seriously, is the demonstration that the sovereign, although *legibus solutus, necessarily* has to be taken to be subject to his own contracts and agreements, even those entered into with his subjects. This is so, we remember, because the sovereign is the guarantor and enforcer of all the contracts concluded in his realm, an essential function the sovereign would not be able to discharge if it were itself *pactis solutum*.

Extraordinary commands (imperia extraordinaria) *and the fall of the Republic*

When discussing the extraordinary commands of the late Roman Republic, Bodin uses them as an example of a delegation of powers from the sovereign—i.e., the People in the case of Rome—to a subject, where, as in the case of the dictator, this does not translate into an abdication of sovereignty. Extraordinary commands are, also like the dictatorship, examples of mere commissions, as opposed to magistracies. This was an extremely important distinction for Bodin. Pompey's command against the pirates, we will remember, which he had received in 67 BC as a private citizen, had been unlimited over the whole Mediterranean and its coasts up to fifty miles inland for at least three years with the mandate

66. For the distinction between sovereignty or state on the one hand and government or administration on the other, see *Commonweale* 2.2, pp. 199–200; Lee, "'Office is a Thing Borrowed'"; see also Hoekstra, "A Lion in the House," pp. 197–198.

to eradicate piracy.[67] This kind of authority, however, does not constitute sovereignty according to Bodin, and not even an ordinary office, but a mere delegation of powers to a commissioner.[68] Bodin explains the distinction thus:

> Now in the definition by our selves proposed, we first said, all officers . . . to be publique persons: who in that differ from privat men. . . . We said also the Magistrats to have an ordinarie charge, whereby to differ from Commissioners, who have also publique charge, but yet extraordinarie, according to the occasions in the occurents of time presented: such as were in auntient time the Dictators. ... And last of all we said, their ordinarie charge to be to them by law limitted and bounded: for the erection of their publique ordinarie charges, erected by the name of offices, which otherwise should be no offices, if there were not for them an expresse edict or law.[69]

These offices are distinct from the officeholders, and are perpetual: they "continue for ever after they be once by edict erected, until that by contrarie edicts or lawes the same offices be againe put downe."[70] They must be established by law (*lege*), written or unwritten, while commissioners serve "with an extraordinarie charge limited unto" them, and "without law (*sine lege*)."[71] The crucial difference is that an "office is a thing borrowed, which the owner cannot demaund againe before the time it was lent for bee expired," while a commission on the other hand "is a thing which one hath but by sufferance . . . which the owner may againe demaund when he seeth good."[72] Here the terminology of the Latin version is revealing. Ordinary office is modeled on *commodatum*, loan for use under Roman private law, where the borrower was allowed to keep the thing for the agreed time, except in cases of misuse in breach of contract, in which case the lender could reclaim it at once.[73] Extraordinary commission, by contrast, is

67. Vell. 2.31.2-4.

68. *Commonweale* 1.8, p. [90]: "Example we have of *Pompey* the great, who was dispensed withal from the lawes for five yeres, by expresse decree of the people, published at the request of *Gabinius* the Tribune, at such time as extraordinarie power was given him to make warre against the pirats."

69. Ibid. 3.2, p. 280.

70. Ibid. 3.2, p. 280.

71. Ibid. 3.2, p. 278.

72. Ibid. 3.2, p. 282; *De republica*, p. 263.

73. *Dig.* 13.6.5.pr.; 17.3; *Cod.* 4.65.3. Cf. Buckland, *Roman Law*, pp. 470–471.

likened by Bodin to *precarium*, a grant of enjoyment of things revocable at will by the grantor.[74] This goes along with the Latin terminology for commissioner, *curator*, and for commission, *curatio*. Guardianship (*cura*) is best attested in Roman law for minors, and at least initially, guardians (*curatores*) were appointed ad hoc for those between fourteen and twenty-five years of age for important, isolated transactions.[75] Bodin says that commissions, too, could be granted by laws, but the "charge, the time, and place being still limitted by commission: as a man may see by the commissions granted unto the Dictators, which were sometime made by the decree of the people." The extraordinary commands given to Pompey against the pirates and Mithridates are given as examples, granted by the *lex Gabinia* and the *lex Manilia*.[76]

Bodin, quoting from Cicero's *Fifth Philippic*, points out that when Cicero urged that Octavian be given a military command (*imperium*), Cicero had to do so explicitly because at that point Octavian was not a regular magistrate, but merely a private citizen. Had Octavian been a regular officeholder, had he been "either Consul or Praetor, *Cicero* would not have used these words, for that he should then by law (*iure*) had the power and commaund of a magistrat."[77] Again, the law (*ius*) by which a consul or praetor would have already had *imperium* was of a *constitutional* nature for Bodin, who took over the terminology of *ius* from his late republican sources. Cicero himself in his speech before the Senate cleverly avoided admitting that this constituted an *imperium extraordinarium*, seeking to make this seem more regular a request than it really was "in order to make the senators agree to his proposal more readily," as Gesine Manuwald points out.[78] Indeed, later on in his *Eleventh Philippic* Cicero, opening himself up to the charge of inconsistency, was trying to argue that the bestowal of *imperia extraordinaria* on private citizens constituted an unconstitutional and exceptional move.[79] Bodin, with extreme clear-sightedness and perspicacity, fills in what Cicero would have preferred to leave out and writes that "therefore *Cicero* persuaded, That the charge for the mannaging of the warre should with power by commission be given unto him." In the Latin version, it becomes clear

74. *Dig.* 43.26.2.2; cf. Buckland, *Roman Law*, pp. 524–525.

75. Johnston, *Roman Law*, pp. 41–42.

76. *Commonweale* 3.2, p. 281.

77. Ibid. 3.2, p. 292; *De republica*, p. 271.

78. Cic. *Phil.* 5.45. Manuwald, *Cicero,* Philippics *3–9*, vol. 2, p. 702.

79. Cic. *Phil.* 11.17-20; cf. above, Chapter 2, p. 104; Manuwald, *Cicero,* Philippics *3–9*, vol. 2, pp. 702–703.

that by "power by commission" Bodin means Octavian's late republican extraordinary command: *Cicero suadet ut cura belli gerendi cum imperio illi extra ordinem detur.*[80] Drawing on Sigonio, Bodin says that the distinction between office and commission was also apparent in the exact wording in which the matter was put before the People in the Roman Republic: for "the magistrat was usually created by vertue of the *lawes before made* [my emphasis]," while commissions were assigned by using the words "If they willed and commaunded that this or that man should have the government in this or that province."[81] He then goes on to adduce the example of Scipio Africanus, discussed above in Chapter 1, who, according to Livy, had been elected to the aedileship before the required age.[82] Commissions, then, are extraordinary commands, and offices, by contrast, are constituted by an existing legal structure and are thus legally independent from the officeholder himself.

The most important difference between commission and office, however, lies, according to Bodin, in the danger posed to the commonwealth by the former: "the greater the charge is given by commission, the more need it is to have it in short time expired; least longer power might give occasion to ambitious minds to take unto themselves the government, and so to oppresse the libertie of the state." Bodin's bases his important claim primarily on the reign of the Ten Men:

> For at such a time as the people of Rome had extraordinarily (*extra ordinem*) created the Decemviri with a yearely and soveraigne power, for the reforming of their old lawes and customes (*legibus ferendis*), and the making of new and more commodious for the state: their commission which should not have passed, a yeare being expired, was againe by the people for another yere proroged, with absolute . . . power:[83] and all other magistrats suspended during the time of their commission; until that out of the best lawes of other cities they had gathered the lawes of the twelve tables. Upon which continuance of bearing rule, these Decemviri tooke occasion to oppresse the libertie of the state (*Reipublicae libertatem*), and to take

80. *De republica*, p. 271.

81. *Commonweale* 3.2, p. 292. Bodin here claims to have solved problems that had occupied Sigonio and Grouchy, but he fails to disclose that he is really following Sigonio, whom he tacitly quotes; see McCuaig, *Sigonio*, pp. 233–234.

82. *De republica*, p. 271. Cf. Livy 25.2.6-7.

83. Knolles has "with absolute and soveraigne power," rendering *cum annua summaque potestate* (*De republica*, p. 262); from Bodin's system it becomes clear that here this means merely absolute, not sovereign power.

> upon themselves the soveraigntie (*imperium*), had it not by force againe bene wrong out of their hands, and that not without the great trouble and turmoile of the citie.[84]

It is most interesting that for Bodin, who is ostensibly neutral as to whether the sovereign should exercise his sovereignty through magistracies and offices established under law or rather by commissioning extraordinary commissioners, now proceeds to give an account of commission that is anything but neutral. The "most cruell and bloodie civill warre that ever was in Rome," that between Sulla and Marius, was caused when Marius "by the working of *Pub. Sulpitius*, one of the Tribunes by him suborned" had the People take Sulla's ordinary command from him "and by extraordinarie commission given unto himselfe."[85] Bodin takes up this theme again in the next book and elaborates on it: Marius had

> passed through all the degrees of honour, and bene six times Consull (which never Roman had bene before him) yet not so content, would needs take upon him the charge of the wars against king *Mithridates* (which by lot was fallen unto Sylla) howbeit that hee was now growne extreame old, to the intent to obtaine the seventh Consulship, and to continue perpetuall commaunding power unto himselfe.[86] But *Sylla* understanding of the commission given to *Marius*, and of the authority by a tumultuous assembly of the people taken from him now absent . . . contrarie unto the law and the custom of their auncestors, straight way returned to Rome with his partakers, seyzed upon the citie, where he made a most horrible massacre; which afterwards in such sort continued, as that all Italie and Spaine was embrued with blood, not onely the captaines and chief commaunders of *Marius* his faction being by *Sylla* slaine, but even his companions, friends, and kinsmen also, being most shamefully proscribed, or els banished, and so the Popular estate brought unto an extreame tyrannie.[87]

Bodin makes it clear that sovereigns handing over power by commissions or even by extended or prorogued ordinary offices run the danger of undermining the state and changing it inadvertently into "tyrannicall governments." This is not, as

84. *Commonweale* 3.2, p. 282. See also *Commonweale* 4.4, p. 481 (*De republica*, p. 434).

85. *Commonweale* 3.2, p. 286.

86. The Latin version makes the claim that Marius aimed at the seventh consulship in order to gain perpetual command *domi. De republica*, p. 434.

87. *Commonweale* 4.4, p. 481.

he sees it, necessarily unconstitutional; he gives the example of Tiberius Gracchus removing his interceding colleague Marcus Octavius, and seems to believe that this was done constitutionally.[88] But there is a tension here in Bodin's thought, as he makes it abundantly clear that at the very least for prudential reasons it is not advisable for the sovereign itself to take over the government or administration of the state and rule by commission; "nothing," Bodin says, "hath ever bene more daungerous, or more ruinated Commonweales, than to translate the authoritie of the Senat or commaund of the magistrats, unto the prince or the people"—onto, that is, the sovereign. The paradoxical lesson Bodin draws here is that "the lesse the power of the soveraigntie is . . . the more it is assured."[89] This is a lesson learned, first and foremost, from the history of the fall of the Roman Republic:

> Neither was the Roman Commonweale ever fairer or farther from civill warres, than when (the maiestie of the people saved whole) all things were done by the Senat and the magistrats: which was from the first Carthaginensian warre, unto the conquest of the kingdome of Macedon. But after that both the Gracchies by their most popular lawes had taken from the authoritie of the Senat and the power of the magistrats, as much as they possibly could, all to encrease the wealth and libertie of the people; there ensued thereof a most miserable change of that Commonweale: neither did the citie of Rome ever after cease from civill warres and sedition, untill that immoderat libertie of the insolent people, was by the power of one oppressed and brought under, and they so brought into extreame miserie and servitude.[90]

Paradoxically, it is the sovereign exercising sovereignty *directly* that leads ultimately to the sovereign's being "spoyled of their owne soveraigne maiestie." Although Bodin is often at pains to claim that the sovereign is perfectly within his (constitutional) rights to exercise sovereignty whichever way he sees fit, there is, sparked by the example of the *constitutional crisis* of the Roman Republic, a built-in normative preference for a sovereign—in this case the Roman People—exercising his sovereignty through magistracies established

---

88. Ibid. 3.3, p. 301; 3.6, p. 350: a tribune could be legitimately removed by the people, Bodin writes—this was, of course, precisely Tiberius Gracchus' revolutionary doctrine, as discussed in Chapter 3.

89. Ibid. 4.6, p. 517.

90. Ibid. 4.6, p. 518. Cf. Montesquieu, *Spirit of the Laws* 11.18, p. 182: the Gracchi and their changes had run "counter to the liberty of the constitution in order to favor the liberty of the citizen, but the latter was lost along with the former."

by law, and not through commissions; a sovereign that does not overstep the limits drawn by *ius* and *mos maiorum*, the major sources of Roman republican constitutional law; a sovereign, in short, whose arbitrary will is hedged in by Roman contract law and whose lawmaking is limited by *ius publicum*. This normative preference is, I submit, the outcome of Bodin's study of the fall of the Roman Republic and its descent into civil wars; and it was this prism of the fall of the Republic which was to provide major political thinkers in Bodin's wake such as especially Montesquieu (but also Walter Moyle, Trenchard and Gordon, Mably, Rousseau, as well as John Adams) with the framework for their constitutional ideas.[91] Bodin's concern with the entrenchment of constitutional norms comes to the fore most prominently in his discussion of the advisability of changing laws and constitutional forms. While lower-level laws "concerning ordinarie policie" may be changed often and subject to necessity, such laws "as concerne the very estate it selfe" should rather "still be most firme and immutable." This is so, Bodin argues, because the laws are made for the maintenance of the commonwealth, not the other way around; and this results in Cicero's phrase from *De legibus*, according to which *salus populi suprema lex esto*, being elevated to the "first and chiefe law of all Commonweales."[92] This is not to be confused with the use of the *salus populi* phrase in the *raison d'état* literature,[93] but rather shows that Bodin is here trying to establish a distinction between malleable everyday legislation and higher-level, more entrenched constitutional norms. Bodin's use of *salus populi* here stands also at the beginning of a way of thinking about *salus populi* which becomes prominent with Thomas Hobbes, where it means, not only peace, but also "commodity of living"[94] and "temporal goods" in general.[95]

For reasons already briefly touched upon in Chapter 7—first and foremost an anti-Sallustian lack of trust in virtue as well as an interest in entrenched constitutional norms and the imposition of peace by way of a legal framework—Hobbes, albeit for obvious rhetorical reasons much less overtly "Roman" and much less republican, may be seen as an important link in the constitutionalist tradition

91. For the later development of this strand of thought, see the Epilogue, as well as McDaniel, *Adam Ferguson*.

92. *Commonweale* 4.3, p. 471; *De republica*, p. 426.

93. For the use of *salus populi* by writers in the *raison d'état* tradition, see Malcolm, *Reason of State*; Meinecke, *Staatsräson*; Münkler, *Im Namen des Staates*; for the difference between Bodin and that tradition, see Lee, " 'Office is a Thing Borrowed' "; Foisneau, "Sovereignty."

94. Hobbes, *Elements* 2.9.3, p. 179.

95. Malcolm, *Reason of State*, p. 117.

between Bodin and Montesquieu.[96] Hobbes shared Bodin's sense of the importance of certain entrenched constitutional norms and seems to have modeled the juridical character of his edifice as well as the emphasis on contractual relations and his conception of *salus populi* on Bodin's work. Bodin's influence on this strand of political thought was thus based on his view of the fall of the Roman Republic; and to the extent that his successors' grappling with the specter of military despotism was owed to this Bodinian framework of a sovereign "waking up" and overstepping constitutional boundaries only to bring about civil war and, ultimately, military despotism, to that extent later political thought, using the Roman example in the seventeenth and especially eighteenth centuries, was deeply indebted to Bodin and his constitutional analysis. This is the tradition of all those thinkers, culminating in Montesquieu, who discounted virtue and looked to *constitutional* reasons to account for the Roman Republic's decline and fall. Bodin, then, is the crucial early modern heir to the late Roman republican constitutional tradition, a constitutional republican in Cicero's vein, all the way down to his terminology.

96. For convincing interpretations of Hobbes as a constitutionalist thinker, see Dyzenhaus, "Hobbes's Constitutional Theory"; Lee, "'Office is a Thing Borrowed'"; id., *Popular Sovereignty*, ch. 6; Foisneau, "Sovereignty."

Epilogue

CONSTITUTIONAL REPUBLICANISM, THE "CANT-WORD" VIRTUE AND THE AMERICAN FOUNDING

A COMPLETE HISTORICAL survey of the ideas of constitutionalism as they emerged from the study of the Roman Republic in the period from Bodin's work to the Revolutions of the late eighteenth century could easily fill at least one other book—a sequel—and would obviously be far too ambitious a task for the remainder of this volume. What I will attempt to do here is to present a bird's eye view of what appear to me to be the most prominent strands leading from Bodin's often-printed and influential work to the mature constitutionalist thought of the late eighteenth century. In keeping with the main topic of this book I will focus on writers who interpreted the crises of the late Republic, not as crises of virtue following rising levels of corruption, luxury, and vice, but rather as constitutional crises amenable to constitutional solutions. Viewed from this vantage point, many of the important political ideas developed in the seventeenth and eighteenth centuries owe their more liberal commitments, perhaps paradoxically, to an examination of the institutional setup and ultimate fall and dissolution of the Roman Republic; for it was not only Cicero and some of his contemporaries who were convinced of the need for a constitution by the increasing recourse to emergency powers and the relatively recent phenomenon of far-reaching extraordinary commands bestowed by the popular assembly. Not confined to Cicero's time, but extending long afterwards, in the strand of thought I have been concerned with in the last part of this book, there emerged out of the crises of the Republic a Roman concept of constitution and a search for the substantive norms and rights that would provide the content of such higher-order constitutional rules. This process saw its culmination in the work of Jean Bodin, and in what follows I propose to look at the subsequent development of constitutional thought through the framework established by Bodin. This will lead us to Montesquieu as the central figure connecting Bodin and the ideas discussed by the Founders and Framers of the American Constitution.[1]

Important recent scholarship such as Vickie Sullivan's on the "liberal republicanism" of key English thinkers from Nedham and Harrington to Trenchard and Gordon has convincingly demonstrated that these thinkers were far from being "classical republicans" as described so impressively by John Pocock, Quentin Skinner, or Gordon Wood. Sullivan envisages a sharp break—very much akin to that postulated by Leo Strauss and his adherents—between ancient and modern political theory, replicating a dichotomy and line of thinking that goes back at least to Montesquieu and found its most famous expression in Benjamin Constant's classic formulation. While I would agree that most of the English thinkers she discusses are indeed committed to a "liberal" interest in law and constitutional institutions and a corresponding lack of interest in virtue, the results of the present book suggest that "classical republicanism" is not really a viable category and should be discarded.[2] In its place we might postulate a *constitutional* republicanism as described here, taking its cue from the crises and fall of the Roman Republic, on the one hand, and a *polis*-centered concern with virtue and political eudaemonism, on the other.[3]

There are early examples of the use of Jean Bodin's constitutionalist ideas in the English Civil War.[4] Writers of the Royalist and Parliamentary cause alike could be found drawing upon some of the categories Bodin had developed in his examination of the constitutional causes of the fall of the Roman Republic as

1. This approach will necessarily leave out many important strands of the reception of Bodin; on the German reception, see Dreitzel, *Protestantischer Aristotelismus*; Stolleis, *Geschichte*; id., *Staat und Staatsräson*, esp. ch. 2; on Hermann Conring's use of Machiavelli and Bodin, see Dauber, "Anti-Machiavellism."

2. See, for a similar view, Nippel, "Klassischer Republikanismus." See also Adams, *First American Constitutions*, pp. 312–314.

3. See Sullivan, *Machiavelli*. My own distinction is not supposed to be exhaustive. As shown in Chapter 7, a Machiavellian concern with glory and the instrumental use of certain virtues, too, can be shown to have had important ancient forebears: Sallust and Tacitus come readily to mind. On the reception and interpretation of the late Roman Republic and early Empire in late Elizabethan and early Stuart literature more generally, covering a wide array of attitudes, see Cox Jensen, *Reading the Roman Republic*; for the use specifically of Lucan in English political culture between 1580 and 1650, with examples of a less republican, and more "ancient-constitutionalist" Lucan than hitherto assumed, see Paleit, *War, Liberty, and Caesar*; but cf. Norbrook, *Writing the English Republic*.

4. Bodin's use of late republican history might add additional perspective to Alan Cromartie's "constitutionalist revolution," whose description of the influence of Bodin on the political theory of James I is compelling: *Constitutionalist Revolution*, pp. 150–154. Cf. also Salmon, "The Legacy of Jean Bodin."

discussed above.[5] Responding to some of Henry Parker's more absolutist claims in favor of parliamentary sovereignty, Sir John Spelman seems to have written in a very Bodinian vein when he said that unconstrained absolute power without "bound, nor limitation" tended to "the destruction of itselfe."[6] Drawing on Bodin's distinction between the state and the administration of the state, Spelman acknowledged that the King was "restrained ordinarily to the mediation of his Judges," who "by their interpretation and judgement then bind both the King and Subject." When it comes to making new law, "the agreement of the King, the Peeres, and the Commons" was said to be necessary by Spelman, who went on to point out that this necessary agreement, far from enfeebling or curbing "the regall power from any due work or office that belongeth to it," rather "close[d] and fence[d] it in, within the bounds of safety and of preservation."[7] The Bodinian pedigree suggests itself. Far from pushing Royalist writers in a more absolutist direction, therefore, Bodin seems to have had a mitigating effect. Indeed, as Glenn Burgess observes, a highly absolutist Royalist such as Griffith Williams went so far as to pronounce Bodin's distinction between an "unmixed" state and an administration curbed by checks and balances as both ridiculous and dangerous.[8] Burgess correctly points out that Spelman did not refer explicitly to Bodin when making his own observations; but, as Burgess himself notes, "Bodin's discussions of Salic law, taxation, and even the implications of a king's promise to abide by law, could have given him [Spelman] material to work with, as indeed could Bodin's discussion of the relationship between the form of a state and its government."[9] The suggestion that Spelman here followed Bodin without referencing him, given his explicit and lengthy use of Bodin elsewhere, does not seem farfetched.

Hobbes cited Bodin only in his early *Elements of Law* (1640) when arguing against divided sovereignty, but there is a Bodinian element even in Hobbes' mature thought, especially in his view of the people as presupposing sovereignty. By creating a representative sovereign, the commonwealth constitutes itself and becomes one. Only when the artificial person of the sovereign is established

5. Parliamentary writers using Bodin in support of a concept of parliamentary sovereignty include Henry Parker, Philip Hunton, and William Prynne. See Burgess, "Bodin in the English Revolution," pp. 401–405.

6. Spelman, *Certain Considerations*, p. 21.

7. Spelman, *Case of Our Affaires*, pp. 3–4.

8. I do not therefore believe, *pace* Burgess, that Bodin's citation by constitutionalist Royalists introduced "a cuckoo's egg into the nest." Burgess, "Bodin in the English Revolution," p. 400.

9. Burgess, "Bodin in the English Revolution," p. 399. I owe the quoted Spelman passages to Burgess' article.

do "the people" start to exist—in the absence of a sovereign they are bound to remain a multitude, "not *One*, but *Many*."[10] Bodin's own definition of *res publica* retained the "lawfulness" in Cicero's definition (*iuris consensus*), but added the requirement that there be a "puissant soveraigntie."[11] The affinity with Hobbes' political theory and especially his highly juridical account of sovereignty as well as his respect for legality and procedure is obvious.[12]

Indeed, as Luc Foisneau has argued in a very perceptive essay, there is evidence for a transformation in Hobbes' hands of Bodin's crucial distinction between state and administration of the state into a parallel distinction between sovereign rights on the one hand and the exercise of those rights on the other. Foisneau convincingly points out that in Hobbes the Ciceronian *salus populi* formula is "not used for the purpose of justifying the *arcana imperii* of princes" as in the Tacitist literature on *ragion di stato*, or in Richelieu's approach, but "in order to protect the rights of the sovereign, which are themselves the foundation of civil peace." Both Bodin's and Hobbes' reluctance to admit a constitutional right of resistance should be read, according to Foisneau, in light of their "strict rejection of 'reason of state' conceived as a warrant to trespass" legal norms.[13]

We have already commented on Bodin's use of the *salus populi* formula and its affinity with Hobbes' interpretation above; Foisneau makes it very clear that neither Bodin nor Hobbes can be seen in any meaningful way as heirs of the tradition of reason of state.[14] Bodin's novel emphasis on the sovereign as lawgiver and legislation as the defining feature of sovereignty as well as his insistence on the sovereign's obligation to live up to his own contracts is completely at odds with Giovanni Botero's *ragion di stato* as put forward in his eponymous book of 1589. For Botero, as well as *raison-d'état* Tacitists such as Guy du Faur de Pibrac, or Richelieu, the prince—be it the Spanish crown acting on behalf

10. Hobbes, *Leviathan*, vol. 2, ch. 16, p. 250. Cf. Hoekstra, "A Lion in the House," pp. 205–206, esp. n. 74; M. Brito Vieira, *Elements*, pp. 163f.

11. Bodin, *Commonweale* 1.1, p. 1.

12. *Leviathan*, vol. 2, ch. 26, p. 428: "every man by recourse to the Registers . . . may (if he will) be sufficiently enformed, before he doe such injury, or commit the crime, whither it be an injury, or not." For a convincing, more constitutionalist Hobbes, stressing the continuities with Bodin, see Hoekstra, "Early Modern Absolutism." See also Dyzenhaus, "Hobbes's Constitutional Theory."

13. Foisneau, "Sovereignty," pp. 340–341. See, for scholarship on reason of state after Meinecke, Baldini, *Ragion di stato*.

14. Similarly Malcolm, *Reason of State*, pp. 114–123; Salmon, "Bodins politische Philosophie," p. 474. Foisneau is taking a convincing stance (p. 326) against Friedrich Meinecke's interpretation of Bodin in *Machiavellism*, p. 59.

of Catholicism or the French king achieving a divinely ordained mission—was justified in extraordinary circumstances to "trespass on the rights of his subjects."[15] This is so because for Botero and the *ragion di stato* tradition, including Machiavelli, the state is the state of the prince and therefore rests on the *virtue* of the prince, while for Bodin and indeed Hobbes the state is built on a constitutional foundation that may be called "jural."[16] It is instructive that Hobbes mentions the Roman dictatorship in the context of his comparative argument for monarchy vis-à-vis popular government; monarchy is ultimately better because the private self-interest of the monarch and the interest of the public he represents are, in Hobbes' estimate, better aligned. The chief argument against monarchy is the "inconvenience" that the "sovereignty may descend upon an infant" or upon someone lacking sound judgment. However, according to Hobbes, popular states *always* find themselves in "the same condition as if the government were in a child." This necessitates "dictators, or protectors of their authority," since the assembled people themselves lack the necessary judgment; as a consequence, however, these popular commonwealths have been "oftener deprived" of their power "than infant kings by their protectors, regents, or any other tutors."[17] The subversion of popular constitutional government is thus in Hobbes' empirical judgment more likely than the subversion of constitutional monarchy, which he argues counts in favor of the latter.[18] Note that this argument implies that the monarchy be *constitutional*—otherwise, why fear the dictator in the first place?

It seems that Polybius' and especially Cicero's specifically constitutional solution to problems posed by justice and political order had an afterlife in those early modern writers who looked to constitutional solutions for their own problems with political order. The very different approaches of Machiavelli and Bodin to the Roman Republic suggest that when considering early modern and modern politics it is indeed necessary, as Foisneau recommends, to take into account not reason of state alone, but also theories of sovereignty, and to consider those as "two *rival* views on [modern] politics."[19] Theories of sovereignty, properly

15. Foisneau, "Sovereignty," p. 335.

16. The term is Henry Sidgwick's; see, for a discussion, Straumann, *Roman Law in the State of Nature*, pp. 86–88.

17. Hobbes, *Leviathan*, vol. 2, ch. 19, pp. 292, 294.

18. I say "empirical judgment" because it is obviously drawn from ancient history; as Nippel points out, Hobbes makes his claim *before* the dissolution of the Rump and Cromwell's assumption of the title of Lord Protector. Nippel, "Saving the Constitution," p. 38.

19. Foisneau, "Sovereignty," p. 323. Emphasis mine.

understood as rivals of *raison d'état* views, are an expression of the Roman constitutional strand of thought we have been examining in this book, especially as they emanate from Bodin's interpretation of the Roman Republic.

The political journalism of Marchamont Nedham provides an oscillating but (especially in America) influential example of how an engagement—however superficial—with the Roman Republic yielded constitutionalist ideas.[20] Nedham, unlike Machiavelli and Harrington, is impressed with constitutional rights and uses Coriolanus to show that the *comitia tributa* had had the power to hold patricians accountable by popular trial; the Ten Men, on the other hand, not having been subject to this kind of accountability provoked unrest and tumults precisely because they robbed the People of this option.[21] The prohibition on the continuation and iteration of office is another constitutional norm of the Republic Nedham admires and points out.[22] A "continued Power in one and the same Hands" is corrosive of liberty, and Nedham proceeds to illustrate this principle with examples drawn from republican history: citing "Kingly aspirers" such as Maelius, "that upstart Tyranny of the *Decemviri*," as well as the extraordinary commands of the late Republic, which had subjected Rome to a monarchy, Nedham concludes that "[i]f this were so among the Romans, how happy then is any Nation, and how much ought they to joy in the Wisdom and Justice of their Trustees, where certain Limits and Bounds are fixed to the Powers in being."[23] Nedham's solution does not look to virtue, but, invoking Cicero and Livy, to constitutional rights and the kinds of checks and balances between powers[24] that went into abeyance in the last century of the Republic: Nedham's concern is indeed with corruption, but corruption of constitutional principle, not corruption of virtue. Unlike Machiavelli, he disdains factions and believes that a "succession and revolution" of the "supreme Powers" is the only (constitutional) remedy against that kind of corruption; note that the end of government is liberty, not expansion. This passage is worth quoting

20. Sullivan, *Machiavelli*, pp. 113–143 provides a good survey; her interpretation is compatible with mine, especially her insistence that, unlike Machiavelli, Nedham makes "the protection of the people's individual rights," not empire, the end of political association (p. 115). She does not pay attention, however, to the constitutional Roman tradition.

21. Nedham, *Excellencie*, pp. 63–64; pp. 100–101. Cf. Livy 2.34–35.

22. Nedham, *Excellencie*, p. 86.

23. Ibid., pp. 21–22.

24. Ibid., pp. 109–113. Nedham refers to Cicero's accounts, in *On Duties* and the *Laws*, of the early arbitrary rule of the Kings at Rome, as cautionary tales of the executive power having legislating powers as well.

in full as it takes up all of the constitutional issues dealt with in the first part of this book, except for the *SCU*:[25]

> Did not *Appius Claudius* and his Junta, by the same means, Lord it over the Senate? Whence was it, that *Sylla* and *Marius* caused so many proscriptions, cruelties, and combustions in *Rome,* but by an extraordinary continuation of Power in themselves? How came it to pass likewise, that *Julius Caesar* aspired, and in the end attained the Empire? and, that the People of *Rome* quite lost their Liberty, was it not by the same means? For, had not the Senate and People so long protracted the Power of *Pompey* and *Caesar;* had *Pompey* had less command in *Asia,* and *Caesar* less in *Gallia, Rome* might have stood much longer in the possession of her Liberty. After the death of *Caesar,* it was probable enough, they might then have recovered their Liberty, but that they ran again into the same Error, as before: for by a continuation of Power in the hands of *Octavius, Lepidus,* and *Antonie,* the Commonwealth came to be rent and divided into three several Factions; two of which being worn out by each other, onely *Octavius* remained; who considering, that the Title of perpetual Dictator was the ruine of his Father *Julius,* continued the Government onely for a set-time, and procured it to be setled upon himself but for ten yeers. But what was the effect of this continuation of Power? Even this, That as the former protractings had been the occasions of Faction, so this produced a Tyranny: for, at the end of every ten yeers, he wanted no pretence to renew a lease of the Government; and by this means so played his Cards, that at length he easily and utterly extinguished the small remains of the Roman Freedom. The Observation then arising from hence, is this, that the onely way for a people to preserve themselves in the enjoyment of their Freedom, and to avoid those fatal inconveniences of Faction and Tyranny, is, to maintain a due and orderly succession of Power and Persons.[26]

The continuation of extraordinary powers, that is to say, violations of the constitutional order, are held responsible for the decay of the Republic and

25. This neglect of the *SCU* is a common feature of the seventeenth- and eighteenth-century reception of late republican constitutional thought. Gordon, despite having translated Sallust, connects the *SCU* formula (*nequid detrimenti respublica capiat*) with the office of the dictator: *Cato's Letters* no. 11, vol. 1, p. 89. Rousseau, however, does allude to it in *Social Contract* 4.6.

26. Nedham, *Excellencie*, pp. 22–23.

for "extinguishing the small remains of Roman freedom." And although Nedham was certainly intent on showing that the Republic had been a popular, rather than an aristocratic, state, he finds fault with the Gracchi, too, for helping to start the constitutional crises that ultimately issued in civil war.[27] His focus on the "supreme powers" within the Republic seems to be indebted to Bodin's analysis, although we do not know whether Nedham used Bodin.[28]

James Harrington wrote his *Commonwealth of Oceana* (1656) under the Protectorate, with a view to presenting a practical constitutional proposal for a republic he vainly hoped would be implemented under Cromwell. Since John Pocock's famous treatment of Harrington in *The Machiavellian Moment* as a prototypical "classical republican" and as the crucial link between English and American republicanism, Harrington has been subjected to much fine-grained analysis in recent years.[29] Harrington's intimate knowledge of the Roman republican institutions and his foray into some of their more intricate details, motivated by their potential usefulness as a model for his own undertaking, make him a prima facie target of our discussion.[30] One of the central problems with Pocock's account was with the status accorded to virtue; classical republicanism, on Pocock's account, was essentially concerned with inculcating virtue to prevent the *polis* from corruption and to allow for a citizenry ready to participate in communal decisions and warfare without giving priority to their narrowly conceived self-interest. While this is, even as an account of Aristotle, rather tendentious and seems to have it back to front—instrumentalizing virtue, while Aristotle, as we have seen, makes *eudaemonia*, and thus virtue of the

27. Ibid., p. 97: "when the *Gracchi,* who were supposed great Patrons of Liberty, took upon them to side with the people, they did, instead of finding out some moderate wayes and Expedients to reduce the Senators to Reason, proceed with such heat and violence, that the Senate being jealous of their own safety, were forced to chuse *Sylla* for their General: which being observed by the people, they also raised an Army, and made *Marius* their General: so that here you see it came to a downright Civil-War."

28. See ibid., p. civ.

29. Fink, *Classical Republicans,* had already put forward a view of Harrington as a "republican" on the basis of his use of a mixed constitution on Polybius' model; for the reasons elaborated in Chapter 4, I do not think that this makes him a "classical republican" in the *Aristotelian* sense; rather, this Polybian allegiance fits well with the interpretation of Harrington as a "modern," as put forward by Paul Rahe and Vickie Sullivan. My own interpretation of Harrington tracks Sullivan, *Machiavelli,* pp. 144–173, apart from her dubious, stark ancient-modern distinction. For an interesting, both more Stoic and more "modern," commerce-friendly Harrington, see Cromartie, "Harringtonian Virtue," esp. p. 999.

30. See Millar, *Roman Republic,* pp. 86–96.

select few, into the main normative *goal* of the *polis*—it most certainly fails to do justice to Harrington's emphasis on constitutional solutions and his corresponding neglect of virtue.[31]

Harrington does exhibit an essentially prudential outlook when it comes to the purpose, or end, of the political order; what his carefully calibrated constitutional set-up aims at is first and foremost stability, and then expansion. To this extent his is indeed a Machiavellian theory.[32] Also, like Machiavelli, Harrington is not interested in liberty or the protection of rights as the purpose of political society, nor does he have a concept of the state of nature; also, Harrington follows Machiavelli in accepting, indeed welcoming, a single man's founding of a republic by extraordinary means. He shares, furthermore, Machiavelli's prudentially motivated qualms about the corrosive effect of prolonged magistracies and extraordinary commands.[33] Yet there is far more stress on the essentially legal character of Harrington's constitutional design in *Oceana* than Machiavelli allows, and this merits our attention as it is a feature deeply indebted to Roman constitutional thought. These rule-of-law characteristics and Harrington's interest in legal accountability almost amount to ends in themselves, which gives *Oceana* a much stronger normative commitment to juridical ideals and procedural justice than the *Discorsi* ever exhibit.

Quite apart from its highly original model of representative republican government, then, *Oceana* may at least partly be read as influenced and constituted by some of the "unit-ideas," that is to say, some of the basic conceptual elements of constitutionalism that were first developed in the constitutional crises of the late Republic.[34] As an example, one may cite Harrington's highly Ciceronian phrasing of the constitutional constraints he believes the executive should be operating under: there is one condition of the magistracy in any commonwealth, Harrington says,

31. For a similar view, see Fukuda, *Sovereignty*, p. 8 and ch. 7. For criticism of Pocock pointing to a Roman tradition of liberty neglected in *The Machiavellian Moment*, see Hexter, "Review Pocock," pp. 330–337.

32. For a more pacifist Machiavelli, see Viroli, *Machiavelli*, pp. 101–102; 139–140. This is not convincing, for reasons pointed out by Sullivan, *Machiavelli*, p. 39, n. 8. For an interpretation of Harrington as a methodological Machiavellian who did not share Machiavelli's values, see Boralevi, "Harrington's 'Machiavellian.'"

33. See *Oceana*, p. 296, referring back to *Discorsi* 3.24, with a quotation of Livy 4.24.4 concerning the importance of time limits on magistracies.

34. For a convincing proposal to revive Arthur O. Lovejoy's concept of unit-idea, see Knight, "Unit-Ideas Unleashed."

> or it dissolves the commonwealth where it is wanting. And this is no less than that as the hand of the magistrat is the executive power of the law, so the head of the magistrat is answerable to the people, that his execution be according to the law; by which LEVIATHAN may see that the hand or sword that executes the law is in it, and not above it.[35]

This should be seen in the tradition of Polybius' and Cicero's constitutional views as laid out above in Chapter 4, especially Cicero's claim in the *Laws* that the magistrate has to be a "law that speaks," and that "just as the laws are in charge of the magistrates, so the magistrates are in charge of the people."[36] This reliance on Cicero's constitutional thought is of a formal nature; Cicero's and Harrington's views of agrarian legislation obviously collide, but they agree on a more basic level on the role of constitutional constraints, institutional remedies and the importance of fundamental law (Cicero's *iuris consensus*) for the commonwealth.

Walter Moyle, a "key figure in the transmission of Harrington's ideas to the next generation of commonwealthmen,"[37] especially to Trenchard and Gordon, was also a key figure in the use and adaptation of the constitutional tradition of the late Roman Republic. In his *Essay on the Constitution of the Roman Government*, written in the 1690s, Moyle expressed exactly the kind of constitutional anxieties discussed in Chapter 3 related to the sovereignty of the comitia and its limits. He believed that certain institutions such as the "law of appeals to the people" constituted the "great fences of liberty," but that the Republic was ultimately undermined by the "mistaken liberty which the people assumed of dispensing with the most fundamental laws of their constitution, as the yearly elections, and the laws against continuation of magistracy."[38] In Moyle's view, the absence of constitutional constraints on the People—which, as we have seen, had been so characteristic of the *popularis* interpretation of the republican order—was an absolutely central concern:

> [A]nd although there was an outward appearance of liberty in the maxim on which this proceeding was founded, to wit, that the last resolution of the people was the undoubted law of the commonwealth;[39] yet nothing can be more certain, than that no constitution can subsist, where the

35. Harrington, *Oceana*, p. 46.

36. Cic. *Leg.* 3.2. Trans. Zetzel.

37. McDaniel, *Adam Ferguson*, p. 137.

38. Moyle, *Essay*, p. 254.

39. This is, of course, the formula reported by Livy (7.17.12) discussed in Chapter 1.

> whole frame of the laws may be shaken or suspended by the sudden temporary counsels of a multitude, and where the laws are governed by the people, instead of the people being governed by the laws.[40]

Moyle's concern with the absence of a constitutional "frame of the laws" and his corresponding anxiety about the "sudden temporary counsels of a multitude" stem explicitly from his examination of the late Roman Republic. Like Bodin, Moyle stresses that the "supreme power of a nation, 'tis confessed, can be bounded or limited by no precedent law; but . . . it would have well become the wisdom of the people to have laid a voluntary restraint on their own authority, and have had recourse to the dictatorian power, or any other expedient, rather than to expose and weaken the great bulwarks of their constitution, by assuming such a dispensing power."[41] This constitutionalist outlook does not depend on the concept of virtue, either as an educational goal for the commonwealth to aspire to, or as something instrumental for the stability of the state. Rather, it is concerned, once again, with the constitutional checks and balances that themselves represent reason. It is an outlook very close to Polybius', Cicero's and Bodin's.[42]

It is telling that some of Pocock's key witnesses for his account of a virtue-oriented, anti-modern classical republicanism and its transmission from Machiavelli to the American Founders, Trenchard and Gordon, are on closer inspection not as concerned with virtue as Pocock claims.[43] Writing as Cato, they draw most of their constitutional thought from the crises of the late Roman republican order. The way these country Whigs talk about virtue is hardly compatible with a Peripatetic outlook:

> And, indeed, it is wisdom in a state, and a sign that they judge well, to suppose, that all men who can enslave them, will enslave them. Generosity, self-denial, and private and personal virtues, are in politicks but mere names, or rather cant-words, that go for nothing with wise men, though they may cheat the vulgar.[44]

---

40. Moyle, *Essay*, p. 255.

41. Moyle, *Essay*, p. 254.

42. For an interpretation of Moyle as close to Machiavelli's "stern, aggressive republicanism," see Sullivan, "Moyle's Machiavellianism."

43. This complements both Sullivan, *Machiavelli*, pp. 227–257, and Jacob, "Eighteenth-Century Republican," p. 13, who convincingly stresses the Hobbesian political psychology underlying *Cato's Letters* as well as Cato's sympathies toward commerce. Cf. Pocock, *Machiavellian Moment*, pp. 467–477.

44. *Cato's Letters*, no. 11, vol. 1, p. 92.

This is however not merely compatible with but quite directly drawn from the late republican constitutional thinking we have been concerned with throughout this book. Gordon makes this clear when he talks about the constitutional norms that lie beyond the reach of positive law-making. Cato's approach is entirely Ciceronian and so is his language, not simply in his invocation of the principle of *salus populi*, but on a deeper level, as Cato interprets *salus populi* in a constitutionalist manner while giving the constitutional norm the status of natural law, exactly as Cicero himself had in the *Laws*:

> *Salus populi suprema lex esto*: That the benefit and safety of the people constitutes the supreme law, is an universal and everlasting maxim in government; It can never be altered by municipal statutes: No customs can change, no positive institutions can abrogate, no time can efface, this primary law of nature and nations. The sole end of men's entering into political societies, was mutual protection and defence; and whatever power does not contribute to those purposes, is not government, but usurpation.[45]

The extraordinary powers invoked by the dictator Cincinnatus and his Master of the Horse to put down the attempted *coup* by Spurius Maelius were thus constitutional, Cato asserts, interpreting these powers exactly as Livy had done. Dictatorship "free and unfettered by the laws" (*leges*) could be used to put down any subversion of the constitutional order, and do so in a way consistent with constitutional norms—*iure*, as Livy had Cincinnatus put it.[46] In an entirely Grotian and Lockean way, this power to punish transgressors against the constitutional order Cato derives from the natural right to punish inherent in everyone in the state of nature.[47]

45. Ibid., p. 87. In the following letter, Trenchard castigates the *unconstitutional* interpretation of *salus populi*: "[B]y the flattery of priests and servile lawyers, the *salus populi*, or security of the state, soon came to signify only the unbounded power and sovereignty of the prince; and it became treason to hinder one, constituted, and grandly maintained out of the people's labour and wealth, for the publick safety, from destroying the publick safety. Our ancestors found, by lamentable experience, that unworthy men, preferred by corrupt ministers for unworthy ends, made treasons free only of the court; that the least attempt to oppose unlimited and unlawful authority, was often called treason; and that the highest treasons of all, which were those against the commonwealth, might be committed with impunity, applause, and rewards": *Cato's Letters*, no. 12, vol. 1, p. 96.

46. Ibid., no. 11, vol. 1, pp. 90–91. (with constant citations from Livy's text). On Maelius and Cincinnatus cf. Chapter 2, pp. 49–51.

47. See, on the natural law tradition asserting such a revolutionary right, Straumann, *Roman Law in the State of Nature*, ch. 9.

That Trenchard and Gordon were thus not in the least relying on "cant-words," such as "virtue," they make very clear in a very perspicacious account of the crises of the late Republic, an account perfectly in line with our constitutionalist theme. It is also an account that owes much to an Epicurean political psychology borrowed from Hobbes, one that is close to Cicero's early accounts of the state of nature such as exhibited in his *De inventione* and the speeches for Sestius and Milo.[48] Writing in a letter dedicated to constitutional constraints on power, Gordon points out that even "Nero had lived a great while inoffensively, and reigned virtuously: But finding at last that he might do what he would, he let loose his appetite for blood." In the absence of constitutional constraints, the virtue counseled by Seneca was ultimately useless. Given human nature, therefore, Cato writes in a very Hobbesian vein, it is "owing more to the necessities of men, than to their inclinations, that they have put themselves under the restraint of laws, and appointed certain persons, called magistrates, to execute them; otherwise they would never be executed, scarce any man having such a degree of virtue as willingly to execute the laws upon himself; but, on the contrary, most men thinking them a grievance, when they come to meddle with themselves and their property." Gordon then goes on to point out, using Tacitus' description of Pompey's consulship without a colleague, that extra-constitutional powers had subverted the Roman Republic: "*Suarum legum auctor & eversor*,[49] was the character of Pompey: He made laws when they suited his occasions, and broke them when they thwarted his will. And it is the character of almost every man possessed of Pompey's power: They intend them for a security to themselves, and for a terror to others." This, Cato says at his most Hobbesian, is because of "the distrust that men have of men; and this made a great philosopher call the state of nature, a state of war."[50] "The world is governed by men, and men by their passions; which, being boundless and insatiable, are always terrible when they are not controuled":[51] hence the necessity of (constitutional) government. Government is conceived as a "mutual contract of a number of men," so that "men quitted part of their natural liberty to acquire civil security." But this remedy often "proved

48. See Chapter 4; as have seen, however, Cicero retained elements of this outlook even in his account in the *Republic*. It is instructive that Bellarmine realized that Cicero had come up with a revolutionary anti-Aristotelian concept of the state of nature, a concept he attacked in a proto-Burkean way: *De Laicis*, ch. 5, pp. 22–23.

49. An unacknowledged reference to Tac. *Ann*. 3.28. Gordon translated Tacitus (as well as Sallust) in 1728-31 and added extensive "political discourses" to these translations, which were widely read in revolutionary America. See Bailyn, *Origins*, p. 22.

50. *Cato's Letters* no. 33, vol. 1, p. 236.

51. Ibid., p. 238.

worse than the disease; and human society had often no enemies so great as their own magistrates; who, where-ever they were trusted with too much power, always abused it, and grew mischievous to those who made them what they were."[52] This leads to the conclusion that the Republic had been free to the extent that there had been constitutional restraints:

> Rome, while she was free (that is, while she kept her magistrates within due bounds) could defend herself against all the world, and conquer it: But being enslaved (that is, her magistrates having broke their bounds) she could not defend herself against her own single tyrants.[53]

The remedy for vice is not virtue, but legal institutions, so that wickedness is made unsafe: the "only security which we can have that men will be honest, is to make it their interest to be honest." This language is as far removed from "classical republicanism" as it is in line with the Polybian-Ciceronian constitutional remedies we examined in Chapter 4. Moreover, as we have seen, Cato has a conception of the state of nature that is very close indeed to Cicero's and John Locke's. He shares with both the notion of pre-political property rights and of a right of resistance in case the government fails to protect those pre-political rights. Most importantly, Cato shares with Cicero and Locke the idea that it is the very *purpose* of the state to protect said pre-political rights.

Is this doctrinal overlap coincidental? Cato was the first of the country Whigs or commonwealthmen to have access to Locke's writings,[54] and he certainly knew his Cicero. We know that Locke, in turn, was intimately familiar with Cicero's writings, especially the *De officiis* (*On Duties*), of which he owned numerous editions and which he recommended as the only other work on ethics next to the Bible.[55] Locke's early *Essays on the Law of Nature* (1663–64) evince close familiarity with the *De officiis*, as does later, unpublished work.[56] Both John Marshall and Phillip Mitsis have made a strong claim that Cicero exerted a "strong and palpable influence" on John Locke's thinking.[57] Mitsis tries to substantiate this influence by pointing to the attraction Cicero's ethical doctrine as

52. Ibid., p. 236.

53. Ibid., pp. 236–237.

54. Sullivan, *Machiavelli*, p. 15.

55. Marshall, *John Locke*, p. 301.

56. Mitsis, "Locke's Offices," p. 54.

57. Marshall, *John Locke*, pp. 157–204, 292–326; Mitsis, "Locke's Offices," p. 51.

expounded in *De officiis* held for Locke; at the same time he admits that there is a basic inconsistency between Locke's hedonism and subjectivism concerning the *summum bonum* and Cicero's anti-hedonistic theory of value.[58] Yet when it comes to Locke's *political* theory, as opposed to his views concerning ethics and the good, there is a much more obvious, palpable direct influence: both Cicero and Locke stipulate pre-political property rights and both claim that it is the very purpose of political society to protect these rights. In another essay, where he is concerned to refute Anthony Long's view that the Stoics had a robust conception of private property rights, Mitsis argues that it amounts to a distortion of Cicero's doctrine of justice to attribute such a Lockean view to him, as Neal Wood has done, but Mitsis' main goal is to deny that the *Greek* Stoics had ever held such a view.[59] Mitsis' argument is as convincing with regard to the early Stoics as it is unconvincing with regard to Cicero.

In Chapter 4, we have seen how Cicero's conception of the state of nature contributed to his considered doctrine of the end of political society. Whether or not this is correct as an interpretation of Cicero, it would certainly seem very plausible to attribute to Locke precisely this kind of reading of *De officiis* and of Cicero's definition of the state in the *Republic*. From what we have learned about Cicero's views on property, natural justice, the end of the state, and his definition of the state, Locke's doctrine "Of the Ends of Political Society and Government" should sound familiar indeed. The "great and *chief end* therefore, of Mens uniting into Commonwealths, and putting themselves under Government, *is the Preservation of their Property*," Locke writes.[60] Cicero had maintained that "commonwealths (*res publicae*) and cities were constituted especially so that men could hold on to their possessions." The "hope of safeguarding their possessions (*spe custodiae rerum suarum*)" made men seek "protection in cities."[61] For Locke, the state is a "Society of Rational Creatures entred into a Community for their mutual good," and the

58. Mitsis, "Locke's Offices," p. 59. From what I am arguing here, it seems that Locke's liberal answer to his skepticism concerning the *summum bonum* was inchoate in Cicero, so that the tension between an ethical theory of the good and a political theory of the right is something Locke could have found already in Cicero. In a sense Cicero reduces a far-reaching conception of the good to one that still claims, formally, that justice is the *summum bonum*—but now in Cicero justice itself is reduced to maintaining existing, pre-political property relations. Locke would then seem to be influenced by Cicero even in his skepticism concerning the *summum bonum*.

59. Mitsis, "Stoics on Property," n. 10; Mitsis does not discuss Cic. *Off.* 2.73. Cf. Long, "Stoic Philosophers"; id., "Cicero's Politics"; Nussbaum, "Duties of Justice"; Annas, "Cicero on Stoic Moral Philosophy"; Wood, *Cicero's Social and Political Thought*, pp. 113–115.

60. Locke, *Second Treatise*, ch. 9, § 124.

61. Cic. *Off.* 2.73.

reason the state of nature cannot guarantee the preservation of their property lies in the lack of an "*establish'd . . . Law*, received and allowed by common consent."[62] For Cicero, in Scipio's famous definition, the commonwealth was a community of people associated (*sociatus*) with one another through agreement about law (*iuris consensu*) and community of interest (*utilitatis communione*).[63] For both Cicero and Locke, agreement about law provides a constitutional framework higher than mere legislation and apt to secure the purpose of the state.

In his chapter on the "Subordination of the Powers of the Commonwealth," Locke differentiates in a Bodinian way between (popular) sovereignty and its administration, pointing out that the executive power as the representative of the commonwealth has "no Will, no Power, but that of the Law." This fiduciary relationship between constitutional powers on the one hand and sovereign on the other is reminiscent of Bodin;[64] and it may not be too fanciful to hear echoes of Cicero's *Laws* in Locke's metaphor of the executive as a mere "image," or "phantom" of the commonwealth and in his insistence that the executive power, even when exercising the famous prerogative, is still bound by the constitutional principle of *salus populi suprema lex*.[65] While hardly ever mentioning the Roman Republic,[66] Locke's constitutional solution to what he identifies with Cicero as the essential purpose of the commonwealth bears a close resemblance to the Polybian-Ciceronian solution discussed in Chapter 4: given human frailty and the temptation to "grasp at Power" and to act "contrary to the end of Society and of Government," the various powers have to be limited by law and separated, that is, they themselves have to be subject to a constitutional framework.[67] With a nod to Bodin and his distinction between "lordly" and "lawful" sovereignty, Locke makes it clear that "even *absolute Power*, where it is necessary, is *not Arbitrary* by being absolute, but is still limited by that reason, and confined to those ends," by which Locke means "that Men might have and secure *their Properties*." The

---

62. *Second Treatise*, ch. 14, § 163; ch. 9, § 124.

63. Cic. *Rep.* 1.39.

64. Locke did not reference Bodin and did not own any of his works, but was acquainted with them. See Laslett's note in Locke, *Two Treatises*, p. 146.

65. *Second Treatise*, ch. 13, § 158; ch. 14. Note the Bodinian history of government at § 162, where all government is said to have originated as mere prerogative without legal constraints; Locke's solution to the problem of how to determine the constitutionality of prerogative is broadly Jeffersonian: Kleinerman, *Discretionary President*, pp. 148–164.

66. Locke does make mention of the Ten as tyranny (ch. 18, § 201), however, and uses the example of the founding of the Roman state as a historical example to show the possibility of an original social contract (ch. 8, § 102).

67. *Second Treatise*, chs. 12–13.

taking of property would be arbitrary, but even absolute power under martial discipline, cannot expropriate its subjects' property but is constitutionally constrained.[68] Bodin's lordly government "without *settled standing Laws*" would violate Locke's account of the purpose of political society; it would amount to "absolute Arbitrary Power," for which men "would not quit the freedom of the state of Nature."[69] "Extemporary Decrees," too, amount to a violation.[70] Locke's "settled standing Laws" are tantamount to Cicero's *ius*: higher-order, entrenched constitutional norms that guarantee pre-political rights.[71]

When we reach the man who was probably the most influential political theorist writing in the eighteenth century, Montesquieu, we find an examination of the constitutional crises of the late Republic leading to the denigration of the importance of virtue and to an acknowledgment of constitutional principles akin to Bodin.[72] Although Montesquieu does have an original, anti-Hobbesian concept of the state of nature that anticipates in some ways Rousseau's, he does not operate with Cicero's or Locke's notion of pre-political rights.[73] Montesquieu does have an underlying normative aim of freedom from despotism and individual rights, however, which supplies him with the end for (constitutional) government. Using the distinction between "lordly" and "lawful" government in the way Bodin had done, Montesquieu in his work *Considerations on the Causes of the Greatness of the Romans and Their Decline* observed that "in Rome, governed by laws, the people allowed the senate to direct public affairs," while "in Carthage, governed by abuses, the people wanted to do everything themselves."[74] Although Montesquieu arrives in his later work at the view that Rome, as an ancient Republic, had been sustained by virtue,[75] he is at the

---

68. Ibid., ch. 11, § 139.

69. Ibid., § 137.

70. Ibid., ch. 9, § 131. Note that Locke here expounds a separation of three powers.

71. Such rights are conceptually identical with human rights; they can be said—*pace* Moyn, *Last Utopia*, p. 13—to be "above and outside" the state, and they "serve as its foundation" only in the sense that for sovereignty to be legitimate, pre-political (human) rights must be respected. Whether such rights can be *enforced* by supranational institutions is a different question, but even today this issue remains unresolved in human rights law.

72. On Montesquieu, see Richter, *Political Theory*; Shklar, *Montesquieu*; Shklar, "Montesquieu"; Sonenscher, *Before the Deluge*, pp. 95–178.

73. *Spirit*, bk. 1, ch. 2. His notion of natural law betrays certain affinities with Cicero's, however, and he was taken by Adam Ferguson to be a Stoic: McDaniel, *Adam Ferguson*, p. 12.

74. *Considerations*, p. 45.

75. By which he means "love of homeland" and "love of equality": *Spirit*, p. xli (this amounted to a retraction added to the 1757 edition, to the effect that by "virtue" he had always just

same time at pains to give an account of the republican order that is heavily institutional and already very similar to his famous account of the English constitution in book 11, chapter 6.[76] It is thus only to an extent that Montesquieu's "aim is to rob Rome of its allure";[77] partly his aim is to give a constitutional interpretation of the fall of the Republic, and show *some* similarities between that Republic and the constitution of England. Indeed, as Paul Rahe has shown, Montesquieu intended to present England as "the only modern analogue to classical Rome."[78] "Corruption" is for Montesquieu not so much the antithesis of virtue; rather, it can be prevented by "the strength of . . . institutions."[79] "The government of Rome," Montesquieu writes, "was admirable" because from "its birth, abuses of power could always be corrected by its constitution," that is to say, by the checks and balances provided by the temperate distribution of power among People, Senate and magistrates.[80] "Free government" can only last if it is "capable of being corrected by its own laws."[81] The "republic was lost" once "the people could give their favorites a formidable authority abroad."[82] Montesquieu is thus an heir, not to the "mixed" constitution in the strict sense, but to the "well-tempered" constitution, balancing separate institutions, as we found it

meant "political virtue"—the idea that monarchies were somehow less amenable to giving rise to private virtue proved highly provocative).

76. My interpretation, as a consequence, differs from Paul Rahe's view that in the *Considerations* Montesquieu had painted a picture of Rome entirely dependent on Machiavelli's *Discorsi*, where "Montesquieu's Rome is a machine designed for conquest—and nothing more": Rahe, "Montesquieu's *Considerations*," p. 73. Cf. also id., "Montesquieu's anti-Machiavellian Machiavellianism." As Rahe himself acknowledges (see the following), Rome appears also as a machine designed for free constitutional government, not too dissimilar from England, apart from the role played by commerce. My interpretation follows Rahe, however, in acknowledging Montesquieu's disparaging view of ancient, "Greek" virtue, and thus runs counter to Eric Nelson's attempt to attribute to Montesquieu an unambiguous admiration for virtuous republics; Nelson, *Greek Tradition*, pp. 127–194. See Rahe, "Review Nelson." Cf. also Sonenscher, *Before the Deluge*, pp. 95–178, where the *Spirit of the Laws* is said to belong to a more monarchical Montesquieu than the *Considerations*.

77. Rahe, "Montesquieu's *Considerations*," p. 77. One may say, with Vickie Sullivan, that Montesquieu's aim is to rob *Machiavellian* republicanism of its allure, describing it as despotic: Sullivan, "Against the Despotism."

78. Rahe, "Montesquieu's *Considerations*," p. 82. Rahe convincingly adduces the first impression of the first edition of the *Considérations* (before Montesquieu was urged to change it) to show this.

79. *Considerations*, p. 98.

80. Ibid., p. 87.

81. Ibid., p. 88.

82. Ibid., p. 92.

described by Polybius and Cicero in Chapter 4—indeed, we should now be able to see the extent to which his celebrated doctrine of the separation of powers is really dependent on the Roman constitutional tradition, as was Locke's before him.[83]

In a fitting description of the Polybian-Ciceronian constitutional synthesis, Montesquieu observes that a "true body politic" is "a union of harmony, whereby all the parts, however opposed they may appear, cooperate for the general good of society—as dissonances in music cooperate in producing overall concord. In a state"—and here Montesquieu is thinking of the Roman Republic when it was still constitutional—"where we seem to see nothing but commotion there can be union."[84] With Sulla, however, we encounter violations of the constitutional order that could not be undone even by Sulla's own "well-designed laws," because "in the frenzy of his successes, he had done things that made it impossible for Rome to preserve its liberty."[85] The extra-constitutional powers—commissions given by the People—of Sulla, Pompey, and Caesar and the ensuing proscriptions and confiscations of property led to the end of the Republic:

> The laws of Rome had wisely divided public power among a large number of magistracies, which supported, checked[86] and tempered each other. Since they all had only limited power, every citizen was qualified for them, and the people . . . did not grow accustomed to any in particular. But in these times the system of the republic changed. Through the people the most powerful men gave themselves extraordinary commissions—which

83. Cf. Riklin, *Machtteilung*, pp. 269–298; Riklin shows convincingly Montesquieu's debt to the classical tradition of constitutional thought and the extent to which the "separation of powers" is not original with Montesquieu, but Riklin tends to subsume this whole tradition under the notion "mixed constitution," which flattens it unduly and neglects the specifics of Polybius' and Cicero's innovative approach.

84. *Considerations*, pp. 93–94. Note the use of musical metaphor; cf. Polybius' and Cicero's use of similar musical metaphors in Chapter 4, and see, on John Adams' use thereof, below.

85. Ibid., p. 101. See also Montesquieu's little known tract *Dialogue de Sylla et d'Eucrate* (*Œuvres complètes*, 1876, p. 342), where Sulla's friend Eukrates says to the dictator that "en prenant la dictature, vous avez donné l'exemple du crime que vous avez puni. Voilà l'exemple qui sera suivi, et non pas celui d'une modération qu'on ne fera qu'admirer. Quand les dieux ont souffert que Sylla se soit impunément fait dictateur dans Rome, ils y ont proscrit la liberté pour jamais." Sulla's example also seems to underlie Adam Smith's distinction between two kinds of leaders in times of civil discord: *Theory of Moral Sentiments* 6.2.2, pp. 231–234.

86. Montesquieu, who writes of "magistratures, qui . . . s'arrêtaient," may have borrowed the idea of "checks" from Bolingbroke.

> destroyed the authority of the people and magistrates, and placed all great matters in the hands of one man, or a few.[87]

This is a perfectly Bodinian analysis—note especially the "extraordinary *commissions*"—of the fall of the Republic, designed to support a constitutionalist solution. In the absence of such a solution, arbitrary Augustan monarchy looms: "There is no authority more absolute than that of a prince who succeeds a republic; for he finds himself in possession of all the powers of a people who had not been capable of imposing limitations upon themselves."[88] There is a continuation in *The Spirit of the Laws*. Montesquieu's famous chapter "On the constitution of England" includes a great many observations on the Roman Republic, and it is fair to say that Montesquieu's presentation of Rome here is of a piece with that given in his earlier *Considerations*.[89] The conventional distinction between Montesquieu's ancient republics which were governed by virtue and the modern, commercial republics governed by constitutional institutions runs the danger of obscuring the extent to which Montesquieu's constitutional views are in fact derived from Roman republican examples, although not from Rome's virtue. The cause of the fall of the Republic is, as it had been in Bodin, of a constitutional nature and Montesquieu uses it to illustrate features of the English constitution:

> The cause of the change in government in Rome was that the senate, which had one part of the executive power, and the magistrates, who had the other, did not have the faculty of vetoing, as the people had.[90]

This had led to the abuse of the powers of the people as described in the *Considerations*; but the power of vetoing itself, and the checks thus introduced on the other powers, was extremely useful and could be found in the constitution of England as well. Montesquieu illustrates the veto with reference to the Roman tribunes, whose veto power however "was faulty in that it checked not only legislation but even execution; this caused great ills."[91] In general, of

87. *Considerations*, p. 103. Note also that Pompey "aspired to the dictatorship, but through the votes of the people."

88. *Considerations*, p. 138.

89. This no less than all the evidence discussed in Part III here makes David Wootton's Venturi-inspired argument that all the classical references in the republican tradition amount to mere ornamentation very implausible: "True Origins."

90. *Spirit*, bk. 11, ch. 6, p. 164.

91. Ibid., p. 162.

course, Montesquieu thought that the power of the people should not go beyond choosing representatives; the people, according to him, should not even legislate directly, let alone "make resolutions for action." The latter should be left to magistrates, the former to a representative body. Montesquieu believes that in the Roman Republic, the People, in "a frenzy of liberty," had gained "exorbitant power" that "should have reduced the authority of the senate to nothing; but Rome had admirable institutions." These institutions consisted in a means to "regulate" the legislative power of the People, and in a means to "limit" it. Montesquieu has in mind the censors, who, according to him "created the body of the people" and thus "exercised legislation even over the body that had legislative power." This constitutional device was joined by the power of the Senate "to remove the republic from the hands of the people, so to speak, by creating a dictator before whom the sovereign bowed and the most popular laws [i.e., the *provocatio* laws] remained silent."[92] We have all the familiar themes, rendered in the language of sovereignty, with a constitutional mechanism, the dictatorship, to check the power of the popular assemblies.[93] Montesquieu sees the crises of the Republic in the perspective of Bodin and describes its dissolution as the unintentional consequence of unconstitutional popular overreach:

> In Rome, as the people had the greater part of the legislative power, part of the executive power, and part of the power of judging, they were a great power that had to be counter-balanced by another. The senate certainly had part of the executive power; it had some branch of the legislative power, but this was not enough to counter-balance the people. . . . When the Gracchi deprived the senators of the power of judging, the senate could no longer stand up to the people. Therefore, they ran counter to the liberty of the constitution in order to favor the liberty of the citizen, but the latter was lost along with the former.[94]

The liberty of the citizen depends, then, on the liberty of the constitution. The way Montesquieu's chapter on the constitution of England is suffused with examples from the Roman Republic as well as the similarities between that

92. Ibid., ch. 16, pp. 176–177.

93. Obviously, the historical accuracy or otherwise of this account is not at issue here; see the discussions in Chapters 2 and 3. The basic problem is already inchoately visible in the Roman sources.

94. *Spirit*, bk. 11, ch. 18, p. 182. Cf. ch. 17, p. 178 for a reference to Polybius' description of the role of the Senate.

chapter and Montesquieu's *Considerations* both suggest that the conventional contrast postulated for Montesquieu between ancient republics and modern constitutionalism might be overdrawn. It seems, rather, that it is ancient imperial virtue and military glory that need to be left behind, according to Montesquieu, while Rome's "admirable institutions" with its inchoate constitutionalism are well worth discussing and betray important "modern" features.[95] Even the strong contrast between modern commerce and the Romans, who are said to have "rarely thought about" commerce is mitigated by Montesquieu himself, who remarks that the "Romans did considerable commerce in the Indies," "even more considerable than that of the kings of Egypt," and thereby introduces a tension into his account. After the "Roman empire was invaded, . . . one of the effects of the general calamity was the destruction of commerce."[96] Even Rome had some commercial traits, and its late republican inchoate constitutionalism deserved the attention of the moderns. Virtue, on the other hand, for Montesquieu, as it was for Trenchard and Gordon, appears to have been a "cant-word"—witness his utterly pejorative description of "virtue in a republic": virtue is a passion for the general order, and the "less we can satisfy our particular passions, the more we give up to passions for the general order. Why do monks so love their order? Their love comes from the same thing that makes their order intolerable to them. Their rule deprives them of everything upon which ordinary passions rest; what remains, therefore, is the passion for the very rule that afflicts them. The more austere it is, that is, the more it curtails their inclinations, the more force it gives to those that remain."[97]

Montesquieu's discussion of virtuous republics, constitutionalism, Rome, and England was formative for later political thought, especially in France, Scotland, and America. In France, Montesquieu's distinction between ancient republics and modern commercial monarchies established "the umbilical connection between 'virtue' and republicanism,"[98] which had crucial consequences for revolutionary politics.[99] For this connection, Montesquieu could of course

95. Rome also provided a focal point for Montesquieu's subtle discussion of standing armies (bk. 11, ch. 6, p. 165), which also served to show the "resemblance between England and the Roman republic," as McDaniel reminds us: *Adam Ferguson*, p. 36.

96. *Spirit*, bk. 21, ch. 14, p. 382; ch. 16, pp. 383–384; ch. 17, p. 386.

97. Ibid., bk. 5, ch. 2, pp. 42–43.

98. Wright, "Montesquieuean Moments," p. 155.

99. Linton, *Politics of Virtue*; Sonenscher, *Before the Deluge*, p. 150. See Rawson, *Spartan Tradition*, pp. 242–245 on Helvétius as an important proponent of glory and Spartan public virtue.

draw upon the rich strand of thought we discussed in Chapter 7, especially upon Augustine's influential notion of Rome's expansionist, imperial glory and pagan virtue. But as we have seen, an important strand of Roman constitutionalist thinking is also characteristic of Montesquieu, and this constitutionalist line can be detected in Diderot's *Encyclopédie*, in the entry of Jaucourt on the Roman Republic, which is lifted word for word from Montesquieu's *Considerations*, complete with its praise of Rome's institutions which held firm even in the face of luxury.[100]

Jean-Jacques Rousseau (1712-1778) famously put the Roman Republic to very prominent use in the *Contrat Social* (1762).[101] On the one hand, the Republic serves as a model for a large republic that legislated without representation, where the sovereign assembled and pronounced its will despite the size of its constituency.[102] The Roman People in the assemblies were thus "genuinely Sovereign both by right and in fact."[103] Drawing the very distinction Constant was to draw between ancient and modern liberty, but favoring the former, Rousseau argues against the very possibility of the representation of sovereignty[104] and claims that once "the People is legitimately assembled as a Sovereign body, all jurisdiction of the Government ceases, the executive power is suspended."[105] Rousseau seems to hold a view akin to Bodin's when he states that ultimately the Roman People came to "usurp" the "most important functions of Government."[106] But even more than in Bodin, there is ultimately no vantage point—notwithstanding the normative coloring of *usurpé*—from which to declare this usurpation wrong, or unconstitutional. Rousseau thinks the dictatorship as practiced in the early and

100. *Encyclopédie* 14, p. 157: "Cependant la force de l'institution de Rome, étoit encore telle dans le tems dont nous parlons, qu'elle conservoit une valeur héroïque, & toute son application à la guerre au milieu des richesses, de la mollesse, & de la volupté; ce qui n'est, je crois, arrivé à aucune nation du monde." The following famous passage, where the importance of individual vice is downplayed and the effect of structural factors stressed, also made it into the article: "Enfin la *république* fut opprimée; & il n'en faut pas accuser l'ambition de quelques particuliers, il en faut accuser l'homme, toujours plus avide du pouvoir à mesure qu'il en a davantage, & qui ne desire tout, que parce qu'il possede beaucoup. Si César & Pompée avoient pensé comme Caton, d'autres auroient pensé comme firent Cesar & Pompée; & la *république* destinée à périr auroit été entraînée au précipice par une autre main."

101. On the importance of Sparta, see Rawson, *Spartan Tradition*, pp. 231–241.

102. *Social Contract* 3.12.

103. Ibid. 4.4. Trans. Gourevitch.

104. Ibid. 3.15.

105. Ibid. 3.14.

106. Ibid. 4.4.

middle Republic with its strict time limit had been a highly useful emergency institution conducive to upholding the republican order; he clearly believes that the dictatorship had not been subject to *provocatio* and finds fault with Cicero and the Senate for not putting it to use against the Catilinarians.[107] Ultimately, however, nothing can hinder the sovereign from ridding itself of any constitutional emergency devices or changing the fundamental laws of the polity: the sovereign is perfectly unbound.[108] Rousseau, it is clear, does not put his trust in institutional devices; criticizing Montesquieu, he writes that it is not only small popular republics that are in need of virtue, but polities in general; it is the sovereign's virtue, nothing institutional, which will guarantee the political order (it is, however, completely unclear how the general will could ever be unjust, or merely corrupt).[109] It is true that in the chapter on the "lawgiver," Rousseau seems to speak of the institutional "machinery" of the state, but it is said, at the same time, that it would take gods to set up this machinery, and that the lawgiver is not supposed to be sovereign; Rousseau wavers as to whether the Ten Men were sovereign, but after some ambiguity seems to deny this. The lawgiver needs to stand outside the polity and his own legislation, but is at the same time expected to "change human nature" and transform the humans who are also, confusingly, supposed to give their sanction to the proposed legislation.[110] There is no room—that much seems clear—for a constitutional framework above and beyond the people acting as sovereign.

---

107. Ibid. 4.6.

108. Ibid. 3.18: "Je suppose ici ce que je crois avoir démontré, savoir, qu'il n'y a dans l'État aucune loi fondamentale qui ne se puisse révoquer, non pas même le pacte social; car si tous les citoyens s'assemblaient pour rompre ce pacte d'un commun accord, on ne peut douter qu'il ne fût très légitimement rompu."

109. Ibid. 3.4: "Voilà pourquoi un auteur célèbre a donné la vertu pour principe à la république, car toutes ces conditions ne sauraient subsister sans la vertu; mais, faute d'avoir fait les distinctions nécessaires, ce beau génie a manqué souvent de justesse, quelquefois de clarté, et n'a pas vu que l'autorité souveraine étant partout la même, le même principe doit avoir lieu dans tout État bien constitué."

110. Ibid. 2.7: "Rome, dans son plus bel âge, vit renaître en son sein tous les crimes de la tyrannie, et se vit prête à périr, pour avoir réuni sur les mêmes têtes l'autorité législative et le pouvoir souverain. Cependant les décemvirs eux-mêmes ne s'arrogèrent jamais le droit de faire passer aucune loi de leur seule autorité. 'Rien de ce que nous vous proposons, disaient-ils au peuple, ne peut passer en loi sans votre consentement. Romains, soyez vous-mêmes les auteurs des lois qui doivent faire votre bonheur.' Celui qui rédige les lois n'a donc ou ne doit avoir aucun droit législatif, et le peuple même ne peut, quand il le voudrait, se dépouiller de ce droit incommunicable, parce que, selon le pacte fondamental, il n'y a que la volonté générale qui oblige les particuliers, et qu'on ne peut jamais s'assurer qu'une volonté particulière est conforme à la volonté générale qu'après l'avoir soumise aux suffrages libres du peuple."

A further fascinating, if ambiguous, case is Bonnot de Mably (1709–1785). The abbé de Mably, whom Benjamin Constant famously grouped with Rousseau as one of the main culprits for having prepared the way for Jacobinism by idolizing "ancient liberty," started out as an enthusiastic defender of monarchy and of the modern party in the *querelle des Anciens et des Modernes*, but revised his views and came to defend, in his *Observations sur les Grecs* (1749) and his *Observations sur les Romains* (1751), a version of ancient republicanism that was beholden, above all, to Sparta's Lycurgan constitution and the proposition that wealth and luxury had corrupted the Roman Republic and thus caused its decline. Johnson Kent Wright has shown that Mably departed from Machiavelli's *Discorsi* in relying on a Polybian separation and balance of powers, on the one hand, and in endorsing a strict pacifism in obvious tension with Roman imperialism.[111] Wright correctly says that the "exact relation" between the doctrine of the separation of powers and that of mixed government is "one of the most vexed questions in the historiography of political thought."[112] He ascribes Mably's account of checks and balances and of separate powers to seventeenth-century English thought, but I think we would be justified in giving credit for this aspect of Mably's thinking to Polybius and Cicero themselves. While Mably indeed conforms to Constant's caricature when it comes to his skepticism toward commerce, his admiration of Sparta and his concern with the corruption of virtue, there are indications that Mably's alleged utopian communism should not be taken at face value and that there is an important strand of Ciceronian natural-law constitutionalism and even the occasional Anglophile sentiment running through Mably's most influential writings, especially the *Des droits et des devoirs du citoyen*, Mably's "script for a French Revolution."[113] In this work, written in the late 1750s or even later, but not published until 1789, one finds a perfectly Ciceronian account of private property as a pre-political, natural right in the state of nature.[114] This stands in tension with Mably's professed Spartan egalitarianism, but as Wright convincingly explains, Mably seems ultimately to dismiss anti-property egalitarianism as

111. Wright, *Classical Republican*, pp. 39–64, esp. pp. 43–50. On Mably's adoration of Sparta, see Rawson, *Spartan Tradition*, pp. 245–267.

112. Wright, *Classical Republican*, p. 43; on the influence of the classical model on seventeenth-century English debates, see Nippel, *Mischverfassungstheorie*; see also von Fritz, *Mixed Constitution*; Gwyn, *Separation of Powers*; Riklin, *Machtteilung*.

113. Baker, "Script." For the Anglophilia, see Acomb, *Anglophobia*, pp. 37-38 (who counts Mably otherwise justifiably among the Anglophobes).

114. Mably, *Des droits*, p. 108. As Wright points out, Mably also uses the Lockean idea of mixing one's labor to acquire property: *Classical Republican*, p. 101.

a chimera and to return to the *parti des modernes* in giving expression to a feeling, inspired by Rousseau, that with the end of Graeco-Roman antiquity and the ensuing corruption, "a whole range of political and social possibilities was closed off for good" and thereby arriving at an entirely "conventional natural rights outlook."[115] This "profound impasse in Mably's thought"[116] we can perhaps explain by pointing to the *ancient* precedent Mably had for this outlook—Cicero's work and the *De legibus* above all.[117]

How to achieve an order where pre-political property rights, "the foundation of order, peace, and public security,"[118] can be guaranteed? In his *Doutes proposés aux philosophes économistes sur l'ordre naturel et essentiel des sociétés politiques* (1768), Mably proposed a *constitutional* arrangement as the solution, one we might term a conventional well-tempered constitutional order. Mably points to the Romans as the model, and beyond the Romans to "a good many *modern* peoples," who "will tell you that it is necessary for powers to balance one another reciprocally, and that it is only by means of this balance that the citizens, despite their inequality of fortune, can draw closer to natural equality, and enjoy the security for which they first entered into society."[119] There is little here that should arouse Constant's objection; of course, this constitutional order is also compatible with the strict regulation of commerce and agrarian laws, but the extent to which Mably relies on constitutional arrangements to achieve this is still remarkable. The other striking aspect of Mably's thought lies in his acceptance of Ciceronian pre-political natural property rights, which seems to push him inexorably, in spite of his original aims, towards acknowledging simply security, including security of property holdings, as the end of political society. Mably went on to play a role in the international debate on the American state constitutions; in 1784 his *Observations sur le gouvernement et les lois des Etats-Unis d'Amérique* saw publication in Holland and immediately provoked controversy. The state constitutions of newly independent America were built, Mably admiringly stated, on the true principles Locke had put forward concerning the natural liberty of mankind. Again, nothing for Constant to worry about, yet there is again a basic tension here between his general admiration

115. Wright, *Classical Republican*, pp. 103–104.

116. Ibid., p. 104.

117. For the impact of Cic. *Leg.* on Mably, see Dyck, *Commentary*, pp. 36–37.

118. Wright, *Classical Republican*, p. 104. The account would have been "endorsed by Grotius, Hobbes, and Locke alike," Wright points out—as well as by Hume and Smith, one might add.

119. Mably, *Collection complète*, vol. 11, pp. 223–224. Trans. Wright, *Classical Republican*, p. 105. Emphasis mine.

for the American constitutions and an almost Hartzian view of their Lockean pedigree, on the one hand, and his ongoing worry about impending corruption through commerce and his preference for the unicameral, egalitarian legislatures of Pennsylvania and Georgia and the latter's agricultural economy.[120] Massachusetts' well-tempered constitution, with checks and balances on the English model, seems but a necessary second-best for a state already subject to a certain amount of corruption.[121]

The extent to which Constant may have been correct when he blamed Rousseau and Mably for the Terror we cannot even begin to gauge here. My remarks above suggest that, at least with regard to Mably, Constant's interpretation was rather tendentious. Whether one agrees with the "revisionist" historians such as François Furet that Rousseau's doctrine of the general will really did influence the Jacobins and their regime,[122] or with Dan Edelstein's recent, provocatively argued view that it was rather a "natural republicanism" indebted to a kind of natural law that was crucial for the justification of Jacobinism,[123] there is an overlap in that both positions claim that the arbitrary executive will of the *Comité de salut public*—the committee of *salus populi*—was committed to a doctrine of virtue that had only contempt for formal institutions and constitutional safeguards.[124] Indeed, the fate of the Constitution of 1793, as well as the Terror, testifies to a prevailing doctrine that regarded the sovereign, whether it be the people or a "general will," as unconstrained and constitutional rules as fundamentally malleable, thereby falling foul of constitutionalism's most essential ingredient, entrenchment. As Edelstein himself concedes, the Montagnards' natural-law doctrine as established in the Convention was of a "very different"

---

120. Note, however, that even in Pennsylvania, when radical Whigs tried to restrict property holdings, the "revolutionary legislature that was ready to experiment with a unicameral legislature rejected this seventeenth-century English classical 'republican' (in the Harringtonian sense of the word) idea in the wide-open American setting. So much for those who try to find civic humanist frugality and fear of corruption by wealth in Pennsylvania in 1776." Adams, *First American Constitutions*, p. 311.

121. I follow Wright, *Classical Republican*, pp. 178–187.

122. See, for a survey of the revisionist interpretation, Van Kley, *French Idea*, pp. 8–9. Cf., for an explanation discounting the role of ideas altogether, Martin, *Violence et Révolution*.

123. Edelstein, *Terror*.

124. This finds further support in Claude Mossé's finding that it was mostly Sparta's "idéal de vertu et d'austérité" and Rome's republican heroism—providing a "modèle de comportements plus que . . . une référence politique proprement dite"—rather than institutional models, that impressed the French revolutionaries; *L'Antiquité*, pp. 154–156. Cf. Parker, *Cult of Antiquity* (where Rome appears as a crucial reference, yet this is clearly subject to Mossé's caution). See also Rawson, *Spartan Tradition*, p. 271. Cf. also Nippel, *Antike*, pp. 166f.

kind from the classic natural-law theories of the seventeenth and eighteenth centuries.[125] This concession surely detracts somewhat from his most spectacular claims. For the "cult of nature" reigning supremely during the Terror was an anti-jural doctrine relying on natural *virtue*, and opposed to institutions and entrenched rules. It was this anti-constitutionalism, therefore, which surely provides the most glaring difference between the ideas of Robbespierre and Saint-Just on the one hand, and the American revolutionaries and constitutional Framers on the other.[126] A further aspect that deserves attention lies, even before the Terror, not only in Rousseauvian but also in Jeffersonian influence on the *Déclaration des Droits de l'Homme et du Citoyen*. Whatever Robbespierre may have thought of Rousseau, Clause Six of the *Déclaration* with its elevation of statute law (*loi*) over any constitutionally entrenched norms (including the *Déclaration* itself) surely bears the fingerprints of the Genevan thinker, and maybe of Jefferson as well.[127]

For the Scottish Enlightenment, Montesquieu had laid important foundations not only by establishing a historical sequence outlining the development and progress of free government and thereby providing a model for the Scots' philosophical history and theories of progress, but also by providing a new status for commerce and even luxury.[128] This Montesquieu achieved by providing a different explanation for the demise of the Roman Republic than the conventional one, which had focused on the Sallustian factor of luxury and on increased agrarian inequality.[129] Luxury was "not in itself a misfortune," Montesquieu held—rather, as we have seen, it was constitutional factors and, ultimately, imperial expansion and military despotism that were to blame for the fall of the Republic.[130] These ideas proved influential with the Scottish writers, who showed a similar view of the role of extra-constitutional powers in the fall of the Roman

125. Edelstein, *Terror*, p. 259.

126. See ibid. for an unconvincing explanation of that difference; see Zuckert, *Natural Rights*, for an account that shows the Americans' interest in theories of natural rights.

127. See McLean, "Jefferson, Adams, and the *Déclaration*."

128. See McDaniel, *Adam Ferguson*, for an excellent survey of Montesquieu's effect on the Scottish writers, especially Ferguson. On the Scottish writers on luxury, see Berry, *Luxury*.

129. As for example in René Aubert, abbé de Vertot's *Histoire des révolutions de la république romaine* (1719); see McDaniel, *Adam Ferguson*, p. 19; Raskolnikoff, *Histoire Romaine*, pp. 29–38. For a subtle account of Rousseau's and Adam Smith's interpretation of the Republic's demise, see now Hont, *Politics*, chs. 4 and 5. For a recent, utterly Sallustian take on the Republic's demise by a classicist, see Wiseman, "The Two-Headed State."

130. McDaniel, *Adam Ferguson*, pp. 15–25.

Republic[131] and an admiration for the constitutional checks and balances, limits on magistracies, and the boundaries between civil and martial law.[132] Indeed, even though Montesquieu owed much to Bolingbroke's country party thought, he is closer to his friend David Hume, who, writing against Bolingbroke, insisted on the importance of institutions and the comparative unimportance of virtue. Hume developed his argument "That Politics may be reduced to a Science" with reference to a period of Roman republican history—the Punic Wars—when "wise regulations" exercised "a considerable check on the natural depravity of mankind," and pointed out that "the ages of greatest public spirit are not always most eminent for private virtue. Good laws may beget order and moderation in the government, where the manners and customs have instilled little humanity or justice into the tempers of men."[133]

In America, political thinkers, above all John Adams and the writers of the *Federalist Papers,* drew extensively on the constitutional tradition described in the present book.[134] Indeed, the pseudonym "Publius" chosen by the authors of the Federalist points to the mythical Publius Valerius Publicola's chief achievement, the introduction of the right of appeal (*provocatio*).[135] The scholarly debate over the relative influence of classical examples has been fixated, for too long, on the relative importance of modern liberalism (or Lockean natural rights) and classical republicanism (or Greco-Roman virtue).[136] Our discussion of the

131. Adam Ferguson, e.g., in his popular *History of the Progress and Termination of the Roman Republic* (1783), although defending Sulla's laying down of the dictatorship as virtuous, really intended to "show that men could not be relied upon to act like Sulla and virtuously renounce dictatorship for patriotic reasons. Rather, emergency dictatorships would quickly become permanent": McDaniel, *Adam Ferguson*, p. 61.

132. McDaniel, *Adam Ferguson*, pp. 173–174.

133. Hume, "That Politics," p. 11.

134. For an excellent discussion of the philosophical ideas underlying the Revolution, see still Lovejoy, *Reflections*; White, *Philosophy*.

135. Livy 2.8.2; cf. Cic. *Rep.* 2.53–54 for the view that *provocatio* had existed already in the regal period.

136. The bibliography is vast. Good places to start are Hartz, *Liberal Tradition*; Bailyn, *Origins*; Wood, *Creation*; id., *Radicalism*; for the role of the classics in late eighteenth-century America, see Bederman, *Foundations*; Chinard, "Polybius"; Gummere, "Classical Ancestry"; Kennedy, "Classical Influences"; Reinhold, *Classica Americana* (criticizing Gummere for putting too much weight on classical references); Wiltshire, *Greece, Rome*; Rahe, *Republics*; Roberts, *Athens on Trial*; Richard, *Founders*; Winterer, *Culture of Classicism*; Shalev, *Rome Reborn*; Hanses, "Antikebilder." Wood's portrait of John Adams as a "classical republican" whose vision was becoming increasingly irrelevant has been influential, but should be challenged on the grounds advanced below. Pocock's *Machiavellian Moment* represents an attempt at providing a historical lineage to the so-called classical republicanism of many of the Founders; Shalev, *Rome Reborn*,

Roman constitutional tradition may prove to be a good vantage point from which to interpret the political debates of the American Revolution. By emphasizing institutions, checks and balances, legal rules, and constitutional entrenchment and suspicion of virtue, we may be able to see the political thought of the Revolution beyond the narrow dichotomy of liberalism versus republicanism.[137] Indeed, if my account of Roman constitutional thought has merit, it should complicate any facile *querelle des anciens et des modernes*. The distinction between the concept of higher-order, entrenched constitutional norms, on the one hand, and faith in public virtue, on the other, and the corresponding distinction between a Ciceronian account of the end of political society and an Aristotelian one may be more fruitful in guiding an investigation into American political thought than a narrow focus on republicanism or the corruption of virtue through commerce. Gordon Wood points out—in some tension with his otherwise virtue-oriented account—that it was precisely the "distinction between 'legal' and 'constitutional,'" between *lex* and *ius*, as our Roman sources would have it, that marked the difference between "American and English constitutional traditions." The American Founders believed that "the fundamental principles of the English constitution had to be lifted out of the lawmaking and other institutions of government and set above them."[138] There is little in the language of the Founders, however, that would confirm that they themselves drew such a firm distinction; like Montesquieu, they looked to the English constitution through the lens of the late Roman republican example. Wood goes on to quote Samuel Adams, who in 1768 in the Massachusetts Circular Letter wrote that in "all free States, the Constitution is fixed; and as the supreme Legislature derives its Powers and

---

gives a fascinating and largely convincing account of the influence of the classics on the American revolutionaries' historical consciousness, but adheres too strictly to the conventional idea of a "republican synthesis" devoted to "public civic virtue" and scornful of commerce and luxury (pp. 5, 15). Cf. Shalhope, "Republican Synthesis"; id., "Republicanism." Hanses, "Antikebilder," relativizes the influence of the classics in the dispute between Federalists and anti-Federalists, but does not pay any attention to John Adams; moreover, to the extent that the tradition we are concerned with here is a) specifically constitutionalist in the sense made clear in Chapter 1 and 4 and b) filtered through many later thinkers, Hanses' argument is not directly relevant to our concern.

137. Mortimer Sellers' *American Republicanism* provides a good contrarian corrective to the prevailing view of the American founding representing a move away from the classics. Sellers shows how deeply and directly indebted the Founders were to Roman political theory and touches upon the Roman constitutional tradition; however, his account suffers from too broad a notion of "mixed government," and he fails to give natural law and natural rights doctrine its due, especially Cicero's, and sees Montesquieu mostly in the service of the Anti-Federalists, in opposition to John Adams. Sellers' work also suffers from its excessive focus on the ratification debates of 1787–1788.

138. Wood, "Origins," p. 176.

Authority from the Constitution, it cannot overleap the Bounds of it without destroying its own foundation."[139] But Adams, of course, was claiming that it was under the "British Constitution" that certain property rights were "irrevocable" and constituted ultimately both "natural and constitutional Rights."[140] Samuel Adams, who at times had also used the pen name "Valerius Poplicola," like the authors of the *Federalist* later on, was hostile neither to the English constitution nor to constitutional values gleaned from the Roman example. Along with his cousin John, Adams was to play a role in the drafting of the Massachusetts Constitution of 1780, which became the first to have been formed in a specially designated convention, thus being properly separated from, and lifted above, mere law and the institutions of government.[141]

John Adams has served as a prime example for "classical republicanism" in many accounts of the American founding and its political thought.[142] Adams is cited as a "puritanical republican" by Forrest McDonald, as a proponent of austere morals, with "public Virtue" as "the only Foundation of Republics."[143] But Adams already in his 1776 pamphlet "Thoughts on Government" had written that "the happiness of society is the end of government, as all Divines and moral Philosophers will agree that the happiness of the individual is the end of man. From this principle it will follow, that the form of government, which communicates ease, comfort, security, or in one word happiness to the greatest number of persons, and in the greatest degree, is the best."[144] Ease, comfort, and security for individuals are certainly not "classically republican" ends of political society, nor are the means by which Adams sought to achieve these ends: a well-tempered balance of powers. Gordon Wood points out that Adams' "Thoughts" became "the most influential work guiding the framers of the new republics," and that the Massachusetts Constitution of 1780, in the framing of which Adams had an important hand,[145] is widely "regarded

139. Ibid., quoting Massachusetts Circular Letter of February 11, 1768 by Samuel Adams, written in response to the Townshend Acts.

140. Massachusetts Circular Letter of February 11, 1768, by Samuel Adams.

141. See Wood, "Origins," p. 178, for the pioneering role of Massachusetts in this regard.

142. See, most recently, Heun, "Die Antike."

143. McDonald, *Novus Ordo*, pp. 71–72. On Machiavelli's influence on Adams, and Adams' criticism of Machiavelli, see Thompson, "Adams's Machiavellian Moment." On Adams, see McCullough, *Adams*; and Diggins, *Adams*.

144. "Thoughts," p. 287.

145. For an account of the drafting of the Massachusetts Constitution, see Adams, *First American Constitutions*, pp. 83–90.

as the most consequential state constitution of the Revolutionary era." His main work, the *Defence of the Constitutions of Government of the United States of America*, written from England and directed against French criticism of American constitutionalism,[146] was "the only comprehensive description of American constitutionalism that the period produced," the "finest fruit of the American Enlightenment."[147] The first volume of the *Defence* was available at the Philadelphia Convention in 1787 and, far from being irrelevant, its ideas became "the central principles of America's new Federal republic,"[148] with Adams being, along with Montesquieu, the most cited writer in the ratification debate.[149]

Adams drew on the writers of the Scottish Enlightenment, especially Hume and Smith,[150] and was very well versed in the classics. He begins the *Defence* by citing from the fragments of Cicero's *Republic*, juxtaposing Cicero's thought with the "Grecian commonwealths" and recommending the former on the grounds that "[h]uman nature is as incapable now of going through revolutions with temper and sobriety . . . as it was among the Greeks so long ago."[151] Adams suspected that Cicero in the *Republic* had "entered more largely into an examination of the composition of monarchical republics than any other ancient writer," and points out, very much in line with our interpretation in Chapter 4, that Cicero, in defending his balanced constitutionalism, welcomed "disputes" within society, as long as they were constitutionalized: "As the treble, the tenor, and the bass exist in nature, they will be heard in the concert: if they are arranged by Handel, in a skilful composition, they produce rapture the most exquisite that harmony can excite."[152] Adams goes on to quote verbatim Cicero's metaphorical move from musical harmony to the balanced constitution as well as Scipio's definition of *res*

146. Namely against Turgot; for French criticism of American constitutionalism and the relationship between Adams and French political philosophers, see Lacorne, *L'invention de la république*; Appleby, "John Adams"; Diggins, "John Adams and the French Critics."

147. Wood, *Creation*, p. 568.

148. Sellers, *American Republicanism*, p. 35; Sellers is arguing here, convincingly, against the "unfortunate title" of Gordon Wood's chapter "The Relevance and Irrelevance of John Adams" in his *Creation of the American Republic*.

149. Ibid., p. 164.

150. On the Scottish influence on Adams, see Lovejoy, *Reflections*.

151. Adams, *Defence*, vol. 1, p. vi.

152. Ibid., pp. xvi–xvii.

publica[153] and dismisses Tacitus' doubts concerning the very possibility of a constitutional order.[154] Adams knows and quotes Augustine's summary of book 3 of Cicero's *Republic*, where *consensus iuris* is made the essential criterion of a constitutional order and where either the king, the few, or the people can thus be rightly called unjust.[155] The "English nation" had implemented this kind of constitutional order, Adams maintains, finding it "the most solid and durable government, as well as the most free," and having "obtained by means of it, a prosperity among civilized nations, in an enlightened age, like that of the Romans among barbarians."[156] Adams draws the conclusion that America, too, is well advised to avail itself of this kind of constitutional order.

Adams agreed with Bodin's institutional analysis of the decline of the Roman Republic. It was "by no means" the "ambition of private men" which began the conflicts, but the fact that the constitutional "balance of power" had been broken by the commons' increasingly "gaining ground." This, not the lack of virtue, had "destroyed the wisest republic, and enslaved the noblest people, that ever entered the stage of the world."

> And to put it past dispute, that the entire subversion of Roman liberty was altogether owing to those measures, which had broken the balance between the patricians and plebeians, whereof the ambition of private men was but the effect and consequence.[157]

The *Defence* represents in essence an argument for bicameralism, as a crucial check on popular representation, against Turgot's unicameralism.[158] According to Adams, the passions of men, which are unlimited, have to be governed, in a

153. Cic. *Rep.* 2.69; 1.39.

154. Adams, *Defence*, vol. 1, p. xvi. Cf. *Annales* 4.33; and see above, Chapter 1, pp. 28–30.

155. Ibid., p. xviii, quoting August. *De civ. D.* 2.21 (cf. Cic. *Rep.* 3.45). Adams goes on to quote August. *De civ. D.* 19.21, taking it also to be a fragment of Cic. *Rep.*

156. Adams, *Defence*, vol. 1, p. xix. See, for a similar assimilation of the Roman Republic with the British constitution, Noah Webster, writing in 1787 as "A citizen of America," *Examination*, where he compares the proposed Constitution with (p. 378) "the two best constitutions that ever existed in Europe, the Roman and the British." See, for a discussion of Webster, Millar, *Roman Republic*, pp. 123–128.

157. Adams, *Defence*, vol. 1, p. 101.

158. Turgot as well as Condorcet and La Rochefoucauld were influenced by the constitution of Pennsylvania and preferred a unicameral legislature.

Ciceronian way, by a well-tempered constitutional system of balances. Adams adopts an almost Hobbesian political psychology but recommends a constitutional "balance of power" as the remedy.[159] Unchecked unicameralism will result in something like the Decemviri or civil war, like that between Pompey and Caesar; long before this result, "the laws, instead of being permanent, and affording constant protection to the lives, liberties, and properties of the citizens, will be alternately the sport of contending factions, and the mere vibrations of a pendulum." [160] Again, the virtues are helpless in the face of constitutional crises—the *decemvir* Appius Claudius' "modesty and decency were found in him but feeble barriers against ambition."[161] Nothing but an entrenched constitution will provide such barriers, according to Adams. Severing Montesquieu's "umbilical connection"[162] between virtue and republicanism, Adams argues, shockingly, that it "is not true, in fact, that any people ever existed who loved the public better than themselves, their private friends, neighbours, &c. and therefore this kind of virtue . . . is as precarious a foundation for liberty as honour or fear: it is the laws alone that really love the country."[163] Indeed, "[e]very page of the history of Rome appears equally marked with ambition and avarice,"[164] but a balanced, well-tempered constitutional machinery need not fear vice or corruption by luxury;[165] Adams doubts the "universality of the doctrine, that commerce corrupts manners."[166]

Property rights, which also figured prominently in the 1780 Massachusetts Constitution,[167] will have to be protected by such constitutional entrenchment, and unchecked popular sovereignty as advocated by Turgot will result inevitably in "the people . . . usurping others rights." Both triumvirates, Adams writes in a Bodinian vein, were created by the People and "there never was a more arrant creature of

159. Adams, *Defence*, vol. 1, p. 130. Adams claims to "agree with Butler rather than Hobbes" or Mandeville (ibid., p. 129), but his psychological account, if not his solution, owes much to Hobbes and Mandeville.

160. Ibid., p. 141. Cf. for the Decemviri vol. 3, pp. 266–270 (against Nedham's unicameralism).

161. *Defence*, vol. 3, pp. 269–270.

162. Wright, "Montesquieuean Moments," p. 155.

163. Adams, *Defence*, vol. 3, p. 491.

164. Ibid., p. 489.

165. Ibid., pp. 348–349.

166. Ibid., vol. 1, p. 212.

167. *Constitution of the Commonwealth of Massachusetts*, Article I.

the people than Caesar."[168] Extraordinary *imperia* emanated from the unchecked, overreaching People: "[w]hen private men look to the people for public offices and commands, that is, when the people claim the executive power, they will at first be courted, then deceived, and then betrayed."[169] A sovereign unicameral representation of the people will thus not be able to guarantee the safety of particular men—"the direct contrary is true." "Every man lived safe, only while the senate remained as a check and balance to the people: the moment that controul was destroyed, no man was safe," except the "triumvirs and their tools; any man might be, and multitudes of the best men were, undone, without rendering any reason to the world for their destruction, but the will, the fear, or the revenge of some tyrant."[170] Like Cicero, Nedham and Cato before him, Adams believes that the killing of Maelius after his attempted *coup* was constitutional: "If the people had been unchecked . . . they would . . . have crowned Melius."[171] But Adams is far from exhibiting simply aristocratic sympathies; attacking the "aristocratical despotism" of his age, he defends what he reckons were Manlius Capitolinus' attempts at remedying the dangerous imbalance of the Roman constitution of his age by adding a third, independent power to that of the Senate and of the People; quoting Livy's account of Manlius' speech to the People with its abolition of the dictatorship and the consulate and its proposal of one chief magistrate, Adams writes that this "is a manifest intention of introducing a balance of three branches" and claims that in "this oration are all the principles of the English constitution."[172] Without a third branch, "some eminent spirit . . . gains an ascendancy," violating term limits in the process, "and then the spirit and letter too of the constitution is made to give way to him."[173]

Adams, while not present at the Federal Convention in 1787, certainly had an important impact on it. Benjamin Rush, writing to Richard Price on June 2, 1787,

---

168. *Defence*, vol. 3, pp. 216–221. Adams takes Turgot to advocate Nedham's views, which may be somewhat tendentious in light of what we have said about Nedham above. Apart from the issue of unicameralism, Adams agrees with Nedham more than he lets on; see the lengthy quotation from *Excellencie* ibid., pp. 408–410.

169. Ibid., p. 499.

170. Ibid., p. 221. Cf. ibid., p. 467: in the last years of the Roman Republic, the "people were now uncontrouled" and "behaved as they always do, when they pretend to exercise the whole executive and legislative power; that is, they set up immediately one man and one family for an emperor, in effect, sometimes respecting ancient forms at first, and sometimes rejecting them altogether."

171. Ibid., p. 244.

172. Ibid., pp. 245–251. Cf. Livy 6.18.5-15. Cf. also *Federalist* 70, where Hamilton uses the Roman dictator as an example of the need for a strong, unified executive.

173. Ibid., pp. 245–246.

observed that "Mr Adams's book has diffused such excellent principles among us, that there is little doubt of our adopting a vigorous and compounded federal legislature," i.e., a checked, bicameral system; Adams' *Defence* "has done us more service than if he had obtained alliances for us with all nations of Europe."[174] His acknowledgment of persistent social conflict, even in the absence of feudal European social distinctions, simply as an expression of certain universal features of moral psychology, found prominent expression at the Convention as well as in the *Federalist Papers*, as did his constitutional remedy. Indeed, Madison's description of America as a "compound republic" and his claim that "ambition must be made to counteract ambition" echo Adams' *Defence*.[175]

Discussion of Roman republican precedent was not confined to Adams' work, however. Other Federalists, such as Hamilton, arguing for an expansive interpretation of presidential power under the Constitution, described the dictatorship in rather favorable terms as a bulwark against tyranny,[176] while Thomas Jefferson was highly skeptical and saw the dictator as a "temporary tyrant," who, "after a few examples, became perpetual."[177] This obviously corresponded to different interpretations of the constitutional authority of the President under the Constitution. Jefferson, who had sympathized with the French Revolution and even shown understanding for the Terror (which he later regretted), was suspicious of the Federalists' trust in a strong government and in the ability of constitutional mechanisms to constrain government's power. Against the *Federalist* and Adams, he insisted on republican

174. Farrand, *Records*, vol. 3, p. 33.

175. See, e.g., Madison's argument for a large-scale republican system: Farrand, *Records*, vol. 1, pp. 134–136; *Federalist* 10. For the "compound republic" and the idea of counterpoise, see *Federalist* 51. Note Madison's Bodinian distinction between undivided popular sovereignty and separation of the powers of government.

176. *Federalist* 70: "There is an idea . . . that a vigorous executive is inconsistent with the genius of republican government," but Hamilton insists that "[e]nergy in the executive is a leading character in the definition of good government" and goes on to say that "[e]very man the least conversant in Roman history knows how often that republic was obliged to take refuge in the absolute power of a single man, under the formidable title of dictator, as well against the intrigues of ambitious individuals who aspired to the tyranny, and the seditions of whole classes of the community whose conduct threatened the existence of all government, as against the invasions of external enemies who menaced the conquest and destruction of Rome": *Federalist Papers*, p. 402. For various viewpoints on the unity of the executive at the Federal Convention, see, e.g., Farrand, *Records*, pp. 64–75.

177. Jefferson, "Notes," p. 254. For a novel account of the way the presidency was created, not from "classical republicanism," but from texts defending (royal) executive prerogative in the English seventeenth-century context, see Nelson, *Royalist Revolution*, esp. introduction and ch. 5. Nelson is right in stressing Montesquieu's and the English writers' importance, but he does not discuss the Roman constitutional background to these ideas.

virtue and saw it threatened by strong federal institutions. The controversies of the Founders concerning the powers of the President under the Constitution fastened on the President's powers in emergencies. Apart from Jefferson, who thought the President had only a discretionary prerogative that could only be politically and retroactively justified, Publius defended expansive presidential powers authorized by the Constitution itself. To various degrees and in various ways, Hamilton, Adams, and James Madison, even when he was writing as Helvidius, agreed that it was a constitutional framework that would define and ultimately constrain the power of not only the executive, but also of the "legislative vortex."[178] This contrasted starkly with Jefferson's and Thomas Paine's suspicion of an entrenched constitutional order and their anti-constitutionalist insistence, drawing on Blackstone, that constitutional precommitment was illegitimate and inconsistent with the sovereignty of the people.[179] Madison famously and forcefully argued against Jefferson's idea of holding constitutional conventions every 18-19 years by pointing to the unintended consequences of such malleability, adapting ideas of tacit consent originally developed by natural lawyers such as Grotius, Pufendorf, and Locke and views on the psychology of convention put forward by Hume.[180] If the constitutional norms are not entrenched and of a higher order, Madison points out, it is likely that future constitutional conventions will allow passion to overrule reason.

The authors discussed in this book were all in a sense motivated by an interest in the fall of the Roman Republic. What unites them is that their answer to the failure of that Republic consisted in putting forward a constitutional framework of entrenched, higher-order norms, not in bemoaning a lack of virtue or

178. The expression is Madison's. For a subtle and illuminating discussion of these authors' approaches to discretionary presidential power, with further literature, see Kleinerman, *Discretionary President*, chs. 3–6. For a subtle discussion of Hamilton's constitutional thought, taking into account the differences between his views in the Federalist and at the Convention, see Stourzh, *Hamilton*, ch. 2 and *passim*.

179. For a good comparison of Paine and Adams, see Adams, *First American Constitutions*, pp. 118–122. For Paine's and Jefferson's radicalism, setting them apart from the constitutionalist tradition, see Wood, "Radicalism of Jefferson," who does not, however, draw a sufficiently clear distinction between these virtue-oriented "radicals" and the constitutionalist Founders. The Founders in general, Wood writes elsewhere, "stood for a classical world that was rapidly dying," and all of them "saw themselves as moral teachers." The Federalists "had not yet abandoned . . . the tradition of civic humanism," had not lost hope "that at least some individuals . . . might be . . . virtuous enough to transcend their immediate material interests": Wood, "Interests and Disinterestedness," pp. 141–142. But as we have seen, this far overstates the importance of virtue, and understates that of constitutionalism, for the Framers and John Adams.

180. *Federalist* 49; "Letter of February 4, 1790." See the excellent discussion in Holmes, *Passions*, ch. 5.

corruption through luxury and vice. This presupposed a certain not too optimistic political psychology that acknowledged that political theory is inexorably, in Thomas Nagel's words, "hostage to human nature."[181] A constitutional order is necessary due to the fact that in the "simple" constitutional orders, in their reliance on virtue, human passions and desires tend to encroach upon moral motivations. Cicero draws the conclusion that reason can govern if it is embodied in a set of constitutional norms that prescribe a well-tempered order. For Cicero, this entailed the need to justify these constitutional norms on grounds of natural law. It would seem that in general, in order to be acknowledged as valid, entrenched constitutional rules require an argument based on either moral realism or prudence. Why otherwise should these rules be entrenched and privileged? Why otherwise should not the sovereign people themselves rule via frequent Jeffersonian constitutional conventions? Cicero and some of his successors, Hobbes and Locke, as well as Locke's natural-law predecessors among them, argue for an entrenched set of constitutional rules on the basis of a normative framework that they hold to be valid even in a pre- or extra-political state of nature. In Cicero's case, these rules are taken over from an existing legal order but defended on grounds of natural law and reason. It is not Burkean tradition that ultimately validates this constitutional order, but natural law. Natural law also plays a—somewhat more muted—role in Bodin, Cato, and Montesquieu, and it is again central for John Adams, who looked to nature and reason as grounds of validity. Adams claimed that the "United States of America have exhibited . . . the first example of governments erected on the simple principles of nature," and that "these governments were contrived merely by the use of reason and the senses."[182]

However, this did not turn Adams and the Federalists into utopians in the sense discussed in Chapter 4. Rather, in contrast with the Jeffersonians and what Adams termed the "democratic Party" in Philadelphia,[183] Adams and the Federalist constitutionalists acknowledged, with Cato, the limits of virtue and put their trust in the kind of constitutional framework Bodin and Montesquieu had sketched in their respective examinations of the fall of the Roman Republic. The American leaders did indeed begin "their Revolution trying to recover" at least *some* aspects—inchoate constitutionalism—of a "vanished Roman republic," but at least the Framers and Adams were not seeking to become an

181. Nagel, *Equality and Partiality*, pp. 26f.

182. *Defence*, vol. 1, pp. xiii–xiv.

183. In Adams' diary, where the term is aimed, among others, at Paine; quoted in Adams, *First American Constitutions*, p. 119.

"incarnation of ancient Rome, a land of virtuous and contented farmers," as Gordon Wood has it.[184] If, as Wood writes (arguing against Bernard Bailyn), "the writings of classical antiquity . . . provided more than scholarly embellishment and window dressing for educated Britons on both sides of the Atlantic," but constituted "in fact the principal source of their public morality and values" so that "all political morality was classical morality," it now appears that this is true only if we do not confound the constitutionalist tradition discussed in this book with a virtue-oriented republicanism.[185]

This book reorients scholarship from stale ideas concerning republican virtue to the rediscovery of the constitutional thought of the late Republic. I have demonstrated that the early modern political thinkers discussed here were less curious about Livy's mythical early Republic and its uncorrupted virtue than they were interested in the Republic's decline and fall, and that the intellectual history of the late Roman Republic played a crucial role in the subsequent development of constitutionalism. Roman constitutional thought, not Roman virtue, distinguished the Roman Republic for many thinkers from the Renaissance onward. The deep and important insight that the crises that had brought about the downfall of the Republic were of a constitutional nature generated the equally deep and important idea of constitutionalism as a remedy. Bodin begets a tradition concerned with the fall of the Roman Republic that no longer trusts Sallustian clichés about the Republic's demise. Constitutionalism, not virtue, is the answer for Montesquieu and John Adams no less than for Bodin. Their new, constitutional republicanism insists on the limits of virtue and is dedicated to avoiding the fate of the Roman Republic: military despotism. To look at the history of political thought more broadly, it is clear that the increasing skepticism concerning virtue and eudaemonistic political theory as well as the corresponding turn to constitutional rules—a turn from teleological good to deontological right, to put it anachronistically—constitutes a crucial aspect of the protohistory of liberalism. We are now in a position to understand the contribution of late Roman republican constitutional thought to the early history of this consequential move.

184. Wood, "Legacy," p. 75.

185. Ibid., pp. 66–67. Cf. Bailyn, *Ideological Origins*, p. 24.

Bibliography

Classical authors and works are cited according to standard editions and methods of citation. The *Oxford Classical Dictionary*'s system of abbreviations has been used throughout. Translations are referenced in the notes; if no reference is given, translations are my own.

Acemoglu, Daron, and James A. Robinson. *Why Nations Fail*. New York, 2012.

Acomb, Frances. *Anglophobia in France, 1763–1789: An Essay in the History of Constitutionalism and Nationalism*. Durham, NC, 1950.

Adams, John. *A Defence of the Constitutions of Government of the United States of America, against the Attacks of M. Turgot in his Letter to Dr. Price, Dated the Twenty-Second Day of March, 1778*. 3 vols. Philadelphia, 1797.

———. "Thoughts on Government." In id., *The Revolutionary Writings of John Adams*. Selected and with a Foreword by C. Bradley Thompson, 285–293. Indianapolis, 2000.

Adams, Willi Paul. *The First American Constitutions: Republican Ideology and the Making of the State Constitutions in the Revolutionary Era*. Trans. Rita and Robert Kimber, with a Foreword by Richard B. Morris. Expanded Edition. Lanham, MD, 2001.

d'Addio, Mario. *L'idea del contratto sociale dai sofisti alla Riforma*. Milan, 1954.

Allély, Annie. *La déclaration d'hostis sous la République romaine*. Bordeaux, 2012.

Ando, Clifford. *Law, Language, and Empire in the Roman Tradition*. Philadelphia, 2011.

Annas, Julia. "Cicero on Stoic Moral Philosophy and Private Property." In M. Griffin and J. Barnes (eds.), *Philosophia Togata*, 151–173. Oxford, 1989.

———. *An Introduction to Plato's Republic*. Oxford, 1981.

———. *The Morality of Happiness*. New York and Oxford, 1993.

———. "Virtue and Law in Plato." In Bobonich, *Plato's* Laws, 71–91.

Appleby, Joyce. *Capitalism and a New Social Order: The Republican Vision of the 1790s*. New York, 1984.

———. "John Adams and the New Republican Synthesis." In *Liberalism and Republicanism in the Historical Imagination*, 188–209. Cambridge, MA, 1992.

Arena, Valentina. "The Consulship of 78 BC: Catulus versus Lepidus: an *optimates* versus *populares* Affair." In Beck et al., *Consuls and* Res Publica, 299–318.

———. *Libertas and the Practice of Politics in the Late Roman Republic.* Cambridge, 2012.

Armitage, David. "Empire and Liberty: A Republican Dilemma." In M. van Gelderen and Q. Skinner (eds.), *Republicanism: A Shared European Heritage.* Vol. 2, *The Values of Republicanism in Early Modern Europe*, 29–46. Cambridge, 2002.

———. *The Ideological Origins of the British Empire.* Cambridge, 2000.

———. "What's the Big Idea? Intellectual History and the Longue Durée." *History of European Ideas* 38, 4 (2012): 493–507.

Asmis, Elizabeth. "Cicero on Natural Law and the Laws of the State." *Classical Antiquity* 27, 1 (2008): 1–33.

———. "The State as a Partnership: Cicero's Definition of *res publica* in his Work *On the State.*" *History of Political Thought* 25 (2004): 569–598.

Astin, A. E. "*Leges Aelia et Fufia.*" *Latomus* 23 (1964): 421–445.

———. *Scipio Aemilianus.* Oxford, 1967.

Atkins, E. M. "'Domina et Regina Virtutum': Justice and Societas in De Officiis." *Phronesis* 35 (1990): 258–289.

Atkins, Jed W. *Cicero on Politics and the Limits of Reason: The* Republic *and* Laws. Cambridge, 2013.

Badian, E. "The Death of Saturninus." *Chiron* 14 (1984): 101–147.

———. "M. Porcius Cato and the Annexation and Early Administration of Cyprus." *Journal of Roman Studies* 55 (1965): 110–121.

———. "Review Kloft, *Prorogation und ausserordentliche Imperien.*" *Gnomon* 51 (1979): 792–794.

———. "Waiting for Sulla." *Journal of Roman Studies* 52 (1962): 47–61.

Bailyn, Bernard. *The Ideological Origins of the American Revolution.* Enlarged ed. Cambridge, MA, 1992.

Baker, Keith Michael. "A Script for a French Revolution: The Political Consciousness of the abbé Mably." In id., *Inventing the French Revolution: Essays on French Political Culture in the Eighteenth Century*, 86–106. Cambridge, 1990.

Baldini, Artemio Enzo. *La ragion di stato dopo Meinecke e Croce: dibattito su recenti pubblicazioni.* Genoa, 1999.

Balot, Ryan K. *Greek Political Thought.* Malden, MA, 2006.

Balsdon, J. P. V. D. "Roman History, 65–50 B.C.: Five Problems." *Journal of Roman Studies* 52 (1962): 134–141.

Bandel, Friedrich. *Die römischen Diktaturen.* Breslau, 1910.

Baron, H. *The Crisis of the Early Italian Renaissance.* 2nd ed. Princeton, 1966.

Bauman, Richard A. "The *Hostis* Declarations of 88 and 87 B.C." *Athenaeum* 51 (1973): 270–293.

Bayle, Pierre. *Dictionnaire historique et critique.* 5th ed. Vol. 4. Amsterdam, 1740.

———. *Historical and Critical Dictionary: Selections.* Trans. R. H. Popkin. Indianapolis, 1965.

Baynes, N. H. *The Political Ideas of St. Augustine's De Civitate Dei.* London, 1936 (rpt. 1968).

Beard, Mary, and Michael Crawford. *Rome in the Late Republic. Problems and Interpretations*. London, 1985.

Beck, H., A. Duplá, M. Jehne, F. Pina Polo (eds.). *Consuls and* Res Publica: *Holding High Office in the Roman Republic*. Cambridge, 2011.

Bederman, David. *The Classical Foundations of the American Constitution: Prevailing Wisdom*. Cambridge, 2008.

Behrends, O. "Tiberius Gracchus und die Juristen seiner Zeit – die römische Jurisprudenz gegenüber der Staatskrise des Jahres 133 v. Chr." In *Das Profil des Juristen in der europäischen Tradition. Symposium aus Anlass des 70. Geburtstages von F. Wieacker*, 25–121. Eberbach, 1980.

Bellarmine, Robert. *De Laicis: or, The Treatise on Civil Government*. Trans. Kathleen E. Murphy. New York, 1928.

Bellen, Heinz. "Sullas Brief an den Interrex L. Valerius Flaccus." *Historia* 24, 4 (1975): 555–569.

Beloch, K. J. *Römische Geschichte bis zum Beginn der Punischen Kriege*. Berlin, 1926.

Benton, Lauren, and Benjamin Straumann. "Acquiring Empire by Law. From Roman Doctrine to Early Modern European Practice." *Law and History Review* 28, 1 (February 2010): 1–38.

Berlin, Isaiah. "The Originality of Machiavelli." In H. Hardy (ed.). *Against the Current*, 33–100. 2nd ed. Princeton, 2013.

Bernett, M., W. Nippel, A. Winterling (eds.). *Christian Meier zur Diskussion*. Stuttgart, 2008.

Berry, Christopher J. *The Idea of Luxury: A Conceptual and Historical Investigation*. Cambridge, 1994.

———. *Social Theory of the Scottish Enlightenment*. Edinburgh, 1997.

Blair, Ann. "Authorial Strategies in Jean Bodin." In Lloyd, *Reception of Bodin*, 137–156.

Bleicken, Jochen. *Die athenische Demokratie*. 4th ed. Paderborn, 1995.

———. *Gedanken zum Untergang der Römischen Republik*. Sonderband der wissenschaftlichen Gesellschaft an der Johann Wolfgang Goethe-Universität Frankfurt a.M. Vol. 33, 4. Stuttgart, 1995. (=id. *Gesammelte Schriften* II. Stuttgart, 1998, 683–704.)

———. *Geschichte der römischen Republik*. 6th ed. Munich, 2004.

———. "*Imperium consulare / proconsulare* im Übergang von der Republik zum Prinzipat." In id. (ed.), *Colloquium . . . Heuss*, 117–133 (=id. *Gesammelte Schriften* II. Stuttgart, 1998, 705–721).

———. *Lex Publica. Gesetz und Recht in der römischen Republik*. Berlin, 1975.

———. "Rezension Meier, Res publica amissa." *Zeitschrift der Savigny-Stiftung für Rechtsgeschichte, Romanistische Abteilung* 85 (1968): 451–461 (=id. *Gesammelte Schriften* II. Stuttgart, 1998, 778–788).

———. *Senatsgericht und Kaisergericht*. Göttingen, 1962.

———. *Die Verfassung der Römischen Republik*. 7th ed. Paderborn, 1995.

———. "Verfassungsschutz im demokratischen Athen." *Hermes* 112 (1984): 383–401.

———. *Das Volkstribunat der klassischen Republik: Studien zu seiner Entwicklung zwischen 287 und 133 v. Chr.* Munich, 1955.

———. *Zwischen Republik und Prinzipat. Zum Charakter des Zweiten Triumvirats.* Göttingen, 1990.

———. (ed.). *Colloquium aus Anlass des 80. Geburtstages von Alfred Heuss.* Kallmünz, 1993.

Blösel, Wolfgang. "*Mos maiorum*: Von der Familientradition zum Nobilitätsethos." In B. Linke and M. Stemmler (eds.), *Mos maiorum: Untersuchungen zu den Formen der Identitätsstiftung und Stabilisierung in der römischen Republik*, 25–97. Stuttgart, 2000.

Boak, A. E. R. "The Extraordinary Commands from 80 to 48 B.C." *American Historical Review* 24 (1918/1919): 1–25.

Bobonich, Christopher (ed.). *Plato's* Laws: *A Critical Guide.* Cambridge, 2010.

———. *Plato's Utopia Recast: His Later Ethics and Politics.* Oxford, 2002.

Bodin, Jean. *De republica libri sex.* Paris, 1586.

———. *I sei libri dello stato.* Margherita Isnardi Parente and Diego Quaglioni, eds. 3 vols. Turin, 1964–1997.

———. *Les six livres de la République.* Paris, 1583, rpt. Aalen, 1961. English trans. K. D. McRae, ed. *The Six Books of a Commonweale. A Facsimile Reprint of the English Translation of 1606, corrected and supplemented in the light of a new comparison with the French and Latin texts.* Cambridge, MA, 1962 (rpt.1979).

———. *Methodus ad facilem historiarium cognitionem.* Paris, 1566.

Boldt, Hans. "Ausnahmezustand." In W. Conze et al. (eds.), *Geschichtliche Grundbegriffe.* Vol. 1, 343–376. Stuttgart, 1972.

Bolingbroke. See St John, Henry, Viscount Bolingbroke.

Boralevi, Lea Campos. "James Harrington's 'Machiavellian' anti-Machiavellism." *History of European Ideas* 37, 2 (2011): 113–119.

Borle, J.-P. "Pompée et la dictature." *Les études classiques* 20 (1952): 168–180.

Bowen, A., and P. Garnsey. *Lactantius: Divine Institutes.* Translated with an Introduction and Notes. Liverpool, 2003.

Brennan, T. Corey. *The Praetorship in the Roman Republic.* 2 vols. New York, 2000.

Bringmann, Klaus. *Die Agrarreform des Tiberius Gracchus: Legende und Wirklichkeit.* Stuttgart, 1985.

———. "Der Diktator Caesar als Richter? Zu Ciceros Reden *Pro Ligario* und *Pro rege Deiotaro.*" *Hermes* 114 (1986): 72–88.

———. *Krise und Ende der römischen Republik (133-42 v. Chr.).* Berlin, 2003.

———. "Das zweite Triumvirat. Bemerkungen zu Mommsens Lehre von der ausserordentlichen konstituierenden Gewalt." In *Alte Geschichte und Wissenschaftsgeschichte. Festschrift Karl Christ*, 22–38. Darmstadt, 1988.

Brito Vieira, Monica. *The Elements of Representation in Hobbes: Aesthetics, Theatre, Law, and Theology in the Construction of Hobbes's Theory of the State.* Leiden-Boston, 2009.

Brooke, Christopher. *Philosophic Pride. Stoicism and Political Thought from Lipsius to Rousseau.* Princeton, 2012.

Broughton, T. R. S. *The Magistrates of the Roman Republic*. Vols. 1–2. 2nd ed. New York, 1960. Vol. 3. Atlanta, 1987.

Brown, Lesley. "How Totalitarian is Plato's *Republic*?" In Erik Nis Ostenfeld (ed.), *Essays on Plato's* Republic, 13–27. Aarhus, 1998.

Bruni, Leonardo. *History of the Florentine People*, ed. and trans. James Hankins. 3 vols. Cambridge, MA, 2001.

———. *Laudatio Florentinae urbis*, ed. S. U. Baldassarri. Florence, 2000.

Brunt, P. A. "The Fall of the Roman Republic." In id., *The Fall of the Roman Republic and Related Essays*, 1–92. Oxford, 1988.

———. "Lex de Imperio Vespasiani." *Journal of Roman Studies* 67 (1977): 95–116.

———. *Social Conflicts in the Roman Republic*. New York, 1971.

Büchner, K. *Marcus Tullius Cicero, De Re Publica. Kommentar*. Heidelberg, 1984.

Buckland, W. W. *A Text-Book of Roman Law From Augustus to Justinian*. 3rd ed. Rev. by Peter Stein. Cambridge, 1975.

Burckhardt, L. A. *Politische Strategien der Optimaten in der späten römischen Republik*. Stuttgart, 1988.

Burgess, Glenn. *Absolute Monarchy and the Stuart Constitution*. New Haven, CT, 1996.

———. "Bodin in the English Revolution." In Lloyd, *Reception of Bodin*, 387–407.

Burnyeat, M. F. "Did the Ancient Greeks Have the Concept of Human Rights?" *Polis* 13 (1994): 1–11 (= id. *Explorations in Ancient and Modern Philosophy*. Vol 2, ch. 14. Cambridge-New York, 2012).

———. "Sphinx without a Secret." *New York Review of Books*, May 30 (1985): 30–36.

Canevaro, Mirko. "*Nomothesia* in Classical Athens." *Classical Quarterly* 63, 1 (2013): 139–160.

Canning, J. *A History of Medieval Political Thought, 300-1450*. London-New York, 1996.

———. *The Political Thought of Baldus de Ubaldis*. Cambridge, 1987.

Carawan, E. "The Trial of the Arginousai Generals and the Dawn of 'Judicial Review.'" *Dike* 10 (2007): 19–56.

Chinard, Gilbert. "Polybius and the American Constitution." *Journal of the History of Ideas* 1, 1 (1940): 38–58.

Christ, K. *Krise und Untergang der römischen Republik*. 3rd ed. Darmstadt, 1996.

———. *Sulla: Eine römische Karriere*. Munich, 2002.

———. "Der Untergang der römischen Republik in moderner Sicht." In id., *Römische Geschichte und Wissenschaftsgeschichte*. I, *Römische Republik und augusteischer Prinzipat*, 134–167. Darmstadt, 1982.

Clarke, Michelle T. "Uprooting Nebuchadnezzar's Tree: Francis Bacon's Criticism of Machiavellian Imperialism." *Political Research Quarterly* 61, 3 (2008): 367–378.

Cloud, Duncan. "The Constitution and Public Criminal Law." In *The Cambridge Ancient History*. Vol. 9. 2nd ed., 491–530. Cambridge, 1992.

Cohen, D. *Law, Violence and Community in Classical Athens*. Cambridge, 1995.

———. "The Origin of Roman Dictatorship." *Mnemosyne* (1957): 303–320.

Cole, Thomas. *Democritus and the Sources of Greek Anthropology*. Cleveland, 1967.

———. "The Sources and Composition of Polybius VI." *Historia* 13 (1964): 440–486.

Coli, Ugo. "Sui limiti di durata delle magistrature romane." In *Studi Arangio-Ruiz*. Vol. 4, 395–418. Naples, 1953.

Colish, M. L. "Cicero's *De officiis* and Machiavelli's *Prince*." *Sixteenth Century Journal* 9 (1978): 81–93.

Condorcet, J. A. N. Caritat de. *Sur l'instruction publique*. Offprint from the Bibliothèque de l'homme public, second year, vol. 1. Paris, 1791.

Constant, Benjamin. "The Liberty of the Ancients Compared with that of the Moderns." In id., *Political Writings*, ed. B. Fontana, 307–328. Cambridge, 1988.

Cooper, John. "Plato's *Statesman* and Politics." In id., *Reason and Emotion*, 165–191. Princeton, 1999.

Cox Jensen, Freyja. *Reading the Roman Republic in Early Modern England*. Leiden and Boston, 2012.

Crawford, M. H. (ed.). *Roman Statutes*. 2 vols. Bulletin of the Institute of Classical Studies Supplement 64. London, 1996.

Crifò, G. "Attività normative del senato in età repubblicana." *Bulletino dell'Istituto di Diritto Romano* 10, 3 (1968): 31–121.

———. "In tema di senatus consultum ultimum." *Studia et documenta historiae et iuris* 36 (1970): 1–15.

Cromartie, Alan. *The Constitutionalist Revolution: An Essay on the History of England, 1450–1642*. Cambridge, 2006.

———. "Harringtonian Virtue: Harrington, Machiavelli, and the Method of the *Moment*." *The Historical Journal* 41, 4 (1998): 987–1009.

Crook, John. "*Sponsione Provocare*: Its Place in Roman Litigation." *Journal of Roman Studies* 66 (1976): 132–138.

Dahlheim, W. "Der Staatsstreich des Konsuls Sulla und die römische Italienpolitik der achtziger Jahre." In Bleicken (ed.), *Colloquium . . . Heuss*, 97–116.

Daube, David. "Das Selbstverständliche in der Rechtsgeschichte." *Zeitschrift der Savigny-Stiftung für Rechtsgeschichte* 90 (1973): 1–13.

Dauber, Noah. "Anti-Machiavellism as Constitutionalism: Hermann Conring's Commentary on Machiavelli's *The Prince*." *History of European Ideas* 37 (2011): 102–112.

Davis, Charles T. *Dante's Italy and other Essays*. Philadelphia, 1984.

———. "Ptolemy of Lucca and the Roman Republic." *Proceedings of the American Philosophical Society* 118 (1974): 30–50.

Deane, H. A. *The Political and Social Ideas of St. Augustine*. New York, 1963.

Degrassi, A. *Fasti Capitolini*. Turin, 1954.

Deininger, J. "Zur Kontroverse über die Lebensfähigkeit der Republik in Rom." In P. Kneissel, and V. Losemann (eds.), *Imperium Romanum. Studien zur Geschichte und Rezeption. Festschrift Karl Christ*, 123–136. Stuttgart, 1998.

De Ligt, L. "Poverty and Demography: The Case of the Gracchan Land Reforms." *Mnemosyne* 57 (2004): 725–757.

de Ste. Croix, G. E. M. *The Class Struggle in the Ancient Greek World*. London, 1981.

Diggins, John Patrick. *John Adams*. New York, 2003.

———. "John Adams and the French Critics of the American Constitution." In H. Belz, R. Hoffmann, P. J. Albert (eds.), *To Form a More Perfect Union: The Critical Ideas of the Constitution*, 104–133. Charlottesville, 1992.

Dreitzel, Horst. *Protestantischer Aristotelismus und absoluter Staat: Die "Politica" des Henning Arnisaeus (ca. 1575–1636)*. Wiesbaden, 1970.

Drogula, Fred. "Imperium, Potestas and the Pomerium in the Roman Republic." *Historia* 56, 4 (2007): 419–452.

Drumann, Wilhelm. *Geschichte Roms in seinem Übergange von der republikanischen zur monarchischen Verfassung oder Pompeius, Caesar, Cicero und ihre Zeitgenossen nach Geschlechtern und mit genealogischen Tabellen*. 6 vols. 2nd ed. by P. Groebe. Berlin-Leipzig, 1899–1929.

Drummond, A. *Law, Politics and Power. Sallust and the Execution of the Catilinarian Conspirators*. Stuttgart, 1995.

Duplà Ansuategui, A. Videant consules. *Las medidas de excepción en la crisis de la República Romana*. Zaragoza, 1990.

Dyck, Andrew R. *Cicero: Catilinarians*, with an Introduction, Text and Commentary. Cambridge, 2008.

———. *A Commentary on Cicero,* De Legibus. Ann Arbor, 2004.

———. *A Commentary on Cicero,* De Officiis. Ann Arbor, 1996.

———. "Evidence and Rhetoric in Cicero's *Pro Roscio Amerino*: The Case against Sex. Roscius," *Classical Quarterly* 53 (2003): 235–246.

Dyzenhaus, David. "Critical Notice of *On the People's Terms: A Republican Theory and Model of Democracy*, by Philip Pettit." *Canadian Journal of Philosophy* 43, 4 (2013): 494–513.

———. "Hobbes's Constitutional Theory." In Ian Shapiro (ed.), *Leviathan*, 453–480. New Haven, CT, 2009.

———. "How Hobbes Met the 'Hobbes Challenge.'" *The Modern Law Review* 72, 3 (2009): 488–506.

Earl, D. C. *The Political Thought of Sallust*. Cambridge, 1961.

Eckstein, Arthur M. *Moral Vision in the Histories of Polybius*. Berkeley, 1995.

Edelstein, Dan, *The Terror of Natural Right: Republicanism, the Cult of Nature, and the French Revolution*. Chicago, 2010.

Ehrenberg, Victor. "*Imperium maius* in the Roman Republic." *American Journal of Philology* 74, 2 (1953): 113–136.

———. *Die Rechtsidee im frühen Griechentum. Untersuchungen zur Geschichte der werdenden Polis*. Leipzig, 1921.

———. *Sophocles and Pericles*. Oxford, 1954.

Elster, Jon. *Ulysses and the Sirens*. Rev. ed. Cambridge, 1984.

———. *Ulysses Unbound: Studies in Rationality, Precommitment, and Constraints*. Cambridge, 2000.

Encyclopédie ou Dictionnaire raisonné des sciences, des arts et des métiers, par une Société de Gens de lettres. Ed. Diderot and d'Alembert. Paris, 1751–1772.

Everson, Stephen. "Aristotle on the Foundations of the State." *Political Studies* 36 (1988): 89–101.

Fantham, Elaine. *The Roman World of Cicero's* De Oratore. Oxford, 2004.

Farrand, Max (ed.). *The Records of the Federal Convention of 1787*. 3 vols. Rev. ed. New Haven, 1937 (rpt. 1966–1967).

The Federalist Papers. Ed. Isaac Kramnick. London, 1987.

Ferguson, Adam. *An Essay on the History of Civil Society*. Edinburgh, 1966 (orig. 1767).

Ferrary, Jean-Louis. "L'Archéologie du De re publica (2, 2, 4–37, 63): Cicéron entre Polybe et Platon." *Journal of Roman Studies* 74 (1984): 87–98.

———. "Cicéron et la dictature." In Hinard, *Dictatures*, 97–105.

———. "The Statesman and the Law in the Political Philosophy of Cicero." In Laks and Schofield, *Justice and Generosity*, 48–73.

Filmer, Robert. *Patriarcha and Other Writings*. Ed. Johann P. Sommerville. Cambridge, 1991.

Fink, Z. S. *The Classical Republicans: An Essay in the Recovery of a Pattern of Thought in Seventeenth-Century England*. 2nd ed. Evanston, IL, 1962.

Flach, Dieter, ed. *Das Zwölftafelgesetz*. With Translation and Commentary, in Collaboration with Andreas Flach. Darmstadt, 2004.

Flaig, Egon. "Volkssouveränität ohne Repräsentation. Zum 'Römischen Staatsrecht' von Theodor Mommsen." In Wolfgang Küttler et al. (eds.), *Geschichtsdiskurs 3*, 321–339. Frankfurt a. M., 1997.

Flower, Harriet I. *Roman Republics*. Princeton, 2010.

Foisneau, Luc. "Sovereignty and Reason of State: Bodin, Botero, Richelieu and Hobbes." In Lloyd., *Reception of Bodin*, 323–342.

Fontanella, Francesca. *Politica e diritto naturale nel* De legibus *di Cicerone*. Rome, 2012.

Fränkel, Max. *Die attischen Geschworenengerichte. Ein Beitrag zum attischen Staatsrecht*. Berlin, 1877.

Franklin, Julian H. *Jean Bodin and the Rise of Absolutist Theory*. Cambridge, 1973.

Friedrich, Carl J. *Constitutional Reason of State: The Survival of the Constitutional Order*. Providence, RI, 1957.

Fritz, Kurt von. "Emergency Powers in the Last Centuries of the Roman Republic." *Annual Report of the American Historical Association*. Vol. 3, 1942 (=id. *Schriften zur griechischen und römischen Verfassungsgeschichte und Verfassungstheorie*, 388–406. Berlin 1976).

———. *The Theory of the Mixed Constitution in Antiquity: A Critical Analysis of Polybius' Political Ideas*. New York, 1954.

Fukuda, Arihiro. *Sovereignty and the Sword: Harrington, Hobbes, and Mixed Government in the English Civil Wars*. Oxford, 1997.

Gabba, Emilio. *Appiani bellorum civilium liber primus*. Introduzione, testo critico e commento con traduzione e indici. 2nd ed. Florence, 1967.

———. "Dionigi e la dittatura a Roma." In id. (ed.), *Tria Corda. Scritti in onore di Arnaldo Momigliano*, 215–228. Como, 1983.

———. *Dionysius and the History of Archaic Rome*. Berkeley, 1991.

Gasperini, L. "Su alcune epigrafi di Taranto romana." In *Seconda Miscellanea greca e romana*, 381–397. Rome, 1968.

Gelzer, Matthias. *Caesar, der Politiker und Staatsmann*. 6th ed. Wiesbaden, 1960.

———. "Das erste Konsulat des Pompeius und die Übertragung der grossen Imperien." *Abhandlungen der Preussischen Akademie der Wissenschaften, philosophisch-historische Klasse*. Nr. 1, 1943 (=id. *Kleine Schriften*. Vol. 2, 146–189. Wiesbaden, 1963).

———. *Pompeius: Lebensbild eines Römers*. 2nd ed. Stuttgart, 1984 (rpt. 2005).

Gentili, Alberico. *The Wars of the Romans. A Critical Edition and Translation of* De armis Romanis. Ed. B. Kingsbury and B. Straumann, trans. D. Lupher. Oxford, 2011.

Gert, Bernard. "Review Skinner, *Hobbes and Republican Liberty*." *Notre Dame Philosophical Reviews* 2008.07.24.

Gigante, M. *Nomos Basileus*. Naples, 1956.

Gill, C. "Rethinking Constitutionalism in *Statesman* 291–303." In C. Rowe (ed.). *Reading the Statesman*, 292–305. St. Augustin, 1995.

Giovannini, Adalberto. *Consulare imperium*. Basel, 1983.

Girardet, K. M. *Die Ordnung der Welt. Ein Beitrag zur philosophischen und politischen Interpretation von Ciceros Schrift de legibus*. Wiesbaden, 1983.

———. "Die Rechtsstellung der Caesarenattentäter Brutus und Cassius in den Jahren 44-42 v. Chr." *Chiron* 23 (1993): 207–232.

Giuffrè, Vincenzo. *Aspetti costituzionali del potere dei militari nella tarda "respublica."* Naples, 1973.

Golden, Gregory K. *Crisis Management during the Roman Republic: The Role of Political Institutions in Emergencies*. Cambridge, 2013.

Goldsworthy, Jeffrey. *The Sovereignty of Parliament. History and Philosophy*. Oxford, 1999.

Gough, J. W. *The Social Contract: A Critical Study of its Development*. 2nd ed. Oxford, 1957.

Griffin, Miriam T. *Seneca on Society: A Guide to* De Beneficiis. Oxford, 2013.

———. "When is Thought Political?" *Apeiron* 29 (1996): 269–282.

Grotius, Hugo. *De iure belli ac pacis libri tres*. Paris, 1625. English trans. R. Tuck, ed. *The Rights of War and Peace*. Indianapolis, 2005.

Grouchy, Nicolas de. *De comitiis Romanorum libri tres*. Venice, 1559.

Gruen, Erich S. *The Last Generation of the Roman Republic*. Berkeley, 1974.

Grziwotz, Herbert. *Der moderne Verfassungsbegriff und die "Römische Verfassung" in der deutschen Forschung des 19. und 20. Jahrhunderts*. Frankfurt a.M., 1986.

———. *Das Verfassungsverständnis der römischen Republik. Ein methodischer Versuch*. Frankfurt a.M., 1985.

Guarino, A. "Senatus Consultum Ultimum." In W. C. Becker and M. Schnorr von Carolsfeld (eds.), *Sein und Werden im Recht. Festgabe für Ulrich von Lübtow*, 281–294. Berlin, 1970.

Gummere, Richard M. "The Classical Ancestry of the United States Constitution." *American Quarterly* 14, 1 (1962): 3–18 (revised version in id., *The American Colonial Mind and the Classical Tradition: Essays in Comparative Culture*, 173–190. Cambridge, MA, 1963).

Gutberlet, D. *Die erste Dekade des Livius als Quelle zur gracchischen und sullanischen Zeit*. Hildesheim, 1985.

Guthrie, W. K. C. *A History of Greek Philosophy*. Vol. 3, *The Fifth-Century Enlightenment*. Cambridge, 1969.

Gwyn, W. B. *The Meaning of the Separation of Powers. An Analysis of the Doctrine from its Origin to the Adoption of the United States Constitution*. New Orleans-The Hague, 1965.

Hagendahl, Harald. *Augustine and the Latin Classics*. 2 vols. Gothenburg, 1967.

Hahm, David E. "Kings and Constitutions: Hellenistic Theories." In Rowe and Schofield, *Cambridge History*, 457–476.

———. "Polybius' Applied Political Theory." In Laks and Schofield, *Justice and Generosity*, 7–47.

Hahn, Istvan. "Appians Darstellung der sullanischen Diktatur." *Acta Classica Universitatis Scientiarum Debreceniensis* 10-11 (1974/1975): 111–120.

Hammer, Dean. *Roman Political Thought and the Modern Theoretical Imagination*. Norman, 2008.

———. *Roman Political Thought from Cicero to Augustine*. Cambridge, 2014.

Handlin, Oscar, and Mary Handlin (eds.). *The Popular Sources of Political Authority: Documents on the Massachusetts Constitution of 1780*. Cambridge, MA, 1966.

Hankins, James. "The 'Baron Thesis' after Forty Years and Some Recent Studies of Leonardo Bruni." *Journal of the History of Ideas* 56, 2 (1995): 309–338.

Hansen, Mogens Herman. *The Athenian Democracy in the Age of Demosthenes: Structure, Principles, and Ideology*. Trans. J. A. Crook. Oxford, 1991.

———. "Athenian *nomothesia*." *Greek, Roman, and Byzantine Studies* 26 (1985): 345–371.

———. *Eisangelia: The Sovereignty of the People's Court in Athens in the Fourth Century BC and the Impeachment of Generals and Politicians*. Odense, 1975.

———. "*Graphe Paranomon* against *Psephismata* not yet Passed by the *Ekklesia*." *Classica et Mediaevalia* 38 (1987): 63–73.

———. *The Sovereignty of the People's Court in Athens in the Fourth Century BC and the Public Action Against Unconstitutional Proposals*. Odense, 1974.

———. "The Theoric Fund and the *graphe paranomon* against Apollodorus." *Greek, Roman, and Byzantine Studies* 17 (1976): 235–246.

Hanses, Mathias. "Antikebilder im 'Federalist'/'Anti-Federalist.'" In Niggemann and Ruffing, *Antike als Modell*, 85–110.

Hantos, Theodora. *Res publica constituta. Die Verfassung des Dictators Sulla*. Stuttgart, 1988.

Harries, Jill. *Cicero and the Jurists. From Citizens' Law to the Lawful State*. London, 2006.

Harrington, James. *The Oceana and Other Works of James Harrington, with an Account of His Life by John Toland*. London, 1771.

Harris, Edward M. (trans.). *Demosthenes, Speeches 20-22*. The Oratory of Classical Greece, 12. Austin, TX, 2008.

———. "Open Texture in Athenian Law." *Dike* 3 (2000): 67–75.

———. *The Rule of Law in Action in Democratic Athens*. Oxford, 2013.

———. "The Rule of Law in Athenian Democracy. Reflections on the Judicial Oath." *Dike* 8 (2008): 157–181.

Harris, William V. "On Defining the Political Culture of the Classical Roman Republic, 200-151 B.C." *Classical Philology* 85 (1990): 288–298.

Hartfield, Marianne. "The Roman Dictatorship: Its Character and Evolution." Doctoral dissertation. University of California, Berkeley, 1982.

Hartz, Louis. *The Liberal Tradition in America: An Interpretation of American Political Thought since the Revolution*. New York, 1955.

Hassall, M., M. Crawford, and J. Reynolds. "Rome and the Eastern Provinces at the End of the Second Century B.C. The So-Called 'Piracy Law' and a New Inscription From Cnidos." *Journal of Roman Studies* 64 (1974): 195–220.

Heikkilä, K. "*Lex non iure rogata*: Senate and the Annulment of Laws in the Late Republic." In U. Paananen, K. Heikkilä, K. Sandberg, L. Savunen, and J. Vaahtera (eds.), *Senatus Populusque Romanus. Studies in Roman Republican Legislation*, 117–142. Helsinki, 1993.

Herzog, Don. *Happy Slaves: A Critique of Consent Theory*. Chicago, 1989.

Heun, Werner. "Die Antike in den amerikanischen politischen Debatten in der zweiten Hälfte des 18. Jahrhunderts." In Niggemann and Ruffing, *Antike als Modell*, 65–83.

Heuss, Alfred. *Barthold Georg Niebuhrs wissenschaftliche Anfänge. Untersuchungen und Mitteilungen über die Kopenhagener Manuscripte und zur europäischen Tradition der* lex agraria *(*loi agraire*)*. Göttingen, 1981.

———. *Ciceros Theorie vom römischen Staat*. Nachrichten der Akademie der Wissenschaften in Göttingen. Philologisch-Historische Klasse, Jg. 1975, Nr. 8, 195–272. Göttingen, 1976.

———. "Zur Thematik republikanischer 'Staatsrechtslehre.'" In O. Behrends et al. (eds.), *Festschrift für F. Wieacker zum 70. Geburtstag*. Göttingen, 1978, 71–89.

Hexter, J. H. "Review Pocock, *The Machiavellian Moment*." *History and Theory* 16, 3 (1977): 306–337.

Hinard, François. "De la dictature à la tyrannie. Réflexions sur la dictature de Sylla." In id., *Dictatures*, 87–96.

———. (ed.). *Dictatures: Actes de la Table ronde réunie à Paris les 27 et 28 février 1984*. Paris, 1988.

———. *Les proscriptions de la Rome républicaine.* Rome, 1985.

———. *Sylla.* Paris, 1985.

Hinrichs, F. T. "Die lateinische Tafel von Bantia und die 'lex de piratis.'" *Hermes* 98 (1970): 471–502.

Hirschman, Albert O. *The Passions and the Interests: Political Arguments for Capitalism before Its Triumph.* Princeton, 1977.

Hirzel, Rudolf. *Agraphos Nomos.* Leipzig, 1900.

Hobbes, Thomas. "Answer to Davenant's Preface to *Gondibert.*" In J. E. Spingarn (ed.), *Critical Essays of the Seventeenth Century.* Vol. 2. Oxford, 1908.

———. *De cive. The Latin Version,* ed. H. Warrender. Oxford, 1983.

———. *The Elements of Law,* ed. F. Tönnies. London, 1889.

———. *Leviathan,* ed. Noel Malcolm. 3 vols. Oxford, 2012.

Hoekstra, Kinch. "Early Modern Absolutism and Constitutionalism." *Cardozo Law Review* 34 (2013): 1079–1098.

———. "A Lion in the House: Hobbes and Democracy." In A. Brett et al. (eds.), *Rethinking the Foundations of Modern Political Thought,* 191–218. Cambridge, 2006.

Hofmann, H. "Diktatur - eine begriffsgeschichtliche Miniatur." In *Recht-Politik-Verfassung: Studien zur Geschichte der politischen Philosophie,* 122–126. Frankfurt a. M., 1986.

Hölkeskamp, Karl-Joachim. "Ein 'Gegensatz von Form und Inhalt.' Theodor Mommsens Konzept des republikanischen 'Senatsregiments'—Hindernis oder Herausforderung?" In Nippel and Seidensticker, *Theodor Mommsens langer Schatten,* 87–129.

———. (ed.). *Eine politische Kultur (in) der Krise? Die "letzte Generation" der römischen Republik.* Munich, 2009.

———. "Eine politische Kultur (in) der Krise? Gemäßigt radikale Vorbemerkungen zum kategorischen Imperativ der Konzepte." In id., *Eine politische Kultur,* 1–25.

———. *Reconstructing the Roman Republic. An Ancient Political Culture and Modern Research.* Princeton-Oxford, 2010.

———. *Rekonstruktionen einer Republik. Die politische Kultur des antiken Rom und die Forschung der letzten Jahrzehnte.* Historische Zeitschrift, Beihefte Neue Folge 38. Munich, 2004.

———. *Senatus Populusque Romanus. Die politische Kultur der Republik – Dimensionen und Deutungen.* Stuttgart, 2004.

Holmes, Stephen. *Passions and Constraint: On the Theory of Liberal Democracy.* Chicago, 1995.

Hont, Istvan. *Politics in Commercial Society: Jean-Jacques Rousseau and Adam Smith.* Cambridge, MA, 2015.

Horn, Christoph. "Politische Gerechtigkeit bei Cicero und Augustinus." *Etica & Politica / Ethics & Politics* 9 (2007): 46–70.

Hörnqvist, Mikael. *Machiavelli and Empire.* Cambridge, 2004.

Hough, John N. "The Lex Lutatia and the Lex Plautia de vi," *The American Journal of Philology* 51, 2 (1930): 135–147.

Hume, David. "Of some Remarkable Customs." In id., *Political Essays*, 179–185.

———. *Political Essays*, ed. K. Haakonssen. Cambridge, 1994.

———. "That Politics May Be Reduced to a Science." In id., *Political Essays*, 4–15.

Hurlet, Frédéric. *La dictature de Sylla. Monarchie ou magistrature républicaine?* Brussels, 1993.

———. "Pouvoirs extraordinaires et tromperie: La tentation de la Monarchie à la fin de la République romaine (82-44 av. J.-C.)." In A. J. Turner, J. H. Kim On Chong-Gossard, F. J. Vervaet (eds.), *Private and Public Lies: The Discourse of Despotism and Deceit in the Graeco-Roman World*, 107–129. Leiden, 2010, 107–129.

Hutson, James H. (ed.). *Supplement to Max Farrand's The Records of the Federal Convention of 1787*. New Haven, 1987.

Irmscher, J. "Die Diktatur – Versuch einer Begriffsgeschichte." *Klio* 58 (1976): 273–287.

Irwin, Terence. *Aristotle's First Principles*. Oxford, 1988.

———. *The Development of Ethics. A Historical and Critical Study*. Vol. I, *From Socrates to the Reformation*. Oxford, 2007.

———. "Morality as Law and Morality in the *Laws*." In Bobonich, *Plato's* Laws, 92–107.

———. *Plato's Ethics*. Oxford, 1995.

Issacharoff, Samuel, and Richard H. Pildes. "Emergency Contexts without Emergency Powers: The United States' Constitutional Approach to Rights during Wartime." *International Journal of Constitutional Law* (2004): 296–333.

Jacob, Margaret. "Was the Eighteenth-Century Republican Essentially Anticapitalist?" *Republics of Letters: A Journal for the Study of Knowledge, Politics, and the Arts* 2, 1 (2010): http://rofl.stanford.edu/node/66.

Jashemski, W. F. *The Origins and History of the Proconsular and the Propraetorian Imperium to 27 B.C.* Chicago, 1950.

Jefferson, Thomas. "Notes on the State of Virginia: Query XIII." In Merrill D. Peterson (ed.), *Thomas Jefferson: Writings*, 235–255. New York, 1984.

Jehne, Martin. "Krisenwahrnehmung und Vorschläge zur Krisenüberwindung bei Cicero." In J.-M. Roddaz et al. (eds.), *Les fondements et crises du pouvoir*, 379–396. Bordeaux, 2003.

———. *Der Staat des Dictators Caesar*. Cologne, 1987.

———. "Die Volksversammlungen in Mommsens *Staatsrecht* oder: Mommsen als Gesetzgeber." In Nippel and Seidensticker, *Theodor Mommsens langer Schatten*, 131–160.

———. (ed.). *Demokratie in Rom? Die Rolle des Volkes in der Politik der römischen Republik*. Stuttgart, 1995.

Johnston, David. *Roman Law in Context*. Cambridge, 1999.

Kahn, Charles. "From *Republic* to *Laws*: A Discussion of Christopher Bobonich, *Plato's Utopia Recast*." *Oxford Studies in Ancient Philosophy* 26 (2004): 337–362.

Kalyvas, Andreas. "The Tyranny of Dictatorship: When the Greek Tyrant Met the Roman Dictator." *Political Theory* 35, 4 (2007): 412–442.

Kapust, Daniel. *Republicanism, Rhetoric, and Roman Political Thought: Sallust, Livy, and Tacitus*. Cambridge, 2011.

———. "Skinner, Pettit and Livy: The Conflict of the Orders and the Ambiguity of Republican Liberty." *History of Political Thought* 25, 3 (2004): 377–401.

Kaser, Max. *Das römische Privatrecht*. 2 vols. 2nd edn. Munich, 1971–1975.

Kaster, Robert A., trans., comm. *Cicero: Speech on Behalf of Publius Sestius*. Oxford, 2006.

Keaveney, Arthur. *Sulla, the Last Republican*. 2nd ed. London-New York, 2005.

———. "What Happened in 88?" *Eirene* 20 (1983): 53–86.

Kellett, E. E. *The Story of Dictatorship From the Earliest Times Till Today*. London, 1937.

Kennedy, George. "Classical Influences on *The Federalist*." In John W. Eadie (ed.), *Classical Traditions in Early America*, 110–138. Ann Arbor, 1976.

Keyes, Clinton Walker. "The Constitutional Position of the Roman Dictatorship." *Studies in Philology* 14 (1917): 298–305.

———. "Original Elements in Cicero's Ideal Constitution." *American Journal of Philology* 42 (1921): 309–323.

Kingsbury, Benedict, and Benjamin Straumann. "Introduction: Roman Wars and Roman Laws." In Gentili, *The Wars of the Romans*, x-xxv.

———. (eds.). *The Roman Foundations of the Law of Nations: Alberico Gentili and the Justice of Empire*. Oxford, 2010.

———. "The State of Nature and Commercial Sociability in Early Modern International Legal Thought." *Grotiana* 31 (2010): 1–22.

Kleinerman, Benjamin A. *The Discretionary President: The Promise and Peril of Executive Power*. Lawrence, 2009.

Kloft, Hans. *Prorogation und ausserordentliche Imperien 326-81 v. Chr. Untersuchungen zur Verfassung der römischen Republik*. Beiträge zur klassischen Philologie 84. Meisenheim am Glan, 1977.

Knight, Carl. "Unit-Ideas Unleashed: A Reinterpretation and Reassessment of Lovejovian Methodology in the History of Ideas." *Journal of the Philosophy of History* 6 (2012): 195–217.

Kraut, Richard. *Aristotle: Political Philosophy*. Oxford, 2002.

———. "Reason and Justice in Plato's *Republic*." In Lee et al., *Exegesis and Argument*, 207–224.

Kremmydas, Christos. *Commentary on Demosthenes Against Leptines*. Oxford, 2012.

Kunkel, Wolfgang. "Bericht über neuere Arbeiten zur römischen Verfassungsgeschichte I." *Zeitschrift der Savigny-Stiftung für Rechtsgeschichte* 72 (1955): 288–325.

Kunkel, W., and R. Wittmann. *Staatsordnung und Staatspraxis der römischen Republik: Zweiter Abschnitt*. Munich, 1995.

Lacorne, Denis. *L'invention de la République. Le modèle américain*. Paris, 1991.

Laks, André, and Malcolm Schofield (eds.). *Justice and Generosity: Studies in Hellenistic Social and Political Philosophy*. Cambridge, 1995.

Lane, Melissa. *Method and Politics in Plato's Statesman*. Cambridge, 1998.

Lanni, Adriaan. "Judicial Review and the Athenian 'Constitution,'" *Harvard Law School Public Law & Legal Theory Working Paper Series,* Paper No. 10-21 (= M. H. Hansen (ed.). *Demokratia – Ancient and Modern*, 235–263. Geneva, 2010).

———. *Law and Justice in the Courts of Classical Athens*. Cambridge, 2006.

Lanzani, C. *Lucio Cornelio Silla dittatore*. Milan, 1936.

Last, Hugh. "Gaius Gracchus." In *Cambridge Ancient History*. Vol. 9, 40–101. Cambridge, 1962.

———. "Review H. J. Haskell, *This Was Cicero*." *Journal of Roman Studies* 33 (1943): 93–97.

Lausberg, Heinrich. *Handbuch der literarischen Rhetorik: Eine Grundlegung der Literaturwissenschaft*. 3rd ed. Stuttgart, 1990. English trans. D. E. Orton and R. Dean Anderson (eds.). *Handbook of Literary Rhetoric: A Foundation for Literary Study*. Leiden, 1998.

Lee, Daniel. "'Office is a Thing Borrowed.' Jean Bodin on Offices and Seigneurial Government." *Political Theory* 41, 3 (2013): 409–440.

———. *Popular Sovereignty in Early Modern Constitutional Thought*. Oxford, 2016.

Lee, E., A. Mourelatos, and R. Rorty (eds.). *Exegesis and Argument: Studies in Greek Philosophy Presented to Gregory Vlastos*. Assen, 1973.

Lefèvre, Eckard. *Panaitios' und Ciceros Pflichtenlehre. Vom philosophischen Traktat zum politischen Lehrbuch*. Stuttgart, 2001.

Lehmann, G. A. *Politische Reformvorschläge in der Krise der späten römischen Republik. Cicero de legibus III und Sallusts Sendschreiben an Caesar*. Meisenheim am Glan, 1980.

Levick, B. M. "Sulla's March on Rome in 88 B.C." *Historia* 31 (1982): 503–508.

Levy, Ernst. *Die römische Kapitalstrafe*. Heidelberg, 1931.

Linderski, Jerzy. "The Augural Law." *Aufstieg und Niedergang der römischen Welt* II.16.3 (1986): 2146–2312.

———. "Review Lintott, *The Constitution of the Roman Republic*." *The American Journal of Philology* 122, 4 (2001): 589–592.

———. "The Surname of M. Antonius Creticus and the Cognomina *ex victis gentibus*." In id., *Roman Questions: Selected Papers*, 436–443. Stuttgart, 1995.

Linke, B., and M. Stemmler (eds.). *Mos maiorum: Untersuchungen zu den Formen der Identitätsstiftung und Stabilisierung in der römischen Republik*. Stuttgart, 2000.

Linton, Marisa. *The Politics of Virtue in Enlightenment France*. Basingstoke, UK-New York, 2001.

Lintott, Andrew. "Cicero and Milo." *Journal of Roman Studies* 64 (1974): 62–78.

———. *Cicero as Evidence: A Historian's Companion*. Oxford, 2008.

———. *The Constitution of the Roman Republic*. Oxford, 1999.

———. *Judicial Reform and Land Reform in the Roman Republic*. Cambridge, 1992.

———. *Plutarch: Demosthenes and Cicero*. Oxford, 2013.

———. "*Provocatio* from the Struggle of the Orders to the Principate." *Aufstieg und Niedergang der römischen Welt* I.2 (1972): 226–267.

———. "The Theory of the Mixed Constitution at Rome." In J. Barnes and M. Griffin (eds.), *Philosophia Togata*. Vol. 2, *Plato and Aristotle at Rome*, 70–85. Oxford, 1997.

———. "The Tradition of Violence in the Annals of the Early Roman Republic." *Historia* 19 (1970): 12–29.

———. *Violence in Republican Rome*. 2nd ed. Oxford, 1999.

Lloyd, Howell A. (ed.). *The Reception of Bodin*. Brill's Studies in Intellectual History 223. Leiden-Boston, 2013.

Lo Cascio, E. "Recruitment and the Size of the Roman Population from the Third to the First BCE." In W. Scheidel (ed.), *Debating Roman Demography*, 111–137. Leiden, 2001.

Locke, John. *Two Treatises of Government*, edited with an introduction and notes by Peter Laslett. Cambridge, 1988.

Long, A. A. "Cicero's Politics in *De officiis*." In Laks and Schofield, *Justice and Generosity*, 213–240.

———. "Stoic Philosophers on Persons, Property-Ownership and Community." In R. Sorabji (ed.), *Aristotle and After*, 13–31. Bulletin of the Institute of Classical Studies, Supplement 68. London, 1997.

Lovejoy, Arthur O. *Reflections on Human Nature*. Baltimore, 1961.

Lübtow, Ulrich von. *Das römische Volk: Sein Staat und sein Recht*. Frankfurt a. M., 1955.

Luce, T. James, Jr. "Appian's Magisterial Terminology." *Classical Philology* 56, 1 (1961): 21–28.

Lundgreen, Christoph. *Regelkonflikte in der römischen Republik. Geltung und Gewichtung von Normen in politischen Entscheidungsprozessen*. Stuttgart, 2011.

Lupher, David. "The *De armis Romanis* and the Exemplum of Roman Imperialism." In Kingsbury and Straumann, *The Roman Foundations*, 85–100.

———. *Romans in a New World. Classical Models in Sixteenth-Century Spanish America*. Ann Arbor, 2003.

Mably, Gabriel Bonnot de. *Collection complète des Oeuvres de l'abbé de Mably*, ed. G. Arnoux. 15 vols. Paris, 1794–1795 (rpt. 1977).

———. "Observations sur les Romains." In *Collection complète des Oeuvres*. Vol. 4. English trans. *Observations on the Romans*. London, 1751.

MacCormack, Sabine. *The Shadows of Poetry: Vergil in the Mind of Augustine*. Berkeley, 1998.

MacDowell, Douglas M. *The Law in Classical Athens*. Ithaca, NY, 1978.

Machiavelli, Niccolò. *Discorsi sopra la prima deca di Tito Livio*, ed. C. Vivanti. Turin, 1983.

———. *Discourses on Livy*, trans. H. C. Mansfield, N. Tarcov. Chicago, 1996.

———. *The Discourses of Niccolò Machiavelli*. Trans. with Introduction and Notes by Leslie J. Walker. With a new Introduction and Appendices by Cecil H. Clough. 2 vols. London-Boston, 1975.

MacIntyre, Alasdair. *After Virtue*. 2nd ed. Notre Dame, IN, 1984.

Mackie, J. L. *Ethics: Inventing Right and Wrong*. Harmondsworth, 1977.

MacMullen, Ramsay. "How Many Romans Voted?" *Athenaeum* 58 (1980): 454–457.

Magdelain, André. *Recherches sur l'"imperium." La loi curiate et les auspices d'investiture*. Paris, 1968.

Malcolm, Noel. "Hobbes and the European Republic of Letters." In id., *Aspects of Hobbes*, 457–545. Oxford, 2002.

———. *Reason of State, Propaganda, and the Thirty Years' War: An Unknown Translation by Thomas Hobbes*. Oxford, 2007.

Malcovati, H. (ed.). *Oratorum Romanorum fragmenta*. 4th ed. Turin, 1967.

Manuwald, Gesine. *Cicero,* Philippics *3-9*. Edited with Introduction, Translation and Commentary. 2 vols. Berlin, 2007.

Markus, R. A. *Saeculum: History and Society in the Theology of St Augustine*. Cambridge, 1989.

Marshall, B. A. *A Historical Commentary on Asconius*. Columbia, MO, 1985.

Marshall, John. *John Locke: Resistance, Religion and Responsibility*. Cambridge, 1994.

Martin, Jean-Clément. *Violence et Révolution: Essai sur la naissance d'un mythe national*. Paris, 2006.

Martin, Jochen. "Die Provokation in der klassischen und späten Republik." *Hermes* 98 (1970): 72–96.

Martino, Francesco de. *Storia della costituzione romana*. 3 vols. 2nd ed. Naples, 1972–73.

McCuaig, W. *Carlo Sigonio: The Changing World of the Late Renaissance*. Princeton, 1989.

McCullough, David. *John Adams*. New York, 2001.

McDaniel, Iain. *Adam Ferguson in the Scottish Enlightenment: The Roman Past and Europe's Future*. Cambridge, MA-London, 2013.

McDonald, Forrest. *Novus Ordo Seclorum: The Intellectual Origins of the Constitution*. Lawrence, 1985.

McIlwain, C. H. *Constitutionalism Ancient and Modern*. Ithaca, NY, 1947.

McLean, Iain. "Thomas Jefferson, John Adams, and the *Déclaration des droits de l'homme et du citoyen*." In R. Fatton, Jr. and R. K. Ramazani (eds.), *The Future of Liberal Democracy: Thomas Jefferson and the Contemporary World*, 13–30. New York, 2004.

McMahon, Darrin, and Samuel Moyn (eds.). *Rethinking Modern European Intellectual History*. Oxford, 2014.

Mehmel, F. "Machiavelli und die Antike." *Antike und Abendland* 3 (1948): 152–186.

Meier, Christian. "Antworten." In Bernett et al., *Christian Meier*, 259–310.

———. *Caesar: A Biography*, trans. David McLintock. London, 1995.

———. Res publica amissa. *Eine Studie zur Verfassung und Geschichte der späten römischen Republik*. 2nd ed. Wiesbaden, 1980 (orig. 1966).

Meinecke, Friedrich. *Die Idee der Staatsräson in der neueren Geschichte*. 3rd ed. Munich, 1963.

———. *Machiavellism: The Doctrine of Raison d'État and Its Place in Modern History*. London, 1957.

Meloni, Giovanni. "Dictatura popularis." In Hinard, *Dictatures*, 73–86.

Meyer, Eduard. *Caesars Monarchie und das Principat des Pompeius*. 3rd ed. Stuttgart, 1922 (rpt. Darmstadt, 1974).

Meyer, Ernst. *Römischer Staat und Staatsgedanke*. 4th ed. Zurich, 1975.

Meyer, Inga. *Von der Vision zur Reform. Der Staat der Gesetze: Ciceros Programm einer Neuordnung der Römischen Republik: 56-51 v. Chr.* Munich, 2006.

Mill, John Stuart. *A System of Logic*. In J. M. Robson (ed.), *Collected Works of John Stuart Mill*. Vols. 7 and 8. Toronto, 1974.

Millar, Fergus. *The Crowd in Rome in the Late Republic*. Ann Arbor, 1998.

———. "Politics, Persuasion and the People before the Social War (150-90 BC)." *Journal of Roman Studies* 76 (1986): 1–11.

———. *The Roman Republic in Political Thought*. Hanover-London, 2002.

———. *A Study of Cassius Dio*. Oxford-New York, 1964.

Miller, Jon. "Stoics, Grotius and Spinoza on Moral Deliberation." In Miller and Inwood, *Hellenistic and Early Modern*, 116–140.

Miller, Jon, and B. Inwood (eds.). *Hellenistic and Early Modern Philosophy*. Cambridge, 2003.

Mirhady, David C. "The Dikasts' Oath and the Question of Fact." In A. Sommerstein and J. Fletcher (eds.), *Horkos: The Oath in Greek Society*, 48–59. Bristol, 2007.

Mitchell, T. N. "Cicero and the *Senatus Consultum Ultimum*." *Historia* 20 (1971): 47–61.

Mitsis, Phillip. "Locke's Offices." In Miller and Inwood, *Hellenistic and Early Modern*, 45–61.

———. "The Stoics on Property and Politics." *The Southern Journal of Philosophy* 43 (2005): 230–239.

Moatti, Claudia. *La Raison de Rome. Naissance de l'esprit critique à la fin de la République*. Paris, 1997.

Molthagen, J. "Die Durchführung der gracchischen Agrarreform." *Historia* 22 (1973): 423–458.

Mommsen, Theodor. *Abriß des römischen Staatsrechts*. 2nd ed. Leipzig, 1907.

———. *Römische Geschichte*. Rpt. with Introduction by Stefan Rebenich. Darmstadt, 2010 (orig. 1854-56).

———. *Römisches Staatsrecht*. 3 vols. Leipzig, 1887-1888 (rpt. 1952).

Montesquieu, Charles de Secondat, Baron de. *Considerations on the Causes of the Greatness of the Romans and Their Decline*. Trans., with Introduction and Notes by David Lowenthal. Indianapolis-Cambridge, 1999.

———. *Oeuvres complètes*, ed. Édouard Laboulaye. Vol. 2, *Le Temple de Gnide, Grandeur et Décadence des Romains*, etc. Paris, 1876.

———. *Oeuvres complètes*, ed. D. Oster. Paris, 1964.

———. *The Spirit of the Laws*, ed. A. Cohler, B. Miller, H. Stone. Cambridge, 1989.

Morgan, M. Gwyn. "Q. Metellus (cos. 206). Dictatorii in the Pre-Sullan Senate and the End of the Dictatorship." *Athenaeum* 79 (1991): 359–370.

Morrow, G. R. *Plato's Cretan City*. Princeton, 1960.

Morstein-Marx, Robert. "Consular Appeals to the Army in 88 and 87: The Locus of Legitimacy in Late Republican Rome." In Beck et al., *Consuls and* Res Publica, 259–278.

———. "*Dignitas* and *res publica*: Caesar and Republican Legitimacy." In Hölkeskamp, *Eine politische Kultur*, 115–140.

———. *Mass Oratory and Political Power in the Late Roman Republic*. Cambridge, 2004.

Mossé, Claude. *L'Antiquité dans la Révolution française*. Paris, 1989.

Mouritsen, Henrik. *Plebs and Politics in Late Republican Rome*. Cambridge, 2001.

Moyle, Walter. *An Essay on the Constitution and Government of the Roman State*. In C. Robbins (ed.), *Two English Republican Tracts*, 201–259. Cambridge, 1969.

Moyn, Samuel. *The Last Utopia: Human Rights in History*. Cambridge, MA, 2010.

Münkler, Herfried. *Im Namen des Staates. Die Begründung der Staatsraison in der frühen Neuzeit*. Hamburg, 1987.

Münkler, H., and M. Llanque. "Diktatur." In *Der Neue Pauly. Enzyklopädie der Antike*, ed. M. Landfester, in association with H. Cancik and H. Schneider. Rezeptions- und Wissenschaftsgeschichte. Vol. XV/2. Stuttgart-Weimar, 2002.

Münzer, Friedrich. *Römische Adelsparteien und Adelsfamilien*. Stuttgart, 1920.

———. "Ti. Sempronius Gracchus." *Paulys Realenzyklopädie der klassischen Altertumswissenschaft* II A2 (1923): 1409–1426.

Nagel, Thomas. *Equality and Partiality*. New York, 1991.

Nedham, Marchamont. *The Excellencie of a Free-State; Or, The Right Constitution of a Commonwealth*. Ed. and with an Introduction by Blair Worden. Indianapolis, 2011.

Nelson, Eric. *The Greek Tradition in Republican Thought*. Cambridge, 2004.

———. *The Hebrew Republic. Jewish Sources and the Transformation of European Political Thought*. Cambridge, MA, 2010.

———. *The Royalist Revolution: Monarchy and the American Founding*. Cambridge, MA, 2014.

Neschke-Hentschke, Ada. *Platonisme politique et théorie du droit naturel dans l'Antiquité*. Louvain, 1995.

Newman, W. L. *The Politics of Aristotle. With an Introduction, Two Prefatory Essays, and Notes Critical and Explanatory*. 4 vols. Oxford, 1887–1902.

Nicolet, Claude. "Consul togatus." *Revue des Études Latines* 38 (1960): 695–716.

———. "Le *de re publica* (VI, 12) et la dictature de Scipion." *Revue des Études Latines* 42 (1964): 212–230.

———. "Dictateurs romains, strategoi autokratores grecs et généraux carthaginois." In Hinard, *Dictatures*, 27–47.

———. "Dictatorship in Rome." In Peter Baehr and Melvin Richter (eds.), *Dictatorship in History and Theory*. Cambridge, 2004, 263–278.

———. *Rome et la conquête du monde méditerranéen: 1) Les structures de l'Italie romaine*. Paris, 1977.

———. *The World of the Citizen in Republican Rome*, trans. P. S. Falla. Berkeley-Los Angeles, 1980.

Niggemann, Ulrich, and Kai Ruffing (eds.). *Antike als Modell in Nordamerika?* Historische Zeitschrift, Beiheft 55. Munich, 2011.

Nippel, Wilfried. *Antike oder moderne Freiheit? Die Begründung der Demokratie in Athen und in der Neuzeit*. Frankfurt a. M., 2008.

———. "Antike und moderne Freiheit." In W. Jens and B. Seidensticker (eds.), *Ferne und Nähe der Antike*, 49–68. Berlin, 2003.

———. *Aufruhr und "Polizei" in der römischen Republik*. Stuttgart, 1988.

———. "Carl Schmitts 'kommissarische' und 'souveräne Diktatur.' Französische Revolution und römische Vorbilder." In Harald Blum et al. (eds.). *Ideenpolitik: Geschichtliche Konstellationen und gegenwärtige Konflikte*, 105–139. Berlin, 2011.

———. "Emergency Powers in the Roman Republic." In Pasquale Pasquino and Bernard Manin (eds.), *La théorie politico-constitutionnelle du gouvernement d'exception*, 5–23. Paris, 2000.

———. "Gesetze, Verfassungskonventionen, Präzedenzfälle." In Hölkeskamp, *Eine politische Kultur*, 87–97.

———. "Klassischer Republikanismus in der frühen Neuzeit: Kritische Nachfragen." In Niggemann and Ruffing, *Antike als Modell*, 23–34.

———. "Macht, Machtkontrolle und Machtentgrenzung. Zu einigen antiken Konzeptionen und ihrer Rezeption in der frühen Neuzeit." In J. Gebhardt and H. Münkler (eds.), *Bürgerschaft und Herrschaft: Zum Verhältnis von Macht und Demokratie im antiken und neuzeitlichen politischen Denken*, 58–78. Baden-Baden, 1993.

———. *Mischverfassungstheorie und Verfassungsrealität in Antike und früher Neuzeit*. Stuttgart, 1980.

———. *Public Order in Ancient Rome*. Cambridge, 1995.

———. "Regel und Ausnahme in der römischen Verfassung." In Bernett et al., *Christian Meier*, 121–141.

———. "The Roman Notion of *Auctoritas*." In P. Pasquino and P. Harris (eds.), *The Concept of Authority. A Multidisciplinary Approach: From Epistemology to the Social Sciences*, 13–34. Quaderni della Fondazione Adriano Olivetti 55. Rome, 2007.

———. "Saving the Constitution: The European Discourse on Dictatorship." In J. Coleman and P. M. Kitromilides (eds.), *In the Footsteps of Herodotus. Towards European Political Thought*, 29–49. Florence, 2012.

Nippel, Wilfried, and Bernd Seidensticker (eds). *Theodor Mommsens langer Schatten. Das römische Staatsrecht als bleibende Herausforderung für die Forschung*. Hildesheim, 2005.

Nocera, Guglielmo. *Il potere dei comizi e i suoi limiti*. Milan, 1940.

Nolte, E. "Diktatur." In W. Conze et al. (eds.), *Geschichtliche Grundbegriffe*. Vol. 1, 900–924. Stuttgart, 1972.

Norbrook, David. *Writing the English Republic: Poetry, Rhetoric, and Politics, 1627-1660*. New York, 1999.

Nörr, D. *Rechtskritik in der römischen Antike*. Munich, 1974.

North, Douglass C. *Institutions, Institutional Change and Economic Performance*. Cambridge, 1990.

North, Douglass C., J. J. Wallis, and Barry R. Weingast. *Violence and Social Orders: A Conceptual Framework for Interpreting Recorded Human History*. Cambridge, 2009.

North, Douglass C., and Barry R. Weingast. "Constitutions and Commitment: The Evolution of Institutions Governing Public Choice in Seventeenth-Century England." *The Journal of Economic History* 49, 4 (1989): 803–832.

North, John. "Politics and Aristocracy in the Roman Republic." *Classical Philology* 85, 4 (1990): 277–287.

Nussbaum, Martha C. "Duties of Justice, Duties of Material Aid: Cicero's Problematic Legacy." *Journal of Political Philosophy* 8, 2 (2000): 176–206.

Oakley, S. P. *Commentary on Livy, Books VI-X*. 4 vols. Oxford, 1997–2005.

Ober, Josiah. *Mass and Elite in Democratic Athens: Rhetoric, Ideology, and the Power of the People*. Princeton, 1989.

O'Daly, Gerard. *Augustine's* City of God: *A Reader's Guide*. Oxford, 2004.

Ogilvie, R. M. *A Commentary on Livy, Books 1-5*. Oxford, 1965.

Osmond, Patricia J. "'Princeps Historiae Romanae': Sallust in Renaissance Political Thought." *Memoirs of the American Academy in Rome* 40 (1995): 101–143.

Ostwald, Martin. *From Popular Sovereignty to the Sovereignty of Law*. Berkeley, 1986.

———. *Nomos and the Beginnings of the Athenian Democracy*. Oxford, 1969.

———. "Was there a Concept ἄγραφος νόμος in Classical Greece?" In Lee et al., *Exegesis and Argument*, 70–104.

Paine, Thomas. *The Rights of Man*. In Moncure Daniel Conway (ed.), *The Writings of Thomas Paine*. Vol. 2. New York-London, 1894.

Paleit, Edward. *War, Liberty, and Caesar: Responses to Lucan's 'Bellum Ciuile', ca. 1580-1650*. Oxford-New York, 2013.

Pani, Mario. *Il costituzionalismo di Roma antica*. Rome, 2010.

Parker, H. T. *The Cult of Antiquity and the French Revolutionaries*. New York, 1965 (orig. 1937).

Pennington, K. *The Prince and the Law, 1200-1600*. Berkeley, 1993.

Perelli, L. *Il movimento popolare nell'ultimo secolo della Repubblica*. Turin, 1982.

Perreau-Saussine, Emile. "Quentin Skinner in Context." *The Review of Politics* 69 (2007): 106–122.

Pettit, Philip. *On the People's Terms: A Republican Theory and Model of Democracy*. Cambridge, 2012.

———. *Republicanism. A Theory of Freedom and Government*. Oxford, 1997.

Pizzorni, R. M. *Il diritto naturale dalle origini a S. Tommaso d'Aquino*. Rome, 1978.

Plaumann, G. "Das sogenannte *senatus consultum ultimum*, die Quasidiktatur der späten römischen Republik." *Klio* 13 (1913): 321–386.

Plumpe, J. *Wesen und Wirkung der auctoritas maiorum bei Cicero*. Bochum, 1932.

Pocock, J. G. A. *The Machiavellian Moment: Florentine Political Thought and the Atlantic Political Tradition*. Princeton, 1975.

Podes, Stephan. "Die Krise der späten römischen Republik und Ciceros Rechtsphilosophie (de legibus): Bedingung der Möglichkeit zur Alternative?" *Archiv für Rechts- und Sozialphilosophie / Archives for Philosophy of Law and Social Philosophy* 77, 1 (1991): 84–94.

Podoksik, Efraim. "One Concept of Liberty: Towards Writing the History of a Political Concept." *Journal of the History of Ideas* 71, 2 (2010): 219–240.

Pollmann, K. et al. (eds.). *The Oxford Guide to the Historical Reception of Augustine*. Oxford, 2013.

Pomtow, H. "Delphische Neufunde V." *Klio* 17 (1921): 171–174.

Premerstein, Anton von. "Commentarii." *Paulys Realenzyklopädie der klassischen Altertumswissenschaft* 4.1 (1900): 726–759.

Ptolemy of Lucca. *On the Government of Rulers. De Regimine Principum*. With Portions Attributed to Thomas Aquinas. Translated and Introduced by James M. Blythe. Philadelphia, 1997.

Pufendorf, Samuel. *De iure naturae et gentium libri octo*. Frankfurt, 1704. English trans. by B. Kennett. *Of the Law of Nature and Nations: Eight Books*. London, 1729 (rpt. 2005).

Quaglioni, Diego. *I limiti della sovranità: il pensiero di J. Bodin nella cultura politica e giuridica dell'età moderna*. Padua, 1992.

———. "The Italian 'Readers' of Bodin, 17th-18th Centuries: The Italian 'Readers' out of Italy—Alberico Gentili (1552-1608)." In Lloyd, *Reception of Bodin*, 371–386.

———. *Politica e diritto nel trecento Italiano. Il "De tyranno" di Bartolo da Sassoferrato (1314-1357). Con l'edizione critica dei trattati "De Guelphis et Gebellinis," "De regimine civitatis" e "De tyranno."* Florence, 1983.

Quaritsch, H. *Staat und Souveränität*. Vol. 1. Frankfurt a.M., 1970.

Rahe, Paul. *Against Throne and Altar: Machiavelli and Political Theory in the English Republic*. Cambridge, 2008.

———. "The Book that Never Was: Montesquieu's *Considerations on the Romans* in Historical Context." *History of Political Thought* 26, 1 (2005): 43–89.

———. "Montesquieu's anti-Machiavellian Machiavellianism." *History of European Ideas* 37, 2 (2011): 128–136.

———. *Republics Ancient and Modern*. Chapel Hill, 1992.

———. *Republics Ancient and Modern*. Vol. 1: *The Ancient Régime in Classical Greece*. Chapel Hill, 1994.

———. "Review Nelson, *The Greek Tradition in Republican Thought*." *The Historical Journal* 49, 2 (2006): 635–642.

Raskolnikoff, Mouza. *Histoire romaine et critique historique dans l'Europe des Lumières: La naissance de l'hypercritique dans l'historiographie de la Rome antique*. Strasbourg, 1992.

Rathbone, D. W. "The Control and Exploitation of *ager publicus* in Italy under the Roman Republic." In Jean-Jacques Aubert (ed.), *Tâches publiques et entreprise privée dans le monde romain*, 135–178. Geneva, 2003.

Rawson, Elizabeth. "The Interpretation of Cicero's *De legibus*." *Aufstieg und Niedergang der römischen Welt* 1.4 (1973): 334–356.

———. "Review Girardet, *Die Ordnung der Welt*." *Journal of Roman Studies* 75 (1985): 310–311.

———. *The Spartan Tradition in European Thought*. New York, 1969.

Raz, Joseph. "Can There Be a Theory of Law?" In *The Blackwell Guide to the Philosophy of Law and Legal Theory*, ed. M. G. Golding and W. A. Edmundson. Oxford, 2005.

———. *Practical Reason and Norms*. Oxford, 1990.

Rech, H. "Mos maiorum. Wesen und Wirkung der Tradition in Rom." Diss. Marburg, 1936.

Reeve, C. D. C. *Philosopher-Kings: The Argument of Plato's Republic*. Princeton, 1988.

Reinhold, Meyer. *Classica Americana: The Greek and Roman Heritage in the United States*. Detroit, 1984.

Rhodes, P. J. "*Nomothesia* in Fourth-Century Athens." *Classical Quarterly* 35 (1985): 55–60.

Richard, Carl J. *The Founders and the Classics. Greece, Rome, and the American Enlightenment*. Cambridge, MA, 1994.

Richardson, John. *The Language of Empire: Rome and the Idea of Empire from the Third Century BC to the Second Century AD*. Cambridge-New York, 2008.

Richter, Melvin. *The Political Theory of Montesquieu*. Cambridge, 1977.

Ridley, Ronald T. "*Leges Agrariae*: Myths Ancient and Modern." *Classical Philology* 95, 4 (2000): 459–467.

———. "Pompey's Commands in the 50's: How Cumulative?" *Rheinisches Museum* 126 (1983): 136–148.

Riklin, Alois. *Machtteilung: Geschichte der Mischverfassung*. Darmstadt, 2006.

Riley, Patrick. "The (Non-) Legal Thought of Niccolò Machiavelli." In E. Pattaro et al. (eds.), *A Treatise of Legal Philosophy and General Jurisprudence*. Vol 9, *A History of the Philosophy of Law in the Civil Law World, 1600-1900*, 355–363. Dordrecht, 2009.

Rilinger, Rolf. "Die Ausbildung von Amtswechsel und Amtsfristen als Problem zwischen Machtbesitz und Machtgebrauch in der Mittleren Republik (342 bis 217 v. Chr.)." In T. Schmitt and A. Winterling (eds.), *Ordo und dignitas: Beiträge zur römischen Verfassungs- und Sozialgeschichte*, 11–76. Stuttgart, 2007 (= *Chiron* 8 [1978]: 247–312).

Robb, M. A. *Beyond Populares and Optimates: Political Language in the Late Republic*. Historia Einzelschriften 213. Stuttgart, 2010.

Roberts, Jennifer Tolbert. *Athens on Trial: The Antidemocratic Tradition in Western Thought*. Princeton, 1994.

Rodgers, Barbara S. "Catulus' Speech in Cassius Dio 36.31-36." *Greek, Roman, and Byzantine Studies* 48 (2008): 295–318.

Rödl, Bernd. *Das Senatus Consultum Ultimum und der Tod der Gracchen*. Bonn, 1969.

Roloff, H. *Maiores bei Cicero*. Göttingen, 1938.

Roselaar, Saskia T. *Public Land in the Roman Republic: A Social and Economic History of Ager Publicus in Italy, 396-89 BC*. Oxford, 2010.

Rossiter, C. L. *Constitutional Dictatorship. Crisis Government in the Modern Democracies*. New Brunswick, NJ, 2002 (orig. Princeton, 1948).

Rotondi, G. *Leges publicae populi Romani*. Hildesheim, 1966 (orig. Milan, 1912).

Rousseau, Jean-Jacques. "Du contrat social." In *Oeuvres complètes*. Vol. 3. Paris, 1964.

———. *The Social Contract and Other Later Political Writings*, ed. and trans. V. Gourevitch. Cambridge, 1997.

Rowe, Christopher. "The *Politicus* and Other Dialogues." In Rowe and Schofield, *Cambridge History*, 233–257.

Rowe, Christopher, and Malcolm Schofield (eds.). *The Cambridge History of Greek and Roman Political Thought*. Cambridge, 2000.

Salamonius, Marius. *Marii Salamonii De principatu libros septem*, rec. Marius d'Addio. Milan, 1955.

———. *Patritii Romani de principatu*. Paris, 1578.

Salmon, J. H. M. "Bodins politische Philosophie. Diskussion." In Horst Denzer (ed.), *Jean Bodin: Verhandlungen der internationalen Bodin-Tagung in München/ Proceedings of the International Conference on Bodin in Munich/Actes du colloque international Jean Bodin à Munich*, 461–487. Munich, 1973.

———. "The Legacy of Jean Bodin: Absolutism, Populism or Constitutionalism?" *History of Political Thought* 17 (1996): 500–522.

Santangelo, Federico. *Sulla, the Elites and the Empire: A Study of Roman Policies in Italy and the Greek East*. Leiden-Boston, 2007.

Sauer, Jochen. "Dichotomie in der Naturrechtskonzeption von Ciceros Schrift *De legibus*?" *Rheinisches Museum* 155 (2012): 65–84.

Schanbacher, Dietmar. "Ius und mos: Zum Verhältnis rechtlicher und sozialer Normen." In M. Braun et al. (eds.), *Moribus antiquis res stat Romana. Römische Werte und römische Literatur im 3. und 2. Jh. v. Chr.*, 353–371. Munich, 2000.

Schmitt, Carl. *Die Diktatur. Von den Anfängen des modernen Souveränitätsgedankens bis zum proletarischen Klassenkampf*. 3rd ed. Berlin, 1964.

Schofield, M. "Cicero's Definition of *Res Publica*." In J. G. F. Powell (ed.), *Cicero the Philosopher*, 63–83. Oxford, 1995.

———. "Cosmopolitanism, Imperialism and Justice in Cicero's *Republic* and *Laws*." *Journal of Intellectual History and Political Thought* 2.1 (2013): 5–34.

———. *Plato: Political Philosophy*. Oxford, 2006.

———. "Social and Political Thought." In Keimpe Algra et al. (eds.), *The Cambridge History of Hellenistic Philosophy*, 739–770. Cambridge, 2005.

Schwartzberg, Melissa. "Athenian Democracy and Legal Change." *The American Political Science Review* 98, 2 (2004): 311–325.

———. "Was the *Graphe Paranomon* a Form of Judicial Review?" *Cardozo Law Review* 34 (2013): 1049–1062.

Seager, Robin. *Pompey the Great: A Political Biography*. 2nd ed. Oxford, 2002.

———. "Sulla's Monarchy: Review Hurlet, *La dictature*." *Classical Review* 44, 2 (1994): 347–348.

Selden, John. *The Table Talk of John Selden*. With a Biographical Preface and Notes by S.W. Singer. 2nd ed. London, 1856.

Sellers, Mortimer N. S. *American Republicanism: Roman Ideology in the United States Constitution*. New York, 1994.

Shackleton Bailey, D. R. *Cicero's Letters to Atticus*. Vol. 4. Cambridge, 1968.

Shalev, Eran. *Rome Reborn on Western Shores: Historical Imagination and the Creation of the American Republic*. Charlottesville-London, 2009.

Shalhope, Robert E. "Republicanism and Early American Historiography." *The William and Mary Quarterly* 39, 2 (1982): 334–356.

———. "Toward a Republican Synthesis: The Emergence of an Understanding of Republicanism in American Historiography." *The William and Mary Quarterly* 29, 1 (1972): 49–80.

Sherk, R. K. *Rome and the Greek East to the Death of Augustus*. Cambridge, 1984.

Sherwin-White, A. N. "Review Bleicken, *Senatsgericht*." *Journal of Roman Studies* 53 (1963): 203–205.

Shklar, Judith. *Montesquieu*. Oxford, 1987.

———. "Montesquieu and the New Republicanism." In G. Bock, Q. Skinner, M. Viroli (eds.), *Machiavelli and Republicanism*, 265–279. Cambridge, 1990.

Sigonio, Carlo. *De antiquo iure civium Romanorum libri duo*. Venice, 1560.

———. *In Fastos Commentarius*. 2nd ed. Basel, 1559.

Simmonds, K. R. "The Gentili Manuscripts." *Zeitschrift der Savigny-Stiftung für Rechtsgeschichte, Romanistische Abteilung* 76 (1959): 534–552.

Skinner, Quentin. *The Foundations of Modern Political Thought*. 2 vols. Cambridge, 1978.

———. *Hobbes and Republican Liberty*. Cambridge, 2008.

———. "The Idea of Negative Liberty: Philosophical and Historical Perspectives." In Richard Rorty (ed.), *Philosophy in History: Essays in the Historiography of Philosophy*, 193–222. Cambridge, 1984.

———. *Liberty before Liberalism*. Cambridge, 1998.

———. *Machiavelli*. Oxford, 1981.

———. *Visions of Politics*. Vol. 3. Cambridge, 2002.

Smith, Adam. *The Theory of Moral Sentiments*, ed. D. D. Raphael and A. L. Macfie. Oxford, 1976.

Sonenscher, Michael. *Before the Deluge: Public Debt, Inequality, and the Intellectual Origins of the French Revolution*. Princeton, 2007.

Sordi, Marta. "Ottaviano patrono di Taranto nel 43 a. C." *Epigraphica* 31 (1969): 79–83.

———. "La sacrosanctitas tribunicia e la sovranità popolare in un discorso di Tiberio Gracco." In id. (ed.), *Religione e politica nel mondo antico*, 124–130. Pubblicazioni della Università Cattolica. Milan, 1981.

Spelman, John. *The Case of Our Affaires, in Law, Religion and Other Circumstances Briefly Examined, and Presented to the Conscience*. Oxford, 1643.

———. *Certain Considerations Upon the Duties Both of Prince and People*. Oxford, 1642.

Steinberger, Peter J. "Analysis and History of Political Thought." *The American Political Science Review* 103, 1 (2009): 135–146.

Stevenson, Tom. "Readings of Scipio's Dictatorship in Cicero's *De Re Publica* (6.12)." *Classical Quarterly* 55 (2005): 140–152.

St John, Henry, Viscount Bolingbroke. *A Dissertation upon Parties*. In *The Works of Lord Bolingbroke*. Vol. 2. Philadelphia, 1841.

Stock, Brian. *Augustine the Reader*. Cambridge, MA, 1996.

Stolleis, Michael. *Geschichte des öffentlichen Rechts in Deutschland*. Vol. 1, *Reichspublizistik und Policeywissenschaft 1600-1800*. 2nd ed. Munich, 2012.

———. *Staat und Staatsräson in der frühen Neuzeit*. Frankfurt a.M., 1990.

Stourzh, Gerald. *Alexander Hamilton and the Idea of Republican Government*. Stanford, 1970.

Straumann, Benjamin. "*Appetitus societatis* and *oikeiosis*: Hugo Grotius' Ciceronian Argument for Natural Law and Just War." *Grotiana* N.S. 24/25 (2003/2004): 41–66.

———. "The *Corpus iuris* as a Source of Law between Sovereigns in Alberico Gentili's Thought." In Kingsbury and Straumann, *The Roman Foundations*, 101–123.

———. "*Ius erat in armis*: The Roman and Spanish Empires and Their Discontents." *International Journal of the Classical Tradition* 13, 4 (2007): 597–607.

———. "Review Allély, *La déclaration d'*hostis *sous la République romaine*." *Klio* 96, 2 (2014): 364–367.

———. "Review Beck et al., *Consuls and* Res Publica." *Classical Review* 63 (2013): 174–178.

———. "Review Golden, *Crisis Management during the Roman Republic*." *Classical Philology* 110, 2 (2015): 168-173.

———. "Review Hammer, *Roman Political Thought and the Modern Theoretical Imagination*." *Perspectives on Politics* 8, 2 (2010): 660–662.

———. "Review Nippel, *Antike oder moderne Freiheit?*" *Bryn Mawr Classical Review* 2008.10.31.

———. *Roman Law in the State of Nature: The Classical Foundations of Hugo Grotius' Natural Law*. Cambridge, 2015.

Striker, Gisela. "Origins of the Concept of Natural Law." In id., *Essays on Hellenistic Epistemology and Ethics*, 209–220. Cambridge, 1996.

Stroh, Wilfried. "*De domo sua*: Legal Problem and Structure." In J. Powell and J. Paterson (eds.), *Cicero the Advocate*, 313–370. Oxford, 2004.

Sullivan, Vickie B. "Against the Despotism of a Republic: Montesquieu's Correction of Machiavelli in the Name of the Security of the Individual." *History of Political Thought* 27, 2 (2006): 263–289.

———. *Machiavelli, Hobbes, and the Formation of a Liberal Republicanism in England*. Cambridge, 2004.

———. "Walter Moyle's Machiavellianism, Declared and Otherwise, in *An Essay upon the Constitution of the Roman Government*." *History of European Ideas* 37, 2 (2011): 120–127.

Sundahl, Mark. "The Living Constitution of Ancient Athens: A Comparative Perspective on the Originalism Debate." *The John Marshall Law Review* 42 (2009): 463–504.

Syme, Ronald. *The Roman Revolution*. 2nd ed. Oxford, 1952.

Tatum, W. Jeffrey. *The Patrician Tribune: Publius Clodius Pulcher*. Chapel Hill-London, 1999.

Täubler, E. *Untersuchungen zur Geschichte des Decemvirats und der XII-Tafeln*. Berlin, 1921.

Taylor, C. C. W. "Plato's Totalitarianism." *Polis* 5 (1986): 4–29.

———. "Politics." In Jonathan Barnes (ed.), *The Cambridge Companion to Aristotle*, 233–258. Cambridge, 1995.

Testard, Maurice. *Saint Augustin et Cicéron*. 2 vols. Paris, 1958.

Thomas, Yan. *Mommsen et "l'Isolierung" du droit. Rome, l'Allemagne et l'État*. Paris, 1984.

Thommen, Lukas. *Das Volkstribunat der späten römischen Republik*. Stuttgart, 1989.

Thompson, C. Bradley. "John Adams's Machiavellian Moment." *The Review of Politics* 57, 3 (1995): 389–417.

Trenchard, John, and Thomas Gordon. *Cato's Letters, or Essays on Liberty, Civil and Religious, and Other Important Subjects*. 4 vols. in 2. Ed. and Annotated by Ronald Hamowy. Indianapolis, 1995.

Tuck, Richard. *Rights of War and Peace: Political Thought and the International Order from Grotius to Kant*. Oxford, 1999.

Turchetti, Mario. "'Despotism' and 'Tyranny': Unmasking a Tenacious Confusion." *European Journal of Political Theory* 7, 2 (2008): 159–182.

Ungern-Sternberg, Jürgen von. "Appians Blick auf Rom." In id., *Römische Studien*, 199–217.

———. "Die beiden Fragen des Titus Annius Luscus." In *Sodalitas. Festschrift A. Guarino*, 339–348. Naples, 1984 (=id. *Römische Studien*, 264–272).

———. "Das Dezemvirat im Spiegel der römischen Überlieferung." In K. A. Raaflaub (ed.), *Social Struggles in Archaic Rome. New Perspectives on the Conflict of the Orders*, 75–97. 2nd ed. Oxford, 2005 (=id. *Römische Studien*, 75–99, with additional notes).

———. "Die Legitimitätskrise der römischen Republik." *Historische Zeitschrift* 266 (1998): 607–624 (=id. *Römische Studien*, 390–404).

———. *Römische Studien*. Munich, 2006.

———. "Romulus-Bilder: Die Begründung der Republik im Mythos." In *Römische Studien*, 30–50.

———. *Untersuchungen zum spätrepublikanischen Notstandsrecht. Senatus consultum ultimum und hostis-Erklärung*. Munich, 1970.

———. "Das Verfahren gegen die Catilinarier oder: Der vermiedene Prozess." In U. Manthe and J. v. Ungern-Sternberg (eds.), *Grosse Prozesse in der römischen Antike*, 85–99, 204–206. Munich, 1997 (=id. *Römische Studien*, 341–357).

———. "Die Wahrnehmung des 'Ständekampfes' in der römischen Geschichtsschreibung." In W. Eder et al. (eds.), *Staat und Staatlichkeit in der frühen römischen Republik*, 92–102. Stuttgart, 1990.

Vander Waerdt, Paul. "Philosophical Influence on Roman Jurisprudence? The Case of Stoicism and Natural Law." *Aufstieg und Niedergang der römischen Welt* II.36.7 (1994): 4854–4856.

Van Kley, D. (ed.). *The French Idea of Freedom: The Old Regime and the Declaration of Rights in 1789*. Stanford, 1994.

Vázquez de Menchaca, Fernando. *Controversiarum illustrium aliarumque usu frequentium libri tres*, ed. F. Rodriguez Alcalde. Vol. 2. Valladolid, 1931.

Vervaet, Frederik J. *The High Command in the Roman Republic: The Principle of the summum imperium auspiciumque from 509 to 19 BCE*. Stuttgart, 2014.

———. "The *Lex Valeria* and Sulla's Empowerment as Dictator (82-79 BCE)." *Cahiers Glotz* 15 (2004): 37–84.

———. "Pompeius' Career from 79 to 70 BCE: Constitutional, Political and Historical Considerations." *Klio* 91 (2009): 406–434.

———. "The Praetorian Proconsuls of the Roman Republic (211-52 BCE). A Conditional Survey." *Chiron* 42 (2012): 45–96.

Viroli, Maurizio. *Machiavelli*. Oxford, 1998.

———. *Republicanism*. New York, 2002.

Vlastos, Gregory. *Studies in Greek Philosophy*. Vol. 2, *Socrates, Plato, and Their Tradition*, ed. Daniel W. Graham. Princeton, 1995.

Volkmann, H. *Sullas Marsch auf Rom*. Munich, 1958.

Walbank, F. W. "A Greek Looks at Rome: Polybius VI Revisited." In id., *Polybius, Rome and the Hellenistic World: Essays and Reflections*, 277–292. Cambridge, 2002.

———. *A Historical Commentary on Polybius*. 3 vols. Oxford, 1957-1979.

———. *Polybius*. Berkeley-Los Angeles, 1972.

Ward, Allen M. *Marcus Crassus and the Late Roman Republic*. Columbia, MO-London, 1977.

Warner, J. M., and J. T. Scott. "Sin City: Augustine and Machiavelli's Reordering of Rome." *The Journal of Politics* 73, 3 (2011): 857–871.

Watson, Alan. *Contract of Mandate in Roman Law*. Oxford, 1961.

Watson, Gerard. "The Natural Law and Stoicism." In *Problems in Stoicism*, ed. A. A. Long, 216–238. London, 1971.

Webster, Noah. *Examination into the Leading Principles of the Federal Constitution* [1787]. In Colleen A. Sheehan and Gary L. McDowell (eds.), *Friends of the Constitution: Writings of the "Other" Federalists 1787-1788*. Indianapolis, 1998.

Wegner, Michael. *Untersuchungen zu den lateinischen Begriffen socius und societas*. Göttingen, 1969.

Weithman, P. "Augustine's Political Philosophy." In E. Stump and N. Kretzmann (eds.), *The Cambridge Companion to Augustine*, 234–252. Cambridge, 2001.

West, D. A. "*Cernere erat*: The Shield of Aeneas." *Proceedings of the Virgil Society* 15 (1975-1976): 1–7.

White, Morton. *The Philosophy of the American Revolution*. New York, 1978.

Wieacker, Franz. *Römische Rechtsgeschichte, Erster Abschnitt: Einleitung, Quellenkunde, Frühzeit und Republik*. München, 1988.

Wiehn, E. *Die illegalen Heereskommanden in Rom bis auf Caesar*. Marburg, 1926.

Wilcken, Ulrich. "Zur Entwicklung der römischen Diktatur." *Abhandlungen der Preussischen Akademie der Wissenschaften zu Berlin, philosophisch-historische Klasse* 1 (1940): 3–32.

Williamson, C. *The Laws of the Roman People. Public Law in the Expansion and Decline of the Roman Republic*. Ann Arbor, 2005.

Wiltshire, Susan Ford. *Greece, Rome and the Bill of Rights*. Norman-London, 1992.

Winkler, Lorenz. *Salus. Vom Staatskult zur politischen Idee. Eine archäologische Untersuchung*. Heidelberg, 1995.

Winterer, Caroline. *The Culture of Classicism: Ancient Greece and Rome in American Intellectual Life 1780-1910*. New York, 2002.

Winterling, Aloys. "Dyarchie in der römischen Kaiserzeit. Vorschlag zur Wiederaufnahme der Diskussion." In Nippel and Seidensticker, *Theodor Mommsens langer Schatten*, 177–198.

Wirszubski, Chaim. *Libertas as a Political Idea at Rome during the Late Republic and Early Principate*. Cambridge, 1950.

Wiseman, T. P. *New Men in the Roman Senate 139 B.C. – A.D. 14*. Oxford, 1971.

———. "The Two-Headed State: How Romans Explained Civil War." In Brian W. Breed, Cynthia Damon, Andreola Rossi (eds.). *Citizens of Discord: Rome and Its Civil Wars*, 25–44. Oxford, 2010.

Witt, Ronald. "The Rebirth of the Concept of Republican Liberty in Italy." In A. Mohlo and J. A. Tedeschi (eds.), *Renaissance Studies in Honor of Hans Baron*, 173–199. Dekalb, 1971.

Wolff, H. J. *"Normenkontrolle" und Gesetzesbegriff in der attischen Demokratie*. Heidelberg, 1970.

Wood, Gordon. *The Creation of the American Republic, 1776-1787*. 2nd ed. Chapel Hill, 1998.

———. *The Idea of America: Reflections on the Birth of the United States*. New York, 2011.

———. "Interests and Disinterestedness in the Making of the Constitution." In id., *The Idea of America*, 127–169.

———. "The Legacy of Rome in the American Revolution." In id., *The Idea of America*, 57–79.

———. "The Origins of American Constitutionalism." In id., *The Idea of America*, 171–187.

———. *The Radicalism of the American Revolution*. New York, 1992.

———. "The Radicalism of Thomas Jefferson and Thomas Paine Considered." In id., *The Idea of America*, 213–228.

Wood, Neal. *Cicero's Social and Political Thought*. Berkeley, 1988.

Woodman, A. J., and R. H. Martin. *The Annals of Tacitus. Book 3*. Cambridge, 1996.

Wootton, David. "The True Origins of Republicanism: The Disciples of Baron and the Counter-Example of Venturi." In Manuela Albertone (ed.), *Il repubblicanesimo moderno: L'idea di repubblica nella riflessione storica di Franco Venturi*, 225–257. Naples, 2006.

Wright, Johnson Kent. *A Classical Republican in Eighteenth-Century France: The Political Thought of Mably*. Stanford, 1997.

———. "Montesquieuean Moments: The 'Spirit of the Laws' and Republicanism." *Proceedings of the Western Society for French History* 35 (2007): 149–169.

Yakobson, Alexander. *Elections and Electioneering in Rome. A Study in the Political System of the Late Republic*. Stuttgart, 1999.

———. "Review Flower, *Roman Republics*." *American Journal of Philology* 132 (2011): 153–156.

———. "Review Robb, *Beyond Populares*." *Scripta Classica Israelica* 31 (2012): 212–214.

Yunis, H. "Law, Politics, and the *Graphe Paranomon* in Fourth-Century Athens." *Greek, Roman, and Byzantine Studies* 29 (1988): 361–382.

Zecchini, Giuseppe. "Die staatstheoretische Debatte der caesarischen Zeit." In W. Schuller (ed.), *Politische Theorie und politische Praxis im Altertum*, 149–165. Darmstadt, 1998.

Zetzel, James E. G. (ed.). *Cicero: De Re Publica*. Selections, with Commentary. Cambridge, 1995.

———. (trans.). *Cicero: On the Commonwealth and On the Laws*. Cambridge, 1999.

———. "Natural Law and Poetic Justice: A Carneadean Debate in Cicero and Virgil." *Classical Philology* 91, 4 (1996): 297–319.

———. "Review Millar, *Roman Republic in Political Thought*." *Bryn Mawr Classical Review* 2002.05.31.

Zuckert, Michael P. *Natural Rights and the New Republicanism*. Princeton, 1998.

General Index

abrogation of laws, 45–46
absolutism, 8, 40, 41, 247, 256, 257, 259, 278, 286, 291, 293, 295, 305
Acton, John Emerich Edward Dalberg-Acton, 1st Baron, 3
Adams, John
  constitutional ideas of, 301, 340, 341
  constitutionality of late Roman Republic and, 19–20
  political thought of, 262, 331, 333–338, 339
  and Quinctius Cincinnatus, story of, 67n13
Adams, Samuel (Valerius Poplicola), 332–333
adiaphora proegmena (preferable indifferent things), 45
Aemilius Lepidus, Marcus, 86, 92, 132, 133, 309
aequitas. *See* justice
Aeschines, 226, 227
Africanus the Elder. *See* Cornelius Scipio Africanus, Publius
age limits of office
  for aedileship, 38, 83, 298
  for consulships, 40, 50, 105, 107
  extraordinary commands and, 104
ager publicus (public land), Gracchus' redistribution plan and, 124n23, 139, 141–144
agraphos nomos (unwritten law), 223–225
agrarian commissions, 64, 124, 141, 178, 263
agrarian crisis, Gracchi and, 124
agrarian laws, 111, 185
agrarian policies, of Gracchus (Tiberius), 16
agrarian reform, private property and, 139–142
Alcibiades, 221n105
alienability, of sovereignty, 288, 293
American Enlightenment, 334
American Revolution, 332
amour propre, 164n55
ancestral custom. See *mos maiorum*
ancient liberty, 3–4, 255
ancient republicanism. *See* classical republicanism
Ando, Clifford, 11
Andocides, 229
Annas, Julia
  on Aristotle's notions of nature, 211, 212
  Cicero, comparison with, 174n96
  on Cicero, 188
  on justice, 192
  on Plato, 195, 199–200, 201
Annius, Titus, 120
Annius Milo, Titus, 93n171, 166–167

annuity of offices, 41, 102, 104, 106, 108, 110, 128
anti-constitutionalism, 330. *See also* Machiavelli, Niccolò
anti-Federalists, 332nn136–137
Antipater of Tarsus, 188
Antonius, Marcus
  Cicero on, 99–100
  Cicero's war with, 56–57
  dictatorship, statute on, 64–65
  extraordinary commands of, 102, 103, 106
  Nedham on, 309
  Norbanus, defense of, 125
appeal, right of. See *provocatio*
Appian
  on Antonius' abolition of dictatorship, 64–65
  on dictatorship, 68, 74–75
  on election of Scipio Aemilianus to consulship, 39–43
  on government collapse (year 88), 33
  on *hostis* declaration, 96
  on land distribution, 140, 141, 143
  on *provocatio*, 71
  on Sulla, 80
Appius Claudius. *See* Claudius Crassus
Appuleius Saturninus, Lucius, 52n106, 89–90, 99, 127
Aratus of Sicyon, 187, 292
arcana imperii, 281n12
Arena, Valentina, 102n224, 132–133, 172n86
Arginusae affair, 10, 225, 233–234, 235, 236
Aristotle, 208–221
  Cicero, comparison with, 235
  constitution, concept of, 216–221
  Lintott on, 152–153
  political anthropology of, 209
  political theory of, vs. early modern political theory, 212–216
  rationalism of, 162
  Striker on, 222–223
Aristotle, views of
  on the good life, 208–209, 215–216
  on hierarchy of norms, 235
  on justice, 210
  on language, 209
  on money-making, 212
  on nature, 211–212
  on private property, 220–221
  on states and individuals, relationship of, 210
  on supreme state authority, 191–192
Armitage, David, 20
Asconius Pedianus, Quintus, 78, 108, 125–127, 167
Asmis, Elizabeth, 44–45, 171
assemblies, popular (*comitia*)
  Bodin on, 279–280
  comitia centuriata, 37, 47, 76
  comitia tributa, 47, 109, 121, 122, 125, 126, 308
  constitutional constraints on, 84, 119–129
  extraordinary commands bestowed by, 104, 105
  imperium of, 279
  Moyle on, 312–313
  as sovereign, Gracchan doctrine of, 295
  sovereignty of, 84, 119–129
  Sulla and, 81, 82
  T. Gracchus on, 16
Athens
  Athenian republicanism, 10
  Constant on, 3–4
  constitutional institutions of, 225–237
  courts of, 229–230
  graphe nomon me epitedeion theinai, 232–233
  graphe paranomon, as judicial review processes, 229–235

graphe paranomon, description of, 225–228
institutional reality of, 10
nomothesia, 231
nomothetai, establishment of, 228–232
Polybius on, 1, 174
positivist constitutionalism of, 234–235, 237
success of, 157
See also Greek constitutionalism
Atkins, E. M., 173n91, 179n112
Atkins, Jed
on balanced constitutions, 176
on Cicero, 149–150, 180, 185
on *De legibus*, 44–45, 178–180
on limits of reason in politics, 182
political theory, work on, 12
Polybius, comparison with Machiavelli, 153–154
on *Pro Sestio*, 168
on Scipio, 171–172, 174n96
Straumann vs., on Cicero's constitutional theories, 171–185, 173n92
Straumann vs., on Polybius, 154–155, 156–158
Atticus. *See* Pomponius Atticus, Titus
Aubrey, John, 275
auctoritas patrum, 23, 126n40
augurs (priests), 55, 182n121
Augustine
Adams, influence on, 335
Carneadean debate and, 261, 265, 266
Gentili, influence on, 273
Machiavelli and, 268–272
Montesquieu and, 325
Ptolemy of Lucca and, 249, 250, 252, 253, 255
on Roman empire, 266–267
on Romulus and Remus, 270
Virgil's influence on, 265n21, 268
See also Machiavelli, Niccolò
Augustus
Augustan order, 17, 117
extraordinary commands for, 297–298
Nedham on, 309
powers of, 115
See also Principate
auspices, constitutionality and, 126, 127, 137, 182n121
auxiliary class (in Plato's ideal state), 192–195
auxilium (tribunes' help to citizens against coercion), 120, 122

Badian, Ernst, 90n152
Bailyn, Bernard, 7, 341
balanced (well-tempered) constitution
as Cicero's preferred constitutional order, 174
existence of, 176
functions of, 179, 182
in Mably's political thought, 328
in Montesquieu's political thought, 320–321
necessity of justice for, 176
Polybius', 155, 156, 159
prudens as metaphor for, 175–176
reason and, 180
Scipio on, 173–174
balance of powers, 327, 333, 335–336, 337. *See also* checks and balances
Baldus de Ubaldis, 258, 259
Balot, Ryan, 12
Baron, Hans, 247, 258
Bartolus of Sassoferrato, 248, 258, 259
Bayle, Pierre, 268
Bellarmine, 315n48
beneficentia, 184n131
Berlin, Isaiah, 8, 269n51
Besold, Christoph, 281n12
bicameralism, 335–336, 338

bills of attainder (*privilegia*), 46, 135–138
Blackstone, William, 339
Bleicken, Jochen
  on *ius*, 54
  on republican constitution, 27
  Mommsen, critique of, 14–15
  on *mos maiorum*, 48–49
  on *nomothetai*, 228–229
  on Senate actions against Catilinarians, 98
  on the state, legal nature of, 15
Blythe, J. M., 255n48
Bobonich, Christopher, 206
bodies politic, Montesquieu on, 321
Bodin, Jean, 278–302
  Adams, influence on, 335
  constitutional framework of, 340, 341
  Hobbes, influence on, 306
  importance of, 19, 302
  Locke, comparison with, 319
  Machiavelli, comparison with, 307–308
  Moyle, comparison with, 313
  natural law in political thought of, 340
  on constitutional contract law and *ius-lex* distinction, 286–289
  on dictatorship, 73
  on extraordinary commands, 295–301
  on lordly vs. lawful rule, 289–295
  on Roman dictatorship, *provocatio,* and sovereignty, 280–286
  political thought of, 262
  Rousseau, comparison with, 325
  salus populi formula, use of, 306
  on sovereigns and sovereignty, 19–20, 306
Bolingbroke, Henry St John, Viscount, 35, 36, 262, 331
Botero, Giovanni, 306–307
Bringmann, Klaus, 87–88, 87n134
Brooke, Christopher, 275, 276n83
Bruni, Leonardo, 258
Brunt, P. A., 27, 28n10, 48n81, 101n212, 124n25
Brutus. *See* Iunius Brutus
Büchner, Karl, 174n96
Burckhardt, Jacob, 3
Burgess, Glenn, 305
Butler, Joseph, 336n159

Caecina Severus, Aulus, 60–61
Caelius Rufus, Marcus, 93n171
Caesar
  Adams on, 337
  on Catilinarians, execution of, 130–133, 135
  Cicero on, 54–55, 128–129, 186
  as dictator, 86–88, 249
  extraordinary powers of, 85–88, 103, 115–116
  Moyle on, 100
  Nedham on, 309
  Pompey, comparison with, 114
  public land, privatization of, 142n122
  SCU and, 91
Callicles (in Plato's *Gorgias*), 223, 224
cant-words, virtues as, 313, 315, 324
capital cases, Cicero on venue for, 46–47
Carbo, Gnaeus Papirius, 56–57
Carneades and Carneadean debate
  Christian writers on, 265–266
  Cicero on, 176–177, 188, 251
  Gentili's *War of the Romans* on, 272
  influence of, 261, 276–277
  as source for anti-constitutionalism, 260
  Zetzel on, 262
Cassius Longinus, Gaius, 105, 116
Catilina and Catilinarians
  Cicero's actions against, 94, 99, 284

Cicero's speeches on, 51, 59, 89–90, 92, 94, 99, 131–132
execution of, debate over constitutionality of, 129–130
Rousseau on, 326
Senate actions against, 98
use of *SCU* against, 92

Cato. *See* Trenchard, John, and Thomas Gordon
Cato, Marcus Porcius, 20, 61n144, 98, 113, 116n302, 133, 134, 250, 267
Catulus. *See* Lutatius Catulus
censors, Montesquieu on, 323
censorship, Cicero's reform of the, 182
checks and balances
Cicero's just balance, 174–175
Locke on, 318
Montesquieu on, 320, 321
Nedham on, 308
in Polybius and Cicero, 160
Polybius on, 151–152, 156

Christian virtue, pagan virtue vs., 268–272
Cicero, Marcus Tullius
actions violating right of appeal, 66
Adams, influence on, 334
Aristotle, comparison with, 235
Augustine on, 267
brutish state of nature of, 161–168
Cato (Trenchard and Gordon), comparison with, 316
constitutional theory of, 2, 20, 25, 168–190
exile of, 128, 135–136, 284
Gentili's references to, 272–273
Harrington, comparison with, 312
lex, use of term, 46
Mably, influence on, 328
moral and political psychology of, 161–162
natural law doctrine, 44–46, 168–189
Opimius and, 90n154
Polybius, comparison with, 160–161
Ptolemy of Lucca and, 254–255
SCU and, 88–89, 91, 93
written constitution of, 44–47
See also political authority, Cicero and legitimacy of

Cicero, Marcus Tullius, views of
on extraordinary commands, 104–105
on goodness, 53
on greatest good, 269
on *hostis* declarations, 99
on justice, 168–169, 184
on land redistribution, 143
on laws passed by force, 31–32
on own exile, 135–136
on property, 118–119, 142, 144, 164, 168–190
on *provocatio*, 77, 242
on reason, 164, 340
on Rullus, agrarian law of, 111–112
on Senate, powers of, 126
on the state, 167–168, 185
on state of nature, 163–166, 170
on Sulla, 56–57, 82–83, 85, 134–135

Cincinnatus. *See* Quinctius Cincinnatus, Lucius
Cinna. *See* Cornelius Cinna
citizens
Caesar on killing of, 133–134
declared as *hostes*, 95–97
as enemy combatants, 97–98
See also Roman People; subjects

civilization, Cicero on origins of, 163
civil justice, natural justice vs., 272–273
civil law (*ius civile*), relationship with natural law, 180–181
civil rights, 5, 6, 71, 83, 169
Civil War (England), constitutionalist ideas of, 304–305
civil wars (Rome), 23–25, 31, 54, 56–57, 78–79, 149

Clapmarius, Arnold, 281n12
classes, within Plato's ideal state, 192–199, 214–215
classical republicanism
 as concept, need for disassembling of, 11–12, 304
 Constant on, 3–4
 modern liberalism, dichotomy with, 6–10, 21
 Pocock on, 310
 problems of, 2–3
classics, influence on American Founders, 331–332nn136–137
Claudius Crassus, Appius, 66, 309, 336
Claudius Marcellus, Marcus, 87
Clodius Pulcher, Publius
 Cicero, actions against, 135–138, 284
 Cicero on, 99
 Cicero's arguments against, 113–114, 127, 129, 136–137
 murder of, 166, 167
 success of constitutional argument of, 98
Cloelius Siculus, Quintus, 69
coercion, 195, 199, 203–204, 221
Cola di Rienzo, 247
collegiality of offices, 50, 102, 104, 106, 108, 128
comfort, as end for political society, 333
Comité de salut public, 20, 329
comitia. *See* assemblies, popular
commands. See *imperia*
commerce
 Adams on, 336
 class divisions and, 195
 Constant on, 328, 329
 corruption of virtue through, 333
 Mably on, 327
 of Roman empire, 320n76, 324
 Scottish Enlightenment and, 330
commissions and commissioners, 282, 296–297, 298, 300–301
commonality of interest (utility (*utilitas*)), 164, 168, 170
commonwealth. See *res publica*
commonwealthmen (country Whigs). *See* Trenchard, John, and Thomas Gordon (Cato)
Commonwealth of Oceana (Harrington), 310, 311
community of interest, 170, 171, 318
Condorcet, Nicolas de, 3, 335n158
conflict (general), 195, 271n60
conflict, constitutional, 152–153, 160, 174n97
Congress (U.S.), enemy combatant declarations and, 97
consensus iuris, 170, 171, 172n88, 176, 178, 180, 276n85, 306, 312, 335
Considerations on the Causes of the Greatness of the Romans and Their Decline (Montesquieu), 140, 319, 322–323, 325
Constant, Benjamin
 on ancient liberty, 255
 on classical constitutional ideals, associations of, 6
 liberty, theories of, 3–4
 on Mably, 327, 328
 political thought of, 304, 328–329
 Rousseau and, 325
 Skinner on, 9
constituent powers, dictators as, 282
constitution (*politeia*)
 Aristotle's concept of, 216–221
 Cicero's written, 44–47
 descriptive concept of, 31, 150, 204, 218–219
 equilibrium of, Polybius on, 154–155
 normative concept of, 13, 18, 21, 151, 191
 politeia as, 204

See also balanced (well-tempered) constitution; conflict, constitutional; Roman constitution; *entries beginning "constitutional"*
constitution (U.S.), 332–333
constitution, Roman concept of, 27–62
constitution, working concept of, 34–39
constitutional conventions, 339
Constitutional Convention (U.S.), 329, 334, 337–338
constitutional crises, 118–145
- Cicero's solution for, 169
- crises of the late Republic as, 30–34
- private property in, 139–145
- right of appeal in, 129–139
- sovereignty of the people in, 119–129

constitutional equilibrium. *See* balanced (well-tempered) constitution
constitutional norms
- contract law as, 290
- *De legibus* as, 46
- entrenchment of, 301, 339
- importance of, 24
- *ius* as, 168
- *ius* as source of, 54–62
- *ius publicum* as, 91
- in jural conception of politics, 25
- lack of higher-order, as cause of Republic's fall, 149–150, 161
- *mos* as source of, 47–54
- natural law, relationship with, 166–167, 178, 179–180
- *salus populi* as, 183
- terms used for, 111
- *See also* emergencies and extraordinary powers

constitutional order
- Cicero on, 116, 151, 163–166
- importance of right of appeal and right to trial for, 138
- Livy on, 76–77
- Machiavelli on, 271–272
- Mill on, 24
- modern defining characteristics of, 33–34
- normative vs. descriptive concern with, 31
- Polybius', 157–159
- Polybius vs. Cicero on, 160
- Virgil on, 274
- *See also* Roman Republic, as constitutional order

continuation of office, 110, 308, 312
contio (informal assembly), 67–68
contractarianism, 173
contract law, 257–258, 286–289, 290
contracts (contractual obligations), 172–173, 283, 287, 293, 294–295
Contrat Social (Rousseau), 325–326
Coriolanus, 308
Cornelius, Gaius, 108
Cornelius Cinna, Lucius, 56, 57, 78, 123
Cornelius Lentulus, Lucius, 103
Cornelius Scipio Aemilianus, Publius
- Appian on election of, 39–40
- in Cicero's *Republic*, 150, 162, 168–171, 173–176, 178–179, 263
- election of, 50, 83
- on *populus*, definition of, 184

Cornelius Scipio Africanus, Publius, 38–39, 171
Cornelius Scipio Nasica, Publius, 52
Cornelius Sulla Felix, Lucius
- Cicero on, 56–57, 82–83, 186, 285, 291
- as dictator, nature of rule of, 74–75, 77–85, 123
- Dio on, 110
- Ferguson on, 331
- Gracchus (T.), comparison with, 122n17
- *hostis* declarations and, 96
- Marius, actions against, 96, 299
- Montesquieu on, 321
- Nedham on, 309

Cornelius Sulla Felix, Lucius (*Cont.*)
- *provocatio* and, 85, 134–135
- Rome, occupation of, 33
- as tyrant, 284–286
- unlawful laws against, 32–33
- use of *SCU* against, 92

Corpus iuris (codification of Roman law), 246, 273
corrective justice, distributive justice vs., 186
corruption, 29, 157, 308, 320
counter-majoritarian difficulty, 234
country Whigs. *See* Trenchard, John, and Thomas Gordon (Cato)
courts
- Athenian, 229–230
- permanent, 59–60
- *quaestio de vi*, 162
- *quaestio perpetua*, 59–60, 82
- Supreme Court (U.S.), 17–18

Crassus. *See* Licinius Crassus
crises, of late Roman Republic, as constitutional crises, 30–34
Cromartie, Alan, 304n4
Cromwell, Oliver, 310
crown lands, 293
Culleo, Q. Terentius, 136
cult of nature, 330
cupiditas gloriae (glory-seeking), 261, 264, 265, 267, 270
cura annonae (care of the grain supply), 115
cura (guardianship), 297
curatio (commissions), 296–297, 298
Curio, Gaius Scribonius, 116

d'Addio, Mario, 259n63
Damasippus. *See* Iunius Brutus Damasippus, Lucius
Dante Alighieri, 248
Davis, Charles Till, 247
debt relief, 66, 186
decemviri. *See* Ten Men
Decius Mus, Publius, 58
Déclaration des Droits de l'Homme et du Citoyen, 330
decrees (*psephismata*), 111, 222, 227, 228, 230
Defence of the Constitutions of Government of the United States of America (Adams), 334–336, 338
delegate conception of representation, 121–122
delegation of powers, 286–287
democracy
- Aristotle on, 216, 217
- Roman Republic as, 279–280
- subversion of, 228

Democritus, 154n17
Demosthenes, 109, 232, 233, 234, 235
depositum (contract of deposit), 281, 283, 286
De regimine principum (Ptolemy of Lucca), 247–255
Des droits et des devoirs du citoyen (Mably), 327
despotism
- Adams on, 337
- Bodin on, 289–290, 302
- Cicero on, 111
- despotic (seigneurial) rule, 289–290
- military, 19, 302, 330, 341
- Montesquieu on, 319
- Pompey's desire for, 111
- regal rule as, 248
- of the Ten Men, 243
- *See also* tyranny

Dialogue de Sylla et d'Eucrate (Montesquieu), 321n85
dictators and dictatorship
- Bodin on, 280–286
- *dictator legibus scribundis et rei publicae constituendae*, 70, 75, 81
- *dictatura sine provocatione*, 87

Hamilton on, 338, 338n176
Jefferson on, 338
Nedham on, 309
nomination of, 55, 80
Pomponius on, 243–244
provision of exceptional powers by, 64–74
Ptolemy of Lucca on, 249
Rousseau on, 325–326
separation of powers in, 80
Sulla and *decemviri* and, 74–88
term limits on, 246
Trenchard and Gordon on, 314
as tyranny, 69
Dictionary (Bayle), 268
Diderot, Denis, 325
Diogenes of Babylon, 188
Dionysius of Halicarnassus
anachronisms of, 241
Bodin, influence on, 280
on dictatorship, history of, 65, 68–69, 70
on Sulla, 74–75, 79–80
Discorsi (Machiavelli), 260, 311, 327
distributive justice, corrective justice vs., 186
dominium eminens (eminent domain), 278n1
Doutes proposés aux philosophes économistes (Mably), 328
dowry, Roman law of, 294
Drogula, Fred, 71
Drummond, A., 90–91, 130
due process, 98–99
Dyck, Andrew, 179n112

economics, neo-institutional, 12
Edelstein, Dan, 329–330
education
in Aristotle's ideal state, 209, 215
in Plato's ideal state, 195–196, 198–200, 202, 207
eisangeliai (impeachments for treason), 228
elections, of consuls, 54–55
Elements of Law (Hobbes), 305
Elster, Jon, 13
emergencies and extraordinary powers, 63–117
in bill on Pompey, 49–50
Bodin on, 286
Caesar and, 85–88
decemviri and, 75–77
dictatorships and, 64–74, 243–244
extraordinary commands, 100–117
hostis declarations, 95–100
overview, 63–64
Polybius on, 62
provocatio, conflict with, 245
senatus consultum ultimum and, 88–95
Sulla and, 74–75, 77–85
See also extraordinary commands and powers
eminent domain (*dominium eminens*), 278n1
emperors (in general), limitations to sovereignty of, 292
Emperors (of Roman State), 245–247, 256, 287–288. *See also* Principate (of Augustus)
empire of the legislator, 4, 8, 10
Enchiridion (Pomponius), 241, 242–245, 256–257, 279, 281
Encyclopédie (Diderot), 325
enemy combatants, 97–98. See also *hostes* (foreign enemies) and *hostis* declarations
England
Adams on, 335
Civil War, constitutionalist ideas of, 304–305
constitution of, 34–35
Roman Republic, similarities to, 320
U.S. constitutional traditions vs., 332
Whig tradition, 7

entrenchment
  clauses for, in Athenian enactments, 225n119
  constitutionality and, 18, 36
  of constitutional norms, 301, 339
  French Revolution and, 329
  jural conception of politics and, 25
  of last decrees, 59
  of *nomoi*, 232, 234, 235
Epicurus and Epicureanism, 163–164, 167, 210, 315
equilibrium, constitutional. *See* balanced (well-tempered) constitution
Essay on the Constitution of the Roman Government (Moyle), 100, 119, 312
Essays on the Law of Nature (Locke), 316
ethics
  Locke's books on, 316
  politics and, 25, 192, 208
  of rulers, Aristotle on, 218
  summum bonum and, 269
eudaemonia, 184, 207, 269, 310–311. *See also* virtue
Euryptolemus, 233–234, 235
euthunai (procedures to hold magistrates accountable), 228
Eutropius, Flavius, 248, 249
expertise, relationship to laws, 202–203
extraordinary commands and powers (*imperia extraordinaria*), 100–117
  Adams on, 337
  and fall of Roman Republic, 101
  Bodin on, 295–301
  examples of, 64, 102–103
  extraordinary constituent power, 83, 84–85, 87–88
  Harrington on, 311
  Machiavelli on, 270–271, 276n82
  Montesquieu on, 321–322
  Nedham on, 308, 309–310
  overview of, 101–102
  of Pompey, 105–113
  private citizens, bestowal of *imperia* on, 104–105
  prorogation vs. bestowal of *imperia*, 103–104
  See also emergencies and extraordinary powers
extra ordinem, Cicero's use of term, 114, 138

Fabius Maximus Rullianus, Q., 41–42, 72, 81n90, 86n126
Federal Convention. *See* Constitutional Convention
Federalist Papers, 19–20, 262, 331, 338
Federalists, 332nn136–137, 338, 340
Ferguson, Adam, 3, 140, 144
Ferrary, Jean-Louis, 175, 179n112
fides (faith), 187, 258
fiduciary obligation, 294, 318
Fifth Amendment, 99
Filmer, Robert, 293n58
Fink, Z. S., 310n29
Finley, Moses, 62
Flavius, Lucius, 125, 143
Florus, Lucius Annaeus, 143–144
Flower, Harriet, 96
Foisneau, Luc, 306, 307
force, 31–32, 166–167, 221n105. *See* also *vis*
Founders, American (Founding Fathers), 332, 333, 339
Fränkel, Max, 230n144
French Revolution, 262, 329, 339n124
Friedrich, Carl J., 254, 286
Fritz, Kurt von, 12
Fulvius Flaccus, Marcus, 89–90

Fulvius Flaccus, Q., 81n90
fundamenta rei publicae, 117n306, 186
Furet, François, 329
Furius Philus, Lucius, 156n27, 176, 177, 178, 180, 251
Fustel de Coulanges, Numa Denis, 3

Gabba, Emilio, 74
Gabinius, A., 106, 108–109, 125, 296n68
Gaius (jurist), 172
game theory, 154
Garnsey, Peter, 12
Gentili, Alberico, 19, 261, 255n45, 265n21, 272–277, 293
Girardet, Klaus, 44, 178–179, 180
Glaucon, 189–190, 260
glory
  Augustine on, as goal of the Republic, 249, 251, 253, 266–267
  Gentili on, 272–276
  glory-seeking, 261, 264, 265, 267, 270
  justice vs., Cicero on, 264
  Machiavelli on, 269, 272
  military, Montesquieu on, 324
  as pagan virtue, 261–268
good life, 208–209, 215–216, 219
Gordon, Thomas, 309, 314. *See also* Trenchard, John, and Thomas Gordon (Cato)
government
  "lordly" vs. constitutional, 289–295
  secrecy of, 281n12
  sovereignty vs., 278–279, 289–290, 293–294, 318
Gracchi and Gracchan crisis
  Appian on, 68
  Bodin on, 300
  Cicero on, 99
  lack of dictator during, 72
  land reforms, 139–144
  Montesquieu on, 323
  nature of, agrarian reforms and, 124
  Nedham on, 310
Gracchus, Gaius (Sempronius Gracchus, Gaius)
  ius provocationis and, 59, 73
  killing of, 58–59, 89, 92
  Mommsen on, 84
  Senate action against, 57
Gracchus, Tiberius (Sempronius Gracchus, Tiberius)
  agrarian legislation, 143
  Cicero on, 167, 263
  crisis of election of, 68
  disapproval of, 16
  friends of, actions against, 95n185
  killing of, 52
  land distribution commission of, 124, 178
  limits of popular power and, 119–123
  Octavius, actions against, 183, 300
graphe nomon me epitedeion theinai, 228, 230n143, 231, 232, 233n157, 234, 237
graphe paranomon, 10, 222, 225–232, 236, 237
greatest good (*summum bonum, telos*), 269, 270, 271, 317
Greek constitutionalism, 191–237
  Aristotle, 208–221
  Athens, constitutional institutions of, 225–237
  Caesar's rejection of, 130–131
  conclusions on, 236–237
  natural law, idea of, 222–223
  Plato, 192–208
  question of, 221–236
  unwritten law and, 223–225
Griffin, Miriam, 293
Grotius, Hugo, 19, 278n1, 328n118, 339
Grouchy, Nicolas de, 279

guardian class (in Plato's ideal state), 192–195, 197–199, 200
guardianship (*cura*), 294, 297
Guthrie, W. K. C., 224

habeas corpus, 97–98
Hamilton, Alexander, 337n172, 338, 339
happiness, 193, 194–195, 202, 206, 333. See also *eudaemonia*
Harrington, James
  on dictatorship, time limits and, 77n61
  and legal accountability, 311
  Nedham, comparison with, 308
  as neo-roman theorist, 8
  political thought of, 262, 310–312
  supposed liberal republicanism of, 304
Helvidius (James Madison), 338, 339
Hesiod, 224
Hexter, J. H., 7n20
hierarchy of norms. *See* norms, hierarchy of
higher-order norms. *See* norms, higher-order
higher-order rules, 258, 290
Hinard, François, 80, 135n87
Hobbes, Thomas
  Aristotle, comparison with, 213–214
  Carneadean debate and, 261
  on Cicero on property rights, 186–187
  classical republicanism and, 4
  on entrenched constitutional rules, 340
  influences on, 275, 305–306
  as link between Bodin and Montesquieu, 262, 301–302
  Machiavelli, comparison with, 271
  Polybius and, 161n48
  on *salus populi*, 301
  Skinner on, 8
  on the state, 307
  on state of nature, 276
  on taxation by lawful sovereigns, 293
Hoekstra, Kinch, 12
Hölkeskamp, Karl-Joachim, 14
Holmes, Stephen, 8
honestum (morally right), 188, 264, 269, 270n56
Hortensius, Quintus, 106
hostes (foreign enemies) and *hostis* declarations, 33, 89, 94–100, 132
human nature, 156–159, 180, 196–197, 199–201, 211–212
Hume, David
  Adams, influence on, 334
  on *graphe paranomon*, 225–226, 227, 236
  Madison, influence on, 339
  Montesquieu and, 331
  political thought of, 262
Hunton, Philip, 305n5
Hurlet, Frédéric, 80, 80n84
Hutcheson, Francis, 155

ideals, utopian vs. Polybian, 158–159
ideal state, 158, 192–199, 215. *See also* Kallipolis; Magnesia
impartial spectator, 155n19
imperia (commands)
  Bodin on, 280, 281, 297, 299
  of Caesar, 101
  of Cassius Longinus, 105
  Cicero on, 112, 263
  of consuls, 88, 174, 279
  of Cornelius Lentulus, 103
  of dictators, 71
  of Emperors, 257
  extraordinary powers as, 49
  imperium domi, 71
  imperium infinitum, 106
  imperium maius, 49
  imperium sine fine, 264

imperium sine provocatione, 72, 82
irregular, 6
of offices, 123
of the popular assembly, 279
of praetors, 55
private citizens, bestowal on, 78, 101, 103, 104, 105
pro-consular, 38
Salamonio on, 259
imperia extraordinaria. *See* extraordinary commands and powers
imperialism, Roman
constitutional rule spread by, 252
Gentili on, 272, 273–274
Ptolemy of Lucca on, 251
inchoate constitutionalism, 23–25, 63, 118, 324, 340. *See also* constitution, Roman concept of; constitutional crises; emergencies and extraordinary powers
indemnati (condemned without trial), 135
institutions
impact of decay of, 25
legal, 199, 316
life of, 15
relative power of, Polybius on, 151–152
intermediate actions (*kathekonta*), 44–45
irrationality, 153, 176, 179
irrational passions, 161, 180
irregular commands (*imperia*), 6. *See also* extraordinary commands and powers (*imperia extraordinaria*); *imperia* (commands)
Irwin, Terence, 197, 271
Isauricus. *See* Vatia Isauricus, Publius Servilius
Isidore of Seville, 249
Issacharoff, Samuel, 97n198
iteration of office, 41, 51, 87, 104, 106, 183n125, 308
Iunius Brutus, Lucius, 265n21
Iunius Brutus, Marcus, 42, 115, 116
Iunius Brutus Damasippus, Lucius, 133
iuris consensus. See *consensus iuris*
ius (constitutional law)
Cicero's use of term, 168
ius civile (civil law), relationship with natural law, 180–181
ius civile (positive legal norms), 188–189
ius gentium, 172, 180, 290
ius provocationis, 237
ius publicum, 91, 129–130
ius rei publicae (constitutional law of the Republic), 138
lex vs., 54, 112, 147, 286–289
property rights and, 186
settled standing laws as, 319
as source of constitutional norms, 54–62
See also constitutionalism; *leges* (laws, statutory laws)

Jacobinism, 327, 329
Jaucourt, Louis de, 325
Jefferson, Thomas, 330, 338–339
Jehne, Martin, 14
judicial review, 34, 229–230, 231–235
Julian (jurist), 246
jural conception of politics, 25
justice (*iustitia, aequitas*)
Aristotle on, 210, 213
Cicero on, 168–169, 184, 263, 264
civil vs. natural, 272–273
coercion and, 203–204
consequences of, 194
distributive vs. corrective, 186
importance to *res publica*, 176
natural justice, 151, 178, 222, 272–273

justice (*iustitia, aequitas*) (*Cont.*)
natural law and, 189
norms of, vs. positive legal norms, 188–189
Plato on, 192–193, 196, 201
Plato on, critiques of, 193–194
as political, 210, 213
political justice, liberal views of, 196–197
Polybius on, 154, 155, 157, 159
as upholding of property rights, 189
zeal for, 250

Kallipolis, 159, 192, 196, 198–199, 200, 207
Kaster, Robert, 163
katalusis tou demou (subversion of democracy), 228
katorthomata (perfectly appropriate actions), 44–45
Keaveney, Arthur, 80
Keyes, Clinton Walker, 183
killings
of citizens, 91–92, 95–96, 133–134
of Gracchus (C.), 58–59, 89
of Gracchus (T.), 52
kingship (*regnum,* monarchy)
Bodin on, 288
constitutional rule against, 42–43
constraints on, 305
decemviri as, 76
Hobbes on, 307
liberty in, 8–9
"lordly" vs. constitutional government, 289–295
Montesquieu on, 322
odium regni, 64
Polybius on, 155
Ptolemy of Lucca on, 253–254
Roman monarchy, 173–174
See also sovereigns
Kraut, Richard, 235
Kristeller, Paul Oskar, 258
Kunkel, W., 72n33, 81–82, 81n92

Labienus, Titus, 94
Lactantius, 261, 265–266
Laelius, Gaius, 169, 176–178, 180, 251, 262
land
demarcation of public vs. private, 141
distribution of, 111, 124
Gracchan land reform program, 124, 139–144, 178, 263
Rullus' agrarian law on sale of, 112
Lanni, Adriaan, 228n133, 229n138, 230n144, 233, 234
Larcius Flavus (Rufus), Titus, 69
La Rochefoucauld, François, duc de, 335n158
Last, Hugh, 88–89
last decree. See *senatus consultum ultimum*
late Roman Republic
Adams and constitutionality of, 19–20
Bodin on constitutional history of, 294
importance of intellectual history of, 341
inchoate constitutionalism in, 23–25, 63, 118, 324
nature of crisis of, 18, 30–34, 79
as state of nature, 100, 150
See also emergencies and extraordinary powers
Latini, Brunetto, 248
law of contracts. *See* contract law
law of nature. *See* natural law
laws. See *leges*
Laws (*De legibus,* Cicero)
Atkins on, 149

constitutional norms in, 169
constitutional proposal in, 162
on consulship, 43
on contracts, 173
dispute over laws in, 178–179
Mably, influence on, 328
on magistrates, 312
on *mos*, 52–53
natural law and, 44–47, 161, 172
natural law constitutionalism of, 129
on natural law doctrine, 223
Ptolemy of Lucca and, 252, 253
on *salus populi*, 301
terminology in, 116
Lee, Daniel, 278, 287
legalis iustitia, 252
legalized murder, 83n107
leges (laws, statutory laws)
Cicero on, 46, 116
expertise, relationship to, 202–203
ius vs., 54, 112, 147, 286–289
leges agrariae, 140
leges annales, 110
leges sacratae, 122n14, 137, 284n22
lex regia, 256–257, 259, 288–289
lex repetundarum, 73
passed by force, question of basis for annulment of, 31–32
People's assemblies as source of, 134
in Plato's ideal state, 200
property rights and, 186
unwritten law, 223–225
See also constitutional norms; *ius; nomoi*
leges (laws), named
leges Aelia et Fufia, 126n39
leges Liviae (Livian laws), 127
leges Porciae, 130, 131
lex Antonia, 64–65
lex Caecilia Didia, 126, 127
lex Clodia, 138
lex Cornelia de sicariis, 134
lex de imperio Vespasiani, 247, 257, 280, 289
lex Gabinia, 101n212, 297
lex Hirtia, 87
lex Hortensia, 245, 279
lex Licinia (Licinian law), 140, 141
lex Manilia, 105, 106, 297
lex Plautia de vi, 162
lex Pompeia de vi, 166
lex Valeria, 80, 82, 284–285, 286
lex Vatinia, 128
legibus solutus, 246–247, 256, 257, 259, 286, 291, 295. *See also* absolutism
legislation
abrogation of earlier conflicting, 37
ius vs., 60–61
legislative procedure (*nomothesia*), 228, 231–232, 236
Cicero's concept of *lex* vs., 46
natural law vs., 44
voiding of, 125–129
See also *leges*
Lepidus. *See* Aemilius Lepidus
Leviathan (Hobbes), 8–9, 213, 275
lex. See *leges*
liberalism
liberal constitutionalism, 4
liberal republicanism, 304
republicanism vs., in political thought of American Revolution, 331–332
rights-based theory underlying, 201
liberty
ancient vs. modern, 3–4
constitutional safeguards and, 9–10
Hobbes on, 8–9
nature of, 323
of the People, dictatorship vs., 71
preservation of, Polybius on, 156
as right of appeal, 70

"Liberty of the Ancients Compared with that of the Moderns" (Constant), 3, 6
Licinianus, Granius, 140, 141
Licinius Crassus, Marcus, 103
Linderski, Jerzy, 20
Lintott, Andrew
  on Aristotle, 152–153
  on dictatorship and *provocatio*, 72
  on Gracchi, actions against, 96n185
  on mixed constitution, 151
  on republican constitution, 27
  on tyranny, characteristics of, 112n279
Lipsius, Justus, 276n83
Livy
  anachronisms of, 241
  authority of the People, privileging of, 139
  on Camillus, 71
  Cato (Trenchard and Gordon), comparison with, 314
  on constitutional order, components of, 76–77
  on *decemviri*, breach of time limit by, 76
  on dictatorship, history of, 65–68, 70–72
  on Fabius Maximus Rullianus, election of, 41–42
  on Iunius Brutus, 42
  on Licinian agrarian law, 140
  Livian laws, 127
  on Manlius, 337
  on popular assemblies, power of, 37, 119
  on *provocatio*, 242
  on Roman Republic, fall of, 2
  on Scipio, election of, 38–39
  on *SCU*, 93, 94–95
Locke, John
  Cato (Trenchard and Gordon), comparison with, 316
  Cicero, knowledge of, 316–317
  doctrine of the prerogative, 254
  on entrenched constitutional rules, 340
  on property rights in state of nature, 187
  on sovereignty vs. administration, 318
  on tacit consent, 339
Long, Anthony, 317
"lordly" vs. constitutional government, 289–295
Lovejoy, Arthur O., 20n66, 311n34
Lucretius, 164, 167
Lutatius Catulus, Quintus (father), 50–51
Lutatius Catulus, Quintus (son), 49–51, 106, 109, 133
luxury, 250, 253, 261, 267, 303, 325, 327, 330, 336, 340
Lycurgus, 156, 158, 173–174

Mably, Gabriel Bonnot de, 301, 327–329
Machiavelli, Niccolò, 260–277
  Augustine and, 266
  Bodin, comparison with, 307–308
  conclusions on, 276–277
  Gentili vs., 272–276
  glory, pagan virtue of, 261–268
  Harrington, comparison with, 311
  Hobbes, comparison with, 276
  Nedham, comparison with, 308
  as neo-roman theorist, 8
  pagan vs. Christian virtue and, 268–272
  Polybius, comparison with, 153–154
Machiavelli, Niccolò, views of
  on agrarian laws, 144
  on Brutus, 265n21
  on peasants, 140
  on Roman Republic, fall of, 77n61
  on Roman Republic, institutions of, 11
  on the state, 307

Mackie, J. L., 173n91
MacMullen, Ramsay, 245n9
Madison, James (Helvidius), 262, 338, 339
Maelius, Spurius, 66–67, 68, 167, 308, 314
magistrates and magistracies
  Aristotle on, 216–217
  Bodin on, 282, 296
  Cicero on, 46–47, 312
  exercise of sovereignty through, 300–301
  Harrington on, 311–312
  Montesquieu on, 321
  power of, vs. Roman People, 123
  sovereigns and, 287
Magna Carta, 7n20
Magnesia (city in Plato's *Laws*), 204–206
mandate (*mandatum*), 257, 286
Mandeville, Bernard, 336n159
Manilius, Gaius, 49, 108
Manlius Capitolinus, Marcus, 71, 92, 95, 337
Manlius Capitolinus, Publius, 70–71
Manuwald, Gesine, 57, 297
Marcius Philippus, Lucius, 132, 144–145, 185
Marius, Gaius
  Cicero on, 50–51, 56, 57, 78, 90
  command against Mithridates, 32–33
  consulship as extraordinary power, 102, 106, 110, 123
  exile of, 96n187
  Moyle on, 100
  Nedham on, 309
  Sulla and, 77–78, 79, 299
  Sulpicius and, 79, 90
Marshall, John, 316
Marsilius of Padua, 248, 258
Massachusetts, Constitution of the Commonwealth of (1780), 333–334, 336
Massachusetts Circular Letter, 332–333
McDonald, Forrest, 333
McIlwain, Charles H., 191
Meier, Christian, 27, 85, 123
Messalla Rufus, Marcus Valerius, 55
Metellus Nepos, Quintus, 91n158, 92, 93n170
Methodus ad facilem historiarum cognitionem (Bodin), 278, 279, 280
Meyer, Eduard, 87
Millar, Fergus, 5, 12, 14, 48n81, 279n6
Mill, John Stuart, 24
Milo. *See* Annius Milo
Milton, John, 5
Mitchell, T. N., 88
Mithridates
  Marius and war against, 299
  Pompey's extraordinary command against, 49, 105, 107, 109, 110n270, 114, 297
  transfer of command against, 32, 79, 123
Mitsis, Phillip, 316–317
mixed constitution (mixed government)
  Atkins on Polybius on, 154
  Bodin on, 279
  Cicero on, 174
  Harrington and, 310n29
  Lintott on Polybius and Cicero on, 151
  of Lycurgus and Roman monarchy, 173–174
  Montesquieu on, 320, 321n83
  Polybius on, 152
  separation of powers and, 327
  Walbank on terminology of, 152n8
Moatti, Claudia, 18, 164n58, 179n112, 179n116
modern liberalism, classical republicanism, dichotomy with, 6–10, 21
modern liberty, ancient liberty vs., 3–4

Mommsen, Theodor
  on Caesar, 86n126, 101
  on dictators, 84–85, 282
  influence of, 14
  on Principate, 101
  on *SCU*, 88
  sources for, 84–85n117
  on statutes, annulment of, 127–128
  supposed anachronism of, 15–16
monarchy. *See* kingship
Montagnards (the Mountain), 20, 329–330
Montesquieu, Charles-Louis de Secondat, Baron de
  on agrarian laws, 144
  constitutional framework of, 340, 341
  constitutionality of late Roman Republic and, 20
  Founders, as bridge between Bodin and, 303–304
  Founders, comparison with, 332
  Founders, influence on, 334
  framework for constitutional ideas of, 301
  natural law in political thought of, 340
  political thought of, 262, 319–325
  on private property, distribution of, 140
  Rousseau's critique of, 326
  Scottish Enlightenment and, 330, 331
moral sentimentalism, 154
More, Thomas, 8
Morstein-Marx, Robert, 12, 78
mos maiorum (ancestral custom), 15, 47–54, 90, 91, 130, 264
Mossé, Claude, 339n124
motivation, Plato on problem of, 205
the Mountain (Montagnards), 20, 329–330
Moyle, Walter, 100, 119, 301, 312–313
Moyn, Samuel, 319n71
Mucius Scaevola, Publius, 125, 126

Nagel, Thomas, 158, 160, 340
National Assembly, proponents of virtue in, 262
natural justice, 151, 178, 222, 272–273
natural law
  Bodin on, 291
  Cicero on, 53, 168–190, 251, 265
  Cicero's code of norms as, 44–47
  civil law, relationship with, 180–181
  constitutional norms, relationship with, 166–167, 178, 179–180
  idea of, in Greek political theory, 222–223
  iuris consensus and, 176
  ius gentium as, 172
  justice and, 189
  as limitation to sovereignty, 292
  Montagnards', 329–330
  mos and *lex* under, 52
  natural justice vs., 222–223
  norms of, 164
  Philus on, 176–178
  Ptolemy of Lucca on, 254
  Salamonio on, 259
  salus populi as, 314
  as validation for constitutional order, 340
  See also state of nature
natural rights, 168–190
natural state. *See* state of nature
nature (*phusis*), 211–212, 222, 223. *See also* state of nature
Nedham, Marchamont, 8, 304, 308–310, 337n168
Nelson, Eric, 3, 192, 320n76, 338n177
neo-Roman theorists, Skinner on, 8–9. *See also* Machiavelli, Niccolò
Neville, Henry, 8

Newman, W. L., 210, 221
Nicolet, Claude, 12
Nippel, Wilfried, 12, 27, 152, 166, 307n18
nomoi (laws)
  Aristotle on, 218–220
  description of, 224
  Dio's use of term, 111
  entrenchment of, 232, 234, 235
  nomon me epitedeion theinai, 228, 234
  nomothesia (procedure of legislation), 228, 231–232, 236
  nomothetai (legislators), 228–229, 231
  phusis, distinction from, 222, 223
  psephismata, comparison with, 228, 230
  See also *ius* (constitutional law); *leges* (laws, statutory laws)
non-domination, 9n28, 275n79
Norbanus Balbo, Gaius, 125
norms, hierarchy of
  in Athenian legislation, 228, 230, 234
  Cicero's constitutional norms vs. legislation, 181–182
  entrenchment and, 36
  of natural law vs. positive legal rules, 188–189
  Pomponius on, 244–245
norms, higher-order
  existence of, in late republican Rome, 40
  extraordinary commands as violation of, 110
  importance of, 19
  lack of, as cause of Republic's fall, 149–150
  legislation vs., 181–182
  need for, 144
  process of searching for, 303
  rule of reason in, 162
  settled standing laws as, 319
Nozick, Robert, 185–186
Ober, Josiah, 12, 229n138
Observations sur le gouvernement et les lois des Etats-Unis d'Amérique (Mably), 328
Observations sur les Grecs (Mably), 327
Observations sur les Romains (Mably), 327
Oceana, Commonwealth of (Harrington), 310, 311
Octavian. *See* Augustus
Octavius, Gnaeus, 56, 57
Octavius, Marcus, 119–123, 183, 300
Octavius Rufus, Gaius, 309
odium regni (hatred of kingship), 64
offices
  annuity of, 41, 102, 104, 106, 108, 110, 128
  collegiality of, 50, 102, 104, 106, 108, 128
  commissions vs., 296, 298
  continuation and iteration of, 308, 310, 312
  See also iteration; term limits; time limits; *specific offices*
"Of the Ends of Political Society and Government" (Locke), 317
oikeiosis, 164, 184
oligarchies, 216, 217, 227–228, 231
Olynthians, 232
On Duties (*De officiis,* Cicero)
  Aratus in, 187
  on fall of the Roman Republic, 150
  Gentili's references to, 273
  on glory vs. justice, 264
  hierarchy of norms in, 188–189
  Locke's knowledge of, 316–317
  on natural justice, 47
  on natural law, 180–181
  Ptolemy of Lucca and, 252, 253
  on purpose of the state, 184–186
  Republic and *De legibus,* relationship to, 185n137

Opimius, Lucius
  Gracchus, killing of, 73
  SCU and, 89, 90, 91
  trial and acquittal of, 57–60, 129
  Valerius, comparison with, 66
optimates, 132–133
order, passion for, 324
ostracism, 235
Ostwald, Martin, 223–224

pacification, 264, 274, 277
pagan virtue, 260, 261–268, 268–272
Paine, Thomas, 34
Panaetius, 184
Papirius Cursor, Lucius, 72
Parker, Henry, 305, 305n5
partnership (*societas*), 171–172, 258
Patritii Romani de principatu libri VI (Salamonio), 256
Peachin, Michael, 117
Pennsylvania
  constitution of, 329, 335
people (*populus*)
  Hobbes on, 307
  Montesquieu on power of, 323
  in political society, 170, 184
  sovereigns, relationship to, 305–306
  sovereignty of, 119–129
  See also assemblies, popular; Roman People; *entries beginning "popular"*
People of Rome (*populus Romanus*). *See* assemblies, popular; Roman People
perfectly appropriate actions (*katorthomata*), 44–45
Peripatetics, 161–162, 182, 184
permanent court (*quaestio perpetua*), 59–60
Pettit, Philip, 3, 9n28, 10–11, 275n79
Philadelphia Convention (1787). *See* Constitutional Convention
Philippus (Lucius Marcius Philippus), 132, 144–145, 185
philosopher-kings, 198
Philus. *See* Furius Philus, Lucius
Pibrac, Guy du Faur, seigneur de, 306–307
Pildes, Richard H., 97n198
Pindar, 224
pirates, as reason for Pompey's extraordinary commands, 110n270, 114, 123, 295–296, 297
Plato, 192–208
  on citizens and states, order of priority of, 206–208
  on happiness, 206
  ideal state of, 158, 192–199
  on justice, critiques of, 193–194
  lack of constitutional concept in, 206, 208
  on lawfulness, 204
  on motivation, problem of, 205
  political theory of, basis for, 196
  rationalism of, 161–162
  Striker on, 222–223
  on women's equality, 200–201
Platonic-Aristotelian framework, 153, 156, 157
Plautus, 49
Plutarch
  anachronisms of, 241
  on Cicero, 133
  Gracchus (T.), biography of, 119–120, 123, 126
  on land distribution, 124
  on Opimius, 73–74
  on Pompey, 109
  on Sulla, 80
Pocock, J. G. A., 7, 304, 310
politeia (polity), 191–192, 204, 218n97, 219–220. *See also* constitution(s)
politeuma (highest magistracy), 217, 219

political authority, Cicero and legitimacy of, 149–190
  overview, 149–151
  Polybius' constitutional equilibrium, 151–161
  private property and natural rights, 168–190
  rule of reason, 161–168
political order, 13, 20, 34, 154–156, 161, 185–186, 198–199, 234, 294, 307, 311, 326
Polybius
  Atkins' vs. Straumann's views of, 154–155
  Cicero, comparison with, 160–161, 167, 173n92, 174
  constitutional equilibrium of, 151–161
  constitutional order, basis for, 155
  Machiavelli, comparison with, 153–154
  pessimism, 6
  political thought of, 262
  rationalism of, 161n48, 162
  terminology of, 152
Polybius, views of
  on checks and balances, 182
  on dictatorship, 73
  on human nature, 156–159
  on justice, 154
  on liberty, preservation of, 156
  on Roman constitutionalism, 11n32, 28
  on Roman Republic, institutions of, 11
  on states, origins and purpose of, 154–155
pomerium (boundary of Rome), 115, 130n60
Pompey (Pompeius Magnus, Gnaeus)
  Cicero on, 54, 112–113, 167
  as dictator, possibility of, 86
  dispute over command of, 49–51
  extraordinary commands of, 64, 102–103, 105–113, 123, 295–296
  Moyle on, 100
  Nedham on, 309
  as proconsul, 93n171
  sole consulship of, 315
Pomponius, Sextus (jurist), 19, 241–247, 279
Pomponius Atticus, Titus, 54–55, 56, 114, 135, 136, 181
Pontiffs (pontifices) college of, 113–116, 136–139
Poplicola, Valerius (Samuel Adams), 332–333
popular assemblies. *See* assemblies, popular (*comitia*)
populares-optimates dichotomy, 48, 57, 134
popularis interpretation of constitution, 133, 312
popular legislation, dictatorships and, 88
popular sovereignty, 244, 246, 278–280, 282, 291
positivism
  positive legal norms (*ius civile*), 188–189
  positivist constitutionalism, 234–235, 237
power
  absolute, 112, 305, 318–319
  balance of powers, 327, 333, 335–336, 337
  Cicero on, 161
  delegation of, 286–287
  of institutions, 151–152, 153n10
  presidential, 338–339
  question of distribution of, 118
  See also sovereignty
precarium (temporary land tenure), 142, 283, 287, 297
pre-political condition, 166–167. *See also* state of nature

pre-political rights, 319, 327, 328
prerogative, Locke's theory of, 254, 318
presidential power, 338–339
Price, Richard, 337–338
primitivism, 212
Principate (of Augustus)
  Caesar's monarchy vs., 87
  on causal forces undermining the Republic, 242
  as extraordinary command, 101
  Mommsen on, 84, 101
  Pomponius and, 244, 245
  provocatio during, 284
  on state's legal nature, 15
private property, 139–145
  Cicero on, 139, 168–190, 317
  Clodius and, 167
  confiscation of, 220–221
  issue of, in constitutional crises, 118–119
  as limit to sovereignty, 289–290, 292, 294
  Locke on, 317
  Mably on, 327
  in Plato's ideal city, 198
  as pre-political, 165, 184
  private property rights, 172–173
  in state of nature, 164–165
privati (private citizens), bestowal of *imperia* on, 78, 101, 103, 104–105
privilegia (bills of attainder), 46, 135–138
producer class (in Plato's ideal state), 192–195, 197–198, 200
property rights
  justice as upholding of, 189
  pre-political, 185, 317
  private property rights, 172–173
  protection of, 186–187, 336
  See also private property
prorogation, 103, 110–111
pro salute patriae (for the public safety), 58, 60
proscriptions, 80, 82, 83, 123, 132, 133–135, 137, 138, 142n122, 186, 284, 285, 309, 321
Protectorate, 310
provocatio (right of appeal)
  Appius Claudius on, 66
  Bodin on, 279–286
  Caesar on Gracchus (C.) and, 59
  Cicero on Sulla's abolition of, 85
  in constitutional crises, 129–139
  consuls and, 183
  dictatorship and, 65, 68, 70–72, 283
  importance of, 77, 118, 174–175
  as limit on consuls, 246
  Maelius' appeal to, 67
  Pomponius on, 244
  senatus consultum ultimum and, 57–58
  source of validity of, 237
  sovereignty and, 242
  under Sulla, 82, 134
  Valerius Publicola and, 331
  See also *senatus consultum ultimum*
prudence
  Cicero on, 108, 188, 340
  Hobbes on, 271, 276
  Hume on, 226
  of rulers, 253
prudens, 175–176, 179
Prynne, William, 305n5
Ptolemy of Lucca, 247–255, 256, 258
public land (*ager publicus*), Gracchus' redistribution plan and, 124n23, 139, 141–144
Publius (*Federalist Papers*), 331, 339
Pufendorf, Samuel, 339
Punic Wars, 104–105, 331
punishment, natural right of, 314

quaestio de vi (jury court on public violence), 162
quaestio perpetua (permanent court), 59–60, 82
querelle des anciens et des modernes, 4, 327, 332
Quinctius Cincinnatus, Lucius, 67–68, 314
Quinctius Flamininus, Titus, 67

Rabirius, Gaius, 59, 91, 93–94
ragion di stato tradition, 306–307
Rahe, Paul, 4–5, 6, 7, 12, 320
raison d'état. *See* reason of state
rationalism, 161–162. *See also* reason
Rawls, John, 194
Rawson, Elizabeth, 12
reason
  application to social life, 154–155
  in balanced constitution, 175n102
  Cicero on, 164, 180, 340
  constitutional norms and, 180
  in individual justice, 193
  rule of, Cicero on, 161–168
  See also rationalism; right reason
reason of state
  Foisneau on Bodin and Hobbes on, 306
  Friedrich on, 254
  Hobbes on, 276
  Roman support for, 261
  theories of sovereignty vs., 307–308
recta ratio. *See* right reason
rectors, 161, 175, 253
redistribution
  of public land, 124n23, 139, 141, 142, 143, 144
  as violation of constitutional norms, 186
Reeve, C. D. C., 198
reficere (reelection), 103
regnum. *See* kingship
religion, *mos* in, 52–53
Remigius of Florence, 248
Remus, 270, 274
Republic (Cicero)
  Adams, influence on, 334
  Atkins on, 149, 168
  Augustine and, 250–251
  Cicero's constitutional theory in, 150, 169–178, 182
  context for, 263
  Gentili's references to, 272–273
  ius in, 61
  Locke's knowledge of, 317
  Ptolemy of Lucca and, 252, 255
  on rule of reason, 162
  Salamonio and, 257
  sources for preservation of, 261
republicanism
  historiography of, 7–8, 10–11
  liberalism vs., in political thought of American Revolution, 331–332
  virtue and, 324
République (Bodin), 73, 278, 282, 283
resentment, 154–155, 158, 159, 160, 161n48
res publica (commonwealth)
  Bodin on, 306
  Cicero on, 61–62, 257, 262, 306, 318
  Scipio's definition of, 169–170
  See also the state
Richelieu, Cardinal Armand Jean du Plessis, 306
Rienzo, Cola di, 247
right of appeal. See *provocatio*
right reason
  in balanced constitutions, 179
  Cicero on, 265
  constitutional norms and, 162
  natural law and, 177
  of *prudens*, 179
  on reason, limits of, 180

rights
in Cicero's thought, 171–172
natural rights, 168–190
property rights, 172–173, 185
sovereign right, 242, 244, 284
of tenure on public land, 142
See also *provocatio*
Rights of Man (Paine), 34
Riklin, Alois, 321
Roberts, Jennifer Tolbert, 12
Robespierre, Maximilien, 330
Rodgers, Barbara Saylor, 109
Roman People
Cicero on, 132
comitia as sovereign, adherence to, 294–295
extraordinary commands, granting of, 107
majesty of, 125
Manlius and, 95
Montesquieu on, 323
Rousseau on, 325
sovereignty of, 37–41, 119–129
tribunes and consuls, rights concerning, 121–123
See also citizens; *salus populi*
Roman Republic, as constitutional order, 241–259
Pomponius and *lex regia*, 241–247
Ptolemy of Lucca and *De regimine principum*, 247–255
Salamonio, early Roman constitutionalism of, 256–259
Roman Republic, Bodin and fall of, 278–302
constitutional contract law and *ius–lex* distinction, 286–289
extraordinary commands, 295–301
lordly vs. lawful rule, 289–295
overview, 278–280
Roman dictatorship, *provocatio,* and sovereignty, 280–286
Roman Republic, fall of
Cicero on, 150
as constitutional crisis, 2
as context for Cicero's political theory, 149
Livy on, 2
locus of sovereignty and, 25
Machiavelli on, 77n61
Montesquieu on, 323
reasons for, 101
Sallust on, 261
state of nature and, 25
Tacitus on, 29–34, 241
See also constitutional thought, rise of, and fall of Roman Republic; late Roman Republic; Roman Republic, Bodin and fall of
Rome, Sulla's occupation of, 33
Romulus, 270, 273, 274
Roscius of Ameria, 82
Roselaar, Saskia, 142, 144
Rousseau, Jean-Jacques, 301, 325–326, 329, 330
rule by commission, 300–301
rule of law, Aristotle on, 218–219
rule of reason, Cicero on, 161–168
Rullus. *See* Servilius Rullus
Rush, Benjamin, 337–338

safety of the people. See *salus populi*
Saint-Just, Louis Antoine de, 330
Salamonio, Mario, 256–259, 286, 288
sales, Roman law of, 188
Sallust
Bellum Catilinae, 130–134
Drummond on, 91
as forebear to Machiavelli, 304n3
on glory-seeking, 261
Machiavelli on, 271n60
political thought of, 262
Ptolemy of Lucca and, 250, 253
on *SCU*, 89, 90

salus populi
Bodin on, 301
Cato (Trenchard and Gordon) on, 314
Cicero on, 183–184
consuls and, 43
in Hobbes, 306
Locke and, 254
Locke on, 318
Machiavelli contra, 271–272
Selden on, 35
sapiens, 44, 179
Saturninus. *See* Appuleius Saturninus, Lucius
Scaevola. *See* Mucius Scaevola, Publius
Schmitt, Carl, 282
Schofield, Malcolm, 62, 194, 199–200
Schwartzberg, Melissa, 225n119, 229
Scipio Aemilianus. *See* Cornelius Scipio Aemilianus, Publius
Scipio Africanus. *See* Cornelius Scipio Africanus, Publius
Scott, J. T., 271
Scottish Enlightenment, 159, 330–331, 334
SCU. See *senatus consultum ultimum*
Seager, Robin, 80
security, as end for political society, 333
seditionis sedandae causa, dictatorship, 70
seigneurial (despotic) rule, 289–290. *See also* "lordly" vs. constitutional government
Selden, John, 35–36, 183
self-defense, natural law and, 165
self-discipline (*sophrosune*), 200
self-interest, 133, 156, 159, 160, 161n48, 164n55, 168, 173n91, 176, 188, 189n159, 205, 276, 307, 310
Sempronian law, 59n139, 131
Senate (Roman)
acting as a court, 135, 138
agrarian bill, opposition to, 125
authority of, 31
on Cicero, restitution to, 136
dictatorship, establishment of, 69, 280
hostis declarations by, 96
land distribution bill, opposition to, 111, 143
legislation, annulment of, 126–127
Manlius, actions against, 95
People, conflict with, 58
Pompey, granting of extraordinary powers to, 112–113
power of, 126, 323
prorogations by, 103–104
representative function of, 246
senatus consultum (decree of the Senate), Pomponius on, 245
senatus consultum ultimum (*SCU*, last decree)
Bodin on, 280n10
hostis declarations and, 88–95
neglect of, in reception of late republican constitutional thought, 309n25
for Pompey, 115
provision of exceptional powers by, 64
as senatorial interpretation of republican constitution, 57–60
voiding legislation via, 127
Seneca, 292–293, 315
sentimentalism, moral, 154
separation of powers, 80, 152n8, 173n92, 319n70, 321, 327, 338n175. *See also* checks and balances
Septennial Act (1716, Britain), 35
Servilius Ahala, Gaius (Master of the Horse), 67, 314
Servilius Glaucia, Gaius, 52n106, 90
Servilius Rullus, Publius, 83, 111

Sestius, Publius, Cicero's defense of, 48, 58–59, 162–166, 167–168
Shackleton Bailey, D. R., 56
Shalev, Eran, 331–332n136
Sidney, Algernon, 8
Sieyès, Emmanuel Joseph, 85n117
Sigonio, Carlo, 86n130, 140, 279, 282
Simonides, 196n22
sine provocatione, 71, 77, 82, 85, 87, 281
Six livres de la république (Bodin), 73, 278, 282, 283
Skinner, Quentin, 3, 8–9, 10–11, 258, 304
Smith, Adam, 155n19, 321n85, 334
sociability, 117n107, 167, 170–171, 173, 184, 190
social contract, 164n55, 259, 318n66
societas (partnership), 171–172, 258
Solon, 225n119
Sophocles, 224
sophrosune (self-discipline), 200
sovereign Comitia, Mommsen's concept of, 128
sovereign right (*summum ius*), 242, 244, 284
sovereigns
  Bodin on, 306
  creation of, 289
  danger of rule by commission by, 300
  Locke on, 318
  people, relationship to, 305–306
  Rousseau on, 326
  subjects, relationship with, 287
  See also kingship
sovereignty (sovereign authority)
  alienability of, 288, 293
  Bodin on, 280–286
  characteristics of, 244
  of *comitia*, 312
  in constitutional debates of late Roman Republic, 19
  constraints on, 259
  criteria for, 283
  of *decemviri*, 241–242
  of dictators, 282–283n17, 283
  of the Emperor, 246–247
  government vs., 278–279, 289–290, 293–294, 318
  lex regia and, 288–289
  of the people, 119–129
  Pomponius on, 242, 246
  popular, 244, 246, 278–280, 282, 291
  public vs. private sphere for, 292
  Roman constitutional thought's concern with, 6
  of Roman People, 37–41
  theories of, 307–308
Sparta, 174, 327
Spelman, John, 305
The Spirit of the Laws (Montesquieu), 322–323
Staatsrecht (Mommsen), 14, 84–85, 128
stability, political, 29, 30, 31, 153n8
stasis, 152–153
the state
  Aristotle on, 212, 216, 219
  Cicero on, 165, 167–168, 184, 185
  death of, vs. of individuals, 262–263
  goal of, 186–187, 310–311
  individuals, relationship to, 210, 211–212
  ius, dependence on, 178
  legal nature of, 15
  Machiavelli vs. Polybius on purpose of, 154
  order of priority of citizens and, 206–208
  preservation of, virtue and, 270–271
  unity of, 193, 194–195
  See also *res publica*
state of nature
  ager publicus as, 143, 145
  Cato (Trenchard and Gordon) on, 316

Cicero on, 163–166, 170, 317
constitutional norms in, 116–117
fall of Roman Republic and, 25
Gentili on, 275
Hobbes on, 213–214, 276
Locke on, 318
Mably on, 327
Montesquieu on, 319
private property in, 142, 185, 328
property holding in, 140
See also natural law
statutory law. See *leges*
Ste. Croix, G. E. M. de, 186
Stoics and Stoicism
in Catilinarian arguments, 132–133
Mitsis on, 317
natural law and, 222–223
natural law theory of, 44
rationalism of, 161–162
on written laws, 178–179
Strauss, Leo, 304
Striker, Gisela, 206, 222–223
Sulla. *See* Cornelius Sulla Felix, Lucius
Sullivan, Vickie, 304, 308n20
Sulpicius Rufus, Publius
Cicero on, 56
Marius and, 299
Sulla's actions against, 77–79, 96
unlawful laws of, 31, 32–33, 57, 79
summum bonum (greatest good, *telos*), 269, 270, 271, 317
summum ius (sovereign right), 242, 244, 284
Supreme Court, 17–18
suum cuique, 186
Syme, Ronald, 13, 28

Tacitus
Adams on, 335
Annals, 28–29
on fall of Roman Republic as constitutional crisis, 30–34, 241
as forebear to Machiavelli, 304n3
on Pompey, 315
on Roman concept of constitution, 28–30
on Roman imperial rule, 274–275
Taylor, C. C. W., 214–215
telos (greatest good, *summum bonum*), 269, 270, 271, 317
Ten Men (*decemviri*)
Bodin on, 283, 298–299
Cicero on, 76
dictatorship, as analogue to, 70
and emergencies and extraordinary powers in constitutional argument, 75–77
extraordinary powers of, 64
Nedham on, 308
Pomponius on, 241–242, 243
provocatio and, 242
Rousseau on, 326
sovereignty of, 242
term limits on, 76, 243, 244
Twelve Tables as laws of, 37
term limits
for consuls, 249
for *decemviri*, 76, 243, 244
for dictators, 70, 75, 82, 244, 281, 282
as limit to sovereignty, 246
Ptolemy of Lucca on, 249
for Ten Men, 283
See also time limits
Terror (French Revolution), 6, 329, 330, 338
Thebes, 1, 157, 174
Thirty at Athens, 133, 228
Thomas Aquinas, 248
"Thoughts on Government" (Adams), 333
Thrasymachus, 197
Thucydides, 227

time limits
  of Caesar's dictatorship, 86–87
  for commissions, 298
  between consulships, 102n225
  See also term limits
Trebellius Maximus, Marcus, 93n171, 123, 125–126
Trenchard, John, and Thomas Gordon (Cato), 20, 262, 301, 304, 309, 312–316, 337, 340
tribunes
  chief function of, 120
  during dictatorship, Polybius on, 73
  dictatorship and, Bodin on, 281
  establishment of, 249
  Gracchus (T.) on, 121–122
  removal of, 300n88
  veto power of, 322
triumvirs (Triumvirate), 88, 115, 336, 337
trusteeship. *See* guardianship
Tuck, Richard, 261, 262
Tuditanus, Gaius Sempronius, 55–56
Tullius Cicero, Marcus. *See* Cicero
Tullius Cicero, Quintus, 45–46, 181, 182
Tullus Hostilius, 72
tumultus decree, 96–97
Turgot, Anne-Robert-Jacques, 334n146, 335, 336, 337n168
Twelve Tables
  Bodin on, 298
  as constitutional document, 37
  Livy on, 36–37
  origin of, 242
  private property in, 139
  on *privilegia*, 137
  salus populi supposedly as part of, 35
  Tacitus on, 29–30
tyranny
  Bartolus on, 259n62
  Bodin on, 280, 284, 290
  characteristics of, 112n279
  coercion vs., 221
  danger of, and continuation of office, 104, 109
  dictatorship as, 69, 70, 74, 75, 80, 280
  Hamilton on, 338n176
  by law (*lege*), 81
  Nedham on, 309
  Rullus' agrarian commission as, 111–112
  of Sulla, 75, 80, 81, 284, 285–286
  of Sulpicius, 79
  Ten Men as, 76, 308, 318n66
  Thirty as, 133

Ulpian (Gnaeus Domitius Annius Ulpianus), 281, 288, 289
unicameralism, 335–336, 337, 339n120
United States
  American Enlightenment, 334
  American Revolution, 332
  Constitutional Convention, 329, 334, 337–338
  early constitutionalism of, 334
  English constitutional traditions vs., 332
  Founders, 332, 333, 339
  Mably on state constitutions of, 328–329
  political thought, debate over historiography of, 7, 331–332
  Supreme Court, 17–18
unit-idea, 20, 311
unity, 193, 194–195, 202
unwritten law (*agraphos nomos*), 223–225
usufruct, 294
utilitas (utility, mutual advantage), 163, 164, 167, 168, 170, 210, 251
utopianism, 149, 153, 158, 159, 327, 340

Valerius Flaccus, Lucius, 80, 90
Valerius Maximus, Manius, 66, 68, 74–75
Valerius Publicola, Publius, 43, 69. *See also* Publius

Vatia Isauricus, Publius Servilius, 86
Vázquez de Menchaca, Fernando, 252n34
Velleius Paterculus, Marcus, 109
Verres, Gaius, 82
Vervaet, Frederik, 80n84, 81, 102n224
Vespasian (emperor), 247, 289
veterans, plans for land distribution to Pompey's, 111
veto power, 121–122, 183, 322
vice
  Cicero on, 53
  in crises of late Republic, 303
  Encyclopédie on, 325n100
  glory as, 253, 267–268
  in late Republic, 340
  remedies for, 316
Vico, Giambattista, 140
violence. See *vis*
Virgil, 261, 262, 264, 265n21, 274–275
Viroli, Maurizio, 3
virtue
  in Adams's political thought, 336
  as cant-word, 313, 315, 324
  in Cato's political thought, 316
  Cicero on, 183–184, 269
  civic virtue, 249–250
  in Federalists' political thought, 340
  in French National Assembly, language of, 262
  generosity as, 221
  in Harrington's political thought, 310–311
  in Hume's political thought, 331
  as lacking power against corruption, 157, 160
  in Montesquieu's political thought, 319, 322, 324, 326
  in Moyle's political thought, 313
  in Rousseau's political thought, 326, 329
  nature of, 269
  in Nedham's political thought, 308
  pagan virtue, 260, 261–268, 268–272
  in *ragion di stato* tradition, 307
  rhetoric of the Mountain and, 19–20, 329
  skepticism toward, 341
vis (public violence), 31–32, 127n44, 162, 165–166
voluntary consent, in constitutional orders, 155
von Ungern-Sternberg, Jürgen, 89

Walbank, Frank, 152–153n8, 152n8, 154n14, 156–167
war, Gentili on, 275
Warner, J. M., 271
The Wars of the Romans (*De armis Romanis*, Gentili), 255n45, 261, 264n17, 265n21, 272–275
Weber, Max, 3
Webster, Noah, 335n156
well-tempered constitution. *See* balanced (well-tempered) constitution
Whigs, 35, 313, 316
Williams, Griffith, 305
Williamson, C., 127n44
Winterling, Aloys, 16
Wirszubski, Chaim, 12, 88
wise man (*sapiens*), 44, 179
Wittmann, R., 72n33, 81–82, 81n92
Wolff, H. J., 232n155
women, Plato on equality of, 200–201
Wood, Gordon, 7, 304, 331n136, 332–333, 339n179, 341
Wood, Neal, 317
Wootton, David, 322
Wright, Johnson Kent, 327–328, 329n121

Yunis, Harvey, 229–230, 230–231

Zetzel, James E. G., 179, 262, 264

Index Locorum

Andocides
(1.85), 231n146
(1.87), 231n146
(1.89), 231n146
Appian
Bella civilia
(1.7–9), 140n116
(1.10), 143n127
(1.15), 68n20
(1.16), 68n19, 71n30
(1.18), 141nn117–119
(1.55), 78n69
(1.55–56), 32n21
(1.56), 102n227
(1.57), 79n77
(1.57–60), 33n23
(1.59), 79n72, 79n78
(1.60), 33n25, 79n73, 79n76, 95n184, 96n187
(1.86), 96n192
(1.97), 82n98
(1.98), 80n85
(1.99), 70n24, 75n50, 80n81, 80n83, 81n88, 81n91, 81n94
(2.13), 103n230
(2.17–18), 103n230
(2.18), 103n229
(2.18.65), 103n231
(2.48), 86n126
(3.25), 65n5
Hispanica
(76), 103n229
Mithridatica
(94), 103n229
(97), 103n229
Punica
(112.531), 39n49
Aristophanes
Aves
(1344–1345), 224n114
Aristotle
Ethica Nicomachea
(1.1094b11), 208n63
(1.1097b21–1098a20), 211
(6.1144b1–12), 211
(7.1152b33–1153a15), 211
(7.1153b7–19), 211
Physica
(193b3–12), 211n77
Politica
(1.1252b27–30), 215
(1.1252b28–1253a4), 209
(1.1253a2–3), 252n36
(1.1253a7–a18), 209
(1.1253a19–a39), 210n68
(1.1253a36–37), 213n83

Aristotle (*Cont.*)
(1.1253a37–39), 213n82
(2.1261a17–31), 200n35
(2.1263b5–14), 221n104
(3.1274b41), 216
(3.1275b20), 216
(3.1276b4–6), 216
(3.1276b10–13), 216
(3.1278b9–15), 216
(3.1279a22–1279b10), 217
(3.1279b20–1280a6), 217
(3.1281a11–24), 220
(3.1281a35–39), 219n100
(3.1282b1–14), 219n101
(3.1284a13–14), 218n98, 235n171
(3.1287a15–1287b35), 218n99
(4), 218n97
(4.1.1289a15), 191n3
(4.11.1295a40), 191n4
(4.1289a32), 218n97
(4.1292a5–7), 220n102, 235n170
(5.8.1307b40–1308a1), 281n12
Asconius
(6C), 89n151
(34C), 92n168, 115n298
(37C), 80n82
(41C), 166n61, 166n65
(58C), 108n259
(61C), 108n258, 108n260
(64C), 78n68
(65C), 109n267
(68C), 126n42
(69C), 127n43
(72C), 108n261, 123, 125n36
(90–91C), 134n84
Athenaion Politeia (Aristotelian)
(29.4), 227n131
Auctor ad Herennium
(3.2), 40n52
Augustine
De civitate Dei
(1.6), 253n37
(2.21), 61n145, 257n56, 273n65, 290n51
(3.10), 274n68
(3.14), 267n38
(5.12), 264n19, 266nn30–31, 266n33, 267nn34–37
(5.13), 253n40, 267nn40–41, 268n42
(5.14), 268n43
(5.15), 267n35
(5.17), 264n19, 268n46
(5.18), 265n21
(15.5), 270n55
(18.22), 250n31
(19.21), 266n29, 335n155
(19.21.1–33), 290n51
(22.6), 262n8
Aulus Gellius
(13.15.4), 55n121

Caesar
Bellum Civile
(1.5), 92n169
(1.5.1), 122n17
(1.5.3), 88n143
(1.7), 92n169
(1.7.3), 122n17
(1.32), 102n221, 102n225
(1.32.2), 115n300
(2.18), 103n229
(2.21.5), 86n126
Bellum Gallicum
(1.10.5), 103n230
(1.21), 103n230
(7.1), 103n230
(7.6), 103n230
Cicero
Brutus
(128), 58n134, 59n136
(168), 96n187
(179), 94n180
(226), 102n220

De amicitia
(37), 95–96n185
De domo sua
(4), 137
(18), 50n93, 113
(19), 113, 114n294
(21), 113
(23), 113
(24), 102n222, 113, 114n291
(26), 114n292, 138nn105–106
(32), 138n107
(33), 138
(42), 137
(43), 82, 83n107, 135n87, 135n88, 137
(44), 135n91
(71), 57n125, 79n71, 126n41
De finibus
(3.50), 45n70
De inventione rhetorica, 163–164
(1.2–3), 164
De lege agraria
(1.42), 82n102
(2.8), 111
(2.10), 135n87
(2.11.3), 135n87
(2.17), 123n20
(2.32–34), 111
(2.35), 112
(2.38–41), 112
(2.56), 135n87
(2.75), 111n277
(3.5), 81, 82n102, 83n106, 84n111, 85n120, 285n32
De legibus, 328n117
(1.17), 46n77
(1.18–19), 45n71
(1.29–30), 45n71
(1.42), 82n102, 84n111, 85n119, 135n87, 160n45, 173n91, 181n120, 285
(2), 150
(2.8), 45n71, 46n75
(2.8–14), 181n120
(2.11), 46n76
(2.14), 45n72, 181n120
(2.21), 182n121
(2.22.3), 52
(2.40), 52–53
(3), 150
(3.2), 43n65, 183n129, 312n36
(3.4.2), 32n19
(3.6), 160n45, 183n128
(3.8), 43n64, 183n126, 183n130, 271n61
(3.9), 120n11
(3.11), 47n79, 182n121
(3.11.3), 31
(3.11.9), 32n20
(3.12), 179n115, 182n122
(3.15–26), 183n124
(3.16), 160n45
(3.16–26), 160n45, 173n92
(3.20), 78n66
(3.24), 16n58, 119, 124n29, 139n112
(3.27), 173n92
(3.42), 32, 125n30, 160n45, 183n125
(3.44), 32n20, 47n80
De officiis
(1.11–12), 170n79
(1.11f.), 184n134
(1.12), 184n135
(1.13), 184n135
(1.20–60), 184n131
(1.21), 142n124, 185n138
(1.57), 253n38
(1.62), 264n16
(1.64), 264n15
(1.68), 264n14
(1.159), 273n67
(2.73), 145n133, 185, 317n59, 317n61
(2.78), 186n140
(2.81), 187n147, 292n55
(2.82–84), 187n148
(2.85), 186n141

Cicero (*Cont.*)
(3.13), 269n50
(3.17), 45n70
(3.19–32), 189n159
(3.21), 189n159
(3.41), 270n56
(3.50–67), 188n149
(3.68–72), 189n156
(3.69), 180n118, 189n157
(3.72), 189n158
De oratore
(1.33), 164n54
(2.106), 58n133
(2.132), 58n130, 58n132, 92n161, 129n57
(2.134), 58n129
(2.167), 125n35
De provinciis consularibus
(15), 103n230
(17), 103n230
(19), 102n225
(39), 128
(42), 103n230
(46), 129nn54–55
De republica, 335n155
(1.39), 61n146, 170, 170n80, 257n56, 276n85, 318n63, 335n153
(1.45), 173n93
(1.54), 173n93
(1.69), 173n93, 174n94
(2.41), 175n102
(2.53–54), 331n135
(2.53–63), 173n92, 175n98
(2.54), 77, 131n66, 160n45, 175n98, 242n4
(2.57–58), 160n45, 174n95
(2.61), 76n54
(2.62), 76n56
(2.66), 150, 175n99
(2.69), 175n102, 335n153
(2.70), 176
(3), 290n51
(3.23), 178
(3.33), 177, 265
(3.34), 262n8
(3.41), 178, 263n12
(3.42), 177
(3.43–45), 171n83
(3.44), 160n45
(3.45), 62n147, 177n109, 290n51
(4.3), 182n123
(6.12), 73n42
(6.13), 171n83
Epistulae ad Atticum
(1.19.4), 111n275, 125n31, 143nn128–129
(3.15.5), 135n92, 136–137n98, 136n94
(4.1.6), 112n280
(4.1.7), 112n281
(4.2.3), 136n96
(4.2.3–4), 127n45
(4.2.4), 136n97
(4.6.1), 128n51
(4.18.3), 86n123
(8.3.3), 103n230
(8.3.6), 79n73
(8.11.2), 114n295
(9.7b.2), 115n298
(9.9.3), 55n120
(9.10.3), 56n122, 78n66
(9.15.2), 54n117, 80n84, 285n29
(9.15.3), 86n127
(10.4.9–10), 87n136, 116n301
Epistulae ad Brutum
(1.3.3), 116n304
(1.8.2), 116n304
(1.10.1–2), 116n304
(1.11.2), 116n304
(1.15.10), 116n303, 116n304
(1.17.6), 115n296
(2.1.1ff.), 116n304
Epistulae ad familiares
(1.10), 103n230

(8.4.3), 86n123
(9.9.2–3), 116n304
(11.13a), 116n304
(12.14), 116n304
(13.68), 87n140
(15.15.1), 116n302
Epistulae ad Quintum fratrem
(2.4.1), 165n59
(2.14.5), 86n123
(3.6.4), 86n123
(3.7.3), 86n123
In Catilinam
(1.3.1), 52n106
(1.4), 90n152, 92n166
(1.5), 130n58
(1.27), 99n203
(1.27.12–28.2), 51n104
(1.28), 99n204
(3.24), 79n71
(4.7–8), 132n68
(4.10), 59, 61n143, 92n162, 99n206, 131n67
In Pisonem
(30), 135n88, 139n110
(35), 100n208
(50), 48n87
In Vatinium
(36), 103n230
In Verrem 2
(2.8), 102n228, 106n246
(3.82), 81n94
(3.213), 102n228, 106n246
(3.213–218), 106n248
(4), 264n16
(5.12), 135n87
(5.141–143), 138n109
(5.143), 129
Orationes Philippicae
(1.3), 64n3
(2.24), 103n230
(2.87), 87n138
(2.91), 64n4
(3), 116n303
(5), 116n303
(5.7–10), 127n46
(5.10), 127n46
(5.45), 297n78
(8.7), 31nn16–17, 33n22, 56n124, 79n71
(8.13–14), 99n207
(10), 116n303
(11), 116n303
(11.17), 40n53, 104nn239–240, 105n243
(11.17–20), 297n79
(11.18), 103n229, 105n242
(11.20), 102n223
(11.28), 25n5, 116, 129n56, 166n64
(13.32), 87n137
Partitiones oratoriae
(37), 172n89
(105), 125n35
(130), 52n108
Post reditum in senatu
(4), 135n88
Pro Balbo
(48), 127n43
Pro Caecina
(70), 186n140
(70–74), 186
(72), 186n144
(74), 186n143
(95–96), 61–62, 82n102, 291
(96), 108n257
Pro Cornelio de maiestate
(1, fr. 30), 123n22
Pro lege Manilia
(52), 103n229, 106n249, 106n252
(60), 50nn96–97, 51n98, 107n255
(61–62), 107n253
(62), 103n229, 107n254
(63–64), 107
Pro Ligario
(11–12), 87n134
(12), 83n107

Cicero (*Cont.*)
Pro Milone
(2), 115n298
(8), 166
(10), 166
(13), 166
(13–14), 167n67
(70), 54, 54n112, 92n168, 115n298, 131n65
(72), 124n29, 167n68
(72–78), 167n67
(74), 167
(77), 167
(78), 167
Pro Murena
(22), 272n64
Pro Plancio
(8), 126n40, 128n50
Pro Rabirio perduellionis reo
(2), 93
(11–12), 94n176
(17), 51n103
(33), 132n74
(33–34), 93
(35), 94n177, 100n209
Pro Sestio
(60), 113n286
(61), 61n144, 113n287
(73), 47n80, 48n82
(91), 163, 172n90
(92), 166n60
(103), 143n126, 187n147
(137), 47–48n81, 126n41
(140), 58n133, 59n135
Pro Sexto Roscio Amerino
(91), 83n104
(125), 82n102
(126), 83n105
(143), 83n104
(153), 82n99
Pro Sulla
(8.2), 32n21
(33), 131n65
Tusculanae disputationes
(1.4), 268n42
(5.83), 265n24
(5.102), 264n16, 268n42
Codex Iustinianus
(1.14.12), 247n12
(4.65.3), 296n73
(8.5.4.4), 288n44
Corpus Inscriptionum Latinarum
(I^2,178), 103n229

Demosthenes
(3.10), 232n153
(20.90), 234n163
(20.94), 234n164
(22.5–7), 235n168
(23.62), 225n119
(24.25), 231n147
(24.34), 233n156
(24.34–35), 233n157
(59.5), 230n140
De origine gentis Romanae
(23.6), 274n69
Digesta
(1.2.2), 281n14
(1.2.2.4), 242
(1.2.2.9–11), 245n8
(1.2.2.16), 244
(1.2.2.18), 244
(1.2.2.24), 243
(1.3.31), 247n11
(1.3.32), 246n10
(1.4.1.pr), 247n12
(13.6.5.pr.), 296n73
(17.3), 296n73
(23.3.7pr.), 294n63
(43.26.2.2), 297n74
Dio Cassius
(4.51.2–3), 65n6

(36.24.4), 123n22
(36.30.1–2), 123n22
(36.31.3–32.1), 110n271
(36.33), 111n272
(36.36–37), 103n229
(36.38), 126n42
(36.39), 102n219
(36.42), 103n229
(37.10.2), 134n84
(37.26.1), 111n273
(37.43.3), 92n167
(37.57.2), 103n230
(38.8.5), 103n230
(38.17.1), 135n90
(39.33), 103n229, 103n230
(39.33.2), 103n231
(39.55.2), 111n273
(40.45.5–46.1), 86n125
(40.49.5), 92n168
(40.51), 102n225
(40.56.2), 103n229
(41.3.3), 92n169
(41.36.1), 86n126, 86n127
(42.20.1), 87n135
(42.21.1–2), 86n128
(43.14.4), 86n132
(43.19.2–3), 87n136
(44.8.4), 87n138
(45.44.3), 111n273
(46.23.4), 111n273
(48.16.1), 111n273
(57.16), 111n273
Diodorus Siculus
(37.29.2), 32n21, 79n72
Diogenes Laertius
(10.150), 210n66
Dionysius Halicarnassensis
Antiquitates Romanae
(5.19.4), 43n63
(5.70), 76n55
(5.70.1), 69
(5.70.2), 69
(5.70.3–5), 69, 280n11
(5.77.4), 70n25, 74n47, 80n80
(7.54–56), 75n49
(7.56.2), 75n49
(12.4.2–5), 67n14

Ennius
Annales
(467), 49n90
Euripides
Hippolytus
(98), 224n114
Supplices
(377–378), 224n114
Eutropius
(1.12), 249n27
(6.17.1), 103n230

Festus
(216L), 281n13
(278L), 137n100
Florus
(2.3.13.7), 144n130
(2.9), 96n187
(2.11.2), 133n77

Gaius
Institutiones
(3.154), 172
(3.162), 257n54
Granius Licinianus
(36), 103n229

Herodotus
(1.29), 225n119
(3.38), 224n118
Hesiod
Opera et Dies
(276–280), 224n114

Horace
  Satirae
    (1.3.98), 210n66
Hyperides
  (4.7–8), 228n132
  (frr. 27–28 Jensen), 232n150, 233n159

Institutiones Iustiniani
  (1.2.6), 247n12
Isidorus
  Etymologiae
    (9.3.6), 249n21
    (9.3.11), 249n25
    (9.3.29), 249n28
    (9.4.18), 249n28
Iulius Exuperantius
  (7), 92n164

Lactantius
  Divinae institutiones
    (1.11.32), 102n228
    (5.16.2–5), 273n66
    (6.8.7–9), 177n107, 265n25
    (6.8.11–12), 266n26
Livy
  (2.1.1), 42
  (2.1.7), 42
  (2.1.9), 42
  (2.8.2), 43n63, 331n135
  (2.18.6), 65n8
  (2.18.8–9), 65n9
  (2.29.9–12), 66n10
  (2.34–35), 308n21
  (3.32.6), 242n4
  (3.34.6), 30, 37, 81n92
  (3.36.5–9), 243n5
  (3.37.4), 81n92
  (3.37.4–38.1), 76n57
  (3.39.8), 76n58
  (3.48.9), 77
  (3.55.4–8), 77
  (4.13.11), 67n11
  (4.14.3–6), 67n13
  (4.15.1), 67n15
  (4.15.2), 68n16
  (4.24.4), 77n61
  (4.48), 140n115
  (6.18.5–15), 337n172
  (6.18.14), 71n29
  (6.19.3), 95n181
  (6.19.7), 95n183
  (6.35.5), 140n115
  (6.38.12), 71n27
  (6.39.1), 70n26
  (6.39.3), 71n28
  (7.17.12), 36–37, 108n257, 119n3, 312n39
  (7.42), 102n225
  (7.42.2), 51n101
  (8.32.10), 72n35
  (8.33.7–9), 72n36
  (9.26.7–20), 73n39
  (9.34.7), 37n42
  (10.13), 102n225
  (10.13.8–12), 41–42
  (25.2.6–7), 38n45, 298n82
  (25.2.7), 83
  (26.18.8–9), 38n46
  (27.5.15–19), 81n90
  (27.6.3–5), 73n40
  (27.22.4–6), 103n234
  (31.20.3–4), 103n232
  Periochae
    (50), 40n53
    (56), 51n102
    (61), 58n133, 59n138
    (67), 51n100
    (77), 32n21, 79n75, 96n187
    (89), 103n229
    (91), 103n229, 106n251
    (97), 102n228, 103n229, 106n246
    (99), 103n229
    (100), 103n229
    (103), 103n230, 135n89

(105), 103n229, 103n231
(109), 92n169
(116), 87n138
Lucan
Pharsalia
(9.190–191), 54n112
(9.190–214), 116n302
(9.204–205), 78n69
Lucretius
(5.1143–1160), 164n55
Lycurgus
Against Leocrates
(36–49), 233n159

New Testament
Acts of the Apostles
(25.16), 250
Nonius
(321.16), 170n80
(342.39), 175n102

Old Testament
1 Maccabees
(8.16), 248n20
Orosius
(6.7.1), 103n230

Plato
Gorgias
(483e6), 223n109
Leges
(6.770c–e), 207n58
(9.874e–875b), 205n49
(9.875a), 205n50
(9.875b–c), 205n51
(9.875c), 205n52
(10.890d), 204n48
(722b4–c2), 221n105
Politicus
(293d–e), 204n46
(294a–c), 203
(295b), 203
(295b–d), 203n43
(295e–296a), 203
(296c–297a), 204
(297a), 203
Protagoras
(337c–338b), 224n114
Respublica
(1.332c), 196n22
(3.389d–e), 200n33
(4.421c), 192n7, 207n57
(4.425a), 195n20
(4.434c), 193n10
(4.435b), 193n11
(4.443a), 196n23
(5.452d–e), 200n37
(5.453e–455a), 200n36
(5.456c), 200n37
(5.457a–c), 200n37
(5.458c–d), 196n24
(5.462b), 202
(5.480a), 158n38
(6.485c–e), 196n23
(6.489a–b), 158n38
(6.499e–501e), 158n38
(6.502b–c), 195n20, 196n24
(7.540c), 200n36
(8.547b–c), 195n18
(9.590c–d), 197, 198n28
Plautus
Trinummus
(1046), 49n91
Plutarch
Caesar
(14), 103n230
(21), 103n230
(28), 103n229
(37.1), 86n126
(51.2), 86n128
Cato Minor
(15.4–5), 134n85
(33.3), 103n230

Plutarch (*Cont.*)
(41.1), 103n231
(45–47), 103n229
Cicero
(30.5–6), 135n90
(32.7), 133n79
Crassus
(15), 103n230, 103n231
(15–16), 103n229
Gaius Gracchus
(4.1), 96n185
(4.2), 96n185
(18.1), 74n43
Lucullus
(34–35), 103n229
Marius
(12), 51n100
(14.6–8), 51n100
(34–35), 32n21
(35.4), 102n227
Pericles
(15.1–2), 133n79
Pompeius
(9.1), 80
(17.1–4), 106n251
(25.4), 106n252
(30.3), 109n265
(30.5), 109n266
(48.3), 103n230
(51–52), 103n231
(54), 103n229
(54.2), 86n124
Publicola
(12.1), 43n63
Sulla
(9.6–7), 79n73
(10.1), 96n187
(10.4), 79n73, 94n180
(33.1), 80, 81n94
Tiberius Gracchus
(8–9), 140n116
(9.2), 144n131
(11.2), 125n34
(13.1), 124n27
(13.2), 124n28
(14.4), 120n7
(14.5), 120n9
(15.1), 120n5
(15.2–5), 121n13
(15.3), 122n16
(19.3), 125nn32–33, 126n38
(20.3), 96n185
(21.1), 124n26
Polybius
(1.1.5), 1
(3.87.7–8), 73n39
(6), 150
(6.3.5), 152n7
(6.4.2), 155
(6.4.3–5), 155n24
(6.5), 154n18
(6.6–7), 154n15
(6.6.4–6), 155n19
(6.6.6), 159n41
(6.6.12), 155n20
(6.10), 155n24
(6.10.7), 152n7, 156n28
(6.10.11), 156n25
(6.10.14), 158n35
(6.15–18), 155n24
(6.18.1), 63, 160n46
(6.18.3), 152n7
(6.43.5), 152n7, 157n33, 174n94
(6.43.5–6.44. 1), 1
(6.44), 157n33, 174n94
(6.44.6), 153n11
(6.46.7), 153n11
(6.47.7–10), 158n38, 159n40
(6.56.11), 156–157n31, 160n47
(6.57.9), 6n14
(10.4–5), 38n45

Quintilian
Institutio oratoria
(5.11.6.), 52n105

Res Gestae, 274n72
Rhetorica ad Herennium
(1.25), 95n184

Sallust
Bellum Catilinae
(7.3), 261n4
(7.6), 266n31
(9.5), 253n37
(11.1–2), 267n37
(29.2), 88, 92n166
(29.3), 90n153
(36.1–2), 99n205
(51), 284n24
(51.1–4), 132, 133n78
(51.6), 130n59
(51.14), 132
(51.18), 133n75
(51.25–43), 133n76
(51.27), 132
(51.30), 132
(51.33), 132
(51.33–34), 134
(51.36), 131
(51.37–39), 131
(51.37–42), 130
(51.43), 132n68
(52.19–23), 261n5
(52.21), 250n29, 253n39
(52.36), 98n202
Bellum Iugurthinum
(95.4), 78n69
Historiae
(1.77.22), 92n165
Seneca
De beneficiis
(7.4.2), 292n57
(7.5.1), 292n57
Epistulae
(64), 116n304
(94), 116n304
Sophocles
Antigone
(450–460), 224n114
Suetonius
Divus Augustus
(28.2), 117n306, 186n140
Divus Iulius
(11), 102n223, 134n84
(22.1), 103n230
(24), 103n230, 103n231
(77), 87n136

Tacitus
Annales
(2.32), 102n220
(3.27), 29n12
(3.28), 315n49
(4.33), 28n11, 30
(13.29), 102n220
Historiae
(1.4), 281n12
(4.74), 275n74
Theognis
(289–290), 224n114
Thucydides
(3.36–49), 132n73
(3.43.4–5), 228n132
(8.67), 227n129
(8.69), 227n130

Valerius Maximus
(1.5.5), 96n187
(3.8.5), 79n73, 79n78, 96n187
(4.7.1), 95n185
(8.15.8), 103n229
(9.7. ext. 1), 32n21,
102n227

Velleius Paterculus
(1.12.3), 40n53
(2.12.6), 106n250
(2.18.5–6), 32n21
(2.18.5–20.2), 79n72
(2.18.6), 79n72
(2.19), 96n187
(2.19.1), 33n23
(2.31.1), 109n264
(2.31.2–4), 50n95, 105n245, 109n263, 296n67
(2.31.3), 103n229
(2.31.3–4), 102n228
(2.33), 103n229
(2.44.5), 103n230
(2.46), 103n230
Vergil
Aeneid
(1.239), 264n17
(6.817–23), 265n21
(6.851–853), 264, 268n46, 274
(6.852), 274n73
(6.853), 253n37
(7.496), 265n22
Georgics
(1.510–14), 275n75

Xenophon
Hellenica
(1.7.16–33), 233n160
(1.7.20–22), 235n169
Memorabilia
(1.2.42–46), 221n105
(1.2.45), 221n105
(2.1.13), 209n64
(4.3.16), 53n111

Zonaras
(10.6), 103n230

The manufacturer's authorised representative in the EU for product safety is Oxford University Press España S.A. of El Parque Empresarial San Fernando de Henares, Avenida de Castilla, 2 – 28830 Madrid (www.oup.es/en or product.safety@oup.com). OUP España S.A. also acts as importer into Spain of products made by the manufacturer.

Printed in the USA/Agawam, MA
July 9, 2026

907524.125